# Stage Lighting Design

## The Art, The Craft, The Life

*Richard Pilbrow*

*Foreword by Harold Prince*

*With Contributions by Dawn Chiang, John B. Read, and Robert Bryan*

*Illustrations by Lucy Gaskell*

**By Design Press**
*an imprint of*
*Quite Specific Media Group Ltd.*
*Hollywood*

**Nick Hern Books**
*London*

*Stage Lighting Design*

First published in 1997 in the USA by By Design Press, an imprint of Quite Specific Media Group
Ltd, and in the UK by Nick Hern Books Limited, by arrangement with Quite Specific Media Group
First US paperback edition in 2000, reprinted 2002, 2008
First UK paperback edition in 2008

Cover image: © iStockphoto.com/Thaddeus Robertson
Cover design: Ned Hoste, 2H

Printed and bound in Canada by Webcom Inc., Toronto

A CIP catalogue record for this book is available from the British Library
ISBN 978 1 85459 996 4 (UK)

Cataloguing-in-Publication data is available from the Library of Congress
ISBN 978 0 89676 235 0 (US)

Quite Specific Media Group Ltd, 7373 Pyramid Place, Hollywood, CA 90046, USA, tel. +1 (323)
851 5797, fax. +1 (323) 851 5798, e-mail. info@quitespecificmedia.com,
www.quitespecificmedia.com
Quite Specific Media Group Ltd imprints: Drama Publishers, Costume & Fashion Press, By Design
Press, EntertainmentPro, Jade Rabbit

Nick Hern Books Ltd, 14 Larden Road, London W3 7ST, UK, tel. +44 (0)20 8749 4953, fax. +44
(0)20 8735 0250, e-mail. info@nickhernbooks.demon.co.uk, www.nickhernbooks.co.uk

*to*

**Molly & Daisy**—*Wife and Daughter*

**Wally Russell**—*Friend & Guide*

**Tony Walton & Harold Prince**—*Friends and Mentors Extraordinaire*

*also to those*

**Master Electricians** *from Len Tucker & Herb Anstett to Greg Husinko,*

*—who have to make it all work…*

# Contents

*Acknowledgments  xi*

*Foreword by Harold Prince  xiii*

*A Memory from Laurence Olivier  xvii*

*Author's Note  xxi*

*Introduction  xxv*

## Part 1 / Design

1. Living Light for Living People  3

2. How to Do It: An Introduction  11
   *Demonstration 1: Typical Box Set  31*

3. Procedure: Preparation  33
   *Demonstration 2: Juno & the Paycock  56*

4. Procedure: Production  59
   *Demonstration 3: Rosencrantz & Guildenstern Are Dead  82*

5. Design Challenges: Color  85

**6.** Design Challenges: Staging  91
   *Demonstration 4: The Storm  104*

**7.** Design Challenges: The Behavior of Light in
   Nature—And Upon the Stage  107
   *Demonstration 5: Four Baboons Adoring the Sun  116*

**8.** Design Challenges: Musical, Ballet and Opera: Lighting in
   Repertoire  119
   *Demonstration 6: Show Boat  140*

**9.** Design Challenges: Widening the Viewpoint  147
   *Demonstration 7: Busker Alley  154*

**10.** Tomorrow  157

# Part 2 / History

**11.** Oil Lamp to Laser  165

A Historical Footnote  189

# Part 3 / The Life

**12.** Training  199

**13.** Andrew Bridge  205

**14.** Pilbrow Story 1: Beginnings  215

**15.** Ken Billington  219

**16.** Pilbrow Story 2: Theatre Projects Begins  227

**17.** Jules Fisher  231

**18.** Brian Gale  241

**19.** Pilbrow Story 3: Starting as a Lighting Designer  247

**20.** David Hersey  251

**21.** Pilbrow Story 4: Meeting "Sir"  259

**22.** Peter Maradudin  263

**23.** Pilbrow Story 5: Hospitality  271

**24.** Luc LaFortune  273

**25.** Pilbrow Story 6: Horror Stories  281

**26.** Anne Militello  285

**27.** Pilbrow Story 7: To Russia With "Sir"  291

**28.** Jim Moody  295

**29.** Pilbrow Story 8: Darkness  305

**30.** Tom Munn  307

**31.** Pilbrow Story 9: America  315

**32.** Tharon Musser  319

**33.** Pilbrow Story 10: Theatre Design  329

**34.** Michael Northen  331

**35.** Pilbrow Story 11: Diversity & Proportion  339

**36.** Chris Parry  341

**37.** Patrick Woodroffe  349

**38.** Pilbrow Story 13: Money  355

# Part 4 / Mechanics

**39.** Introduction: Light & Electricity  361

**40.** Color: Additive and Subtractive Mixing  364

**41.** Color Media  366

**42.** Control Systems  373

**43.** Instruments

   *Profile Spots  385*

   *Follow Spots  398*

   *P.C. Spotlights  402*

   *Fresnels  405*

   *Beam Projectors or Beamlights  410*

   *PAR and Reflector Lamps (PAR cans)  412*

   *Floodlights and Striplights  416*

   *Projectors  419*

   *Moving Lights  422*

   *Color Scrollers, Etc.  429*

   *Ultraviolet Lighting  431*

**44.** Instruments Symbols and Drafting Techniques  433

**45.** Calculation of Lighting Angles  436

**46.** Lighting Software  438

**47.** The Lighting Installation  440

**48.** Lighting Positions  442

**49.** Production Lighting: Scale and Power  447

**50.** Control Rooms  450

**51.** Rigging Techniques  452

**52.** Projection  457

**53.** Optical Effects  460


*Stage Lighting Bibliography  465*
*Index  467*

# Acknowledgments

This book owes a great deal to my very patient extended family and many colleagues. My wife, Molly, and daughter Daisy have been endlessly understanding with my absences—both in the darkened theatre and in my workaholic head. Molly has also helped a lot with editing and assistance. My grown-up kids, Abigail and Fred, grew too used to my disappearance. I thank them and their mother, Viki, for a great deal.

Dawn Chiang, my associate lighting designer, has been a constant support with lighting projects and this book. She's a fine designer in her own right but graciously consented to work in my support as well. She is creative and frighteningly efficient; I owe her a lot. Lucy Gaskell has provided a profusion of lighthearted illustrations. I wanted this book to be fun—life should be—and Lucy, a lighting designer herself, has made a great contribution, adding both information and character. Talking of character, thanks, too, to Peter Copley—one of England's special character actors. His variously lit face graced the 1970 book and continues to do so today, as does Peter himself on the stages of the Royal Shakespeare Company at a ripe age indeed.

My thanks must go also to Ralph Pine, my patient publisher. It was Ralph who for many years complained that *Stage Lighting* was always out of print at the beginning of the scholastic year and who finally took over control of its publishing. He had the temerity to reprint the old book in its last manifestation, commissioned this new version, and then waited as deadline after deadline for its completion passed. I'm most grateful to Tonia Payne, his super-diligent copy editor, and Karl Ruling, who has reviewed part 4 for technical accuracy. All remaining errors are solely my fault.

I've spent forty years so far working for the firm I began, Theatre Projects. Many colleagues have contributed to this book. Recently Don Guyton, Tom Kostusiak, David Taylor, Alan Kibbe and David Hall have contributed to editing and technical information. The book's foundations owe much to earlier "mates": Robert Ornbo, Robert Bryan, John B. Read, William Bundy, David Hersey, and many others.

Lighting design is a wonderful profession. While we're all in competition with each other in some way, we all share parallel dreams, frustrations and hopes. Every designer from whom I've sought help has given it with great generosity. Part 3, "The Life," is enriched by the contributions of those listed. I thank them. But many others have contributed, if unwittingly, so here's thanks to them, too. In particular, Eric Cornwell, Macintosh genius and lighting designer, has assisted with his insight into computer software. Part 4, "Mechanics," has a lot of technical information. I must thank all those manufacturers who both supplied information and helped to verify my interpretation of that information. Mistakes here, too, are now mine alone.

We're part of a continuum. Who was that first torch-bearer in the cave? Key figures of recent times who've played important roles in my life must include Basil Dean, the director who lit the flame of modern lighting in Britain; Joe Davis, who in my eyes was one of the great lighting artists of England; and Frederick Bentham, who pioneered so much of the sophistication in control systems we take for granted today. In the United States, Ed Kook, founder of Century Lighting, put his weighty influence behind our emerging profession, Jean Rosenthal, Tharon Musser and Jules Fisher all welcomed me to Broadway, the latter even introducing me to my wife. Thank you all.

Four men require special mention. Tony Walton, an extraordinary genius of a stage designer, whose uncanny grasp of spirit on the stage first brought me to America, and Harold Prince. Hal made Tony and me his producing partners in London, when we were just newly out of the cradle. He gave me the big breaks of my life. He has profoundly influenced musical theatre everywhere. I, and several of us in the theatre profession, owe him.

Finally I must thank two friends who exited the stage too early. Michael Elliott was a director and friend whose insight into the absolute essence of theatre was an inspiration that is constantly with me. Wally Russell was a friend. If I was faced with a problem, Wally was always there—and always right. His grasp of the essentials, his insight into character, his vision and his commitment to those he discovered and supported have quickly become legend in the lighting world. He was the most unflashy person you could meet. He thought a lot. He talked to you, or himself, around your problem right through the night. He was very deep.

It's fantastic to know people who change things.

# Foreword by Harold Prince

I began working in the professional theatre in 1948, interning for the then preeminent Broadway director of musicals, George Abbott. At that time, which (contrary to what many of Richard Pilbrow's readers might think) was not so long ago, lighting a musical was the assignment of the chief electrician. He worked from the lighting boards backstage, rarely coming into the house to join the director. There was no designer and no design credit.

The director's requirements were limited to "Lights up!" for a scene, "Lights down!" for a musical number and up again as it built to a finish. For comedy scenes, the lights were beefed up another notch. And if that wasn't enough, hard-edged spotlights converged on the actor speaking the funny lines. I well remember Abbott saying, "You can't get a laugh in the dark."

Times have changed. For the past forty years, Richard Pilbrow has been instrumental in creating that change.

It wasn't until I coproduced *West Side Story* in 1957 that I actually observed an artist lighting a show. Jerome Robbins, its director, had been exclusively a choreographer, designing dances on bare stages using minimal costuming, so lighting was the paramount design element. Jean Rosenthal designed most of the lighting for his ballets.

It was through *West Side Story* that I met Richard Pilbrow. A mutual friend, the scenic designer Tony Walton, introduced us, suggesting that we might eventually present shows in England together. Two years later, I produced *A Funny Thing Happened on the Way to the Forum* in New York, with sets and costumes by Tony Walton and lighting by Jean Rosenthal. A few years after that, I reproduced it in partnership with Messrs. Walton and Pilbrow in the West End.

This was the beginning of a collaboration as coproducers and/or director and lighting designer that endures to this day, with our latest, the Oscar Hammerstein-Jerome Kern musical *Show Boat*.

The theatre as a collaborative medium tests the patience of writers, directors, designers and performers, bringing into play not only the stimulating interchange of *ideas*, but, less glamorously, the need for patience, discipline, politic coercion and often, eventually, compromise.

Richard Pilbrow's vision is boundless. Miraculously, it is matched by a clear, no-nonsense approach to the realities of collaboration. He has the curiosity and enthusiasm to have kept apace of technology. All this new computer stuff clearly tickles him.

Over the past forty years, I have been directing and/or producing plays, musicals and operas. I have worked with a number of brilliant designers. I believe I am less patient than many (most, perhaps). I am quick to create and quick to judge.

I use a microphone during technical rehearsals (most of my colleagues do), but how many hang a whistle around their necks to cut through the cacophony of orchestras tuning up, singers vocalizing, and department heads exploding? I recognize that the whistle is a poisonous addition to the mix. (Once, in Vienna at the State Opera, I was politely asked by the chorus master to please jettison it. I did. I regretted it because I lost my voice trying to be heard.)

Richard is used to this. He remains unruffled. Unlike some of his peers, he manages to get the work done swiftly and to quiet this anxious director without patronizing him.

I first read the original *Stage Lighting* in 1970, during a period in which Richard and I worked together almost every year. The fact that I read it willingly and *understood* it, specifically that it clarified information about the process a lighting designer goes through, is testament to Richard's easy, congenial writing style.

No wonder that this book has remained in print for twenty-five years.

In 1992 Richard and I went back to work on a vast project—a revised view of *Show Boat*, the musical first presented in 1927 and reproduced every decade since, either in the U.S. or the West End. I agreed to direct it only on condition that I could rethink its structure, particularly in act 2.

I wanted to capitalize on the epic sweep of forty-five years in the lives of three families. Technology gave an incredible jump-start to the quality of life during those years. The electric light, the steam engine, telephones, automobiles and movies made their appearance at that time—and all of this ran parallel with traumatizing social problems, which remained unaltered.

Designers, directors and choreographers like to work with metaphor. A strong visual metaphor provides the underpinning for many of the most successful theatrical projects. *Show Boat* was no exception. "Ol' Man River"— the Mississippi—had always dominated the first act of that musical. Then it disappeared to be replaced by Chicago, only to reappear abruptly in the last ten minutes of the play.

In our version, Richard, Eugene Lee, our set designer, and I chose to keep it omnipresent. So throughout the second-act sequences in Chicago—when steel has replaced wood—the rippling current of the Mississippi moves in shadow through the scene changes. Time is the river.

As a director, I am obliged to accept a diversity of roles: idea man, stimulator, editor, even drama coach. The ideal collaboration is that in which I present an idea and wait to see what I get in return. If I get back exactly what I asked for, I have failed. After all, I'm not a designer, I'm not an actor, I'm not a playwright. I want something larger, more creative. I want a surprise. Richard Pilbrow has never failed to deliver that surprise. In this book, you'll see how he goes about delivering.

January 1997
Harold Prince

# A Memory from Laurence Olivier

I can't really grasp how an electric bell works. I once said as much to George Kaufmann, who replied, "The *hammer* is a mystery beyond *my* comprehension." The word *candlepower* is the only one among electronic jargon which has ever reflected in my understanding the faintest glow of appreciation. And now if I can't make out the meaning of the word *transistor*, I at least know what it aims to mean. To my brothers and sisters who wallow in even deeper ignorance than that which I enjoy, let me say that it means battery, or a kind of battery, or battery as a means of driving power. "A transistor radio," for instance, is a phrase I bandy about quite carelessly now. Sorry if I'm showing off, but watts, ohms, amps, gnodes, lux, lumens, condensers, thyristors, integrated circuits, digital analogue conversions, ferrite core stores, chips, bits, gates and pots are secrets which are all too safe with me.

But I could once upon a time light a show and do it pretty nicely in the days when this skill was expected of a stage producer, when, if a specialist was brought in, our colleague would be smugly if politely looked down upon by the rest of us.

Only Ingmar Bergman do I know who persists in still practicing this lost aspect of our craft. "Of course I must do my own lightning," he insists. "Lightning is *Blixt*," I explain, "*Belysning* is lighting." But Ingmar is a Swedish genius and Swedish geniuses are as stubborn as they come, particularly when they have kept up the technicalities, and he has.

*Part 1 of this book is based upon my earlier work, Stage Lighting, first published in 1970. Lord Olivier wrote that foreword and for sentimental reasons I include it again. It's also a great piece about lighting.—Richard Pilbrow*

As we used to have it before the invasion of the experts, twelve on no. 1 spot bar or sixteen if possible, ditto in FOH, should provide "a warm" and "a cool" from each side of the house—together with floats, plus no. 1 batten for interior, plus more battens as necessary for exteriors, plus, of course, special effects, hanging pageants or acting areas for streams of sunlight, moonlight, sunset. Special lamps plugged into the dips all round, special "baby Dietz" in the footlights, for candlelit scenes, through the fireplace, in the piano, the bookcase, or underneath tables, assisted in the smoothing-out artifice laid on by the practiced hand of the leading lady of long standing.

Gentle fades and gentle increases have from time immemorial been employed to accentuate the mood of the scene; also, very commonly indeed, to highlight the entrance of a leading player. I remember an auntie of mine years and years ago saying to me, "My dear, Henry Irving was such a very great actor that, do you know, whenever he made his entrance you would swear that the entire stage seemed to light up." (Another example of this very dear lady's memory of the great man came out after a matinee of the Thorndike/Casson production of *Henry VIII* at the old Empire in Leicester Square, in which Wolsey was played by Lyall Swete, "...you see, my dear, Henry Irving wore a gown of real silk and this man had nothing of the kind....How do I know? Why, my dear, before Irving's every single entrance for several seconds you could hear the swish, swish, swish of the real silk as he walked towards his entrance!")

But I am departing from my subject, which is lighting, and when I say "my subject" I am attempting to speak of ground which I have already yielded. It is no longer my subject, though it still fascinates me, but it most definitely is Richard Pilbrow's subject. His work, which follows this lame introduction, is of astonishing completeness and a magnificent exposition of sheer masterliness in the difficult craft that this has grown to be.

It may perhaps be of interest to note the reason behind the beanstalk growth of this aspect of the theatre. It exists in the relation of one sense to another, or the governing of one by another. The effects brought about by Irving and Belasco (incidentally, Belasco would shine his spots upwards into a mirror so that a softer glow would fall upon the form and features of Miss Maud Adams) were, according to A. J. Munnings for instance, more soft, more realistic and more plastic than the hurtful glare offered to more modern eyes.

I was caused to reflect upon this when I played in Australia in 1948. In Perth we were, I believe, the first live actors to be heard or seen for some twelve years; none of our audience could understand what we said in the first half of the play, but all expressed gratitude to us for speaking up better in the second half. This, of course, does not represent the facts as they were, but it illustrates the degree to which amplification had been surreptitiously deadening human hearing.

In other words, in Irving's day the lighting could afford to be soft, quiet, more atmospheric, offering denser differences of light and shade, because the audience's ears were sharp and perfectly responsive to the simple impact of the normal human voice and quiet light playing upon the speaker. It is since the development of habitual amplification that more and more complaints have been made concerning the level of the actor's speech and this has only been eased by the ever-increasing voltage of light thrown upon a subject. In other words, you have to see better in order to hear better. The perception of the eye has been deadened along with the sharpness of the ear.

If the same indulgence as that of oral amplification were provided for the eyes, the race would soon be walking about with binoculars strapped to their faces. One may wring one's hands at the pity of these conditions but along with so many other things in civilization, in order not to despair it must be shrugged off in the lame utility cliché of "progress." That this situation has been met is thanks to Richard Pilbrow and his like. Your old friends, the actor-managers, would not have had the electronic knowledge necessary to satisfy the senses as it is required these days. The difference is just about the same as that of flying before and during the War "by the seat of our pants" and the technological expertise required for handling the jumbo jets of today.

June 19, 1970
Laurence Olivier

# Author's Note

This is a new *Stage Lighting*. It might be described as the fifth version of a book that began in 1970, but hopefully the reader will find so much new "stuff" that he or she won't mind the old chestnuts that remain. The world changes at an ever greater rate, but some things do stay the same. Sex, politics, and the behavior of light seem to possess certain immutable principles that bear repetition for another generation.

Of course for many readers 1970 will be more than a lifetime ago. I often meet people who as teenagers seem to have been turned on to stage lighting by earlier versions of this book, then studied it in college. They are often amazed to find the author actually still alive. So am I.

Thirty-eight years ago, as a hopeful young lighting designer, I had the temerity to challenge the monopoly of Strand Lighting in London. In order to earn a living, I started the only independent lighting rental and design company in the U.K.: Theatre Projects. My timing was, to put it mildly, lucky. Who could have foreseen what our industry would be like in 1997? There are literally thousands of lighting designers earning their living from this crazy craft. Leading lighting designers are famed around the world. Even quite small manufacturers are global companies trading on every continent. There are hundreds of suppliers in an ever expanding arena. Trade shows such as LDI and PLASA bring exhibitors regularly in both directions across the Atlantic. And as we all know, the global world of entertainment and information in which we live hasn't yet begun.

A book is a strange child to bear. It has a life of its own and can gather a reputation that, to the author at least, seems out of all proportion. The original book contained some ideas about the philosophy and approach to lighting design that had emerged, almost by accident, during my early lucky career. Almost immediately after it had gone to the printer, I began to wonder whether any of it was true.

I personally find it very difficult to teach stage lighting. I even find it hard to explain to an assistant on a production what I am up to. I find the process of design very intuitive, very subconscious, very...well...private. Of course it all has to be organized. Of course it all has to be plotted, written down and planned. But in truth it is all about realizing visions. Dreams that float—if you are lucky—in your head. Dreams that have to be translated into three-dimensional light through electricity, wires, electronics, color....Will the vision work? Will the director like what you've done; will the costume designer throw a fit at your color choice? Will the shift from moment A fit unseen alongside moment B? Each and every time I find that the actual process of lighting is very frightening: creating your vision under the scrutiny of all your peers, all of whom wish you'd bloody well hurry up. Every time I seem to temporarily forget the answer to the nerve-wracking question: can I actually do it?

Yet at the same time, there's nothing so invigorating as creating a whole world from the production desk. There's always a moment when you are certain that this time it won't work; it will be an embarrassing disaster. But then time passes. You refocus a bit. You tidge about a bit. It begins to look acceptable to you. Then first night arrives. It's OK.

Obviously it's a thrill for me to meet those who've found some help or inspiration from the first book over its twenty-five-year life so far. That's why there is this new book.


## PART 1/DESIGN

Part one deals with the role that lighting has to play in a production, the lighting designer's place in the theatrical team, and the processes and procedures that he has to go through in designing the lighting of a show.


## PART 2/HISTORY

This is based on a brief history I wrote for the *Cambridge Companion to the Theatre*. I'm grateful for their permission to use much of it here. In 1970 I actually thought that stage lighting began with electricity. It didn't. I was very young. It's a noble calling that has been around for hundreds of years. So to put the record straight, here's the story in brief. From flickering candle in the cave, via Frederick Bentham and Ed Kook, to Vari*Lite and beyond.

## PART 3/THE LIFE

People have often asked me how the politics of lighting design works, how relations with others shake out. Some stories might help. How do you get a job, make a living, deal with crisis or career changes, seek opportunity? This section contains personal anecdotes about some of those good moments that led to the production desk, as well as some bad ones. To broaden the canvas, my friend Dawn Chiang and I sought help on this section by interviewing a selection of other lighting designers, young and old. Many were very generous with their time. Their experiences have greatly enriched the mix.

## PART 4/MECHANICS

This section is in the form of a designer's notebook and covers briefly some of the technical equipment that the working designer needs to know about. The equipment surveyed is representative of English and American practice, with some examples from other countries. It does not pretend to be comprehensive. For real detail see manufacturer's catalogues. The present rate of technological change cannot truly be captured in a book (so please wait for the CD-ROM version!). This section is an introduction to the necessary knowledge of the craft and its tools that must lie at the center of any practice in the art of stage lighting.

Throughout the book I've added some new or recent production examples. I've also retained some pretty old ones, as I think they still continue to offer some interesting or relevant examples.

In 1970 I wrote, "For the serious enthusiast anxious to learn more of lighting, I can recommend three courses of action. (Today I've added a fourth.) First, reading (a wealth of accumulated experience will be found in the bibliography). Second, the study of plays. The first interest of the lighting designer should be in the plays that he is called upon to illuminate. The reading of plays and an interest in other productions of every sort can form the best background to one's own practice. Third, practice itself. A lighting designer can only truly learn his trade by doing some lighting. If it is not always possible to find a real stage on which to practice, a model can provide a tremendously rewarding start. From a very small Pollock's Toy theatre, I gradually build a most elaborate, half-inch-to-the-foot scale model, with a 120-channel switchboard and with an almost professional quantity of spotlights. These little lanterns, made by Robert Stanbury (former tutor in stage lighting at the Wimbledon School of Art), really did give an amazingly accurate representation of the various types of beams to be obtained from focus lanterns, acting areas, pageants, and so on (the lights of the time); and one could set up an almost complete professional lighting layout. I remember a production of *Richard II* at the Old Vic, directed by Val May, set designed by Richard Negri, on which we set up every scene and tried out every cue on the model. The production was hauntingly successful from a visual point of view, and every effect had been seen, in miniature, beforehand and discussed." In more recent times Patrick Woodroffe, with his Four to One studio in London, created a quarter-scale model where many major rock-and-roll tours were "pre-lit." Tomorrow holds the promise of the digital model, where lighting will be created in virtual reality.

But the fourth "tip" for the beginner is to learn to use your eyes. Look around at the wonders that surround us. Light reveals the world, and to use light on the stage, we must employ those eyes in our heads that so many of us take for granted.

## SCOPE OF THE BOOK

The fascinations of stage lighting are many. The designer needs first and foremost imagination, the ability to conceive visions. Next, he or she needs the creative and practical ability to turn these visions into reality with light. And finally, the designer needs dedication. Theatre demands from its servants teamwork, cooperation and commitment. The lighting designer will be required to give peak effort at any hour of the day or night, often in the most unreasonable circumstances. It is at the ever growing number of such complicated, perhaps crazy, enthusiasts that this book is aimed! Throughout the book I have used the term *designer* when referring to the lighting designer. He or she may be solely concerned with the lighting design or may also be the director, set designer, technical director or electrician. He or she is, however, the person responsible for organizing the use of light upon the stage.

For greater brevity I should add that throughout the book from this point on he means she—and vice versa. Let all be aware that the best lighting designers are usually women. There are a lot of male and female electrical things in lighting—here we are genderless. Unless specific reference is made to a particular type of dramatic presentation, the word *play* may be assumed to include any type of live performance, that is, musical, opera, and so on. *Theatre* is also used in an inclusive sense. It means any place of presentation of such a performance. Finally, regarding language: this book is written by an English immigrant to the U.S.A. I know our nations are "separated by a common language"—years of working with Hal Prince have made me accustomed to the confusions. Now even I don't know which is which. My daughter Daisy speaks a wondrous mid-Atlantic tongue: this book attempts the same.

# Introduction

Stage lighting is a remarkable part of modern theatre. Remarkable because, although theatrical productions have been presented for many thousands of years, the new ability to accurately and sensitively control light has led to stage lighting's emergence as an ever more significant element in the creation of theatre.

For centuries people have performed plays: they have spoken, sung, acted or mimed stories to an audience surrounding them. Various rituals have accompanied these performances; styles of presentation have changed. Shapes of theatres and various types of scenery, costume, properties and machinery all have come into and gone out of fashion. Most so-called innovations are basically only a repeat of something that has gone before: however, the use of electricity and electric light and the control of the illumination by which players are seen have meant a true revolution in the theatre.

It is only in the last four or five hundred years that theatre has generally been performed indoors and artificial light has had to be used to illuminate the stage and the players. Candles, oil lamps and gas light each in turn contributed slightly more sophisticated means of producing this light and allowed some degree of effect. Electricity, when it first arrived, merely imitated its predecessors. Rows of lamps, sometimes of different colors, could be dimmed or made brighter as required. After the First World War the introduction of the spotlight and the development of dimmer control broke through the traditional limitations and led to a new awareness of what controlled lighting had to offer to the theatre and the dramatist.

Without light nothing can be seen: it is one of the primary stimuli to the human brain, and we are immensely sensitive to its every nuance. The most hackneyed example is perhaps that of waking in the morning and throwing open the curtains. There are few people who do not react in some way to the prospect of a gray, cloudy, drizzly winter morning or a clear, sharp, brilliant, sunlit day. The actual landscape can be identical. The difference is only in the light, which appears to create the quality of the air surrounding us.

Our lives revolve around the daily cycle of light and dark. Dark has an immediate subconscious and conscious impact upon us. Variations of light and shade affect nearly every move we make. I find as I write these words that I am sitting by a window: it would be inconceivable to work in the far corner of the room away from the light.

The spotlight and the dimmer have given us a new control over light. Within any given space we can create artificially any shape and feeling of light that we desire. Unlike at any time in the past, this light can be created at a distance from its actual source. We can fill a space with the atmosphere of dull day or sparkling morning: we can use these effects naturalistically or abstractly. We can fill the stage three-dimensionally as if creating the air that the actor breathes. Yet this new degree of power over light is still in its infancy, despite the everyday advances in technique, despite the theories that have been endlessly discussed, and despite the marvelously imaginative use that has already been made of this new medium.

An aspect of theatre less than a century old, the new lighting has already influenced the shape of theatres themselves. The interest in open staging, breaking through the proscenium frame, has been strongly influenced by developments in lighting.

For centuries men have written into their plays the light they have experienced in their lives: now this light can be manipulated on the stage. Its visual and emotional effect can be used to accompany and influence the action: its dramatic potential, as new horizons of technique appear, is boundless.

# Part One

# Design

# Chapter One

# Living Light for Living People

A dolphe Appia and Edward Gordon Craig were the prophets of modern stage lighting and production. Appia defined stage lighting as he found it in the nineteenth century as *Helligkeit*, which means general illumination. This was produced by rows of border and wing striplights and footlights. For centuries, candles, oil lamps and gas lights illuminated the stage in this way. Appia found this pitifully inadequate and foretold a new kind of light: *gestaltendes licht*, a "form revealing light." This three-dimensional, directional, moving light would give objects their natural roundness, shape and significance.

Light in nature may, broadly speaking, be divided into two categories: general indirect light (sky light, or the light of an overcast sky) and specific direction light (sunlight). By filling the space of the stage within which the actor moves with an appropriate balance of these two kinds of illumination, the lighting designer creates "living space."

The essence of theatre is its liveliness. Alone among the other media, live theatre presents real live actors to a real live audience. The excitement generated by the participation of this living audience with the performer creates the unique magic that is theatre. Modern lighting creates a world of light that enwraps the actor, linking him with his environment. Lighting provides the glue that joins all elements of the production together and thus helps to underline for the audience the full emotion and meaning of the play.

*"If all the world's a stage—
I want better lighting"
—Anon*

3

In this chapter I shall draw upon previous works on lighting, particularly several from America that are listed, among others, in the bibliography. I do this because, even today, too often the fundamental principles of lighting, which are set forth in these books, are disregarded. In the United States one can take an M.F.A. in lighting design. (David Hersey suggests "an M.F.A. in Hook-up Plots 1947–51" as a potential specialty.) Because of this formal education the lighting process has been codified and the rules of the game have been established, both of which factors have done much to raise the general level of quality lighting design. But rules are made to be broken. Any designer worth his salt will make up his own. I'm going to present some of my own personal recipes for your consideration. But fundamentally the rules do remain useful models and the lighting designer ignores their principles at his (or the theatre's) peril.

## THE PROPERTIES OF LIGHT

The two types of lighting described above can be said to possess four controllable properties: *intensity, color, distribution,* and *movement*

### Intensity

Intensity is the brightness of light. It is variable over a vast range from a mere glimmer to the limits of brightness that the eye can stand. In the theatre brightness depends upon the number of light sources, their type and size, and whatever switches, dimmers, color filters or masks are used. There are certain points to remember about brightness.

a. *Subjective impression of brightness.* Illumination can be measured in a number of scientific ways, which are of only academic interest to the stage lighting designer. He is more concerned with the subjective impression of brightness upon the audience: that is, not how bright the light is but how bright it appears. A single candle lit upon a dark stage will appear to be bright, while a 1,000-watt spotlight upon a bright stage may appear dim. Contrast powerfully affects the impression of brightness. The color and texture of scenery, costumes, properties and, indeed, the actors' faces also affect apparent brightness. The same illumination will give quite different effects on black-and-white settings.

b. *Adaptation.* As the brightness changes, the eye of the observer adapts. A bright scene will appear even brighter by contrast if it follows a dim one. But it will gradually appear less bright as the eye adapts to the new level. It might, therefore, be desirable to creep up the actual intensity during such a scene to counteract this effect. Conversely, if prior to a dim scene the houselights are slowly lowered, the audience's eyes will adjust more easily, and they will see more clearly what is happening on the stage.

c. *Visual fatigue.* Too much light (glare), too little light or too many rapid changes of intensity may prove tiring to the observer.

d. *Visual perception.* The amount of illumination needed to allow an object to be clearly seen depends upon the color, reflective quality, and size of the object and its distance from the observer. With a theatre audience, consideration must be given to those in the back of the house as well as those in the front rows. The farther away the spectator, the more light is needed upon the stage.

e. Intensity and mood associated with brightness. Bright light, allowing greater visual acuity, makes an audience more alert. The old rule of "bright light for comedy" has much to recommend it.

f. *Bright as day!* The stage in 1996 is significantly brighter than it was only twenty years ago. In the 1970s two or three hundred instruments in a big show was a lot. Today a thousand might not be a surprise. But lots of lights do not make great lighting. More is not better. It is how imaginatively the lights are employed that counts. But why not the brightness of sunshine on our stages? A greater range of brightness from stage lighting instruments will surely emerge. We used to light the stage with rows of candles, then gas jets. These in turn were replaced by incandescent lamps in striplights, then spotlights—even 2,000 or 5,000 watts each. New light sources, giving new possibilities of powerful light with greater contrasts—deeper shadows—have arrived, and hopefully will allow stronger characterization of light, not just provide an ever brighter blaze of overall illumination.

## Color

Every color in the visible spectrum is at the command of the lighting designer. The eye only perceives an object because it acts as a reflector of light. Color on the stage is the product of the color of light, the color of every object and the resultant reflected impression upon the eye. Delicate tints of colored light may be used to enhance the actors' faces or to "color-wash" the whole stage. Realistic or stylized color may be called for by the play, or color can be used to emphasize, modify or enrich the pigment in costumes or scenery. The proliferation of color-changer devices (automated instruments, scrollers, etc.) allow greater boldness of color choice. But this freedom must be used for a purpose, to enrich the visual and emotional atmosphere of the stage.

a. *Visual perception.* The eye sees more clearly in the yellow–green zones of the middle spectrum rather than at the red and blue ends.

b. *Color and mood.* Warm colors and tints are often associated with comedy; cool or strong colors, with tragedy. Color is a tremendously potent instrument for triggering the imagination.

c. *White light.* Light in nature is predominantly white. But the whiteness of the sun is endlessly modulated by the time of day or the state of weather and it arrives filtered by the atmosphere. The richness of color on the stage must be used with discretion. Too often stage lighting can be a sickly pinky soft mush. Color must be used as the play demands, but when in doubt, cleanness and clarity are qualities that have much to commend them.

## Distribution

All light has form and direction, ranging from a soft shadowless diffusion to a stark sharp shaft of light. The angle of a beam of light and the resultant shadow may be endlessly varied. The eye only provides distinct vision within two or three degrees; beyond that, peripheral sight is established by fairly crude stereoscopic vision. *The eye is invariably attracted to the brightest object in the field of vision.*

a. *Distribution and accuracy.* The right light from exactly the right angle lies at the heart of good lighting. Only one point in stage space will position that light to create that illumination on that detail of the face. One lamp in the right place is worth several dozen everywhere else. Moving lights must be treated with caution and respect. Their ability to refocus at will is fantastic, but beware falling back on compromise angles. The light should strike the face at an angle that is right for the whole lighting composition, not just one you can achieve because your moving light happens to be hung there. Truthfully, a light that waggles around a fixed point is a wonder, but only a step toward the day when powerful remote-control light sources that can be moved through three-dimensional stage space will be a reality.

## Movement

Each of the first three properties—intensity, color and distribution—may be altered either quickly or slowly. A room may grow darker, the setting sunlight slowly changing color and finally disappearing into the soft diffused light of dusk. This can be achieved on the stage realistically or in any more-abstract style that the designer chooses. Nature has conditioned us to an infinite variety of "effects," to which we tend to become immune in our day-to-day life. Some of these effects—dawn, stormy sunset—however startlingly beautiful, would appear outrageous on the stage. The music video with its barrage of moving visual images has even further overloaded our sensibilities. Moving lights bring a second revolution to stage lighting, offering a new ability to alter light of three-dimensional character, filling stage space in real time in new and changing ways.

## THE OBJECTIVES OF STAGE LIGHTING

The aims of stage lighting are fivefold. By keeping them in mind the designer may judge every moment of his lighting. The aims can be used as a checklist by which all stage lighting can be evaluated.

## Selective Visibility

The designer's first and most important task is to achieve visibility. The cardinal rule is: *Each member of the audience must be able to see clearly and correctly those things that he is intended to see.* Those parts of the stage to which his attention should not be drawn can be less brightly lit or left in complete darkness.

Ninety-nine percent of the time it is the designer's duty to light the actors clearly so that everyone can see them. Only for very particular dramatic effects can the actor be underlit. If the audience has to strain to see the actor who is speaking or singing, the lighting—no matter how beautiful it may look—is a total failure. It is said that an actor who cannot be seen cannot be heard. In fact if an actor cannot be seen the audience can hear, but they soon become weary and gradually begin to pay less attention.

Not only must the actor—and every other object upon the stage that should be seen—be clearly illuminated, but each must receive proportionally the correct amount of illumination, and the lighting must reveal them correctly.

As we have already noted, the eye will naturally look toward the brightest part of the stage. This brightness is determined by: *a. the amount of light*, and *b. the amount of reflection from the object.* Thus a black object upon a bright stage will appear dark, whereas a white object will appear bright even if only dimly lit. For most practical purposes we have an easy reference point, which is the face of the actor. Faces, however, vary in tone: a pale face or make-up will appear lighter than a ruddy or suntanned one in the same lighting. Different ethnic skin coloring requires different consideration.

Almost all the time we will want to make the actor's face appear to be the brightest object upon the stage in order to focus the attention of the audience upon him. This requirement determines almost all the basic principles of stage lighting.

During the action of the play different parts of the stage may become more important, different actors may need to appear more dominant. So the balance of visibility may be changed, either subtly or sharply. The balance of lighting may move from one side of the stage to another; an actor in an important speech may be gradually highlighted. In this way the lighting acts as a pointer to the audience, telling them where to look. The well-known follow spot in a musical is an obvious example of this type of "indication." With the advent of moving and remote-control color-changing lights, the means of changing a composition differ. No longer is brightness the only element that can be rebalanced by varying dimmer levels. Now instruments may shift their focus or color to achieve a new balance.

In a naturalistic production of a Chekhov play, there may be many cues shifting the balance of intensity around the stage, none consciously "seen" by the audience but all of which subliminally direct their attention toward the key point of the scene. In films or television the camera can track or cut to a close-up for a dramatic moment. On the stage the whole audience sees the play all the time in "long shot." Adjustment of the balance of visibility helps to focus their attention.

We must also remember that color, which allows greater visual acuity toward the middle of the spectrum, plays a role in determining the visibility balance.

## Revelation of Form

General illumination alone may produce an even visibility over the whole stage but everything will appear flat and uninteresting. To make an object appear naturally in three dimensions there must be a "form-revealing" light. Appia said, *"Shade and shadow are equal in importance to light itself."* The third property of light discussed above was distribution. What the audience should see must not only be lit adequately, but also correctly. Everyone knows the moon is a sphere, but dependent upon the angles of the sun (the light) and the earth (the spectator) it will appear to be a flat disc or a crescent. All objects on the stage may be seen correctly or they may be distorted, their shape flattened or revealed, depending upon the distribution of light and shade. Most importantly, the three-dimensional shape of the actor and the details of his face may be emphasized and set apart from the scenery behind, thrusting the performer into appropriate prominence.

## Composition

"Painting the stage with light" is always the most obvious and enjoyable pursuit for the lighting designer. Here the overall visual aims of the set designer are realized and perhaps extended. The intensity, color and distribution of light create compositions of light, shade and color over the setting and around the actors.

However, it is clearly the lighting designer's duty never to try to achieve an attractive visual picture at the expense of visibility. He has to ensure that the overall pictorial effect is what is intended, and that at the same time everybody in the audience can see clearly and correctly what should be seen. It is quite easy to create dramatic visual effects with shafts of colored light, psychedelic projections, dazzling neorealistic sunsets. It is comparatively difficult to do this and at the same time ensure a clear and correct balance of visibility. This is the principal challenge of stage lighting design.

The possibilities of creating dramatic compositions in light are, of course, infinite. A study of the use of light in the paintings of the great masters will be rewarding. The "new lighting," made possible by electricity, throws open the challenge of working, not in paint, as they did, but in light itself. Furthermore, this is light and shade in *four* dimensions.

Light is used as an element of design in space, but this design is not static, as in painting or sculpture. Lighting design is visual design in space *and* in time. The controlled compositions of light may change and follow the play like a musical accompaniment.

*Stage Lighting Design*

## Mood

Finally, there is the creation of mood. Often one sees the inexperienced designer striving to create mood at the expense of almost everything else. Mood should, in fact, be the result of having successfully achieved the first three objectives. Light has an undeniably powerful effect upon our state of mind. Almost nothing has such a direct impact upon our emotions. For millennia human life has been shaped by the light of nature and the cycle of the seasons. For modern man, clear warm brightness still makes most people feel good and vice versa. The playwright uses this instinctively in his writing, making day and night, good and bad weather contribute to the dramatic effect.

> How sweet the moonlight sleeps upon this bank!
> Here will we sit, and let the sounds of music
> Creep in our ears; soft stillness and the night
> Become the touches of sweet harmony.
> Sit Jessica. Look how the floor of heaven
> Is thick inlaid with patines of bright gold.
> (*Merchant of Venice* 5.1)

Shakespeare's poetry often sets the designer quite a challenge! Such moments of verbal beauty cannot be visually matched. Every production will have to make its own decision about how to treat them.

The designer, by using intensity, color, distribution and movement, can exploit the fundamental emotional and psychological effects inherent in light and underline appropriately the dramatic effect the playwright intends.

## Information

To my friend and colleague Robert Scales, I owe this new 1997 "objective": the conveying of information. Theatre today, perhaps influenced by the speedier world in which we live, tends often to speak in shorthand. Plays no longer observe the Grecian unities of time and space; scenes jump through place and period as rapidly as the imagination of the playwright will allow. Lighting can support this fluidity by rapidly conveying to the spectator a sense of place and time. Lighting supports the storytelling process and by grounding the scene in its environment of the moment in the play, the designer is contributing to the performance's impact.

## A Summing-Up

The two types of lighting (general indirect and specific directional), possessing four controllable properties (intensity, color, distribution, movement), used to achieve traditionally four, but now five, objectives (visibility, composition, form, mood and information), are equally valid no matter what style of production may be embarked upon, no matter what type of theatrical presentation is intended and no matter what shape of stage and auditorium are used. Classical opera, naturalistic arena drama, anti-illusionistic staging, dance, circus or open-air musical concert, all can benefit from the designer having consciously applied these yardsticks to his work. The content of the play and production style chosen for it by the director and the design team will dictate how these criteria are employed.

# Chapter Two

# How to Do It: An Introduction

**T**he Black Box and an Experiment in Visibility

Assume that the stage is contained within a large black box. All light is excluded. Darkness. How do we best go about lighting this space dramatically?

First, try an experiment. Stand an actor in the middle of the stage. Take a spotlight and shine it on him from above and from the front. He will be seen quite clearly, even from the back of the theatre, sitting in a pool of light surrounded by darkness. Now turn on all the general "flooding" lights in the theatre: battens, striplights, footlights, even the worklights and the houselights. Obviously there will be much more light upon the actor but, strangely, he will appear no more brightly lit; indeed, if there is a light-colored background he will probably appear less bright, his face and outline tending to disappear against his light surroundings.

From this we may deduce two things. First, the spotlight is of great value for lighting the actor since it allows us to light him separately from his surroundings. This makes him more visible. Second, we learn that contrast of light and shade is an important factor in determining apparent brightness.

**The Angle of Light and Its Associations**

Continue the experiment. Observe more closely how the appearance of the actor is altered as the position of the spotlight is moved: from below the actor

*1. The spotlight*

*2. General light*

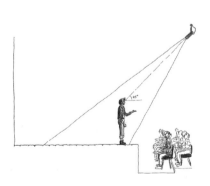

*3. Lighting the actor—section*

to the front, the side, 45° above, overhead, behind, and so on. About 45° to 55° above appears to reveal the face most naturally. Now try the same angles moving around toward the side of the actor. The most "natural" angle will be seen to be about 45° above and to the side. Further around to the side the light will appear more dramatic or perhaps more harsh.

As the theatre is using the human being as a yardstick, and the human situation as the usual basis of its drama, so in theatrical lighting, natural light is the yardstick by which the audience will (subconsciously) react. Thus natural light must be the designer's continual guide.

## Lighting the Actor

We have found that to light the actor's face most naturally the spotlight should be placed roughly 45° above and 45° to the side. But this alone will still cast rather harsh shadows, particularly when he turns his head away from the front. So next we will want to place another spotlight at an equivalent angle on the other side. Two units 90° apart, 45° above the actor and to the side, will illuminate him adequately. He will be free to move around within the limits of the spotlights beams and still be reasonably lit.

## "The Method"

Since a spotlight beam will seldom exceed eight or ten feet in diameter when it reaches the stage, how do we go about lighting the whole scene? We'll begin with an exploration of what has been termed a "Method" of stage lighting. This was first put forward by the late Stanley McCandless in the United States. In rewriting this book in the mid-1990s, I thought long and hard about whether to continue to refer to this sixty-year-old Method, and finally decided to do so. The Method suggests a basic formula for setting about lighting a scene and, as such, still provides a useful framework. However, in common with most dogma, by its very nature it introduces the danger that its rules will be too rigidly adhered to. Certainly the creators of the Method have always preached that the formula should be loosely and freely interpreted. It is regrettably true that some very dull lighting can result from following it too closely. But, a word of warning: while an individual designer should employ his own individual approach, varying it for each production, he would be foolish to forget the basic precepts of the Method. Let him vary his approach to lighting (as indeed I will later suggest), but let him beware at all times of ignoring the basic disciplines the Method provides for the fulfillment of the objectives of lighting. It divides the lighting of a scene into eight categories.

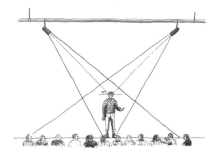

*4. Lighting the actor—elevation*

## 1. LIGHTING THE ACTING AREA

Let us return to the lit actor on the stage. We next have to light the space around him—all the space in which the actors will want to move during the play.

We must first divide the stage into areas of a size that a spotlight beam at the throw available can fill, and yet not so large as to limit flexibility in their control. We will probably decide on a module of about 6–10 feet (2–3.5 meters). If we have a proscenium stage 24 feet (8 meters) wide, we might divide it across its front edge into three parts. With an acting area 16 feet (5 meters) deep it will be two areas deep. For convenience we will letter these areas A–F.

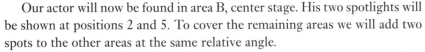

*5. Lighting the actor—plan*

Our actor will now be found in area B, center stage. His two spotlights will be shown at positions 2 and 5. To cover the remaining areas we will add two spots to the other areas at the same relative angle.

Spotlights 1–6 will be placed in the auditorium, while 7–12 will very likely be hung on the first pipe (spotbar) behind the proscenium. The distance of these instruments in plan from their areas will depend upon their height above the stage (see Part 4/Mechanics).

*If the audience is to see the front of an actor, some light at least must come from the front,* that is, from the general direction of the audience. In figure 6 it will be seen that half the illumination is actually coming from the auditorium.

If the two spotlights into each area are both at full intensity, the result may be rather flat. We can vary the balance attractively either by altering their intensity slightly or by putting a different tint of color on one side or the other, perhaps a very pale blue or cold tint in those lamps on the actor's left and a warm gold tint or no color on the right. There are endless variations of this, but it should always be remembered that these units are lighting the actor's face, and they should be subtly colored to avoid distorting his appearance.

Let us apply this acting-area lighting to a simple set to be lit naturalistically. It is a realistic interior box set with a French window stage left, a fireplace on the right and entrance at the back.

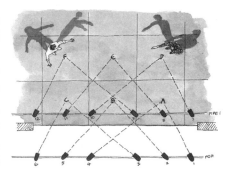

*6. Lighting the acting area*

left: 7. Typical box set
middle: 10. Section with ceiling
right: 11. Section without ceiling

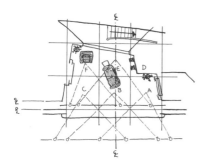

8. Typical box set—plan

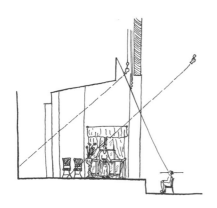

9. Typical box set—section

The acting areas are laid out in the manner described earlier, and we see that area F will light the armchair by the fire and areas B and E, the sofa. Note that area D is much reduced by the shape of the setting. Suppose the scene takes place on a sunny morning: we shall assume the main source of light will be sunlight from the window. Accordingly, the acting-area spots on stage left will be of a light warm tint—gold, pale yellow, or possibly no-color "open white"—while those on the right will be a cool tint, taking the color tone of the walls of the room. (This light from the right would, in nature, be a reflection of the sunlight from the walls.)

A later scene at night may be required, with moonlight coming through the window and two lamps lit in the sofa area. The warm light in the room should now appear to come from the table lamp at center, the cool of the night from stage left. With a fire in the fireplace, the stage-right area C may need warm firelight from the right and lamplight from the left, while area A will want cool moonlight from the left and lamplight from the right. If then the curtains are drawn, the moonlight will have to go, being replaced by another sort of reflected light, this time a reflection of the center lamps from the walls and closed curtains. To cope with these complications we might double-up the acting area spotlights in various tints for each contingency. In a plot with a smaller number of instruments we would choose compromise colors, which, at various levels of brightness, could be accepted as apparently warm or cool, as necessary.

In principle, then, acting-area lighting builds up a pattern of basic illumination around the actor. This pattern is divided into areas as the designer requires, so that each part of the stage can be separately controlled. Into each of the areas we beam two spotlights, from the most suitable angles for the human face, and by varying their color and intensity, we achieve some variety in the composition and mood of the scene. The size of individual areas need not, of course, be identical, and may have to be adjusted to accommodate the position of scenery, furniture, and action.

We must, of course, ensure that each spotlight is spread sufficiently to overlap its neighbor. It is also usually advisable to focus spotlights with a soft diffuse edge to the beam. This will avoid dark spots between the areas and any distracting hard edges of light across the actor's face. The transition from one area to another must be unseen. If after careful focusing there are still dark patches, we have obviously made the areas too large, and they must all be readjusted.

12 and 12a. Below—front

## Moving into three dimensions

With the foregoing we have probably gone some way toward satisfying objective 1—"selective visibility."

If the setting of the play is indeed like the interior box set we have discussed, with a ceiling over it, it might be that the front-of-house (FOH) and first pipe positions we have chosen are the only places we are able to put lighting equipment. Obviously we cannot backlight the actor if there is a ceiling over his head, but suppose the ceiling were not there, or suppose we were lighting the actor on a bare stage, would we gain anything by using more angles than the two at 45° to his front?

The answer is an unqualified yes. Light is three dimensional: it fills space, and its angles, the angles of light and shade and of composition, can be infinitely varied around the actor to enormous advantage. We have already discussed the 45° angles, which were enough to illuminate the human face pleasantly. Let us now examine in more detail the effect of various lighting angles upon the face.

## Light from below (Figs. 12 and 12a)

Light from below casts shadows upward and appears unnatural, because in nature it is an uncommon angle of light. It is probably the least useful lighting position, which is not to say that it should be scorned entirely.

Footlights are a relic of the old days when the lighting of the stage came from rows of candles. The candles were superseded by oil lamps, then gas jets and, finally, electric lamps. Before the days of spotlighting, the footlights, being on the front edge of the stage (and obviously closer to the actor than the chandeliers hung overhead) were a principal source of light. Then spotlights began to be placed in the auditorium; these lit the actor at the front of the stage far more adequately and from a more natural angle. So footlights lost their prime function.

But in nature some light does come from below. The childish game of holding a buttercup beneath someone's chin to see the yellow reflection ("Do you like butter?") should remind us that everything reflects light. A man in a green field on a sunlit day will be "uplit" in green light. The shadows under the eyebrows, nose and chin will be tinged with green. We might want this effect on the stage. Footlights, or lights from below, can be used at a subdued level to color-tone the stage and set. A warm or cool tint can subtly color shadows, walls and ceiling.

For the simulation of artificial light or for a dramatic effect we often need a low angle of light. Obviously a scene played around a candle or lantern on the floor or on a table should be lit from below. This is often difficult to achieve without casting unwanted multiple shadows. However, we can be satisfied that footlights and/or spotlights from below the actor will be needed on occasions—occasions that are demanded by the play or by the type of presentation.

### Eyelevel from the front (Figs. 13 and 13a)

This angle flattens out the actor's features almost completely and he tends to merge with the background. On its own this is an unimportant angle but, nevertheless, it can be useful. An actor with deep-set features may be too harshly lit from the 45° angle. A lower angle of light from the front of house will fill in over-severe facial shadows, if used with discretion. Again, if footlights are not used (for example on an open stage), this low frontal light can be employed for color-washing the stage. A front light washing or spotlighting scenery (particularly far downstage, such as frontcloths) may be necessary.

### Low level from the side (Figs. 14 and 14a)

As the source of light is moved around to the actor's side, his face will be more sharply and dramatically lit. Obviously if he looks away from the light only the back of his head will be seen; but if he is facing front or toward the source, he will be sharply edge lit. As the angle between the spectator and the light increases, the effect becomes more dramatic. Contrast and shadows increase until the actor is in complete silhouette. Examine some of Rembrandt's paintings to see the effective use of sidelighting as a dramatic device. A danger inherent in low sidelight is that one actor will tend to cast shadows upon another; it is therefore often more useful to employ a sidelight from above head height. A low sidelight can, however, be very powerful, particularly in lighting ballet or modern dance, as it reveals fully the plastic three-dimensional values of the moving figure.

*13 and 13a. Front—horizontal*

*14 and 14a. Low sidelight*

*15 and 15a. Basic area angle*

### The angle horizontally and vertically around 45°—the "ordinary" or basic acting area angle (Figs. 15 and 15a)

Of course there is some flexibility about the 45° vertical angle. Often a slightly higher 55° angle will give good facial light with less "spill" light beyond the performer. Beware, however, of the actor with deep-set eyes, who may need some fill light to lessen shadows.

### The angle between 45° and 85°, horizontally or vertically

As the angle through to 90° (i.e., overhead and/or to the side) increases, so the contrasts and shadows grow more pronounced; the light becomes more dramatic and the modeling stronger. As the angle becomes steeper, this edge light can powerfully highlight or accent the features of the face. Side or edge lighting and even "rim" lighting (in which the light is farther behind the actor) are highly potent for their dramatic value. *These will be the most important angles for modeling the actor in three dimensions.*

### The light overhead—downlight (Figs. 16 and 16a)

This cannot contribute much to illuminating the features but it can add a dramatic highlight. Of almost equal use dramatically is backlight.

16 and 16a. Downlight

17 and 17a. Backlight

*18 and 18a. High sidelight*

*19 and 19a. High side backlight*

*20 and 20a. Low side backlight*

### Backlight (Figs. 17 and 17a)

Backlight is angled from above and behind the actor. The beams fall upon the actor's head, hair and shoulders, creating a halolike impression that makes him stand out from his background.

### High and to the side (Figs. 18 and 18a)

Light from this angle has much of the dramatic value of a low sidelight, while lessening the risk of actors shadowing each other.

### Above, behind and to the side (Figs. 19 and 19a)

High side backlight is an angle that mixes the qualities of back- and sidelight and is particularly powerful when used as the dominant motivating "key light" of a scene.

### Low side backlight (Figs. 20 and 20a)

This angle is used for special effect. Again, it is a dramatic angle used for key light and special effect to mold the body three-dimensionally.

21.

## Summary of lighting angles (Figs. 21, 21a and 22)

Having looked briefly at the values of these angles individually, let us now consider them in combination. The ten possibilities divide simply into three groups, each of which can contribute to three-dimensional lighting.

1. Lights to the front. These light the face of the actor, and roughly 35°– 55° horizontally and vertically is preferred for facial illumination. Steeper angles may be more dramatic, but beware a loss of facial visibility.

2. Lights from the side. These finely model the actor. A high angle avoids the shadowing problem.

3. Lights from above (and behind). These complete the modeling and make the actor stand out from the background.

We thus find that to satisfy both "selective visibility" and "revelation of form" with our basic layout, we need to employ not just two but as many as five spotlights in each area. Figure 21a shows this combination in one area. Elaborated over the whole stage it would ensure a highly flexible and exciting lighting set-up.

Once again it must be stressed that this is only a basic method of work. Some plays need backlight, some do not. Some settings allow backlight, others do not. *But if possible the actor should always be lit three-dimensionally* (Fig. 22). The lighting designer, by thinking in terms of all around light, will try to encourage the set designer to create his set so as to allow the appropriate light to be used for the play.

Changes in technology assist in allowing greater variations of sharp yet subtle modeling light. The new moving lights—particularly the new silent Vari*Lite VL6s and VL5s, allow a multiplicity of "specials." These can be used to sharpen the modeling light on an actor in an infinite number of ways. On my recent show *Busker Alley,* the Tommy Tune musical, I have coined for myself the phrase to "sharpen the actor," much like one sharpens a pencil. Adding precise three-dimensional modeling light to any actor at any moment in any position brings him into sharp focus.

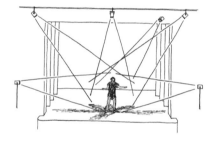

21a. 3D lighting elevation

## 2. SUPPLEMENTARY ACTING AREA

If we look back to the plan of the interior set (Fig. 8) we will note that the acting-area spotlights have adequately covered most of the stage area. But there are certain places on the stage outside the six areas. For example, the arch upstage is beyond area E and an actor standing outside the French windows would be out of area A. In these cases we would need to supplement the acting-area units with "specials." Remembering the 45° principle, we would set two spotlights into the arch area upstage. These would probably come from the first pipe and be placed next to units 8 and 11 (see Demonstration 1). A single unit focused into the French window would probably suffice, again from the first pipe, adjacent to unit 9 (Fig. 23). Both these positions should be lit three-dimensionally, especially the area by the window, with light from outside the room. With these positions covered we have achieved complete illumination of the stage, and wherever an actor may go, we would be able to light him.

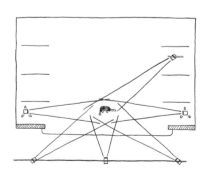

22. 3D lighting plan

*Stage Lighting Design*

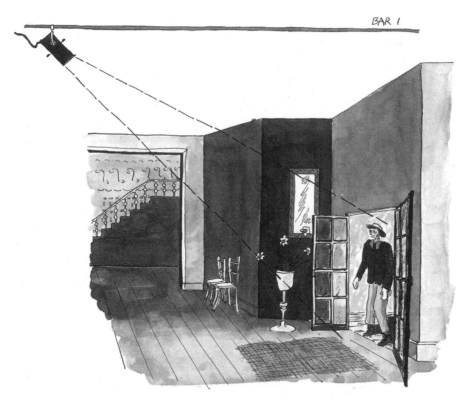

*23. Window special*

## 3. BLENDING AND TONING THE ACTING AREA

In a small installation with very limited equipment it may not be possible to allow even two spotlights into each of an adequate number of areas. It is likely in this case that some flooding equipment will be needed to wash light softly over the acting area, filling any irregularities there may be. This equipment could be a striplight hung beneath the first pipe or perhaps some floodlights—500 watts or smaller—on the pipe itself. It will be useful to have hoods on these lamps so we can direct the light where we want it—on the actor, not lighting the top of the scenery.

Flooding equipment in this subsidiary role can also be valuable on the larger stage, without a loss of the selective quality of spotlighting. A wash of light and color can act as a fill light, affecting the color tone of the whole stage. Particularly in opera and ballet, wings, borders and backcloths may need soft illumination. The PAR or reflector-lamp striplight can be useful here. These units, providing a broad sheet of shadowless illumination, can color and blend the acting area without unwanted spill on the surroundings. Even more potent is the sheet of light from a Svoboda low-voltage "light curtain." Named for the famed Czech scenographer, Josef Svoboda, who pioneered their use, these units give a dazzling strip of down- or backlight, which powerfully lights the air around the performer, providing a visible wall of light. Remote-control color change, tilt and even sideways "pitch" on these light curtains make them very powerful tools for high-key broad brush strokes of light, particularly in the spectacular musical.

## 4. LIGHTING THE SCENERY

A rather amazing rule to begin with is *don't*—or perhaps, *don't unless you have to.*

If the lighting of the acting-area has been carried out as meticulously as it should have been, much of the set will be well lit by reflection. But some scenery will certainly need its own special light. An area of sky, a cyclorama, an effect of sunlight striking a wall—these and many other effects will call for special treatment.

Returning to the interior set example, we will almost certainly find that the walls of the room itself will need no special lighting. The acting-area color tints should have been chosen with due consideration for the painted color on the walls, and reflection should do the rest. But the backing outside the window will need some units, as will the hallway beyond the upstage arch. Three floods (two for day, one for night) should go outside the window, with perhaps two smaller ones in the hall. These should be fixed as high as possible to avoid casting shadows of actors crossing backstage on the backings. The space in front of the window backing should not be forgotten. This is the area that is supposed to be outdoors. It is within sight of the audience, and frontlight, downlight and backlight of the actor will probably be needed (Fig. 24).

We should not always think in terms of using floodlights for lighting scenery, for very often spotlighting will be more effective. The view outside the window may be a painted cloth of countryside, and, if facilities permit, its appearance could be enhanced and the illusion of distance increased if parts of it, for example the horizon, are subtly spotlighted.

The designer in his early meetings with the set designer will need to consider a) Do I have to light the scenery specially? and b) If so, how? Is it to be frontlit? If so, is there any texture on the set that would be enhanced by lighting from a particular angle? If there is, does that angle contradict any other motivating angle of light called for by the script? If the scenery is translucent or transparent, should it be rearlit? From what angle? Should the color of light subdue or enhance the color in the set? Are the colors chosen by the set designer suitable to be lit in every way demanded by the play? (For example, it would be unwise to design a green set that is used only in a scene described by the author as lit by a blood-red sunset.)

These and many other questions will have to be posed and answered with regard to sets, props, costumes and everything that makes up the environment surrounding the actor.

## 5. MOTIVATING LIGHT

Now we must consider (at least with any play that is remotely naturalistic) the motivating light. This means any light sources used on the stage: candles, gas lamps, oil lamps, electric fittings, fires, chandeliers, braziers and natural sources such as the moon and stars. A direct sight of the sun itself is (luckily) not often called for, since its brightness would be impossible to imitate, but a setting sun or sun seen through mist or cloud would come into this

*24. Window exterior light*

*25. Window sunlight*

category. The designer will often have to re-create the artificial light source electrically. If, for example, a candle is required, since most fire authorities will only allow real flame on the stage in exceptional circumstances, the designer will have to use his ingenuity to provide a substitute that is acceptable to the audience. Reasonable imitation candle flames, that appear to flicker randomly can be obtained, but larger flames from fire or torch are almost impossible to imitate realistically. Electronic controllers to create random flickering effects, as if from candle or flame, can be effective.

The motivating light, that is, the source or sources of light on the stage, will often be the key to the lighting composition of a scene. It is important that the director and the designers of both set and lighting consider carefully the placement of these sources in relation to the blocking of the actors. Even more important is the fact that, once decided upon, these light sources should in turn influence the movement of the actors. Behavior is influenced by light. One sits by a light or by a window to read a book. These considerations are too often forgotten in the daylit rehearsal room.

## 6. MOTIVATED LIGHT

Next in importance from the point of view of composition is motivated light. This includes all the special lighting required to give the illusion of a light coming from a chosen source. This may be one of the motivating light sources (see above) or it may be a source from offstage. Very often we will assume that the sun is the offstage light source, and so the motivating light will suggest the sun's rays. On the interior set example, sunshine is supposed to be coming through the window at left. For this we will probably use one or maybe several very bright lamps, either hung overhead or on tall stands, shining through the window. The rays of the sun are virtually parallel and are quite the hardest thing to reproduce on the stage, but we can no doubt assume artistic license and use 1kW or even 2kW instruments. If available, perhaps the best thing would be to use several parallel-beam lanterns, such as narrow angle PAR cans, and some low voltage beamlights or beam projectors. Only with these can one truly simulate a parallel shadow of the window into the room (Fig. 25). Banks of low-voltage light curtains can give a powerful impression of the parallel beams of sunlight from overhead.

Available stage-lighting equipment needs to be supplemented by a broad range of these parallel-beam lanterns, and I suspect their size should not be limited to 1kW or 2kW—for why should we not be able to achieve a really blistering shaft of sunlight? Use of low-voltage or nonincandescent light sources, such as more efficient discharge lamps, should be considered, particularly for the larger theatre.

If the time of day in a scene changes—for instance to sunset—we will need some other motivated light. A similar type of unit but hung lower down would cast the longer shadows of evening across the room. Obviously the motivated light is going to be the dominant light. The acting-area units will be balanced on their dimmers to reinforce the illusion that the sunlight is in fact the source of light. Once again we should see that the director and his team have chosen the position of the window itself with care, and that the director has placed his actors on the stage bearing in mind that his main light source will be coming from the window.

We move on to the next scene. Night has fallen and the lamps are lit. Perhaps we will want to suggest moonlight outside using similar units to those for sunshine but differently colored and much much lower in intensity. The lamplight itself, from the fittings onstage, will be insufficient, so we will hope to color and set the acting-area units in such a way that they will give the illusion of light coming from the fittings. But it may be necessary to set one or two specials on the sofa area to reinforce this impression.

On a more ambitious installation we will use two more spots to supplement each light fixture. We must remember that we are trying to give the impression of light coming from the fitting. An actor standing by a lamp should have the warm light, apparently from the fitting, on the near side of his face. At the same time we must also beware of casting a shadow of the fixture itself on any nearby surface (Fig. 26).

We must then consider other, perhaps less important, sources of light. We may want a glow from the fire: for this we can conceal a small spot or flood in the fireplace. This might be supplemented from an adjacent low tormentor-boom side position. If realism calls for this firelight to be animated as if from flame, an animation disk or twin-spinning gobo in an ellipsoidal spot will give a good impression.

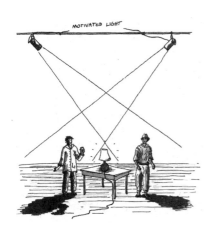

26. Lamp specials

Last, let us imagine a hanging fitting on the landing at the top of the stairs. If we have a spotlight hung above and beyond the landing, it will back-light the actors as they go up or down.

Motivated light might employ gobos or templates to cast a shadow as if from an offstage light source. The shape of a window, arch or doorway may add interest. Sunlight as if through the leaves of a tree may give dappled light across the stage.

## 7. SPECIAL VISIBILITY

We have now noted most of the types of lighting that might be used for illuminating the actor or his setting. This category is for all "specials." In our interior example, the last scene may end with one actor left alone on the sofa at a dramatic moment. The director would like everything to fade except a light on the actor's face. The acting-area units will be set too wide for this, so we must focus a special spotlight for the job. A nonrealistic production may use dozens of such specials, beams of arbitrary light. Moving lights provide the potential for many specials from a single instrument. Follow spots would be included in this category, and we must remember that such spotlights can range from the bright hard-edge front follow spot of a big musical to the most delicately handled softly focused light (perhaps from the side), which might be almost unnoticed by the audience.

## 8. SPECIAL EFFECTS LIGHTING AND PROJECTION

The reader may be surprised to find these being considered so low in priority. Special effects include all the wonders and illusions of the rock-and-roll world or disco, swirling color, fire and flame, ghosts, clouds, lightning, snow and explosions. These, one might suppose, are the essence of stage lighting. Nothing could be further from the truth. They are fun and games to the designer, effects that have to be handled with expertise and precision, but that must nevertheless be considered as secondary to the job of lighting the actor dramatically.

An important aspect of special effects is projection. The projection of scenery is constantly becoming more and more practical and exciting as equipment becomes more powerful. Cycloramas, backcloths, rear-projection screens, all can be covered with powerful projections of real or stylized images. Great possibilities of projection on to other surfaces—the floor, three-dimensional objects, scrims, mirrors and so on—create new dimensions in scene and lighting design. (For more details see Chapter 6.)

### The Creative Concept—"Pilbrow's Philosophy"

The categories we have just explored are the framework of the classic Method of lighting. However, I must confess that, much as I admire the Method, it is not the way in which I actually approach my own work. My own "method" has parallels but places different emphasis on the various categories.

My approach stems from a desire to create a three-dimensional atmosphere of light around the actor. It is founded upon the inspiration of natural light, although the way in which it is developed will allow any type of production style. In practice I take two sections of the Method and consider them in a different way.

First must come the "Idea." What is the intent of the visual effect of the stage? What is the look or feel we intend to create? How will it support or underline the storyline of the play? Out of discussion with director and scene designer and study of the play there emerges an idea of what every moment in the play might be—how lighting might enwrap the actor, shape the visual and emotional environment of the play and help in the telling of the tale. Then this "dream image" in your head has to be translated into a lighting design.

Whether we are in a realistic situation or not, the category of light the Method describes as "motivated light" is the *dominant key light* of the scene. Just as sunlight dominates natural lighting, so the dominant key light of a scene should influence everything else.

When working on a production with a great number of scenes, the discipline of the Method is still valuable. However, where my approach differs is in the degree of priority given to motivated light and the acting-area light. The Idea comes first and will be expressed principally through the dominant motivated light. This will be the pivot around which the rest of the composition revolves.

So we combine the acting-area and motivated lighting and then divide them into:

1. dominant lighting

2. secondary lighting

3. rim lighting

4. fill lighting

The dominant lighting should set the dramatic key of the scene—the Idea (I often call this light the key light). If the scene requires it, it should have a clearly pronounced direction, intensity and color. It might be highlight from the sun through a window, from moonlight, the light from a lamp or fire, or a perfectly abstract shaft with no particular naturalistic significance. It might equally, of course, be a soft indefinable misty light without apparent direction or form.

Our earlier investigations into the effect of varying angles of light tell us a lot about how the key light might best be considered. It may come from the front; it may, indeed, be from one of the acting-area 45° angles. A frontal angle will give a soft but generally flattening effect. As the angle between the audience's vision and the direction of the key light increases, the dramatic effect is also increased. The most powerful angles will be found at the side, above and behind the actor.

This key light is all important: it provides the basic construction upon which the remainder of the composition can be built. It can create shadow (which is all too often lost when we start our composition with the acting-area light) and everything can be balanced appropriately to the level we choose for the keylight.

Next we consider the secondary lighting. This is a mix of the acting-area and supplementary acting-area lighting of the Method. It is supplementary to the key light and may be quite complex, coming from various angles at different intensities. We will note that conventional acting-area angles alone will provide only limited modeling to the face. Steeper overhead or stronger side-light will more powerfully model the face and make the performer stand out from the surroundings. But secondary light will be a counterfoil to the key light in naturalistic schemes, functioning as the reflections created by the key light. The amount of shadow that the key light creates will be determined by the secondary lighting; the brighter this is, the less will be the effect of contrast. It determines, therefore, how dramatic the key light effect is and it creates a balanced composition. For an exterior scene, in which the key light is sunlight, the secondary light will be the light from the sky and reflections from the ground or any adjacent walls.

The key light for a night scene may be the light from a practical lantern, and the secondary light may be moonlight as well as reflections from secondary surfaces. The moonlight could be considered a key light but, due to the composition of the scene, it is making a secondary contribution.

The final two categories are intended to accentuate the actor and model the face. First is rim lighting. This is the highlighting from the high top, back or sides of the actor. It will usually be at a higher intensity than the rest of the secondary lighting if its modeling is to be apparent. It will give highlights to the actor's hair, dramatic edge lighting to the face and will rim light him to separate him from the background. Sometimes this separation will be neither necessary nor desirable, but whenever it is needed it enhances the actor's dramatic appearance.

Lastly, there is fill lighting. Fill light is light, generally from the front, that softens the shadows and blends the key and secondary lighting. It will only be used if needed to enhance the actor's appearance. It may also be a toning light for the setting. Fill light from a low frontal position can do this and at the same time perform another task, that is, provide lighting into the actor's eyes from a low level to soften any shadows that may result from the overhead lighting.

## Summary of "Pilbrow's Philosophy"

These two theories—one demanding an original approach for each production, the other supplying a discipline for all—may be combined to produce a new checklist, a program for organizing your lighting design :

1. the dominant key light

2. lighting the acting area with

   (a) secondary light

   (b) rim light (if required)

   (c) fill light (if required)

3. supplementary acting area

4. blending and toning the acting areas—if not already dealt with under 2(c)

5. lighting the scenery

6. motivating light source

7. special visibility

8. special effects, lighting and projection

Lighting is not a mechanical process; it is neither simply a matter of illumination nor of making effects. The art of creative lighting is to begin with an *idea* based upon a play and upon the concept decided upon by the design team. This idea is of light and shade and *space* that enfold the actor and help him project his story to his audience. Therefore, the designer must have a mental image of the overall visual effect of the stage, filled with actors and scenery. This image must be in three dimensions, and in the fourth, too—in time—as the lighting ebbs and flows and changes with the drama.

With this idea in mind the designer must start work on the technical realization of his plans, constantly testing in his mind his duty to the actors and the objectives of lighting. He remembers too that it is frighteningly easy to produce startling visual images and that the real task of the designer is to do this as required and at the same time to light the actors perfectly, "in balance" with them.

With a clear dramatic and visual concept painstakingly carried through, the designer's work should fit in to the whole production perfectly. Except in unusual circumstances, it will probably go almost unnoticed by the public, but his reward will be a personal satisfaction. His colleagues, the director and set designer will have had their concepts too—the lighting designer hopes to satisfy their wishes and give them that little bit extra, the ten percent extra of which they didn't quite dare dream.

# DEMONSTRATION 1 — *Typical Box Set*

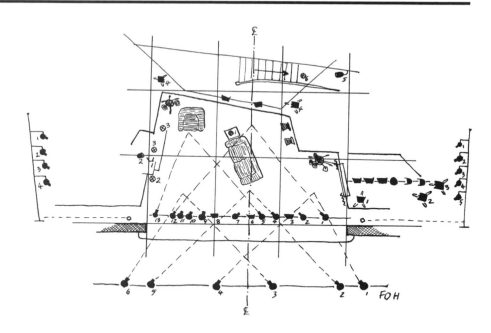

| Position | Unit | Instrument Type | Function |
|---|---|---|---|
| FOH | 1 | 6x12 Leko | Area A |
| (Front-of-House) | 2 | 6x12 Leko | Area B |
| | 3 | 6x12 Leko | Area C |
| | 4 | 6x12 Leko | Area A |
| | 5 | 6x12 Leko | Area B |
| | 6 | 6x12 Leko | Area C |
| Electric 1 | 1 | 6x9 Leko | Area E |
| | 2 | 6x9 Leko | Arch US |
| | 3 | scoop | Soft light |
| | 4 | 6x9 Leko | Lamp special |
| | 5 | 6x9 Leko | Area F |
| | 6 | scoop | Soft light |
| | 7 | 6x9 Leko | Window special |
| | 8 | scoop | Soft light |
| | 9 | 6x9 Leko | Arch US |
| | 10 | 6x12 Leko | Lamp special |
| | 11 | 6x12 Leko | Sofa special |
| | 12 | 6x9 Leko | Area E |
| | 13 | 6x9 Leko | Area F |
| Electric 2 | 1 | beamlight | Sun to window |
| | 2 | beamlight | Sun to window |
| | 3 | 6" Fresnel | Downlight exterior |
| | 4 | scoop | Cloth |
| | 5 | scoop | Cloth |
| | 6 | scoop | Cloth |

| Position | Unit | Instrument Type | Function |
|---|---|---|---|
| Boom L | 1 | 6x12 Leko | X Light warm |
| | 2 | 6x9 Leko | X Light warm |
| | 3 | 6x12 Leko | X Light cool |
| | 4 | 6x9 Leko | X Light cool |
| | 5 | 6x9 Leko | Night |
| Boom R | 1 | 6x12 Leko | X Light warm |
| | 2 | 6x9 Leko | X Light warm |
| | 3 | 6x12 Leko | X Light cool |
| | 4 | 6x9 Leko | Fire X Light |
| Stage L | 1 | scoop | Flood cloth (8'6" stand) |
| | 2 | 8" Fresnel | Sunset (4'6" stand) |
| | 3 | 8" Fresnel | Moon (8'6" stand) |
| | 4 | 6" Fresnel | X Hall (4'6" stand) |
| | 5 | 6" Fresnel | Downstairs wall bracket |
| | 6 | practical | Hanging fitting |
| Stage R | 1 | scoop | Fire glow |
| | 2 | 6" Fresnel | Firelight |
| | 3 | practical | Fire |
| | 4 | 6" Fresnel | X Hall (8'6" stand) |
| Onstage | 1 | practical | Tablelamp |
| | 2 | practical | Wall bracket |
| | 3 | practical | Wall bracket |

# Chapter Three

# Procedure: Preparation

## THE ROLE OF THE LIGHTING DESIGNER

Once upon a time there used to be a discussion about who should be in charge of lighting the stage. Many years ago the English professional theatre traditionally held the director responsible. In America it was the set designer's prerogative. But lighting is now established, in both these and many other countries, as a separate element of production, under the control of the lighting designer.

The reason for this is obvious. Lighting has grown increasingly more complex. More sophisticated technology has been introduced, with the result that the lighting process has taken more time and has cost more money. With more elaborate facilities, more elaborate and sophisticated effects have been made possible. A desire for these effects and an ever growing recognition of the dramatic potential in lighting have led in turn to increasing demands being made by the director. New technical possibilities extend artistic horizons; greater creative demands prompt new technological developments. Voices have been raised against this seemingly inevitable increase in complexity but nothing has stopped it. It is interesting to note that most of this elaboration in lighting has come out of the American and English commercial theatre, which is hardly an area that encourages unnecessary or frivolous expenditure. Yet for many years hard-headed producers have paid out ever more substantial sums of money for their lighting. They may have been reluctant, but in the end they have found it necessary—and worthwhile. The specialist lighting designer has emerged; part artist, part technician, he must possess the imagination to grasp the director's and set designer's concept of the production and have the vision to contribute something of his own. He must also have at his command the ability to plan and use light as well as a knowledge of stagecraft and electricity in order to realize his vision. Finally, in our seemingly ever faster society, he must work ever more efficiently and economically.

Theatre lighting design is a profession of its own. In England the Association of Lighting Designers, formed in 1963, absorbed the other design areas and became the Society of British Theatre Designers. It is the professional body devoted to ensuring the working conditions of its members and through British Actors' Equity, it negotiates minimum wage agreements with management. The lighting design professional body devoted to the raising of standards of work and the improvement in quality is the Association of Lighting Designers, founded in 1981. Its membership is responsible for perhaps eighty percent of the major professional lighting in the United Kingdom.

In the United States, professional lighting designers must be members of the lighting section of the United Scenic Artists, Local 829 (USA 829). To join this union the applicant must pass an entrance interview process and/or a practical lighting exam, each of which are held annually in New York, Chicago and Los Angeles. USA 829 is divided into three regions—the Eastern, Central and Western regions. Each region oversees the work in that third of the United States. The offices for each of the regions, respectively, are New York, Chicago and Los Angeles.

The lighting exam committee for each region arranges its own procedures regarding the lighting exam. Therefore, some regions may offer the exam as an interview only, or some regions offer an interview and practical. (The practical typically involves lighting a brief scene, under limited time and equipment constraints, with a panel of judges reviewing the process as you work.) Check with the regional office in your area for details. They usually have general information available to potential applicants year round.

Lighting candidates can also join USA 829 under the professional category. This is a mechanism by which designers who are already scheduled to work at a venue that requires a major USA 829 contract, such as Broadway or the Metropolitan Opera, can become members without having to wait until the next union exam. The producer can request in writing to the union that the designer be allowed to join 829. The designer will then be interviewed by the union. If the interviewing committee recommends membership, the recommendation is then voted on at the next general membership meeting.

In the U.S. the union now ensures that every Broadway production has to employ a lighting designer. A standard contract of employment, a minimum fee, working conditions, program credit and so on are established. There is also a standard minimum contract for working at most of the League of Regional Theaters (LORT).

Fees are negotiable, but minimums in February 1995 were:

*Broadway/West End*

| | USA Lights | USA Lights in $1=£1.6 | (scenery) | UK Lights | (scenery) |
|---|---|---|---|---|---|
| Musical, Multiset | $17,883 | £11,177 | $23,843 | £1,430 | £2,858 |
| Musical, Unit w/Phases | $10,305 | £6,440 | $13,741 | £1,111 | £2,223 |
| Musical, Single Set | $5,627 | £3,516 | $7,501 | £825 | £1,652 |
| Weekly Fee | $250 | £156 | $250 | £51 | £85 |
| Commercial Tour Dramatic, Unit Set | $10,305 | £6,440 | $13,741 | £735–£409 | £1,672–£1,331 |
| Small Scale | $5,627 | £3,516 | $7,501 | £197 | £723 |

*Freelance*

| | USA Lights | USA Lights in $1=£1.6 | (scenery) | UK Lights | (scenery) |
|---|---|---|---|---|---|
| National /RSC* | | | | £979–£489 | £3,041–£1,825 |
| LORT A | $3,065 | £1,916 | $4,475 | £409–£197 | £1,561–£669 |
| LORT B+ | $2,685 | £1,678 | $3,645 | £245–£197 | £1,256–£609 |
| LORT B | $2,190 | £1,386 | $2,850 | £197–£181 | £723–£457 |
| LORT C-1 | $1,645 | £1,028 | $2,255 | | |

Scary figures—particularly for the British designer. For mainstream Broadway and regional theatre the USA designer gets seven or eight times the fee.

But frankly, all the fees are low when considered in terms of the hours of effort. The very fortunate designer will get a hit show that pays the weekly rate or (if the designer can command more) a percentage of the gross receipts, which might range from one quarter to one percent of the gross receipts. This way a few, a very lucky few, have made lighting design at last a profession that can provide a good living. Regional theatre is a very different situation. Fees are appallingly low, royalties almost nonexistent, and a living can only be made by taking on more shows than are probably sensible for health, sanity or family life.

*National Theatre Company/Royal Shakespeare Company

In England the working conditions of the profession are generally worse than in the U.S. There are all too few designers able to live exclusively off the proceeds of lighting design. Shows are still presented with no one person responsible for the lighting, but these decrease in number. About ninety percent of London productions credit a lighting designer. Royalties are still only grudgingly given to top designers. Since a fee may cover three or four weeks' work, a large part of which will be over weekends, sometimes at night, it is obvious that money is not a great temptation to the designer.

In England there is still a need for improved training in lighting design. Whereas in the United States many universities offer courses in stage lighting, in England there is little that is comparable. For the first time in 1995 a B.A. course in theatre lighting design was offered by the Rose Bruford School in London. Other lighting training is associated with either scene and costume design courses such as those offered by the Wimbledon or Croydon Schools of Art or stage management and technical theatre courses at the London Academy of Music and Dramatic Art or the Central School of Speech and Drama.

It is as an assistant that many designers get their break. Properly organized lighting needs to be documented appropriately. An assistant can help with all the drafting and paperwork preparation, keep plots up to date as things change in the theatre, and preserve the designer's sanity by acting as his second eyes and ears. A good assistant with the personality to match will soon be indispensable. Then the opportunities will arrive. The lighting may have to be repeated by the assistant when his principal is unavailable; the producer, director or designer may notice this "keen young thing" next time around. Assistants get their foot on the rung of a career ladder that can lead to…who knows where?

## The Production Team

Theatre is teamwork, and the director is the leader of the team. It is quite useless for the designer to pursue an idea of his own that is at variance with the director's intention. Wherever there may be disagreement, the lighting designer can, of course, try to persuade his colleagues to his way of thinking, but if he cannot then he must bow to the director's wishes. It is also clearly no part of his job to do anything but enhance the appearance of the set and costumes. A costume designer has every right to expect the true colors of the costumes to be seen on the stage. The lighting should do this, unless by so doing it is conflicting with the overall intention established by the director.

## Planning Begins: Analysis of the Script

Ideally the designer will start work at the very outset of the production. It is far from satisfactory to start work when the set has already been completely designed and the actors are in rehearsal. The lighting designer should be in on the early conferences and discussions between the director and the scenic

**SHOWBOAT**
Produced by Garth Drabinski
Directed by Harold Prince

**Script Analysis**
Scenery by Eugene Lee
Costumes by Florence Klotz
Lighting by Richard Pilbrow

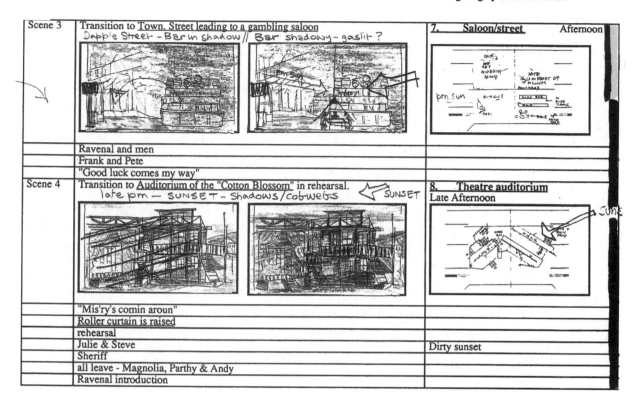

| Scene 3 | Transition to <u>Town. Street leading to a gambling saloon</u><br>Dapple Street - Bar in shadow // Bar shadowy - gaslit ? | 7. **Saloon/street** Afternoon |
|---|---|---|
| | Ravenal and men | |
| | Frank and Pete | |
| | "Good luck comes my way" | |
| Scene 4 | Transition to <u>Auditorium of the "Cotton Blossom"</u> in rehearsal.<br>late pm - SUNSET - shadows/cobwebs ← SUNSET | 8. **Theatre auditorium**<br>Late Afternoon |
| | "Mis'ry's comin aroun" | |
| | <u>Roller curtain is raised</u> | |
| | rehearsal | |
| | Julie & Steve | Dirty sunset |
| | Sheriff | |
| | all leave - Magnolia, Parthy & Andy | |
| | Ravenal introduction | |

designer. He will probably be able to make a positive contribution, perhaps pointing out how lighting might influence the staging of a particular scene or suggesting how a solution with light might help overcome a particular scenic problem. The most successful productions are usually those on which the director and all of the design team have collaborated closely.

Since every facet of the lighting will come in one way or another from the play itself, the first step, obviously, is to read the script. I like to first read a script through quite rapidly to get the feel and atmosphere of the play and then go through it again, painstakingly making a lighting synopsis of the action. In this scene-by-scene breakdown, every reference, either in the text or in the stage directions, to any lighting effect should be noted, as well as those scenes in which the lighting may make a special contribution. The time of day of each scene, any reference to the weather or season of the year and any indication as to whether the lighting should change during the act with the passing of time or to underline any change of atmosphere should also be recorded (Fig. 27).

When every detail has been extracted from the script itself, discussions can proceed. It is terribly important to truly listen to your director. Each person will have preconceptions from their first reading of the play. It is vital

*27. Scene synopsis*

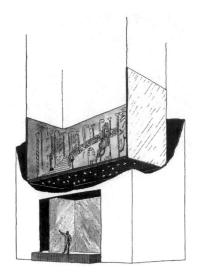

*28. The flying* Sunset Boulevard *drawing*

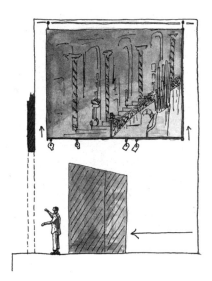

*29. The flying* Sunset Boulevard *section*

that your antennae are attuned to listening to your director's thoughts and hopes, which must form the central basis for your own developing concept. First, it is vital to establish why and how the play is going to be staged. What is the intention of the director and what style has he chosen for his staging? Is it to be realistic or naturalistic? Stylistic or expressionistic? It is unlikely that the style can be labeled in any of these convenient ways, but it is important that each person knows clearly what is in the others' minds.

Each scene will be discussed and the lighting designer may suggest how the light called for by the author in a particular scene could influence how or where it will be played and how the set may best be used. The director and set designer and the set and lighting designers will need to meet separately on details that only concern themselves, but there should be a continuous interplay of ideas until the time when the final decisions are made. I like to keep the lighting synopsis up to date with the evolving discussions, adding thumbnail sketches to explore the possibilities of each moment.

Using the model, the set will be discussed in great detail and the lighting designer must ensure that whatever is being designed is practical from his point of view. He must see that sufficient space is left for lighting equipment and that the set is correctly fitted to the proposed stage. It would be foolish to allow the set designer to cover the whole stage with a huge ceiling right down to the proscenium wall if it is absolutely essential that overhead lighting be used. It is no use, except in extremely unusual circumstances, to allow the designer to design a part of the set that makes it impossible to light the stage. If the intention of the production is that the actors should be very harshly crosslit to make them stand out sharply from their surroundings, then the designer must allow space for the sidelighting.

Every now and again a production crops up where there appears to be almost no way of fitting in the lighting equipment at all. One such was the musical *Jorrocks* at the New Theatre, London (director Val May, set designer Disley Jones), which had such an enormous quantity of complicated flown scenery that there was no room for overhead lighting pipes at all. Most of the flown scenery consisted of solid-built pieces, and eventually I reached a solution whereby the lighting pipes were built in to the underside of these. When the scenery was in use at stage level, the lighting pipes were touching the floor, but when the piece was flown out the pipes became convenient overhead lighting positions. An example of 1994 vintage would be Andrew Lloyd Webber's *Sunset Boulevard*. John Napier's massive interior box set filled the stage and, when not in use, stored above in the grid. Lighting for other scenes was built into the underside of the flying set by lighting designer Andrew Bridge (Figs. 28 and 29).

**Rehearsals**

As soon as possible the designer must watch rehearsals. I personally like to go to the very first read-through of the play. You've already lived through the drama in your head many times as the design evolved. To sit at the reading and

*Stage Lighting Design*

first see the actors in person always brings a new perspective to your vision. The director will have discussed how he intends using the stage, but he has to have absolute freedom to do what he likes once he begins work with the actors themselves. As rehearsals develop, the designer should log in his script all the moves around the stage. By the time he comes to the lighting rehearsals onstage, he should know the actors' positions as well as the director does. During rehearsals he may find that the director has staged a scene in a way that is not only contrary to the original intention, but so different from it as to make it almost impossible to light as intended. Conditions in the rehearsal room will seldom remind the director of any lighting conditions that may affect blocking, and actors struggling with their developing characters will have no idea of the lighting environment. The designer should point these things out, for it may be that the director has simply overlooked the change, or he may have deliberately wanted to do something quite different. The designer, having made his comment, will adapt his plans according to the director's wishes.

### The Theatre and Its Equipment

Many shows in the commercial theatre are planned and rehearsed before the actual theatre space is arranged. Of all the departments on a production, the lighting is probably most affected by the theatre in which the show is staged. The theatre will affect not only space on and around the stage and the position of much of the lighting in the front of house, but also may affect the type and size of control system that might have to be used. In the United States this is less of a problem, as each show will travel with its own control board, but in England, where the control is usually permanently installed, the lighting designer is often dependent on what he finds at the theatre. The designer should find out as soon as possible which theatres may be visited if there is to be a tour. He should then obtain accurate plans and sections, on which he can double check the position of the set and the places where he can rig his equipment. He will need to know the details of the permanent lighting, the type of control, the number of circuits and how they are distributed, and what, if any, extra power is available.

### Paperwork, Plots and Plans

Now the formal process of design can begin. The designer will have a clear idea of what the play is about and the contribution that his lighting can make to the production ideas of his colleagues. He might have seen some early rehearsals and he will know what facilities and space he can expect in the theatres that the show is going to visit. As well as all this, he must have some idea of the scale upon which the lighting is conceived. Obviously every production has its limits. A school production of *Julius Caesar* with a twelve-way control board might, if it is a gala occasion, use as many as twenty or thirty spotlights; a major Broadway musical might use over twelve hundred. Everything has to be considered in proportion, but the same rules of good lighting apply to all productions.

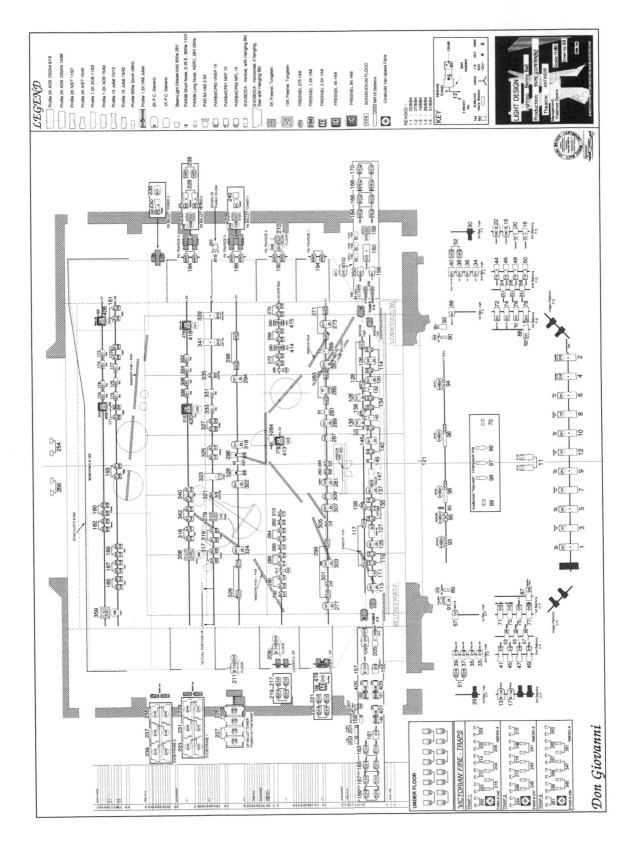

*Don Giovanni*

*Stage Lighting Design*

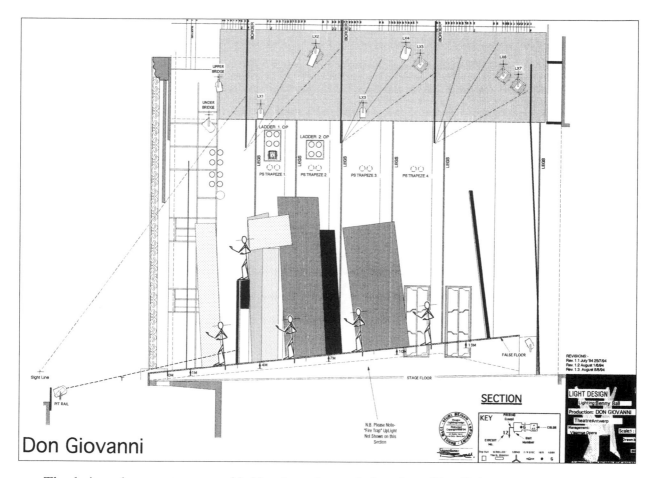

SECTION

Don Giovanni

*Facing page*
*30. Lighting layout plan*

*Above*
*31. Lighting layout section*

The designer has now to convert his ideas into plans and plots that will allow his equipment to be prepared. The process of lighting is a strange contradiction. In performance we are dealing with a totally insubstantial medium: light is so difficult to contain, describe or confine. Yet when we employ it in the theatre, it is essential that every detail be precisely planned in advance. Every single part of the lighting can be calculated and considered. Only by preparing all the physical aspects of the lighting—that is, the equipment—in great detail can we get sufficient creative freedom on the stage itself. Sloppy and inefficient planning will only lead to confusion on stage: time and money will be wasted and both will always be at a premium. The first priority in any theatre is for the actors to have sufficient time to rehearse: they should not have to wait for a designer who has not done his homework. Furthermore, good planning will ensure that the designer is able to spend the maximum available time on the creative part of his lighting. The lighting design, set down on paper, can be described in four documents.

1. The Lighting Layout Plan (Fig. 30): a plan of the stage and the set on which the layout of equipment will be marked accurately and to scale.

2. The Lighting Layout Section (Fig. 31): a cross section of the stage showing vertical sightlines and the position and height of all lighting equipment.

*Procedure: Preparation*                                                         41

# SHOW BOAT

| CHN | LOCATION | NO. | TYPE | WATTS | FOCUS | COLOR |
|---|---|---|---|---|---|---|
| 367 | Low Booth | 1 | Pani BP 1.2/f=33 | 1.2kw HMI | Snow (Loop 1197) | R65+R119 |
| 371 | Low Booth | 2 | Pani BP 1.2/f=33 | 1.2kw HMI | Ripple | |
| 368 | Low Booth | 3 | Pani BP 1.2/f=33 | 1.2kw HMI | Cloud (Loop1191) | R65+R119 |
| 372 | Low Booth | 4 | Pani BP 1.2/f=33 | 1.2kw HMI | Ripple | |
| 370 | Low Booth | 5 | Pani BP 1.2/f=60 | 1.2kw HMI | Moon + Cloud | |
| 373 | Low Booth | 6 | Pani BP 1.2/f=33 | 1.2kw HMI | Ripple | |
| 369 | Low Booth | 7 | Pani BP 1.2/f=33 | 1.2kw HMI | Cloud (Loop1194) | R65+R119 |
| 294 | Low Booth | 8 | 1KL6/12° | 1kw | Showcloth River | R06 |
| 551 | Low Booth | 8 | TWIN SPINNER | 100w | Showcloth River | *** |
| 294 | Low Booth | 9 | 1KL6/12° | 1kw | Showcloth River | R62 |
| 551 | Low Booth | 9 | TWIN SPINNER | 100w | Showcloth River | *** |
| 102 | Balcony Rail | A | 1KL6/12° | 1kw | Chi Legs US-Day | NC |
| 103 | Balcony Rail | B | 6x16 | 1kw | Chi Legs-Night | L143 |
| 257 | Balcony Rail | 1 | 6x16 | 1kw | Chicago Legs Day | NC |
| 288 | Balcony Rail | 2 | 6x16 | 1kw | Showcloth sepia | G370 |
| 290 | Balcony Rail | 3 | 6x16 | 1kw | Showcloth color | G370 |
| 288 | Balcony Rail | 4 | 6x16 | 1kw | Showcloth sepia | G370 |
| 295 | Balcony Rail | 5 | 1KL6/12° | 1kw | Cotton sky | R99 |
| 290 | Balcony Rail | 6 | 6x16 | 1kw | Showcloth color | G370 |
| 292 | Balcony Rail | 7 | 1KL6/12° | 1kw | Showcloth sky | G370 |
| 258 | Balcony Rail | 8 | 6x16 | 1kw | Chicago Portal Top Day | NC |
| 296 | Balcony Rail | 9 | 1KL6/12° | 1kw | Cotton sky | R99 |
| 259 | Balcony Rail | 10 | 6x16 | 1kw | Chicago Portal Top Night | L143 |
| 293 | Balcony Rail | 11 | 1KL6/12° | 1kw | Showcloth sky | G370 |
| | Balcony Rail | 12 | | | | |
| 258 | Balcony Rail | 13 | 6x16 | 1kw | Chicago Portal Top Day | NC |
| 292 | Balcony Rail | 13A | 1KL6/12° | 1kw | Showcloth Sky | G370 |
| 292 | Balcony Rail | 14 | 1KL6/12° | 1kw | Showcloth Sky | G370 |
| 293 | Balcony Rail | 15 | 1KL6/12° | 1kw | Showcloth sky | G370 |
| 259 | Balcony Rail | 16 | 6x16 | 1kw | Chicago Portal Night | L143 |
| 296 | Balcony Rail | 17 | 1KL6/12° | 1kw | Cotton sky | R99 |
| 258 | Balcony Rail | 18 | 6x16 | 1kw | Chicago Portal Top Day | NC |
| 292 | Balcony Rail | 19 | 1KL6/12° | 1kw | Showcloth sky | G370 |
| 291 | Balcony Rail | 20 | 6x16 | 1kw | Showcloth color | G370 |
| 295 | Balcony Rail | 21 | 1KL6/12° | 1kw | Cotton sky | R99 |
| 289 | Balcony Rail | 22 | 6x16 | 1kw | Showcloth sepia | G370 |
| 291 | Balcony Rail | 23 | 6x16 | 1kw | Showcloth color | G370 |
| 289 | Balcony Rail | 24 | 6x16 | 1kw | Showcloth sepia | G370 |
| 257 | Balcony Rail | 25 | 6x16 | 1kw | Chicago Legs Day | NC |
| 103 | Balcony Rail | 26 | 6x16 | 1kw | Chi Legs US-Day | NC |
| 102 | Balcony Rail | 27 | 1KL6/12° | 1kw | Chi Legs-Night | L143 |
| 41 | 2 Cove | 1 | 1KL6/12° | 1kw | Warm L | R321 |
| | 2 Cove | 2 | | | | |
| 48 | 2 Cove | 3 | 1KL6/12° | 1kw | Auditorium Wash R | R70 |

| CHN | LOCATION | NO. | TYPE | WATTS | FOCUS | COLOR |
|-----|----------|-----|------|-------|-------|-------|
| 48 | 2 Cove | 3 | 1KL6/12° | 1kw | Auditorium Wash R | R70 |
| | 2 Cove | 5 | 1KL6/12° | 1kw | Auditorium Wash R | R70 |
| 49 | 2 Cove | 7 | 1KL6/12° | 1kw | Auditorium Wash L | R70 |
| | 2 Cove | 9 | 1KL6/12° | 1kw | Auditorium Wash L | R70 |
| 50 | 1 Cove | 1 | 1KL6/12° | 1kw | Apron L - a | R321 |
| 51 | 1 Cove | 17 | 1KL6/12° | 1kw | Apron R - a | R321 |
| 52 | 1 Cove | 2 | 1KL6/12° | 1kw | Apron L - b | R64 |
| 53 | 1 Cove | 16 | 1KL6/12° | 1kw | Apron R - b | R64 |
| 54 | 1 Cove | 7 | 1KL6/12° | 1kw | Apron L - c | R47 |
| 55 | 1 Cove | 11 | 1KL6/12° | 1kw | Apron R - c | R47 |
| 56 | Truss-Btm | 19 | 6x12 | 1kw | X Apron L | R3204 |
| 57 | Truss-Btm | 7 | 6x12 | 1kw | X Apron R | R3204 |
| 58 | Truss-Btm | 1 | 6x12 | 1kw | Apron L-Dn | R99 |
| 59 | Truss-Btm | 25 | 6x12 | 1kw | Apron R-Dn | R99 |
| 60 | 1 Box Boom L | 6 | 6x12 | 1kw | Apron L | R3409 |
| 61 | 1 Box Boom R | 6 | 6x12 | 1kw | Apron R | R06 |
| 62 | Truss-Btm | A | 6x12 | 1kw | Apron L - Day | R3409 |
| | Truss-Btm | 10 | 6x12 | 1kw | Apron L - Day | R06 |
| 63 | Truss-Btm | 16 | 6x12 | 1kw | Apron R - Day | R3409 |
| | Truss-Btm | 26 | 6x12 | 1kw | Apron R - Day | R06 |
| 64 | Truss-Btm | 5 | 6x12 | 1kw | Apron L - Night | R65 |
| | Truss-Btm | 9 | 6x12 | 1kw | Apron L - Night | R65 |
| 65 | Truss-Btm | 17 | 6x12 | 1kw | Apron R - Night | R70 |
| | Truss-Btm | 21 | 6x12 | 1kw | Apron R - Night | R70 |
| 66 | 1 Box Boom L | 10 | 6x12 | 1kw | Forestg L-Wm | NC |
| | 1 Box Boom L | 15 | 6x12 | 1kw | Forestg L-Wm | NC |
| 67 | 1 Box Boom L | 2 | 6x16 | 1kw | Forestg R-Wm | NC |
| | 1 Box Boom L | 5 | 6x16 | 1kw | Forestg R-Wm | NC |
| 68 | 1 Box Boom R | 2 | 6x16 | 1kw | Forestg L-Wm | NC |
| | 1 Box Boom R | 5 | 6x16 | 1kw | Forestg L-Wm | NC |
| 69 | 1 Box Boom R | 10 | 6x12 | 1kw | Forestg R-Wm | NC |
| | 1 Box Boom R | 15 | 6x12 | 1kw | Forestg R-Wm | NC |
| 70 | 1 Box Boom L | 9 | 6x12 | 1kw | Forestg L-Cool | R61 |
| | 1 Box Boom L | 14 | 6x12 | 1kw | Forestg L-Cool | R61 |
| 71 | 1 Box Boom L | 1 | 6x16 | 1kw | Forestg R-Cool | R61 |
| | 1 Box Boom L | 4 | 6x16 | 1kw | Forestg R-Cool | R61 |
| 72 | 1 Box Boom R | 1 | 6x16 | 1kw | Forestg L-Cool | R61 |
| | 1 Box Boom R | 4 | 6x16 | 1kw | Forestg L-Cool | R61 |
| 73 | 1 Box Boom R | 9 | 6x12 | 1kw | Forestg R-Cool | R61 |
| | 1 Box Boom R | 14 | 6x12 | 1kw | Forestg R-Cool | R61 |
| 74 | 2 Box Boom L | 5 | 1KL6/12° | 1kw | DL Color-a | R70 |
| | 2 Box Boom L | 7 | 1KL6/12° | 1kw | DL Color-a | R70 |
| 75 | 2 Box Boom L | 1 | 1KL6/12° | 1kw | DR Color-a | R70 |
| | 2 Box Boom L | 3 | 1KL6/12° | 1kw | DR Color-a | R70 |

*Procedure: Preparation*

*Proceding pages:*
*32. Instrument schedule*
*33. Hook-up schedule*

3. The Instrument Schedule (Fig. 32): a list of each piece of equipment, instrument by instrument, giving details of its type, wattage, the use to which it will be put, the color media it will require, the way in which it will be rigged and plugged, details of any special accessories that might be required and the number of the dimmer and control channel to which it is connected.

4. The Hook-Up Schedule (Fig. 33): a list of all the control channels and dimmers, showing which instruments are connected to which and their type, wattage, function and color. In the United States this plot is mandatory, but its more optional equivalent in England would be a "plugging schedule." Particularly with a large installation, it is helpful to have this list of channels with the instruments connected to them. It can be helpful at a lighting rehearsal when one cannot in an instant, perhaps, locate a particular number on the layout plan.

I usually work from a half-inch-to-the-foot scale plan and section of the stage, or, with a large installation, quarter inch to the foot. (In the U.K. a ratio of 1:50 or 1:25 is used.) Once I have decided from where I will be lighting each area, I draw on the plan the pipes (bars) from which the equipment will be hung. There are several different ways of indicating instruments on a ground plan, and there is an internationally recognized set of symbols that can be used. I prefer the system that I introduced in England long ago (copied from American practice) of using stencils that provide accurate scale representations of each instrument. This accuracy is of great importance when a large quantity of units have to be stacked together along a pipe. By drawing each to scale, one can tell exactly how they will be fitted into the space available.

With stencils, ground plan and section, the designer can begin to build up a pattern of lighting equipment. Each scene has to be carefully considered with regard to the key light and acting-area lighting for each part of the stage that is used in the action, the motivated, motivating lights and so on. When all this has been considered and roughly noted scene by scene on the drawings, the designer will probably find that he has an enormous quantity of equipment; perhaps far more than the budget will allow, and possibly more than he can fit onto the dimmers in the theatre concerned! Now he must go back over each scene, rationalizing and simplifying and compromising as he goes. It is very likely that several instruments provided for one purpose in one scene can quite satisfactorily perform another function later on. Some cool acting-area spotlighting in a night scene could double as a shadow fill light in a bright midday scene. Through this type of planning the designer can reduce his layout to the minimum with which he is confident he can achieve his objectives.

Of course this process of planning, drawing and scheduling may be carried out on paper or with a computer. Computer-aided drafting may be combined with various custom software products to speed the design process along. It certainly makes changing what has been drawn much faster.

Software varies in cost and functionality. It can be divided into two broad types. Drafting software automates the process of drawing plans and sections

*Stage Lighting Design*

and provides an electronic equivalent of the stencil. Good software also allows the designer to instantly view his design from any angle and may provide further information. For example, on paper the coverage of a beam from a spotlight drawn in plan can be calculated in section, as can its brightness, but it takes a few minutes. On the computer the beam from any spotlight may be instantly viewed in section through that beam, or in front or side elevation. That view, together with information about the instrument's brightness, throw and beam spread can be a speedy aid to the thinking process.

The second category of software is that which automates the paperwork and preparation of schedules. Instrument, hook-up schedules, color and equipment lists may be easily generated in standard or customized forms. At the top end of the market these schedules may be directly linked to the drawings through a database, so that any alteration to the drawing is automatically carried through to all the paperwork. Some designers prefer to separate the schedule process to retain a physical and personal check. Either way, many hours of toil are saved. Specialist software is not mandatory. Few designers can afford the sophistication of a fully professional drafting package such as Autocad, for which a specialized stage lighting add-on program is available. A general-purpose drawing program can be used for drafting and a standard database or spreadsheet program will automate the otherwise very laborious paperwork process.

Of course advances in available software increase exponentially. Low-cost programs allowing instrument performance to be examined in three dimensions are a valuable aid to the designer. The future will see design programs that link the designer's drafting through full three-dimensional modeling to the lighting control system itself. (See the description of some available software in Part 4/Mechanics.)

When the layout has been completely rationalized and every instrument is doing as many jobs as possible, the designer employing manual drafting methods will begin to draw them out carefully on a working plan and section. Now that he knows how many will need to be hung in each position, he will lay them out as neatly as possible. It is helpful to the electrician to space them regularly, but if for any particular reason the spacing is irregular, this should be made clear and appropriate dimensions indicated.

While the plan is taking shape, the designer must also work out how each instrument will be connected to the dimmers. If the number of circuits available is limited, he may have to loop several together onto shared circuits. If some instruments are only used in one or two scenes, he may need to have these patched, replugged or cross-switched. This should be kept to a minimum, however, for the more circuits that have to be changed during the performance, the more likely it is that a mistake will occur and the wrong instrument connected.

When working out which instruments should be fed from which dimmer, it is advisable to consult your electrician, who will know the most sensible layout. His opinion, the designer's knowledge of the play and how the lighting will be used combine to produce the most rational and practical layout of dimmers and control channels.

When the plan and section are complete, the instrument schedule can be prepared. This is a detailed analysis of the layout and functions as work instructions to the electricians preparing the equipment. Particular care must be paid to any nonstandard items. If the designer wants to use some special instrument made for the production, he must note this on his schedule and, probably, supply working drawings for its construction. Any practical light fixtures used in the show, such as chandeliers or oil lamps, must also be listed. The set designer will probably want to select these, but the lighting designer must liaise closely with him to make sure that whatever is chosen is suitable from a lighting point of view, and he must then make sure that appropriate electrical arrangements are made.

### Obtaining the equipment

Each production will, of course, have different needs regarding equipment. A production in a major regional theatre will probably be equipped entirely from the organization's own resources. A commercial show in the West End of London, Broadway and many amateur or school productions will need to hire equipment. This can be obtained from various companies. (Some of these are listed in Part 4/Mechanics.) A clear and precise shop order must be completed by the designer.

### Shop orders (section contributed by Dawn Chiang)

A shop order must specifically itemize all equipment, accessories, perishables and miscellaneous items that are required from the lighting supply vendor. As with any order that a customer places with a supplier, what you specify is what you get, no more and no less. Therefore, a lighting equipment shop order must be a complete and accurate document of all lighting and electrical equipment required for the production. In the U.S. most shop orders include the following information.

*Cover Page*

The cover page lists general information regarding the rental:

- Name of production
- Name of theatre: where to deliver equipment. If the rental shop may not be familiar with the location of the theater, be sure to include the theater address on the cover page.
- Shop load-out date: When does the equipment leave, or load out, of the rental shop. Equipment rental usually begins the day the equipment loads out of the shop. If the rental shop is in a different city than the theatre, then trucking time needs to be factored in, which can add one or more days to the rental.
- Load-in date: When does the equipment load in to the theater.
- Closing date: This date aids in determining when the equipment will be returned to the rental shop, which is usually when the rental period stops.

Time for striking the equipment and trucking to the shop must be added on to the closing date to determine the actual date the equipment arrives back at the rental shop.

- Producer

- General Manager

- Production Manager: Who is renting the equipment; who is paying the bills. Who to talk to regarding money issues.

- Lighting Designer

- Associate Lighting Designer

- Assistant Lighting Designer: Who is designing the show and generating the equipment list. Who can answer questions regarding the shop order.

- Production Electrician: Who should be contacted regarding technical questions regarding the shop order.

Here's an example:

**Electrical Equipment List**
**for:** Four Baboons Adoring the Sun
**at the:** Vivian Beaumont Theatre

|  |  |
|---:|:---|
| Date: | January 13, 1992 |
| Load-in date: | January 31, 1992 |
| Announced closing: | April 5, 1992 |
| Producer: | Lincoln Center Theatre Company |
|  | 150 West 65th Street |
|  | New York, NY 10023 |
|  | (212) 362–7600 |
| Lighting Designer: | Richard Pilbrow |
|  | (Address) |
|  | (Telephone) |
| Associate LD: | Dawn Chiang |
|  | (Address) |
|  | (Telephone) |
| General Manager: | Steve Callahan |
| Production Manager: | Jeff Hamlin |
|  | (Telephone) |
| Production Electrician: | Jimmy Maloney Sr. |
|  | (Address) |
|  | (Telephone) |

*General Notes*

Any notes applicable to the entire shop order can be listed under an opening section called General Notes:

**General Notes**

1. All units must be painted FLAT BLACK.
2. All units to be supplied with appropriate lamp, gel frame, C-clamp and safety cable.
3. All gel frames to be painted black (front and back).
4. No tinted (green) lenses are acceptable.
5. Cable, power distribution, spares, additional hardware, rigging, perishables per production electrician.
6. All Lekos and Fresnels to be supplied with quartz lamps.
7. All Lekos to be axial mounted.

(N.B. Leko is used as a generic term for an ellipsoidal reflector spot.)

*Equipment Totals*

Next follows totals of all equipment required by the production.

**Intruments**

| | | |
|---|---|---|
| 1 | 5° Lekos | 1kW |
| 48 | 10° Lekos | 1kW |
| 4 | 12° Lekos | 1kW |
| 12 | 20° Lekos | 1kW |
| 12 | Lee Zoom Mini 40/65 Lekos | 600W |
| 6 | Altman 6x9 Lekos | 1kW |
| 246 | Altman 6x12 Lekos | 1kW |
| 58 | Altman 6x16 Lekos | 1kW |
| 2 | Altman 6x22 Lekos | 1kW |
| 13 | 6" Ianiro Fresnels | 2kW |
| 4 | 8" Ianiro Fresnels | 5kW |
| 8 | PAR 64/VNSP | 1kW |
| 24 | PAR 64/NSP | 1kW |
| 10 | Reiche & Vogel beamlights | 500W |
| 6 | Mini-10 worklights | 1kW frosted |

All other equipment is then categorized and listed. Note the level of detail used when specifying equipment. For example, a template holder for a 20°

Leko is different than the template holder for an Altman Leko, therefore, these two types of template holders should be listed separately.

## Accessories

All accessories to be painted FLAT BLACK, inside and out.

| | |
|---|---|
| 18 | Tophats for 10° Lekos |
| 2 | Tophats for 12° Lekos |
| 12 | Tophats for 20° Lekos |
| 290 | Tophats for Altman 6" Lekos |
| 12 | 4-way barndoors for Ianiro 2kW Fresnels |
| 5 | 4-way barndoors for Ianiro 5kW Fresnels |
| 8 | Template holders for 20° Lekos |
| 12 | Template holders for Altman 6" Lekos |

## Control

| | |
|---|---|
| 4 | Racks of 96 x 2.4kW dimmers, ETC/LMI (including 1 dimmer capable of dimming neon sign having dimmable ballast) |
| 1 | 48 x 2.4kW dimmers |
| 1 | 6 x 6kW dimmer pack |
| 10 | Non-dims at 10 amps each |
| 1 | Strand Light Palette V6E |
| 10 | Disks for Light Palette |
| 1 | Electrician's hand-held remote |
| 1 | High-speed printer, 250 characters per second minimum Voltage regulators, control interface, control cable, per production electrician. |

## Production Table

| | |
|---|---|
| 1 | 4' x 8' Plywood table |
| 2 | Video monitors; underscan, video cable per production electrician |
| 4 | High intensity "Little Lites" with dimmer and stand |
| 1 | Apple Macintosh IIci computer and monitor with: 4 megabytes internal memory 20 megabyte hard disk keyboard mouse |
| 1 | Apple Imagewriter II printer, with interface cable for Macintosh IIci |
| 1 | Plugging strip |

## Pipe (Schedule 40 or Schedule 80 pipe)

| | |
|---|---|
| 1 | 32'0" curved pipe for No. 1 Electric |
| 1 | 38'0" curved pipe for No. 2 Electric |
| 1 | 38'0" pipe for No. 5 Electric (tailed down) |
| 1 | 23'0" pipe for No. 3 Grid |
| 1 | 12'0" pipe for No. 5 Grid |
| 2 | 8'0" (approx.) pipes for position vom entrance L & R |
| 1 | 4'0" (approx.) pipe for addition box boom row |
| | Additional pipe as per electrician |
| | Provide all necessary rigging hardware and stiffeners |

## Hardware

| | |
|---|---|
| 4 | 21'0" threaded schedule 40 boom pipe with 18" diameter base, boom locking hardware, and ring top |
| 12 | floor mount plates for Lee Zoom Minis |
| 10 | floor mount plates for Altman 6" Leko |
| 36 | 18" single-tee sidearms |
| 38 | 24" single-tee sidearms |
| | Additional hardware as per electrician |

## Other

| | |
|---|---|
| 14 | Rosco Animation Motors #3510, 5 rpm, fixed speed |
| 12 | Rosco Animation Discs #1012, "Radial" |
| 2 | Rosco Animation Discs #1019, "Flicker" |
| 2 | Optec "Moon Flower" units with 200W HMI lamp fitted with: |
| 2 | Optec "Moon Flower" units colorwheels, customized as per designer |
| 2 | Scene Machine 3-way EPM prisms |
| 2 | Scene Machine 5-way EPM prisms |
| 2 | Howard Eaton flicker wheels mounted on: |
| 2 | Lobsterscope motors, 30rpm, fixed speed |
| 2 | Tubular ripple machines, 2kW |
| 1 | Great American Beamer #6010 with: |
| 1 | Solo Power Supply with joystick |
| 1 | Joystick |
| | 5-wire Beamer head cable |
| | Cable as per electrician |
| 4 | Muffin fans with mounting brackets |

Color and template list under separate cover

*Equipment Breakdown by Position*

Listing equipment by position provides a variety of information that is useful for cross-checking equipment totals, verifying that all accessories have been itemized, and provides the electrician with a quick checklist. Equipment for large productions is often packed by location, that is, crate #4 is packed for all lighting fixtures for the No. 2 and No. 3 electrics. An equipment breakdown by position provides a quick list by which to pack the crates. Another example:

---

## NEW YORK CITY OPERA AT SARATOGA PERFORMING ARTS CENTER 1989

Equipment Breakdown by Position

### No. 2 Box Boom Right

| 11 | 6x16 1kW Lekos |
| 6 | 24" sidearms with 2 sliding tees |
| 11 | 6" Leko colorframes |
| 11 | 6" Leko top hats |
| 4 | Twofers |
| 11 | Safeties |
| 7 | 20-amp circuits required |

### No. 3 Box Boom Right

| 10 | 6x22 1kW Lekos |
| 5 | 24" sidearms with 2 sliding tees |
| 10 | 6" Leko colorframes |
| 10 | 6" Leko tophats |
| 4 | Twofers |
| 10 | Safeties |
| 6 | 20-amp circuits required |

### No. 1 Electric

| 4 | 6x12 1kW Lekos |
| 24 | 6" Ianiro 2kW Fresnels |
| 1 | Worklight, 750W quartz |
| 28 | 12" sidearms with singe sliding tee (must fit 2" pipe) |
| 4 | 6" Leko colorframes |
| 48 | 6" Ianiro 2kW Fresnel colorframes |
| 1 | 60' x 18" Xetex |
| 1 | 60' Light Bridge (provided by Saratoga Performing Arts Center) |
| 1 | Wire Rope Ladder (provided by New York City Opera) |
| 28 | 20-amp circuits required |

---

On major productions this list is provided by the electrician. On smaller shows, the lighting designer may be expected to provide this list. The list should be provided in a cable summary format as well.

Since there is an item listed in the cable breakdown "jumpers as necessary," there will be an additional list that itemizes the number of jumpers at each length required for the production (for example, a list of jumpers for one production might include fifty 5-foot jumpers, fifty 10-foot jumpers, thirty 25-foot jumpers and five 50-foot jumpers).

---

**New York City Opera at Saratoga Performing Arts Center 1989**

Cable breakdown by position

**Booth**

| 1 | 2 x 400' bundle |
|---|---|

**Balcony Rail**

| 16 | Permanent House Circuits |
|---|---|
| 5 | Twofers |
| 2 | 6 x 175' / 185' Bundles |
| 2 | 5 x 150' / 160' Bundles |
| 2 | 5 x 125' / 135' Bundles |

Pick-ups:

| 1 | 50' Multicable |
|---|---|
| 1 | Female Breakout |

Jumpers as necessary

**Cove**

| 40 | Permanent house circuits |
|---|---|
| 9 | Twofers |

Pick-ups:

| 2 | 50' Multicables |
|---|---|
| 2 | Female breakouts |

Jumpers as necessary

**Box Booms Left**

| 24 | Permanent house circuits |
|---|---|
| 8 | Twofers |

---

## Electrics Bids

As with renting any type of equipment for a period of time, the producers may be interested in obtaining rental bids from more than one lighting rental supplier. Depending on the location of the theater, there may or may not be multiple lighting suppliers in the vicinity who can handle the shop order. In some particular cases, having equipment trucked in from out of town or even out of state may be a feasible option.

Consult with your electrician to determine how long he estimates it would take to prepare and assemble the shop order as listed, then work back from that date to plan sufficient time to submit a shop order to all the desired rental shops, allow them time to prepare a bid, and time to award the shop order to the desired shop. As a courtesy, be sure to call the other rental shops back that are not awarded the shop order, so that they know they are free to rent the equipment to other productions.

Wherever the equipment is coming from, the designer and his electrician must make every effort to ensure that it is delivered to the theatre ready for speedy erection. Providing that the designer has done his planning homework, almost every part of the equipment can be preset by the supplier before it is delivered to the theatre. Pipes and booms can be prepared and marked up with all the clamps and feed cables in the right position, instruments, color, accessories can be packed or crated pipe by pipe so that everything that is required is immediately to hand. If a show is to tour for a long period it may be worthwhile to make up all the equipment so that the instruments are not even taken off the pipes or trusses. When moving the pipes are simply broken up into manageable lengths, dropped into crates and packed off to the next date.

## Planning the Tour

If the production is going on tour, one has to face some complications. Obviously it is unlikely that any two theatres will be the same. The designer must find out what facilities he is going to meet at each date and shape his plans accordingly. He may have to talk to his director about compromising on some of his effects at some of the less well-equipped theatres. If a compromise has to be made, the designer must remember that, no matter how fond he may be of any particular visual effect, the one thing that cannot be compromised is the lighting of the actors.

## Final Rehearsals

During the last few days before the production weekend, the designer must get to see as many rehearsals as he can. He knows that right up to the last minute the director may be making changes in his handling of the actors and he must be up to date on every development. The problem is that he will have had to finalize his equipment requirements long before the actors have finalized their performances. He will thus have to make sufficient allowance for any reasonable changes that may occur.

At the final rehearsals the designer will be able to make a note of the probable timing of his lighting cues and approximately how much time there will be between each cue. This will allow him to update his lighting synopsis into a lighting cue synopsis (Fig. 34). This is a list of all cues in the production, scene by scene, with each cue number, ideally stating the time to be taken with the cue, the effect to be achieved, and noting how long after one cue the electrician will have before the next. This cue synopsis will be used as a guide by the designer during the lighting rehearsal, and a copy should also be given to the stage manager and the board operator. The stage manager will have it for information and the board operator will need it so that throughout the lighting rehearsal he will know where he has got to in the show; he will know which cues are very close to each other and how long he has to prepare for the next sequence of changes.

When all is finally ready the designer can pack his bags for the first production weekend. Plots, plans, whisky, glucose and patience! If he takes his pajamas, he must remember he may not need them. (I cannot resist leaving these final sentences in from the 1970 edition. The patient reader will be amazed that it referred to: 1. the custom in England of serving cocktails at the production desk during the tech period in the theatre—not customary in the USA—and 2. the habit in the sixties of working all night, loading in, rigging and lighting. The advance of unions—or civilization—make all-nighters less common today. The reader will have his, or her, own more personal reasons for packing pajamas—or not.)

| CUE | TIME | WHEN | DESCRIPTION | PG. | V*L CUE | TIME |
|---|---|---|---|---|---|---|
| Q99 | 0.4 | 2nd verse | Tighten to 4 | 1.8.42 | Q99 | 6 |
| Q100 | 6 | End "He Has A Way" | Recover | 1.8.42 | Q100 | 6 |
| Q101 | 8 | Start "Moonlight Bright in Brighton" | Blue cyc | 1.8.44 | Q101 | 8 |
| Q101.5 | 4 | Trunk to C | | 1.8.44 | Q101.5 | 4 |
| Q102 | 4 | Move DC | | 1.8.44 | Q102 | 6 |
| Q103 | 2 | End "Moonlight Bright in Brighton" | Spread RC between 2 & 3 | 1.8.45 | Q103 | |
| Q104 | 4 | | Poster R, Lamp 1,8,9 | 1.8.45 | Q104 | 4 |
| Q104.5 | 0.4 | Start "Crazy Happy Tears" | Gobos out | 1.9.46 | | |
| Q105 | 5 | Charely & Libby x DC | Gobos R | 1.9.46 | Q105 | |
| | FOLLOW .7 | | | 1.9.46 | | |
| Q105.2 | 2 | | Add Posters SR | 1.9.46 | | |
| | FOLLOW .7 | | | 1.9.46 | | |
| Q105.3 | 2 | | Add Posters C | 1.9.46 | | |
| | FOLLOW .7 | | | 1.9.46 | | |
| Q105.4 | 2 | | Add Posters L | 1.9.46 | | |
| | FOLLOW .7 | | | 1.9.46 | | |
| Q105.5 | 1 | | Red+Lamp post downlights | 1.9.46 | Q105.5 | 5 |
| Q106 | 5 | Music break DC | DC Post & red b/l | 1.9.46 | Q106 | 5 |
| Q106.5 | 3 | Libby's Charleston solo | Close tight | 1.9.46 | Q106.5 | |
| Q107 | 5 | Charley & Libby dress | Close to dressing | 1.9.48 | Q107 | 5 |
| Q107.5 | 1 | Charley & Libby x DC with smocks | Isolate | 1.9.48 | Q107.5 | 1 |
| Q108 | 3 | Group leaves C | Build lamps & red | 1.9.48 | Q108 | 4 |
| Q109 | 0 | "Went to me folks" | Down to #4, red low key | 1.9.48 | Q109 | 0 |
| Q109.1 | 1 | "asked who died" | Restore | 1.9.48 | D109.1 | 1 |
| Q109.2 | 0 | "The undertaker told me" | Down to #4, red low key | 1.9.48 | D109.2 | 0 |
| Q109.3 | 1 | "Crazy Happy Tears" | Restore | 1.9.48 | Q109.3 | 1 |
| Q110 | 3 | Dance break | | 1.9.48 | Q110 | 3 |
| Q111 | 4 | | Passage of time | 1.9.49 | Q111 | 4 |
| Q112 | 0.4 | | V*L's out, F/S only | 1.9.49 | Q112 | 4 |
| Q115 | 4 | Boys entry | Return red | 1.9.49 | Q115 | 5 |
| Q116 | 3 | Boys UR march DL | Add DS V*L diag R | 1.9.49 | Q116 | 3 |
| Q117 | 0.4 | Boys UL march DR | Add V*L diag L | 1.9.49 | Q117 | 2 |

*34. Lighting cue synopsis—Busker Alley*

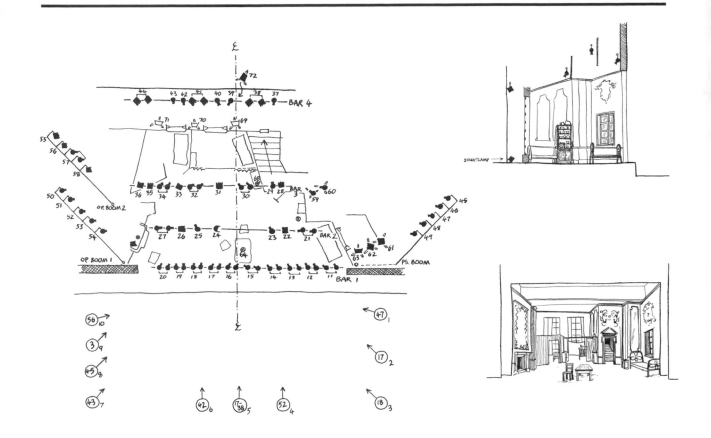

National Theatre of Great Britain, London
Director  Sir Laurence Olivier
Designer  Carmen Dillon
Lighting  Richard Pilbrow

CUE SYNOPSIS (ABRIDGED)

ACT I    Living room of the Boyle family in a Dublin tenement.
         Morning. Sunlight from back right bright clear.
Fire burning. Motive light.
         Joxer/Boyle scene. Close to table DC. Lose sunlight.
         Exterior colder foreboding.
         (Keep door area L)
         Will reading—recover sunlight

ACT II   Few days later. 6 P.M. Sunset from low back left.
         Light from window left cross table to fire.
         Warm afternoon.
         Through scene slow fade to twilight.
         Table lamp lit and dresser lamp.
         Gas brackets lit

*Follow on* slow fade exterior to night.
Close to table/fire acting area.
Cheat in cool bed area DL for Johnny.
Streetlamp below back on (uplight onto ceiling to
create strange false dimension).
*Follow on* cheat up interior acting area for "party."
Start fade to cool funeral—emphasize door left.
X-fade to cold reality—Johnny and the Moblizer.
Very gaunt skeletal—emphasis to fire right.

ACT III  2 P.M. November. Cold grim gaunt. Table/sofa door.
         Mrs. Boyle entry fade—close to centre.
         Furniture men. Fade 2. Very shadowy. X-light window.
         Johnny taken. Lose sunlight to cold silhouette.
         Clock strikes.
         X-fade to very low sunset from left.
         Mrs. B. exit. X-fade to night.
         Joxer and Boyle just seen at table.
         Fade to very low level bed left to table.
         Room dark, stark, empty.

**by Sean O'Casey**

| Unit | Position Type | Instrument | Function | Color (Cinemoid) |
|---|---|---|---|---|
| 1 | FOH Sides | 2 patt 264 | X light DS | 47 |
| 2 | FOH High side | 6 patt 264 * | Acting areas DS | 17 |
| 3 | FOH High side | 2 patt 264 | Night wash DS left | 18 |
| 4 | FOH Front | 3 patt 264 * | Warm frontlight | 52 |
| 5 | FOH Front | 3 patt 264 * | Cool frontlight | 17-38 |
| 6 | FOH Front | 2 patt 264 | Twilight wash DS | 42 |
| 7 | FOH High side | 2 patt 264 | Night wash DS right | 43 |
| 8 | FOH High side | 3 patt 264 * | Acting area | 45 |
| 9 | FOH High side | 5 patt 264 * | Acting area | 3 |
| 10 | FOH Sides | 2 patt 264 | X light DS | 56 |
| 11 | ELECTRIC 1 | 2 patt 23 | Acting area | 67 |
| 12 | | 2 patt 23 | Acting area | 3 |
| 13 | | 2 patt 23 | Acting area | 52 |
| 14 | | 2 patt 23 | Acting area | 67 |
| 15 | | 2 patt 23 | Acting area | 3 |
| 16 | | 2 patt 23 | Acting area | 17 |
| 17 | | 2 patt 23 | Acting area | 50 |
| 18 | | 2 patt 23 | Acting area | 17 |
| 19 | | 2 patt 23 | Acting area | 50 |
| 20 | | 2 patt 23 | Acting area | 3 |
| 21 | ELECTRIC 2 | 2 patt 264 | Night backlight DS | 18 |
| 22 | | patt 223 | Lamplight C | 4 |
| 23 | | patt 264 | Cool US | 17 |
| 24 | | beamlight | Sun X to bed DL | 50 |
| 25 | | patt 264 | Warm fire to chair | 9 |
| 26 | | patt 223 | Lamplight C | 4 |
| 27 | | 2 patt 264 | Night backlight DS | 18 |
| 28 | ELECTRIC 3 | patt 223 | Hall & stairs shadow | 27-47 |
| 29 | | patt 23 | Stairs | 60 |
| 30 | | 2 patt 23 | Acting area US | 17 |
| 31 | | patt 223 | Acting area US | 56 |
| 32 | | 2 patt 23 | Lamp on dresser | 2 |
| 33 | | patt 223 | Night US | 18 |
| 34 | | 2 patt 23 | Acting area US | 67 |
| 35 | | patt 223 | Acting area US | 55 |
| 36 | | patt 223 | Bed alcove UR (shadow fill) | 38 |

| Unit | Position Type | Instrument | Function | Color (Cinemoid) |
|---|---|---|---|---|
| 37 | ELECTRIC 4 | patt 264 | Backlight stairs | 17 |
| 38 | | 2 patt 243 | Sunset to windows L & R | 47 |
| 39 | | patt 264 | Moon to windows L | 40 |
| 40 | | patt 264 | Cool sun to windows L | 17 |
| 41 | | 2 patt 243/2kW | Sun to windows L | 50 |
| 42 | | patt 264 | Moon to windows R | 40 |
| 43 | | patt 264 | Cool sun to windows R | 17 |
| 44 | | 2 patt 243/2kW | Sun to windows R | 50 |
| 45 | BOOM L | patt 264 | X light DS cool | 67 |
| 46 | | patt 264 | X light DS lamplight | 3 |
| 47 | | patt 264 | X light DS night | 18 |
| 48 | | patt 264 | X light DS fill/shadow | 55 |
| 49 | | patt 264 | X light DS sunset | 47 |
| 50 | BOOM R1 | patt 264 | X light DS cool | 17 |
| 51 | | patt 264 | X light DS lamplight | 2 |
| 52 | | patt 264 | X light DS night | 43 |
| 53 | | patt 264 | X light DS fill/shadow | 56 |
| 54 | | patt 264 | X light DS firelight | 4-B 11 |
| 55 | BOOM R2 | patt 243 | X light US night | 18 |
| 56 | | patt 243 | X light US sun | 50 |
| 57 | | 2 patt 23 | X light US lamplight | 3 |
| 58 | | patt 223 | Bed alcove UR | 9-56 |
| 59 | STAGE L | patt 264/stand | X stairs | 17 |
| 60 | | patt 264/stand | X stairs | 47-60 |
| 61 | | patt 243/stand | Through DL window sunset | 53-56 |
| 62 | | patt 243/stand | Through DL window cool | 60 |
| 63 | | patt 49/stand | DL window backing | 60 |
| 64 | ONSTAGE | practical | Table lamp | |
| 65 | | patt 123 | Firelight | 4-B 11 |
| 66 | | practical | Fire | |
| 67 | | practical | Votive lamp | |
| 68 | | practical | Dresser lamp | |
| 69 | BACKSTAGE | patt 49 | Backcloth | 18 |
| 70 | | patt 49 | Backcloth | 60 |
| 71 | | patt 49 | Backcloth | 18 |
| 72 | | patt 223 | Streetlamp shadow on ceiling | 17-50 |

\* = On separate circuits          B = broken color

# Chapter Four

# Procedure: Production

## The Load-In/Get-In and Hang/Fit-Up

The day of the load-in arrives. All the weeks of theoretical work are over and theory has to be turned into reality .

In the professional theatre the time taken between the closing of one show and the opening of another has to be kept to a minimum. Every night the theatre is "dark" an audience is lost. This can mean that the fitting up of scenery and lighting may go on around the clock, day and night, until complete. With the high cost of crew overtime, a well-planned production will try to work to a more rational timetable, but in any event speed and efficiency are essential. The crew must have reasonable breaks for rest and meals, whether or not such breaks are mandated by any union involved.

Since the lighting always has to be done after everything else, the lighting designer has to become used to working at any hour. All too often he will find himself focusing his lamps at the end of a long day, even perhaps at four o'clock in the morning. After hours on his feet, he may have to start lighting the production, beginning the really creative work, in a dirty, hungry and exhausted state. The wise designer will ensure some refreshment for himself and his crew, but ideally he will try to see that a program is arranged that avoids the need for this manic effort.

*35. The fit-up*

There is, however, one advantage in having to light late at night or in the small hours. At this time most other people have gone home. If one of the problems the designer has to face is fatigue, the other is interruption. Only on one show in twenty will he be able to get on with his job quietly and without interference.

All too often the scenery takes longer to put up than anticipated, or something else will have gone wrong. The designer, first focusing and then doing the actual lighting, will be constantly hindered. The electrician's ladder will be used by someone else; a painter will be working in the very place the designer needs to reach; he starts focusing as an electric saw merrily shatters the eardrums. A special piece of scenery may need to be flown in to have a lamp focused on it—but all the flymen have broken for a visit to the nearest bar. Eventually, with the laborious job of focusing finished, he starts lighting. He calls for darkness; a horde of people will produce imperative reasons why they must have some work light. At last, he begins—and with a sickening crash some zealous stage hand, "tidying up," crashes a flat into a lovingly focused boom—and so on. I repeat, there are many advantages to doing the lighting when everybody else has gone home!

There is, of course, a better solution: a well-planned accurate timetable, ably supervised by a team who work well together and who help each other—stage manager, carpenters, electricians, scene and lighting designers.

For the purpose of this chapter we shall assume that we are working on a production in a theatre like those in the West End of London or New York's Broadway, where little or no permanent equipment is installed. In other words, we must take all the equipment into the theatre and rig it according to our plan before we start lighting.

*Stage Lighting Design*

During the load-in and fit-up, the designer, if he is working with a good electrician, will have little to worry about. But he should know what is going on and, since on a very small production he may be acting as his own electrician, he should know how to do the work himself.

As we discussed in the last chapter, the major part of the preparation of equipment should have been done before it arrives at the theatre. The only thing now left to be done is to take the equipment in and to rig it speedily.

It is important to bring the scenery and lighting into the theatre in a logical manner and to place it where it will be most convenient to hand when wanted. A large part of the lighting equipment will be hung over the stage. It is therefore usually possible to hang it out of the way before the carpenters start on the scenery.

If the production uses a false floor with a revolve or sliding wagons, it is convenient to lay the floor first. Next, the flown lighting should be hung while the engineers are rigging any mechanism under the stage; then the sets should be built and the side lighting rigged. Finally, the set should be dressed with props and portable lighting equipment placed on stage. Any lighting equipment in the auditorium can be rigged either when the floor is being laid or as the scenery is erected—in other words, the whole fit-up is planned as a "leapfrog" process (Fig. 35).

The first step is to measure out the set accurately on the stage. Obviously in a well-run theatre there will be plans and sections of the stage showing the exact position of all the hanging lines. From this the designer will have worked out which set of lines or which counterweight pipe is to be used for each lighting pipe. It is always worth checking the accuracy of positioning of these before actually starting. It is ridiculous to have to move a lighting pipe after it is flown. The master carpenter will be asked for the first pipe wanted and the flyman will fly it in. The designer should have told him the number of instruments that he is going to hang on it. If he has not, he should give him an indication of the weight he can expect, so he can begin to load the counterweights.

In collaboration with the carpenter he will decide in what order the hanging should be done. Perhaps the electrical work could start downstage with the carpenter's work at the back or vice versa. In order to work as quickly as possible, the pipe can be first laid out on trestles, the instruments hung from the pipes, cables connected and neatly strapped along the pipe's length.

Before the pipe is flown out each instrument should be carefully checked for the following :

1. The instrument has a lamp and is working correctly.

2. Any shutters, colors, and accessories are fitted and working easily and correctly.

3. The clamp holding the instrument to the pipe is fitted solid and tight.

4. The safety chain and feed cable are fitted with sufficient slackness to allow movement of the instrument in any direction.

*36. Erecting the scenery*

*37. Almost ready*

*38. Focusing*

5. The offstage ends of all feed cables have been tested through and clearly marked with the circuit number.

6. Nuts or locking handles are firm and correctly tightened. Much time is wasted on focusing if some enthusiast has so tightened the locking nuts that the instrument is immovable.

I find that it saves time later to "rough set" each instrument—pointing it in the direction you expect it to go. This is particularly important on a very tightly packed pipe, since it allows you to check that each instrument is sufficiently clear of its neighbor. If the equipment has been correctly prepared in the shop, it will only take a matter of minutes to assemble and prepare each pipe; each instrument can then be quickly checked and rough set and each feed checked before the pipe is flown out. There is nothing more frustrating than being held up in the middle of focusing by an electrician perched twenty-four feet up a ladder trying to find a fault in a circuit, clear a jammed shutter, or loosen an instrument that has been tightened as solid as the Rock of Gibraltar. Three minutes' work and foresight on the ground can save half an hour on the top of a ladder.

Once all the overhead equipment is flown out of the way—well out of the way, to clear any scenery being hung—the stage crew can take priority on the stage (Fig. 36). The electrics staff can probably split into groups (if there are more than two, that is) and work elsewhere. One pair of crew members can probably begin to rig any extra equipment in the auditorium; one pair can begin to make ready any sidelighting equipment such as booms (tormentors) or ladders, and one pair can start to plug up the overhead flown equipment, connecting it to the dimmers.

In the commercial theatre in the United States all the dimmers will also be installed afresh for each show. Setting these up is a big task, and all cables have to be fed from the boards to each instrument. In Europe it is more common for the theatre to have a permanent control system installed. This will be wired out to sockets around the theatre, thus reducing the lengths of temporary wiring needed.

When the erection of the scenery is almost complete (Fig. 37) the electrics crew can rig the sidelighting equipment and any lights or electrical effects actually fitted on the scenery, such as practical lamps, and so on. Then every circuit should be tested individually. When all is working the designer is ready to start.

### Focusing (Fig. 38)

Accurate focusing is the key to successful lighting. Each instrument has to be directed with great care to do its chosen job, and this has to be done quickly. Every minute saved now becomes valuable rehearsal time later.

Obviously the easiest show to focus is the one on which the instruments are all in easy reach, the stage floor is flat and uncluttered and there is a permanent set on which to focus. If the instruments are high out of reach,

*Stage Lighting Design*

another way of getting to them must be devised. A way of getting a man up to a high bar is to pull him up in a bosun's chair (Fig. 39). At its simplest this is a seat like a child's swing hung from the grid by two or more hemp lines. Under the supervision of a senior flyman, the electrician is lifted alongside the bar and, by taking up or letting out the appropriate lines, he can be moved across the stage. This is obviously a dangerous operation and it must be well supervised. While a man is aloft, the stage should be in silence and one man alone must give the orders. At all times, at least two ropes must take the weight and these ropes must be in first-class condition. (I shall never forget trying to catch my friend and colleague Robert Ornbo when he fell thirty feet in a bosun's chair because of a broken line. The flyman had allowed the second line to go completely slack. By a miracle his fall was broken and he survived uninjured, but, as in all theatre work, it was a never-to-be-forgotten reminder of the need for care and discipline.)

There are several variations on the bosun's chair. A focus track (Fig. 40) provides a movable cradle suspended from a track flown alongside the lighting pipe. If a very high bar has a lot of instruments on it, it may be well worth hanging alongside it such a focus track or a temporary scaffolding bridge along which the electrician can work. If the stage floor is not level, but obstructed by ramps, platforms or rostra, it can present a further hazard to the conventional ladder, although a tallescope or Genie air lift (Fig. 41) with adjustable legs will cope with reasonable angles or differences of level.

Whenever a man is working on an air lift, ladder, tallescope, scaffolding tower or suspended cradle, all must be aware of the dangers. Too many accidents happen too often. If the device is intended for use with outriggers, use them. If a man is high on an A-frame, there must be sufficient ladder crew to hold him. If an instrument is just out of reach, stop and move closer

*left: 39. Bosun's chair*

*middle: 40. Focus track*

*right: 41. Air lift*

rather than take unnecessary risks. The number of serious accidents that occur in even the most professionally run theatres should reinforce the constant need for vigilance and discipline.

A complication arises with a multiscene show. An instrument may be used for a different purpose in each scene. Some may be used only in one scene, some only in another. Obviously one doesn't want to have to change the set every time there is a move from one instrument to another. The designer will have to work out which instruments can be focused in one set, where focusing by calculation will do for another, and which instruments must be focused specially onto a certain set—or piece of it—when it is in position.

It is important to realize how long the focusing is going to take. An average show might take two minutes for each unit. If access is good and the focusing straightforward, this should be reduced to one and a half minutes or less. Most shows will have a complication somewhere. For every pipe on which you can rattle along at great speed, there will be an awkward lamp that is just out of reach.

With a big show and a tight schedule it may be possible, if hardly desirable, to focus with several teams at once. Hopefully, with your assistant helping, several crew teams can work concurrently, one team upstage and one downstage, for example, or one stage left and the other stage right.

Much credit for the speed at which the job can be done will, of course, go to the electrician doing the work. Here should be true teamwork: the designer on stage, quite clear about the function of each instrument; the electrician at the top of the ladder, his equipment prepared, the appropriate tools to hand, his ladder crew holding him firmly and ready to move him at his orders, his board operator prepared to bring in the next channel immediately when it is required.

The lighting designer or assistant must have direct talk-back communication with the control board when calling for circuits. The less shouting the better. Even better will be a hand-held rigger's control, which gives direct onstage access to each channel.

While focusing an instrument I prefer to use hand signals to indicate my detailed requirements. When the first channel is called for and the working lights are extinguished, I stand on the spot where I wish the beam to fall. So that I will not be blinded, I stand with my back to the instrument and by signals show the electrician where to set it, until the centre of the beam is on the back of my head (Fig. 42). When set, a thumbs-up signal will tell him to tighten the locking nuts so the unit is fixed solid. Further signals can indicate a widening or narrowing of focus or movement of shutters until the beam is exactly adjusted. The whole process is carried out in silence.

As the designer focuses he is rapidly reconciling the actual effect of the light, which he is seeing for the first time, with the image of it he has carried in his head through the planning stages. Now he can begin to tell if it will contribute to the overall effect he imagined. Has he chosen the right instrument;

*42. The focus position*

*Stage Lighting Design*

is it the right color and at the right angle? He must calculate how it will fit with other settings and combine with other lights. Quite possibly he will have to modify or alter slightly his original intention as he goes along to meet some unforeseen eventuality.

He must remember all the various uses to which the instrument will be put. While each will normally be set head high, there are also sitting or even lying-down positions to be remembered. Usually each spot has to be set so that it blends unobtrusively with its neighbor. For this the edges have to be softly focused and the beam has to be large enough to provide an overlap. In some places the beam of the spot will fall upon part of the set. Unless the designer deliberately intends to preserve the resultant hard edge of light, it will be best to soften it. The designer has to remember that some instruments, for example the Fresnel or focus lantern, become less bright the wider the beam is spread.

Lamps depicting sunlight pouring through a window not only have to look right, they have to light an actor standing in a certain position in a certain scene. The designer must also ensure that any mirrors, panes of glass or pictures with glass in them are not casting unpleasant reflections into the audience; also that any instruments offstage are not revealed by reflection. Lights on backings or lamps offstage must not cast unwelcome shadows of actors who might be waiting to make entrances or cause hotspots on them as they walk onto the stage.

Next comes the setting of the front-of-house instruments (Fig. 43). The designer must be quite sure how high or how far upstage he wants them to be set—particularly those with beams coming straight onto the stage from the front of the balcony. In order to avoid shadows on the back wall, he will probably want to set these lamps fairly low but he must be careful that they light actors sufficiently far upstage. If the FOH instruments are set so low that they only light the very front edge of the stage, the area upstage will only be lit from the spotbar overhead and, without fill light, may appear to be too toplit; the actors' eyes will disappear in shadow and faces will look distorted.

Sidelighting from the front of house must be carefully judged (Fig. 44). In a multiscene production some lamps may need to be cut off at different depths of the stage for different scenes. As each lamp is set, the designer

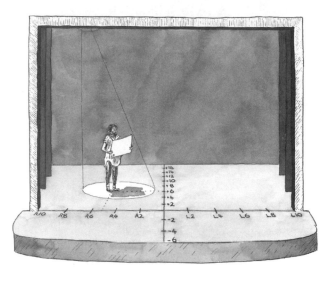

*left: 44. Focusing box booms*

*right: 45. Plotting focus*

should double-check that no spill or ghost light is coming from it. Unwanted glows on the proscenium or a border or box front must be avoided. An incorrectly focused profile spot may send a ring of spill light onto an adjacent backcloth, or a faulty instrument may send an irritating leak of light almost anywhere. If this is not corrected while focusing, it may cause embarrassment at the lighting rehearsal while the designer tracks down the cause of that unwelcome spot of light.

l am continually surprised, even in a show using hundreds of spotlights, at how accurate one has to be with focusing. Even a few inches of error can show up later. Indeed, however carefully the focusing session is carried out, I find that after the first rehearsal one has to go back and readjust several instruments to secure the exact desired effect.

If the lighting is going to be used more than once, it is very important to record the exact position of each spotlight. In a long run, units may get knocked; in repertoire they will probably have to be reset continually. The only way to log the setting of an instrument is by the painstaking plotting of its position. Let us now consider a useful method of doing this.

The stage is measured off in two-foot squares and calibrated accordingly, upstage from the setting line and left and right of the center line (Fig. 45). This grid is shown on the layout plan and marked on the stage on the center line and the proscenium or plaster line. A resourceful designer or assistant will have tapes marked in two-foot increments, which can be laid out across the front of the stage and up the center line, thus avoiding the need to mark the stage.

On the focus schedule we will now be able to log the exact position of each instrument. If the first spot is aimed at position A, we will describe this as being set to +6R5.

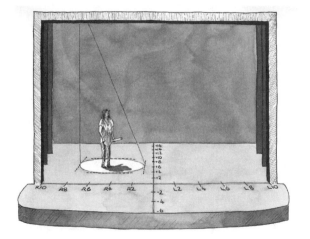

Position   B +4L5
        C -4L3
        D +5CL

| CHN | LOCA-TION | PLUG WITH | TYPE | FOCUS | COLOR & NOTES |
|---|---|---|---|---|---|
| 266 | 7 Elec-Top 1 | Window above Convent | 6x12 / 1kw | Chruch R · Sharp · L- · R- · DS- · US- | R37 |
| 267 | 7 Elec-Top 2 | L | 6x12 / 1kw | Church L Sharp · L-SR SL · R- · DS- · US- | R16 |
| 268 | 7 Elec-Top 3 | | 6x12 / 1kw | Chi Windows LC Sharp · 3:Palmer Hse Window · L- · R- · DS- Tight to us windows | B13 NC |
| 269 | 7 Elec-Top 4 | Windows Above Palmer | 6x12 / 1kw | Chi Windows C/LC Sharp SR SL · DS- Tight to window · US- | R13 |
| 270 | 7 Elec-Top 5 | Hse CS | 6x12 / 1kw | Chi Windows C/C Sharp SR SL · DS- Tight to window · US- | R16 |
| 271 | 7 Elec-Top 6 | | 6x12 / 1kw | Chi Windows C/RC Sharp Palmer Hse Window L SR SL · DS- Tight to window · US- | R13 |
| 272 | 7 Elec-Top 7 | Windows Above Reaming | 6x12 / 1kw | Chi Windows R1 - Sharp L-SR SL R- · DS- Tight to Windows · US- | R11 |
| 273 | 7 Elec-Top 8 | Hse SR | 6x12 / 1kw | Chi Windows R2 Sharp SR SL · DS- Tight to window · US- | R13 |
| 274 | 7 Elec-Top 9 | | 6x12 / 1kw | Chi Windows R3 Sharp R SL · DS- Tight to window · US- | R16 |

Windows Above Hse SR

*left: 46. Shutter cuts*

*right: 46a. Focus plot*

This will describe the center of the beam at head height. If there are no alterations to the beam shape, this indication of position may be sufficient, with a note as to how wide or narrow, soft or hard the focus should be. If the beam has to be shaped we need more detail (Fig. 46).

Let us take our first example. We are standing at A, described as +6R5. Next we describe the top of the beam, the bottom, the left, then the right:

| Unit No. | Position | Focus |
|---|---|---|
| 5 | +6R5 | R8/R1/+4/+8 soft |

If the beam is of a complex shape and cut at a diagonal, a small plan sketch may help to clarify it.

If the focus is related to any object, such as a wall, door or piece of furniture, this can obviously be more easily described. The description "Stand behind center of sofa/cut at left end" is probably quite sufficient. Any combination of grid numbers and description can be satisfactory.

While the designer is focusing, he or an assistant can note the settings (Fig. 46a). I usually prefer to plot the focus in detail after the show has settled down, when time is not at such a premium, and when the lighting has been finalized.

Although speed is essential, the electrician should always be allowed enough time to make sure each lamp is securely locked before moving on to the next. It can be somewhat irritating to find during later rehearsals that all the beams of light are slowly sinking toward the floor.

A word on focusing moving lights: these can be focused by the designer giving instructions to the control board from anywhere in the theatre at any time. But in fact it's an incredibly time-consuming process to focus all the many different positions that may be used throughout a production. It's prudent to carry out preset or target focusing before lighting proper commences. Unlike a fixed-focus instrument, a moving light has many different parameters to record; pan, tilt, color, perhaps zoom, edge, gobo and sometimes more. All these take time—and much thought. Establishing key target positions for moving lights before lighting begins will save hours of fiddling later. Most moving lights require a separate board operator. Many of these specialist operators are highly skilled and, once shown the principles of moving-light usage in the show, will be able to lay-in preset focuses. A walker can stand in at each prefocus point while the operator sets each unit to it. Hopefully with the advance of computer technology, control of moving lights will improve and speed up the presently tiresome process. A glimpse of such a possibility is the Wybron Autopilot. This is an infrared, ultrasound device that allows a moving light to track a tiny transmitter that may be attached to an actor. While this might provide an exciting unmanned follow spot capability, a more mundane use might be for speedily setting prefocuses of many moving lights.

When all focusing is complete two things remain to be checked. First, the practical fittings: the designer should see that each practical is working and that the lamp being used in it is sufficiently bright. If it's not connected to a dimmer that is suitable for its small wattage, he should ensure that it is not in fact too bright. Second, all the lights that are placed offstage should be turned on to see that the set is "light tight," in other words, that no light is leaking through holes or gaps in the scenery or glowing through the scenery itself. If there are any problems, the scene designer or master carpenter should be able to help solve them.

### The Lighting Rehearsal (Fig. 47)

Should there be a lighting rehearsal at all? The traditional way of lighting was to do it with a set on the stage and stage management to represent the actors, while the designer with the director and the scene designer sat in the empty auditorium and called up lighting states until all were satisfied. With the use of memory controls this practice has changed. Once focusing is complete, the actors can begin to work onstage, getting accustomed to the scenery and theatre, while the lighting designer lays in his lighting—at least in broad strokes—around them. Certainly I much prefer to work this way. Instead of hours spent with an empty stage, trying to imagine it full of actors, one has the whole cast acting as their own stand-ins. The designer must work quickly, for the director won't want to wait around for the lighting. But these first hours onstage for the performers, getting used to the

*47. Lighting rehearsal*

*48. Lighting desk*

*Stage Lighting Design*

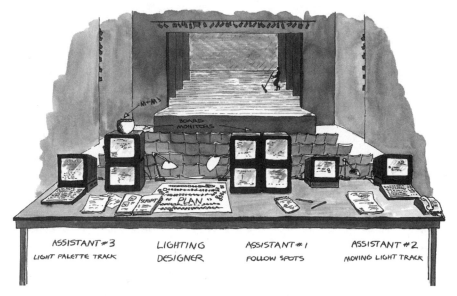

ASSISTANT #3 | LIGHTING | ASSISTANT #1 | ASSISTANT #2
LIGHT PALETTE TRACK | DESIGNER | FOLLOW SPOTS | MOVING LIGHT TRACK

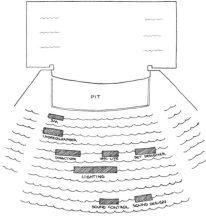

*left: 49. Big lighting desk*
*above: 50. Desk proliferation*

scenery and practicing movements, entrances and exits, will usually allow plenty of time, providing the designer has done his homework and knows what he is about. The ability to instantaneously record any lighting state frees the designer to take a "snapshot" of perhaps several variations of any moment. After this initial rough-in of the design with the cast, a detailed tidying-up session can allow the necessary detailed decisions to be made and the fine-tuning to be carried out.

But let's begin in the conventional way with the lighting rehearsal. All is focused, the first set is onstage and we're ready to begin lighting. The designer will have equipped himself with a desk from which to work, which he will place either in the orchestra stalls or first circle, where he has an ideal view of the stage (Fig. 48). I prefer doing the initial lighting from an orchestra position, but wherever the designer chooses, he should remember that in later rehearsals he must move around the theatre and check that his lighting is correct from every part of the house. The desk should be large enough to take his layout plan, plots, script and other amenities such as cups of coffee, bottles of whisky, etc. (Alcoholic refreshment is frowned upon at the American production desk!) If they don't have desks of their own, it is also hospitable to provide a little extra space for the stage manager or director to use when necessary (Fig. 49). (It's amusing to ruminate upon the increase of complexity of the production desk set-ups to be found in modern theatre. For epic musicals like *Miss Saigon* and *Show Boat* in New York, no less than eleven desks were distributed across the orchestra, many laden with computers, control desks, telephones, modems, intercoms, P.A. systems—and refreshment [Fig. 50].)

Most important, however, are the facilities for communicating with the crew who are actually going to operate the lighting. The lighting process requires thought and concentration, and these qualities are not ideally mixed with the need to bellow instructions. As already mentioned, the best communication is some form of talk-back. Modern lighting control desks are portable and can often be operated from anywhere in the theatre. Either the main control or a portable section of it may be available and can be set up next to the lighting designer's desk. This is an ideal situation, where the designer can sit right next to his operator and communicate directly with him as the lighting is developed. Ideally the operator is a partner in the design process. That way the operator can share in the creative work and fully understand the intentions of the designer. Particularly with moving lights, such a partnership with the operator can yield real results.

If the production is a complex one, the designer will have to be in touch with other parts of the theatre—the lighting bridges, follow-spot operators, etc. It will also be useful for the designer to be in talk-back contact with the stage manager (although this link should be used sparingly during rehearsals, when the stage manager may be involved in giving other vital instructions).

Finally, of course, the designer has to be able to see at his desk, so shaded lights must be provided. Lights must be on dimmers so that their brightness can be adjusted to match that of the stage.

Now the designer is at his desk, the operator will be ready at the control board, equipped with pencil and paper to take notes; and the stage manager or assistants will be on stage, armed with the prompt script in case any information about actors' movement is needed.

A word about time. Lighting rehearsals are, by tradition, rather prolonged affairs. They can be very absorbing to the designer and director and, if correctly conducted, a busy time for the board operator. It is important that everyone in the theatre knows what is going on and what is going to happen next. If sets have to be changed, the stage management should be warned well in advance of when the designer is going to be ready. The designer must also remember that everyone working in the theatre is human; everyone needs to eat, sleep and take occasional breaks; bars close and last trains sometimes run on time. It is surprising how much more can be achieved if problems of this nature are taken into account, and a break at the right time can often mean that much better work is done afterward. Of course in many situations union requirements will dictate working hours, and following these rules precisely should create a collaborative working atmosphere.

It is usually best to start from a blackout, with all the work lights turned out, any doors to the outside closed, all lights in the auditorium off. In other words, start with a blank slate. A note of warning here. It is wise to turn on any emergency lights or exit lights that will have to be kept on during a performance. Similarly, if the show has an orchestra, the pit lights should be turned on before lighting starts, otherwise some quite unexpected and probably unpleasant light spill may come as a surprise later.

Once darkness has been achieved, it is a good idea to check quickly through one channel at a time. This is the final assessment that everything is working, and it allows the designer to see for the first time, from the auditorium, the effect that each spotlight is going to give. He must make a note of anything that looks like a possible problem: any too-obtrusive color, any spill light that escaped his attention, any hard edge of light where it is not wanted. Then he should tell the board operator that he is going to start and call for the first state of lighting according to the cue synopsis. Presumably, he is starting from the beginning of the show, and he must explain to the board operator exactly how it will start. He may want to take the curtain up on a dark stage and then fade in the lights; or the curtain may rise on a scene with preset lighting. We may have an open stage with the set seen in a lighting preset while the houselights are on and as the audience arrives. Whichever is the case, the designer will start by plotting the first state of light.

There are, of course, as many different ways of lighting a show as there are different results, so the following can only be an expression of my own personal preferences.

We would begin by calling for those lights that represent the key light of the scene. Thus, taking the simple example in Chapter 2 (the interior realistic set), we would first call for the exterior lighting, the sunlight coming through the window and the light representing skylight illuminating the backing. These circuits have to be brought up to the intensity at which they are likely to be used. If we are starting the play with all the lights coming up to a bright level in which the actors can perform, we should probably set the key light to a level that appears very bright when seen on its own, remembering that when all the other lighting in the room is added it will probably look correctly in balance. If the play starts with a more atmospheric opening, to enhance the pictorial effect we may keep the lighting within the set to a lower level. This will probably allow us to create a more dramatic visual picture; then, as soon as the curtain has risen, we can slowly creep up the acting-area lighting until the level is sufficient for the action of the play. With our example, supposing the play is a bright cheerful comedy, it is likely that the sunshine will be used at full; but at this initial stage it is perhaps best to set it to 80 percent on the dimmer so there is some extra brightness in reserve.

When the exterior is balanced for the best visual effect, we can begin to build the secondary lighting. We will bring up each circuit on the acting-areas, all the while attempting to keep the correct balance, using the key light through the window and trying to make the effect of the acting area spots carry through the feeling of daylight coming from that side of the room. As soon as we feel we have roughed in a balance of lighting over the stage, one of the stage managers can walk through each actor's moves in the scene. We may discover that the whole thing is a little too dim for the play at this point and we will have to make the acting-area slightly brighter. In this case it can be done without undue alarm, because the backing and sunlight can also be brightened to avoid losing the pictorial balance.

Any soft light or fill light from FOH instruments or perhaps footlights should then be added. Too much will tend to flatten out the stage picture, indeed too much light from below may cause distracting shadows over the upper part of the set: too little will mean the desired color-toning effect is not achieved.

Once this is done, the stage manager can again cover all those parts of the stage that the actors use. We should then find that, wherever they are, they are correctly, attractively and appropriately lit, and that even from the farthest part of the auditorium they can be seen clearly. As they walk toward the window they come more obviously into the direct light of the sun; and the side of the face away from the sunlight will look as if it is lit from the natural reflection in the room. As they move around the stage there should be no feeling that they are going from spotlight to spotlight; indeed, all the beams should merge together, creating the three-dimensional feeling of real space and real air that we have been attempting to achieve.

If there are parts of the stage that are not used, we need not be afraid to leave them underlit, provided that this does not detract from the atmosphere of the scene. Remember that shadow is as much a part of interest in lighting as is light itself (provided we do not have actors walking through quite unnatural black spots). In the less-important parts of the stage a shadow can give depth to the scene, and these "natural" areas of shadow may be made even more interesting by the subtle addition of a complementary or contrasted color tone. We must ensure that all the colors used blend together suitably and that there are no sudden or unnatural changes. If there are, it may be a question of adjusting the intensity of the offending lamp, or even of changing the color we are using.

If any part of the stage is very bright—a light fitting or a bright sky-backing, for instance—it may be that an actor standing in front of it will appear underlit by contrast. It may be possible to cure an underlit point on the stage by reducing the brightness elsewhere.

Most lighting control is computerized, and each lighting state is stored in the computer's memory. With a manual board, as each circuit was called for, we had to make a note, so that as the picture on the stage built up there was a record of the circuits used and their intensity. The most convenient low-tech way of doing this was to have a pad of cue sheets, (Fig. 51) each of which had a list of all the numbers of the lighting channels. As each was called, note was made against it in pencil of the level to which it was brought. It's tremendously helpful, while looking at the stage and considering the picture that I have created, to be able to see at the same time the channels in use and their levels (it is almost like seeing an X-ray of a body). This can show up a discrepancy—some instrument that has been left on unnecessarily or one that is too bright or too dim—when a look at the stage will merely indicate that something is not quite right. A control system that has a VDU (visual display unit) showing channels and their levels obviously provides this information instantly.

When everything is to the designer's satisfaction, the opening light is complete. The electrician should then be told to "plot" it. Of course memory

```
  1   2   3   4   5   6   7   8   9  10  11  12  13  14  15  16  17  18  19  20
  .   .   .   .   .   .   .   .   .   .   .   .   .   .  \0  \0   .   .   .   .

 21  22  23  24  25  26  27  28  29  30  31  32  33  34  35  36  37  38  39  40
  .   .   .   .   .   .   .   .   .   .   .   .   .   .   .   .   .   .   .   .

 41  42  43  44  45  46  47  48  49  50  51  52  53  54  55  56  57  58  59  60
  .   .   .  /30 /30 /30  .   .  /30  .   .   .   .   .   .   .   .   .  /50 /60

 61  62  63  64  65  66  67  68  69  70  71  72  73  74  75  76  77  78  79  80
  .   .   .   .   .   .   .   .   .   .   .   .   .   .   .   .   .   .   .   .

 81  82  83  84  85  86  87  88  89  90  91  92  93  94  95  96  97  98  99 100
  .   .   .  /70  50   .   .   .   .   .   .  \0   .   .   .   .   .   .   .   .
```

```
101   2   3   4   5   6   7   8   9  10  11  12  13  14  15  16  17  18  19 120
  .   .   .   .   .   .   .   .   .   .   .   .   .   .   .   .   .   .   .   .

121  22  23  24  25  26  27  28  29  30  31  32  33  34  35  36  37  38  39 140
  .   .   .   .   .   .   .   .   . /50   .   .   .   .   .   .   .   .   .   .

141  42  43  44  45  46  47  48  49  50  51  52  53  54  55  56  57  58  59 160
  .   . \30   .   .   .   . /60   .   .   .   .   . /70   .   .   .   .   .   .

161  62  63  64  65  66  67  68  69  70  71  72  73  74  75  76  77  78  79 180
  .   .   .   .   .   .   .   .   .   .   .   .   .   .   .   .   .   .   .   .

181  82  83  84  85  86  87  88  89  90  91  92  93  94  95  96  97  98  99 200
  .   .   .   .   .   .   .   .   .   .   .   .   .   .   .   .   .   .   .   .
```

```
201   2   3   4   5   6   7   8   9  10  11  12  13  14  15  16  17  18  19 220
  .   .   .   .   .   .   .   .   .   .   .   .   .   .   .   .   .   .  FT.  .

221  22  23  24  25  26  27  28  29  30  31  32  33  34  35  36  37  38  39 240
  .   .   .   .   .   .   .   . /50   .   .   .   .   .   .   .   .   .   .   .

241  42  43  44  45  46  47  48  49  50  51  52  53  54  55  56  57  58  59 260
  .   .   .   .   .   .  40 /70   .  50   .   . 30 /50   .   .  40  40  40

 61  62  63  64  65  66  67  68  69  70  71  72  73  74  75  76  77  78  79 280
 40   .   .   .   .   .   .   .   .   .   .   .   .   .   .   .   .   .   .

281  82  83  84  85  86  87  88  89  90  91  92  93  94  95  96  97  98  99 300
  .   .   .   .   .   .   .   .   .   .   .   .  25  25  25   .   .   .
```

```
301   2   3   4   5   6   7   8   9  10  11  12  13  14  15  16  17  18  19 320
  .   .   .   .   .   .   .   .   .   .   .   .   .   .   .   .   .   .   .   .

321  22  23  24  25  26  27  28  29  30  31  32  33  34  35  36  37  38  39 340
  .   .   .   .   .   .   .   .   .   .   .   .   .   .   .   .   .   .  10   .

341  42  43  44  45  46  47  48  49  50  51  52  53  54  55  56  57  58  59 360
  .   .   .   .   .   .   .   .   .   .  20  20   .   .   .   .   .  10  10

361  62  63  64  65  66  67  68  69  70  71  72  73  74  75  76  77  78  79 380
 20  20   .   .   .   .   .   .   .   .   .   .   .   .   .   .   .   .   .

381  82  83  84  85  86  87  88  89  90  91  92  93  94  95  96  97  98  99 400
  .   .   .   .   .   .   .   .   .   .   .   .   .   .   .   .   .   .   .   .
```

```
401   2   3   4   5   6   7   8   9  10  11  12  13  14  15  16  17  18  19 420
  .   .   .   . /15   .   .   .   .   .   .   .   .   .   .   .   .   .   .   .

421  22  23  24  25  26  27  28  29  30  31  32  33  34  35  36  37  38  39 440
  .   .   .   .   .   .   .   .   .   .   .   .   .   .   .   .   .   .   .   .

441  42  43  44  45  46  47  48  49  50  51  52  53  54  55  56  57  58  59 460
  .   .   .   .   .   .   .   .   .   .   .   .   .   .   .   .   .   .   .   .

461  62  63  64  65  66  67  68  69  70  71  72  73  74  75  76  77  78  79 480
  .   .   .   .   .   .   .   .   .   .   .   .   .   .   .   .   .   .   .   .

  1  82  83  84  85  86  87  88  89  90  91  92  93  94  95  96  97  98  99 500
  .   .   .   .   .   .   .   .   .   1   .   .   .   .   .   .   .   .   .
```

*51. Cue sheet*

control systems make the tedious business of actually writing out the plot unnecessary. Now the electrician plots a cue by simply pressing a button to record it. This speeds up the whole process, but it also demands that the designer work faster than he used to in the olden days. In those distant days of manual control, during the time when the electrician was laboriously plotting, the designer could be double-checking what he had done so far and getting himself ready for the next cue. However, times have changed, and the advantages of instant recording and accurate reproduction are very well worth a little extra mental agility.

The electrician should be able to see from his synopsis how the cue is to be operated, its duration and the time between one cue and the next. The designer must make this clear anyway, and if rehearsal time is not too limited, he may want to go back and have the cue rehearsed several times to get the timing exactly established.

When the board operator is ready, the designer can continue with the next cue. First, he must tell the operator what he wants to achieve—that is, whether it is a fade, a build or a cross-fade and how long it should take—and then rebalance the lighting on the stage accordingly. It is at this point that some knowledge of the control system and how it operates may become desirable. A good electrician can probably perform almost any cue on a control board that he is used to, but there are some boards on which it may be difficult to achieve certain effects. The designer must have enough knowledge to be able to judge what is possible. It is obviously useless spending hours plotting a complicated series of cross-fades if they are beyond the ability of the operator or the capability of the machine. However, many cues that at first sight seem appallingly complicated on a manual board can, after a few days' practice, become quite simple. Memory systems obviously make the instant operation of almost any movement quite simple, but multipart cues and effects cues may still need the designer's help.

Lighting with a memory system brings another change to the lighting process. With a manual board each individual circuit is called for and brought up separately until a balanced picture is achieved. With a memory board it is just as easy to call up a memory of prerecorded circuits for use, so the cues can be created using blocks of lighting as well as individual circuits. This means, for example, that all the motivating light, all the light coming through our window stage left, which is perhaps seven channels, may be combined onto a single memory or "group." Each acting area may be recorded as a group. All the FOH lighting from, say, the left, might be a group, and the right side another. By intelligently grouping the lighting into usable blocks, very rapid changes may be easily accomplished. Once a state of light is roughed in using groups, one can always go to the individual circuit within a group to adjust it.

When working with groups of light rather than single channels, it becomes impractical to write down the movement of each circuit. Indeed, with memory systems generally one can go at such a speed as to make manual plotting impossible. Most memory systems allow a paper copy of the whole lighting plot to be printed out. Providing this printing is done regularly it will be a sufficient record. (Needless to say, a memory system—like any computer—can loose its memory. It must be backed up frequently to avoid disaster). A software program is available that allows the designer or assistant to plot the lighting straight into a Macintosh computer, directly emulating the operation of the lighting console. This provides the additional security of a totally independent journal of every detail of the lighting should the main board crash. More significantly to the designer, it gives him the complete lighting plot in a form that may be examined in many different ways. He can, for example, compare the state of one cue directly with another to see exactly which channels have moved and by how much. He can see how often a channel is used and at what levels. This ability to analyze the structure of lighting states is a valuable aid to the designer. It provides information management capabilities to the designer, a resource obviously the computer is well able to offer. It is hoped that such facility will increasingly be built into control boards of the future.

Pursuing this process, using individual channels or groups of light, the entire show is worked through, cue by cue, state of light by state of light.

During lighting it is much better if the director and the scenic designer sit alongside the lighting designer. They should comment freely and positively about what the lighting designer is doing. They should all have confidence in one another as a team, and the lighting designer should simply be putting into practice what they have all visualized. The director will naturally be interested in how well the actors can be seen, and the set designer will be biased toward thinking that the only priority is the look of his set on the stage. The lighting designer has to satisfy both their demands. Inevitably there will sometimes be conflict, and on many occasions he must attempt to reach a compromise. The creative designer is the one who can overcome a problem with a new solution that is more satisfying to every one.

The designer should always remember that a lighting rehearsal is only a rehearsal; it is a waste of time to spend hours and hours fiddling in tremendous detail, trying to achieve absolute perfection. This first session is much better thought of as a roughing-in process. The old days of the lighting rehearsal that went on hour after hour and day after day are best forgotten. The aim of the first session is to broadly achieve all the desired results; inevitably when the actors are seen on the stage, certain things will have to be altered.

Whether there is a proper lighting rehearsal or not depends upon the designer and his director. It also, of course, will often depend upon economics. Lighting through the first technical with the actors onstage is the method I prefer, but it will only succeed if the lighting design has been carefully considered in advance. If this has been done, and if the show has been carefully and well focused, the designer can go into that first rehearsal with actors and light with a good deal of confidence. Memory control systems allow the designer to improvise his lighting more freely and more creatively alongside the actors, but success will still stem from a carefully planned and prepared design.

Unfortunately, working with moving lights is not so simple at present. While time is saved by not having to focus moving lights by hand, the comparative crudity of moving-light control boards to date makes the programming process painfully slow. Preset focuses, the ability for one or more lights to "follow" another and off-line editing with a computer model all will hopefully develop, so as to allow the designer to once again "busk" his lighting "on the fly."

## Technical Rehearsals

Each production period will be planned in a different way, but if the play has complex scene changes, a formal technical rehearsal should be held before the dress rehearsal. The "tech" is a stopping rehearsal, held either with or without the actors, to practice the set changes and to try out the lighting and sound cues. It is valuable for the lighting designer, for it may be the first time that he will have had a chance to run through the lighting cues in rapid succession. After a long extended first lighting session he may have mistakenly lit a scene with too great a contrast to the one preceding or following it. While the stage crew and technicians are rehearsing their part, he will now have a chance to see the thing as a whole, going from scene to scene without pause. Now he can also see how the timing of changes works (allowing time for the possibly missing dialogue), and he can supervise any physical movement of instruments that has to be done on stage. Instruments may have to be repositioned or moved from scene to scene, and now is the moment to see that the assistant electricians know their job and can reposition them with the necessary degree of accuracy.

## The Dress Rehearsal (Fig. 52)

This will be the first time that the designer will see the whole thing come together: actors, setting, costume, lighting and sound. First, he must remember one vital point: this will also be the first time that the electrical staff have worked the show with the actors performing on the stage and with their cues coming at them in rapid succession, as they will during performance. While the actors may have been rehearsing for several weeks, the electrical staff will have only rehearsed once or twice before. The designer must be patient with any mistakes and defend them from the possible impatience of others. It may be hard for the director and producer or even the actors to appreciate that people with such vital roles as the board and spot operators are coming to the show afresh. They will have to be given time to rehearse, just as the actors have had time; the designer must ensure, on behalf of his operators, that the rehearsal is not so rushed that it sends them into a panic.

Follow-spot operators may have complex cues to learn. In a big musical an assistant might well be assigned to organize the follow-spot plot and instruct the operators.

*52. The dress rehearsal*

This will probably be the first time that the designer sees the lit actors in costume. During rehearsals before costumes are used, I usually find myself getting depressed. The stage looks rather dreary. But if all the homework has not been in vain, when the costumes come on the stage, everything suddenly fits into place: the whole thing begins to take on the expected degree of sparkle and brightness. Some things however, may still not be working. A lighting color may conflict with the delicate tones in a costume. Some scenes may look too bright with the actors in costume and some not bright enough. Adjustments will have to be made. The timing of cues will be seen for the first time, maybe a two-minute fade is a little too fast, or maybe a build at the beginning of the scene is a little too slow. All must be corrected. The designer must also ensure that the stage manager calls the cues in exactly the right place. Perhaps the moment a cue is given may have to be altered slightly to accommodate a new piece of business or different timing onstage. The director will probably want to go back and try various parts of the play again. On pre-memory switchboards it is sometimes difficult to go back two or three cues. The designer must resist any impatience and help the board operator find his place in the plot.

During dress rehearsals the lighting designer must go all over the theatre. He must see his lighting from the orchestra stalls and every other part of the house, ensuring that everything he means to be clearly visible is clearly visible from the farthest seat. Whenever he is in doubt, let him err on the side of visibility; rather overlight for the first few rows than underlight for all the rest.

During dress rehearsals and previews, lots of people will comment upon the lighting, some informed and some, perhaps, ill-informed. Lighting is a subject about which almost everybody can have an opinion. A designer should pay scrupulous attention to the comments of his colleagues in the team, the director, the set designer and so on. If he finds himself in disagreement with them, he may attempt to persuade them to his own point of view. If he fails with the director he must accommodate him, for the director is finally in charge, and his wishes have to be realized. Comments from other people may well be much less important. The designer must always remember his initial concept of the lighting. He must remember that this concept was produced as a result of collaboration with and understanding of his director's and set designer's intentions, and he must continually question his own fidelity to these intentions. But he must be understanding, flexible and accommodating about any changes introduced by his colleagues. The best of directors will want to try new ideas and will restage parts of a production even late in the process. A piece of theatre is never a static and final piece of work; it is alive and open to change. The designer must be continually aware of this and receptive to it, even if it means altering his own carefully considered plans. He must adapt to change and must at the same time apply his own standards of good lighting, seen always in the context of what the production needs and what the production is all about.

Indeed it must be said that for all the best-laid plans, some of the most exciting moments will come almost accidentally out of improvisation in rehearsal. Perhaps because of all that careful thought, true creativity will often flourish, and new ideas will supersede first thoughts in the cut and thrust of production. For many designers there are few moments like those spent behind the lighting desk. The play is onstage before you. The set and costumes are in place. Your director and the actors are developing their performances, and you are bringing the whole to life, adding the quality of the air the actors breathe, completing the world of the play around them.

A word about self-criticism. Nobody will know more about the lighting than you do. It is your job to make it as special as possible. No matter how tired you are, no matter how stressfull the circumstances may be, no matter how irritating your colleagues may be, great lighting is your responsibility—yours alone. Keep at every detail until it's as good as you can make it. Then do it better!

During the dress rehearsals the designer should not forget such practical details as the handling of the houselights, the lighting of the curtain before the show and in the interval, and the curtain calls. He should remember that the speed at which the house lights are dimmed will affect the impression the audience gets when the curtain rises. He should also remember the effects of a sudden change of light and the rules of contrast. The house curtain warmly lit before the performance will build (in the audience) a feeling of theatrical warmth and anticipation; and the color chosen can affect the coloring of the scene immediately following. All these details contribute to a smooth and efficiently run show, and thus add to the audience's enjoyment.

*53. Curtain up*

## The First Night (Fig. 53)

Before every performance the crew must check that every instrument is functioning, colored and focused correctly. This must be a routine that is followed nightly, and the designer must ensure that it is done.

When the curtain rises on the first night, the lighting designer's job is virtually over. Perhaps the most important thing he can do now is to keep calm. The performers will all be on edge, and so will the stage management and the electrical crew. If minor mistakes are made, it is always best to leave them; simply note the error and discuss it the following day. In the case of a major problem, for example if the working light or the house lights are left on when the curtain is taken up, then obviously something must be done. If the error is one that is really going to spoil the whole scene, the designer should act rapidly but calmly, telling the stage management or the operator exactly what is wrong in a clear and concise manner. Before doing so he should make quite sure that they are not engaged in any other cue at the time, never interrupting if there is a danger that by so doing he will upset the show even more. In the days of manual boards, some were difficult to work, especially when it came to correcting a mistake. Memory control makes the reproduction of lighting both more accurate and more reliable, so emergencies are a rarer occurrence. What can occur is that the board can crash—lose memory or function. This regrettably happens too frequently. As with any computer, it is essential to back up all the information on a floppy disk—and multiple copies will be a wise investment. Hopefully, control systems will improve in reliability; it's really absurd that high-price systems still fail too often.

*54. The control room*

Finally a last and pleasant duty. Your crew will have performed feats that only a short time before seemed impossible. The stage management will have got every split-second cue "on the button." Thank them.

### The Show Is On (Fig. 54)

After the first night, if the show embarks on a run or goes into repertoire, the designer must check that all his plots, plans and paperwork are up to date and that all the last-minute alterations have been included. He must make sure that copies of these are given to those people responsible for the standard of lighting throughout the run of the play. These will normally be the electrician and the stage manager. Both should be given copies of the up-to-date lighting layout plan, schedule and hook-up, a focus schedule and a cue plot. With this paperwork the staff on the production must double-check the lighting before each performance and correct any problems that occur.

It is useful when a production has been lit to reconcile all the cues to see how much use is made of each circuit and whether any instruments can be eliminated. The cues on a memory system can be printed out and used as the final authority. One can also check which instruments are contributing to each moment. This is informative to the designer and essential if the lighting is ever to be reproduced elsewhere. If any further changes are made to the lighting during the run, these changes too must be noted in the master plots. Thereafter the designer must ensure that he visits the theatre regularly. Lighting can so easily change: instruments can be knocked or move slightly out of position, remote-control instruments drift, the timing of manual cues can, over a period of weeks gradually alter. The designer must be quite clear that only he can be finally responsible for maintaining the standards that were set for the first night (Fig. 55).

*Stage Lighting Design*

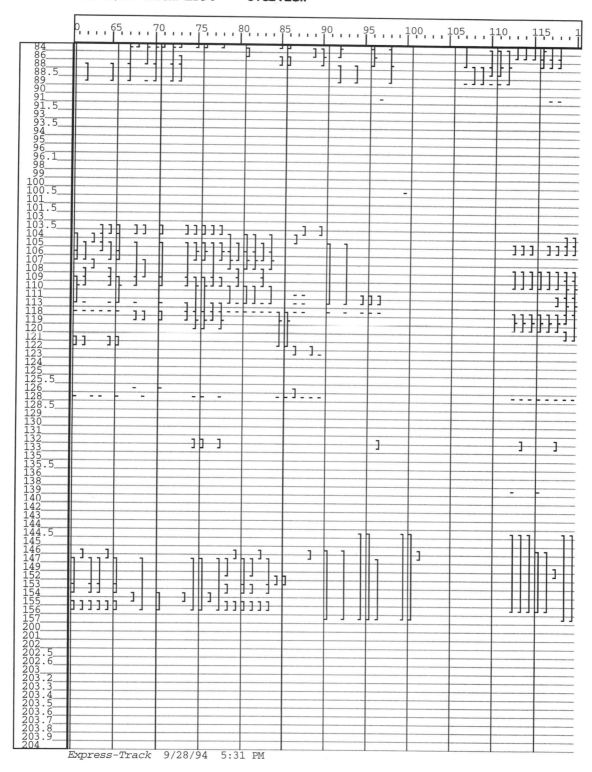

"ET 9/27 from LP90"   **Overview**

Express-Track   9/28/94   5:31 PM

*55. Cue graph plot*

*Procedure: Production*

81

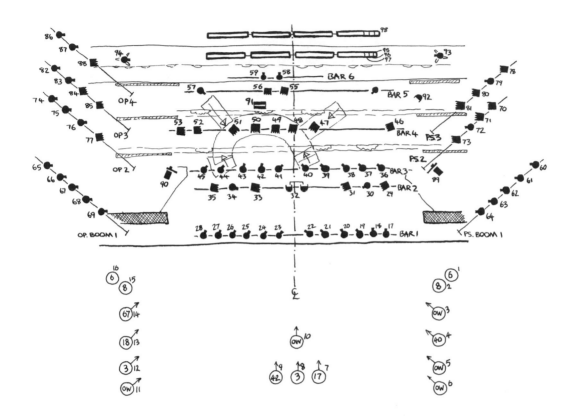

National Theatre at the Old Vic Theatre, London and
Alvin Theatre, New York
Director  Derek Goldby
Designer  Desmond Heeley
Lighting  Richard Pilbrow

CUE SYNOPSIS (ABRIDGED83)

ACT 1   A deserted place. Misty. Limbo. Cold.
    Build bleak empty day. Moorland.
    Players entry. Warm toward sunset.
    Fade to "exaggerated" twilight.
    End scene. Fade to night.
    Build castle. Flickery lamplight, ghostly. Golden chiaroscuro.
    Increase forestage to bright "battle of the wits."
    Return to court.

ACT 2   Snap on to full court.
    X-fade to "rehearsal." Weird hot red.
    Close to death mime.
    Court. Dark night. All-revealing sunrise.
    X-fade to exterior with distant castle. Cold, bleak.
    Close to *Hamlet* tableau.

ACT 3   Start in darkness.
    Build to ship. Sail. Golden morning.
    Sunset through to night—exchange of letters.
    A new day. Players discovered.
    Battle with pirates. Hot. Smoke. Confusion.
    Black out.
    Restore ship. Late afternoon.
    "The sun's going down."
    Fade sunset. Continue to surrealistic red dream.
    Nightmare of players' dominance.
    Mime of deaths. Intensify to low backlit red on Player King.
    Rosencrantz and Guildenstern in pin spots, face only at prosce-
    nium.
    Restore to court. Night all blue and cold. "Purged" for *Hamlet*
    ending.
    Very slow to darkness.

*Note: PS means prompt side—an old way of describing stage left in Britain*
*(where the prompter used to sit). OP means opposite prompt, i.e., stage right.*
*OW means open white, i.e., without color—in the United States this is*
*described as NC, i.e., no color.*

| Unit | Position Type | Instrument | Function | Color (Cinemoid) |
|------|--------------|-----------|----------|-------|
| 1 | FOH LEFT | beamlight | "Nightmare" red forestage RC | 6 |
| 2 | | 3 patt 264 * | Sunset left | 8 |
| 3 | | 6 patt 264 * | Acting areas DS | OW |
| 4 | | 2 patt 264 | Night wash forestage | 40 |
| 5 | | 1 patt 93 | Rosencrantz pinspot DR | OW |
| 6 | | 1 patt 93 | Guildenstern pinspot steps R | OW |
| 7 | FOH CENTER | 3 patt 264 * | Front wash cool | 17 |
| 8 | | 3 patt 264 * | Front wash warm | 3 |
| 9 | | 2 patt 264 | Front wash twilight violet | 42 |
| 10 | | 2 beamlights | Front dawn | OW |
| 11 | FOH RIGHT | 1 patt 93 | Guildenstern pinspot DL | OW |
| 12 | | 3 patt 264 * | Acting areas DS warm | 3 |
| 13 | | 2 patt 264 | Night wash forestage | 18 |
| 14 | | 5 patt 264 | Acting areas DS cool | 67 |
| 15 | | 3 patt 264 | Sunset right | 8 |
| 16 | | beamlight | Red forestage LC | 6 |
| 17 | ELECTRIC 1 | patt 264W | Acting area left | 3 |
| 18 | | patt 264W | Acting area left | 17 |
| 19 | | patt 264W | Acting area center | 3 |
| 20 | | patt 264W | Acting area center | 17 |
| 21 | | patt 264W | Acting area right | 3 |
| 22 | | patt 264W | Acting area right | 17 |
| 23 | | patt 264W | Acting area left | 17 |
| 24 | | patt 264W | Acting area left | 3 |
| 25 | | patt 264W | Acting area center | 17 |
| 26 | | patt 264W | Acting area center | 3 |
| 27 | | patt 264W | Acting area right | 17 |
| 28 | | patt 264W | Acting area right | 3 |
| 29 | ELECTRIC 2 | patt 243 | Night backlight forestage | 18 |
| 30 | | 2 patt 264 | Backlight forestage verbal battles | OW |
| 31 | | patt 243 | Backlight court rich gold | 4 |
| 32 | | 2 beamlights | Downlight red forestage | 6 |
| 33 | | patt 243 | As 31 | 4 |
| 34 | | 2 patt 264 | As 30 | OW |
| 35 | | patt 243 | As 29 | 18 |

| Unit | Position Type | Instrument | Function | Color (Cinemoid) |
|------|--------------|-----------|----------|-------|
| 36 | ELECTRIC 3 | patt 264W | Rostra L cool | 17 |
| 37 | | patt 264W | Rostra C white | OW |
| 38 | | patt 264W | Players' rehearsal "spook-light" | 1 |
| 39 | | patt 264W | Rostra warm court | 3 |
| 40 | | patt 264W | Rostra warm court | 2 |
| 41 | | patt 264W | Rostra R cool | 17 |
| 42 | | patt 264W | Rostra court | 38 |
| 43 | | patt 264W | As 38 | 1 |
| 44 | | patt 264W | As 37 | OW |
| 45 | | patt 264W | Rostra C cool | 17 |
| 46 | ELECTRIC 4 | patt 243 | Court backlight X RC | 4 |
| 47 | | patt 243 | Red backlight | 6 |
| 48 | | patt 243 | Night downlight LC | 40 |
| 49 | | patt 243 | Court downlight | 38-60 |
| 50 | | patt 243 | Night downlight RC | 40 |
| 51 | | patt 243 | Red backlight | 6 |
| 52 | | patt 243 | Court backlight X LC and sail | 4 |
| 53 | | patt 243 | Rostra X light | OW |
| 54 | ELECTRIC 5 | patt 264 | Opening rostra high side/ backlight | 17 |
| 55 | | patt 243 | Backlight rostra | 17 |
| 56 | | patt 243 | Backlight sail | OW |
| 57 | | patt 264 | As 54 | 17 |
| 58 | ELECTRIC 6 | 2 patt 23 | Light arches above gauze cool | 17 |
| 59 | | 2 patt 23 | Light arches above gauze warm | 52 |
| 60 | PS BOOM 1 | 2 patt 264 | X light forestage warm | OW |
| 61 | | 2 patt 264 | X light forestage cool | 17 |
| 62 | | 2 patt 23 | X light forestage night | 40 |
| 63 | | 2 patt 23 | X light forestage court | 38 |
| 64 | | 2 patt 23 | X light forestage sunset | 34 |
| 65 | OP BOOM 1 | 2 patt 264 | X light forestage warm | OW |
| 66 | | 2 patt 264 | X light forestage cool | 17 |
| 67 | | 2 patt 23 | X light forestage night | 40 |
| 68 | | 2 patt 23 | X light forestage court | 38 |
| 69 | | 2 patt 23 | X light forestage sunset | 34 |
| 70 | PS BOOM 2 | patt 223 | X light below rostra warm | OW |
| 71 | | patt 223 | X light below rostra night | 40 |
| 72 | | 2 patt 23 | X light below rostra cool | 17 |
| 73 | | patt 223 | X light below rostra sunset | 34 |

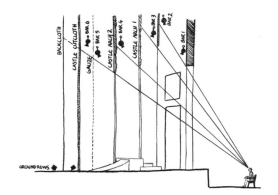

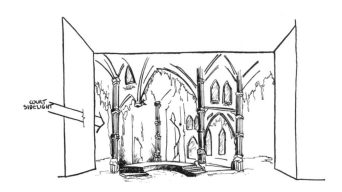

| Unit | Position Type | Instrument | Function | Color (Cinemoid) |
|------|---------------|------------|----------|------------------|
| 74 | OP BOOM 2 | 2 patt 264 | X light front court arches | 2 |
| 75 | | 2 patt 264 | X light front court arches | 18 |
| 76 | | 2 patt 23 | X light below arches cool | 17 |
| 77 | | patt 223 | X light below arches sunset | 34 |
| 78 | PS BOOM 3 | patt 243 | X light rostra court | 2 |
| 79 | | patt 264 | X light rostra cool | 17 |
| 80 | | patt 243 | X light rostra night | 18 |
| 81 | | patt 243 | X light rostra sunset | 34 |
| 82 | OP BOOM 3 | 2 patt 264 | X light middle court arches | 2 |
| 83 | | 2 patt 264 | X light middle court arches | 18 |
| 84 | | patt 243 | X light rostra cool | 17 |
| 85 | | patt 243 | X light rostra sunset | 34 |
| 86 | OP BOOM 4 | 2 patt 264 | X backlight court arches | 2 |
| 87 | | 2 patt 264 | X backlight court arches | 18 |
| 88 | | patt 243 | X backlight court arches sunset | 34 |

| Unit | Position Type | Instrument | Function | Color (Cinemoid) |
|------|---------------|------------|----------|------------------|
| 89 | STAGE L | patt 252 | Cloud effect on gauze (opening) | 17 |
| 90 | STAGE R | patt 252 | Cloud effect on gauze (opening) | 17 |
| 91 | STAGE C | tubular ripple | Ripple effect on gauze (ship) | 15 |
| 92 | STAGE L | 3 beamlights | Low side backlight to Player King's death (end ship) | 6 |
| 93 | STAGE L | patt 264 | X light above gauze off cloth | 17 |
| 94 | STAGE R | patt 264 | X light above gauze off cloth | 17 |
| 95 | BACKSTAGE | ground row | Frontlight cloth | 32 |
| 96 | | ground row | Frontlight cloth | 34 |
| 97 | | ground row | Frontlight cloth | 17 |
| 98 | BACKSTAGE | ground row | Rearlight cloth | OW |

\* = On separate circuits

# Chapter Five

# Design Challenges: Color

The next chapters discuss various design challenges that will arise with different types of production being staged in several types of theatre. Before getting down to specifics, we must discuss one important subject that applies to every sort of show in every sort of theatre. It is color.*

The use of color and colored light is an important part of lighting. With it the designer can suggest the time of day or the season of the year. He can underline the mood of a scene and he can enhance or destroy the effect of the scenery and costumes. Indeed, to a great many people stage lighting means color, and the fact that the best-selling color is red (by a substantial margin) indicates how brashly color is all too often used.

In the professional theatre the use of rich color seems to ebb and flow with fashion. At one time there was a call, stimulated by the Brechtian theory of stagecraft, for a return to the use of white light.** Color has been considered by some directors as anathema and a symbol of everything that was old fashioned. Sir Tyrone Guthrie, in his *A Life in the Theatre*, protested against stages bathed in a "weak solution of apricot jam." The reaction,

---

*Color identification in the earlier examples in this chapter will be Cinemoid unless otherwise mentioned. Lee colors employ a similar number scheme with a 1 before double digits, i.e., Cinemoid 17 becomes Lee 117. A comparative color chart will be found in Part 4.

** Bertold Brecht called for a hard white bright light on the stage to "alienate" the audience, making them witness the play as dispassionate observers rather than emotionally involved participants.

typified by work at London's Royal Court Theatre in the sixties, was a healthy one. As with so many things in life, l suspect the real truth lies somewhere in the middle. No doubt far too many plays used to be performed bathed in a soup of pale gold. On the other hand, how does one actually define "white" light? The light produced by the conventional theatre spotlight is a very different white from that of an English sunlit winter morning, and the colors of a natural sunset often far outdo the most lurid theatrical effect. In fact, I happen to be writing this chapter while on holiday in the Hebrides. As I write the sun is setting, and there's a large bank of storm cloud building in the east. The last rays of the sun fill the air with a color closely akin to the once well-known No. 8 (a Cinemoid color remembered by the more mature lighting designer with much nostalgia—it's never been matched). The shadows are warm blue, the sea two quite separate colors, ranging from a greeny-blue to a deep purple-brown under the almost indigo storm clouds. I would hesitate before offering any director such a Technicolor vision on the stage!

When thinking about how much or how little color to use, the choice may seem to be between stark Brechtian whiteness, a psychedelic morass of multicolored sensation, or an attempted distillation of the colors of nature. The guideline seems to lie in the simple rules that we have tried to follow throughout this book: first, what does the playwright call for, and second, how does the director intend to re-create the work on the stage? Taking the natural world as our inspiration we can certainly assume that there need be little call for the "apricot jam" solution.

For *Love for Love* at the National Theatre in London, director Peter Wood and set designer Lila de Nobili wanted very deliberately to create a varnished, crusted, "old-master" feeling over the stage. Here the apparently clear sunshine was 50 or 50–50 (Cinemoid colors); the shadows, 52, 53–7 and even 42; the sunset, various combinations including 8, 7, 47; and lamplight, 3, 2 and even 4 and various complications thereof. This was an example where one strove deliberately for the marmalade effect! By contrast, I remember a production of *Richard III* for the Royal Shakespeare Company at Stratford-on-Avon for William Gaskill, with a set by Jocelyn Herbert. For this the effect of white "Brechtian" light was wanted. The result, with which I think we were all pleased, was part white but part variations of 17, 67, 55, 50, 60, and so on. The off-white tints were used to model and modify the "real" white light, which in fact appeared quite yellow. This complex mixture of off-whites combined to give the stark effect required, and yet provided a very subtle degree of visual variety.

Many years ago I had the privilege of working with the Berliner Ensemble when they did a season at the Old Vic Theatre in London. Their famous version of "white light" was very different from that imagined by most English Brechtian disciples. First, although they found that the Old Vic permanent equipment provided them with the brightest stage area that they had met outside their own theatre, they nevertheless boosted this with some thirty or forty kilowatts of twenty-four-volt beamlights. Then, every lantern on the stage was colored with 67 Cinemoid. This was the authentic version of Brechtian whiteness. Rather sadly it also almost entirely blotted out the marvelous textures of the scenery, but this, we found later, was the unfortunate result of the rushed conditions under which they were working on their tour. Many years later in their Berlin home, I saw the Ensemble use a lot of steely-blue "white" light from batteries of low-voltage instruments, but the lighting was strongly textured and highly dramatic and theatrical—as were their stunning performances.

I approach color from an entirely subjective point of view. I have no preconceived ideas about how it should be used, and few predetermined color choices: all must stem from the play, the style of its presentation stemming from the director's intention. I normally have vague thoughts of color at the back of my mind as I begin to lay out the lighting design. First it's usually a matter of how many variants of color are needed from each direction in each category of instrument. For example, what about the acting area? Will one color suffice or will double coverage be needed? The whole plot must be worked through considering every use of each instrument.

After everything on the plot has been roughed in, the decisions on color must be made. I like to use swatch books from all the principal manufacturers. I often cut up small samples and assemble a palette of the colors I've selected for that particular project on one reference sheet. Perhaps with a section for motivating light, another for acting areas, another for lighting the background. Samples of color can be tried out for the eye using a small spotlight to check for the effect on costume samples or skin tone.

Remember of course, that most colors will be seen in combination with others from other angles. Always remember that white light is made up of all the colors of the spectrum. As colors or tints are added together, they'll tend to become paler. I find it useful to have to hand or to visualize a color triangle with white light at the center and the primaries and secondaries at the edges. The tints are found as colors become desaturated toward the center. Choices of tint need to be imagined bearing in mind how they will mix together and bearing in mind what effect they'll have upon the lit object.

The choices are infinite. For instance, how many different variations of blue might be used? A cold steely blue might be balanced against a greener, moonlight tint or a richer royal warm blue. What will be the effect upon skin tone or costume color. How might the variants work together, will they set each other off, harmonize or jar, reveal shape and dimension or flatten? Every color, tint, hue or density may be considered. Once chosen, every color may then be thought about at every level of brightness. What will be the effect of dimming the instrument with your chosen color? An incandescent source will become redder as it drops in brightness. It's through the enormous mix of such variables, that eventually, "magic" can be created.

With increased availability of color scrollers, the color horizons from a single instrument can be greatly widened, but their expense can only be justified where there is a really potent reason to utilize a change of color. If available, a scroller not only allows a wider choice of color, it can be used dynamically to change color "in view." Wonderful effects of sunset or dawn can be achieved with well-chosen series of hues in a slowly moving color string. Similarly, of course, automated fixtures liberate the designer. Some allow the slow (or rapid) cross-fading from color to color for dramatic effect.

Some notes on the basic laws and rules about color and its use are found in Part 4/Mechanics. The various demonstrations throughout the book will illustrate some actual uses on productions—they worked for me at the time!

Apart from rules about how colored light and pigment behave, what are the other things that influence the designer in his thoughts about color? Of the four properties of light discussed in Chapter 1, color is probably the most potent when it comes to evoking an emotional or psychological response in the audience. Changes of intensity, the distribution of light or its movement have, of course, an emotive effect, but color, which can be applied so subtly and with such complexity, provides an unparalleled opportunity.

An interesting production from this point of view was *Rosencrantz and Guildenstern Are Dead* for the National Theatre of Great Britain in London and on Broadway, by Tom Stoppard, directed by Derek Goldby, set designed by Desmond Heeley, lighting by me. The setting was a curved, textured, low platform, standing in front of a backcloth. Into this area there was flown, for the Elsinore scenes, a series of three-dimensional arches, and for the ship scene, an enormous sail. The production had a bizarre, theatrical quality; the two protagonists seemed to pass through a sort of wonderland. We evolved a scheme whereby the lighting would take the strange shifts of mood and, largely through the use of color, amplify them.

For example, the play opens in a "no-man's land" on a barren heath. The light slowly built from darkness with a suggestion of gray mist, and the stage was gradually lit in a cold, mysterious, mournful tone. This slowly lightened, until the entry of the group of players who were to become a pivotal element in the development of the play. They brought on with them their own new light, but a light that was still keyed to the composition of the deserted moorland. It increasingly added warmth, suggesting a setting sun through the mist and then twilight. As the play became more bizarre and the spell of the players seemed to enfold Rosencrantz and Guildenstern, so the lighting became hotter and more aggressive. When the players went on their way, the scene ended; there was almost a feeling of relief as the stage disappeared into an other-worldly blue backlight of night. Out of this came the court: dusty, mysterious, encrusted arches dimly seen as if by a flickering torchlight. At other times Rosencrantz and Guildenstern moved almost in a world of their own, with brilliant games of verbal tennis, in a style that was little short of music hall. For this the lighting in which they worked grew clearer, whiter and brighter, as if cocooning them in a sharp clear light of their own. When the players again intruded, the lighting took their hot bizarre tone, eventually, at the play's climax and the players' deaths, resorting to stark shafts of pure red, cutting across the stage from weird angles (see Demonstration 3). This play used color aggressively, perhaps outrageously, and yet it proved to be in tune with the director's intention. Its success in London and New York perhaps proved the lighting's justification. At the other end of the scale, the most subtle variations of white—cool white, warm white, brown-white, gray-white, green-white—called for by many plays, can all build toward a thrilling result.

A very obvious note of warning here: the designer should use strong color only with the greatest care, remembering that the first function of lighting is selective visibility. Under normal circumstances an actor cannot be considered truly visible if he has a bright green face. Only in exceptional circumstances can there be any justification for using anything but the subtlest color on the acting area, except as an underlying deep-color wash to affect the overall tone of the stage. When the designer comes to lighting the setting or background, he can obviously take more license, provided that he is enhancing the work of the set designer and not simply trying to "improve" it without reference to the original intention. Designers have every right to expect to see their scenery and costumes the way they intended them to appear.

## Color Mixing on Backcloth or Cyclorama: Additive Mixing

The designer frequently has to decide whether to light a cyclorama with a single color medium to give exactly the color required or whether to blend several colors, for example the primaries, until the desired tint is achieved. The answer to this depends upon the degree of variety of color that one has to achieve. If a cyc has to go through every color in the spectrum, a three-color mix of the primaries is worth considering. If, on the other hand, all that is needed is a blue sky that fades to a sunset, it would be far more economical to have two circuits of blue, perhaps one light and one dark, and one circuit of a sunset color. An additive mix of deep colors is very wasteful of light since, while the result may be white or a light tint, it is only achieved with a small part of the light from each circuit coming through the saturated color medium. Wherever possible, it is best to use the palest colors that are consistent with providing the required range of effect.

## Subtractive Mixing

Subtractive mixing means that if one combines several colors in a single frame for a single spotlight, a new color is created that will have been subtractively mixed in the same way as one mixes pigment. The colors in each color manufacturer's range provide for most of the color variations that a designer may require; however, it can be rewarding to experiment and develop one's own color from combinations of these. Subtractive color mixing is an experiment that can be done at home, and there are many fascinating combinations of color to be found. The 1959 production of *Brand* at the Lyric Theatre, Hammersmith, London, directed by Michael Elliott and set designed by Richard Negri, used a great deal of subtracted color. The play, which was set almost entirely in the Norwegian mountains, seemed to call for a wide range of pale colors—grays, browns, greens, blues and yellows, most of which were combinations of color. The range of standard colors available from manufacturers today is far wider. Even so, interesting variations can still be derived from subtractive mixing.

## Broken Color

This means that instead of using two different pieces of color in front of an instrument, one cuts either or both of them in a certain pattern so that each color can be seen both separately and in combination. Different types of spotlight will react to this in different ways, depending on their lens systems, but great variety can be obtained. I found it particularly effective in the Royal Shakespeare Company's *As You Like It* (again with Michael Elliott and Richard Negri). I used a considerable number of units with broken color in combinations of various greens and yellows. These, together with a quantity of gobos, produced an enchanting forestlike impression.

## Fluorescence

Fluorescence provides a way of changing the light of one wavelength into that of another, longer wavelength. We usually see this used with ultraviolet (UV) light. These rays, which are almost invisible, will cause certain substances to fluoresce in various vivid colors. Fluorescent pigments are available in paints, dyes and stage makeup. Some of them are visible under white light but change in quality under UV. Some are almost invisible and only appear in UV light. Particularly exciting use was made of UV in the National Theatre's production of *Loves Labour's Lost* for the National Theatre at the Old Vic, London (directed by Sir Laurence Olivier and designed by Carl Toms). The set was a formalized pattern of trees that were moved into various formations from scene to scene. The trees were green and leafy as if in full summer, but their trunks and branches were invisibly painted with fluorescent paint. At the very end of the play, as the stage faded to night and the last haunting words were heard, the normal stage lighting faded out, leaving only the UV lamps. The entire scene was magically transformed: the trees were stripped of their leaves and looked as though they were covered in snow.

# Chapter Six

# Design Challenges: Staging

## Backdrops, Frontcloths and Cycloramas

Backdrops, frontcloths, and cycs usually need special lighting treatment. Sometimes, when used as a neutral background to the stage, they can be left unlit, but usually they will represent sky, a distant scene or some purely visual piece of design.

Cloths hung toward the back of the stage are usually lit from battens (striplights) or multiple floods on a pipe. Which of these methods is used depends upon the brightness required and the amount of space available between the lighting position and the cloth. If considerable brightness is needed and if the space is five to six feet (about 1.6 meters) or more, then a flood bar can be used. Closer than this, it will probably be found that the cutoff from each flood will show in a series of ugly lines that can only be removed with difficulty by using a heavy frost diffuser. The striplight will give a good color mix at a much closer range but with less brightness (Fig. 56). Miniature striplights (Zipstrips) with MR16 lamps allow a cloth to be well lit in extremely shallow circumstances.

When space is limited or when the cloth is a very high one, it is always difficult to get the light down to the middle of the cloth. This can be overcome in various ways: a second batten with a more directional light pattern, for example, using PAR lamps (Fig. 57) can be hung alongside the first or on its own, or the center of the cloth can be spotlighted from the top, sides, or the

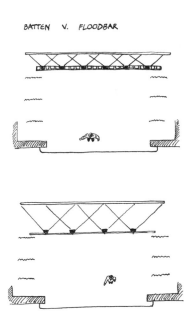

BATTEN V. FLOODBAR

*56. Batten v. floodbar*

*above: 57. Par batten to cloth bottom*

*right: 58. Spotlighting a cloth*

front (Fig. 58). We have noted already that the low-level circle front lighting position can be very useful for flooding a downstage cloth (Fig. 59).

We may find that we do not want to flood a backcloth overall with even light and subtle spotlighting can be useful. Soft-focus profiles or Fresnels can provide accents as needed.

The cyclorama, wrapping itself around the sides of the stage, presents a different and more complex problem. It is extremely difficult to light it from nearby. For a large cyc it is essential to get well away and to use powerful floods and/or Fresnels. If the cyc is of limited height and has to be combined with borders it is almost impossible to get a satisfactory match of intensities between each border. This combination is best avoided by set designers. The best position from which to light a wraparound cyclorama is well downstage (Figs. 60 and 61).

*Stage Lighting Design*

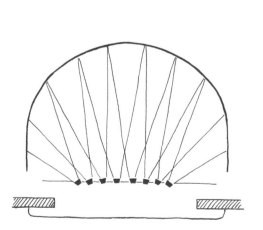

*above: 59. Spotlighting a cloth from FOH*

*left: 60 and 61. Cyclorama lighting*

## Scrims or Gauzes

Theatrical gauze (scrim) has been aptly described as "holes tied together with string." Different types of scrim offer choices of opacity or transparency. It has the quality of appearing solid when lit from the front but transparent when a scene behind it is lit. The description quoted is a good reminder of how to use it. The holes are always there, and it is the careful control of light that gives different results. If the front of the scrim is flooded, a lot of light will go through the holes and also illuminate the area behind it. If the scrim is to be completely opaque it should be lit carefully from an oblique angle that will not send spill through into the scene behind (Fig. 62). Similarly, when the scrim is to be transparent, the light behind has to be very tightly controlled (Fig. 63). To make quite certain of the opacity of a scrim (for example, if a scene change has to take place behind it), it is best to back it with another cloth. Black velour is best, and this can be flown out or opened just before we wish to dissolve.

Scrim has other uses apart from that of creating spectacular effect. Used in front of a cyc or backcloth it will give a misty quality of distance. Used as part of a standing set it can create rooms or acting areas that can be made to appear and disappear at will. In all cases the techniques for lighting are the same.

Scrim used with projection can be fascinating. A front projection shone through a scrim will give the effect of a double image, the projection being seen both on the scrim and on the surface behind it. I once saw a remarkable production of *Under Milk Wood* in Berlin. In this a suggestion of the wooded hillside around the little Welsh village was projected onto a vast cyclorama, and a series of scrim borders were very slowly dropped in. As each came into sight it caught and repeated the projected image until the whole stage was wrapped in an abstract pattern of foliage, creating a most extraordinary three-dimensional visual effect.

A dark scrim in front of a rear-projection screen will slightly darken the whole picture, but it will also make the blacks in the projected image stand out with greater contrast and reduce the amount the picture is dissipated by spill reflection from the acting area.

There are several types of scrim in common use. One, very thin and delicate, is known as "English gauze" or bobinette, and should be used when its chief function is its transparency. The other is known as "sharkstooth" or "Hanson" gauze. This has much thicker "string" and should be used if the primary purpose of the gauze is to appear to be solid. Filled scrim is similar in appearance to sharkstooth but with the "holes" filled in. It can make a good material for backlit cloths, providing the lights behind are out of audience sightline.

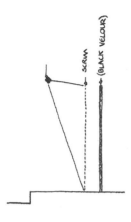

62. *Opaque scrim—frontlight*

63. *Transparent scrim—rearlight*

*64 and 65.* Brand *rearlighting*

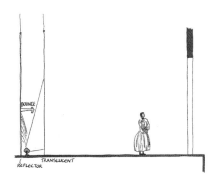

*66. Reflector drop*

## Translucency

Another important scenic device is the translucent cloth that is lit from the rear. This uses a translucent material that can be obtained in very wide widths to avoid unwanted seams appearing in the design. The uses to which translucency can be put are endless. The section on musical lighting in Chapter 7 mentions two uses of the technique that are typical of much American musical scenic design. Equally fascinating are the variations one can achieve with an almost blank translucent screen and varied lighting. The ideal surface is a plastic rear-projection screen, but various other materials make a satisfactory substitute. Revues and ballets often give the opportunity for exciting and startling variations of back light; the use of gobos, perhaps with color-changers creating moving shapes and colors of light on the screen, can be fascinating.

On a more sober note was Ibsen's *Brand*, for the 59 Theatre Company (Figs. 64 and 65). For this production the predominant scenic effect was a plain white translucent cloth hung behind a dark gauze. Behind these a series of cut out shapes were suspended that, used singly or in combination and backlit, gave a staggering impression of misty views of the mountains and fjords of Norway. Pairs of 500-watt profile spots were used to suggest the sun or moon as seen through mist: one was focused to give a hard circle and its partner focused softly to create a watery halo. They were set to coincide with the clefts in the silhouette shapes. Out of nothing but light, the shadow of unpainted cut-outs and the translucent screen, all the required mysteries of Norway were evoked. Perhaps much may be learned from the traditional Indian or Indonesian shadow play, in which, using delicately cut out puppets, stories of extraordinary beauty are told.

A translucent cloth can be partly painted with transparent dye, and partly opaqued on the rear. Through a combination of back- and frontlighting great variations and illusions of depth can be obtained. A translucent cloth is always helped by hanging a white reflector drop upstage of any backlighting. This can be a plain white cloth or even the back wall of the theatre if it is painted white: by its reflection of any spill light it will substantially increase the brightness of the translucency (Fig. 66).

## Mirrors

Have fun exploring the use of mirrors onstage. Josef Svoboda, the Czech scenic designer, does some extraordinary things with mirrors. His version of Verdi's *La Traviata*, an outdoor production at Macerata, used a massive 30-meter wide by 15-meter high mirror at varying angles, reflecting both designs created with carpet on the floor and the audience itself. I remember an industrial show for the British fiber-optic company STC that I both designed and lit. This used a ceiling mirror covering the stage. When the audience entered, the mirror was lying on the floor—the stage was a black void, with no sign of scenery or lighting. As the show began, to suitable outer-space music the whole black floor/mirror lifted into the air accompanied by flashing lights, color, smoke and lasers until it hung overhead. The floor beneath was a checkerboard of multicolored light boxes and *all* the show lighting was on the floor around the perimeter of the central light box platform. The performers were entirely lit from overhead by reflection in the mirror. The inspiration for the concept was the subject of the industrial show, fiber-optics with their total internal reflection, and it worked to turn a rather dry presentation of technology into quite a stunning event. Mirrors can be surprisingly interesting and useful.

## Scenic Projection

The success of projection depends on an exceptional degree of collaboration among the design team and an understanding of projection's problems and limitations.

There was a time, many years ago, when projection was considered a rather dangerous venture. Projectors were limited in power, the results were rather fuzzy and diffuse, and the pictures never quite came out as predicted.

During the late 1950s, having read books the 1930s about scene projection, I became determined to see it satisfactorily used again. Visits to Germany had shown me that a large and comparatively bright picture could be obtained, and I refused to believe that the smaller theatres and different lighting conditions in England meant that projection could never work there satisfactorily. My theory was, on the contrary, that a small theatre could be a positive advantage because, assuming that sufficiently wide-angle projection could be achieved, the projector would be placed so close to the screen that the image would be very bright indeed.

We therefore imported a German projector, the largest then available, of 5,000 watts, from Reiche and Vogel of Berlin. The production was a revue for Michael Codron called *One Over the Eight*, and it was to be staged at the Duke of York's Theatre in London. The stage was only about twenty-five feet deep; front projection was mandatory and eventually, together with Tony Walton, the designer, I evolved a scheme whereby two projectors, situated on high towers built into a false proscenium on either side of the stage, would shine onto the opposing sides of a curved cyclorama (Figs. 67 and 68). The resulting image was twenty-five feet high by about fifty feet wide. The next step was the preparation of the slides. We wished to project about forty or fifty different scenes. They were all to be in color, some were cartoon-like and some were abstract paintings by Tony. The traditional method of making slides, which the German experts also used, was to set up the projector in the position where it would be in the theatre, shine a blank slide onto the cyclorama and then mark the slide until the correct shape required on the stage was established. Unfortunately, in our case the production was starting on tour and we were only able to start assembling our projectors in the theatre on the Sunday morning before the Monday night on which the show was due to open. In the thirty-six hours at our disposal there was no

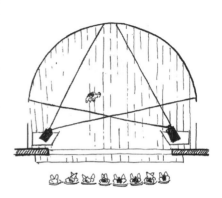

*67 and 68.* One Over the Eight *projection*

time to establish the required distortion by trial and error; but I was convinced it could all be done photographically and checked mathematically. Our German advisers were sceptical (one might almost say hysterical!).

To cut a long story short, it worked. Robert Ornbo, friend, colleague, artist and mathematician, helped photograph and manufacture the slides. Then, with our hearts in our mouths, we tried them out. Each picture, projected from its acute angle, came out fair and square. The short throws of the projectors produced a bright and clear-cut picture and the considerable gamble (there was no other scenery had the projection not worked) came off. The critics, almost without exception, praised "the multitude of brightly colored backcloths." Many people were not even aware that projection was used at all: the show indeed appeared to be backed by an amazing quantity of highly colored cloths. Since then, of course, equipment has improved dramatically, and an enormous amount of projection has been used, some successfully and some with disappointing results. Strangely enough, the failures can usually be attributed to the same series of problems that we managed to overcome on that first attempt.

The first problem to solve is intensity of image. If a picture is to be crisp and decisive, it must be bright. There are usually complaints about the lack of brightness in projection equipment, which are often justified. High intensity is badly needed, and instruments with nonincandescent light sources, such as the Pani HMI projector range, are now available. But even with advanced equipment one has to extract the maximum power out of what is available. This can be done in two ways. First, one can control the artwork, that is, of the picture to be projected (the lighter the picture, the more light travels through the slide on to the screen: the more contrasted the picture, the more effective the result will be). Second, and more importantly, the inverse square law must be remembered: the closer the projector can be placed to the screen the brighter the picture will be. Consequently a very-wide-angle projector is necessary as well as, of course, a large slide, the German/Austrian 18 centimeters (approximately 7 inches) being most satisfactory.

Besides a powerful projector placed as close as possible to the screen and the right artwork, certain other factors contribute to success with projections. One must also ensure that the rest of the light on the stage has the minimum of effect on the projection. It is absolutely essential that as much as possible of the spill light from the acting area is cut out before it hits the screen. In *One Over the Eight* the stage had no other scenery, and the action took place right up to within five feet of the screen. To cut any bounce-light down to an absolute minimum, the floor was covered with inverted hardboard (Masonite)—the rough side up—which was then painted a matte brown-black.

An effective method of reducing spill is to place some scenic element between the stage and the projection. In *A Funny Thing Happened on the Way to the Forum*, the American musical seen on Broadway and in London, again designed by Tony Walton, there were several high ground rows around the acting area that effectively caught most of the bounce light. As this was an American musical, lit in New York by the late Jean Rosenthal, the acting area was extremely bright; but even so the projections stood out vividly whenever they were required.

The angle of light into the acting area is obviously important to the success of projection. Whenever possible, light should be directed so that it will not bounce toward the screen. With a screen across the back of the stage, sidelighting becomes particularly important. Finally, of course, the sheer quantity of light has to be carefully controlled and balanced in proportion to the screen. As we have seen throughout this book, the impression of brightness is not necessarily achieved with actual brightness.

It goes without saying that the darker the acting area, the more effective the projection can be. Svoboda has often demonstrated the enormous potential of projected scenery, yet, at home in Prague, he often achieved these effects with very low light levels onstage. While I was lighting for him in London, I was reminded of the need to achieve a balance that illuminates the actors adequately and at the same time avoids the projection becoming dominant. Svoboda's hauntingly beautiful sets for Ostrovski's *The Storm* (Demonstration 4), directed by John Dexter at the National Theatre, used a series of screens, some of scrim, some opaque, set at various angles, and a large number of photographic projections of trees, water and sky. These fused into a fascinating mosaic, creating a luminous and haunting atmosphere around the story; but on occasion the projections had to be subdued to keep them in correct balance with the action. Projection, like every other aspect of lighting, is a matter of balance, proportion and taste.

The ultimate success of projected scenery depends upon the use to which it is put and the skill with which it is employed. Projection cannot be considered a cheap way of producing scenery (indeed it is probably only cheap if an enormous number of scenes are required); it is simply another way of creating visual images. But projected images always seem to have a certain luminosity and character, and their ability to dissolve from image to image provides a uniquely fluid scenic environment.

The surface upon which the projection is thrown needs careful thought. It is useless having a powerful projector if too much light is wasted on an inefficient screen. Different types of screen have different reflective and transmission characteristics. A few hours' experiment are the answer. I have found that a very white and highly efficient screen brings its own problems because it often reflects, with equal efficiency, the spill light from the acting area.

Finally, remember that projection doesn't have to be used only on flat surfaces. Images across three-dimensional scenery can be stunning. *The Magic Flute* for the Los Angeles Opera (director Peter Hall, designer Gerald Scarfe and lighting by the author) used projection not only on a huge rear-projection screen but also front projection across a great pyramid that moved around the stage (see color plates).

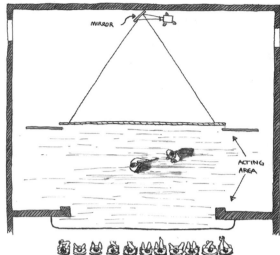

## Rear Projection (Fig. 69)

Rear projection requires a greater stage depth than does front projection, but when the production only requires a small acting area, rear projection comes into its own. This means that a rear-projection screen can be placed far enough downstage to allow the projector to stand behind it. If space is limited, the projection can be diverted by means of a mirror, although some light is lost in the process (Fig. 70). An advantage of rear projection is that it gives a brighter picture than front projection because light is transmitted through the screen rather than reflected off it. *Four Baboons Adoring the Sun*, set designed by Tony Walton, projection by Wendall Harrington, for the Vivian Beaumont Theatre at Lincoln Center in 1992, used rear projection on a large scale: four kilowatt Pani HMI projectors behind a forty-eight-foot wide screen provided enormously powerful images that could match almost any level of brightness onstage.

A drawback to the use of rear projection in the theatre arises from the width of the viewing angle from the auditorium. Most rear-projection screens tend to transmit the light in a straight line through the screen; thus from a position directly facing the projector one gets a clear bright image, while from the sides of the auditorium the image tends to fade. A careful choice of screen can reduce this problem but, generally speaking, be careful of a rear-projection screen at the side of the stage or at too steep an angle to the stage front.

## Multiscreen Projection

If the space available for rear projection is limited, if multi-image projection is required, if small projection screens (perhaps combined with other scenic elements) are to be employed or, finally, if only a low-brightness image is needed, a smaller projector or a number of them can be used. The most commonly employed small projector is the Kodak Carousel, and variations of this excellent unit are available with higher powered light sources ranging from 1,200-watt incandescent to xenon. Two advantages become immediately apparent: first, the projector is small and compact; second, and most importantly, it can be easily operated by remote control with eighty slides in a magazine as standard. Custom-built remote slide changers for large 7-inch slides were developed for the musical *On the Level* in London by Theatre Projects in 1968 and are now available for Pani projectors from Production Arts in New York. But using a small, commonly available projector can often make economic sense, as it allows projectors to be used in hitherto inaccessible positions, and allows far more complex multiscreen effects to be achieved, due to readily centralized operation.

Two complex multiscreen productions will serve as examples. First, *I and Albert*, a musical by Charles Strouse and Lee Adams, at the Piccadilly Theatre, London, directed by John Schlesinger, set designed by Luciana Arrighi, with lighting and projection by Robert Ornbo (Fig. 71). This musical was a pageant of the life of Queen Victoria and had dozens of scenes that had to flow with a filmlike quality from one to another. The design concept was for a semipermanent set that created levels and staircases, backed by a three-dimensional "wall" of variously shaped rear-projection screens (Fig. 72). All the forward screens were shaped like picture frames—square, rectangular, oval—while behind them hung a large rear-projection screen containing holes shaped to coincide exactly with the "pictures" in front. Thus, some or all of the pictures could be rear-projected to produce, for example, a gallery of royal portraits hanging in space. Most ingeniously, another battery of projectors could rear-project on the "wall" surrounding them, thus providing, among other effects, a richly patterned wallpaper upon which the pictures appeared to be hung; at the end of a scene this could dissolve to another wall or vanish. The pictures could dissolve individually, collectively, or in a rippling or random manner to another image, or each could disappear. Furthermore if a single image were projected across all the screens, the "pictures" vanished and the whole back of the stage became a single vista, used to much effect for a scene set in the Crystal Palace. Finally all the screens could fly out, as they did at the end of act 1. The thunder of the Crimean war burst across the theatre as the stage filled with smoke, the screens miraculously disappeared, and thirty-eight projectors projected a massive Union Jack flag through the flickering, swirling smoke, right out into and enveloping the audience. The projectors comprised nineteen pairs of 1,200-watt Carousels stacked on a scaffold against the theatre's rear wall. Because of the noise from their thirty-eight fans, a sound-absorbing wall with glass projection ports had to be built downstage of them.

Our second example is the sadly short-lived musical *Shelter* in New York, set designed by Tony Walton with lighting and projection by myself. A new series of problems required different solutions. The musical told of a young TV advertising executive who was so obsessed by his work that he lived on the job. He lived in a small house with a garden, all artificial and built (for filming commercials) in a TV studio. The studio was run by a computer—a friendly

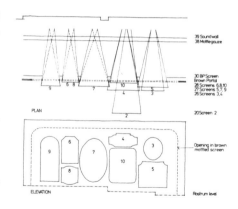

71. I and Albert *plan and elevation*

72. I and Albert *gallery, detail gallery, and Khyber Pass*

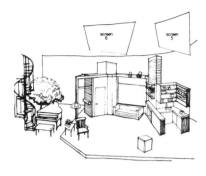

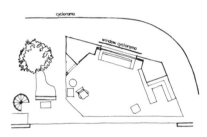

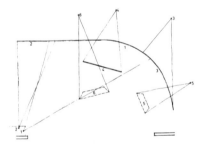

*73.* Shelter *elevation*

*74.* Shelter *plan*

*75.* Shelter *plan projectors*

computer. Here our hero was sheltered from the world, his wife, and other complications: for with the aid of the studio's computer technology he could transport the house and change its environment to anywhere in the world —or universe. The stage set was a mock TV studio, with the grid extending through the proscenium, galleries and spiral stairs, video and sound equipment and all around a cyclorama upon which could be projected literally any image or environment. The house, taking up two thirds of the stage, was a realistic TV setting with a window and a porch; the garden had grass and a willow tree. At a word from our hero the whole scene could appear to be set on a sunlit day in New England, a moonlit night in the Bahamas (good tactics, this, for the new girl friend) or in a blizzard at the top of Mount Everest. Scale could be enlarged or reduced and every sort of image, realistic or phantasmagoric, summoned up.

So far so good—and great fun. Then technical problems emerged. The stage was very shallow: most of the cyclorama had to be front projected, but parts of it could not be reached. The water tank above the house and the willow tree were a partial obstruction. The house window had to be almost touching the cyc, but luckily there was a minute amount of space behind it. So a combination of front and rear projection was involved (Figs. 73-77). The stage right part of the cyc (No. 2) and the top above the house (No. 1) were each covered with two 5-kilowatt projectors mounted high on a stage right downstage tower, using 18-centimeter slides, predistorted for the horizontal and vertical angles and the curved screen and to avoid shadows of tree and house. The left end of the curved angle cyc (No. 3) was rear projected from pairs of high-power Carousels placed upstage left, and the window (No. 4) from up-stage center. (Note the window screen is cheated downstage of the main cyc to obtain sufficient throw.) All those different projectors from different angles and different throws, some front, some rear, merged together to create what was apparently a single vista. Two additional small screens hung over the stage at angles, showing images merging with or counterpointing the main action. These were rear projected by pairs of Carousels concealed in a dummy air-conditioning duct running beneath the TV grid. It was an amusing show with charm and lots of visual humor, but it closed within a week. Such is theatre.

The world of industrial shows and commercial conferences uses audiovisual and slide/sound multiscreen techniques with ever greater complexity. Multimedia "experiences" seem to proliferate in many aspects of entertainment. In the music industry, pop and rock shows have broken almost all the boundaries of theatrical light, sound and projection staging. Projection, which is light literally creating the whole visual image, is a valuable element of modern stagecraft.

## Film and Video

There are many problems—technical, but perhaps more important, artistic— surrounding the use of film and video in live theatre. The occasions on which it is used successfully are all too rare. Svoboda, with his spectacular in Prague, *Laterna Magica*, achieved amazing effects mixing live action and film but succeeded in part by using very low light levels on the stage. Jules Fisher in his production of *Elvis* used large-scale front film projection with film projectors developed by Bran Ferren that could track and zoom images across the stage. Maybe the largest difficulty is that of divergence of scale and the mixing of projected with live action. But as with slide projection, the first step toward success with film is a powerful projector, correctly placed, in conjunction with very sympathetic lighting. Video is employed using conventional TV monitors, projection or multiscreen video walls. The same problems encountered in still projection of keeping light from diluting the image apply. Every designer will dream of a budget to match the Rolling Stones Sony Jumbotron screen on their "Voodoo Lounge" tour. Superb and enormous video images seemed to extend the imagery of the lighting, seamlessly welding the parts into a visual whole.

For the revival of *How to Succeed in Business Without Really Trying* in New York, a wall of screens at the rear of the stage provided a powerful vista of a changing cityscape rendered by video and computer graphics.

## Optical Effects

A whole series of optical effects—fleecy clouds, storm clouds, waves, flame and smoke—have become so much a part of the theatre and television scene that they are now no more than clichés. I have found that the only way to make an optical effect work is to muddle it up. One flame effect looks quite ridiculous, four look better and twenty can look superb; add a little smoke, a few flickering lamps and perhaps some fluttering silk or mylar and the result can be dazzling. Lionel Bart's *Blitz*, which was infamous for its fire-raid sequence, used quite simple effects. (Noel Coward was reported as saying that it was twice as effective as Hitler's original.) The secret was that there were lots of flame effects from all directions. The same applies to clouds and snow: jumbling up quantities of projections will achieve the most effective results. I should like to make here another point arising from the *Blitz* example: in all the roaring of air-raid sound effects, whirring of effects motors, trundling of vast scenic units, pumping of smoke, way at the back of the stage there was a rear projection of the silhouette of Saint Paul's Cathedral, a famous news photograph from the blitz itself. That simple and familiar image stirred the memory and imagination of many in the audience, filling in and making allowances for the comparative crudity of the remainder. Effects are illusion and illusion is trickery. Something very simple can often be the key that captures the imagination of the audience.

Effects have traditionally been achieved with optical-effects projectors and effects disks or film loops. Ellipsoidal spotlights with gobos and either animation disks or twin-spin gobo rotators can produce marvelous moving effects too. Water, flames and a wide variety of moving and shimmering images can be obtained with efficient low-cost units. (More information is found in Part 4/Mechanics.)

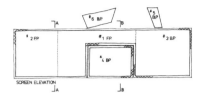

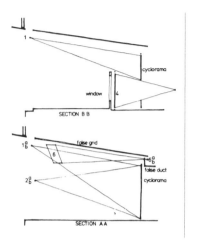

*76.* Shelter *screen elevation*

*77.* Shelter *two sections*

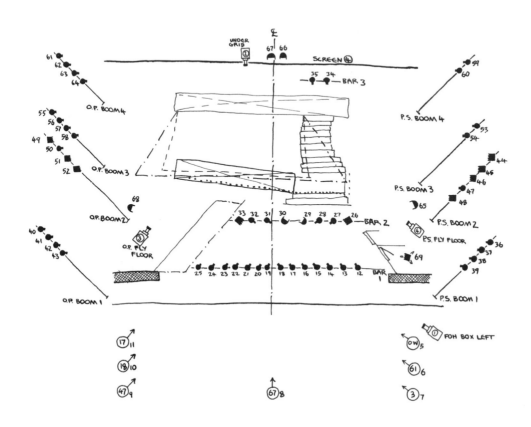

**National Theatre of Great Britain, London**
Director John Dexter
Designer Josef Svoboda
Lighting Richard Pilbrow

## CUE SYNOPSIS (ABRIDGED)

ACT 1   A public garden high above the Volga. Evening
         Fade to evening. Close to Katerina bench L.
         Cheat in ramp US. Fade toward storm. Lose bench.
         Close foot of steps Katerina.
         Fade to projections.

ACT 2   Room in the Kabanov house. Interior bright sun through
Scene 1   small window (beam light frame).

ACT 2   Street in front of Kabanov house. Evening.
Scene 2   Fade to twilight.

ACT 2   A small overgrown ravine and a wicker gate. Late the same
Scene 3   evening to night.
         Very romantic, poetic. Lovers meet.
         Close to love scene center.
         X-fade to parting picture.

ACT 3   An arcade around an old decaying building. A storm
Scene 1   coming up.
         Rain passes and scene brightens.
         Storm again. Lightning.
         Lightning fade to severe storm

ACT 3   A public garden. Bleak cold evening.
Scene 2   Close to Katerina. Suicide attempt.
         Crowd on with torches center.
         Close to Katerina body center.

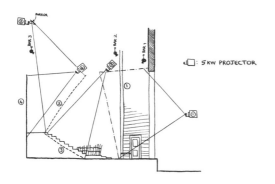

⌐□: 5KW PROJECTOR

○ : SCREEN NUMBERS

| Unit | Position Type | Instrument | Function | Color (Cinemoid) |
|------|---------------|------------|----------|------------------|
| 1 | FOH CIRCLE L | 5kW projector | Screen 1 | |
| 2 | UNDERGRID | 5kW projector | Screen 2 | |
| | (back gallery) | | | |
| 3 | OP FLY FLOOR | 5kW projector | Screen 3 | |
| 4 | PS FLY FLOOR | 5kW projector | Screen 4 | |
| 5 | FOH L | 6 patt 264* | Acting area DS | OW |
| 6 | | 2 patt 264* | Night gobo wash DS | 61 |
| 7 | | 1 patt 264* | Katerina body lamplit C | 3 |
| 8 | FOH C | 4 patt 293* | Cool front fill | 67 |
| 9 | FOH R | 2 patt 264 | Sunset/warm DS fill | 47 |
| 10 | | 2 patt 264 | Night gobo wash DS | 18 |
| 11 | | 6 patt 264* | Acting areas DS | 17 |
| 12 | ELECTRIC 1 | patt 264W | Center (Katerina body) | 3 |
| 13 | | patt 264W | Gobo around bench RC | 40 |
| 14 | | patt 264W | Acting area LC/L | OW |
| 15 | | patt 264W | Acting area LC cool | 40 |
| 16 | | patt 264W | Acting area C | OW |
| 17 | | patt 264W | Acting area RC/R (bench) | OW |
| 18 | | patt 264W | Acting area RC cool | 40 |
| 19 | | patt 264W | Acting area L cool | 17 |
| 20 | | patt 264W | Acting area L warm | 51 |
| 21 | | patt 264W | Acting area C cool | 17 |
| 22 | | patt 264W | Acting area C warm | 51 |
| 23 | | patt 264W | Acting area R cool | 17 |
| 24 | | patt 264W | Acting area R warm | 51 |
| 25 | | patt 264W | Gobo all LC | 40 |
| 26 | ELECTRIC 2 | patt 243 | Night forestage | 18 |
| 27 | | patt 264 | Cool storm backlight | 17 |
| 28 | | patt 264 | Leaf downlight gobo | 61 |
| 29 | | beamlight | Lightning shaft | 17 |
| 30 | | beamlight | Lightning shaft | 17 |
| 31 | | patt 264 | Leaf downlight gobo | 61 |
| 32 | | patt 264 | Cool storm backlight | 17 |
| 33 | | patt 243 | Night forestage | 18 |
| 34 | ELECTRIC 3 | patt 264 | Backlight stairs day | OW |
| 35 | | patt 264 | Backlight stairs night | 40 |

| Unit | Position Type | Instrument | Function | Color (Cinemoid) |
|------|---------------|------------|----------|------------------|
| 36 | PS BOOM 1 | 2 patt 264 | X light forestage cool | 67 |
| 37 | | 2 patt 264 | X light forestage warm | 52 |
| 38 | | 2 patt 23 | X light forestage sunset | 47 |
| 39 | | 2 patt 23 | X light forestage night | 40 |
| 40 | OP BOOM 1 | 2 patt 264 | X light forestage cool | 17 |
| 41 | | 2 patt 264 | X light forestage warm | 3 |
| 42 | | 2 patt 23 | X light forestage sunset | 47 |
| 43 | | 2 patt 23 | X light forestage night | 40 |
| 44 | PS BOOM 2 | patt 223 | X light foot stairs night | 40 |
| 45 | | patt 223 | X light foot stairs cool | 17 |
| 46 | | patt 223 | X light foot stairs warm | 3 |
| 47 | | 2 patt 23 | X light center warm | 52 |
| 48 | | patt 223 | X light center night | 40 |
| 49 | OP BOOM 2 | patt 223 | X light center to steps | OW |
| 50 | | 2 patt 23 | X light center warm | 51 |
| 51 | | patt 223 | X light center cool | 17 |
| 52 | | patt 223 | X light center sunset | 47 |
| 53 | PS BOOM 3 | patt 264 | X light bridge warm | 52 |
| 54 | | patt 264 | X light bridge cool | 17 |
| 55 | OP BOOM 3 | patt 264 | X light bridge to L | OW |
| 56 | | patt 264 | X light bridge to L | 61 |
| 57 | | patt 264 | X light bridge to RC | 50 |
| 58 | | patt 264 | X light bridge to RC | 47 |
| 59 | PS BOOM 4 | patt 264 | X back rostra day | OW |
| 60 | | patt 264 | X back rostra night | 40 |
| 61 | OP BOOM 4 | patt 264 | X back rostra night | 61 |
| 62 | | patt 264 | X back rostra day | 50 |
| 63 | | patt 264 | X back rostra sunset | 47 |
| 64 | | patt 264 | X back rostra night UR | 8 |
| 65 | FLYS L | beamlight | Lightning shaft forestage | 67 |
| 66 | FLYS BACK | beamlight | Backlight cloud | 67 |
| 67 | FLYS BACK | beamlight | Backlight cloud | 67 |
| 68 | FLYS R | beamlight | Lightning shaft C | 67 |
| 69 | STAGE L | patt 223 | Window DL | 3 |

* = On separate circuits

# Chapter Seven

# Design Challenges: The Behavior of Light in Nature— And Upon the Stage

One of the most wonderful ways of studying lighting is to open your eyes and look. Light is all around us, all the time, and we only have to be aware of it. Moonlight on water, neon reflected in a filthy window, the soft glow from a deep-set window at twilight…there is a world of magic just waiting to be seen.

In this chapter we shall be concerned with an extension of the ideas on lighting naturalistic settings discussed in Chapter 2 and the matter of style in theatre lighting.

In dwelling first on natural light and how it might be realized upon the stage I am not suggesting that natural light is the only inspiration for theatre lighting. It is merely an important one—one of a vast array of possibilities for the expressive use of dramatic lighting. After all, we have real human beings walking the stage, and the real world will often inspire the design of their environment.

## The Interior—Natural Light

I should like to explore further the question of motivating light and its effect on our design ideas for this type of setting.

Once inside our room, we should observe carefully how light behaves. All the light in the room should appear to originate from the window. The wall on the side opposite the window will be brighter than the others. This may need a special lift from a supplementary instrument on the first pipe or from the first boom position. The surface of the ground outside the window will also affect the pattern of light in the room. Supposing the ground is covered in snow, the ceiling inside will be brighter than normal because of the reflection from it. If we are by a lake or river, the reflection might even be a moving impression of reflected ripples.

Since we are attempting to be realistic, we should be fastidious in choosing the angles of light. Sunlight should not come streaming in through windows on opposite sides of the same room at the same time; and a dawn on stage left should not come from the same direction as a sunset. I suspect that reactions to natural light are so deeply ingrained that more people notice such discrepancies, if only subconsciously, than is sometimes realized.

As evening falls in our room the exterior dominant light can cross-fade to the lower angles and warmer tones of sunset. Within the room the shadows should lengthen, the color perhaps change softly as the level of reflected light naturally drops. The acting area and fill lighting should be reduced, leaving a greater emphasis on the key lighting perhaps supplemented by cross-lighting from the side, which would be at an angle more in keeping with the sunset.

What if the day is dull, or if the scene is in cold early morning? The overall color tone should be colder, and the overall level softer. We want to create the impression of an overall diffusion of light. The key light, which should now be in a cold tone from the window, will be hardly any brighter than the light in the room. It certainly should not show as a clear shaft.

### Interior Artificial Light

If the action calls for one or more artificial light sources to be turned on (table lamps, wall brackets or a chandelier), we shall have to supplement their light from our stage lighting and yet somehow maintain the impression that all the light is radiating from these fittings.

In the case of a chandelier—or anything above head height—this can be done comparatively easily. The production of *The Three Sisters* for the National Theatre at the Old Vic had a large chandelier hung upstage in the dinner party scene. This was supplemented by eight instruments, some upstage of it, some downstage, which cast a pattern of light that appeared to radiate from the chandelier itself. We should not ignore the light that comes from the fitting itself. This can be as bright as we can afford to have it without dazzling the audience. We can cheat and have an especially bright light in a fitting, partially masked to avoid glare to the audience, with an aperture, hidden to the audience, throwing light onto the actors. Sometimes a real light fitting will cast light where we don't want it: for instance, a table-lamp shade will often send a lot of its light straight up to the ceiling. As we want to keep the attention of the audience at stage level, we can cheat and mask out the top of the fitting without this being visible from the audience. Fittings on tables or below eye level are the most difficult to reinforce, because most of the spotlighting comes from overhead. It may be possible, if we need it, to conceal some small unit in the furniture adjacent to the fitting.

All light fittings that have to be switched on during the action should actually be switched from the control board. The actor simply mimes the operation, while the switchboard does the work. This is the only way in which one can achieve a really satisfactory coordination between the fitting and its covering spots. A battery-operated oil lamp should be fitted with a rheostat for the actor to use rather than a switch. Lamps that have to be carried around the stage probably present the greatest problem, since our lighting has to "follow" and this necessitates a series of rapid overlapping cues. Here we have an argument for positioning the board operator where he can see the stage, see what the actors are doing and coordinate the lighting changes with the action.

It is always difficult to produce a battery-powered lamp that is bright enough, particularly if it has got to stay on through a long scene. I recall a production of *The Father* with Trevor Howard, directed by Casper Wrede, set designed by Malcolm Pride, where an oil lamp had to be carried on, placed on a table and burn for almost forty minutes. It was impossible to get a battery lamp strong enough to remain bright for that length of time, and eventually we constructed one that ran on both battery and mains. It was carried on under battery power and placed on two mains contacts fixed in the table. The mains supply was then faded in to take over from the battery.

Particularly in a dramatic production such as *The Father,* one can afford to be bold about how little covering light is needed in an artificially lit scene. Light from the front should be reduced to an absolute minimum and a truly claustrophobic effect achieved within the room by restricting the illumination to the pool of light from the fitting. This is a moment where the 45° angle becomes positively undesirable. Perhaps my favorite lighting moment was in a production of *Measure for Measure* for Michael Elliott at the Old Vic. In this, one entire scene (five minutes of dialogue) was played around a lantern on a table: the only illumination came from this lantern. Inside was a 25-watt lamp, the light of which was only allowed to escape from two little holes on either side, which only just illuminated the two hovering conspiratorial faces.

## Moonlight

As with sunlight, one should try to suggest the parallel rays of natural light, but in this case it should be very low-key and of a cool tint, probably avoiding some of the more flagrantly romantic colors that sometimes pass as moonlight on the stage.

## Firelight, Candle and Oil Lamps

Shimmering firelight can add sparkle and interest to a scene. The impression of real fire may be of less importance than the light it emits, as the "fire" may be masked from the audience by its grate or stove. The light from the fire can be imitated by well-concealed miniature spots. Several small lamps will be more effective than one larger one, for it must be remembered that firelight spreads out across the room. The color of fire is not red but rather yellow and amber. I often use broken color, and a mixture of Lee 104 or 105 with broken 110 or 111 can be useful. It can be best to avoid movement in the firelight itself, for this can be distracting, but a few neon flicker lamps built into the fire and partially obscured can be effective. Softly shimmering light from the fire can be well simulated with twin-spin gobos or an animation disk for a Leko. For something special, this, together with some smoke and some strips of silk or mylar blown by a fan, can be almost as realistic as the real thing. But I must stress the word *almost*. Wherever possible, real flame, if permitted by the authorities, is always best.

In the 1994 *Show Boat* revival, perhaps my favorite scene is the Cotton Blossom theatre in performance. Intended to be primarily lit by guttering oil lamps in the footlights and around the auditorium, the spectators, packed in the gallery and orchestra, are lit with low cross-light from Lekos with twin-spin shimmering gobos.

The advance of technology—as candle gave way to kerosene, then gas to electricity—always gave rise to regrets that some intangible quality was lost in the advance of brightness. The loss of heat and smoke was probably not missed, but movement...? There is something wonderfully alive about fluttering candlelight. Maybe this was real "moving light."

### Exteriors

The realistic lighting of exterior scenes is always difficult, for here the light really has to be used in three dimensions. That the effect so often falls short of the designer's intention seems to me confirmation that lighting design is still in its infancy. How can we hope to suggest the sun itself with 1- or 2kW instruments? In nature on a sunlit day, everything is lit up, but the human eye does not see everything; it only looks at what it wants to see. On the stage, we have to direct the audience's attention as necessary. We are attempting to create the essence of sunlight.

Ideally the set is so designed that it allows us to strike a part of it with a very powerful shaft of sunlight and to create shadow. If the side of a house or a piece of wall can be strongly sunlit, this will be the key for the remainder of the scene. For *Four Baboons Adoring the Sun*, by John Guare, at the Vivian Beaumont Theatre the strong sunlight of Sicily had to be evoked (see Demonstration 5). The thrust stage had acting-area lighting from four angles with supplementary lighting from four more. Add to this cold downlight over the whole stage and a high-key "sunlight" from a mix of 5kW Fresnels and 1kW PAR 64 NSPs. The actors literally blazed in a quite Sicilian fashion. Nonincandescent light sources can provide a high-key powerful "motivating" source. HMI Fresnels have a higher color temperature than incandescent lamps, and this colder, whiter light can more effectively cut across the stage picture.

A dull day can present even greater problems. Without a dominant light to present the idea to the audience, it is all the more difficult to prevent the scene looking artificial and "stagey." With spotlighting (or perhaps the addition of some soft fill light) we have to create the effect of reflection and diffusion. A cool color will be needed with a very delicate balance of light from all directions. Real reflected light and truly diffused light might seem the ideal solution, though I've personally never found this so. For even under these circumstances the illumination still has to be selective, and truly diffused light would illuminate everything indiscriminately.

When creating the illusion of dawn or sunset, it is important to decide where the sun is coming from. Is it from the sides, the back or front of the stage? Dawn and sunset are all too often associated with rather technicolor shafts of light. My favorite "dawn" was in the production of the musical *Jorrocks*. In a scene set on a deserted heath (a bare stage in front of a large wraparound backlit cyclorama) darkness gave way to a low-lying, very cool greeny-gray diffused light that was gradually, in its turn, cut across by a faintly growing glassy yellow-white low sidelight.

## Exterior Night

Realistic exterior night scenes are among the most difficult to light because they should, in nine cases out of ten, actually be dark! The lighting designer obviously has to effect some compromise between reality and what is needed theatrically to allow the audience to see. The larger the stage area, and the darker the surrounding scenery, the easier is his task. Whenever possible, the designer should try to introduce some clearly defined source of light, be it a lamp, streetlight, fire or whatever. If the eye has one light source on which to focus, the remainder of the stage will appear darker by contrast. Similarly, a few stars in the night sky, with just a faint touch of deep blue, can make the whole scene recede in the imagination. If moonlight is called for, the parallel beams of natural light will be needed again. Several instruments with parallel beams will be far more effective than a single large one dimmed very low, unless the setting is a very open one with a cyclorama, when it may be possible to suspend an instrument sufficiently far away to give the impression of almost parallel rays and hard-edge shadows.

## Style in Lighting

I've not previously written about the issue of style in lighting, other than to suggest that everything must stem from the nature of the play—the source material and the approach of the creative team led by the director. I find that while one can talk about process and perhaps about problems encountered, it's very hard to talk about art. Each production should have its own unique qualities. Of course each lighting designer will bring some personal qualities to his work. Most of us can recognize an element of "trademark" in our colleagues' work.

Mark Henderson, accepting the 1992 Olivier Award for Best Lighting, spoke of his lighting for the National's production of *A Long Day's Journey Into Night*. He was seeking "extremely enhanced realism": "A long sunset came through big side windows. There was strong contrast of light and dark—people went into and out of light—the light choreographed the action. The key is to make a good stage picture and make it work within the play."

One of the most eloquent dissertations upon style in lighting I've heard was delivered by the Australian lighting designer Nigel Levings, giving a paper at the 1991 Pro Sound and Light Expo in Melbourne. For me, it made the long trip worthwhile. He has kindly allowed me to quote from an edited version of his remarks:

> I have been struck by the exquisite uniqueness of certain moments of time. A particular combination of sun and smells and sound, of wind and warmth can instantly recreate a moment in my life. It is this *particularity* of moment that I am trying to capture. It may not be that the dawn light I portray is exactly the dawn light you yourself experienced the first time you spent all night in bed with your own Romeo or Juliet. I hope at least that I manage to convey something of the uniqueness of that moment for them as well as to suggest the other elements that this dawn stands for, the cold light of day dawning on the last conscious moments they will spend together. At these "hinge" moments I try to suggest some strong and at times surrealistically stretched version of reality. For an audience this shift works almost subconsciously.

> These are the fragments of time I long to capture on the stage. The attempt to do so involves an intuitive response to the work based upon a careful study of text, direction, design and music.

> We can consider lighting analogous to painting, except we do it in 4D. Most of our lighting has been from some intensely fastidious school of naturalistic painting....but what about the lessons of more modern painters? We should examine how naturalism has constrained us. Why is it always night when we most want to see things? Why has that bloody Rodolfo blown out the candle before he pockets the key to Mimi's apartment, just when we want the back row of the gallery to see him do it?

> Some years ago I did *A Midsummer Night's Dream* with Jim Sharman, in which the night was half a dozen mercury vapour-floodlights. In 1974 I saw Nick Chelton do night in a suburban backyard lit by a sodium vapour streetlight. The point I am trying to make is that even in naturalism our range can be extensive.

> I want to find a language of light for the stage where a light is a light and nothing more. It is not the sun or a door shaft or a candle's glow, it is simply a light illuminating a performer in an interesting way. A simplicity of gesture and an abstraction from the naturalistic world are what I search for in my lighting. Rock lighting does not suggest sun or moon. A light is a light; in most cases what it looks like in the rig and what it does in the air are more important than what it does when it hits a performer. I'm not suggesting we should incorporate the "whizz-bang" effects in their entirety into theatre, in fact these are elements I hate most; design of the "Hey! Look at me, aren't I fantastic" school of

fascistic lighting. The aspect of sidestepping naturalism is what interests me intensely.

Another influence is the hyper-realism of the German school, which insists that if you are to have sunlight through a window it must be the right color temperature and the right lux level. Mount a 4kW HMI outside the cottage window. Facial fill is out, entire productions are in nothing but backlight. The faces are a little undernourished for our tastes. Set against this is what I think of as the British school of lyrical naturalism. Beautiful stage pictures, exquisitely modeled and shaped. I feel that despite their innovations, such as the architectural rig on British stages, a lot of the work of the "white light" designers fall into this category.

A major area of cross-fertilization is film lighting. I have long borrowed the techniques of film noir to handle night scenes. Now we are seeing film adopt stage techniques.

A paper I would love to see would be "Rock Lighting—Abstract Kitsch and the Fascist Influence": Light as a symbol of power—sexual, social and egotistical.

Light can also act as other sorts of symbols in more meaningful ways. Images of light as blaze of truth or knowledge.

We will all find numerous examples of all these influential styles of light among the work of our favorite designers.

But if Nigel spoke eloquently, let us turn back to Robert Edmond Jones over fifty years ago. In 1941 in his book *The Dramatic Imagination* he wrote most brilliantly on lighting:

Future historians will speak of this period as the spotlight era. Once upon a time our stages were lit with gas jets: before that by kerosene lamps, and before that by tapers and torches. But today our productions are characterized by conical shafts of colored light which beat down upon actors from lamps placed in the flies and along the balconies of the theatre. Lighting a play today is a matter of arranging and rearranging those lamps in an infinite variety of combinations. This is an exercise involving great technical skill and ingenuity. The craft of lighting has been developed to a high degree and is kept to a high standard by rigorous training in schools and colleges. It has become both exacting and incredibly exact. The beam of light strikes with the precision of a mot juste. It bites like an etcher's needle or cuts deep like a surgeon's scalpel. This wonderful invention has become part of the general expertise of Broadway. We handle our spotlights and gelatins and dimmers in the theatre with the same delight and the same sense of mastery with which we drive a high-powered automobile or pilot an aeroplane.

But at rare moments, in the long quiet hours of light rehearsals, a strange thing happens. We are overcome by a realization of the livingness of light. As we gradually bring a scene out of the shadows, sending long rays slanting across a column, touching an outline with color, animating the scene moment by moment until it seems to breathe, our work becomes an incantation. We feel the presence of elemental energies.

There is hardly a designer who has not experienced at some time or another this overwhelming sense of the livingness of light. I hold these moments to be among the most precious of experiences the theatre can give us. The true life of theatre is in them. We catch disturbing glimpses of a theatre not yet created.

Slowly, slowly, we begin to see lighting in the theatre, not only as an exciting craft, but as an art, at once visionary and exact, subtle, powerful, infinitely difficult to learn. We begin to see that a drama is not an engine, running at full speed from overture to final curtain, but a living organism. And we see light as a part of that organism. And we see light as part of that livingness.

Our first duty in the theatre is to the actors. It is they who interpret the drama. The stage belongs to them and they must dominate it. In nine cases out of ten our problem is simply to make the actors and their environment clearly and fully visible.

Visible, yes. But in a very special way. The world of the theatre is a world of sharper, clearer, swifter impressions than the world we live in. The actors who reveal the heightened world of the theatre should move in a light that is altogether uncommon. Perhaps the word lucid best describes this light. A lucid light. Everything is perceived here; everything is known.

Lighting a scene consists not only in throwing light upon objects but in throwing light upon a subject. We have a choice of lighting a drama from the outside, as a spectator, or from the inside, as part of the drama's experience. We reveal the drama. We use light as we use words, to elucidate ideas and emotions. Light becomes a tool, an instrument of expression, like a paintbrush, or a sculpture's chisel, or a phrase of music. We turn inward and at once we are in the company of the great ones of the theatre. We learn from them to bathe our productions in the light that never was on land or sea.

A rare light of imagination is poured over the scene, fresh and disturbing and strangely tender. A new theatre draws near, bathed in "the nameless glow that colors mental vision."

Lucidity, penetration, awareness, discovery, inwardness, wonder: these are the qualities we should try to achieve. And there is a luster, a shine and a gleam that befits the exceptional occasion. Last of all, there is a quality of secularity, a bold firm stroke, an authority that puts an audience at its ease. Here in the little circle of radiance, the life of the theatre is going on.

In illuminating dramatic action we must concern ourselves not only with light but also with shadow. How shall I explain to you the meaning of shadow in the theatre—the primitive dread, the sense of brooding, the blackness, the descent into endless night? At heart we are all afraid of the dark, and our fear goes back to the remote beginnings of the human race. See the mood of the audience change, hear them chatter or fall silent as the lights in the theatre are raised or lowered. It is such instinctive responses that give light its dynamic power in the theatre. We are practicing an art of light and shadow that was old before the pyramids, an art that can shake our dispositions with feelings beyond the reaches of our souls.

The creative approach to the problem of stage lighting—the art, in other words, of knowing where to put light on the stage and where to take it away—is not to be found in textbooks or precepts. There is only a goal and a promise. We have the mechanism with which to create this ideal, exalted, dramatic light in the theatre. Whether we can do so or not is a matter of temperament as well as technique. The secret lies in our perception of light in the theatre as something alive.

Does this mean that we are to carry images of poetry and vision and high passion in our minds while we are shouting out orders to electricians on ladders in light-rehearsals?

Yes. This is what it means.

# DEMONSTRATION 5 — *Four Baboons Adoring the Sun*

Vivian Beaumont Theatre, New York
Director  Sir Peter Hall
Designer  Tony Walton
Lighting  Richard Pilbrow
Projection  Wendall Harrington

CUE SYNOPSIS

Preset. Glowing disk of sand.
Messenger emerges from primordial ooze.
Palermo airport. Neon and fluorescent light.
The family arrive.
Car park. Blazing Sicilian sun.
The van. "Real Sicily. See the poppies."
Cafe by the sea. Hot sun and sea.
The dig at Muculfa. Hot white, brown blaze.
Flashbacks: The Met museum, a hotel, Paris by moonlight,
the Louvre.
A bedroom. The kids discovered.
Camping trip. Campfire. Sunset to night.
Volcano erupts. The earth cracks open.
Wayne and Halcy flee up the mountain. "The air is on fire."
Climbing the stone.
Vision of a deer. "The moon reflects in the pool of water."
They appear transformed in white and gold.
Wayne steps into the sky.
Cold dawn of grief.
Departure as "Mount Etna spews out its lava."

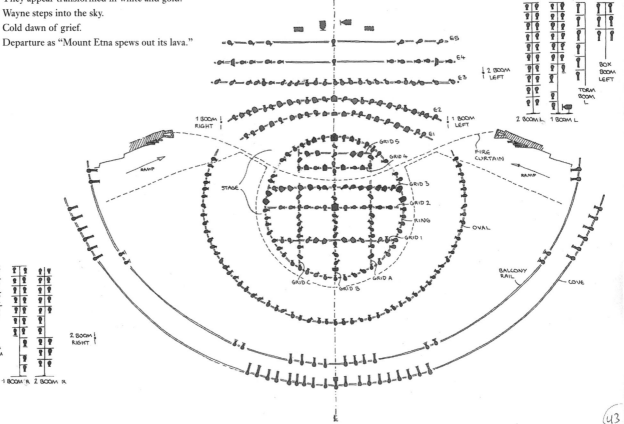

by John Guare

| Position | Instrument Type | Function | Color | Notes |
|---|---|---|---|---|
| COVE LEFT | Leko 10° | X DS Hot | G343 | |
| | Leko 10° | Night fill | G730 | |
| COVE CENTER | Leko 10° | Front acting area left | R60 | |
| | Leko 10° | Front acting area right | R07 | |
| | Leko 10° | Front fill twilight | R57 | |
| | Leko 10° | Front fill night | R81 | |
| COVE RIGHT | Leko 10° | X DS Hot | G343 | |
| | Leko 10° | Night fill | G730 | |
| BALCONY RAIL | Leko 20° | Sunset X | R321 | |
| | Leko 20° | Flame | R41-10 | gobo R7785 |
| | Leko 20° | Sea kids | G680 | |
| | Leko 20° | Scrim gobo | R41 | gobo R7811 |
| | Leko 20° | Scrim gobo | R13 | gobo R7811 |
| | Leko 20° | Scrim gobo | R81 | gobo R7788 |
| | Leko 20° | Twilight | R57 | |
| BOX BOOM LEFT | Leko 10° | X Tan | G380 | |
| | Leko 10° | X cool | G730 | |
| | Leko 10° | Sunset | R321 | |
| BOX BOOM RIGHT | Leko 10° | X Tan | G380 | |
| | Leko 10° | X cool | G730 | |
| TORM BOOM LEFT | Leko 10° | X Tan | G380 | |
| | Leko 10° | X cool | G730 | |
| | Leko 10° | Sunset | R321 | |
| TORM BOOM RIGHT | Leko 10° | X Tan | G380 | |
| | Leko 10° | X cool | G730 | |
| VOMITORIUM LEFT | Leko 6x12 | Eros | R60 | |
| | Leko 6x12 | Flame | R41-20 | gobo R7785 |
| | Leko 6x12 | Fire | R30 | |
| VOMITORIUM RIGHT | Leko 6x12 | Flame | R41-20 | gobo R7785 |
| | Leko 6x12 | Fire | R30 | |
| OVAL | Leko 6x12 | Acting area left back | R08 | |
| | Leko 6x12 | Acting area left front | R60 | |
| | Leko 6x12 | Acting area right back | R07 | |
| | Leko 6x12 | Acting area right front | R3206 | |
| | Leko 6x12 | X Gobo | G690 | gobo R7788 |
| | Leko 6x12 | Sidelight left cool | G885 | |
| | Leko 6x12 | Sidelight left warm | G365 | |
| | Leko 6x12 | Sidelight right cool | G790 | |
| | Leko 6x12 | Sidelight right warm | G520 | |
| RING | PAR64/NSP | Moon X-light | L118 | |
| | Leko 6x12 | (as Oval) | | |
| | Leko 6x12 | Eros bed | R62 | |
| | Leko 6x12 | Specials | | |
| | PAR 64/NSP | Sun DS | G470 | |
| | Leko 6x16 | Baboon specials | NC | |

| Position | Instrument Type | Function | Color | Notes |
|---|---|---|---|---|
| GRID 1 | 2kW Fresnel | Mauve wash | R50 | |
| | 2kW Fresnel | Rose wash | R81 | |
| | 2kW Fresnel | Sepia wash | G330 | |
| GRID 2 | Leko 6x12 | Sidelight left cool | G885 | |
| | Leko 6x12 | Sidelight left warm | G365 | |
| | Leko 6x12 | Sidelight right cool | G790 | |
| | Leko 6x12 | Sidelight right warm | G520 | |
| | Leko 6x12 | Backlight | R62 | |
| | 5kW Fresnel | Center pool | | |
| GRID 3 | PAR 64/NSP | Moon X-light | L118 | |
| | PAR 64/NSP | Gold splash | R20 | |
| | PAR 64/NSP | Red splash | G250 | |
| | Leko 6x12 | Voms left & right | R08 | |
| | PAR 64/NSP | Sun DS | G470 | |
| GRID 4 | 2kW Fresnel | Red wash | R26 | |
| | 2kW Fresnel | Blue wash | R77 | |
| GRID 5 | PAR 64/NSP | Moon X-light | L118 | |
| | PAR 64/NSP | Sun DS | G470 | |
| GRID A | Beamlights | Shafts | R62 | |
| | Leko 6x12 | Sidelight left cool | G885 | |
| | Leko 6x12 | Sidelight left warm | G365 | |
| GRID B | Beamlights | Shafts | R62 | |
| | Leko 6x12 | Specials | | |
| GRID C | Beamlights | Shafts | R62 | |
| | Leko 6x12 | Sidelight right cool | G790 | |
| | Leko 6x12 | Sidelight right warm | G520 | |
| 1 ELECTRIC | Leko 6x12 | Acting area left back | R08 | |
| | PAR 64/NSP | Moon X-light | L118 | |
| | Leko 6x12 | X Gobo | G685 | gobo R7788 |
| | PAR 64/NSP | Purple splash | R49 | |
| | PAR 64/NSP | Red splash | G250 | |
| | PAR 64/NSP | Sun DS | G470 | |
| 2 ELECTRIC | PAR 64/NSP | Moon X-light | L118 | |
| | Leko 6x12 | Ruin DL | R08 | |
| | 5kW Fresnel | B/L blue green | R93 | |
| | PAR 64/NSP | Sun DS | G460 | |
| 3 ELECTRIC | Leko 6x12 | Kids left | R62 | |
| | Leko 6x12 | Disk front night | L118 | |
| | Leko 6x12 | Disk front gold | R13 | |
| | Leko 6x12 | Kids high | R60 | |
| | Leko 6x12 | Deer | R87 | gobo R7805 |
| | Leko 6x12 | Kids right | R62 | |
| 4 ELECTRIC | Leko 6x16 | Wayne top | R62 | |
| | Leko 6x12 | Disk rim | NC | |
| | Leko 6x12 | Disk top | R60 | |
| | Leko 6x12 | Disk sun | G460 | |

| Position | Instrument | Function Type | Color (Cinemoid) | Notes | | Position | Instrument | Function Type | Color (Cinemoid) | Notes |
|---|---|---|---|---|---|---|---|---|---|---|
| 5 ELECTRIC | Leko 6x12 | Disk moon | L118 | | | 2 BOOM RIGHT | Leko 6x12 | X disk gold | R13 | |
| | Leko 6x12 | Disk edge | R13 | | | | Leko 6x12 | X disk cold | R62 | |
| | Leko 6x12 | Disk top | G470 | | | | Leko 6x12 | X disk moon | R71 | |
| | Leko 6x12 | Disk sun | G460 | | | | Leko 6x12 | Kids front | R60 | |
| 1 BOOM LEFT | Leko 6x12 | Sun X | R04 | | | | Leko 6x12 | Disk | G470 | |
| | Leko 6x12 | Night X | R70 | | | | Leko 6x12 | Disk sunset | R321 | |
| | Leko 6x12 | X ruins | R04 | | | | Leko 6x12 | Disk center sunset | R23 | |
| | Leko 6x12 | Sunset | R321 | | | | Leko 6x12 | Disk night | R62 | |
| | Leko 6x12 | Flame | R41-20 | gobo R7785 | | | Leko 6x12 | Disk center night | R62 | |
| | Leko 6x12 | X ruins | R3408 | | | | Leko 6x12 | Disk gold | R14 | |
| 1 BOOM RIGHT | Leko 6x12 | Sun X | R04 | | | | Leko 6x16 | Disk uplight | R3408 | |
| | Leko 6x12 | Night X | R70 | | | STAGE | Zoom Mini 40/60 | Salmon | R41 | |
| | Leko 6x12 | X ruins | R04 | | | | | Sea blue | R71 | |
| | Leko 6x12 | Sunset | R321 | | | | | Straw | R13 | |
| | Leko 6x12 | Flame | R41-20 | gobo R7785 | | | | Blue | R62 | |
| | Leko 6x12 | X ruins | R3408 | | | DISK | | Deer uplight | | |
| 2 BOOM LEFT | Leko 6x12 | X disk gold | R13 | | | | | Center white | | |
| | Leko 6x12 | X disk cold | R62 | | | | | Center red | | |
| | Leko 6x12 | X disk moon | R71 | | | | | Inner white | | |
| | Leko 6x12 | Kids front | R60 | | | | | Outer red | | |
| | Leko 6x12 | Disk | G470 | | | NEON SIGN | | | | |
| | Leko 6x12 | Disk sunset | R321 | | | UNDER FLOOR | Leko 6x9 | Earthquake | R41-20 | |
| | Leko 6x12 | Disk center sunset | R23 | | | UPSTAGE | Tubular ripple | Lava on RP | R18-44 | |
| | Leko 6x12 | Disk night | R62 | | | | Moon Flower | Lava on RP | | |
| | Leko 6x12 | Disk center night | R62 | | | | | | | |
| | Leko 6x12 | Disk gold | R14 | | | | | | | |
| | Leko 6x16 | Disk uplight | R3408 | | | | | | | |

# Chapter Eight

# Design Challenges: Musicals, Ballet and Opera: Lighting in Repertoire

The musical can encompass many different styles of production. The designer may be called upon for pure dance light, for the naturalism of straight drama, or for all the effects of grand opera. However, there is generally a demand for brightness and sparkle, a need to make the actors stand out vividly from their background. The late Jean Rosenthal, the brilliant American lighting designer, described the lighting of the musical as an attempt to make the actors appear "jewel-like."

In 1970 I wrote "no other country could compete with America when it comes to producing musicals; and the lighting of the best American musicals would seem to have reached a pinnacle within the genre." How times have changed. The 1980s saw the emergence of Andrew Lloyd Webber and Cameron Mackintosh and with them a renaissance of British scenic and lighting design.

What happened? The heyday of the American musical had immense influence in London. *West Side Story*, directed by Jerome Robbins, scenery by Oliver Smith and lighting by Jean Rosenthal, revolutionized many peoples' view of the musical as a form of theatre to be taken seriously. It was produced by Harold Prince. His later productions, many of which he directed,

---

There is often confusion about the use of the words repertory and repertoire. In this book the word repertoire refers to a theatre using a production pattern of daily change of performance, as opposed to repertory, where weekly or biweekly change of production is employed.

included *Cabaret, Company, Fiddler on the Roof* and *A Little Night Music.*
Each set new standards of excellence for the musical in London. They led
directly to *Evita* (David Hersey's first major lighting success). The phenomenal success of *Cats,* followed by *Les Miserables* and *Phantom of the
Opera,* might be described as an extraordinarily successful combination of
two strains: the best of Broadway in the Hal Prince tradition, with the best
of a flowering of English Arts Council-supported classical production and
design quality (Trevor Nunn, John Napier, Maria Bjornson, etc., with lighting designers David Hersey and Andrew Bridge).

The fifties were a golden period for American lighting. With an acceptance of lighting design as a distinct discipline, the emerging specialist
designers, such as Abe Feder, Peggy Clark and Jean Rosenthal, were following in the footsteps of visionary scene designers (Robert Edmond Jones, Lee
Simonson, Jo Mielziner) who had pioneered advances in the design of lighting. The principal manufacturer, Century, was led by Ed Kook. He saw the
commercial value of this emerging specialization and supported the new
young profession. Finally, American lamp manufacturers seemed to possess
a more pioneering spirit than their European counterparts. The supply voltage in the United States is 110 volts, which produces greater lamp efficiency. Thanks to this, the ellipsoidal spotlight offered a range of flexible and
powerful instruments, which together with the PAR lamp became standard
tools in that country. Thus supported by a greater appreciation by producers of the role of lighting in a production, larger budgets for lighting rental
became common, which meant that the American designer had greater
quantities of more powerful equipment at his disposal in those early days of
modern lighting.

The shape of Broadway theatres also used to only allow front-of-house
lighting from a very low frontal position on the balcony rail and from booms
in boxes to the side of the stage. Without an acting-area lighting position in
the front of the house, the tendency developed toward using rail lighting
straight into the stage as a frontal fill light, while all the modeling was
achieved by units adjacent to or behind the proscenium. The first and second pipes, immediately behind the proscenium or show portal, usually provided acting-area lighting, both edge lighting directly downward to the
forestage as well as toward areas farther back. The instruments were almost
always double hung, that is, instead of having one at either side of each area,
there were two, making four lamps each, one pair in one color tone and one
pair in another (probably warm and cool). This was supplemented by sidelighting (ellipsoidal spots or beam projectors), which added plasticity, giving
extra color effects and linking the acting areas together. Downlighting
and/or backlighting was also added, with ellipsoidal spots, beam projectors
or PAR battens (striplights). Together this multi-instrument complexity
produced the jewel-like lighting described by Jean Rosenthal.

A large musical used as many as twelve or fifteen spot bars and six or eight
tormentor booms on either side. This added up to a very considerable

amount of equipment, more than was customary in Europe at that time. In the skilled hands of such designers as Jean Rosenthal, Jules Fisher, Martin Aronstein and Tharon Musser, the results were often superb.

The quality of lighting in these big Broadway productions was evident when they came to London. There the best lighting designers were then working with Theatre Projects, often for the newly emerging National Theatre, the Royal Shakespeare Company and the major regional theatres— all with a dramatic orientation. The combination of American musical tradition and practice and American-style multi-instrument rigs with English classical scenic and lighting design proved a powerful combination. It only needed the musical talent of Andrew Lloyd Webber and the entrepreneurial brilliance of Cameron Mackintosh to create the resurgence of the English musical that has since swept the theatre world.

Today the best musical lighting stretches the art to the uttermost on both sides of the Atlantic. Andrew Bridge in *Phantom of the Opera* and *Sunset Boulevard*, David Hersey in *Cats*, *Les Miserables* and *Miss Saigon*, Jules Fisher in *Grand Hotel* and *Will Rogers' Follies*, Paul Gallo in *Crazy for You*, employing complex resources, remote focus instruments, color scrollers, low voltage follow spots—each demonstrates in an individual way great artistry and sensitivity with light.

A great deal of use has been made in musicals of the translucent backcloth. It was used to particularly good effect in *Fiddler on the Roof,* directed by Jerome Robbins, set designed by Boris Aronson. A sky cloth in front of which was hung a gauze with applied cut-outs represented the village of Anatevka. This was lit in London from the rear by PAR battens at the top and bottom. Since the bottom lamps had to be struck to allow scenery to be set from the back of the stage, the battens were hung from a counterweight bar, with the lamps shining upward instead of downward, and the bar was lowered right to the stage floor. This ground row could then be struck in a matter of seconds by flying it away (Fig. 78).

David Hersey has pioneered the use of the low-voltage striplight, or light curtain, in the musical. For *Miss Saigon* he added to the conventional fixed light curtain remotely controlled tilt capability and a twenty-color scroller. The effect of being able to move a wall of light and change its color is very powerful. For the Hal Prince *Show Boat* revival on Broadway (lighting by myself), a second direction of movement—sideways pitch—was added, making these units even more effective as instruments to create focusable, parallel-beam walls of light—a good simulation of sunlight on the stage.

Remote-controlled spotlights have become commonplace in the big musical. Pioneered in the music industry for rock and roll, an increase in reliability has made them an essential tool. Quite apart from their capability to move dynamically through the show, as seen in almost every music video, the capability of being able to constantly refocus and recolor special after special is amazing. Again, David Hersey used them with great subtlety in *Miss Saigon*. Conventional Vari*Lites were supplemented by Vari*Lites mounted on

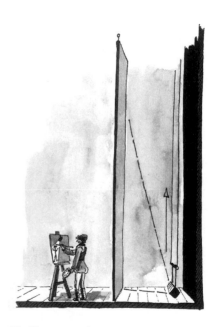

78. *Flown ground row*

tracks, able also to slide from side to side overhead and vertically at the sides of the proscenium. Surely this is a foretaste of where remote-control instrumentation will go.

It has long been customary for musicals to use follow spotlights on the principal artists. This quite arbitrary method of illumination seems to some people to convey a theatricality that contributes to the excitement of the evening. The way in which follow spots are handled (and the decision whether or not to use them at all) depends upon the subject and content of the show. A bright, sparkling, lighthearted entertainment can certainly benefit from an obvious and glamorous follow spot, whereas in a dramatic musical, the follow spots if used at all should be extremely subtle. If subtlety is required, the follow spots might be best worked from a side, front-of-house, or proscenium position (from the old "perch" position rather than from the conventional rear of the auditorium). *The Man of La Mancha* and *Golden Boy* employed this technique effectively. David Hersey in *Evita* began the use of 24-volt 1,000-watt beam projectors in a high side position as follow spots of great intensity. He describes their ability as being able to achieve a "white-out."

Today the side follow spot is as common as that from the front. A big musical such as the *Show Boat* revival may use two or three conventional frontlights, one follow spot from either side in a high box-boom position, as well as one or even two from either side of the stage. We might well compare today's practice with that common almost one hundred years ago when, for David Belasco, multiple follow spots from all around the proscenium on bridges and side perch platforms were standard—long before the days of multiple spotlights and computer-controlled moving lights had arrived. Perhaps this is another example of "back to the future."

## Lighting Ballet and Dance

*In conversation with John B. Read (lighting designer to the Royal Ballet, London, England)*

One of the fascinations of lighting for dance is that here, more than in any other branch of theatre, the lighting designer's role has advanced furthest. The process of staging ballet and, perhaps most particularly, modern dance is almost a collaboration between partners, the choreographer and the lighting designer.

Lighting the dance gives the designer almost total freedom. His role is to manipulate light in space. That space however, will be filled with a continually changing number of people. Dancers use their entire bodies as instruments, and lighting has to mold and sculpt the whole person. The dancers become a series of moving sculptures, and revealing these visually to the audience in a dramatic or appropriate way is the lighting designer's task.

However, by referring to the dancer as a moving sculpture, one could be in danger of ignoring the most important ingredient: that is, the individual personality of the dancer himself and the interaction between the individual personalities of all the dancers involved, the choreographer and the lighting designer. The interplay between personality and the physical movement that results from it should determine the sort of lighting and make it seem almost inevitable.

I turn up at the rehearsal studios at least twenty minutes before the run-through of the piece is due to begin. I need to sense the ambiance among the group and to be accepted by them. There has to be a realization of all the most subliminal factors that show me how to light it. It is absolutely vital to sense and understand the inner interpretation that lies beneath the movement. I take down everything the choreographer says. Some, of course—Glenn Tetley, Robert Cohan, or David Bintley—I have worked with a lot, and one goes in with some sense of their intentions, but every view or thought expressed may go toward understanding. The choreographer will usually have a feeling of what he wants and the style he asks for is usually right, but occasionally I find a choreographer who asks for something that is belied by the work that he later produces. Sometimes it's difficult to talk about the lighting: indeed, it may be the last thing that he wants to discuss. Perhaps it's rather like a cat stalking a mouse; you talk about everything else except the subject under discussion. I try to find something constructive to say, then talk about something else until I can cheat my way into the subject. I cannot force them; there's sometimes insecurity to be overcome. I slowly work toward understanding.

I do not like intruding on rehearsals in the very beginning, but I try to see the work when it's almost ready, to get an overall impression of the impact it will make on an audience. I plot all the movement diagramatically straight away, almost touch-typing it on to paper. Simultaneously I time with a stopwatch all the rhythms and changes and most importantly have all my senses attuned to getting the emotions I feel that underlie the dance. I need all the explosions to happen in my head that first time—to get the inspiration going.

Some companies have a visual image or style that to some extent might be dictated by the circumstances in which they work. For example they might have a semipermanent touring rig, and the need to do two or three pieces in one evening will provide some framework or limitation. But I try to start from scratch with every new piece. The style has come from the director and every item has to have the appropriate degree of individuality.

The movement is everything. I think that the lighting should be totally unselfish. I hate tricks; all the light should be on the body, and the thing I perhaps most dislike is overdesign. Trick changes out of context can destroy the concentration of the dancer and the audience.

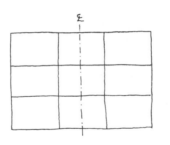

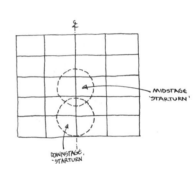

79. *Nine-part acting area*

80. *Twenty-part acting area*

terms of physical layout of the equipment, much will depend on the company. For example, for a contemporary dance company I might use a toplight in areas, a three-color choice from a high side position at the end of the overhead pipes, a sidelight at eye level, mid-level above and a shin buster (just above floor level). In addition I use a heavy backlight position but no spot bar, very little FOH and consequently no conventional acting-area lighting. In addition to this I will have perhaps twenty specials. The whole thing adds up to about two hundred units on eight pipes and is controlled by a touring eighty-way memory board. Other companies are like this with fewer specials, perhaps with less backlight. For classical ballet I use more, softer acting-area light at the conventional 45°, and less toplight and sidelight, largely because of the problems that are thrown up by girls in tutus. Too much toplight can make them look dwarflike. Of course for the really big shows in the classical repertoire, I might do a specific, fairly elaborate rig.

A lot of dance involves touring, and touring brings with it the need for great practicality. We need to use rugged equipment that can take rough handling.

If I divide the stage up into conventional areas, there can be nine (three rows deep of three across) or twenty (five rows deep of four across; Figs. 79 and 80). In the latter case I often create one or two center positions: one downstage "star turn" position and one midstage. I will also divide the stage up into strips across—in one, in two, in three, in back—and an end pipe side high light will go from center stage to the far side in each one of these strips (Figs. 81, 82 and 84). Backlight will cover perhaps two strips, but in sections across the stage. I will probably use a minimum of four sidelights: one lamp over three meters, one just below, one at eye-level and one shin buster (Figs. 85 and 86). Another common movement that can mean special crosslight will be diagonal from downstage to upstage on the opposite side (Fig. 83). The "acting areas" I have mentioned for modern dance will usually only have a toplight; this might be a single lamp or possibly two quite closely mounted together, but for classical "tutu" type dance, conventional spot bar coverage will be added.

*Stage Lighting Design*

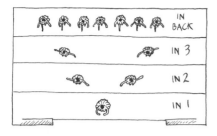 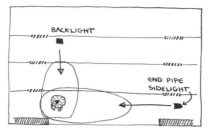 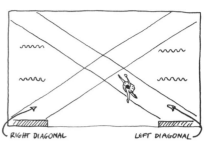

81. *Dance strips*

82. *Back and sidelight*

83. *Dance diagonals*

84. *Dance strips*

The thing that I have to be careful of is the problem that classical dancers call "experience with eye-level side lighting." This can easily disorient them when doing spins, pirouettes and turns, and they sometimes need an establishing light at a low level of brightness in some permanent position in the theatre. Also, sudden change has to be used with great care and must always be before any difficult sequence a dancer is about to go into. If a big lighting change, of level or direction or height, happens during a complicated movement, this can disorient the dancers completely. I always remember, in *Giselle*, the Queen of the Wilis's entrance. She looks far the best very dramatically cross-lit. However, her dance demands she be able to see the floor or she is completely lost—and so a certain amount of toplight at a very low level is essential. Quite often one has to make the stage look totally dark even when parts of it are lit for purely technical dance reasons.

Color is an essential part of dance lighting. Used with care it can create mood and atmosphere. It can help with the feeling of space around the dancer. For modern dance it can be used quite freely, but for

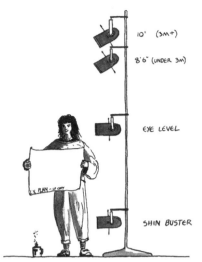

*85 and 86. Dance sidelight*

classical work it must be used with extreme care. A heavy selection of color, like strong toplight, can distort the image of the dancer.

The biggest lantern I usually use is a 5kW, but I often wish for some special effect of far greater intensity. I have used a whole cluster of PAR 64 lamps to build a pyramid of light upon the stage, and I seek a greater range of brightness than is presently possible. Sometimes a 2.5kW HMI Fresnel will be a good special toplight and in Germany a 4kW HMI from a ten- to fifteen-meter throw can be effective. Their large size, however, makes them difficult to fit into a permanent rig.

All too often in the olden days ballet was performed in enormous open areas with acres of canvas background lit by rows of battens and border lights. It is infinitely more exciting to see all the light emphasis on modeling the dancer in space, with the scenery taking its place discreetly in the background.

The lighting designer has the greatest scope in the field of modern dance. He can allow his imagination virtually total freedom when the dance, no longer restricted to storytelling, concentrates upon the evocation of mood and emotion through sheer movement. The lighting itself can dance with the performer, weaving its pattern around him, revealing every moment and conveying every mood.

New developments in lighting control offer the dancer a new partner able to react as fast as quicksilver or as fast as light itself.

### Lighting Opera #1

*In conversation with William Bundy, O.B.E. (former technical director of the Royal Opera House, Covent Garden, London)*

In the previous section on lighting the dance we saw that the battle for establishing the place of the lighting designer seems to have been won. In the world of lighting for opera it still rages.

One of the fascinations of operatic lighting is how little there is of it. Opera after opera seems to take place in Stygian darkness. Yet the scene has been changing; the old European style has given way to the new American-influenced style of lighting in which the lighting designer's role counts and is appreciated.

In many ways the new style of lighting was pioneered in the U.K. Under the old regime, the director, the set designer and the chief electrician got together and in an all too often haphazard manner decided how they would light the scenery and, when necessary, the singers. In the early fifties Tyrone Guthrie and Peter Brook both worked at the Royal Opera House, Covent Garden, and tried to bring the light they were used to in dramatic productions into the world of opera. Frankly, however, they were beaten by the system. The system is one largely influenced by the German opera example. The equipment consists of very little front of house, a very heavily equipped proscenium bridge manned by electricians, who would move large-wattage lamps from position to position between scenes, and the rest of the stage primarily lit by rows and rows of battens. This was still prevalent until quite recently in many of the world's great opera houses, and indeed in some it is only now beginning to change.

The lighting in opera is motivated by the music. On the whole, the stories are rather idiotic, but the music is not. The overall trend has been away from a purely vocal and musical performance toward presenting a totally theatrical experience. With the productions of Visconti and Zeffirelli in London, a demand was placed upon the singers for them to act as well as sing. Movement and performance became part of a total picture. Light was used to create atmosphere so that the stage was a whole, and directors with the power of imagination and stagecraft, put their stamp on their productions. Gradually the more outstanding conductors also began to realize that opera was more than just the music, and men such as Solti and Guilino began to take a keen interest in the overall staging and lighting in particular.

Opera calls upon a total emotional commitment, the power of the music draws in the spectator and makes operatic theatre the ultimate creative visual, aural, all-involving experience.

Wieland Wagner in Bayreuth demonstrated sensational possibilities for imaginative operatic lighting because he threw away all the clutter that traditionally had come to surround Wagnerian production, and made a statement with simplicity and the power of light that fitted perfectly with the music.

A director such as Zeffirelli took another route, often employing enormous realistic sets that, with the lighting, created an all-embracing atmospheric surround to the musical sound. With monumental, realistic, atmospheric staging (such as in *Tosca*—my favorite) an overwhelming impression could be made. The great designer Svoboda took yet another direction, providing not a complete environment but a powerful fragment of that environment with highly dramatic lighting.

Opera often includes large groups of people on the stage. They have to be able to sing and they have to be able to see the pit where the conductor holds the whole performance together. The audience doesn't need to see every face among the chorus, so darkness and light can be used with greater freedom than is often possible in a dramatic theatre. A picture can be created with shadow and darkness to convey atmosphere. Of course, in the new-style opera, with singers being expected to act better and look better and not just be voices, they can be lit properly and appropriately, so opera is really moving toward the dramatic style of lighting—three-dimensional lighting selectively revealing and concealing, shaping and creating atmosphere around the stage in sympathy with music.

Opera seems to have inherited immense problems. Everything is large. Sets are huge and cumbersome, and time is limited. Opera singers cannot sing on consecutive nights and usually want a two-day break between performances. They cannot rehearse and play the same opera in a single day, therefore there is an immense repertoire changeover problem. Even so, and despite the difficulties, operatic lighting is moving toward the three-dimensional. No longer is the front bridge sufficient, and although it took me seven years to get a backlight established at the Royal Opera House, Covent Garden, in the famous production of *Cav and Pag*, this is the direction in which things are going. In 1965 Covent Garden went toward a dramatic multilantern complex of equipment. This has been widely appreciated by all the visiting foreign directors and scenographers and increasingly has an influence on the Continent.

Of course, since operatic lighting leans so heavily upon the music, subtlety and complexity of timing are of great importance. The lighting designer works as one of a team with the director and designer. He must be fluid and flexible, creating as the work develops. Only through the closest collaboration can lighting make its contribution toward a totally coherent visual product that supports and uplifts and surrounds the musical and emotional experience.

So the days of the flapping backcloth revealed by rows of border lights are ever more surely numbered. Opera is traditionally the most hidebound of the theatrical arts, but the realization grows that to reveal the music fully, staging and lighting must be brought up to date. It is by lighting the singers, not leaving them in the dark, and by using what the new dynamic lighting has to offer that opera production can enter the twentieth century.

## Lighting Opera #2

*In conversation with Robert Bryan (past lighting director the Royal Opera Company, London, and the Glyndebourne Opera)*

Music is the key to all operas, an obvious statement to make but one which needs to be said many times, because if we lose sight of this fundamental, any work in opera is meaningless. It has been said that lighting opera is rather like lighting a very large play with anything from one or two players on up to as many as three hundred onstage, sometimes going from one to the other within the space of a few seconds. This is as accurate a summary as is possible, given that opera is music drama. It is simplistic to say that the difference between drama and opera is one of scale; however, it is not a bad idea to hold on to. One thing that is very true is that the lighting rules of drama (if there are any) apply equally to the operatic world. The rationale behind lighting for opera has not changed since Bill Bundy's writings in the 1970s. Music and the emotions always have and always will coexist. It is simply not possible to have music without emotion. That lighting reflects emotional commitment is as true today as it always has been.

What has changed is the recognition in opera of the lighting designer as an indispensable member of the production team. This development has indisputably led to an improvement in the visual aspect of opera. Gone are the days of Stygian gloom! With this recognition, of course, comes an expansion in the number of lighting designers (LDs) involved. Of particular interest in this expansion is the spread of lighting design in mainland Europe. Probably the most significant factor in the recent past has been the emergence of lighting designers from the Continent. As in the U.K., there was great reluctance by European managements to recognize the significance of the lighting designer. In a remarkable mirrored pattern, the U.S./U.K. lighting design influence has been repeated with a U.K./European design input. For some years now, LDs such as Robert Ornbo, John B. Read, David Hersey and myself have been lighting various types of theatre on the Continent. Our working methods, style, and so on have shown a way of lighting design so that our "brothers in light" over there have begun to chart careers. As a result, distinctive French, German and Italian styles have emerged. Understandably, these styles reflect the stage/set-design styles of their respective countries. To give an example of their influence, I think it true to say that our French and German colleagues have in many ways pioneered the use of HMI and fluorescent light sources, particularly in the operatic field. Two LDs currently working in the U.K., Jean Kalman from France and Wolfgang Goebbels from Germany, have influenced their British counterparts in rejection or acceptance of this European lighting style.

The other enormous influence in opera lighting has come from our television colleagues. Televising opera directly from the theatre has brought us into close contact with TV lighting designers, and a very healthy dialogue has developed between us. This dialogue has helped to persuade manufacturers to develop and modify equipment to our mutual benefit. Thus, the television need for high-powered, high-intensity Fresnel luminaries has helped theatre designers enormously; conversely, the theatre requirement of more efficient tungsten and HMI profile luminaries has greatly interested TV designers. Together, I suspect we have helped to push manufacturers into the twentieth or twenty-first century more than they otherwise would have done. The extraordinary paradox in all this is that the new generation of TV cameras is able to function with far less light than was formerly imagined.

Technically, the larger opera houses in the U.K. and mainland Europe have gradually restructured their lighting rigs into a healthy amalgam of old-style big luminaries of the "European" style and the multilantern rigs favored by British and American theatres. The extremely welcome research and development done by such manufacturers as Robert Juliat (France), Niethammer (Germany), and Pani (Austria) to develop highly efficient profile and projection luminaries has given us all an enormous range of equipment from which to choose. This is not to forget the excellent Italian range currently available. The flexibility of the multilantern rig, with the ability to have specials of whatever "hue," is certainly still much favored by the touring companies in the U.K.

Such companies as the Welsh National Opera, Opera North, and Scottish Opera, have by and large superseded the large houses in terms of operatic innovation relative to both production and design. The monoliths of Covent Garden, the Bastille, Vienna State Opera, and so on, have become so constipated with their over-large production scale, the subsequent costs, and the undoubted encouragement of a star system that they have lost sight of the true nature of opera, which is that it is music drama of the highest order. Thus it is that the trio of aforementioned touring companies have been in the vanguard of the best that opera has had to offer the public for some time now. Indeed, Opera North, based in Leeds, commissioned and produced the first football opera this year (1994) [*Playing Away* by Benedict Mason and Howard Brenton].

This all begs the question: Will the size of international opera productions continue to get even bigger as the years go by? I suspect not. Budgeting restraints are beginning to show through. The idea of mounting coproductions is now spreading, as is the practice of renting productions between companies. None of this addresses the physical size of productions, of course.

We now come to the vexed question of the operatic repertoire system. The demands of this system, in which a different production is mounted every day of the week, is one which is slowly driving companies to the brink. (The brink of what I will leave to your imagination.) With the increasing size of productions, there is a consequent increase in setup time required. In order to relieve the demands on technical time, some houses (such as The Royal Opera) have established the practice of having a nighttime changeover. This is in order to have the stage ready for morning rehearsals. The six- to eight-hour night shift does ease the pressure on technical staff the following morning, and gives a decent chance for a morning rehearsal with full set, lighting and costume. However, at the end of such a morning rehearsal, there comes a changeover for the evening performance. In many instances, this setup is less than satisfactory in that the daytime strike and reset has less time than the night changeover. It seems to me that opera companies using this system are in great danger of becoming rehearsal companies and not performance companies. Where is the logic behind that, I wonder? Possibly this will all ultimately be resolved through financial restraints: by default and not by planning. The one element that suffers day by day is the lighting, since by its very nature it is almost always "last on." This puts enormous pressure on lighting teams. One tremendous help in this area will be the more sophisticated automation systems currently on the drawing board; which will undoubtedly be the next step forward for opera lighting in the technical sense. Quiet color-scroll systems are already helping. What we cannot allow are noisy systems—it would be unforgivable to have, say, at the end of act 3 in *Cosi* that sublime musical trio interfered with by the next lighting state getting into position.

Many companies do not follow a repertoire system, for example Chatelet Theatre, Paris; Opera de Monte Carlo, Monaco; Bologna, Nice; and so on. Others, such as the main touring companies in the U.K., close down to setup and technically rehearse new shows. In the former case, the shows are undoubtedly the better for not having repertoire constraints put upon them. In the latter case, the concentrated time element gives the production and technical teams a good chance to a) get a production they are satisfied with and b) get a production the company can fit into a working repertoire.

One of the most endearing qualities of opera is the durability of many classic productions lasting over decades in time. These are often associated with a particular design. I think of the Caspar Nehar *Wozzeck* and the Zeffirelli *Moses* at the Royal Opera House and the David Hockney *Rakes Progress* at Glyndebourne. The nature of the operatic beast is such that it will continue to both excite and irritate us all; lighting designers at their peril will ignore the dictates of the music.

## Problems in Repertoire

One of the problems of major operas and classical ballets in England is that they are usually performed in repertoire (that is to say that a different

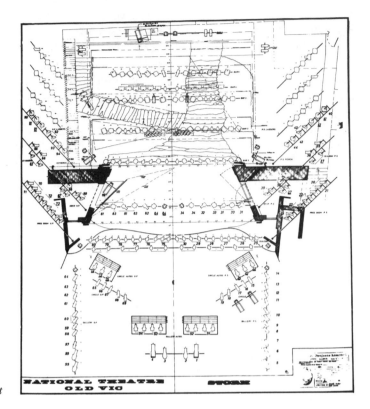

87. *Repertoire layout*

production will be performed every night). This same problem has been more recently encountered in the leading English dramatic theatres, the Royal National Theatre and the Royal Shakespeare Company in particular. However, this is a tremendously expensive way to operate, and in these stringent times companies are moving to reduce the number of changeovers.

A large part of this book has been about the lighting process, the way in which the lighting is created. It may have seemed rather complex and, indeed on a professional scale, lighting can be extremely complicated. In the West End of London or on Broadway, hundreds of spotlights and man-hours are involved in creating the sort of lighting that I have attempted to describe. It is not difficult to appreciate, therefore, that considerable problems arise when such complex lighting setups have to be changed between one performance and another.

Germanic practice has solved the problem to a certain extent by placing as much equipment as possible in positions that are accessible. Their stages are large, the instruments are suspended on lighting bridges, and sufficient manpower is available to focus the instruments during the performance. This solution cannot apply in English and American dramatic theatre for three reasons. The first is that the stages are usually much smaller and the necessary flying depth for a lighting bridge is simply not available. Second,

*Stage Lighting Design*

manpower today is increasingly expensive, and the normal theatre budget cannot cope with the large number of electricians needed.

Third, the use of light put forward in this book is based upon American and English theory and practice. This is a concept of light used in three dimensions and one that, for all its popularity in the English-speaking world, is still comparatively new on the Continent. There, the five functions of lighting are given less consideration, and lighting is more often designed only for illumination and effects. The scenery may be beautifully and atmospherically lit, and the effects, spectacular, but the actors themselves will be lit almost crudely, often with follow spots. There is little attempt to bring the four component parts together and to link the actor with his setting through a three-dimensional use of light. This means that the use of multiple banks of spotlights—for backlight, sidelight and downlight—is reduced, and the problem of handling and rehandling quantities of instruments is automatically lessened. But the obvious solution to the repertoire situation—much simpler lighting with fewer units—can only be considered a backward step.

I believe the only way to achieve an ambitious and complex lighting plot, of the standard seen in London's West End or on Broadway, in this situation is by following the principles that I have tried to outline in this book. First, the lighting has to have method; second, it has to be carefully planned.

The designer has to provide a repertoire theatre with a basic permanent layout of equipment. This layout has to provide all the acting-area and standard lighting that might be required. These instruments may account for about half of the installation and should be focused and locked tight, never to be moved again—for that season at least. Then there should be a liberal supply of "specials." From each angle a range of equipment should be available that can be shared between productions: some set permanently and some to be reset between performances. In the old days battens (striplights) and footlights provided basic illumination, but this is now obsolete in these days of total spotlighting. The repertoire theatre, using good planning and an organized approach, must provide a basic spotlight illumination that each designer can use.

For the National Theatre Company, when it began at the Old Vic all those years ago, I designed a layout of equipment that was described at the time as a "saturation rig" (Fig. 87). A proportion of the equipment, particularly in the front of house, was permanently focused. Accessible instruments could have their colors changed, but only a number of specials were refocused from show to show. Over the stage, general coverage was fix focused, and specials were divided across the repertoire, allowing each show to focus their own units, which then remained fixed while that show was in the repertoire.

Today the same approach is probably wise, but tomorrow? The availability of reliable, high-quality, quiet, remote-control instruments will soon revolutionize lighting in repertoire. Instantly refocusable units will make the problems of yesteryear only a memory.

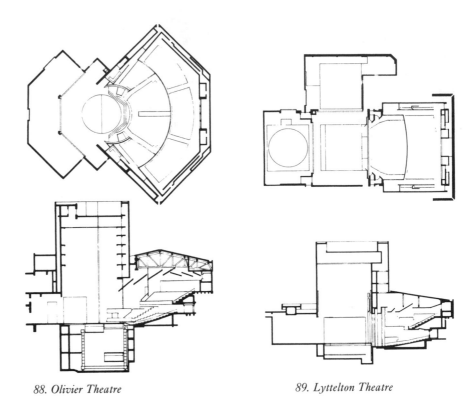

88. *Olivier Theatre*

89. *Lyttelton Theatre*

## The Royal National Theatre, London

In 1976 the new Royal National Theatre of Great Britain opened. In fact the building and its technical installations were largely designed in the period from 1966 to 1970. This is now a long time ago. Since then, I have been involved in the design of many theatre spaces and their equipment. However, few projects provide the opportunity to truly move the limits of their time forward, and it's interesting, more than twenty years later, to review what was thought necessary then and how things have worked out. It's also somewhat depressing to realize that no other theatre complex since then has made such comprehensive preparations for lighting drama in repertoire. Even the new Glyndebourne Opera House, which opened in 1994, acknowledged using the same fundamental approach.

The National includes three auditoria: the Olivier, the Lyttelton and the Cottesloe. The Olivier Theatre has an open stage set in the corner of a room, with the stage partially surrounded by the audience seated in a semicircle. The modified thrust stage has space at the rear capable of being opened out to form a surrounding "space" stage (Fig. 88). The Lyttelton is a comparatively conventional proscenium theatre, only with a Germanic-style semi-cruciform stage for production changes in repertoire and an exceptionally flexible proscenium opening (Fig. 89). The third theatre, the Cottesloe, a studio theatre, is a galleried flexible space that, in deliberate contrast to the two main theatres, is equipped comparatively simply.

The concept of the two large theatres was arrived at by the architect Sir Denys Lasdun, guided by the National Theatre Building Committee, a group of the wise and great theatre people of the time, led by Sir Laurence Olivier, and including Peter Brook, George Devine (whom this author replaced on his death), John Dexter, Michael Elliott, Bill Gaskell, Sir Peter Hall, Norman Marshall and Tanya Moiseiwitsch. The committee spent most of its time debating the design of the Olivier Theatre, which was seen as by far the most important. It attempted to develop upon the experience of the Chichester Festival Theatre and the Guthrie thrust stage, then a source of great interest. The proscenium theatre was hardly discussed; it was assumed that everybody knew how a proscenium theatre worked. How wrong the great and the good can be.

With the wisdom of hindsight, the buildings are indeed products of their time. Architecturally designed with enormous integrity, they are in the brutalist, then "modern," concrete style, sadly out of fashion even before the building opened. The guiding committee were all inexperienced in designing and building theatres. They knew the frustrations of working in the then-prevalent Victorian and Edwardian West End theatres. The virtues of these were hardly appreciated. Much attention was paid to issues such as "point of command," of "actor/audience relationships," of sightlines, acoustics and technology. Little thought was given to the very special values of intimacy, emotion, audience encirclement and involvement, all qualities commonplace in those nearby West End theatres of the pre-First World War period. The result in the larger two theatres is spaces that lack these values. Efficient places for theatrical production they may be; places hospitable to human communication for the conveyance of intimate emotion they are not. The smallest theatre, the Cottesloe, was almost an afterthought, primarily designed by Iain Mackintosh of Theatre Projects, who were the theatre consultants. It was a forerunner of theatres to be designed through the next two decades, that sought to restore intimacy and audience intercommunication as the primary virtues of theatrical space.

But from a lighting standpoint, particularly in the two larger theatres, the latest advances of the time were employed. Both theatres are elaborately equipped in order both to allow first-class lighting to be achieved within the repertoire pattern of perhaps a twice-daily change of production and to provide superlative facilities for the lighting designer. What did this mean in terms of the design of the building and its equipment?

First, a comprehensive range of lighting angles was made a top priority. Both the main auditoria have ceilings that contain five lighting bridges to achieve a wide variety of coherent acting-area angles to the stage. Two to five vertical lighting positions are built into the side walls. In the Olivier Theatre, owing to the configuration of the ceiling (which curtails the width of the bridges), lighting was also mounted on four "chandeliers," which are vertical lighting positions hung through and below the ceiling. All these positions are accessible from above, and a series of walkways connect through the roof void from the front-projection room (at the rear of the circle) right to the fly floor and the stage.

The stages are surrounded by galleries for lighting or the handling of scenery. All rails throughout stage and auditorium are of $1^{29}/_{32}$-inch (50 millimeter) diameter pipe to allow instruments to be fixed in any position.

Over the stage in the Lyttelton theatre the lighting is hung from conventional counterweight pipes. All feed cables are dropped from the grid by windlasses that automatically take in or let out cable as the lights are raised and lowered. Over the Olivier stage, because the stage equipment is particularly designed for the use of three-dimensional scenery (which is suspended by 140 electronically synchronized computer-controlled point hoists), lighting was suspended BBC-TV style on short, 8- to 10-foot (2 to 3 meter) long hoists. This was intended to allow lighting to be hung at varying heights across the stage and also to allow sections of the rig to be flown out to the grid in order to clear a piece of scenery positioned up- and downstage at any angle. Subsequent to the theatre's opening seasons, the bulk of the overstage lighting was placed on a semipermanent lighting bridge around the rear of the mainstage, thus allowing personnel access to much of the overhead lighting equipment.

The electrical installation followed the principle of the "saturation rig" that we had previously developed for the company at the Old Vic Theatre. At every potential lighting position a number of socket outlets were placed to allow a sufficient number of instruments for every standard demand made by the current repertoire (Fig. 90). Some instruments were dedicated to a permanent focus and merely recolored for each production. The minimum number of specials were available for refocus.

A point of historic interest is that many of the profile spots (manufactured by CCT) had a shutter assembly that was easily removable from the instrument like a cartridge. When set, the shutter position could be locked, and thus for a small beam-shape adjustment the unit itself could be left undisturbed, and only its shutter assembly changed, which was as easy as changing a color filter.

Every socket had its own dimmer, at the time an innovation in such quantity. Thus there were 600 dimmers in the Olivier Theatre and 470 in the Lyttelton. No patch panel was involved; all dimmers were connected to the computer lighting-control system in each theatre, which was named Lightboard. Lightboard was designed by the author and Theatre Projects Consultants and engineered by Rank Strand Electric. Two were installed at the National; others—later at the Burgtheater, Vienna, the Royal Opera House, Covent Garden, the Deutsches Oper and the Schaubuhne, Berlin, and the Hamburg Opera—attested to the advanced facilities Lightboard offered at the time. More important, Wally Russell, then head of Strand Century in the U.S., was so impressed with the control that he initiated the development of an American version built around microprocessor technology, which he named Light Palette (after a section within the Lightboard

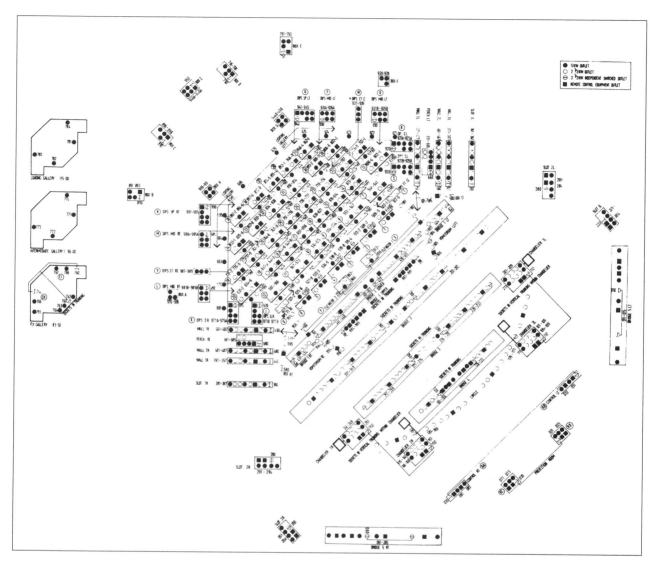

*90. Olivier lighting socket layout*

desk). This became virtually the standard lighting control in North America and has influenced almost every theatre lighting-control system since.

Lightboard took the early principles of memorized lighting control and advanced them. Other systems allowed the memorization of lighting pictures and the ability to add, subtract or cross-fade from one to another. Most boards at the time, however, allowed this process to happen at a comparatively limited number of speeds. But light is, by its nature, the most fluid and ephemeral of substances; it shifts and changes subtly or blatantly, slowly or quickly, sometimes in an instant. Lightboard acknowledged this and provided an instrument that could be played by the operator, allowing different groups of light to be under his fingertip control simultaneously and also allowing different groups of light to travel to any new intensity simultaneously at many different speeds. The control allowed access to override the speed of light movement in twelve simultaneously running cues. Multitime movements could be started together or separately and travel at their own speeds—yet all or any part was always under the immediate control of the operator.

Operation of one or a multiplicity of lights was through a calculator-type keyboard, which a proficient operator could operate by touch while watching the stage. But no longer was it necessary to think in terms of single dimmers or channels; lighting could be conceived in blocks, pictures or "groups" of light that could be mixed, interwoven and balanced. Within each block, the operator could still summon a single channel, but he had equal ease of access to one light or to any group. A group was composed of any prerecorded memory or cue channels, but with or without the destination levels, that is, as a group, any prerecorded lighting state could have its level increased or decreased proportionally. The operator had the ability to instantly collect all or any part of the lighting under his control. The state of lighting upon the stage (or in any recorded memory) was displayed on video monitors that showed all channels, or all channels in use, and their levels together with their source of control. There were many other auxiliary facilities designed both to speed the lighting process and to extend the possibilities open to the designer. One section of Lightboard was portable and could be operated from the center of the orchestra stalls or elsewhere. Another allowed any channel to be connected to a sound-to-light-effects control for automatic flashing or fading, light movement synchronized to sound, or random light modulation.

Finally, Lightboard allowed orientation control—the remote control of luminaires (pan, tilt and focus), color change (at that time up to eight colors) and projector control (random-access slide change and focus). This system was multiplexed around the theatre via a data highway (a forerunner of today's DMX), so an appropriate unit could be connected anywhere and respond to the operator's instructions. These orientation commands could be memorized on any cue, with or without an intensity change occurring before or after the physical movement. Sadly, the mechanized lanterns themselves were even then too expensive, so their number was limited to twelve—at least initially. Today, lighting controls are still moving toward the seamless integration of instrument movement, color change and intensity control that Lightboard began twenty years ago.

Another innovation first seen with the National was in the area of worklight control. For the first time, all control for all the differing states of worklight needed—rehearsal, daytime fit-up, show running lights, and nighttime security—were all brought together under relay control to the stage manager or lighting control. No longer did an assistant stage manager (ASM) have to be sent to the grid to turn off a forgotten worklight. This improved the efficiency of running the stage in myriad small ways. Such a system is now commonplace, operated with much more economical solid-state logic controllers.

Lightboard and the National represented a move forward on then-current methods and technology. Since then, of course, technological advance has been overwhelming. The Lightboard and computer hardware was replaced with the more reliable microprocessor-based Galaxy system from Strand, which incorporated most of the original operational features. But the techniques we were able to develop for the National still seem relevant today.

Remote control instrumentation will change the repertoire situation entirely. To date, however, even the finest equipment available isn't versatile enough, nor do today's instruments offer the range of light quality needed to replace conventional instruments entirely. The first steps will be for hybrid systems, which mix fixed and moving lights.

A new opera house in Toronto was planned recently for the Canadian Opera and the National Ballet of Canada. Complex provisions were made to facilitate changeover from ballet to opera in repertoire. Provisions included overhead lighting hung on short cross-stage pipes, which could track up- and downstage between the wires hanging the motorized scenery suspension points and be trimmed at different heights across the stage. Instruments throughout were to be a combination of automated and fixed instruments. Access for focusing or maintenance was to be from hydraulic cherry-picker work platforms. These were suspended below a track below the grid on either side of the stage and could be maneuvered to allow an electrician to reach any point onstage at any height. Sidelighting was to be from lighting ladders suspended from tracks below the grid. These could be individually raised and lowered and moved to any position up- and downstage. Finally and most radically Toronto was to have a cross-stage moving rigging bridge. This tracked between fly floors up- and downstage and effectively divided the stage into two working areas, above and below. When positioned over the stage, it was to provide a working platform from which overhead lighting pipes or instruments could be changed over or simply maintained, as well as to allow overhead cloths, borders and draperies to be set and struck, while the stage below was clear for work. This was a concept first developed by Theatre Projects for the Royal Opera House, Covent Garden, as long ago as 1971. The distinguished German technical director Helmut Grosser regarded the concept of the horizontal division of the fly tower as one of the most significant of modern developments in stage machinery, and his enthusiasm influenced its inclusion in the Bastille Opera in Paris.

All lighting relies upon cooperation between all disciplines. Lighting in repertoire can be assisted by new ways of approaching the mechanical handling problems of repertoire logistics.

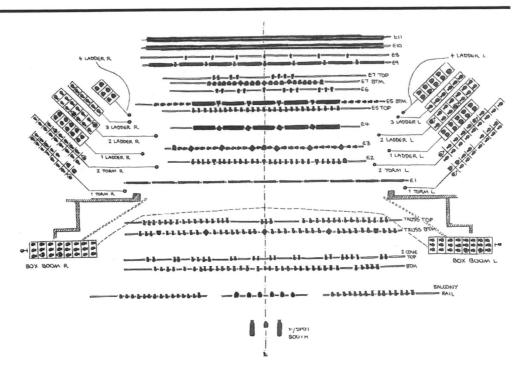

Director  Harold Prince
Designer  Eugene Lee
Lighting  Richard Pilbrow

"Epic" was the word that director Harold Prince first used when talking to me about lighting *Show Boat*. The show is perhaps the classic American musical. Its glorious Jerome Kern score illuminates the story of three generations of a showboat family on the Mississippi River amid a time of constant social change.

Today *Show Boat* allows us a glimpse of a world that has past: a world of richness and poverty, of bigotry, ignorance and fortitude. By following the fortunes of Magnolia, in her growth from innocence to independence; Ravenal, her errant husband; Captain Andy and his tyrannical wife, Parthie; the ill-fated Julie; Queenie, the cook, and Joe, her husband; and others of the Cotton Blossom troupe, we are taken on a journey through time, through an America changed by technology and progress yet witnessing the constancy of human emotion. Just as the river inexorably rolls on, so too the ebb and flow of time finally heals all heartache. The tale is wonderfully emotional, and the music, glorious, with such immortals as "Ol' Man River," "Can't Help Lovin' Dat Man," "Make Believe," "Why Do I Love You," "Life upon the Wicked Stage," "You Are Love," and many others.

*Show Boat* was first produced by Florenz Zeigfeld in 1927. Since then it has been performed around the world. I lit the Harold Fielding revival at the Adelphi Theatre in 1971, which, with 910 performances, was, at that time, the longest run the show ever enjoyed. But this new production was to be different. Hal determined to strip away the varnish of show-business glossiness typified by the 1951 MGM movie. He suggested that I return to the original novel by Edna Ferber for inspiration. The fundamental themes of family, tradition and racial intolerance were to underpin the production. Ferber's novel is still a wonderful read. Particularly for the lighting designer, her descriptions of storm and light are immensely evocative. The play encompasses forty years. In scenes of summer and winter, sunshine and storm, dawn and sunset, rain and snow, the constant passing of time is accompanied by technological change in artificial lighting from oil, gas and limelight to electricity. The scenery by Eugene Lee, the more than six hundred costumes by Florence Klotz and the lighting were to reawaken a world of the past but with a new reality and grittiness against which the drama would unfold. Real materials—wood, steel—would be used to recreate the world of *Show Boat*.

The lighting would follow through this evocation of reality. The humid heat of the Mississippi would be followed by a Chicago winter. Sun, moon and candlelight would be used, sometimes in a theatrical epic Brechtian style, exposing the tough grittiness of the play's physical environment. At other moments the stage would be filled with the visual and emotional richness of a *Gone with the Wind*–type movie.

There's a lot of "stuff": dockyard, saloon and the levee at Natchez, cotton bales, a three-deck Cotton Blossom, with galley, theatre and decks seen from every level and angle, the Molly Able—a tugboat— carts, carriages, superseded by the streets of Chicago with automobiles, nightclubs and a rooming house. Many meetings with Eugene and my associate Dawn Chiang sought to fit this huge array of three-dimensional scenery onto the stage. The show was to open at the new Performing Arts Center at North York in Toronto before moving to the Gershwin Theatre on Broadway.

The play's first act is on or around the showboat in Natchez. The Mississippi is constantly present and indeed it is the first image as the curtain rises as well as a metaphor that runs through the evening. We needed to evoke a lot of water. Experiment led us to finally employ a mixture of Pani front projectors with wave machines, Great American twin-spin gobo rotators with ripple templates from DHA, tubular ripple machines and some real water troughs in traps below the stage reflecting MR16s concealed below the floor up onto the transom of the Cotton Blossom to give the effect of floating reflections. In New York we substituted a more effective simulation for the real water. This simulation is made using two cross-stage traps below which are mounted pipes of Lekos lighting upward onto fluttering ribbons of Mylar.

The second act of the show is principally set in a very real turn-of-the-century Chicago, with a choreographed transition spanning the passage of twenty years to 1927, and a return to Natchez for the finale. (Susan Stroman's constantly inventive choreography is a treat to light!) The many variations of natural light—sun, moon, dawn and sunset—seemed to require strong motivating light. An early problem that appeared was that with so much three-dimensional flying scenery, there was little room for overhead lighting. Clearly there was no room for very large luminaires. David Hersey's Digital Light Curtains had excited me in *Miss Saigon*. Their ability to both move and color-change (twenty colors) a powerful sheet of light at any speed was impressive. Could they be modified to travel in another dimension? I sketched an idea for a light curtain that would both tilt up- and downstage and pitch from side to side, and sent it to Philip Nye of DHA. He thought it made sense and so we decided to try it out. Three rows of "pitching" light curtains (later reduced to two for economy) would allow strong backlight and high side/backlight from a variety of angles, capable of emulating sun or moon. Most importantly, this apparently powerful light source would take up only fifteen inches of flying space. Philip came to Toronto to commission the prototypes. From the moment we plugged them in they have performed without mishap, this despite being quite frequently knocked by passing scenery.

The huge variety of scenes and times of day and night suggested the need for a variety of instrumentation and color. Vari*Lite VL2Bs, VL2Cs and VL5s provide myriad specials and vast gobo and color potential. These are augmented by Wybron color scrollers (with thirty colors on Lekos and twenty on 5kW Fresnels) all of which of course are capable of fast or very slow color change through a scene. These are particularly effective in the first of two scenes in the Cotton Blossom theatre. It's late afternoon and evil is afoot. One of the showboat's stars, Julie, married to the leading man, is revealed by a rejected suitor as being a colored girl. Miscegenation (marriage between the races) was a crime in Mississippi

then, and this dramatic scene is the hinge around which the whole rest of the story revolves. Five kW Fresnels and 500-watt beamlights with scrollers pursue a relentless color changing sunset—time marching inexorably on—as the ugly drama unfolds amid the bigoted mortals.

Act 1 begins in the oil-lamp era. We then move through gas to electricity. A second scene in the showboat theatre—this time in production—has flickering oil, foot and wing lamps (the latter with Victorian-style color change), and a limelight follow spot. Thanks to Lindsay Lambert, an enthusiastic historian of the days of limelight and a citizen of neighboring Ottawa, my associate Dawn witnessed his demonstration of real limelight. We sought to faithfully reproduce its characteristics. In fact—and perhaps not surprisingly—a realistic reproduction was far too dim for modern eyes, and the limelight's wooden case was later converted to contain a Reiche & Vogel 24-volt 500-watt beamlight. The many actually flickering and guttering light sources are supplemented by more twin-spinners casting flickering light across the scene—hopefully somewhat reminiscent of a Sickert painting. Incidentally, apart from the "prop" limelight, the show uses six follow spots, two from the front, two from a high box-boom position and two from a high side perch position onstage.

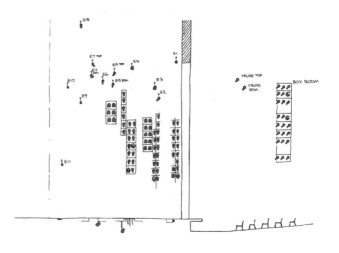

The show is a big one. It opened on Broadway in October 1994. The very big production was managed electrically with consummate efficiency thanks to the high skill of the lighting crew led by Greg Husinko. They bring the world of *Show Boat* to life by filling the stage, the world of actors, with light.

## *Show Boat* — Instrument Schedule - synopsis

| Position | Instrument | Function | Color | Notes |
|---|---|---|---|---|
| Spot booth | Pani BP 2.5kW | Rain/snow | | AS-100 Scroller |
| | 2 Xenon | | | |
| | super troupers | | | |
| Rail | 6x16 Leko | Showcloth sepia | G370 | |
| | 6x16 Lekos | Showcloth gobo | G370 | |
| | 6x16 Lekos | Cotton drop sky | R99 | |
| | 6x16 Lekos | Showcloth sky | G370 | |
| | 6x22 Lekos | Trocadero paintings | NC | |
| | 6x16 Lekos | Chicago portal day | G370 | |
| | 6x16 Lekos | Chicago portal night | L143 | |
| | 6x16 Lekos | Showcloth river | R06 | G271+R7394 twin-spin gobo |
| | Pani BP 1.2kW | Ripple | | Wave F/X + Slide changer |
| | Pani BP 1.2kW | Cloud | | |
| | Pani BP 1.2kW | Moon & Cloud | | |
| | Pani BP 1.2kW | Snow | | |
| 2 Cove | 6x22 Lekos | DS Color wash warm | R70 | |
| | 6x22 Lekos | DS Color wash cool | R18 | |
| | 6x22 Lekos | Apron left warm | R321+R119 | |
| | 6x22 Lekos | Apron left cool | R64 | |
| | 6x22 Lekos | Theatre gobos | R73 | R7805 |
| | 6x22 Lekos | Theatre cobweb | R70 | R7788 |
| | 6x22 Lekos | Bedroom | R76 | |
| | 6x22 Lekos | Kitchen | R99/R72 | |
| | 6x22 Lekos | Rooming house | R57/R77 | |
| | 6x16 Lekos | Waterside top | R69 | |
| Truss | 6x16 Lekos | Gobo warm | NC | R7805 |
| | 10" 5kW Fresnels | Bash Left & Right | Scrollers | |
| | 6x16 Lekos | Gobo cool | R73 | R7764 |
| | 6x16 Lekos | Areas left | R3409 | |
| | 6x16 Lekos | Areas right | R06 | |
| | 6x16 Lekos | Apron left warm | NC | R7805 |
| | 6x16 Lekos | Apron left cool | R73 | R7764 |
| | 6x16 Lekos | Apron night | R65 | |
| | 6x16 Lekos | Theatre specials | R69 | |
| | 6x22 Lekos | Waterside windows | R60 | |

| Position | Instrument | Function | Color | Notes |
|---|---|---|---|---|
| Box Boom Left | 6x16 Lekos | X Forestage cool | R61 | |
| | Super Arc 400 | Follow spot | | |
| | 6x16 Lekos | X Forestage warm | NC | |
| | 6x16 Lekos | Apron left | R3409 | |
| | 6x16 Lekos | Rooming house | R38 | |
| | 6x16 Lekos | Bedroom | R15 | |
| | VL5 | Vari*Lite | | Stipple |
| | 6x16 Lekos | Kitchen | R62 | |
| | 6x16 Lekos | Gobo wash X | NC | R7805 |
| | 6x16 Lekos | Color wash a | R18 | |
| | 6x16 Lekos | Color wash b | R99 | |
| | Source 4 19° | Flame | R13 | G267+G271+ R7394 twin spin |
| | Source 4 19° | Fishing | NC | G267+G271+ R7394 twin spin |
| | Pani BP 1.2kW | Ripple | | Wave |
| Box Boom Right | 6x16 Lekos | X Forestage cool | R61 | |
| | Super Arc 400 | Follow spot | | |
| | 6x16 Lekos | X Forestage warm | NC | |
| | 6x16 Lekos | Apron right | R3409 | |
| | 6x16 Lekos | Rooming house | R36 | |
| | 6x16 Lekos | Bedroom | R15 | |
| | VL5 | Vari*Lite | | Stipple |
| | 6x16 Lekos | Kitchen | R62 | |
| | 6x16 Lekos | Gobo wash X | R65 | R7805 |
| | 6x16 Lekos | Color wash a | R18 | |
| | 6x16 Lekos | Color wash b | R99 | |
| | Source 4 19° | Flame | R13 | G267+G271+ R7394 twin spin |
| | Pani BP 1.2kW | Ripple | | Wave |
| 1 Electric | MR16 Strips | Chicago portal | R07 | |
| | MR16 Strips | Chicago portal | R99 | |
| | MR16 Strips | Chicago portal | R71 | |
| 2 Electric | J+M PAR 64 Strobes | | Lightning | R64 |
| | 6x12 Lekos | Areas left | R3409 | |
| | 6x12 Lekos | Top Cotton Blossom cool | R60 | |
| | 3 VL5s | Top color and toning | Vari*Lite | |
| | Source 4 19° | Ripple | R60 | R7833+G271+ R7394 twin spin |
| | 6x12 Lekos | Areas right | R06 | |
| | 6x12 Lekos | Top Cotton Blossom warm | R06 | |

| Position | Instrument | Function | Color | Notes |
|---|---|---|---|---|
| 3 Electric | 6x12 Lekos | Gobo cool | R73 | R7764 |
| | 6 VL2Cs | Accent lite & gobos | Vari*Lite | |
| | 6x12 Lekos | High X-lite warm | R3408 | |
| | 6x12 Lekos | High X-lite cool | R63 | |
| | J+M PAR 64 Strobes | Lightning | R64 | |
| 4 Electric | Light "Pitcher" | Downstage light curtains | Scroller | |
| | 4 VL2Cs | Accent lite & gobos | Vari*Lite | |
| 5 Electric top | Source 4 26°s | River day | R3216 | R7833+G271+ R7394 twin spin |
| | Source 4 26°s | River night | R63 | R7833+G271+ R7394 twin spin |
| | Source 4 26°s | River sparkle | R3216 | RP sparkle+ G271 + R7394 twin spin |
| | 6x9 Lekos | Train | NC | |
| 5 Electric bottom | 6x12 Lekos | High X-lite warm | R3408 | |
| | 6x12 Lekos | High X-lite cool | R63 | |
| | Light "Pitcher" | Mid-stage light curtains | Scroller | |
| | 4 VL5s | Top color and toning | Vari*Lite | |
| 6 Electric (fly with Chicago) | 6x12 Lekos | Street backlight warm | G365 | |
| | 6x12 Lekos | Street backlight cool | G720 | |
| 7 Electric top | 6x12 Lekos | Church left | R16 | |
| | | Chicago windows | R37/R11/R16 | |
| 7 Electric bottom | PAR 64/VNSPs | Hi-side backlight left | Scrollers | |
| | PAR 64/VNSPs | Hi-side backlight center | Scrollers | |
| | PAR 64/VNSPs | Hi-side backlight right | Scrollers | |
| | 3 VL2Cs | Accent backlite & gobos | Vari*Lite | |
| 8 Electric (to fly with river) | 6x12 Lekos | Model boat | R62 | |
| 9 Electric | MR16 Strips | Upstage drop front | G370 | |
| | MR16 Strips | Upstage drop front | R67 | |
| | MR16 Strips | Upstage drop front | R76 | |
| | 6x12 Lekos | Model train | R71 | |
| 10 Electric | MR16 Strips | Upstage drop rear top | R77+R104 | |
| | MR16 Strips | Upstage drop rear top | R3407+R104 | |
| | MR16 Strips | Upstage drop rear top | R3202+R104 | |
| | MR16 Strips | Upstage drop rear mid | R99 | |
| | MR16 Strips | Upstage drop rear mid | R76 | |
| | MR16 Strips | Upstage drop rear mid | R81 | |

| Position | Instrument | Function | Color | Notes |
|---|---|---|---|---|
| 11 Electric | MR16 Strips | Groundrow drop rear mid | R09+R104 | |
| | MR16 Strips | Groundrow drop rear mid | R47+R104 | |
| | MR16 Strips | Groundrow drop rear mid | R73+R104 | |
| | MR16 Strips | Groundrow drop rear btm | R09+R104 | |
| | MR16 Strips | Groundrow drop rear btm | R47+R104 | |
| | MR16 Strips | Groundrow drop rear btm | R73+R104 | |
| 12 Electric | PAR 64/MFL | X Town drop day | R23 | |
| | PAR 64/MFL | X Town drop night | R71 | |
| | PAR 64/MFL | X Town drop night | R321 | |
| 1 Torm Left | 6x16 Lekos | X Apron color | Scroller | |
| | 6x22 Lekos | X Chicago portal | R66 | |
| | 6x16 Lekos | X Apron warm | NC | |
| | 6x16 Lekos | X Apron cool | R61 | |
| | 6x12 Lekos | X Gobo | NC | R7805 |
| | VL5 | X color | Vari*Lite | |
| | PAR 64/VNSPs | X color | Scroller | |
| 1 Torm Right | 6x16 Lekos | X Apron color | Scroller | |
| | 6x22 Lekos | X Chicago portal | R66 | |
| | 6x16 Lekos | X Apron warm | NC | |
| | 6x16 Lekos | X Apron cool | R61 | |
| | 6x12 Lekos | X Gobo | NC | R7805 |
| | VL5 | X color | Vari*Lite | |
| | PAR64/VNSPs | X color | Scroller | |
| 2 Torm Left | 6x16/12 Lekos | X warm | NC | |
| | 6x16 Leko | X rain | L117+L117 | |
| | 6x16/12 Lekos | X cool | R61 | |
| | 6x16/12 Lekos | X color | Scroller | |
| | VL5 | X color | Vari*Lite | |
| | 6x12 Lekos | X gobo | NC | R7805 |
| 2 Torm Right | 6x16/12 Lekos | X warm | NC | |
| | 6x16 Leko | X rain | L117+L117 | |
| | 6x16/12 Lekos | X cool | R61 | |
| | 6x16/12 Lekos | X color | Scroller | |
| | VL5 | X color | Vari*Lite | |
| | 6x12 Lekos | X gobo | NC | R7805 |
| 1 Ladder Left | 6x16 Leko | X Waterside top | R64 | |
| | PAR 64/VNSPs | X light color far | Scroller | |
| | PAR 64/VNSPs | X light color mid | Scroller | |
| | PAR 64/VNSPs | X light color near | Scroller | |

| Position | Instrument | Function | Color | Notes |
|---|---|---|---|---|
| 1 Ladder Right | 6x16 Leko | X Waterside top | R64 | |
| | PAR 64/VNSPs | X light color far | Scroller | |
| | PAR 64/VNSPs | X light color mid | Scroller | |
| | PAR 64/VNSPs | X light color near | Scroller | |
| 2 Ladder Left | 6x16 Lekos | X Boat high warm | R13 | |
| | 6x16 Lekos | X warm | NC | |
| | 6x16 Lekos | X Boat high cool | R61 | |
| | 6x16 Lekos | X cool | R61 | |
| | 6x16 Lekos | X color | Scroller | |
| | VL5 | X color | Vari*Lite | |
| | 6x12 Lekos | X Boat low warm | R13 | |
| | 6x12 Lekos | X Boat low gobo | NC | |
| | 6x12 Lekos | X Boat low cool | R61 | |
| | VL5 | X color | Vari*Lite | |
| 2 Ladder Right | 6x16 Lekos | X Boat high warm | R07 | |
| | 6x16 Lekos | X warm | NC | |
| | 6x16 Lekos | X Boat high cool | R61 | |
| | 6x16 Lekos | X cool | R61 | |
| | 6x16 Lekos | X color | Scroller | |
| | VL5 | X color | Vari*Lite | |
| | 6x12 Lekos | X Boat low warm | R07 | |
| | 6x12 Lekos | X Boat low gobo | NC | |
| | 6x12 Lekos | X Boat low cool | R61 | |
| | VL5 | X color | Vari*Lite | |
| 3 Ladder Left | 6x16 Lekos | X Boat high warm | R13 | |
| | 6x16 Lekos | X Boat high cool | R61 | |
| | 6x16 Lekos | X Boat high color | Scroller | |
| 3 Ladder Right | 6x16 Lekos | X Boat high warm | R13 | |
| | 6x16 Lekos | X Boat high cool | R61 | |
| | 6x16 Lekos | X Boat high color | Scroller | |
| 4 Ladder Left | PAR 64/VNSPs | Auditorium top | Scroller | |
| | PAR 64/VNSPs | Auditorium mid | Scroller | |
| | PAR 64/VNSPs | Auditorium low | Scroller | |
| | PAR 64/VNSPs | X light color far | Scroller | |
| | PAR 64/VNSPs | X light color mid | Scroller | |
| | PAR 64/VNSPs | X light color near | Scroller | |
| 4 Ladder Right | PAR 64/VNSPs | X Boat top | Scroller | |
| | PAR 64/VNSPs | X Pilings mid | Scroller | |
| | PAR 64/VNSPs | X Dawn | Scroller | |
| Spot Platform Left | J+M PAR 64 | Lightning | R64 | |
| | Strobe | | | |
| | Super Arc 400 | Follow spot | | |
| Spot Platform Right | J+M PAR 64 | Lightning | R64 | |
| | Strobe | | | |
| | Super Arc 400 | Follow spot | | |

| Position | Instrument | Function | Color | Notes |
|---|---|---|---|---|
| Orchestra Pit | Tubular Ripples | Apron ripple | R71 | |
| | 6x9 Lekos | Theatre shadow | R13 | |
| Proscenium Left | KL 6/30° | Candle flicker | R13 | G267+G271+ R7394 twin spin |
| Proscenium Right | KL 6/30° | Candle flicker | R13 | G267+G271+ R7394 twin spin |
| Deck Left | Gas Pump | | | |
| | 8" Fresnel | Rover | R17 | |
| Deck Right | 8" Fresnel | Rover | R17 | |
| Downstage Trap | T-10 | Gunnel glow | R60/R61 | |
| Mid-stage Trap | 6x9 Lekos | Reflection day | G520 | |
| | 6x9 Lekos | Reflection night | G440 | |
| Upstage Trap | Tubular Ripples | River ripple | G730 | |
| Train Truss | Neon Indicator | Radio tower lights | | |
| | Grain of wheat 9v | Stars | | |
| Box Office Truck | MR16 | Posters | R16 | |
| | MR16 | Box office window | R16 | |
| | Candle sconces | | R07 | |
| Boat Truss | Model boat | | | |
| CB Theatre | Stage footlights | | | |
| | Stage winglights | | | |
| | Stage foot-shadowlights | | | |
| Convent | Wall brackets | | | |
| Cotton Blossom | 1927 string lights | | | |
| | Cove lights | | | |
| | Marker lights | | | |
| | Navigation lights | | | |
| | Understair lights | | | |
| | Sign chase | | | |
| Molly Able | Port light | | | |
| | Garlands | | | |
| | Steam calliope | | | |
| Newstand | MR16 | Newstand interior | | |
| | | Practical | | |
| Trocadero | Brad "Imperial" fittings | | | |
| Palmer House | PAR 64/MFL | Door top | | |
| | PAR 64/MFL | Door bottom | | |
| | PAR 64/MFL | Snow | | |
| | Sconces | | | |
| | Canopy downlights | | | |
| | Neon | | | |
| Pilings | Streetlamps | | | |
| Rooming House | Gas fixture | | | |

| Position | Instrument | Function | Color | Notes |
|---|---|---|---|---|
| Saloon | Sconces | | | |
| | Bar uplights | | | |
| | Hanging lamp | | | |
| Stardrop | Fibre optics | | | |
| | Fibre optics fan | | | |
| | Fibre optics color wheel | | | |
| Train truss | Train | | | |
| | City lights | | | |
| Waterside | Water barrel lamp | | | |
| | Windows | | | |

Lighting Team

Associate Designer  Dawn Chiang

Production Chief Electrician  Greg Husinko

Vari*Lite Programmer  Douglas Gentile

| | New York | Toronto |
|---|---|---|
| 1st Assistant (Vari*Lite tracking) | Eric Cornwell | James Milburn |
| 2nd Assistant (Express-Track) | Alan Hahn | Charles R. Kaiser |
| Chief Electrician | Don Lawrence | John Beirne |
| Head Follow spots | Mike Barrette | Brent Oakley |
| Vari*Lite Operator | Greg Chabay | David Baer |

# Chapter Nine

# Design Challenges: Widening the Viewpoint

Lighting has had a real influence upon theatrical space. In the fifties and sixties there was a widespread rejection of the traditional proscenium form of theatre. The apparent separation of audience and actors into two rooms divided by a proscenium was much disliked. In this author's view, this animosity was fueled by the particularly unpleasant proscenium arch form that had developed prior to and after the Second World War. This was the fan-shaped auditorium that, rejecting the multiple boxes and balconies of the past, sought to ensure "perfect" sight-lines and a more democratic auditorium by placing the audience on one or two levels in a fan-shaped plan with all seats facing the stage. Despite the overwhelming popularity of this "cinema-style" form around the world, the problems inherent in it soon emerged. The greater proportion of the audience was to the rear of the theatre. The lack of overhanging balconies pushed the rear seats even further backward. The lack of side-box seating and substitution of blank side walls resulted in a loss of a sense of audience participation.

Sir Tyrone Guthrie pioneered the rediscovery of the open stage (Figs. 91–94). After his work at the Assembly Rooms in Edinburgh for that city's festival, he was invited to Stratford, Ontario, to build a Festival Theatre to a design of his choice. He and his designer, Tanya Moiseiwitsch, elected to build a thrust-stage theatre, with the audience on three sides around a stage

*91. Proscenium*

*92. Arena*

*93. Thrust*

*94. Extended forestage*

like a tongue stuck into their midst. If the proscenium theatre shut its actors in a room separated from the audience behind a proscenium arch, the actor now would be liberated from his frame. Returning to the classical theatre of the Greeks for inspiration, they recreated the thrust stage surrounded by its audience. The theatre was a great success and influenced several decades of theatre design around the world. The thrust stage, arena (with audience 360° around the stage) and many other variants of open stage, that is those without a proscenium, became the forms of choice for many theatre people, particularly in the world of drama.

Guthrie himself had little regard for stage lighting as he knew it. As previously noted, he disliked what he saw as an all-prevailing "pale apricot jam" colored lighting around the actor. He called for bright, stark, all-revealing white light. Initially at Stratford the stage was brightly illuminated with white light, rejecting any attempt to have light contribute atmosphere or pictorial quality. But in fact, the new ability of light to illuminate space remote from its source with spotlights contributed significantly to the open stage's popularity. No longer was a proscenium needed to mask the striplights used to light the players. The spotlight allowed the illuminated stage to be placed within the auditorium, while the audience could be effectively in the dark as modern fashion dictated.

It wasn't long before people realized that an open stage could be lit with white light or any other form or style of light. Almost immediately the rejection of visual effect was dismissed. Why, just because audience and actors were seated in a new and more dynamic relationship to each other, had the theatre to reject all the richness of visual effect possible? If, in life, we are influenced by the visual environment around us, why was the suggestion of environment to be lost on the open stage? Open-stage lighting was soon required to fulfill all the needs for pictorial or emotional storytelling support that had developed on the proscenium stage.

At first sight it appeared that lighting a stage partially or fully surrounded by audience posed new and unique lighting problems. In a practical sense it did. But fundamentally the principles of lighting developed for the proscenium stage continued to be relevant. If the design of light is circumscribed by the behavior of natural and artificial light in the real world, allied with the availability of current technology, but serving the demands of the playwright, then the shape of the stage is of little relevance.

There is one obvious difference. The viewpoint of the audience is greatly widened. Instead of sitting only to the front, they may be placed on two, three, or four sides of the stage. Thus, since we know that an actor's face must be lit from the front, this "front" may now extend all around the stage. Furthermore, an actor anywhere on the stage will need to be lit from this all-encircling front. Thus an actor standing right on the edge of the stage, with his back to the nearby audience, must have his face lit from the onstage side. This light must also be at such an angle as to not shine into the eyes of the audience behind him.

*Stage Lighting Design*

In the proscenium theatre we have been striving to think of our lighting in three dimensions. Now we have an absolute commitment to think in depth. In a well-lit proscenium production, when a scene is successfully lit, the lighting will appear almost as good from the back of the stage as from the front. When we come to the open stage, we simply have to ensure that every seat is getting a three-dimensional view of the stage that is perfectly lit with complete actor-visibility lighting.

This creates interesting problems, which have some affinity to the problems found with TV lighting for multiple camera angles. What appears to be marvelously dramatic backlight for one viewing angle becomes frontlight for another. Isolating one performer in a tight spotlight may require light from three or four directions, thus widening the resultant pool of light.

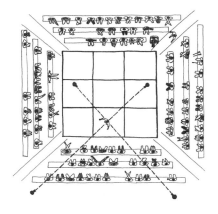

95. Arena acting area

## The Arena Stage

First let us take the example of an arena stage, or theatre in the round. Here the audience is seated right around the stage, and actors' entrances are probably through the audience, down the aisles. Arena stages are usually quite small, with an acting area about sixteen to twenty-five feet wide (Fig. 95). How can our basic lighting organizational thinking be applied?

When lighting the acting area, the basic position for frontlight was seen to be approximately 45° vertically and 45° to either side of the front of the actor. This is obviously not sufficient for the arena stage, and the simplest and most successful expedient is to duplicate those two unit positions at the other two points of the compass. Thus the stage will be divided into the usual acting areas and into each we will direct a spotlight from 45°, 135°, 225° and 315°. These are all shown in plan view in figure 95. The height of these units will be calculated in the same way as for the proscenium stage. Those lights coming from the outer edge of the stage, that is, from over the audience, may need to be lowered slightly to light into the actor's eyes. Alternatively we may decide to use lower-level fill lights but we must beware of glare into the audience's eyes sitting opposite.

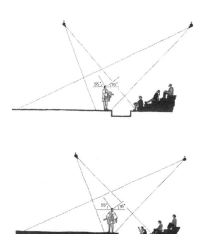

96 and 97. Arena sections

The lights over the stage, which are pointing outward to light actors' faces standing at the stage edge, have to be treated even more carefully. We have to light the actor but avoid dazzling the spectators immediately behind him. To do this we may need to lift this inner angle to as much as 55°. It is likely that any problem of shadowing below the eyebrows will usually be alleviated by bounce light from the stage-floor reflection from other units (Figs. 96 and 97).

These four units into each area provide the basic acting-area lighting, but it will be noticed that they are actually doing more than their equivalent in a proscenium theatre. For example, if we sit to the front of an actor right between the spots at, say, 45° and 135°, the two instruments on the farther side of the stage will be backlighting him; similarly, if we sit beneath the 45° instrument, those at 135° and 225° will be directly sidelighting him, and the fourth instrument will be a backlight. This many seem a daunting complication, but in fact it merely adds to the excitement of lighting the open stage, which can be considerable. No two people have exactly the same view, either of the actors or of the lighting. To create a series of different pictures for each side of the stage, and yet to hold each as a valid expression of that moment in the play, is a fascinating experience.

On top of the basic acting-area lighting we may, of course, add all the other instruments that we need. The rules of dominant key and secondary light apply with equal force: motivating lights, blending and toning, special visibility, effects, and so on, all may have their appropriateness as before. All we have to remember is the varying effect that each might have seen from any angle. What may be a dramatic shaft of backlight from one section of the audience may be rather flat frontal illumination for those on the other side of the stage; everything has to be tempered and judged from all parts of the auditorium.

It's been theorized that open-stage lighting should revert to bold simple beams and patterns of light, or that we should return to the simplicity of a single powerful shaft of light. If the play demands this treatment of course it should have it, but with an audience surrounding the stage, nothing could be more difficult. A single dramatic shaft will almost certainly only look dramatic to that section of the audience that sees the actor in profile; to the others he will either appear flatly lit or in almost total darkness. Except for rare and brief moments of stillness on the stage, each actor has to be lit from more than one direction to ensure basic visibility. Here a complication arises. If we are lighting from a reasonable angle for the face of about 45°, the light to a standing actor will throw a beam about six feet beyond him. If this has to be repeated in two directions at least, a single actor, quite tightly lit, will be surrounded by a pool of light twelve or fourteen feet in diameter. The inability to confine light tightly is a loss, but the enterprising designer will find many other compensations in his work on the arena stage.

The theatres in which open-stage work takes place are so varied that one cannot give general rules for the placement of instruments. It will be clear, however, that most of the lighting will come from overhead, and some form of grid over the entire area is usually the best solution. Obviously a large part of the lighting is going to come from over the audience. This can be masked by catwalks to an extent. But much equipment will be over the stage, and will be impossible to mask. Some form of open "egg-crate" ceiling (Figs. 98 and 99) can be very useful. Low-level light must not be ignored however. Lighting from over vomitorium entrances may be useful. If the space has balconies, as the superb Royal Exchange Theatre in Manchester, the balcony-front positions are useful for special low cross-light effects.

Color on the arena stage has to be used with particular care. Since there are usually fewer instruments coming in from each direction, they are not as "mixed up" as they often are on the proscenium stage. Therefore colors chosen should be usually very subtle. With four acting-area instruments I've found that a flexible solution is to use pairs opposite each other in contrasting

*98 and 99. Egg-crate grid*

*Stage Lighting Design*

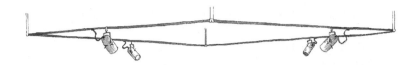

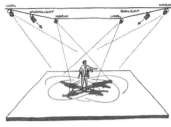

tones, one perhaps warm, the other in open white or a cool tone. In this way we can get an overall warm stage by bringing up all the opposing acting-area instruments with the warm colors, using the others at a lower level as fill light, and vice versa (Fig. 100). Added variety can be achieved by adding further instruments at, say, 90° or 180° in plan. If those on one side are chosen to act as dominant light—say, sunshine—they might be open white or very pale yellow. Used with the warm acting-area pairs, the stage will be hot; used with the cool it will be very fresh. Conversely the instruments on the other side might use cool tones suggestive of moonlight. When used with different combinations of acting area lighting, varying results will ensue. Add to this, overhead downlight in various color tones and rich variety can be achieved (Fig. 101).

In addition to any other special effects or visibility lights required on the stage itself, we may have to light into the aisles of the auditorium. The director will know when he wants his actors to be seen on their entrances or exits.

## The Thrust Stage

With the thrust stage the audience is placed on three sides of the stage. On the fourth is usually a scenic back wall that can either be a permanent background or more usually can be used with scenery. In principle the same lighting variations apply as to the arena stage, the exception being that it is possible (although in my experience not at all desirable) to reduce the number of acting-area spotlights to three per area, which can be placed at 120° in plan from each other instead of 90°. This is a possible economy when demanded, but I find it limits the extent of flexibility obtainable, particularly with color, with the four instrument approach (Fig. 102).

*above: 100. Open stage color layout*

*left: 101. Open stage layout*

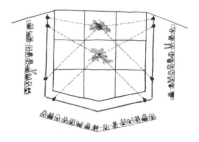

*102.  Thrust stage*

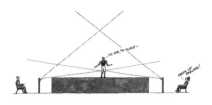

*103. Open stage footlights*

The scenic back wall will usually require some special lighting—in many ways it is like a shallow proscenium stage. Often it is in fact too shallow, because the architect will have failed to appreciate that a scenic wall will require space behind for lighting through entrances and openings and onto backings. Directors will often use upper levels over the upstage parts of a thrust stage. These need lighting consideration as perhaps do those parts of the stage below any such platforms.

It is common for actors to approach the stage from the front, through the aisles or up vomitorium entrances. Every opportunity for low-level lighting positions should be taken in these entrance positions. The production of John Guare's *Four Baboons Adoring the Sun* at New York's Vivian Beaumont Theatre (director Sir Peter Hall, designer Tony Walton, lighting by the author) used strong light from the vomitoria, cross-lighting the stage, both to provide a strong sunset and later to simulate the flickering light from a real campfire. As the stage floor later split to create a raging onstage volcano, this low-level cross-light became even more useful.

Some thrust stages have a lowered trench around the perimeter of the stage, these can provide a lighting position for special effects. A production of *Hamlet* lit by John B. Read at the Edinburgh Festival used uplight effectively for Hamlet's soliloquies; he appeared to almost hang in space above a completely dark floor, with the beams of light lost in the dark ceiling above (Fig. 103).

Gobos and projections can be powerfully employed on the thrust stage. In the National Theatre production of John Arden's *Armstrong's Last Goodnight* (directed by Bill Gaskill, designer Rene Allio, lighting the author) at the Chichester Festival Theatre, exciting forest scenes were created by multiple leaf-pattern gobos giving an impression of dappled sunlight through the trees of the Scottish lowland woods.

Ellipsoidal spots are the principal lighting unit of the open stage, where the usual requirement is the need to contain light to the stage as much as possible. Fresnels are usually best left to the subsidiary role of color washes and downlight. However for *The Heliotrope Bouquet* by Eric Overmeyer at Baltimore's flexible Head Theatre (directed by Stan Wojewodski, designer Chris Barreca, lighting by the author) 5kW Fresnels provided powerful key-light across a number of scenes, and banks of PAR cans provided powerful back cross-light to the stage. There really are no rules.

## Other Forms of Stage

There are many other variants of stage. Indeed an actor and a group of spectators anywhere can create theatre. Some of the most exciting theatrical events happen in converted lofts, cellars, churches or warehouses. The audience can sit on two sides of the stage, facing an end stage platform, or the action of the play may be all around the room with actors in the middle. I think all of these configurations can be well or poorly lit.

*104.* Mystery Plays

One of the most thrilling theatre events of a theatrical lifetime for me was the National Theatre's cycle of *Mystery Plays* (directed by Bill Bryden, designer Bill Dudley), first presented in the Cottesloe Theatre. This was a "promenade" production without any seating in the courtyard orchestra area, and had actors and audience all mixed up together (Fig. 104). As the action moved about the room, so the audience moved into new configurations. The production was a re-enactment of medieval mystery plays, presented as if by fifteenth-century guilds. What little scenery there was consisted of agricultural instruments and tools affixed to the encircling balconies. The lighting was all soft light, glowing from simulated oil lamps concealed in drums, cans, and lanterns hung at random over the whole space. There was only one spotlit moment in the entire nine-hour epic production. In Gethsemane when the angel spoke to Christ, a single 24-volt 500-watt beam-light hit a round mirror held by the angel, who cast its shaft of light onto Christ below. Great lighting.

Director  Tommy Tune
Designer  Tony Walton
Lighting  Richard Pilbrow

As I write this, I'm lighting a new musical starring Tommy Tune. Directed and choreographed by Jeff Calhoun, designed by Tony Walton, with costumes by Willa Kim, the show is based upon the 1938 British movie *St. Martin's Lane*, which starred a very young Vivien Leigh and Charles Laughton.

The wonderful score by Richard and Robert Sherman (of *Mary Poppins* fame) and book by A. J. Carothers tell the tale of an English busker—a street performer—in pre-World War II London. Charley falls for a young, amoral and ambitious streetgirl, Libby, and brings her into the troupe only to lose her to the glamour of the "proper" indoor theatre.

It's a different musical for 1995. Melody, romance and color supplant massive technological construction. Tony Walton's spare yet colorful settings evoke London of the thirties through the eyes of the buskers. A permanent surround of London's skyline, wall posters and city lights enclose skeletal set pieces evoking each locale. Exquisitely colored costumes and boldly colored lighting create a special world of the imagination.

The show opened in Louisville, Kentucky, and is to tour for six months before reaching New York. The show and particularly the lighting has to be designed for an arduous schedule, loading in on Monday and opening on Wednesday.

There's another problem. A fundamental feature of the set is lampposts. Eleven of them, eighteen feet high, are spaced all over the diamond-shaped stage, which itself juts out over the orchestra pit. The show takes place below, in front of, behind and all over lampposts! The dancers use the lamps as swings, vaulting horses, and climbing poles. And no multiple shadows over everything—please.

I'm not sure that any show for me has had such preproduction heartache. Hours over a drawing board (actually the computer, using Argus and MacLux Pro) examining every permutation of the problem:

effectively a thrust-stage show with vertical obstructions all over the stage at about eight-foot intervals, and flying scenery interlacing the lampposts for each scene, all to be dealt with on the road, with unpredictable front-of-house lighting positions and minimum load-in time.

An obvious solution—a forestage truss—was deemed impractical for the tour schedule. But local box booms in various positions couldn't be relied upon to provide the precise angles necessary to get around the lampposts. So a basic feature is a three foot square "dance tower" twenty-six feet high, which sits either side of the proscenium at the front of the stage. From this we are able to focus acting-area light around the front lampposts, cross-light to the forestage and color instrumentation to the downstage areas.

To overcome the shadowing problem, acting-area lighting is from four angles, 45°, 135°, 225° and 315°. Every part of the stage also has cross-light avoiding the lampposts, in warm and cool colors, and broader strokes of rich cross-light color comes from two ladders of narrow-angle PAR lamps with Wybron color scrollers.

The most significant instruments are the new Vari*Lites. For me this is the first major use of the new VL6, a fine addition to their range. Very small, very very bright and absolutely silent, the VL6 provides twenty-four colors or gobos (we use about half of each) in two wheels. Lamps can zoom and dissolve focus from one wheel to another. Photographically etched glass gobos allow half-tone and color gobos. For the first time in my experience here is an instrument that allows the designer to precisely place a dagger of very bright light or a soft textured wash to any part of the stage space at any moment...astonishing. Less dramatic, but equally marvelous, is the VL5, with a new dichroic color range. The first VL5 had color limitations; the new dichroics offer a virtually complete spectrum in any hue or tint, and the ability to dissolve from one color to any other...dreamy! Sixteen VL6s are overhead and on the top of the forestage towers, providing a multitude of specials—with and without gobos—and powerful down and backlight able to flow with the movements of dance. In one scene, a view from backstage in a real theatre,

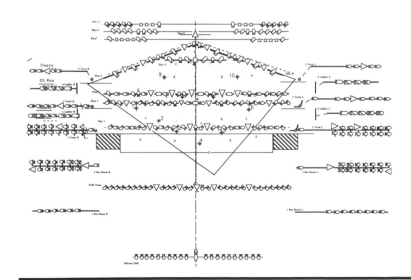

the upstage VL6s act as pseudo followspots, following the stars in a recreation of a 1930s musical number. The VL5s are distributed between overhead and the side tormentors, giving powerful color-wash capability to each setting, the dancers, and across the ever present lampposts.

All the time spent over the computer paid off. In production the lamppost "problem" disappeared, the multiple acting-area and proscenium-tower approach worked. The Vari*Lites and color scrollers allowed each scene and moment of many stunning dance images to be sculpted in colored three-dimensional light. Jeff Calhoun, as choreographer, was wonderful to work for—combining imagination with concern for every detail. Tony and Willa's bold designs were something of a treat to sculpt into a constantly refreshing series of images.

A final nice VL6 characteristic: rotating the gobo or color wheels as

an effect can produce some wonderful moments. Counter-rotation of gobos and colors creates a wonderful shimmering moving light like... butterflies fluttering in the ether. Dreamy again.

Stop Press: Six months of tour, multiple changes, lots of re-lights, a greatly revised book and new songs...all the wonderful lunacy of pre-Broadway "on-the-road." And it actually seemed to be working with improved business and ever more enthusiastic audiences. Dawn and I were to begin pre-hang at the St. James' Theatre for the Broadway take-in when disaster struck. Tommy Tune onstage breaks a bone in his foot. An indefinite postponement. All that work, almost a year's worth! There's no business like show business.

## *Busker Alley* — Instrument Schedule - synopsis

| Position | Instrument | Function | Color | Notes |
|---|---|---|---|---|
| Spot booth | 2 Xenon Super Troupers | | | |
| Rail | Source 4- 19°s | Frontlight L,C,R | G363 | |
| | Source 4- 19°s | Charley's place | L103 | |
| | Source 4- 26°s | Charley's scrim | G842 | gobo R7764 |
| | Source 4- 26°s | Charley's scrim | G105 | gobo R7764 |
| | Source 4- 19°s | Front lamps | G365 | |
| | Source 4- 19°s | Frontlight L,C,R | G130 | |
| 2 Box Boom L | Source 4- 19°s | Areas left | G920 | |
| | Source 4- 19°s | X DS Cool | G847 | |
| | Source 4- 19°s | X DS Warm | G320 | |
| | Source 4- 19°s | Lamp specials | G159 | |
| | Source 4- 10° | X Lamp ripple | G540 | twin spin R7833/G271/R7394 |
| 2 Box Boom R | Source 4- 19°s | Areas right | G364 | |
| | Source 4- 19°s | X DS Cool | G847 | |
| | Source 4- 19°s | X DS Warm | G320 | |
| | Source 4- 19°s | Lamp specials | G159 | |
| | Source 4- 19°s | XDS Color | G290 | |
| 1 Box Boom L | VL6 400W | Vari*Lite specials | | |
| | Source 4- 19°s | Areas L | G920 | |
| | Source 4- 19°s | X above lamps | G159 | |
| | VL5 1000W | Vari*Lite—color | | |
| | Source 4- 19°s | X Color to right | | scroller |
| | VL5 1000W | Vari*Lite—color | | |
| | Source 4- 26°s | X Color to right | | scroller |
| | VL5 1000W | Vari*Lite—shin | | |
| 1 Box Boom R | VL6 400W | Vari*Lite specials | | |
| | Source 4- 19°s | Areas L | G364 | |
| | Source 4- 19°s | X above lamps | G520 | |
| | VL5 1000W | Vari*Lite—color | | |
| | Source 4- 19°s | X Color to right | | scroller |
| | VL5 1000W | Vari*Lite—color | | |
| | Source 4- 26°s | X Color to right | | scroller |
| | VL5 1000W | Vari*Lite—shin | | |
| 1 Electric | Source 4- 26°s | Acting areas left | G920 | |
| | Source 4- 26°s | X DS Cool | G840 | |
| | Source 4- 26°s | X DS Warm | G343 | |
| | VL5 1000W | Vari*Lite—color | | |
| | Source 4- 26°s | Lamp specials | G920 | |
| | VL6 400W | Vari*Lite specials | | |
| | Source 4- 26°s | X DS Cool | G730 | |
| | Source 4- 26°s | X DS Warm | G343 | |
| | Source 4- 26°s | Acting areas right | G364 | |
| 2 Electric | Source 4- 26°s | Acting areas left | G920 | |
| | Source 4- 26°s | Acting areas left back | G510 | |
| | VL6 400W | Vari*Lite specials | | |
| | Source 4- 26°s | X gobos | G720 | R7764 |
| | Wildfire UV Flood | UV drops | | |
| | Source 4- 26°s | X gobos | G720 | R7764 |
| | VL6 400W | Vari*Lite specials | | |
| | Source 4- 26°s | Acting areas right back | G885 | |
| | Source 4- 26°s | Acting areas right | G364 | |
| 3 Electric | Source 4- 26°s | X DS Cool | G840 | |
| | Source 4- 26°s | X DS Warm | G343 | |
| | Source 4- 26°s | Acting areas left back | G510 | |
| | Source 4- 19°s | Lampost backlight | L103 | iris |
| | VL6 400W | Vari*Lite specials | | |
| | Wildfire UV Flood | UV drops | | |
| | VL6 400W | Vari*Lite specials | | |

| Position | Instrument | Function | Color | Notes |
|---|---|---|---|---|
| | Source 4– 19°s | Lampost backlight | L103 | iris |
| | Source 4– 26°s | Acting areas right back | G885 | |
| | Source 4– 26°s | X DS Cool | G730 | |
| | Source 4– 26°s | X DS Warm | G343 | |
| 4 Electric | PAR 64 /NSP 1kW | X backlight blue | G915 | |
| | Source 4– 19°s | Lampost backlight | L103 | iris |
| | 10" Fresnel 5kW | Back wash | Scroller | |
| | Source 4– 19°s | Lampost backlight | L103 | iris |
| | PAR 64 /NSP 1kW | X backlight blue | G915 | |
| 5 Electric | PAR 64 /NSP 1kW | X backlight blue | G915 | |
| | 10" Fresnel 5kW | Back wash | Scroller | |
| | VL6 400W | Vari*Lite specials | | |
| | Source 4– 19°s | Lampost backlight | L103 | iris |
| | Source 4– 26°s | Gobo US | G720 | Gobo R7764 |
| | MR16 75W Zipstrip | Backlight panels | R383 | |
| | MR16 75W Zipstrip | Backlight panels | R81 | |
| | MR16 75W Zipstrip | Backlight panels | G925 | |
| | MR16 75W Zipstrip | Backlight panels | G940 | |
| 6 Electric | PAR64 /NSP 1kW | X backlight blue | G915 | |
| | 10" Fresnel 5kW | Back wash | Scroller | |
| | VL 6 400W | Vari*Lite specials | | |
| | Source 4– 19°s | Lampost backlight | L103 | iris |
| | Source 4– 26°s | Gobo US | G720 | Gobo R7764 |
| | MR16 75W Zipstrip | Backlight panels | R383 | |
| | MR16 75W Zipstrip | Backlight panels | R81 | |
| | MR16 75W Zipstrip | Backlight panels | G925 | |
| | MR16 75W Zipstrip | Backlight panels | G940 | |
| 7 Electric | Source 4– 36°s | Backlight posters | R87/R55/R38/R21 | |
| | 8" Fresnels 2kW | Backlight panels | R80 | |
| 8 Electric | 24v 500W beamlight | Audition backlight | NC | |
| | Source 4– 36°s | Sky backlight | R65 | |
| | Source 4– 36°s | Backlight posters | R17/R54/R321/R70/R18 | |
| | Source 4– 26°s | Backlight windows | R11 | |
| 9 Electric | Source 4– 19°s | Backlight windows | R11 | |
| | 8" Fresnels 2kW | Backlight Sky | R65 | |
| 1 Torm Left | Source 4– 19°/26°s | X stage warm | R385 | |
| | Source 4– 19°/26°s | X DS warm | R385 | |
| | Source 4– 19°/26°s | X stage cool | G740 | |
| | Source 4– 19°/26°s | X DS cool | G740 | |
| | VL5 1000W | Vari*Lite X color | | |
| | Source 4– 26°s | X Gobo | G720 | R7764 |

| Position | Instrument | Function | Color | Notes |
|---|---|---|---|---|
| | VL5 1000W | Vari*Lite X color | | |
| | Source 4– 26°s | Shinbuster | G720 | |
| 1 Torm Right | Source 4– 19°/26°s | X stage warm | R385 | |
| | Source 4– 19°/26°s | X DS warm | R385 | |
| | Source 4– 19°/26°s | X stage cool | G740 | |
| | Source 4– 19°/26°s | X DS cool | G740 | |
| | VL5 1000W | Vari*Lite X color | | |
| | Source 4– 26°s | X Gobo | G720 | R7764 |
| | VL5 1000W | Vari*Lite X color | | |
| | Source 4– 26° | Shinbuster | G720 | |
| 2 Ladder Left | PAR64 /VNSP | X Color R,C,L | Scroller | |
| | PAR 64 /VNSP | X Color Down R,C,L | Scroller | |
| 2 Ladder Right | PAR64 /VNSP | X Color R,C,L | Scroller | |
| | PAR 64 /VNSP | X Color Down R,C,L | Scroller | |
| | Source 4– 26°s | X Alley DRC | NC | |
| | Source 4– 26°s | X stage door | NC | |
| 3 Torm Left | Source 4– 19°/26°s | X stage warm | R385 | |
| | Source 4– 19°/26°s | X stage cool | G740 | |
| | VL5 1000W | Vari*Lite X color | | |
| | Source 4– 26°s | Shinbuster | G720 | |
| 3 Torm Right | Source 4– 19°/26°s | X stage warm | R385 | |
| | Source 4– 19°/26°s | X stage cool | G740 | |
| | VL5 1000W | Vari*Lite X color | | |
| | Source 4– 26°s | Shinbuster | G720 | |
| 4 Ladder Left | PAR 64 /VNSP | X Color R,C,L | Scroller | |
| | PAR 64 /VNSP | X Color Down R,C,L | Scroller | |
| 4 Ladder Right | PAR 64 /VNSP | X Color R,C,L | Scroller | |
| | PAR 64 /VNSP | X Color Down R,C,L | Scroller | |
| 5 Ladder Left | Source 4– 26°s | X US cool | G740 | |
| | | X US warm | G385 | Gobo R7764 |
| 5 Ladder Right | Source 4– 26°s | X US cool | G740 | |
| | | X US warm | G385 | Gobo R7764 |
| Pit | Tubular Ripple | Arthur's ripple | G710 | |
| | Diversitronic Strobes | Flashlamps | NC | |

## Lighting Team

| | |
|---|---|
| Associate Lighting Designer | Dawn Chiang |
| Assistant Lighting Designer | Stan Pressner |
| Production Electrician | Jimmy Fedigan |
| Chief Electrician | Mark Davidson |
| Frontlight | Joe Beck |
| Vari*Lite Programmer | Douglas Gentile |
| Vari*Lite operator | Lonnie McDougal |

# Chapter Ten

# Tomorrow

Too many farewell performances can get to be embarrassing. This book is the final version of one that began its journey in 1970. By a happy irony I'm writing these words on my Macintosh PowerBook Duo, once again sitting on the grass outside a cottage on the Isle of Coll in the Scottish Hebridean islands. The sun is blazing, light clouds scud across a blue sky, sheep and lambs nibble the grass around me, unaware of the advance of technology that puts this whole book, indeed my whole office, into a four-pound laptop. I finished the 1970 book here as well—but on pen and paper.

Within my sight absolutely nothing has changed. The rocks, beach, birds, animals and sky appear identical. Only if I look in a mirror are there real, rather hurtful, signs of time passing.

Not too long ago in New York I saw Rick Fisher's lighting for J. B. Priestley's *An Inspector Calls*, a superb vision carried out with wonderfully appropriate, searingly revealing cross-light. Weeks before that I was thrilled by Paul Pyant's superbly colored lighting for *Carousel*. Another pair of British lighting sensations and another British entry to take New York by storm, thanks to a combination of Cameron Mackintosh and the National Theatre.

How dumbfounded would my father have been to hear that two "theatricals," Cameron and Andrew Lloyd Webber, have joined Britain's "richest men" club. How amazed we would all have been twenty-five years ago to witness Britain's domination, through really two men's work, of Broadway and the whole American touring theatre scene, with shows seen by millions. And fancy a Royal National Theatre that, despite its concrete obstacles, continues to produce some of the greatest theatre in the world.

Shouldn't we celebrate the fact that the Arts Council of Great Britain, through a joyous period, fertilized the British theatre's rebirth, and how a small amount of money (in National terms) transformed the weekly reps of my youth into a true theatrical renaissance? Don't we have to wonder about the values of society, that today (here on the radio in Coll) announced the successful trial of Britain's submarine nuclear *deterrent* (is this a joke I wonder?), purchased from America, while the arts in Britain are reeling under cutbacks and "economies." Luckily my neighbour sheep aren't aware of, never mind frightened by, Britain's nuclear capability any more than they appreciate Britain's theatrical glories.

But the only compensation for witnessing time pass is the possible acquisition of some perspective and awareness.

The crystal clear sunlight in Coll hasn't altered much, nor I believe have the principles of good stage lighting. I've tried to give the book more perspective by adding both my own and other's war stories from the production desk. Also some history of lighting through the ages, which I hope the enthusiast will enjoy.

I've been privileged to live through a thrilling period of theatrical change and of change in lighting. The books that I grew up with were about the thirties. My early equipment was the patt 44 focus lantern. (This was a wonderful instrument because if you tilted the reflector out of alignment behind the lamp, you could get two beams of light for the price of one.) The regional theatre was weekly rep, the National was only a dream, lighting design was effectively unknown.

Joe Davis and Michael Northen began it for us in Britain. Now there are several hundred members of the Society of British Theatre Lighting Designers. Many designers, led by such as Patrick Woodroffe, David Hersey and Andy Bridge, are stars of our profession who are known around the world. In America, where lighting design really began, thousands earn their living in theatrical lighting, whether on stage, in video, music concerts, architecture, interior design, museums, theme parks or virtual reality.

Technically what has happened? As usual with instruments there are some modest advances while some things stay the same. I believe Reiche & Vogel still make the best beamlight, which seems almost impossible to copy. But the best low-voltage PAR lamps now come pretty close and are much cheaper. The little MR lamps are a delight. New light sources are allowing some exciting ellipsoidal developments. Led by ETC and Dave Cunningham, the Source Four sets new standards of efficiency and ease of handling, with Altman and their Shakespeare range coming close, providing high-quality die-cast instruments and 575-watt lamps that out-perform the older 1,000-watt equivalents.

Obviously, moving lights are the major development of the nineties. The music industry had the wealth to move them forward, with Vari*Lite in the vanguard, thanks to the group Genesis. It is worthy of note that an ex-sound company brought new thinking to an old dilemma and broke through to a practical range of robotic lights. The new range of the soft-edge color-dissolving VL5 and the precise ellipsoidal-style VL6 are truly revolutionary. They are silent, the VL6 is extraordinarily bright, and its etched gobos provide a new "gray-scale" subtlety. They are extremely precise. They are economical and reliable. In the professional theatre it's hard to conceive of lighting without them, and I think soon they will be found in almost every theatre. Their delicacy and accuracy provide an entirely new fluidity and precision to lighting design. And there are some amazing new developments around the corner.

But Vari*Lite is only one company producing remarkable instruments. Not to say that there aren't many advances yet to be made. All this technology is surely still young. Costs must come down and reliability improve. More subtle and accurate coloration is still needed. Furthermore, all the moving-light control systems seem to me extraordinarily crude. The stage lighting profession spent four decades developing approaches to the control of light intensity alone. I hope it won't be as long before pan, tilt, focus, zoom, color and all the rest can be as fluidly manipulated.

The computer is with us. My Duo wasn't even dreamt of ten years ago when the Macintosh was invented. A pocket Personal Assistant has more memory than did Lightboard. It's a happy juxtaposition of events that when the designer's overworked brain must cope with up to twenty variables per instrument, computing power seems ready to help. The next generation of lighting controls will surely not only handle the physical movement of light in all dimensions but also become an integral assistant to the design process.

On this same Duo in the Hebrides, I have the whole plot of my current lighting for *Show Boat* in New York and all the paperwork and all the board plots from *Show Boat* in Toronto. Now I need to put the whole thing together. Information technology is all about enabling the brain to handle a complex world around us. My aging brain certainly needs all the help it can get.

I'm still rather proud of Lightboard. Almost everything in control since then has stemmed in some way from its advances. But the days of punching in numbers on key pad, wheels, VDU screens of confusing digits, are surely numbered. I want to *feel* lighting. As Brian Gale says, to "smell it." I certainly want to think it, paint it, sculpt it, manipulate it—play it. Fred Bentham was right in principle when he sought a light "organ" that could be played like a musical instrument.

At the moment moving lights are more difficult to program than their fixed predecessors. This is not surprising. But it's also not right. We must (and will soon) develop a totally intuitive interface between the vision in the head and that onstage.

In 1970 Fred Bentham mocked my dream of a control that would handle three hundred lights to three hundred levels at three hundred speeds. Yet within twenty years that was achieved. Now such performance is almost commonplace. The next aim must be to free us from the tyranny of numbers, must allow control as we wish of any number of moving (or old-fashioned) lights in every dimension. They must be manipulable in the design studio as easily as upon the stage.

We first "take control" of the device—or devices—we wish to handle. A number is really not very informative. The eye sees light, but the brain needs an instrument, or more likely, a group of instruments. The old concept of "grouping" lights seems to be still relevent. But instruments will constantly change their group allegiance depending upon many factors that might be addressed: area, angle, color, attribute. The need to collect and recollect instruments into ever changing groups is increasingly necessary.

Why pick a channel with a calculator keyboard? In the sixties they offered the skilled operator (or accountant) a heads-up way of collecting digits and consequent lights. Surely the process should be more intuitive. I favour a visual representation of the stage and layout and the option to touch with finger, mouse, voice or brainwave any channel or group thereof, then to have instant hands-on manipulation, to touch and drag to collect the needed group, drag to level or to select color or create movement. Eventually manipulating a three-dimensional model of stage space. Touch the tiny instrument and it, with its chosen "mates," will track to the selected position. Touch a point in stage space, and the appropriate instruments will fade in, move or recolor. As we "stroke" our lighting into its new composition we'll instantly see the results, onstage and on-screen. Light beams, with color and gobos or projections, will fill our digital model. Interrogate a channel, group or submaster, and the on-screen visualization will instantly reveal its contribution to the whole picture.

Now, of course, we're dealing also in the fourth dimension: time. As usual, we in the theatre can look to other industries to see glimpses into how the movement of light might be manipulated. The music and audiovisual industries are very familiar with the "timeline." Ours will be complex, needing layer after layer of detail. A group's representation must be able to be expanded into its component channels and instruments, then in turn into each attribute. Any or all must then be advanced or delayed, stretched or contracted in time—on-screen. A new "musical" notation language is needed to graphically describe the ebb and flow of light.

Perhaps we can envisage a touch-sensitive flat video screen as our true lightboard, maybe with monitors and/or heads-up display. Upon this surface of light we'll be able to paint our pictures. We'll want to see our light in three-dimensional space as well as in plan and section. We'll want to rotate our model and peep in behind the scenes, to perhaps prepare a part of the stage temporarily obscured to the audience. At the same time we'll want to see our "time map" and watch as script or score unfolds with our lighting, played as if by a musical instrument. This could be fun.

After that we can move on to the total freedom to not just waggle lights but move them through stage space in any dimension. Scene designers have for decades infuriatingly demonstrated the usefulness of the "anglepoise" lamp. Now maybe we'll have our twenty-first-century equivalent.

So in twenty years? If medical science keeps me going, will I be able to light Broadway on my flexible light-emitting polymer "lightblanket" wrapped round my knees in the Hebrides? Well, let's hope the lightpen will be passed to the next generation. The technology will surely be dazzling. (Let's at the same time express the 'green' hope that the consumption of electricity will be more modest.)

And then where shall we be? Simply nowhere without the magic ingredient—imagination. Light is one of the most marvelous elements in nature. Its ability to reveal and support the action on our stages is thrilling. It takes the designer's imagination to dream dreams and to possess the skills to translate them into reality.

Let's lower the houselights, stand at the production desk and face the darkened stage. It waits.

# Part Two

# History

# Chapter Eleven

# Oil Lamp to Laser

S tage lighting, particularly in the one hundred years since the first use of electricity in the theatre, has had a real effect upon staging, scenery, styles of production and acting and even upon the shape of the theatre building itself. But its impact must be seen against a continuum that takes us back centuries.

Theatre has always used the technology of its period. But stage lighting did not begin with electricity. Its important role in the theatre has been recognized at least since the sixteenth century. During the days of candle, oil lamp, and gas, great ingenuity was employed to illuminate the stage and provide atmosphere and effects. Many principles concerning the placement of lighting, the basic types of instruments and even the intentions of the lighting designer were conceived a surprisingly long time ago.

Theatre began outdoors: God said, "Let there be light," and he liked what he saw. Jehovah, Apollo, Osiris—all religions have recognized light as a fundamental element, the one that enables us to see. From the most ancient times, light and its primeval influence on our every thought, emotion and action has been seen as a harbinger of things to come, as a messenger from the supernatural and as a constantly changing companion that shapes all life on earth.

The theatre evolved from religious ritual. The moving of the sun across the sky, the waxing and waning of the moon, the wheeling firmament of stars, the seasons, all played important roles in the life of early man.

*"Candle—oil—it sounds so untidy. But we lose so much when we want everything as we have it now, and fail to understand that many a thing as it was then, was excellent...and so different from what we suppose. Open a door which leads into a seventeenth- or eighteenth-century room gilded or silvered and strike a match. The place will seem to go off like a firework. The lights in the Malvezzi Theatre (1733) were sufficient. They were soft, well-placed and reflected from the gold that was everywhere (on the dresses even)—from the lustres and the looking glasses, from the sparkling fans, and from the thousands of spangles which in the evening found their way, in those days, on to everything and gave a glow and a sparkle against colour that was rich."*
*—Edward Gordon Craig on candlelight (1922)*

Primitive theatre used this natural light. As the open-air theatres of ancient Egypt, Crete, and Greece developed and became more formalized, the cycle of natural light would play a part.

The more comfort-loving audiences of ancient Rome were protected from the weather by colored awnings that could be drawn over the semi-circular auditorium. Presumably, daylight was still the predominant light source, although after dark, torches, braziers, fires, and oil lamps were put to theatrical use, for they were the only means of dispelling darkness. (Nero's "concert lighting" became the stuff of legend.)

The earliest custom-built theatres of England were also open to the elements and natural light. These theatres had a flexible but usually thrust-shaped stage surrounded by the audience. The stage roof space concealed the hoisting machinery for the descent of gods and visions, and the ceiling was painted to represent the heavens. (Light was also represented in this way in the surprisingly similar forms of theatre across the world in China.) The beauty of light has never been more exquisitely described in words than by Shakespeare, but surely even he used torches and tallow candles to illuminate a gloomy winter matinee, or to enhance the drama.

In *Seven Deadly Sins of London* (1606), Thomas Dekker described a shuttered city "like a private playhouse, when the windows are clamped down, as if some nocturnal or dismal tragedy were presently to be acted." Indoor performances must also have taken place, and perhaps had done so since the cave dwellers. No doubt, light was admitted or shuttered out and artificial light kindled or extinguished, according to the show, the time of day and the ingenuity of the ancient organizers.

The church was very organized indeed (Fig. 1). Religious ceremony has always employed the symbolism of light. But the fifteenth century marks a significant expansion in the employment of artificial light: a Russian bishop described a performance by Brunelleschi (1377–1446) of *The Annunciation* in the church of San Felice, Florence. A revolving globe surrounded by circles of light illuminated translucent clouds, which supported eight cherubim. From this globe was lowered another internally lit globe, containing the angel Gabriel. This could be darkened by remote control (we have to wonder how) as he stepped out to speak to Mary. As the angel returned and rose into the air, the light blazed forth again. Other descriptions of the period reveal more spectacular effects—using more than one thousand oil lamps, diagonal and tracking movements of tableaux and lighting, rays of fire, glistering fireworks and glowing clouds—all recreating in three dimensions the wonders of Renaissance painting and pointing the way to the stagecraft that was soon to come.

But in the open-air performance of the mystery plays in more northern Europe, how was light evoked? The mansion or wagon depicting Hell's mouth belched out real flame and smoke (Fig. 2). A stage direction of 1501 in the Mons Passion reads, "See to it that the painter goes to Paradise to paint Raphael's face red." In the same play Christ is described with gold

*1. Fra Angelico.* The Coronation of Mary

*Stage Lighting Design*

2. *The Valenciennes Play, 1547. Miniature by H. Cailleau and J. de Moelles.*

hands and feet, and "let there be a big sun behind him." Painting the actor's features and using metal reflective halos or even a brightly polished basin to reflect the sunlight were common practice.

The Italian Renaissance theatre became the cradle of stage lighting. Artificial light must have possessed great power over people's imaginations. For most of the population, darkness, which began as the sun set each day, was only occasionally broken by flame, torch or guttering smoky candle.

The courts of sixteenth-century Italy provided the opportunity to expand the capabilities of artificial light. First, in 1514 a description of Peruzzi's design of *La Calandria* gives us one of the earliest views of the use of perspective on the stage. "One cannot imagine how in so narrow a space he could build up so many palaces....With great knowledge he also arranged the sources of light, the inner light that increases the perspective illusion." In 1580 we have the author Guarini extolling the virtue and economy of good lighting for his plays: "Without artificial lighting, the scene will be deprived of its beauty. ...Besides, expenses will be reduced...for the beauty that can be created by light can be made up only by great expense in adorning devices."

A pupil of Peruzzi, Serlio (1475–1554), built a theatre in Vicenza during the 1530s and in 1545 published *Architettura*, which describes contemporary theatrical methods. His drawings of a semicircular theatre with shallow perspective scenes are part of theatre history (Figs. 3 and 4). His lighting descriptions, which are less well known, bring his woodcut renderings to life. He describes "General stage light," which lights the whole stage, and "Mobile light," which often simulates the sun or moon moving across the sky (thus pre-dating Appia by four hundred years). General light was achieved by torches and chandeliers hung above and to the front of the stage, but the chandelier had reflective glass vessels filled with liquid to aim the light toward the stage. "It is better to illuminate the scene from the middle because of the greater power of light hanging in the center," he states, but he also mentions, "A large number of lights are placed leaning at the front of the scene." Is this the first mention of footlights?

The first recorded stage lighting instrument was the *bozze* (Fig. 5). These were glass vessels that came in various convex and concave shapes and were

3 and 4. *Serlio, Scena satyrica and Scena comica, 1545*

5. *Bozze. Used in original lighting of Teatro Olympico*

6. *Teatro Olympico, Vicenza*

filled either with oil and a wick when used as lamps or with colored liquids when used as color media, lenses, or reflectors. Examples still existing in Vicenza are about three inches in diameter. These *bozze*, fixed to boards behind holes in the scene, lit up the windows of the perspective street or the many colored silk transparencies of the pastoral scene (Fig. 6).

When a strong light was needed, Serlio says "you put a torch behind a glass and behind, a barber's basin well burnished." Thus, the spotlight had also arrived. The stage, glowing with multicolored flickering light, shining with encrusted and translucent scenery and costumes that shimmered with jewels, must have been an astonishing and lovely spectacle.

In about 1565 Leoni di Somi (1527–1592), a dramatist and stage designer of Mantua, anticipated Gordon Craig by 350 years and wrote *Four Dialogues on Scenic Representation* in which his protagonists discourse upon mood and atmosphere. They discuss the transition from a stage expressing joy, brightness and life, using brilliant and glowing colors, to the onset of tragedy, in which much of the lighting is dimmed or put out. "This created a profound impression of horror...and won universal praise."

Di Somi pointed out that the colored lenslike *bozze* not only colored the light effectively but also reduced glare. He recommended the use of mirrors to amplify the lights and also to allow them to be placed farther from the stage, hidden from view behind the wings, to reduce obnoxious smoke. Smoke and heat were severe problems for hundreds of years.

Finally, Di Somi championed the darkened auditorium: "A man in the shade sees more distinctly an object illuminated from afar." Further: "You obviate smoke fumes and render the seeing clearer." Lastly: "You save the Duke fifty ducats in respect of the torches usually set."

Truly, stage lighting had begun!

*Stage Lighting Design*

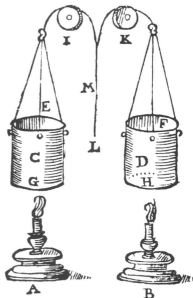

7. *Buontalenti.* First Intermezzo,
*Florence, 1589*

8. *Sabbattini's dimming mechanism*

Angelo Ingeneri (1550–1613) was the scene designer for the famed Teatro Olympico in Vicenza in 1585. He described lighting in 1598 as "one matter of supreme theatrical importance." He also said, "The darker the auditorium, the more luminous seems the stage." He wanted light sources to be concealed and was concerned that the actors' faces must be well lit. To this end, he proposed the first flown lighting position over the front of the stage: "A valance...on the inner side fitted with lamps having tinsel reflectors." Ingeneri described the use of gauze to give an effect of mystery, and he stressed the creative use of light and darkness to enhance the drama.

Also in Italy, Bernardo Buontalenti (1536–1608) worked on a stage at Uffizi, which used about one hundred oil lamps with four wicks each, including footlights, behind an ornamental balustrade (Fig. 7). The lighting crew were told to take great care in trimming the wicks and refilling the lamps.

Stage lighting was becoming systematized, and Sabbattini (1574–1654), in his *Manual for Theatrical Scene and Machines* (1638), describes the system in words and drawings. He evaluates the merits and problems of oil lamps and candles and sketches the fittings. He illustrates a method of remote dimming by lowering tin cylinders on cords over each light (Fig. 8). He describes proscenium lights, footlights, and sidelights behind the wings ("lights must be strongly fixed so they do not shake during the dances"). Sabbattini started a discussion on the problems of footlights that was to last over three hundred years. "The disadvantages outweigh the advantages. You believe that you make the stage brighter, but it actually becomes darker. Heat, dazzle, and smell force the actors backward, their legs and costumes are brighter than their pale and haggard faces, and a haze of smoke creates a barrier to clear vision." Sabbattini also mentions a concealed upstage row of lamps, parallel to the footlights, to light ground rows and backcloths. A German, Josef

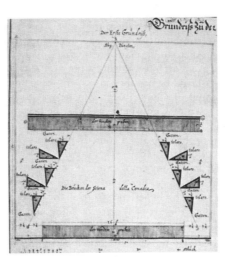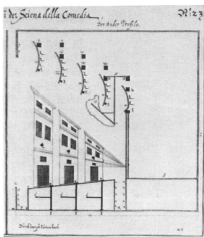

*9 and 10. J. Furttenbach. Plan and section of stage with periaktoi, 1640*

*11. J. Furttenbach. Candle with reflector, 1663*

Furttenbach (1591–1667), who studied in Italy and published *Architectura Recreationis* in 1640 (Figs. 9, 10 and 11), gives a detailed description of lighting that includes *bozzi* with reflectors in a seven-foot-deep upstage pit as well as, for the first time, rows of lamps overhead "between the clouds." This completed the repertoire of Renaissance lighting that created precedents for patterns of thought and practice that still pertain today.

As the Renaissance transformed itself into the elaborations of the Baroque period, Italian influence spread across Europe, with each country emphasizing one aspect or another according to its own theatrical tradition.

In England Inigo Jones (1573–1652) bought and used some *bozze* in 1609. He opened up the English theatre to Italian-style spectacle and employed multicolored lights in profusion. He used translucencies vividly and produced extraordinary effects of nature, but he also used old-fashioned flambeaux torches, which damaged the ceiling paintings in the Whitehall Banqueting Room, after which theatrical performances there were stopped.

The Puritan Revolution brought English theatre to a halt, but the future King Charles II, living in France, saw much theatrical development in the French court. In 1660 Richard Flecknoe, in *A Discourse of the English Stage*, said, "We in England are only scholars and learners yet...especially not knowing how to place our lights for the more advantage and illuminating of the scenes."

With the Restoration, London theatres were built and restored but were now indoors. The Cockpit (1660) had two chandeliers and five pairs of sconces. Tin lanterns and reflectors are described as having existed in the Hall Theatre (1665) but a few years later these were supplanted by 130 candlesticks with reflectors. Footlights too are described as being there in an account of February 1670. A sketch of the Red Bull Theater (1672) shows an indoor stage with an almost Elizabethan thrust lit with chandeliers and footlights (Fig. 12).

In France the court led the way to innovation. In 1581 the *Ballet Comique de la Reine* was performed (Fig. 13). The famous sketch of this production shows a courtyard space with audience on three sides, but the settings are

*Stage Lighting Design*

12. *Red Bull Theatre, 1672*

13. Ballet comique de la Reine. *Petit Palais Bourbon, 1581*

14. *Cardinal Richelieu's Theatre in the Palais-Royal, 1640s*

15. *Molière frontispiece of the Comedie Française, 1726*

simultaneously spread through parts of the hall like medieval "mansions." Detailed descriptions tell of scenery glittering with gold and jewels, shining in the light of many lamps. Gauzes and glowing translucencies, transparent colored glasses—all the techniques of Renaissance lighting must have made a magical spectacle, which sadly only comes to us today through an inadequate black-and-white engraving.

In 1641 in Paris Cardinal Richelieu commissioned construction of the horseshoe-shaped Palais-Royal theatre, where Moliere was later to perform. The width of the proscenium was only 31 feet (9.5 meters), but the stage depth was 58 feet (17.55 meters; Fig. 14). In 1687 Nicodemus Tessin, a Swedish architect touring Europe, described the lighting. Footlights with fifty lamps, each with five flames, supplemented candles on vertical lighting poles at either side of the stage and chandeliers in the auditorium. The French theatre blazed with light throughout, unlike the Italian, where the auditorium frequently was darkened to increase the impact of the stage (Fig. 15).

Tessin also wrote of his experiences in the Italian theatre. He visited the San Giovanni Grisostomo in Venice. The lighting there was developed from the principles of Sabbattini. The chandeliers at the front of the auditorium were hoisted out of sight to darken the auditorium and the footlights could be raised or lowered gradually. Side lighting was on turnable poles to enable the brightness to be varied, and portable lighting strips could be attached to wing trolleys or set pieces.

The Italian stage rapidly grew in width and depth. A scene could be created up to 130 feet (40 meters) in depth. Wings, sliding in grooves, could be swiftly changed, and backcloths could be flown in to vary the depth of the

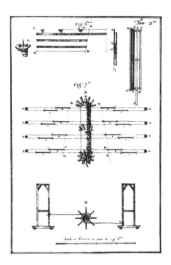

16. *Fabrizio Carini Motta. Movable lighting frames, Mantova, 1688*

17. *F. Bibiena. Ballet of* L'Età dell'oro, *Parma, 1690*

18. *F. Juvaro. Sketch for palace décor, early 18th century*

stage. Machines could move huge tableaux with performers and lights up and down and diagonally. Mirrors, glass and translucencies made spectacular effects. In 1688 Fabrizio Carini Motta, architect and engineer to the duke of Mantua, described in a series of *Discourses* how to design stage machinery, scenery and lighting for the theatre of his time. "I have tried various methods of lighting the stage, both movable and stationary, and have found some difficulties in all of them, for the obstructions they create are as great as the inconveniences in moving them." He goes on to detail in sketches and notes exactly how to mount torches or candles with tin reflectors on vertical posts behind each wing. These lighting "tormentors" could slide on- and offstage, dependent upon the position of the wings, and the level of illumination desired. An optional extra is to mount the lights on rounded shafts on which they could be rotated to dim the light for nighttime (Fig. 16).

Contrasts of light and shade enhanced the sense of depth of the stage, and asymmetry and oblique-perspective scenery became increasingly popular. Ferdinando Bibiena (1657–1743) and his family led the movement that produced astonishing vistas on the stage (Fig. 17). Asymmetrical scenery, with great columns or trees in the middle of the stage behind which lights could be hidden, must have greatly improved the possibility of lighting the darker middle of the backcloth (Fig. 18).

An Italian who worked extensively in Paris, G. N. Servandoni (1695–1766), further developed the use of distorted perspective and transparencies to create the impression of vast distances and spectacle. In 1738 he opened his "Spectacle d'optique" in the Salle des Machines, Paris, with a stage 40 meters deep. From a darkened auditorium, spectators watched performances depicting mythological events, which used live and painted figures in gigantic settings. Two complementary observations were: "A large number of lamps were so well arranged that it all resembled a tableau of a perfectly arranged chiaroscuro" and "That which is perfectly arranged is daylight." Servandoni himself observed that expense for the lighting had been no less than ten thousand francs, but that the admission fees had yielded nearly twenty thousand francs. Outside the conventional theatre such spectacles, under the direction of leading stage designers such as De Loutherbourg (in 1781) and Daguerre (in 1822), proved their popularity time and again. Their value as places of experiment, returning benefit to the theatre, has parallels for today, when high-budget industrial theatre, theme parks or rock-and-roll spectacle provide similar opportunities for development.

England's great actor and director David Garrick (1717–1779; Fig. 19) traveled to the Continent in 1765 and returned determined to modernize lighting at his Theatre Royal, Drury Lane. A friend, Jean Monnet of the Paris Opera-Comique, sent samples of stage lighting equipment to London. They were a success: "The public were agreeably surprised to see the stage illuminated with a strong and clear light, and the rings removed that used to supply it." Garrick introduced wing- and footlights with reflectors and removed the overhanging chandeliers (Fig. 20). Garrick's great scene

*Stage Lighting Design*

designer was P. J. De Loutherbourg (1740–1812), a master of creation of atmosphere who used color-changing silks on his side lighting. In 1772 he wrote to Garrick, assuming that he was to be responsible for lighting his designs at Drury Lane. At the Comedie-Francaise, a designer, Ferdinando Quaglio, stated that he needed one whole day to arrange the scenery and lighting: "The illumination should be to my taste and regardless of expense, particularly during the first two or three nights." He also stipulated his desire for billing on the posters. The management was grudging. They might provide billing, but the lighting would be arranged by the theatre "as was habitual." However, Quaglio "could have access to the stage, provided no other performance was jeopardized."

In 1790 George Saunders wrote *A Treatise on Theatres*. He recommends placing "reverberators" (Fig. 21) on the front of the near-stage boxes and mentions these front-of-house spotlights being used successfully at several theatres, including Blenheim.

Stage lighting was continually growing brighter. At the Comedie-Francaise in 1719, 48 tallow candles were used in the footlights. In 1783 there were 128 of the more efficient but more expensive wax candles. In 1784 the Argand lamp was developed. This was an oil lamp but, for the first time, with a chimney. It was as bright as about a dozen wax candles. Used with reflectors, it created new conditions on the stage, which contributed toward the reduction of makeup, new styles of costume, and encouraged another step toward more naturalistic acting (Fig. 22).

In 1803 the Lyceum Theatre, London, was the scene of a historic demonstration: lighting by gaslight. But it was not until 1817 that the stage of the same theatre became the first in England to be lit entirely by the new substance. A month later the stage of Drury Lane blazed with the new light, but across the Atlantic, the Chestnut Street Theatre, Philadelphia, had installed gas the year before. The owners "flatter themselves that its superior safety, brilliance and neatness will be satisfactory."

*19. Garrick's* Macbeth. *Drury Lane. Painting after Zoffany*

*20. Covent Garden Theatre in 1763*

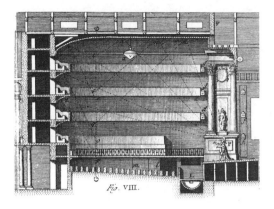

*21. Front-of-house reverberators (lighting) from Patte,* Essai sur l'Architecture théatrale, *1782*

*22. Wing lights on the German stage, 1794*

*23. Paris Opera's* Hernani, *1830*

*24. Vertical gaslights with wire guards*

*25. A. von Menzel.* Souvenir du Gymnase, *1856*

For a long time gaslight was to burn with a bare flame, for the mantle was not invented until the end of the nineteenth century. Depending on the quality of the gas, it could burn brighter and whiter than even the Argand lamp. It burnt without changing intensity and required no trimming and no wicks and, most vitally, it was easier to control. The brightness could be varied by regulating the gas supply, and the "gas table," which allowed control of separate parts of the stage, became the first stage "switchboard." At the Paris Opera in 1822 the former ballet-master wrote, "This light is perfect for the stage. One can obtain gradation of brightness that is really magical" (Fig. 23). But there were problems. The smell of gas could be offensive, and the danger from heat was more serious than ever. Bare gas jets next to wood and canvas presented a major fire hazard. The aforementioned Chestnut Street Theatre disappointed its owners and was one of the first of hundreds of theatres to be burnt down.

As the use of gas became more widespread, it was principally used to replace the former oil lamps and candles (Fig. 24). Perhaps the only significant change in lighting positions was the increase of overhead battens of lights. It was easier to light a row of gas jets than a greater quantity of candles high in the air. Brightness again increased and opened up new possibilities. *The Corsair* at Her Majesty's Theatre, London, in 1856, removed the customary wings and employed a panoramic cyclorama. Once again, styles of acting, scenery, costumes, and make-up that had seemed acceptable under murky candles and oil lamps now seemed overblown, vulgar and garish (Fig. 25).

Gaslight could not provide a beam or shaft of light any better than its predecessors. But in 1826 a new light source, limelight, was invented. Charles Macready tested it in his pantomime *Peeping Tom of Coventry* at Covent Garden in 1837. Limelight used a block of quicklime heated by a flame of oxygen and hydrogen to provide an intense point source that could be installed in a hand-operated spotlight (Fig. 26). This was used to provide strong accents of light across the stage for the first time,.

The practice of darkening the auditorium during the performance was introduced in England by Sir Henry Irving (1838–1905; Figs. 27 and 27a), who was a great innovator in stage lighting. He said, "Stage lighting and

26. *Improved limelight burner*    27 and 27a. *Irving's* Corsican Brothers, *Lyceum Theatre*

groupings are of more consequence than the scenery." He further explored the subtleties of color mixing and sought to enhance his productions with the imaginative use of light and shade. Bram Stoker, his lighting assistant, said, "It became an easy matter to throw any special part of the stage into greater prominence." Irving had extensive lighting rehearsals, without actors but attended by the staff, which included his thirty gasmen and eight limelight operators (Fig. 28). In 1889 the French director Antoine wrote of his admiration for Irving's lighting.

28. *Irving's* Macbeth. *Lyceum Theatre, 1888*

Stage lighting had spawned a service industry to the theatre. Walter Kerr (1809–1893) became the "king of limelight" in the London theatre. Employing dozens of technicians, his firm serviced most of the principal theatres of London with staff and equipment (Fig. 29). Upon his death one of his crew said, "He was the 'Father of Limelight.' At one time he used to do all the business. Contracted all the theatres, and laid by, they say, quite 30,000 pounds. Old Kerr was the grandfather of us all, so to speak."

In 1857 Charles Garnier's new Paris Opera opened (Fig. 30). It contained a lighting system with twenty-eight miles of piping feeding 960 gas jets from a gas table of eighty-eight stopcocks. A Parisian lighting catalogue of 1877 contains details of many types of instrument, including carbon-arc spot-lights, which ranged from the largest, which could flood the whole stage, to small hand-held follow spots. A multitude of special effects and projection apparatus was used, and the climax of the age of gas certainly employed massive resources, often to spectacular effect (Fig. 31).

In 1881 the Savoy Theatre in London opened with an electric lighting installation. One thousand one hundred fifty-eight incandescent lamps were used, of which 824 were on the stage, controlled by six dimmers. Richard D'Oyly Carte appeared before the curtain and demonstrated the new safety of electricity by smashing a lit lamp wrapped in muslin. This was greeted with tumultuous cheers.

The electrical revolution quickly spread across the world. Belasco states that the first theatre in the U.S.A. to be equipped with electricity was the California in San Francisco.

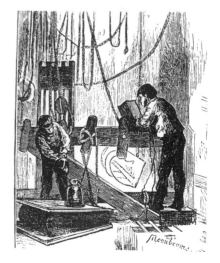

29. *Limelightmen, 1874*

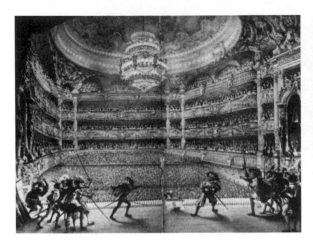

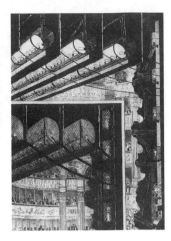

30. Garnier's new Paris Opera, 1875

31. Offstage view of gaslit stage

32. Electric battens and wing lights with the gas they replaced. Paris Opera, 1887

However, for many years electric light was only used to replace the gas jets that preceded it. Footlights, battens, and vertical strips at the sides of the stage were converted to electricity (Figs. 32 and 33). It was brighter, had no smell and was much safer. (A Captain Shaw noted that the temperature in the grid of the Savoy was 68° Fahrenheit, while at the Alhambra, lit with gaslight, it was 105°.) It has been estimated that the electric lamp was perhaps a third brighter than the gas jet. Despite frequent criticism of excessive, harsh brightness, theatres rapidly increased the number of lamps used. By 1902 the Prinzregententheater in Munich had a four-color system using 1,542 onstage lamps in footlights, battens and wings, 770 lamps in movable standards (floor stands) and lengths (striplights) and 12 arc lamps (Fig. 34).

Despite being cumbersome, flickering and often noisy, arc lights were still required to provide accent (Fig. 35). It was some years before the spotlight, coupled to the dimmer, began to offer new opportunities. Even today, the arc lamp is still in use as the brightest long-range follow spot, although newer discharge light sources increasingly replace the carbon arc.

Meanwhile, in reaction against the flat glare of early electric light, two men, Gordon Craig (1872–1966) and Adolphe Appia (1862–1928), dreamt of a new stage lighting. Both rejected the increasingly realistic scenery of their time and both—inspired by the beauty and evocative power of natural light—imagined a stage with the actor in an environment unified by three-dimensional light. Appia said, "Light is to space what sounds are to time" (Fig. 36). Craig wrote of a "master of the art and science of the theatre," the stage manager, who would unify all the arts of theatre into a harmonious whole (Fig. 37).

Craig and Appia were more influential through their writings than through their all-too-few productions. Others, although perhaps without realizing it, took up the challenge that their inspiration posed.

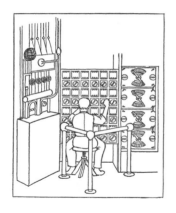

*33. Electric switchboard. Paris Opera, 1887*

*34. The first theatre in Germany with electric light, at the Electro-Technical Exposition, Munich, 1882*

*35. Gas orchestra lights and bunch light*

In the U.S.A. David Belasco (1858–1931) was the first director of the twentieth century to pay great attention to lighting (Fig. 38). Lighting rehearsals for his productions could take weeks, and he established a "laboratory" to plan the lighting in advance. His lighting engineer was Louis Hartmann, who for twenty-eight years worked with him and was responsible for the development of the first incandescent spotlights (Fig. 39). They also introduced indirect overhead lighting by shining spotlights into reflective silver-coated bowls, which produced a soft naturalistic impression of light from the sky (Fig. 40). Today, a multiplicity of carefully focused spotlights create an equally soft and potentially naturalistic impression, but with the "advantage"—we believe today—of more precise control.

Hartmann, a great innovator, was truly a man of theatre (Fig. 41). "Why should we suppose that a radical change is necessary in the theater?" he wrote. "The glory of a sunrise or sunset is just the same today as when the first human beheld it. Our emotions have not changed. Let us use our modern devices to enhance the value of the text; and 'hold, as 't were, a mirror up to nature'" (Fig. 42).

In 1917 Hartmann's baby spotlights were first brought to England from the U.S.A. by the director Basil Dean (1888–1978). He, like Belasco, was intensely concerned with stage lighting and also introduced German equipment, such as the acting-area flood. In 1923 he installed a Schwabe cyclorama system at the St. Martin's Theatre, London, and in *R.U.R.* used scene projection in England for the first time (Fig. 43). In 1939 he directed J. B. Priestley's *Johnson Over Jordan*, devising, with his electrician, Bill Lorraine, an English version of Hartmann's reflected light (Fig. 44). Another significant innovator was director Terence Grey, who created a theatre in Cambridge that combined a classic horseshoe-shaped auditorium with an

*36. A. Appia. Wagner's* Die Walkure, *act 3*

*37. E.G. Craig.* Scene, *1906*

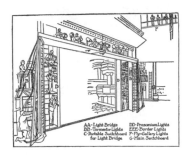

38. *Lighting scheme for* The Return of Peter Grimm. *Belasco Theatre, 1911*

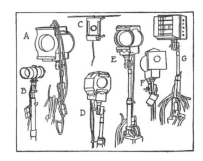

39. *Louis Hartmann. Lens lamp types*

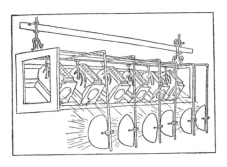

40. *Lighting with reflectors*

41. *Belasco and Hartmann*

open-end stage and accomplished striking lighting with his associate, Harold Ridge (Fig. 45).

The director Max Reinhardt (1873–1943) was a giant of the German theatre who also shared Belasco's conviction about the importance of lighting. His versatility made him a master of the stage in the tradition spoken of by Gordon Craig, with productions that ranged from the vast and spectacular, like *The Miracle,* to the most intimate, such as his work at the Redoutensaal recital room in Vienna. "Lighting must replace the decorations," he wrote in 1901.

Since the mid-nineteenth century German theatres had been lavishly appointed, aided by substantial funding from the court or state (Fig. 46). The practice of repertoire, with a different performance every night, led to large stages equipped with bridges hung over the stage to carry the lighting, which could thus be readily reached and reset by electricians. Equipment was large but finely engineered. High-quality optics and spacious stages encouraged developments in large-scale scene projection. Linnebach, Hasait and other German engineers developed a pattern of stage lighting, which, beginning in the twenties, was to remain largely unchanged for many years. Meanwhile, in the U.S.A. and later in England, lighting that at first consisted of electric lamps in rows of striplights or battens and footlights, imitating the soft overall lighting of the age of gas, began to change.

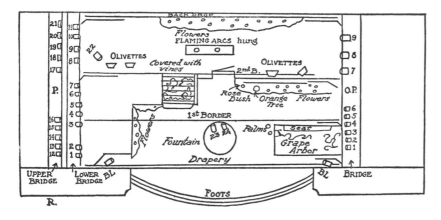

42. *Belasco:* The Rose of the Rancho *lighting plan*

43. *Schwabe cloud projection machine*

44. Johnson over Jordan

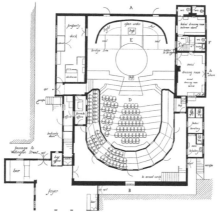

45. *Terence Grey's lighting at Cambridge 1926*

The oldest specialized stage lighting manufacturer is Kliegl Brothers of New York, founded in 1896. Siemens of Germany and Clemançon in Paris were early pioneers but counted the stage as only one of many areas. Strand Electric was founded in England in 1914 by two theatre electricians and remained the leading British company in the field for more than eighty years (Fig. 47). Innovation for many years was largely under the direction of Frederick Bentham (b. 1911; Fig. 48). He led the development of many modern English instruments, but his major achievement was in the field of lighting control.

Intensity control of electric light was achieved with dimmers (Fig. 49), either the variable-resistance type or auto-transformers, the movement of which was synchronized by increasingly sophisticated mechanical linkage systems. A grand-master control allowed dimmers to be connected via shafts and clutches to a central lever or wheel (Fig. 50). Bentham, inspired by a life-long enthusiasm for "color music"—mixing light to music—conceived that

46. *Proscenium lighting of the Städtische Oper, Berlin*

47. *Strand Pattern 43, 58 and 76 lanterns*

48. *Frederick Bentham*

49. *Kliegl 12-way piano board*

50. *Liverpool Empire Grandmaster and Charlie Bristow*

lighting should be controlled in a way that was analogous to music. He developed the Light Console, which employed a console derived from the cinema organ driving remote motor-driven dimmers (Fig. 51). An alternative way of miniaturizing lighting control, with multiple presets, was developed using thyratron valves (Fig. 52). These were later replaced by silicon control rectifiers (SCR). On the Light Console a skilled operator was able to "play" the lighting in a remarkably fluid manner. One man—instead of many—could control several hundred dimmers. This led to remote control systems being installed by West End commercial managements a decade before such systems were adopted by Broadway in the U.S.A (Fig. 53). The emerging—and wealthy—TV industry in England adopted the principle of dimmer control for each light and installed similar control systems. The advent of the computer led to the first memory control.

In the U.S.A. Edward Kook (1903-1990) founded Century Lighting (Fig. 54). He developed the compact ellipsoidal spotlight, often colloquially called the Leko, after himself and his partner, Levy (Fig. 55). More significantly, Kook supported the emergence of the new profession in the theatre, the lighting designer. While in England between the wars lighting was the province of the directors working with their electricians, in the U.S.A. lighting remained the designer's responsibility. Lee Simonson, Norman Bel Geddes, Robert Edmond Jones, Donald Oenslager and Jo Mielziner all extended the use of lighting as an integral part of their scene designs.

In 1925 Stanley McCandless was appointed to teach stage lighting at Yale University. In *A Method of Lighting the Stage*, he formulated a structured approach to the new lighting design process. Specialists in lighting design, such as Abe Feder, Peggy Clark, and Jean Rosenthal, emerged and began to establish a professionalism around the lighting process.

In England in the late thirties Joe Davis (1912–1984) was an electrician with the leading theatrical producers, H. M. Tennent. His lighting for hundreds of productions demonstrated a rare sensitivity. Productions such as Christopher Fry's *The Lady's Not for Burning* evoked the scudding light of an English

*Stage Lighting Design*

51. *Strand Light Console*    52. *Strand Thyratron Control*    53. *Strand CD Control*

spring with extraordinary beauty (Fig. 56). His work reproducing American productions that transferred to London in the 1950s demonstrated the advances that had been effected by the professional lighting designer in the U.S.A. Michael Northen, another pioneer designer, did much work for the Shakespeare Memorial Theatre, at Stratford, and Covent Garden before becoming one of the leading designers of English musicals in the 1960s.

Two men with remarkable influence upon the modern English stage were designer Sean Kenny and director Stephen Joseph. Sean designed Lionel Bart's *Oliver!* (Fig. 57), *Blitz!* and *Maggie May*; sensationally, at the time, exposing all the lighting equipment to view. Stephen became the leading protagonist of arena staging in Britain, founding his theatre in Scarborough, which became the base for author and director Alan Aykbourne.

As mentioned before, your author founded Theatre Projects (TP) in 1957. I introduced American methods of preplanning lighting and imported equipment from America and Germany, widening the spectrum of technology then available. I also developed a team of lighting designers, which included Robert Ornbo, Robert Bryan, John B. Read, David Hersey, Andy Bridge, Nick Chelton, and others who were to have a profound influence upon English stage lighting. Through the 1980s with the emergence of Cameron Mackintosh's worldwide work as producer of the English "mega-hit" musicals, this lighting influence went international, particularly that of David Hersey *(Cats, Les Miserables* and *Miss Saigon)* and Andy Bridge *(Phantom of the Opera* and *Sunset Boulevard)*. These spectacular productions demonstrated dramatic stage lighting, employing all the resources of modern technology but enhancing and underpinning the drama of story and song.

Just as designers of the eighteenth century took their work outside the theatre, so today the lighting designer's skills find a wider audience. Designed lighting in architecture has been strongly influenced by theatre practitioners, as has lighting for television. The fields of rock-and-roll concert lighting, industrial theatre, theme parks, museums and exhibitions have led to an explosion in lighting opportunities as they continue to become

54. *Edward Kook*

55. *Lekolite ca. 1965*

56. The Lady's Not for Burning. *Globe Theatre*

57. *The original* Oliver!

increasingly theatrical and complex. Concert lighting in particular employs amazingly elaborate resources, and much ingenuity was displayed by the pioneer designers and technicians who introduced techniques that were later in their turn to influence theatrical practice.

In the 1970s and 1980s the expansion in government financial support of regional theatre in the U.K. in general and the Royal National Theatre and the Royal Shakespeare Theatre in London led to considerable improvement in British stage design and lighting. New theatres with new sophisticated installations and new demands from directors and producers brought new designers to the forefront. By the mid-1990s the work of English designers such as Chris Parry, Paul Pyant, Benny Ball, Mark Henderson, Rick Fisher, Mick Hughes, Jean Kalman, Mark Brickman, Patrick Woodroffe and hundreds of others was seen around the world. In lighting equipment manufacture the field has also exploded. In 1957 there were less than half a dozen companies in the field; in 1994 nearly two hundred firms are members of PLASA—the Professional Lighting and Sound Association—and many of them are major equipment suppliers internationally.

In the U.S.A., unlike England, major universities offer training in stage lighting design. Outstanding designers such as Tharon Musser, Jules Fisher, Jennifer Tipton, Roger Morgan, John Gleason, Ken Billington, Richard Nelson, Howell Binkley, Paul Gallo and Marc Weiss lead a profession rich in numbers and talent. As in England, the proliferation of regional theatres has led to a widening of opportunity for the lighting designer. The major regional theatres and opera companies utilize lighting of the highest quality with designers such as Peter Maradudin, Pat Collins, and Tom Munn.

*Stage Lighting Design*

Architectural lighting as a vital part of the architectural design scene is more strongly established in the U.S.A. than elsewhere, in large part due to the early influence of theatre lighting designers such as Abe Feder and Jean Rosenthal, who have been followed by such outstanding practitioners as Paul Marantz, Howard Brandston and William Lam. Chip Mounk, Jeff Ravitz, and James Moody are three of the pioneers of rock-and-roll lighting, which has had an important influence upon theatre techniques, but which has also probably become the widest known market for theatrical lighting, opening the eyes of millions to the excitement of lighting through live concerts and music videos.

In Australia lighting was initially influenced entirely by productions imported from Europe and the United States. Equipment followed overseas practice with locally made battens, footlights and resistance dimmer boards accompanied by often second-rate copies of imported equipment. Strand established a local subsidiary in 1952 under Alec Brown. The company was later led by Dennis Irving, who played an important role in modernizing lighting in that country. The sixties saw the development of indigenous theatre. Permanently staffed National Opera and Ballet Companies, originally part of the Australian Elizabethan Theatre Trust, and resident repertory companies in Melbourne, Sydney, and later Adelaide had an effect upon lighting design. The National Institute of Dramatic Art, founded in 1959 began production courses in 1961. Stefan Haag and John Sumner were capable directors and lighting designers, and Roger Barrett, Bill Akers, Jamie Lewis and Nigel Levings became established lighting designers. In 1973 Adelaide opened the first major National Arts Center, to be followed by others in Melbourne and elsewhere. Each had major modern lighting installations. Bill Akers and Dennis Irving pioneered the specification of the Galaxy lighting control, based on the National Theatre's Lightboard but utilizing microprocessor technology, which became the international standard for Strand. Strand closed their direct operation in Australia in 1992, and the lighting industry is now served by a number of smaller companies, including Bytecraft Ltd., Q Engineering, LSC Electronics, Prolite Queensland and Dynalite Controls.

Lighting in Canada was similarly influenced by European and American practice. Wally Russell, technical director of the Canadian Opera Company and the National Ballet of Canada, was a lighting designer and theatre consultant for the National Arts Center in Ottawa. He became head of Strand Lighting in Canada and then in the United States. As lighting designer for the Los Angeles Opera Company's *Tristan and Isolde* (designer David Hockney; Fig. 58) he was the first to light an opera using only Vari*Lite moving lights. A number of fine theatre design courses are available in Canadian universities, and the high quality of staging across the country is influenced by such lighting designers as Michael Whitfield and Rob Thompson.

A 1990 study by lighting designer Lee Watson estimated that there might be as many as 50,000 individuals worldwide working in lighting or associated

*58.* Tristan and Isolde, *First complete installation of moving lights in opera. The Los Angeles Opera. Director: Jonathan Miller. Scenery: David Hockney*

industries. Among these were some 260 members of the United Scenic Artists Union (New York, Chicago, Los Angeles and Florida lighting designers), 400 architectural lighting members of the International Association of Lighting Designers, 200 members of the Hollywood American Society of Cinematographers; the British Association of Theatre Lighting Designers had 120 members (up to 300 by 1994); British TV lighting associations, 400 members; Canadian TV, 120 members; professional lighting designers, 100 members; Australian TV, 120 members, and so on. Altogether, Watson estimated 3,000 lighting designers worldwide with others involved as educators, technicians, manufacturers or suppliers.

English and American techniques have increasingly merged since the early 1980s. Lighting is achieved with a multiplicity of spotlights (largely ellipsoidal or profile spots that allow the beam of light to be shaped at will), which may be colored with a choice of hundreds of different shades of plastic color media. Accent light is usually provided by low-voltage beam projectors or PAR reflector lamps. Instruments are still usually positioned overhead on pipes or trusses in rows across the stage and vertically at the side. In the 1950s probably two hundred instruments were commonplace in a single rig, but in 1995, 600 to 1,200 units are commonly found, of an average power of 575 to 1,000 watts. Major spectaculars, such as the big Las Vegas shows, employ as many as 4,000 units. Swings of theatrical fashion seem to dictate whether or not the lighting should be hidden from the sight of the audience or be prominently incorporated into the scenic design.

Until the late 1980s instrument design had advanced little since the principles were established in the 1930s. In England CCT first developed ellipsoidal reflector (profile) spots with a variable zoom beam angle. Advances in lamp manufacture and in reflector design, such as found in the new dye-cast ellipsoidal units from ETC and Altman, continue to allow improvement in instrument efficiency. The use of new light sources, such as metal halide and xenon, continues, but the theatre's need to have smooth dimming from full brightness to black out is a restraint. Highly efficient discharge-lighting sources that utilize mechanical shutters to fade out the light are used most commonly in Germany. Will new light sources emerge? Of course the answer must be in the affirmative. As 1995 drew to a close, news arrived of the development of highly efficient microwave lamps providing what is virtually a point source.

New advances in remote-control moving lights have become increasingly available from the concert music business. In the early sixties firms such as Century in the U.S. and Pani in Austria had developed spotlights with motorized focusing and color change, but usually at great cost. Led by innovations from Vari*Lite of Dallas, Texas, the world of rock and roll began using computer-controlled remotely resettable spotlights successfully. Helped by a fall in prices, this movement has spread into the theatre. Now fluid control over not only the intensity of light but also its movement about the stage and its color is possible—all capable of sudden or subtle change as the action unfolds.

The improvement in brightness of projection equipment developed in Austria and France has encouraged renewed interest in scenic projection. Projections of enormous power are now possible—almost able to compete with daylight—together with computer control of the image changer.

The advent of the computer brought the ability to memorize at the touch of a button a complete lighting picture, initially by recording the level of dimmer channels but later by recording the position of remote-controlled spotlights and color changers. Lightboard advanced Bentham's "playability" of light, with a new freedom to mix prerecorded lighting images or groups (Fig. 59). Only in the mid-1990s, as a consequence of the constantly greater memory, speed and cheapness of microprocessors, does the prospect of another quantum leap forward in lighting control appear. Computer power will be used to handle the ever increasing complexity of lighting systems, without the endless proliferation of numbers and digits; rather using graphics and computer-modeling techniques to close the loop between the visual image on the stage and the mind processes of the designer.

59. Strand lightboard

The age-old argument about footlights and the need for light from the front and above the actor is long over. Front-of-house spotlighting was first mounted on the front of the balconies, then invaded the audience boxes, and now hundreds of instruments may be used in the auditorium. New theatres make elaborate provision, with bridges in the ceiling and slots in the walls, to allow light to reach the stage with the greatest possible freedom of angle.

In Europe, even in Germany, lighting design has generally been slower to make creative advances, except in the work of some exceptional artists. Wieland Wagner (1917–1966), in directing his grandfather's operas at Bayreuth, created memorable images with light (Figs. 60 and 61). Josef Svoboda (b. 1920) has opened new vistas with light (often low voltage) and projection (Fig. 62). The emergence of the professional lighting designer has been slow to gain acceptance in central Europe, in part due to union traditions, but this is finally changing in the 1990s due to the pioneering work of designers such as Munich's Max Keller as well as the influence of visiting British designers.

In her book *The Magic of Light* Jean Rosenthal wrote, "Light is quite tactile to me. It has shape and dimension. It has an edge. It has quality and it is an entity. It is the one miracle of creation without which, to me, the others would be meaningless."

Today, the stage is a space that can be filled with any shape, pattern, texture, feeling, or atmosphere of light that the performance requires. Opera, ballet, dance, musicals, drama, popular music, each make particular demands on theatrical lighting. Each can be well or poorly lit. That judgment must be a summation of how expressively and purposefully light has been used to illuminate the stage appropriately, how the performers are three-dimensionally revealed, the composition of the lighting within the overall visual intent of the scenic picture, and finally the degree to which the stage is charged with the correctly evocative atmosphere. Each of these qualities will stem from the content and intended style of the production.

*60 and 61. Wieland Wagner. Scenes from* Parsifal, *1956, and* Lohengrin, *1958, Bayreuth*

*62. Josef Svoboda.* King Oedipus, *Prague*

Each step of technological progress in lighting, candle to oil lamp, oil lamp to gas, and gas to electricity, has brought change. More light, safety and greater facility for control have been achieved and yet always accompanied by complaints of over-brightness. But greater brightness has had to be followed by more subtle acting technique and ever more subtle and often more realistic scenery, costumes and makeup. By the 1990s the twentieth century has seen the passing of many styles of production. Realism has given way to many other -isms, and the wheel of style continues to revolve. But the new lighting, the ability to fill stage space with light of character, remote from its source, has had an effect that is perhaps more profound than ever before.

The scenic environment surrounding the actor has become more three dimensional. Physical thickness, depth and texture, used with light, have replaced much of the painted detail of previous ages. Often scenic elements have become large, and backstage areas have had to accommodate consequently bulkier scenery.

But the most significant change has been in the theatres themselves and in the relationship between the actor and the audience. Throughout most theatre times the players performed among their audience and both were lit throughout the performance. As we have seen, every period produced innovators who wished to darken the auditorium, but only in the late nineteenth century did this become the norm. The desire for increased naturalism and audience concentration on the stage made dimming the houselights the symbol of the play's commencement. The actor had to perform upstage of the proscenium lighting in order to be seen, and a gulf grew between him and the darkened audience. Almost immediately, visionary directors realized that this broke the fragile bond of communication that lay at the heart of live theatre, which is the living interaction between performer and spectator.

*Stage Lighting Design*

The coming of the spotlight, which illuminated space from a distance, not only allowed the actors' faces to be lit from the auditorium, it allowed the actor to work in lit space that could be placed *within* the audience. So, a re-examination of antique and new forms of theatre began. Theatre-in-the-round, thrust, transverse, environmental, open stages all became legitimate means of theatrical expression. All were enabled by lighting to place actor and audience in the same space, but allowed the proper focus of attention to remain with the performer. Once more, the actor is able to be at the heart of his audience. Once more, he can be seen as a living, three-dimensional human being in intimate communication with his audience. At a period in theatre history when new electronic means of storytelling challenge the live theatre as never before, this rediscovered intimacy, this living contact, continues to give theatre its uniqueness in a world of ever more dazzling media.

At the same time theatre's ability to offer the unique impact of the live performer can be enhanced with the enriched spectacle that creative lighting affords. Lighting, as an element in the theatre, has had a long and often unrecognized history. Just as stained glass in a Gothic cathedral brought wonder to the beholder, so, since the Renaissance, lighting has played its part in bringing magic to the stage. Today, the lighting designer has at his fingertips computer-controlled intensity, movement and color. These things were imagined by our theatrical ancestors, but electronics have brought them within our grasp. The speed of technological change is still accelerating. The challenge of the future must be to match technical development with a creativity that is always sensitive to the theatre's essentially human needs, so that lighting plays its appropriate role in the service of the living theatre.

# A HISTORICAL FOOTNOTE

---

**S**tage Lighting Control—A Snapshot of Change over Thirty Years

For fun and historical reference I'm including a modest survey of some "out-dated" control boards. Some will still be found in theatres.

I remember well a theatre in Cheltenham, England, where I once lit a show for the famous director Frith Banbury. The theatre had been renovated—so the manager proudly told us. But not, apparently, backstage.

The countryman/board operator was charming. He sat with his spaniel dog at his ancient grand master on a platform above stage right. We began to light. After several cues I began to inquire as to the level of certain dimmers. "Number 10?" "At half," came back the reply. "No, full please." Two minutes later: "Number 10?" "At half," again. "No, at full." After several such goes, I walked onstage to the platform. The dog looked down. "Jack," I said, "When I say full, I mean full, until I want it to move." He showed me the problem. After his hand was removed from any handle, due to its own weight gravity would slowly reduce the intensity level. I sighed and asked him to try to overcome this defect. Walking back to the production desk on the intercom I heard Jack say to his dog, "Aaarh, these people down from Lun'non should modify their ideas a bit."

It's fun to see how the world has changed.

This selection cannot be comprehensive, for much blood—and money — was spilt on the way to today. This story begins in the fifties.

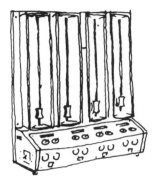

*63. Strand Junior 8*

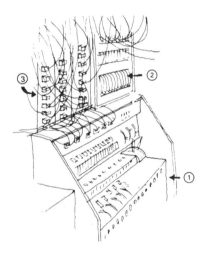

*64. Pianoboard and presets*
*1. Piano board*
*2. Pre-set boards*
*3. Rugguy box*

## HISTORIC CONTROLS
### Strand Junior 8 (Fig. 63)

This is where I started: four slider resistance dimmers on the wall. Officially eight channels could be controlled, but I found that with plenty of three-way socket adapters, you could pile up enough to cook an egg before the fuses blew.

### Water Dimmers with Tracker Wire Control

Betraying my age, I will actually admit that I did light one of my first professional shows at the Savoy theatre in London when they still had some water dimmers. I was told that, when in doubt, one peed in them to top up the mixture. "Turn off the electricity first," was the helpful tip.

### The Piano Board and Presets (Fig. 64)

It's hard to believe, but prior to *A Chorus Line's* arrival on Broadway, all that wondrous Broadway lighting was done on these giant cookers. Looking like battered upright pianos, they contained twelve 6,000-watt or fourteen 3,000-watt resistant dimmer plates. Dimmers could be linked to a shaft, and one man usually operated two boards placed opposite each other with hands, feet, teeth and other adjacent extremities. Placed on top were auxiliary or preset boards. Containing eight 750-watt or twelve 500-watt dimmers for individual instruments these would "preset" levels before being brought up by their master dimmer in the piano board below. Stacks of plugging boxes allowed channels to be ganged or "patched" together as needed. Adding to the fun—and heat—the lighting load on resistance dimmers had to be exactly balanced to the dimmer's rated capacity. In other words, a 100-watt lamp had to have 2,900 watts of something else (like an electric fire!) connected in the basement. How easy life is today! But miracles of lighting could be manipulated with skill, dexterity...and considerable dedication.

### The Grandmaster

This was the way of controlling lots of lights in a permanent installation before electronics began, consisting of mighty mechanical monsters of wheels and shafts, gears and bevels to drive resistance dimmers or autotransformers to their destined levels. Locking dimmers to shafts and shafts to grandmaster, one man and an assistant could wreak miracles on even 120 channels. Who remembers George Andrews at the Theatre Royal Brighton?

### Strand Light Console

Fred Bentham's great invention for British theatre was first installed in the San Carlos Opera in Lisbon in 1940. Seeking to play light like one played music, Fred had the brilliant idea of actually using an organ console. He linked the organ stops and keys to resistance dimmers or autotransformers driven via electromagnetic clutches to a motor. Extraordinarily fluid and rapid movement of light could be achieved using fingers and feet. The difficulty was hitting accurate dimmer levels. Basically on and off was easy, quarter, half or three-quarters could be done, but anything more sophisticated than that...forget it.

*65. Strand Century C-I control*

### Strand Century C-I Control, 5- or 10-Scene Preset (U.S.A.; Fig. 65)

An early U.S. remote-control board developed by George Izenour for Century Lighting was installed in Yale University in 1947. Utilizing twin thyratron valves, the master control ran multiscene presets with one lever per channel per preset. Thus, a 100-channel 10-scene board had 1,000 levers, requiring a miracle of dexterity per cue. A master fader would cross-fade all lighting from one scene to the next. It was reported that one man could only really run 50 channels, with big productions requiring total resetting of every preset ten times. Boards like this were commonly installed in American universities while Broadway continued to cook on piano boards. But the physical impracticality of moving thousands of tiny levers to effect any light change made the multiscene preset an unlikely candidate for the future.

### Strand Electronic Control

The way forward lay in flexible grouping. It was nonsense to have to wipe and reset a whole preset if only ten channels were to move. Another Strand invention to rival Fred Bentham's was the Electronic two-scene preset board developed by J. T. (Woody) Wood. This allowed the accurate presetting of dimmer levels, unlike the Light Console, but had two groups within each preset as well. A two-way switch above each dimmer lever allowed assignment of any channel to one of two group masters. This principle was to guide future developments. Unfortunately the thyratron valves cooked at high temperatures and quickly destroyed themselves.

### Strand CD Control (Fig. 66)

Dimmer level preset limitations of the Light Console and unreliability of the thyratron led to the CD, a control of motorized dimmers (akin to the Light Console) but with remote manual dimmer levers to allow accurate level setting instead of the console's organ keyboard. A motor-driven dimmer maintains its level until instructed to move. A "move" cue changes the level of channels selected to move but ignores those not selected, as opposed to a "cross fade" in which every channel changes from the old level to a new level. This reduces the need to constantly reset every preset dimmer lever required on an exclusively "crossfade" board. This principle of "inertia" in the system inspired the principle of the "move" cue that characterized British control until today's Galaxy. But the problem of the CD was the insensitivity of the grinding motor drive and the complexity of its operation. Genius operators were really required, and theatre owners in the U.K. never thought of paying a decent living wage to their staff. They did, however, cut

*66. Strand CD control desk*

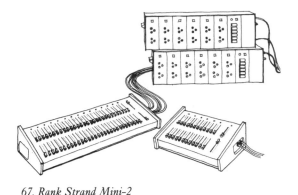

67. Rank Strand Mini-2

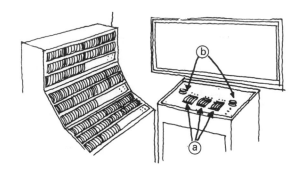

68. Strand LP: a. Master faders, b. Grand masters

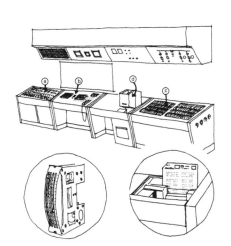

69. Siemens Regulator

their crew costs by installing one-man operation remote-control boards as standard in the London theatre in the fifties—long before Broadway.

### Strand Mini-2 (Fig. 67)

This was sophistication for the modest installation—the arrival of the SCR dimmer! A two-preset control of dimmers providing up to thirty-six 2,000-watt channels.

### Strand LP (Luminous Preset) (Fig. 68)

The Strand LP was a nifty control from the sixties that employed two or three presets but with group switching selection effected by a switch in the illuminated scale of each channel lever. By touching the scale, a channel could be selected to a group, and twenty or forty groups were possible. Presets of groups could be recalled by pressing push buttons. Only channels with lit scales were preset for any cue in which they would move, allowing the electronic equivalent of the "move" cue. A special version with independent grouping per preset was installed for the National Theatre at the Old Vic and was a small step toward some of the Lightboard thinking.

### Siemens Regulator (Germany; Fig. 69)

The Mercedes of European lighting, this board consisted of a desk with one motor-driven lever per channel. Upon operating a master control, all the dimmer levers would motor to their preset levels—an amazing sight in the control room, apart from any effect onstage. Presets were achieved with tiny levers (four per channel) that could mechanically be brought forward to be preset. Punched-card equipment later allowed automation of this process.

### Thorn Q-File (Fig. 70)

Strand got into trouble in the early days of the computer with unreliable punch cards, ferrite cores, and so on. Memory was the obvious way to go, but

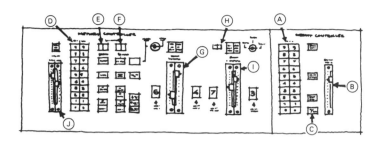

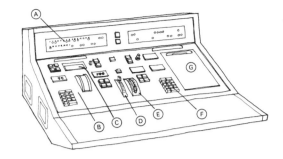

70. Thorn Q-File
   a. Selector
   b. Level fader
   c. On/off switch

d. Memory selector
e. Stage store
f. Preset store
g. Speed control A-B

h. CD indications
i. Speed control
j. Master

71. Strand Compact

how? While they struggled—and in so doing, lost their corporate independence to Rank—Thorn, a major lighting-industry company, stepped in. Led by Tony Isaacs, a rare boffin, they started from scratch on a control for the new generation of TV studios needed by the BBC. At my urging they modified their first controls for theatrical usage. Up to a thousand channels could be handled from a two-foot-square board. For the first time, individual channels were accessed with a keypad to a motorized lever. Selecting a channel number instantly drove the lever to its level. Touch-of-a-button recording of levels became a reality, and multiple pictures of light could be cross-faded, added, subtracted or mixed at will.

## Strand DDM

This was Strand's technological recovery, first installed in the Royal Shakespeare Theatre at Stratford-on-Avon in 1971. A memory system that worked, it used an internally illuminated rocker switch per channel. Press the top and the circuit faded up, the bottom and it faded down. The rocker was an interesting idea, but hardly as wonderfully "playable" as the light console keyboard, and the only indication of channel output was on or off, which was insufficient.

## Strand Compact (Fig. 71)

An interesting portable control with some innovations, this board had a calculator style keypad for channel selection and a wheel to set level. I think that this too had the first "@" key to set level and the first "&Memory" key to mix individual channels with prerecorded memories (or cues).

## Kliegl Performance (U.S.A.)

Another powerful and innovative portable system in a small package, Performance featured a "thru" button to assemble a collection of channels and twenty-four group masters and electronic patching.

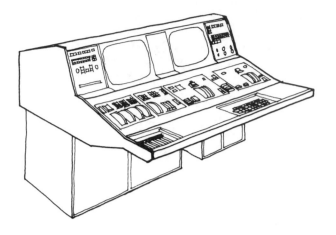

72. Rank Strand Lightboard

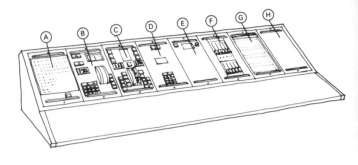

73. Rank Strand MMS

### Skirpan Autocue (U.S.A.)

The first U.S. minicomputer control used a touch-sensitive video screen to access channels, set levels and record memories with a light-pen (an idea whose time might yet return?).

### Rank Strand MMS (Fig. 72)

The MMS was a popular control, built in modular sections, with channel or memory selection by keypad and wheel, video display, submasters and multiple playbacks. Martin Moore was the principle designer, who also made a great contribution to the Strand Lightboard.

### Rank Strand Lightboard (Fig. 73)

This was my baby. I was frustrated by DDM's limited channel-level display and convinced that the next control had to allow equal ease of access to any light or any group of lights. With memory control, the individual channel was no longer very important. Lightboard set forth some basic parameters. 1. It had to be fundamentally simple in its basic operation (no unnecessary buttons!). 2. It could be "played" by a skilled operator "heads-up." 3. A prerecorded group was equally available as any channel, indeed any memorized cue could be summoned up as a group. 4. A lighting "palette" with six submasters could be loaded with any combination of channels, groups or cues to allow balancing of lighting. 5. Lighting could move at many concurrent speeds, while always being capable of being overtaken manually when necessary. 6. VDUs displayed full channel information in different formats, particularly showing only those channels in use. 7. Control of remote-control instruments—pan, tilt, focus, color and slide change—was integrated in the console. 8. It introduced dimmer-per-circuit to the U.K., eliminating the patch panel, and provided for a layout of channel numbers identified by their geographic location, useful for repertory work. 9. A special-effects auxiliary panel allowed chases and complex sound-to-light modulation effects.

*Stage Lighting Design*

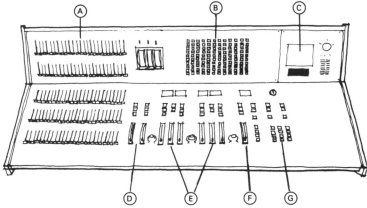

74. *ADB Memolight*

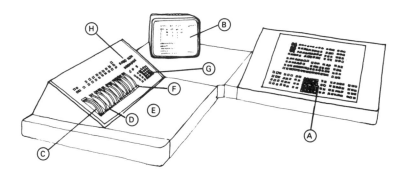

75. *Siemens Sitralux*

### Berkey Colortran Channel Track (U.S.A.)

This high-end American control introduced the ability to view the performance of channels across multiple cues on the VDU.

### ADB Memolight (Belgium; Fig. 74)

This European memory control provided push-button or manual-fader channel selection. Operation of the fader would lower any light level, while the push-button would allow an increase in level.

### AVAB Elektronik AB AVAB 2000 (Sweden)

This was a minicomputer control that introduced dimmer feedback, telling the operator of faults or lamp usage, burning time and failure.

### Siemens Sitralux B30 (Germany; Fig. 75)

The top-end German control of the seventies this had a push-button mimic control that allowed alternate channel access to the keyboard. Multiple submasters allowed complex multispeed movement.

# Part Three

# The Life

# Chapter Twelve

# Training

This section of the book consists of some personal recollections of my life in lighting design, interspersed with a number of interviews with some distinguished colleagues, some of which were conducted by Dawn Chiang.

*Those included are:*

| | | |
|---|---|---|
| Andrew Bridge | Luc LaFortune | Tharon Musser |
| Ken Billington | Peter Maradudin | Michael Northen |
| Jules Fisher | Anne Militello | Chris Parry |
| Brian Gale | Jim Moody | Patrick Woodroffe |
| David Hersey | Tom Munn | |

*"Awake! for Morning in the Bowl of Night*
*Has flung the Stone that puts the Stars to Flight:*
*    And Lo! the Hunter of the East has caught*
*The Sultan's Turret in a Noose of Light."*
*—The Rubaiyat of Omar Khayyam*

One of the most frequent comments made about training for the lighting designer is that it usually ignores the realities of day-to-day life in the profession. No books give even a hint about "how to survive." I think these tales of life in the trenches will be "illuminating." It's fascinating to me how many parallels there are to be found in this selection of lives, no matter how different our backgrounds or fields of specialty. It's quite moving to get an insight into the battles, struggles and excitements that each individual has encountered.

The rich diversity of experience that these stories cover is a cross-section of many of the problems, challenges and opportunities a designer will meet in his or her career.

## TRAINING

We're going to start with training. We all have to migrate from school or amateur theatre to the profession. Training can be crucial. I felt my drama school in London to be a sham. Technical students were there to sweep the stage and set furniture for acting class. This made me so angry that many years later I started the Theatre Projects Trust Technical Training Course, which ran for twenty years at the London Academy of Music and Dramatic Art.

One of the clearest introductions to the challenging task of choosing a training establishment was written by Sarah Nash Gates in *TCI*, February 1993. (Ms. Gates is a former president of USITT; she teaches costume design at the University of Washington in Seattle.) This is specifically about training in America, where the choice is very wide, but the principles are universal. With her kind permission I'm going to quote it.

### Choosing a Design Program

So you want to go to graduate school for theatrical design? Here are some points to consider when choosing a school.

First of all, should you go to graduate school at all? Even if you are your college's all-star techie, that does not mean you were meant to be a designer. If you lack talent, imagination, and intelligence, no school can turn you into a good designer. If you are not skillful with your hands, school cannot turn you into an artisan. On the other hand, be realistic about your potential; remember that artisans and craftspeople often can make a living when designers cannot.

If several reputable schools turn you down, perhaps they are sending you a message you should heed. For that matter, graduate school is not the only way to learn your profession. A lot can be learned on the job, in the time-honored master-apprentice system. In graduate school, you pay to get opportunities to practice your craft. In the real world, you can get paid while getting on-the-job training, though you will have to work your way up before you get the opportunity to design.

There are many valid reasons to go to school: You will make professional contacts, strengthen your skills, learn new skills, gain valuable experience, and get to know your field. You will also get the degree often required to teach at the university level. There are many invalid reasons to go to grad school: The college or university will pay you to go, or you just finished your undergraduate degree, so might as well go to the next step.

While it is true that the school you attend will not necessarily make or break your career, it can have a significant impact on the rest of your professional life. Investigate your options and weigh all the factors carefully before making a choice.

The 1960s and 1970s saw a proliferation of MFA programs in the U.S. Finding a good one can be difficult. One third to one half of the MFA programs do not do their job properly. Graduates from these programs are not prepared to work at a professional level. Just because an MFA program exists and offers scholarships and/or assistantships does not mean that it is worthwhile.

## So how do you find the good programs?

1. *Talk to working designers and craftspeople.* Don't be afraid to call and introduce yourself to perfect strangers. Most professionals are willing to talk to students and offer advice about what skills are useful. They also are aware of what sort of "product" some programs are turning out.

2. *Go to the library and do some research.* Find one or more of the following books, which contain annotated lists of graduate programs: *Directory of Theatre Training Programs*, ed. Jill Charles, Theatre Directories, Dorset, VT (published annually); *Directory of MFA Programs of Theatre Arts 1990*, Li Bin, Cal. State Long Beach; *Directory of Graduate Programs in Theatre Design and Technology*, ed. Robert Lewis Smith, USITT, 1978. Consult your faculty members, but remember that they don't know every program.

    Each program—and the names that follow are only some of the good schools available—has its own personality, strengths, and weaknesses. You want one that suits your needs, aspirations, and personal style. For example, do you want to work in or near New York City? Try Yale or NYU. Do you want to work in the Northeast but don't like New York City? Look at Boston University, Brandeis or Carnegie. Or you prefer warm weather and a less hectic pace? UC San Diego, University of Texas at Austin, and North Carolina School of the Arts are options. Do you like Chicago? Northwestern or the Theatre School at DePaul are worth checking out. Are you a football fan? Florida State or the University of Washington might be for you.

3. *Check out schools that interest you.* Once you have a list of possibles, investigating the following can help you avoid the truly bad programs.

    *Faculty*: Do they have professional experience and are they familiar with current professional practice? Or did they work for one or two area theatres twenty years ago and now rarely, if ever, work off-campus?

    *Staff*: Do they have professional experience? What is the quality of the work produced in the shops? If you want to improve your skills, the level of craft must be higher than what you are used to.

    *Facilities*: The importance of first-rate or new facilities is frequently overrated. You only have to look at the less-than-perfect facilities at Yale School of Drama to understand that the quality of the minds involved is vastly more important than the number of theatres or when they were built. However, you do need enough space in which to work.

*Equipment*: The age and amount of equipment available in a program is important. However, the age factor varies in importance. Thirty-year-old industrial sewing machines are no problem if they have been maintained properly. On the other hand, the presence of some cutting-edge equipment in sound, lighting, and computers is essential.

*Access to professionals*: It is critical that you experience a wide variety of first-rate professional work on a regular basis. You also need contact with the professionals who make that work. A graduate program located in an active theatre community obviously is a plus. Other programs can solve the problem by hosting touring companies and bringing in guest artists. Some programs cannot or do not offer these experiences in any meaningful way. Avoid them.

A note of caution: Find out how often working professionals and guest artists are found on campus. If they only make rare appearances, you will not have much contact with them.

*Curriculum*: What courses are required and what is their content? Titles like "Scene Design I" and "Scene Design II" are pretty vague. Can requirements be waived or substitutions be made? Some schools cover subjects through independent studies, which is not always made clear in the catalog. Do not assume a course is unavailable just because it is not in the catalog. On the other hand, don't assume everyone must offer a scene-painting class; find out for yourself. Don't be impressed with the number of courses offered and/or required. If you are taking eight or nine courses each semester or quarter, that might be too much or reflect a superficial approach in several areas.

*Library*: What is the size and quality of the collection? Ease of access is significant, too. Do not overlook this; often a design is only as good as the research behind it. Remember, you will be using the art, architecture, and engineering collections as well as the theatre collection.

*Size*: Some people thrive on competition and like groups, others do better in a tutorial situation. Consider what size of program will suit you best. Also, consider your potential classmates; the quality of them will affect your education.

*Productions*: Some programs offer little or no actual production work, while others seemingly do nothing but produce shows. However, there is a fine line between a rigorous production program, which challenges a student, and one where the student becomes a pawn in the production machine. You need time for homework as well as production work, or you might as well get a job in a theatre and be paid rather than pretend you are getting an education.

4. *Visit potential schools.* Once you have established a short list of possible schools, call and talk with students and members of the faculty. (If a school won't give you contact information for some current students,

forget the school.) Then pick the schools you want to visit. You will get a much better feel for the place this way.

If you follow these steps, you will be able to make an informed choice of graduate programs. Good luck with your search. Remember that there is no substitute for doing a thorough investigation—it's your career that's at stake.

**Author's Note:** This is U.S. practice—what profusion of choice. Maybe, with proliferating opportunities in lighting for the entertainment and communications industries, the U.K. and elsewhere will seek to catch up.

## Chapter Thirteen

# Andrew Bridge

A ndrew Bridge won the Tony, Drama Desk and Outer Circle Critics Awards (NY), Dora Mavor Award (Canada), and the Los Angeles Critics Award for his lighting designs for Phantom of the Opera, which has been seen in Britain, the U.S.A., Japan, Austria, Canada, Sweden, Germany, Australia, Switzerland and Holland. He was awarded the Los Angeles Critics Award and Ovation Awards and the Tony Award (NY) for the Sunset Boulevard lighting.

His designs can now be seen at the Siegfried and Roy spectacular in Las Vegas and at EuroDisneyland's Buffalo Bill's Wild West Show in France.

His London credits include Sunset Boulevard, Joseph and the Amazing Technicolor Dreamcoat (and U.K., U.S.A., Canadian and Australian tours), Five Guys Named Moe (and U.K., U.S.A., and Australian tours), Aspects of Love (and Broadway), Carte Blanche, An Evening with Tommy Steele, Bing Crosby and Friends, Oliver! (and Broadway), The Boyfriend, Billy Bishop Goes to War, Tomfoolery, Little Me, Blondel, The Hunting of the Snark, and Torvill and Dean on Ice.

For ten years Andy was lighting designer for Shirley Bassey in Concert. In London he was the exclusive lighting design consultant to the production company Imagination for international presentations, industrial theatre and architectural projects. He was responsible for the floodlighting of the famous Lloyds of London building (National Lighting Award).

Andy lives in London with his wife, Sue, and children Oliver, Alex and Tessa.

*Richard:* How did you start?

*Andy:* You taught me.

*R:* Oh, you've got to do better than that.

*A:* My dad was a producer in theatre so I got dragged along. There wasn't a lot of excitement in those days. It was like "cue one," up it went, and "cue two," down it went. I thought that if I was wanting to do something in theatre, what would I want to do? No way would I want to act. No way could I have the patience for scenery. The next thing was lighting and the power and the emotion of what it could do. In England we didn't have a teaching route, until you started it off. We all bumbled along strong on experience but not on procedure. In America they seemed to have a learning route which was strong on procedure but not on experience.

I actually don't like interns sitting on my shoulder, because they ask serious questions and I can't answer them. To me it's gut emotion, and I don't know why. I also think I'm quite insular and introverted. I hate going up on stage during rehearsals and getting caught in the light and all that. I'd rather stay in the dark and watch what goes on. The power of lighting is exhilarating.

I went to Bryanston School. They had an arts center there, and if you didn't want to do Friday chemistry you could go and help in the theatre. That was the way I started—hands on.

My first job was flyman at the Palladium for a pantomime. Then it was flyman for *Promises, Promises*. Then I was a follow-spot operator. A lot of showman jobs to get the smell of it. I had no idea how you control lights, but I knew they were beginning to be very important. I toured around Europe with Led Zeppelin, Chicago and some weird groups and then would go to Glyndebourne Opera in the summer as an electrician.

I went to LAMDA; it was more stage management than lighting, but I got a flavor of the industry and then delved into lighting with your company, Theatre Projects Lighting, and working with the nuts and bolts. I knew how to put a patt 23 together, how many screws there were, self-tapping thingies and all that stuff. Then some guy adapted a PAR lamp in a biscuit tin at the Rainbow Theatre in London, that was the moment when the power of lighting hit me.

*R:* What were the first solo things for you?

*A:* Things that *you* couldn't do. [Laughter.]

*R:* You did that wonderful thing with the staircases, what was that called?

*A: Rock Nativity*. That was one of many shows I did for Cameron [Mackintosh]. That was probably the first British show that utilized more rock-and-roll thinking with PAR cans and overdone smoke. I did lots of little plays and lots of flops. Then I faced a change of direction and went into industrial theatre and conferences.

It used to be theatre people moonlighting, all a bit of a lark, dancing around a deodorant can. But to the people who made the deodorant, it was serious. Eventually it became a big industry, and with Imagination, the company in London, for me it became a profession. We injected theatre, rock and roll and retail expertise together. Now the conference industry is leading the way in technology because of the money they've got and the time span they don't have.

I was always freelance, but on industrials I guaranteed I'd work for Imagination only. I still dabbled in the concert world, and I picked up Shirley Bassey's contract. She didn't tour much, but visited some weird and wonderful venues, no rigs, house rigs, huge, petite, all live, hands-on control. As with the conference industry you had to be able to operate. Half the job was not the design but the way you operated it. If things didn't go to plan you hit that preset and went for it. You only had one chance. The speed of growth in that world severely muted my theatre career. Also in those days in the West End it was really hard work to get anything done. You had to go to the pub with the chief electrician for half a day, get smashed out of your mind on whiskey, which I hated, to get a ladder out to focus a lamp. "Would you mind awfully if..." and it drove me nuts! The conference industry was so efficient and instant in comparison, it certainly taught you how to adapt—that nothing was impossible.

The big break—I don't know. There wasn't *one* thing. Obviously *Phantom* was great for me, which I must admit, I have to thank you for, because you couldn't do it with the date change.[1]

*Phantom* clicked. Somehow it just clicked. I don't believe any one aspect steals it; everything is right on *Phantom*. All the production values make it successful. The lighting style is dramatic but always storytelling. With *Aspects of Love* it was a more impressionistic look; I could only squeeze in a few lamps. My concert background showed through with *Five Guys Named Moe*, which had a classy, cartoony, cabaret feel, and with the big brash stuff like the Las Vegas *Siegfried and Roy*. That one is a real lighting toy shop. The trouble is, when you do something really good, sometimes you can't understand how you did it. On each show I see and do, I feel the lighting's success is down to a different discipline. It's all to do with focus, beautiful focus, it's absolutely smooth as butter, it's wonderful, no joins. On others, it's the cueing. Look at that snap, look at the way that builds. Then its the color; it's the way you colored the show. I am constantly changing my priorities.

R: What's the worst experience of a life time, when you've been like a cockroach with a pin through it? Have you had any horrendous nightmares?
A: All of them. [Laughter.] Some shows haven't quite worked artistically. But I don't always blame myself. Everybody's been in the shit, but you get out of it somehow. The play's not getting the laughs because it's not bright enough—bad writing. The lighting's not telling us where we are—bad scenery. We need more cues for this dance—dodgy choreography. There have been some nasty moments, more to do with politics and schedule than with what I've done. I'm always very serious and concentrated on one production at a time. I don't like double booking, so I don't ever turn up and

suddenly realize that there are three acts and I've only lit two. But within each production there are some horrible moments. Some of the *Phantoms* have been a bit wacky, technically. The opening of the show, half the scenery is on the floor and at the beginning of the first major scene change everything flies out. On a few of the dress rehearsals we've done, the flies took the lights with them. Then you think, "Christ, we've got another two hours and the rig's pointing up in the grid."

And engineering disasters: there was a time when a large travelator severed a mains cable and it caught the piece alight, and afterward we got notes about too much smoke, which in fact were the fire extinguishers. On *Siegfried and Roy* a giant dragon took a serious bite out of the rig. There have been some real cock-ups where we've run out of cues because the operator wiped the discs. I've relit *Torvill and Dean on Ice* three times in one day because the discs were wiped three times. The third time was quite good, because it was a much cleaner version of what I originally did. There have been horrendous moments, but we're getting better at avoidance.

The science master at my six-year-old's school couldn't do the summer play the other day, and I got called in to do it. I had five minutes prep time. I was worried sick. The night before I was absolutely panicked. I had my cue sheets, I phoned my electrician to get color for me. I got my tool kit out, I put a ladder to top of my car. I had to do it seriously; I couldn't just go in and busk it. Twelve faders. And I couldn't move the rig because he set it up last Christmas for *Oliver!*, a show in July, and he didn't want me to move it. I do get worried.

I'm locked into musicals at the moment, but I do intend to break free. Musicals demand an incredible amount of different feelings and scenery moves, so it's quite a challenge. The problem nowadays is that we have to give the audience more than they get from movies or TV. This tends to make scenic designs rather monstrous and complicated. It gets to be a bit of a problem fighting to keep enough space for lighting opportunities. On *Sunset* I originally felt it should be done with 10kW Fresnels, in the movie style. You get one great backlight down the staircase; you get all the shadows. Clean and dramatic shadows. Then you look at the set and no way José, can you get more than a 500-watt Fresnel up there if you're lucky. In a way it's a shame when you're not involved from the outset. But if everybody was involved at the initial procedure, there would never be a finished result. So in a way it's best to let the set designer do his business, and then come back and nibble away at it at a reasonable time and hope that he's not too bigheaded to take some suggestions.

Politics is an important extra accessory that designers now have to have. You can be a great technician, you can be a great artistic person and you can be a brilliant lighting designer, but if you don't understand the political maneuvering and the time structures and the negotiation side of things, you'll be dead in the water. I am constantly dealing. "If I move my boom would you lift the border?" "If I cut this equipment can I have another follow-spot operator?" "If the deck is painted tonight, I need the morning session." "The energy in this scene is magnificent, but can you move the actor downstage?" "Sir Lloyd Webber, I think your ending is marvelous, but is it possible to give us three seconds more?" It's politics! It's a nuisance, but it's there. The other thing is to totally surround yourself with good people who can defend you. Sometimes the positioning of the lighting desk is very important. Depends on what show you're on. You don't want to be too near the political power, but sometimes you want to be in the middle and have associates either side so that the person who is being a bit awkward and wants to talk about every single lighting cue cannot physically get to you without having to trip over things. And eventually they will leave you to get on. I almost believe if they don't like what you do, they shouldn't have hired you. People know styles now.

R: Can people recognize your lighting? You used the word style before.

A: I have no idea. I have just had twin babies. *I* can't recognize them, but they look like me. It's weird, because in the industry, you hear the gossip about other lighting designers: this guy's this and this guy's that, and whatever. I wish I could hear the good bits! I think one of the things people may say is that I was quite good at heavy color. If they looked at my rigs originally, there was quite a bit of heavy color, but now it's calmer but with a sprinkling of automated gear. I feel my style reflects my lighting education. *Sunset* or *Phantom:* dim, dramatic, operatic. Then you look at something like *Siegfried and Roy, Torvill and Dean* or *Five Guys Named Moe*—they're totally the opposite, rock and roll coming through. I'm split. Because of industrial theatre, I can adapt. So I suppose I don't know my style.

Personality-wise, I think people think I'm very easy to get on with. But underneath I can get very wound up and angry. I get home and sometimes I could kill that bloody electrician. I don't suffer fools. On *Sunset* in London, for instance, I was sweet as pie, until I let rip on someone who used my focused boom as a ladder. I made sure that lots of people heard my exaggerated outburst to overstate the importance of our rig. You are head of a big and expensive department, you have to have some authority. I do believe in America the lighting designer gets more recognition than in Europe. You are number three or four in the creative team and even at the stage door they almost say "sir" to you. I like the respect for the profession. Over in London, it's, "Oh, who are you? Don't know if we'll let you come in here." In terms of equipment the only difference in the States, for some reason—maybe to do with voltage or something—the Fresnel is absolutely useless. In England you light shows with Fresnels. PAR cans are generally brighter than profiles over here, but in America that is the opposite. But with most equipment, other than a few technical terms, like *gobo* and *template*, *wrench* and *spanner*, *torch* and *flashlight*, it's not really that much different. The only thing is that it's a proper industry. The difference in America is *hesitancy*. If you seem hesitant in the States, you lose that street credit. So sometimes I've been on shows where the chief flyman or master carpenter would test me out:

"What height do you want that pipe at?"

"I don't know, maybe it should be just behind the boom, but I'm not sure because the scenery's not ready yet and maybe we should do it...I think we'll have to leave it till later." Now that's the English way.

The American way, which I adopt is, "Twenty-eight foot, six!" And you haven't a clue what height you want. [Lots of laughter.] But they think, "Shit, this man knows what he's doing."

New generations of lighting designers are going to have to deal with a whole new problem: moving lights. As a designer, you can design your plot on paper in half an hour and go to lunch, with lots of moving lights—lots of symbols—finished. Unless you discipline yourself to go that extra distance of how you're going to use them before you get to the theatre, you'll suddenly become a crock; you'll be overswamped, because moving equipment is easier to design and a lot more difficult to use. Because every cue you have to get your piece of paper out, focus the lights, color them—and then do the stupid cue. In fact, it's *slower*, and that's the problem for all the new people coming up. The new technology is making the design process quicker and easier, but in the theatre basically it takes longer to program with moving lights than it does with "steam" lights. It's a worrying factor that moving lights can make you complacent with the design on paper and then you're stuck with it in the theatre. And you can see people who use moving equipment like: scene 1, every bit of equipment is used. How the hell do you get to scene 2? Are you going to see them all move? Is there going to be a blackout and then move them and they come up? The problem is the transition.

There's a lovely old producer of the English theatre who did the lighting as well. At the Palladium he put scene 1 scenery up and focused everything to scene 1 and lit it. Got the scenery boys to move to scene 2 and refocused it all and lit it and at the end of the show, he couldn't understand why scene 1 didn't look like it used to. Eric Delzeney, the electrician, tells those stories. That was a man way ahead of his time with moving lights!

So generally, I like to have my basic rig, which is what we call "steam" lights, then the high-technology stuff sprinkled around to get you out of trouble.

I think the direction the moving-light companies are going in is still not exactly helpful for theatre use. The cost and maintenance complications, let alone the union problems, are one thing, but the color temperature of the discharge lamps is not that easy; the dichroic colors of some are horrendous. With the mirror types, placement is difficult, and then of course there's noise and spill. I'm a bit upset that some of the more traditional theatre lighting companies haven't got on to moving-yoke technology properly and haven't adapted some really good theatre units to do it.

The other thing is the frustrations of the production schedules. We used to watch a show in rehearsals, look at the set, go away and do the lighting design, watch rehearsals again, then do a focus call when the set was up and then a technical and then the actors come on and you do a dress rehearsal, then previews and then you open. Nowadays you design the rig before you've seen one rehearsal because the budgets have to be done. You then have to light the show before you've seen anything. And you light it after the technical, because the technical is so difficult they normally like work-light for it. So you light it during the technicals and dress rehearsals and focus time is out the window. I'm looking forward to the time when you just turn up on opening night! You have to learn how to focus on a building site with the worklight on. You have to rough it in, get it there and use your intuition about where the light is. You have to keep going. Just keep your own schedule and not say you're ready before you are.

The future: I think there will eventually be some form of light, a profile-type unit, that will be connected to a computer screen that you can shutter—I mean do precision shuttering. You'll be able to do any shaping remotely, dial in a gobo shape by liquid crystal or something. It would be an automatic projector. That'll probably be the next technology. Moving stuff will probably go on and be a bit more smooth and more reliable. Now for general theatre use, they're too much like an Indy Formula One car—they're too delicate. They have to have pit crews tweaking them to make them work. What we need is the old banger, that can take a few knocks and that anybody can operate. That will come. Intelligent lights should be more obedient; that will come. The first color scrollers were absolutely the most delicate things out. Now you can smack them anywhere. Moving equipment will become the norm.

In England, *maintenance* is not a high-profile word. Over in America it is; they like to be able to write everything down to be able to reproduce it and maintain it properly. They get paid very well to do it, and they're proud of their maintenance. But they need the paperwork. And the paperwork for moving lights is quite a nightmare. But computer technology will help, with CAD and the like.

In drafting a design I like to slow down and put some breaks in the procedure, because you can zap out a rig on CAD in no time, but I prefer to actually have to draft out the first version (by hand). I like to be able to pencil it in and then, in the English way, use ink and pens. It's quite slow, therefore you're forced to think about every lamp; what does it do, is it really needed? To slow down physically means you're really thinking about it. If you do it straight on the computer, you can make a very pretty picture very quickly, and with moving equipment, you're finished. All done, looks lovely, wonderful! But you haven't thought about it. It doesn't have that earthy feel that you've actually really focused it in your head.

Assistants are vital. I like to make sure that they know that their input and ideas are welcome. But I do like them to get me a cup of coffee occasionally.

We will only survive as a team. I hate bad vibes, I hate a bad atmosphere, it makes me so tense. I like to have a friendly crew around me. When you go to the bar at night you want to bitch with them about the set and the producer and your problems and you want to be able to off-load. So the team is very important to have around to support you. They also should be able to cope on their own and not ask too many bloody questions. And it's great when they say, "I'm just going up on stage and refocus this because its been knocked." And you think *"Great! Do it! I didn't even see that!"* This independence is great when you're reproducing shows around the world. You can actually sit down and do the essence of lighting design, rather than cloud yourself with the logistics of scheduling, rehearsals, focus crews. It allows you to look at a show afresh—is that cue too big, too small, wrong, right. It's great rather than worrying about the tiny details, that you can do later.

The other interesting thing now is the world market for musical theatre. It used to be only megahits that made it around some of the big cities. But now most of the cities in most countries can take musicals and have the technology and people who can run them now, because of *Les Miz, Cats, Phantom* and so on, and it's really amazing that you can get a semihit that can go around eight countries. That's a challenge and a worry with personnel. You have to have great associates who can do it on their own. It's quite exciting to see your show in Japanese or Swedish.

*R:* How many *Phantoms* have you done now?

*A:* I think fourteen. Each one is different. The end result may look the same, but I'm not complacent. Each starts with a blank sheet of paper and you know roughly what you're trying to achieve, but whether you have six spot bars or four and how they're configured, each rig is different. Some of the widths go from thirty feet to sixty-five feet. It's a challenge. The unsung heroes and the people you really need to get friendly with are the production managers. They manipulate the budget and control the schedules, which are precious to you.

*R:* Do you have an agent?

*A:* I know in America lawyers are the norm. I actually have a good theatrical agent, and we consult lawyers when we have to. It used to be a hand shake and a phone call. But now because of the international possibilities of a major musical being a hit in so many countries, the basic contract is now twenty-nine pages long, half of which you cannot understand. We seem to be consulting more and more. The royalties are very important to negotiate, there's a sort of set rate. But the thing is, you don't get the royalty you negotiate, because you have things like, you don't get it until double recoupment, you have a ceiling on the gross, you get paid net, you get it after the union, or you get company share, which is a new one. There are probably eight or ten ways of not paying your royalty. My theory is, they should pay you back once the show's paid off. But double recoupment, company shares, caps: you name it, we've had it. With all this, you don't see any money from a major musical for two years.

*R:* But most of the profession aren't working in the Big Time and doing that sort of show. How do people make a living doing regional theatre at $2,000 a time? You can't do many more than twelve a year. It's a frightening business.

*A:* I've been extremely lucky. I worked hard in the commercial market and did many shows a year, from shop windows to car launches. But my heart and enjoyment was always in lighting, so it helped me struggle on. I've done enough financially successful shows now that I don't have to do absolutely everything that comes along. I suppose many survive in other industry areas: teaching, architectural, retail, equipment production.

*R:* Do you ever have desires to do other things?

*A:* I do. I've done some goofy stuff. The Lloyds Building in London was one. Focusing four hundred feet up in the fog. After I did Lloyds, it opened up the English market immensely. The phone didn't stop ringing: would you come light my brick wall? I don't want to light it, I don't even know what the equipment names are. Would you like to do Harrod's windows? No, because you only have four lamps a side and I can't do much with that. It's like, do you want to light the school play? Well, I will if you give me sixteen circuits instead of twelve.

I'm very lucky. At the moment the income is enough to make me not sweat, the shows that I'm doing are busy reproducing themselves, and I don't have to sweat too much, so I've got six months that I can actually have a holiday or do all the planning for the stuff I've got to do.

*R:* You must go home occasionally.

*A:* Twenty years I've worked extremely hard and had heartaches of trying to have personal telephone conversations in the stalls. "Well, Darling, I am coming home one day but they've delayed previews." "Are you sure the dishwasher's broken?" "The printer's done what?" And you're having all these personal dramas unfold while you sit calmly watching some dance number being reblocked. Then the director says, "Well, that looks like shit." And you want to break his neck.

*R:* It's tough being married to one of us isn't it?

*A:* Hey, we've raised a great family despite it all. I do love the industry, but nowadays I could walk away from it without regrets.

*R:* Finally, you must get asked, "How do I become a lighting designer, can you give me some advice, what should I do?" What's your answer?

*A:* It's weird, you see. I suppose you have to know procedures up to a point and then you have to put that away and just put your hands in and do other things and love the theatre. You have to learn in the small pubs, the bars, the shop windows, and the university theatres or school plays. Just learn your trade, love the theatre and light.

*R:* Are there any women designers in England now? It's a woman's profession in America.

*A:* That's because you can go to a university and exit a designer. In England you become a designer by the electrician route and not the design route. The main way is up the ladder...literally. That's supposed to be a man's job, therefore a lot of women don't survive the journey.

*R:* Any last words?

*A:* Be a market gardener, it's easier. Lighting is a very antisocial world, sitting in the dark talking to faceless people on headphones. Very long hours, a lot of traveling and working in uncomfortable positions. I have an incredible bad neck and shoulder problem and an osteopath said, "Tell me, what do you do?" "Well, I tense up over a drawing desk for a week or so and then I go into a theatre and wedge myself in between seats—on my knees in amongst dusty seats—and then I rush down in the dark, hitting my shins on the seats, and go up on stage and then I grind my neck muscles around. So, Doctor, why am I so sore?"

But you have to live, you have to eat.

*Chris Parry,* The Plantagenets (Henry VI)
*Theatre: Royal Shakespeare Theatre, Stratford*
*Director: Adrian Noble*
*Scenery: Bob Crowley*

*Robert Ornbo,* Back to Methuselah
*Theatre: National Theatre, Old Vic, London*
*Director: Clifford Williams*
*Scenery: Ralph Koltai*

*David Hersey,* Cyrano de Bergerac
*Theatre: Haymarket, London*
*Director: Elijah Moshinski*
*Scenery: Michael Yeargan*

*Rick Fisher,* An Inspector Calls
*Theatre: Royale, New York*
*Director: Stephen Daldry*
*Scenery: Ian MacNeil*
*Photo: © Joan Marcus*

*David Hersey,* Mother Courage
*Theatre: The Barbican, London*
*Director: Howard Davies*
*Scenery: John Napier*

*Richard Pilbrow*, Rosencrantz and
Guildenstern are Dead
*Theatre: National Theatre, Old Vic,*
*London, and Alvin, New York*
*Director: Derek Goldby*
*Scenery: Desmond Heeley*

*Rick Fisher*, The Picture of Dorian Gray
*Theatre: Lyric, Hammersmith, London*
*Director: Neil Bartlett*
*Scenery: Ian MacNeil*
*Photo: © Sheila Burnett*

*Max Keller*, Der Snob
*Theatre: Münchner Kammerspiele, Munich*
*Director: Hans-Reinhard Müller*
*Scenery: Jürgen Rose*
*Photo: © Moritz Nauschütz*

*Max Keller*, Der Snob
*Theatre: Münchner Kammerspiele, Munich*
*Director: Hans-Reinhard Müller*
*Scenery: Jürgen Rose*
*Photo: © Moritz Nauschütz*

*Richard Pilbrow,* The Three Sisters
*Theatre: National, London*
*Director: Sir Laurence Olivier*
*Scenery: Joseph Svoboda*
*Photo: © Richard Pilbrow*

*Richard Pilbrow,* The Life
*Theatre: Barrymore, New York*
*Director: Michael Blakemore*
*Scenery: Robin Wagner*
*Photo: © Lewis Lee*

*Scott Zielinski,* The Tempest
*Theatre: Guthrie, Minneapolis*
*Director: Jennifer Tipton*
*Scenery: John Conklin*
*Photo: © Michael Daniel*

*Anne Militello*, A Matter of Faith
*Theatre: Theatre for New York City*
*Director: Maria Irene Fornes*
*Scenery: Donald Eastman*

*David Taylor*, Oedipus Rex
*Theatre: Sutherland Studio*
*Director: Mark Baker*
*Photo: © David Taylor*

*Pat Dignan*, The Cabinet of Dr. Caligari
*Theatre: LaMama Annex, New York*
*Photo: © Pat Dignan*

*Mark Henderson*, Absence of War
*Theatre: National Theatre, London*
*Director: Richard Eyre*
*Scenery: Bob Crowley*
*Photo: © Mark Douet*

*Dawn Chiang,* The Three Sisters
*Theatre: Guthrie, Minneapolis*
*Director: Liviu Ciulei*
*Photo: © Timothy S. Streeter*

*Richard Pilbrow,* Heliotrope Bouquet
*Theatre: Head, Center Stage, Baltimore*
*Director: Stan Wojewodski*
*Scenery: Chris Barreca*
*Photo: © Richard Pilbrow*

*Peter Maradudin,* Oedipus Rex
*Theatre: San Jose Repertory*
*Director: Timothy Near*
*Scenery: Joel Fontaine*
*Photo: © Joel Fontaine*

*Richard Pilbrow,* Four Baboons Adoring the Sun
*Theatre: Vivian Beaumont, New York*
*Director: Sir Peter Hall*
*Scenery: Tony Walton*
*Photo: © Richard Pilbrow*

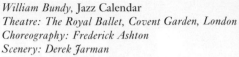

*William Bundy*, Jazz Calendar
*Theatre: The Royal Ballet, Covent Garden, London*
*Choreography: Frederick Ashton*
*Scenery: Derek Jarman*
*Photo: © Zoe Dominic*

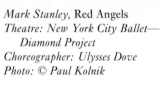

*Mark Stanley*, Red Angels
*Theatre: New York City Ballet—*
*Diamond Project*
*Choreographer: Ulysses Dove*
*Photo: © Paul Kolnik*

*Pat Collins*, Sleeping Beauty
*Theatre: The Royal Ballet, Covent Garden, London*
*Photo: © Zoe Dominic*

*Heather Carson*, Link
*Theatre: The Joyce, New York*
*Choreography and scenery: Elizabeth Streb*
*Photo: © George Mott*

*Benny Ball*, Don Giovanni
*Theatre: Vlaamse Opera (Flemish Opera)*
*Director: Guy Joosten*
*Scenery: Johannes Liecher*

*Heather Carson*, Don Giovanni
*Theatre: Chicago Lyric Opera*
*Director: Christopher Alden*
*Scenery: Paul Steinberg*
*Photo: © George Mott*

*Anne Militello*, Djamileh/La Nava Presse
*Theatre: Connecticut Grand Opera*
*Director: Christopher Alden*
*Scenery: Paul Steinberg*

*Ken Billington*, Madam Butterfly
*Theater: Chicago Lyric Opera*
*Director: Harold Prince*
*Scenery: Clarke Dunham*

*Tom Munn*, The Midsummer Marriage
*Theatre: San Francisco Opera*
*Director: John Copley*
*Scenery: Robin Don*
*Photo: © Ron Scherl*

*Tom Munn*, William Tell
*Theatre: San Francisco Opera*
*Director: Lotfi Mansouri*
*Scenery: Gerard Howland*
*Photo: © Marty Sohl*

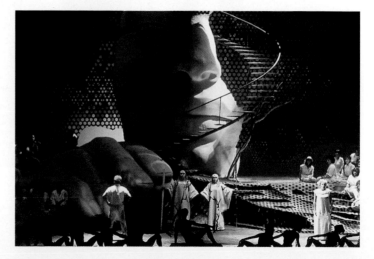

*Jean Kalman*, Il Re Pastore
*Theatre: Nederlandse Opera, Nederlandse*
*Director: Pierre Audi*
*Scenery: Chloe Obolensky*
*Photo: © Deen Van Meer*

*Hans Toelstede*, Moses and Aaron
*Theatre: New York City Opera*
*Director: Hans Neugebauer*
*Scenery: Achim Freyer*
*Photo: © Carol Rosegg*

*Nigel Levings*, La Traviata
*Theatre: The Australian Opera*
*Director: Elijah Moshinsky*
*Scenery: Michael Yeargan*

*Michael Whitfield*, Death in Venice
*Theatre: Canadian Opera, Toronto*
*Director: Lotfi Mansouri*
*Scenery: Wolfram Skalicki*
*Photo: © Robert C. Rafdale FRPS*

*William Bundy,* Tosca
*Theatre: Royal Opera, London*
*Director and scenery: Franco Zeffirelli*

*Jean Kalman,* Orpheo
*Theatre: Nederlandse Opera, Nederlandse*
*Director: Pierre Audi*
*Scenery: Chloe Obolensky*
*Photo: © Ruth Waltz*

*Brian Gale,* Halyx
*Theatre: Disneyland Space Stage*
*Director: Mike Post*
*Scenery: Claire Graham*

*Andrew Bridge,* Phantom of the Opera
*Theatre: Her Majesty's, London*
*Director: Harold Prince*
*Scenery: Maria Bjornson*
*Photo: © Clive Barda*

*Tharon Musser,* A Little Night Music
*Theatre: Adelphi, London*
*Director: Harold Prince*
*Scenery: Boris Aronson*
*Photo: © Zoe Dominic*

*Ken Billington,* Sweeney Todd
*Theater: Uris, New York*
*Director: Harold Prince*
*Scenery: Eugene Lee*

*Jim Moody,* Madam Mao's Memories
*Theatre: Keck, Glendale, California*
*Director: Robin McKee*

*Jules Fisher,* Will Rogers Follies
*Theatre: Palace, New York*
*Director: Tommy Tune*
*Scenery: Tony Walton*
*Photo: © Tony Walton*

*Tharon Musser,* Dreamgirls
*Theatre: Imperial, New York*
*Director: Michael Bennett*
*Scenery: Robin Wagner*
*Photo: © Martha Swope*

*Nigel Levings,* The King and I
*Theatre: Adelaide Festival, Australia*
*Director: Christopher Renshaw*
*Scenery: Brian Thompson*

*Richard Pilbrow,* Blitz!
*Theatre: Adelphi, London*
*Director: Eleanor Fazan*
*Scenery: Sean Kenny*

*Richard Pilbrow*, Fiddler on the Roof
*Theatre: Her Majesty's, London*
*Director: Jerome Robbins*
*Scenery: Boris Aronson*
*Photo: © Zoe Dominic*

*Richard Pilbrow*, Busker Alley
*Theatre: U.S. National Tour*
*Director: Tommy Tune*
*Scenery: Tony Walton*
*Photo: © Tony Walton*

*Richard Pilbrow,*
    A Funny Thing Happened
    on the Way to the Forum
*Theatre: Strand, London*
*Director: George Abbott*
*Scenery: Tony Walton*

*Richard Pillbrow*, Show Boat
*Theater: Gershwin, New York*
*Director: Harold Prince*
*Scenery: Eugene Lee*
*Photo: © Lewis Lee*

*Howell Binkley*, Kiss of the Spider Woman
*Theatre: Broadhurst, New York*
*Director: Harold Prince*
*Scenery: Jerome Sirlin*
*Photo: © Jerome Sirlin*

*Richard Pilbrow*, The Magic Flute
*Theatre: Los Angeles Opera Company*
*Director: Sir Peter Hall*
*Scenery: Gerald Scarfe*
*Photo: © Ken Howard*

*Richard Pilbrow*, One over the Eight
*Theatre: Duke of Yorks, London*
*Director: Paddy Stone*
*Scenery: Tony Walton*

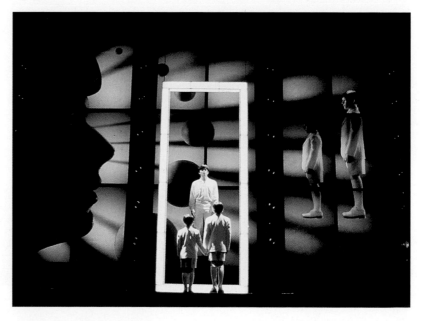

*Chris Parry*, Tommy—The Who
*Theatre: St. James, New York*
*Director: Des McAnuff*
*Scenery: John Arnone*
*Projection: Wendall K. Harrington*
*Photo: © Peter Cunningham*

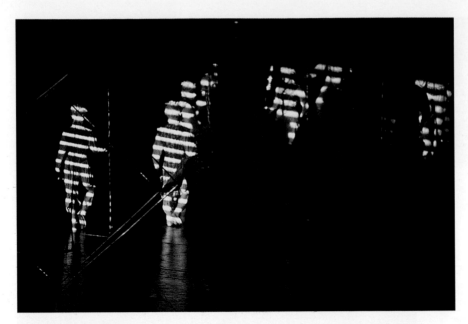

*Luc Lafortune,* Allegria
*Theatre: Cirque du Soleil*
*Director: Franco Dragone*
*Scenery: Michel Crête*
*Photo: © Al Seib*

*Luc Lafortune,* Allegria
*Theatre: Cirque du Soleil*
*Director: Franco Dragone*
*Scenery: Michel Crête*
*Photo: © Kevin Kolczynski*

*Marc Brickman*, Genesis 1992 Tour
*Photos: © Lewis Lee*

*Patrick Woodroffe*, Phil Collins 1994 Tour
*Scenery: Jeremy Railton*
*Photo: © Lewis Lee*

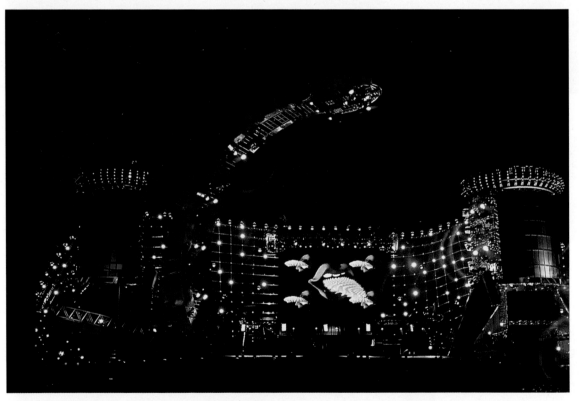

*Patrick Woodroffe*, Rolling Stones "Voodoo Lounge" Tour
*Scenery: Mark Fisher / Jonathan Park*
*Photo: © Paul Natkin*

# Chapter Fourteen

# Pilbrow Story 1: Beginnings

"Mum, I'm bored!" was a frequent whine around the house I grew up in Beckenham. I forget all my mother's ingenious solutions to alleviate that problem, but one of them was to take me up to the big city, London, from the suburbs. We went to the theatre. For six shillings, a pit seat at the New Theatre opened a door to the Old Vic Company in their wartime home, and to a world that dazzled me.

It was backstage that fascinated. At age twelve I had a card-file database (computers in 1946 were not common!) of all the suppliers to the leading London theatres. Culled from the program acknowledgments: "Cigarettes by Abdulla" and "Lighting by Strand Electric and Engineering Co. Ltd." had a special resonance. Perhaps it began at age five. Granny took us all to the Bromley Rep Christmas pantomime, *Robinson Crusoe*. I was awestruck at the mile-long vista of white sand with the waves crashing onto the beach, a perfect illusion in my imagination. Can you imagine what that weekly rep flapping backcloth actually looked like? How it was lit in 1938?

On just an ordinary afternoon my class at prep school (now age eleven) were summoned to the school hall to watch "the play." I forget what it was. I don't forget its impact on me. I suppose since then I've seldom thought of anything else (for very long, that is).

In 1944 (that's age eleven as well) I wrote, directed, lit and starred in a family performance of an original dramatic revue. This was certainly the first theatre I designed. Staged on the first floor of the large Victorian house in which we lived, the landing was divided by a velvet curtain, behind which my mother's parents had a flat. Their hall became our stage. The auditorium had raked seating, asymmetrical of course, because half went upstairs and half down. Among other parts, I played my hero (then and now), Nelson. This was a commercial venture, and we charged relatives for tickets. Cousins donated their services for free. The profits were sent to the Aid to Russia Fund. I still have the letter from Lady Churchill, Winston's wife, congratulating me on the success and donation to our "gallant allies, the Russians."

My other theatre was "the model." Begun as a Pollock's Toy Theatre, it grew and consumed many hours of childhood. My father, seriously seeking to give me the education that he had been denied, sent me to boarding school at age thirteen. This I really hated. Terror and hunger became a way of life until I rediscovered the drama. An early career move—walking-on for the school Drama Society—didn't last. The elderly English master thought he knew more than I did. As an exile I started my own rival company, persuaded another house master to lend me an old barn and thus began my second theatre, The Barn Theatre, complete with monthly theatre magazine, *The Globe*. As this was before the age of Xerox, the magazine was reproduced on a gelatin tray. The establishment relented, and I rejoined the Drama Society and rose to become secretary, designer, technical director, producer and lighting designer. My farewell production employed over half the school population. After my departure such spectaculars were banned.

What saved my teenage years was actually down the road from school. A truly remarkable man named Anthony Thomas ran the National Association of Boys Clubs Arts Centre. Intended for somewhat deprived inner-city boys, it ran summer courses in the performing arts. I hung around and finally was taken on, became odd-job man, small-part player and lighting director. Every weekend I escaped from school hell and eventually gave up going home in the holidays to do theatre.

One day my father found out that this unhealthy interest was becoming a passion. I even wanted to do it for a career. He demanded to meet this man Thomas and end the rubbish. This prospect was depressing, as I had watched Tony Thomas quite cruelly quash many a young aspirant's hopes of a theatrical career. The meeting took place in London. Total silence ensued. Eventually my mother told me that Tony Thomas had in fact been cautiously supportive. He normally strongly opposed adolescent enthusiasms for the theatre, but in my case he thought I might be sufficiently determined to succeed.

I tried to get into the Old Vic Theatre School. They said I was too immature. Instead I went into National Service, the Royal Air Force, where

I proved them correct. My production of *Worm's Eye View* at the camp cinema was very irreverent of service values. The Group Captain was not amused.

Finally I went to drama school, the Central School of Speech and Drama, then resident in the upper reaches of the Albert Hall. I was at last a stage-management student. Unfortunately, it seemed we were there only to sweep the stage and set the props for acting class. Desperate, I turned to girls. A fellow (actually a girl) student was Viki, whom I was later to marry and who was my partner through the early years of Theatre Projects.

The good outcome of Central was its ending. The pass-out show was at Her Majesty's, a real West End theatre. At the end of the matinee, Robert Stanton, the stage manager of the evening show, *Teahouse of the August Moon*, offered me a job. Central had brain-washed us all into believing that our careers had to start with twenty years of weekly repertory. Here was me with a job on Monday in the West End. I gave in my notice four weeks before the end of term. I was rewarded with a Class C diploma. The profession beckoned.

# Ken Billington

*en has more than sixty Broadway productions to his credit including* Meet Me in St. Louis, On the Twentieth Century, Side by Side by Sondheim, Lettice and Lovage, Tru, *and* Sweeney Todd. *Off-Broadway productions include* London Suite, Annie Warbucks, Lips Together Teeth Apart, The Lisbon Traviata, What the Butler Saw, *and* Fortune and Men's Eyes, *to name a few. Since 1973 Ken has been principal lighting designer for Radio City Music Hall, where he created the lighting for the world-famous Christmas and Easter Spectaculars. Other projects include everything from* Turandot *at the Vienna State Opera to nightclub acts for headliners Ann-Margret, Shirley MacLaine, and Liberace. At Disneyland Ken's lighting is part of the magic of the nightime extravaganza* Fantasmic. *His architectural designs can be seen in prominent restaurants and clubs from New York to Asia. Ken has been nominated for five Tony Awards, received two Los Angeles Drama Critics awards and has won the Ace Award for his television designs.*

Lighting is actually all I ever wanted to do, since I was in the fourth grade and ran the lights for the play and got applause for a moment. We did a blackout; Sherry Zimmerman slammed some cymbals at the same time, and the other children applauded. I've been doing it ever since. In junior high school I had a real theatre and ran the lights and joined the Community Players. This was just outside of New York City and one of the directors of the Community Players was Phil Mathias, who had been Rodgers and Hammerstein's production stage manager. He was married to Alice

Hammerstein. They lived there, and he directed the Community Players and taught me how to light legitimately. When I was in ninth grade I used to sit at a production desk in the middle of the auditorium, lighting. When it got to performances, I'd go back and run the board, because that was the fun part. I never knew there was another way of doing it. I got out of high school, went to summer stock, went to Lester Polokov's studio in New York—did not go to college—and started working as Peggy Clark's assistant in 1966 and as Tharon Musser's assistant in 1967. I assisted Tharon for a long time. Maybe too long, because everybody knew me as an assistant. Then in the early 70s I stopped assisting. By then I had assisted everybody in the business: Tom [Skelton], Jennifer [Tipton], and Pat Collins, Bill Ritman. It was a different time then, less complicated—we sent the road company of *Mame* out with fourteen dimmers—so it was good training. I had no formal training other than I learned to draft at Lester Polokov's and took a lighting class there too, with Tom, Peggy, and Chuck Levy.

My first break was an off-Broadway show called *Fortune in Men's Eyes* that Ken Waissman and Maxine Fox produced. They had been the production assistants on a bunch of musicals I had done, and they produced their show and took all of their chums, who were the other production assistants. That was successful. My first Broadway show was a revival of *The Visit*, which Hal Prince directed. Tharon had done the season at the Phoenix Repertory Company the year before and didn't want to do this. I had been doing the Phoenix side shows—which were staged readings that ran for two weeks—so Tharon said, "Hire Ken, he's good." So my first show was a Hal Prince play that was a huge hit, and I got a Tony nomination. And, knock wood, I haven't been out of work since. That was 1973.

Having done twenty shows with Hal Prince, there are a lot of highlights. Even the unsuccessful ones are highlights. Shows that I have particularly liked and liked my work on are, plays first: *The Visit;* and *Foxfire*, a play I did with Hume Cronyn and Jessica Tandy; and *Lips Together Teeth Apart*, which was off-Broadway. Musicals would be *Sweeney Todd*; a flop called *Working*; and things like *Grind*, and *Rosa*, which not many people saw, but I thought looked rather exceptional. I do Radio City; the Christmas show is great fun to work on. I love ice shows. I'm very lucky in that I do a little of everything.

I've done sixty shows on Broadway and I forget a lot of them. I never thought I'd ever forget any of the shows I had done. But I was down in Coconut Grove, doing a play called *The Big Love* and there were all these saturated colors left from the last show. And I said, "What was the last show?" And they said, "*Blues in the Night*," and I said, "Oh, what's that about?" And they started telling me the plot, and then I realized I had designed it on Broadway. So I figure I'm getting older.

An example of a hard show for me was *On the Twentieth Century*, with Hal. Also a show called *Perfectly Frank*, with Ron Field, who made life really difficult. And I remember doing *A Winter's Tale* with Michael Kahn.

*Stage Lighting Design*

I would say *On the Twentieth Century* looked spectacular and *Winter's Tale* at Stratford, Connecticut (1974), with an all-white set, was really breathtaking. During *On the Twentieth Century* I set myself up to be the victim, because I didn't fight hard enough, because I was so impressed with being with all these stars of the theatre, lowly little lighting designer Ken. Robin Wagner left no room for the lights and all those things that happen if you don't sit and fight. I learned from that.

I remember on *Perfectly Frank* when Ron wouldn't stop yelling at me and carrying on nastily, the show looked fine, but it didn't look right. And I said, wait a minute, let's pretend they've hired me to come in and fix it. So I got seats in the fifth row, sat down and watched the show and knew exactly what was wrong with it; came in the next day and fixed it. But I had to say to myself, "I know how to do this." I put on another hat saying, OK, I'm the savior now. It was all the wrong color, much too saturated; everything else was right. I had a gel call and we re-gelled every light. The cues stayed the same. So I learned a big lesson there.

When we were in Boston with *On the Twentieth Century*, pieces of scenery kept bashing into each other as they were flying out. Pete Feller, the head carpenter, took Robin and me on stage and he pointed up to a place in the flies where there were lights and scenery and he said, "Listen, it's eleven o'clock now. We go to lunch at noon; at one o'clock we're taking down either a pipe of electrics or scenery. You two fight it out. At one o'clock you give me an answer. Since I'm the carpenter, I'm going for the electrics." Robin and I fought it out. The scenery came down. Set designers know what they want, but they don't know what you really need. Some do, others don't, and you have to negotiate for all that. And if you don't negotiate and you're sitting there at the production table, and the director asks for something and you can't give it to him, even something as simple as visibility, then you haven't done your job. The director doesn't want to know that ten weeks ago you should have said, "We need to cut scenery." Then everyone would have dealt with it. Or they would have known it was going to be dark.

I would say the greatest influence on me was Tharon, because I assisted her. I would say I went to Musser University. Jeannie Rosenthal was still alive then. When Jeannie passed on, Tharon sort of took over that vocation in the world of lighting. I was her assistant at the time, and we were doing the biggest shows and a lot of them—five or six Broadway shows a year as well as all the other things she did. So it was a fabulous way to learn. I learned from someone who doesn't get angry, who fights for what she believes is right, who everyone in the theatre loves—the crews, the directors. Sure there were disagreements, but the shows looked good. That's really what I learned from.

And then working with everyone else. Working with Tom Skelton a lot. It was a different way of designing. And when I had to move shows for him, I copied his style exactly. I didn't like his style; not that they didn't look good, but I didn't like the way they got there. I didn't like his "five jewel" lighting (where an area down center would be lit from box left and box right, top of torm left, top of torm right, and third electric, all on one dimmer). I didn't understand it. So I really put all those experiences together, with mostly Tharon's influence, and came up with my own style.

My career broadened with somebody asking me to do something. All I ever wanted to do was be a Broadway designer. Then Hal asked me to do an opera. I had assisted Tharon on some operas, but I was never very keen. But Hal asked me to do an opera and it was pretty interesting. So I got known as an opera designer. There've been years where I've done five or six operas.

While I was doing an opera with Hal, Liza Minnelli was sitting at the dress rehearsal. She came running up to the table at intermission and said, "Hi, I'm Liza Minnelli." And I said, "Hi, I'm Ken Billington." And she said, "You have to light my act. It's the best lighting I've ever seen." So I started lighting Liza's act. And after that Shirley MacLaine called me, and then Ann-Margret, then Liberace—and it just went on and on. And because I did one and made it look good, everybody said "Oh, he's good at that." Radio City called one day. They were doing *Snow White and the Seven Dwarfs* on stage and they had never had a lighting designer there. They called three designers: John Gleason, Tharon and me. Tharon didn't want to do it, John was teaching, but I said sure. I didn't know then how to make Radio City work, but I learned.

So people have called me to do things and I haven't said no. The one thing I've always said is, the worst thing they can do to you is fire you. They don't take you out back and shoot you. So if you really screw up, they'll fire you, and somebody else will come in and do it, or you'll figure it out. But it won't be that terrible.

My non-theatrical [work] is the architectural lighting. Again, somebody called me. A friend was opening a restaurant and said, "Light it." I did and it looked great. I didn't do much more after that. Then a friend recommended me to do a night club in New York called The Red Parrot. I didn't know how to do a disco, I'd never done one. I didn't like blinking lights and black light, and UV and all those things that discos were in 1979. I said I won't do it like that. So I got the first Performer II, which was unheard of in a night club, put in three hundred dimmers, and lit it like a show, and changed what disco lighting looked like. I won the Lumen Award, which is the architectural award. All of a sudden I was an architectural lighting designer, and people were calling me all the time. I still don't know all those things that engineers know. But I know how to make it look good. What I didn't know, I learned.

I've worked in Japan, in Europe, all over. That's always a challenge. I got called yesterday to do a musical in Istanbul—in a tent. That's pretty interesting. International work is another challenge. What I've found is that everybody is a professional in their own theatre. There may be different ways of doing it, but it all ends up the same. The shows are presented to an audience in a professional manner, and maybe a little crude and not as slick because the technology here is so good. It's just learning how to deal with the different personalities and the mores of the country.

I don't know how you define good lighting, unless it's: *if it works for the play*. I always say if nobody ever knew I was in the theatre, I probably did well. Maybe that's changing now that we're getting into spectaculars and because, since the light shows of the sixties, people are aware of lighting. Before that nobody knew what a dimmer was; now every bathroom in America has a dimmer. Everyone is a lighting designer. People are more conscious of lighting. The best story about that is, I did a TV show many years ago for HBO called *Sherlock Holmes*. We taped it at Williamstown, Massachusetts. There were five full stage sets. It's written in five acts, each about fifteen or twenty minutes long. We taped it in front of an audience, but it was made for television. We had audiences in for rehearsals and the taping. We'd do an act, bring the curtain in, the curtain warmers would come up, the house lights would come up, and then after about two minutes, we would take the curtain out and with work lights on: the audience would watch the scene shifts. Sometimes we'd be refocusing specials and a guy would go around with a fog machine or cobweb machine, and then we'd bring the curtain down and they'd seen it all in worklight. Then we'd start the play again. Every performance, the curtain would go up on the act and you'd hear the audience go "Huuh!" You'd hear them gasp because they knew all there was about the set, but they hadn't seen it lit. The best compliment I got, at the table in the back of the house, a lady came up and said "Who's Ken Billington?" She was in her middle to late sixties. I said, "I am." She said, "I must tell you, I have been going to the theatre my entire life and I never knew what the lighting designer did until today. I'm embarrassed to say that I didn't know, because I didn't realize how important you were." I thought, that's good. So people don't know what I do. Maybe good lighting means they shouldn't know. But we should turn on the work lights every once in a while and let them find out.

As I get older, I find out that I usually know somebody on the creative team, so I'm not flying blind. I think it was harder when I didn't know everybody. You read the play and get a feeling for it. I always read it just to see if I like the play. Then from there, I start getting visual images, whether the set is designed or not. Sometimes there's a sketch or the name of an artist or something, so I'll have a visual image. And I'll think about it. I'll give my ideas to the set designer, if it's something that needs ideas. Then when I see the scenery, I look at it, go away, think about how it should look. When I've worked it out in my head, the mechanics are the easy part. In my head I have designed the show, then I'll sit down at a drawing board and come up with the mechanics of how we create that look. Somebody will draft it up, I'll focus it and hope I guessed right.

Everybody asks where do I start when I do a light plot: area lights. I always put the area lights in first because when all else fails, you've got to see the people. So once you've seen them you can only make it better. The next thing I go for is backlight, then pipe ends, then sidelight. Now that we have color changers, the technology is wonderful. I've never been afraid of technology. I remember for years we would do a musical with three colors of backlight. But now, with color changers, your pallet is so broad, that you can solve a myriad of problems. Some people just put a lot of toys in the air and then try to figure out what to do with them. That takes time. I know exactly what I'm going to do with them. I might try the light amber, then the darker amber, but I know it's going to be amber.

I turn stuff down all the time, which is scary. I actually turn down Broadway shows, which I thought I'd never do. The show may be bad, or they won't pay you enough money. Yeah, I'm a workaholic. I never wanted to be a big business, but I do have an office with a number of people to pay. So there are financial obligations. I often wonder if I'd make as much money if I still worked out of my bedroom. So I work a lot. But things are challenging. I don't ever do anything I really don't want to do or hate. I go off and do shows I think are going to be fun. I love doing the ice show and when Radio City calls, that's great. If it's fun, I'll try to do it. Why not.

I don't think we know where technology's going. I think we're getting better—great strides with control and dimmers. Dimmers are pretty sophisticated now. Control is immensely sophisticated. It will get more sophisticated as computers and operators get more sophisticated. With the new Source Fours I think equipment is finally catching up with everything else. Where are we going? Everybody says, "Oh we're going to get fully automated." I don't think we are. I think we're going to be more efficient and we're going to have better lighting. Now with memory boards as sophisticated as they are, if I ever see a light hit a curtain when a drop is going out then somebody did something wrong. The designer didn't know how to run the board, or the stage manager called the cue in the wrong place. But you should never see those little things, because there's nothing stopping you from making it perfect, whatever perfect is. I just see us becoming more efficient. The one thing we can never get rid of is the time it takes to do the show. It may take two or three months to load them in now, but the tech period is still a week. That's never going to get smaller. Using moving lights, it takes a long time to program them. So the technology maybe has made the product better, but it hasn't sped up the amount of time it takes to create it. It may have cut down on operation costs. So there's a give and take there.

Somebody has to come up with the definitive moving light console that is user friendly and that is a pleasure to work on.

I think *passion* is absolutely the most important thing. If you really don't want to starve to get there, then you probably don't have the passion to do it. If you will go any place to light a show or work on a show or to see a show, that will help fill that passion. What I see is a lot of kids coming out of school, and they come in with resumes and want to work for me—then they realize they just spent six or seven years of their lives and zillions of dollars going to university, and now they're going to make $350 a week— they hold back. But you have to do it. I think you have to work as an assistant or an associate or work with other master designers, people who have done it. That's a good way of learning. And you have to light, you have to do it. Even if it's with seventeen cans in a basement on seven dimmers, you have to learn how to do that and make your mistakes. Luckily, when I did community theatre they gave me a huge lighting budget and I had professional directors. And I screwed up a lot, but I learned from those things, so I always think doing it helps. You have to admit you don't know anything and that you're going to learn it all.

I don't recommend being an electrician to survive. I think you always have to think of yourself as a designer. Some people are designer/technicians. That's fine, but if you want to be a designer, you have to work as a designer. It doesn't mean you can't go and help your friends hang a show once in a while, but you can't be the head electrician at a theatre. I know it's different in England, but in this country, you get pigeonholed very quickly. So I think you have to assist and maybe wait tables or do something different than work in an electric shop. You just have to find the work. The Broadway shows are few and far between. There are twenty of them at one time. And we can count on one hand the people who are going to do them. I'm going to do a couple, and Jules will do a couple, and you're going to do a couple, and Beverly Emmons and the same folks. You don't see the new kids, because when a producer is spending $2 million to do a play they'd rather hire us, pay the extra money and know what they are getting than take a chance on a new designer.

There's a much bigger world out there than there used to be. Lighting isn't just in New York. There's all that regional theatre out there and those other things. The guys who do concert lighting and rock and roll are artists; they're pretty spectacular. I don't know how to do that. I couldn't light Pink Floyd. I don't have an affinity for the music. I would struggle trying to do that. But they would struggle trying to do *Hello Dolly*. That concert stuff is a real part of lighting. There are a lot of guys out there making a real good living doing that and doing some real good stuff. The same with television.

## Chapter Sixteen

# Pilbrow Story 2:
# Theatre Projects Begins

F alling straight into a long-running West End success was like going to heaven. Never shall I forget passing though the stage door that first time. Never shall I forget the welcome given a naive ASM by the veteran crew of Her Majesty's.

However, heaven didn't last. All too soon I found that stage managing a hit show was not what I had read in Gordon Craig. I was not "The Master of the Art and Science of the Theatre" but the junior junior dogsbody. Unlike actors, who had the stimulus of a new audience every night, I found the prompt corner crashingly boring. But after six months *Teahouse* was sent out on tour, and I was promoted to deputy stage manager. We were to open at the Lyceum Theatre, Edinburgh. As the show was being hung I noticed that the production carpenter was hanging the borders on the wrong side of the lighting pipes. I mentioned this to Bob Stanton, who was directing the touring company. Then we started to focus. Bob thought the electrician was to light. The electrician was surprised. Even worse, nobody seemed to have brought the plots. Yours truly, being young and ambitious, had of course copied all the plots into his Lefax. To cut a story short, I lit the show and we opened successfully.

Next day I was summoned by Bob to take tea at the North British Hotel to meet the real boss, William Styles, general manager of the producers, Williamson Music (the Rogers and Hammerstein London production office). Apparently I had saved the day. Not only did I get tea, I was told that they would both benevolently look after my career. They did—a thousand fold.

We toured for nine months. It was the definitive learning experience. My boss, the company stage manager, was a drunk who disappeared for every crisis. I had to handle the cast, the business, and the stage. Then Bob and Bill called me back to London for another show at Her Majesty's, this time *No Time for Sergeants*. This ran eighteen months and it, too, became seriously boring. Confusingly, a lifetime ambition had turned to ashes.

What to do? I really wanted to be Max Reinhardt. But directing seemed far away to an ASM who hadn't made university. Lighting had always been my hobby. Most of what I saw in London seemed boring (except for the work of the unique Joe Davis, which I worshiped, and that of Michael Northen). I found a book in Samuel French's, *Theatrical Lighting Practice* by Americans Joel Rubin and Lee Watson on lighting design as a profession. Good heavens! Maybe that's what I could do. But how to live? What would I use for money?

An idea emerged. There was really only one lighting rental company in the whole of Britain: Strand Electric. I'd been a loyal customer for years. If I could find, beg, borrow or steal some lights, I could rent them to people at a keen price, offer my services as a lighting designer almost free and live off the hardware. The words "Theatre Projects" had been a childhood fantasy. I always knew the short-term plan was just a small step toward the Theatre Projects International Corporation! More practically, calling the company something other than Pilbrow Associates would allow me to more easily resist blandishments to give equipment away for nothing and at the same time would make it easier for me to bring in colleagues when it came time to expand. Even then I had a feeling that several minds collaborating together would be the key to success.

My general manager, Bill Styles, controlled a large pile of old lighting equipment left over from *Oklahoma*, which lay under the stage at the Theatre Royal Drury Lane. He could sell it to me for £60. My father, overcoming a decade of suspicion of things theatrical, very kindly offered to lend me the money. Our first office was under the stage of Her Majesty's Theatre. There, next to the Victorian stage machinery,[2] I rebuilt my latest model theatre to demonstrate my prospective skills. Then, just around the corner from Her Majesty's, I stumbled upon a tiny room for rent on the third floor. My father's accountant formed a company and lent me the fare back to the West End after I'd signed the papers. We were away.

I enlisted a colleague, Brian Kendall, my assistant stage manager, as partner, and we took a classified advertisement in the *Stage:* "New Lighting Company."

Next day the new phone rang: "This is Cotterill, Strand Electric." I stood to attention. I knew the name, a director of the great firm. "I'd like to pay you a call, Pilbrow." Half an hour later he arrived, bowler hat and umbrella, and sat on our borrowed chair. "What do you think you're doing, Pilbrow?" I told him. He was not amused. Finally, "Where is your money coming from, Pilbrow?" This was no business of his, I thought. Standing on my dignity, I suggested the meeting was over. He left with disdain. "I suggest you give up, Pilbrow. Strand Electric *are* stage lighting. There's no room for anybody else."

This was a good moment. Outrage fueled our survival through many months of near starvation. But our timing was good. Within a few weeks we had our first client, seeking a bargain and getting a lighting designer. One show led to another. Our lighting got noticed, our reputation began to grow.

# Chapter Seventeen

# Jules Fisher

I n a celebrated thirty-year career Jules Fisher has lit more than 150 Broadway and off-Broadway shows as well as film, ballet, opera, television and rock-and-roll concert tours. He has received fourteen Tony nominations and seven Tony awards for lighting design, for Pippin (1972), Ulysses in Nighttown (1973), Dancin' (1978), Grand Hotel (1990), The Will Rogers Follies (1991), Jelly's Last Jam (1992) and Bring in da Noise, Bring in da Funk (with Peggy Eisenhauer; 1995), as well as Drama Desk awards for Frankenstein, Grand Hotel and Jelly's Last Jam. His other theatre credits include Victor Victoria, Angels in America (Millenium Approaches and Perestroika), Death and the Maiden, Two Shakespearean Actors, La Cage aux Folles, Hair, Jesus Christ Superstar, Lenny, No No Nanette, Chicago, Butterflies Are Free, Beatlemania and American Buffalo.

His credits as a producer include The Rink; the award-winning Lenny; Bob Fosse's Dancin'; Rock n' Roll! The First 5000 Years; Elvis, an American Musical; and Dangerous Games. He designed the lighting for Kevin Kline's production of Hamlet for WNET-TV and lit productions of Porgy and Bess and A Midsummer Night's Dream at the New York City Opera. In the world of rock music Jules was production supervisor for tours of the Rolling Stones, Kiss and David Bowie and the concert tour of Tommy. His other lighting design work has ranged from Crosby, Stills and Nash, Whitney Houston, and the Simon and Garfunkel concert in Central Park to the Radio City Music Hall presentation and subsequent national tour of the Teenage Mutant Ninja Turtles; from the 1977 Academy Awards show to the concert lighting for Barbra Streisand's film A Star Is Born. He lit the Quincy Jones Reunion on the

*Mall concert celebration for President Clinton's inaugural, which was nominated for an Emmy Award.*

*Jules is a graduate of Carnegie Mellon University. He also serves as a theatre consultant to architects and performing arts groups and practices magic in his spare time.*

When I was eight years old I was introduced to magic. I was just enamored of the idea of what was making things appear and disappear: slight of hand, legerdemain, the performing of magic. I started to perform as a child. I met a magician who taught me quite a bit and then I read everything I could. I performed in school and the local clubs, like the Elks and the Moose and the Veterans of Foreign Wars. I went to Fort Dix Army Hospital, the local insane asylum, all these little fraternal clubs in town. Seen in hindsight, I was dreadful, I think. But I still practice magic and love it. And now I think I have a better understanding of what it is. Now I'm interested in the psychology of it.

I was not a very good student, but I liked science—the idea of science. I liked the idea that physically you pushed this lever and that happened. I think the two things, liking science and liking magic, led to my going into lighting.

At the end of my last year in high school (Norristown, Pa.) I applied to a new theatre being built, an arena theatre called Valley Forge Music Fair. I went there that first summer as an apprentice and became an assistant stage manager. The last week of the season, the stage manager left and I took over. So I learned a lot that summer, probably more than I did the rest of my career. It was all new to me and I loved it. I looked at the lighting, which was very crude, done by the electrician at the time, and I thought "I can do that." From that moment on, I changed schools and went to Carnegie Mellon in Pittsburgh, which was Carnegie Tech at the time. I worked in summer stock for the next nine summers, three of which were at the Music Fair. Every summer I was doing eight, nine, ten shows, for nine summers.

My last year at Carnegie, a student who had graduated the year before, Mark Schoenburg, called and said, "I'm directing a new play in New York." It was *All the Kings Men* by Robert Penn Warren. "Would you come to New York and light it?" The school finally said, "Yes, go to New York." I went to New York and did the lighting for this off-Broadway play, which was successful. I went back to school. Then a few months later, the designer for that play, Gary Smith, who is now a well-known television producer, called and said, "I am designing a new musical off-Broadway called *Parade* written by Jerry Herman. Would you like to come to New York and light that?"

This was 1959 or 1960. The school let me out again, getting a little tired of me traveling to New York and missing classes. Someone from that show called me, the manager Marvin Krauss in this case, and said, "I'm doing a play, would you come and do it?" So I went to New York three times before I left school. When I graduated, I came directly here. I already had

*Stage Lighting Design*

some acquaintances; I knew either designers, managers or directors. Every time I worked on a production, I met three more. That just expanded, and that's how my career took off.

The great icons in lighting when I started were Abe Feder, who I still look up to, Jean Rosenthal, Jo Mielziner. I think they were the ones who were really special. I saw a play early on that Abe Feder lit, *Three Sisters* for the Actors Studio, and it was brilliant. I remember it to this day. I remember seeing light cues of people walking across the stage with candles, obviously in the era of resistance dimmer boards. I was aware of what somebody must be doing backstage, how many hands it took to make it so fluid. I'd seen a lot of the ballets that Jean Rosenthal had done, very delicate things. All of Jo Mielziner's work: I never saw a production of his where I thought the lighting was poor. Because of his relationship with the scenery, it was all of a piece. Perhaps because he designed both, his shows were the most integrated. His productions had a feeling he was trying to tell the story.

So then I went directly to New York after another summer of stock. I began working off-Broadway, did many shows, one after the other. There were only five days of previews and only four days of technicals. I built things out of tomato cans on a wooden board to make a "broadlight" of nine PAR cans, a three-by-three source of 150-watt PARs to be sunlight coming in a window. But I built those because they didn't exist, or the producer couldn't afford to rent them from the Broadway lighting shops. There weren't many off-Broadway lighting shops. The only one I remember using was Altmans, who was willing to rent equipment for a very low price and supported all my endeavors.

Then I did an off-Broadway play for the producer Kermit Bloomgarden; it was called *Moon on a Rainbow Shawl*, a West Indies play. It had James Earl Jones and Cecily Tyson and a wonderful cast. I had a good time doing it. The producer called me six months later and said, "I'm doing a Broadway musical, would you come and light it?" Now that I look back on that, I think, "What an adventuresome producer!" There aren't many today who would use someone who had only worked off-Broadway. I was not in the union, which was a stumbling block. That also says a lot about the producer. It was called *Nowhere to Go but Up*. The director was Sidney Lumet, and the scenic designer was Peter Larkin. So I started to work on this musical. One thing I remember happening was that Kermit, the producer, got a rental price from Century Lighting, from Ed Kook, our friend. Kermit said, "This is ridiculous, what is all the lighting equipment for?" And I remember having a meeting with him and Ed Kook, who came over. And I took the lighting plot and explained to Kermit what each light was for. I can't picture a producer today doing that. He wanted to see if I knew what everything was for, and at the end of the meeting, he said, "Fine, order the lights." We went forward on the production until the union, United Scenic Artists, was unhappy with the fact that I was not a member. And I think they used some influence to encourage Kermit to use someone else and I did not light the show.

I had taken the union exam twice and failed it twice, at which point I said, "I'm not going to do this anymore." I said, "You're preventing me from earning a living and I think I'm capable of lighting a show." I'd already done quite a few. They did take me into the union at that time.

Richard, you and I met in 1963 because I was lighting a discotheque called Arthur with David Balding and Mike Nichols. Tony Walton was called in to design something for it. And he said, "What if it had projections everywhere? I know a person who knows all about projections. I'll bring him here to meet you." And it was *the* Richard Pilbrow. That was on East Fifty-fourth Street.

Our mutual friend Ed Kook was a fan and a smart business man. He was also a generous man to me. Some people didn't like him. He was a tough, street-smart, born-in-New York kid who fought his way to the top. He loved the theatre. That overrode all the other aspects of him. He loved doing theatre, he loved supporting theatre, he loved all designers. Especially scenic designers; he encouraged scenic designers to learn about lighting. I saw immediately he was saying, "Tell me what you need and I'll develop it, I'll build it, I'll invent it, I'll solve the problem because you, the artist, need it." Look at things like projection. He had, in the very early years, a scenic projector, the Projectorama—a 5,000-watt projector for large-format glass slides. Now he was not going to sell many of those. How many companies today would be willing to put the investment in something they know they're not going to sell a lot of? They did. And they did it all down the line. Sure they also made strip lights, which made a lot more money. So that's an example where I felt Kook's personal influence— he *was* the company. I was with him on some occasions where he *gave* equipment to designers without them knowing about it. I was impressed with that: a great man.

I was invited to join the union because I was doing operas at the City Center. There was Hans Sondheimer, the technical director, remember him? He was at the City Center. I remember doing a *Porgy and Bess* there, a large-scale production. Because of typical opera schedules—changing over after an evening show—the only time for lighting was after midnight till five or six the next morning. Roger Morgan was my assistant. We were working all night long. While we were doing cyclorama changes of an atmospheric sky, Hans Sondheimer said, "Don't just do a cue that goes from here to here, break it up into three cues." And that from someone you think of as a very technical person. He was right; it made it much more interesting. That was my first union job.

Then I was asked to do a play on Broadway called *Spoon River Anthology*. It was nine people sitting on stools. I had a lot of fun. I had 5–12-plate, 500-watt resistance preset boards. There were lots of people doing monologues, so lots of specials for each person in each area, and thus loads of presets. That was my first play on Broadway, and it got very good notices and it ran, oddly enough. I found that over the years, the odds of a play running are slim. I've done maybe ten plays for every one that is a success. To have the first one be a success was unusual, or luck. And I think luck played a lot in my career. I've met a lot of wonderful people. I've had a lot of wonderful assistants over the years. Most of them are successful lighting designers today. And that's got to be luck. I just found these people, or they'd come to me, and I'd hire them or not: Beverly Emmons, Roger Morgan, Craig Miller, John McClain, Natasha Katz, Marc Weiss, Peggy Eisenhauer, loads of them. They've all become very good lighting designers.

My first Broadway musical was a year later, and I got asked to do two musicals almost at the same time. I'll never do that today. First, *Anyone Can Whistle* by Stephen Sondheim and Arthur Lawrence, Herb Ross directing, Bill and Jean Eckert doing the set and Theoni Aldridge doing the costumes. Then, almost simultaneously, *Blythe Spirit* as a musical called *High Spirits*, with Noël Coward directing. So there I was working in the same year with all those great people.

*Hair* was a wonderful musical for its time. The show opened in 1968. It captured the spirit, the elements of the sixties—the sexual revolution, the political revolution, the freedom of speech and behavior. It was also the first Broadway show that Tom O'Horgan directed. It was very powerful. It had not very good reviews, it won no awards, no Tonys, and was all done on resistance dimmer boards. It was a case where lighting could be flamboyant, yet told the story. It was to do with the explosion of the peace movement in this country and the anger against the war. I remember at the time not quite understanding some of the things Tom O'Horgan was trying to do. For the song "Good Morning Star Shine" he had the cast climbing out into the audience and in the balcony and singing in the back of the theatre. And I'd say, "Tom, doesn't that split the focus everywhere?" And now it's second nature, everybody does things like that. So the staging was very special. I remember he said, "Is there any other way we can bring the audience into the theatre other than the front door?" He wanted to break their expectations of what the theatre experience was going to be. And of course because of fire laws we weren't allowed to. But he was right. He didn't want us to go into a red roped, red velour theatre. He was saying this is something unusual. A great learning experience for me.

I then had the chance to do *Jesus Christ Superstar* with him, also in many different productions. And then, jumping to the other end of my career, *Angels in America* and *Jelly's Last Jam*, both with the brilliant scenic designer Robin Wagner. These two are really at the other end of the spectrum, with loads of junk in between and lots of wonderful shows and wonderful people and wonderful experiences. But not enough really good theatre. When *Angels in America* came along, I thought, "This is a rare play." Seven and a half hours of material, and nobody ever left before the final curtain. People sat riveted through the entire play: extraordinary, and on a tough subject. I really cherish that experience, because the director, George C. Wolfe, cared to take the time and direct it precisely and to give us the time to allow light cues to be set very meticulously. Now we're into the era of computer boards and moving lights and we have so many more decisions to make with every light cue, which takes more time. We have to educate the producers that it takes more time if they want lighting of quality. Since, as with many things in life, you can't go backwards, you can only strive to do better lighting with each successive play you design. You, as an artist, can't afford to do anything but the best lighting, which takes time.

I'm frustrated by how long it takes, but I think it's necessary for the other collaborators and the directors to plan in advance and to know what they want. It's going to take longer with a director who looks at it and then says, "I don't like that"—and you have to redo it. With moving lights, the computer needs to know where the light was three cues ago or it's not going to get where you want it in a smooth fashion. So I think it does take time. One solution might be if we could work on a miniature set with miniature lights and a miniature computer where we could work off-line so we aren't tying up musicians', actors' and stagehands' time. To set a beautiful light cue we now have hundreds of parameters that we did not have to worry about years ago. As an example, we have color scrollers, or color changers, including variable dichroics. Before, we used to have the problem of putting *a* color in *a* lamp; what color is it going to be out of a gel book of fifty or sixty colors? Now we're into tints and shades of hundreds of choices, and we can make that choice with every single light cue. That's our obligation now, to make that choice with every cue.

People say I seem so composed when I work. I look calm. But I'm not calm. I'm nervous, I'm often insecure. I'm there thinking, "Is this a mistake? Did I pick the right color?" I often have a sense that I don't know the right way to light the cyc. Is this right for the play? Those few insecurities, I live with them and haven't found a way to get rid of them. No amount of experience has solved it for me. I still look at it and think, "The wrong light is at the top of the cyc, it's not smooth." Not technically but aesthetically the wrong light.

I started a company to do theatre consulting because, as I traveled and did touring shows, I ran into many theatres that had ridiculous mistakes built into them and I was shocked. I started a theatre consultation business in 1963. It was just me to start with. I enjoyed it and realized it was fun to help shape a theatre, to build something that did not thwart the artist years later and to make a theatre that would function. So that began the business, and I do it to this day under the name Jules Fisher/Joshua Dachs Associates.

Eventually, people came to me, including Steve Sondheim, who said he was remodeling an apartment, and could I help him light the space? And I said, "Sure." So I started to do architectural lighting on my own. But I didn't have any training in this. Very quickly I found a partner in Paul Marantz, and he and I joined forces. At the time, he was working for

Century. He liked theatre as well. So we could trade off our creative ideas and we worked together as a company. I thought both companies would give me a base of creativity and finance, which they did. I really believe in working with other people.

I think lighting must be beautiful. If the quality of light on an actor isn't really beautiful, I don't like that. A quality of lighting, a dimension perhaps, is to see actors well, not just see them. But is the face lit in a way that relates to the play? I see plays where it's not. There may be light on the actors and you can see them, but they're not modeled beautifully or they aren't colored properly. So I like to see good basic lighting on the performer be beautiful. And then I think it must help the story emotionally. We now have the ability to have motion, which relates to timing. I think it's wonderful "that light is always moving"—Edward Gordon Craig was talking about this at the turn of the century, and it is now true. Therefore it's timing, the timing we had a lot of experience with in rock-and-roll lighting. It was a great chance to do emotionally powerful timed moves. Without a director coming and saying I want a light cue here, the rock-and-roll bands depended more on the lighting designer. The rhythmic timing of the lighting can be a powerful, emotional tool. It's referred to in Stanley McCandless's definition of lighting. But I don't think many people understand it yet. I've had a couple of instances on Broadway with creators being unable to deal with that on musicals.

*Richard:* I think you're the master of that, Jules. I gasp at some of your work.

*Jules:* I want to credit Peggy [Eisenhauer] with a lot of that. She is much more musical than I am. She was a pianist and has a photographic memory. So she can go to rehearsals and hear music and she knows it, in one rehearsal.

By the way, talking about moving lights moving: my partner, Paul Marantz, and I did a number of discotheques. We did Studio 54 and The Palladium in 1984. The Palladium had the first permanent use of Vari*Lites, on battens that went up and down. So they were moving lights moving. They stayed there for eight years, I think. They were used non-stop. That was my first experience with them. There are going to be lots of companies making moving lights, which is exciting. They're going to get lower in price and friendlier and quicker to cue.

I've had the luck to work with an interesting array of rock artists, from Laura Nyro, Simon and Garfunkel, The Rolling Stones, David Bowie, Kiss, Crosby, Stills and Nash, and Whitney Houston, and many lesser-known ones in between. The biggest thing of interest for me was the use of scale—scale in ideas, scale in physical size: to design for ten thousand people instead of one thousand in a theatre. So the chance to work with scale was exciting, to do visual things that could only work in an arena, that could only work where lights could be fifty feet away from a performer. And then composition in the air—essential because there wasn't any scenery for the early rock-and-roll shows. Rock and rollers allowed lighting designers to be more like scenic designers: the production designer. Many of the rock-and-roll shows invited theatre designers to do them: Robin Wagner did The Rolling Stones, Mark Ravitz did David Bowie. But it was a chance to use scale, scale in movement, scale in color. You could do things in rock and roll that might be outrageous in a theatre production because it would be too overpowering.

The theatre process is almost predictable, but it is a format that works, and we don't break it very often. Rock and roll allows for more flights of fancy and a little more craziness in the design. And in rock and roll, I also had the chance to build some physical things that the theatre wouldn't have allowed me to build because of cost. There's bigger dollars involved in rock and roll because they're playing to ten thousand people a night. Bowie knew that no matter where he played, he'd sell out. It was a fact. So he could say, "OK, what do you want to do? We can afford it."

I like thinking something can't be done and then finding a way to solve it with interesting devices. That's something to do with my interest in magic. It's all connected.

I produced *Beatlemania* and *Rock and Roll! The First 5000 Years*, and *Elvis. Elvis* became visually wonderful, with the use of very high-powered movie projectors, where you'd get the brightness on stage. A mixture of theatre and film is very difficult. I think one of the problems is that it requires all artists in the project to think together. Historically, slide or film projects are thought of as an adjunct. "Oh well, let's add projections." Or, "We can't afford scenery, so let's use projection." So the imagery is not used for a purpose that is amenable to the material. I think on a production where you have a director who understands what projections can do, a projected image can take you to secret places, mystical and magical places that almost nothing else can do, in the same way that movies in a twenty-fourth of a second can take you anywhere.

I never assisted anyone. By accident, by luck, I just started. But I do know that the people that I've had work with me, and God knows there are a lot of them, were all wonderful. Peggy and I have now worked together ten years, we hardly use any assistants. With two of us, we can almost handle everything ourselves and—this is personal, but there is something almost prideful in keeping it to ourselves. We don't have to sell it to anybody else in the moment of creativity. We write down our own follow-spot tracking, our own everything. The board strokes are recorded on disc by the electrician and they're printed out the next day. I'm not somebody for having five assistants or table after table of computers tracking things that I'm not sure you really need to track. I'm not sure you really need to know on paper where the Vari*Lites are at every moment. The computer needs to know. But I see other designers having some kind of measurement of quality based on the number of feet of tech tables. We have very little.

So how does one get to be an assistant? We interview a lot of people, because I'm also looking for people for theatre consulting and architectural lighting. We ask to see drawings. This may be my head buried in the sand, but I still like to see a hand-done drawing. When we draw, we think—spatially, creatively—as artists. Those who have avoided perfecting drawing skills may not relate to our process. I think there's some beauty in that. I relate to the Bibienas. To see a drawing done by a computer lacks a little warmth, charm. That's not to say I'd reject an assistant because he couldn't draw, but there's something nice about drawing skills. I guess I look for someone who's personable, who can be quiet and who has knowledge and is willing to learn. I think it probably is one of the few ways you can learn the mechanics of the business. I think assistants have learned a lot working on our productions about how we deal with stagehands, how we deal with producers. I ask them to remember that what they witness in the course of things is private, because I need the freedom to be myself in front of the director. I don't want to have to think of the assistants, will they go and repeat something I've said to somebody else. I want to feel the intimacy I need with a director.

Look at the change in the expenditure of money for shows. More money's at risk, therefore there's more pressure to do it faster. You have to be more prepared, have your stuff together, know what you're doing.

The future? We're certainly in the infancy of moving lights. They've made vast leaps in ten years. Imagine what they'll do in the next ten years—with technological advance and the competition? Competition is going to be real big. I encourage small companies. I think it's important for the art to not put all our eggs in one basket. I try to help smaller companies or ones not doing as well. I think we need them. We need the competition.

My advice to the newcomer is *"See everything you can."* See every play, every musical, every ballet, every museum exhibit. Get a life. Work as much as you can. Get a job. Don't hold out just to be an assistant on a Broadway show. Light an off-Broadway show, go touring, work in summer stock, get *experience* doing it somewhere. I think the decisions made to light a puppet show are the same as lighting a Broadway show. The dealing with humans may be different, but the artistic decisions are pretty similar.

## Chapter Eighteen

# Brian Gale

**B**rian Gale currently holds a position as a principal show lighting designer with Walt Disney Imagineering.

Brian's most recent WDI lighting designs include Mannequins, The Adventurers Club and four other nightclubs at Pleasure Island at Walt Disney World, as well as the "Indiana Jones Stunt Spectacular," "Superstar Television," "Let's Make a Deal" and the "Honey I Shrunk the Kids Adventure" at the Disney MGM Studios and "Honey I Shrunk the Audience" at EPCOT Center.

He started his Disney career with the Entertainment division at Disneyland in Anaheim, California, in 1977 and has recently designed productions for Disney Entertainment in New York's Central Park and Radio City Music Hall as well as many Disney corporate productions in North America.

In addition to his Disney work, Brian has maintained a theatrical lighting design career.

Among the theatres that Brian has worked with are: the New York Shakespeare Festival, The Mark Taper Forum/Center Theater Group, Berkeley Repertory Theater, Seattle Repertory, South Coast Repertory, as well as the Los Angeles Theater Center.

Recent industrial show clients include IBM, Redken Labs, Sebastian International, Drexel Burnham, Roland and Disney Home Video.

Brian is a member of USA, IATSE, USITT and IES. He is married to fellow Imagineering lighting designer Casey Cowan.

I never thought I would be a lighting designer, you know. I mean I never consciously thought, "Right, that's it! I'll be a lighting designer!"

It just happened. I was an acting student in college with one basic technical theatre class under my belt when the staff TD/designer, Aubrey Wilson, told me I was going to light this little show.

Having previously been studying architecture I went to my collection of colored pencils and started laying out a "plot" by using different colored pencils for the different colored lights. You know how hard it is to find gels to match colored pencils? What did I know. Nothing! But I absolutely loved the experience.

Even now, one of my favorite things about lighting design is the drawing. Just the interaction of pencil and paper is...neat! Forget about all of the mumbo-jumbo and philosophical musings on art and communication. Just the act of striking a line on a blank piece of paper or finding the right path for a note with a leader line is...fun. Now of course I use a computer and plotter, but the feeling is still there.

So after that first experience I began to split my interest between lighting and acting until finally I chose to design the lighting for a production of *The Rimers of Eldritch* rather than be cast in it. I guess that was it. I don't remember hearing trumpets or the Hallelujah Chorus or anything. But looking back...Don't you think that life should come with a sound track so that you'd know when important stuff happens?

I began going to class less and less while working in the university theatre more and more as the "lighting guy"—you know, lighting everything that came through: band concerts, rock concerts, dance recitals, lectures, operas, you name it. I think this is where I learned the most about light and space, time and money. Usually I had a minimal crew and the client had a minimal budget. The theatre tech teacher (and one of my best) made me light within the budget and refused to let me do anything extra for free. Better than any lab class I ever had. A whole theatre to play with, a place to make discoveries and mistakes. I can't imagine a better education.

Soon I was dropping out of college and going to work for the Center Theater Group as an unpaid "production assistant/lighting guy." I also began to design small theatrical productions around Southern California and eventually had a modest career as a professional theatrical lighting designer and all the poverty that that entails. At the same time, in order to make a living, I became a member of the IATSE local, which led to many rock and theater show calls and eventually to a job at Disneyland as an electrician/stagehand.

There I was again, a Disneyland "lighting guy." Most of the talent booked in the park had no lighting designer. Usually we booked acts that were either on the way up or on the way down; in neither case could they afford a lighting designer. So I did a lot of design for up-and-coming or down-and-going pop acts.

At this time, through my theatrical work, I realized that the process of melding my work with that of other designers, the director, playwright, actors (when it works) was what I enjoy the most. This collaborative process is the ultimate high. I understand now why some people in the theatre over concentrate on the process and forget the product. It can be addicting.

I was beginning to do a large amount of industrial work, where I found myself becoming a basic theatre professor. "No, believe me, we've been doing it this way for hundreds of years, it will work." And though the budgets (and fees) I was dealing with began to increase, the collaborative process was more and more scarce.

I've decided that more than the collaboration, the most attractive thing about lighting design is the technical rehearsal. There you sit with the headset on and all of these production team members swirling around you asking, telling, advising, creating. You sit in the absolute center of the creation of the show. Is it no wonder that I (and most lighting designers) am bored with the show come opening night? It is a pretty powerful and rare production that can compete with the adrenaline rush of tech and first preview on headset.

I do not consider myself an academically trained lighting designer. I suppose I am what the military calls a mustang, one who came up through the ranks. I find myself having once been the IA electrician or spot operator with the big thumbs now required to sit on the other side of the headset and play a different role. I now interface with the creative disciplines, straddling the technical and ephemeral worlds. I find great pleasure in sitting down with the creative, nontechnical people and helping to create a vision that I then have to interpret for the nuts-and-bolts electrons-and-lightbulbs people.

After ten years with Disneyland Entertainment I moved to Walt Disney Imagineering where I actually have a title with the words *lighting designer* (imagine trumpets here) in it. Here, I find that the technical and creative disciplines are formally separated into distinct divisions: Engineering, Finance, Production, Project Management on one side of the house, Art Direction, Show Design, Show Production, Writing, et cetera, on the other side. This reflects the original duality in the company structure. Walt was the head-in-the-clouds visionary while Roy was the financial how-do-we-do-it reality check.

And which side of the Imagineering house does Show Lighting fit into? Neither. Show Lighting along with other theatrical disciplines sits in a separate division altogether. This reflects the bridging of the technical and creative role that lighting designers play.

At Imagineering, and at Disney in general, the show and the story is all-important. It's the most important thing we do, so even the schedulers and the planners and the estimators—when the show person says, "Well, we're going to tell this story," or "It has to look like this"—they just say, "Oh, OK." There's no questioning. There's an unwritten law.

Lighting design in Imagineering has traditionally been a nuts-and-bolts operation, where we've been classed with engineers for years and years and years. We're currently going through the process of dragging our show lighting forward, making it current and encompassing, or being the cutting edge.

One of our main problems is maintenance. Maintaining theatre, seven shows a week, is a lot different than seven shows a day or fifteen shows a day. "Indiana Jones" in Florida runs five or six shows a day. More people see the "Kids of the Kingdom Show" in Disneyland than have seen any Broadway show that ever ran.

Not only is the money scale completely different, but the time scale is even more so. Having made a theatrical career out of four- to eight-week commitments, on a theme park project you may not see the finished product for two to five years—that's hard.

You go through two years of discussion with air conditioning people and structural people, estimators and planners, and you're the only one who knows or cares what it looks like, so it's trying to hang on to what you're trying to create over those two years of nuts and bolts—it's hard.

Every time you go back, even the worst theatre experience has some of the ego thing that we all like in theater. I'm sure what every lighting designer, whether they admit it or not, most enjoys is sitting at the tech table at the center of the show. Everything comes through you. You become this traffic cop of creativity. The director is saying, "It should be more cinnamon," or something—and you translate: that means channel 8 at 7. And someone says, "That didn't move right," and you become the focal point. You just need that.

The solo part of it is the picture you create—thinking a picture in your head, using all the tools, renting the gear, planning it out, scheduling it. That's all fun, but getting into the theatre and coming back to the picture that was in your head, or discovering a picture that was never there, that's more fun.

Creating a mood and then experiencing it, feeling it, breathing it in, smelling it: it's like, "Look what I did. Look what we did. Look at how my stuff works on his stuff and her stuff works with my stuff." That costume in that cross-light is incredible. And just enjoying it—it's a visceral thing: a neuron between your eyes and your taste buds that goes, "Wow, that's neat!"

I remember how shows smell. You use that bluish-green backlight that makes everything look wet, and it smells wet, and I smell this in my head forever. An empty stage that's lit for dance, just...you smell the dust in the air—it's all part of it. And the excuse is that you're the lighting designer, and you wouldn't be in that position, you don't get to smell the smells and feel the moods unless you're that particular person in that space.

In my view lighting design—drawing the light plot, doing schedules and paperwork, and going to meetings—is just buying the paints at the paint store. It has nothing to do with lighting design. Lighting design is manipulating the light and shaping the space, and you obviously can't call yourself a lighting designer if you never walk into a theatre and cue a show or set a preset or change a color.

It's fun to be a technical person in a marshmallow world. When you sit there and you have show designers and writers who come to you and say, can we do that? And you can look them in the eye and say, "I can do that." That's kind of fun too. I can do that—that's no problem. If you've got the checkbook, I can do it.

The best experiences, the best show experiences I've had, inside Imagineering and in theatre, it's when there's a clear vision that we're all trying to achieve. And when you execute the vision, it comes together, and that's where the satisfaction comes. Even at the extended scales we have at Imagineering, when the vision holds through and you do successfully create the mood, the look, the feel, you generate your own satisfaction in that.

You'd think lighting designers would be much more of a type. But to make a blanket statement about what the personality of a lighting designer is would be completely wrong. So here I go: I suppose there are two types of lighting designers that I see. There are people who love to organize and plan and plot and schedule, because there's a tremendous amount of logistics involved with lighting. So, they're the supply officer lighting designer. And then you have the people who don't want to deal with the paperwork, who want to create the vision and get right into the theatre and make it happen, and all the steps in-between and all the junk you have to do to get there is not very fun. This is the field marshall lighting designer. Occasionally, you find a lighting designer who likes both. But within those two generic types—introverts and extroverts, loud and soft, big and small—the variety is just amazing.

I was recently reading an article in, I think, *Time* magazine where it said they think that the reason some people have a better sense of direction than others is that there's more magnetite in their heads. OK? Does that mean that *we* have more rods and cones? [Laughing.] It's genetic—is there something in there? It's possible—we all lived too close to the nuclear reactor and we all became lighting designers.

When I did theatre for two years solid, I couldn't wait to get my hands on a rock show. When I did rock shows, I couldn't wait to get my hands on an industrial show. It's hard for me to fashion a career out of only theatrical lighting. It's not just hard, in that it would be hard to be happy with it, but it's hard to create a career of longevity without having to teach someplace or without having to run a company with a hundred productions to manage: hard to make a living and have a family and have a house with a backyard and be a theatrical lighting designer all your life. Maybe you could do it in teaching theatrical lighting design, but again I would call that being a lighting designer-teacher. You can't just do one kind of lighting. Theatrical lighting is financially too hard to do and temperamentally too hard to do—as the only thing you do.

Gilbert Helmsley said, "The worst thing that ever happened to me was to become a Broadway show lighting designer at thirty-two," because all his life he said, "My goal in life is to be a Broadway lighting designer," and he got there. "What do I do now?" Naturally, if you aspire to something, you have to have goals that you maybe can't quite reach easily.

Lighting designers, like all human beings, reach a time when they want to be stable, when they want to create a life, and it's extremely hard to do in theatre, no matter where you are in theatre, it's extremely hard to do. I got to a point where I wanted to have a life, and I didn't think I could do that or wanted to do that on the road and not know when the next check was coming. So, it's actually odd that I married a lighting designer. I guess it's an attempt by both of us to make a life coming from the same place. But every human being will come to a point where they have to make a life, and deal with what that does to a career and how you find an outlet—either that or you get totally out of it.

Somewhere inside me it said this was the right move to go with. So, it happened that Disney happened to offer me something that has stability at a time when inside I must have needed it. I went into it thinking, "This is just another freelance job. If I don't like it, I'll just move on." And here I am seventeen years later. I must like it. But the big advantage with free-lancing is that you don't have to go back. This is America. You can leave and go on to something else. So, we'll see.

Whenever I get too philosophical and high and mighty about the Art of it all, I remember a technical director I once worked with.

A few years ago I was sitting in a small theatre in L.A. talking with the assistant director and the tech director. Eventually the conversation got around to how and why we got into theatre. The AD explained how she was really an aspiring actress and was in love with the theatre and addicted to the limelight; full of flowery descriptions of the art and spirit of the theatrical medium.

I told of being in love with the look of the solitary spotlight piercing the dark. The magic of the theatrical space and how I had been in love with the theatre from the first play I saw.

When it came the TD's turn, he paused and said, "I was arrested for drunk driving in Santa Monica and the judge sentenced me to serve in this theatre. That was two years ago and I'm still here."

Chapter Nineteen

# Pilbrow Story 3: Starting as a Lighting Designer

Innocence was the key for me. I had no idea what you couldn't do. Nobody had ever taught me how to light. I'd read all the books I could find: Fred Bentham, Ridge and Aldred, Gillespie Williams. I'd seen Joe Davis's work using, for those days, a lot of equipment. *Teahouse* and *Sergeants* were American big-rig shows. *West Side Story*, with lighting by Jean Rosenthal, had been an inspiration. Owning my own rental shop not only supported a very modest life style, it allowed me to slip extra equipment into a show without the producer knowing (free of course!). In truth this was a serious advantage. Minimum-budget shows got all the equipment we had left in the store.

My passion for theatre and lighting was backed by years of school and amateur design. All these things combined to make me sense that lighting must envelop the actors and create a new world. The fact that normally, in London theatre at that time, there were only twelve instruments on a pipe was irrelevant. I would add some more to complete the mosaic. I purloined the idea of drawing lighting plots to scale from the drawings in the Rubin/Watson book to prove to reluctant electricians that more lights could be squashed into less space. Of course lights had to come from the back and the sides to fill three-dimensional space. For a first assignment at the Old Vic in 1960 I had to add lighting pipes upstage for the very first time there, albeit to the chagrin of the stage carpenter.

I never knew what I wasn't meant to do.

The other "gift" provided by the rental business was the ability to explore new equipment from sources other than Strand. TP's very modest income was usually spent on buying one (or sometimes two) new lights from overseas rather than on our salaries. Initially in 1960 came the 500-watt 24-volt beamlight from Berlin's Reiche & Vogel (for Vanessa Redgrave's *As You Like It*) giving a shaft of light that could cut across any stage picture—and still my favorite instrument. (Also the Hersey/Bridge follow spot of choice in 1994). Next we got projection equipment from Berlin and later Lekos from Century. A very small quantity of something different distinguished the TP rental stock and expanded our market.

The breakthrough came on almost the very first show: *Lady at the Wheel* at the Lyric Hammersmith. Meeting the designer, Richard Negri, who later led me to director Michael Elliot and the 59 Theatre Company at the same theatre. Richard and Michael are two of the few real geniuses of my lifetime and proved an inspiration to me for two decades. Our next show together, Ibsen's *Brand*, was an enormous success and led to all my work in the busy sixties.

I remember that every show was a new adventure. Every one was a new process of discovery. I knew no rules, so made them up as I went along.

The time was obviously ripe. In fact probably too much came too soon. It quickly became clear that it was impossible to run the business, service the equipment, drive the van with deliveries, draw the plots, light the shows, and write out delivery notes and invoices. I was the only full-time member of staff. Bryan had a night job, and Viki, my wife, worked in TV during the day. We all derusted equipment at night. We needed help. First Jack Ritchie came to work on the equipment and then Robert Ornbo, to be my lighting assistant. Luckily he joined the week that three shows had to be lit at once. We joke that he arrived for work on Monday and went home three weeks later.

From those beginnings the firm developed. Inventory grew, with new and sometimes esoteric special equipment. Innovation became very important to me. Stencils for drafting lighting layouts, Lekos and PAR lamps from the U.S., beamlights and projectors from Germany. Designing and building an automatic 7-inch slide changer in 1966 was a big investment. So was exploring fiber-optics.

But in hindsight, the most important development was the lighting design team. I started with the conviction that if I lit a show, I lit it. Not an assistant. Assistants started in the rental shop to earn their keep. If I couldn't personally commit, then I would initially do a joint design, sharing credit, then try to ensure that my assistant graduated to full designer. Robert quickly made his own reputation and was soon joined by Robert Bryan, John B. Read, Nick Chelton, John Harrison, Michael Wilson, David Hersey and others, Andy Bridge and Benny Ball being two of a later generation.

The excitement among this growing group was something else. We lived, ate and drank lighting—sometimes too much of the latter. There was little or no jealousy, which is amazing. We all shared opportunities and problems, how to achieve such and such. What was the impact of that color? What could you do to cope with that situation? Wow, this director is hopeless, what do I do next? It seemed a Renaissance-like excitement, and the success of the group in their later lives is something of which I'm very proud. It may also suggest that a community of designers is a very productive idea.

Well, TP Lighting grew on. I sensed that our changing world could learn much from the emerging rock-and-roll business. We took over Brian Croft's TFA to lead us into concert lighting. Fast rigging led into industrial theatre and audiovisual and video technology. From the early days we had added a similar pioneering service in sound under David Collison. I became a producer in theatre, film and television. Theatre Projects Consultants began and gradually consumed my time.

It all began to get less personal. Commercial people came in to run the companies in a "businesslike" manner. Finally, by the early eighties there were two hundred or more staff. The lighting team drifted apart. Design was disliked by the management types, and I failed to support it. In truth I had begun to have reservations. Lighting was very important, but perhaps not *that* important. I had begun to sense that for some of the team it had become an obsession, out of proportion to the role that lighting should play in a production. Also for some, life at TP had become too much of a sinecure. Design opportunity came through the door and was allocated to you automatically. Perhaps our designers would do better independently, out in the real world. In any event we encouraged designers to go freelance, and most did profit from that independence. But sadly, a unique laboratory atmosphere was lost.

To finish that story, TP finally severely overreached itself. The commercial management types proved themselves to have feet of straw and perhaps sticky fingers. Over-expansion had built up unsustainable debt. We sold the lighting and sound businesses to the Samuelson Group. Theatre Projects Consultants retained its independence through a management buyout. TP Lighting is now happily a very successful part of Vari*Lite International. Who knows but their future with one of the world's most enterprising lighting companies may again present opportunities to push forward the boundaries of lighting and its design.

Chapter Twenty

# David Hersey

S ince moving from New York to London in 1968, David has been recognized as one of Europe's
leading lighting designers. He has designed the lighting for some two hundred productions for
most of England's major theatre, opera and ballet companies. His recent work is represented in
the West End by Cats, Starlight Express, Les Miserables, Miss Saigon and Oliver! Other
West End musicals include Song and Dance (sets and lights), Marilyn (sets and lights), Evita,
The King and I, The Sound of Music, Camelot, Metropolis, Chess and The Little Shop
of Horrors. On Broadway he has lit Evita, Merrily We Roll Along, Nicholas Nickleby, Cats,
Starlight Express, Les Miserables and Miss Saigon. For ten years he was lighting consultant to the
National Theatre, during which time he lit some twenty-six plays including the opening productions of
the Olivier and Lyttleton Theatres. He also lit the Royal Shakespeare Company's opening at the
Barbican as well as other productions for the RSC in London and Stratford. He has lit numerous
operas and ballets for the Royal Opera House, Birmingham Royal Ballet, English National Opera,
Glyndebourne, Ballet Rambert, London Contemporary Dance and Scottish Ballet. He is founder of
DHA Lighting, which concentrates on the design and manufacture of specialist lighting equipment and
effects. From 1984 to 1986 he served as chairman of the Association of Lighting Designers. His work
has been recognized by the following awards: Los Angeles Drama Critics Circle: 1979, Evita; Drama
Logue Critics Award: 1980, The Crucifer of Blood; Tony Awards: 1980, Evita, 1983, Cats, 1987,
Les Miserables; Drama Desk Awards: 1983, Cats, 1992, Miss Saigon; Maharam Foundation Design
Award: 1982, Nicholas Nickleby; Dora Mavor Moore Award: 1984, Cats; Civic Trust Award: 1985,
Exterior Lighting of the Old Vic Theatre.

I was born in upstate New York. As a child, I used to go out into the garden and pick up arrowheads, which was really quite wonderful.

By the time I got to high school I had moved to New York City. The shock of going from relatively country suburbia to the Village was a great awakening. I went to Oberlin College to study political science and international economics. I discovered the theatre in school. I acted, directed and even wrote a sequel to *The Tempest*. It's one of the things you can do when you are twenty. I did almost every job in the theatre except lighting. It was a mystery to me. In the background there were lots of levers that did things.

My parents wanted me to get a proper job and be a responsible citizen, and a life in the performing arts was not thought of in those terms. I did a bit of acting, a bit of stage management. Then I appeared as the stage manager in a production of *Six Characters in Search of an Author* at the Martinique Theatre, off-Broadway. A year later there was a bus-and-truck university tour. I did everything except drive the bus, including lighting. The show was originally lit by Jules Fisher, and not knowing anything about lighting, I had to reproduce some semblance of what he had done in eighty one-night stands around the country. We would arrive in the afternoon and do a show that evening: proper theatre. I'm sure it was absolutely awful, but by the end of it, something had begun to stir. I got involved in summer stock. I became a technical director. I directed a couple of shows and occasionally played a small part as a sort of token gesture. You could be in the wings, throw a cue, go out and do the scene, come back off and throw the next cue. By the time the late sixties came, I had done about seventy-five various regional kinds of productions. I was ready to come to New York.

This was 1968. Before settling down to life in the commercial theatre, I wanted to see what else was around, so I went to England. I didn't know anyone there. [To the author] I had your name. We met because Mike Wilson [a TP Project Manager] had done something with Paul Marantz. I had a phone number. I rang Mike, who said I should meet you.

I didn't know anything about you. It was funny. I'd been to the theatre the night before. We were chatting, and you asked if I'd seen any shows. I'd seen this production, *Wise Child*, with Alec Guinness. You asked me what I'd thought of the lighting, and I'd been rather off-hand about it. I discovered at the end of the conversation that you'd actually lit it. You had the good grace to offer me a job—I'll never forget this—for the princely sum of twenty-two pounds a week, rising after three months to twenty-five. But, of course, that was a turning point.

Being an American, I hadn't realized how much we are all Anglophiles. Anyway, soon came the opportunity to work with you at the Old Vic, and meet Olivier. My very first job, I assisted you on *Triple Bill*, with Tony Walton and all those slides. I remember staying up all night putting all those slides into the show, and Olivier coming and seeing it, and my staying up all night taking most of them out again. I knew that if I did decide to join your band of merry men, it meant being serious about lighting for at least a couple of years, at least to the exclusion of everything else, and one had to be prepared to do it on that kind of basis. Now, a couple of decades have gone by, and I'm still lighting.

What's turned out to be interesting is that I was occasionally a musician. I had a little group to help earn money to pay the way through school. I did do everything else first: some writing, some directing, some acting, a couple of sets, spent time calling cues in the corner—all those things, which are a huge help for lighting. The all-around thing is essential. I do actually believe that lighting is the big unifying element. It is, ultimately, the glue that can hold everything together. The fact that you are sensitive to all the aspects of it is absolutely essential. You can't apply it unless you have an instinctive, intuitive grasp of everything. These kids in America get so trained. You can get a master's degree in hook-up charts...from 1947 to 1951.

We jointly lit *Oh, Calcutta*. I moved it to various theatres in the West End. The first big show for me was *Evita*. I think I left TP in about 1971. In the end I felt constrained. I'd lost contact with you. You were very busy. So I went out on my own. I always believed you had to have a company as a lighting designer. You had to have something to fall back on. So, that's when I started DHA. When I first came to TP, if you wanted a gobo, you had a funny little man somewhere down Tottenham Court Road who would stamp them out by hand for a pound. Very expensive. So we at DHA started doing gobos, using the technology of other industries, just applying it to our needs. I didn't set out to be in business. I just wanted something so I had to go out and make it.

Then came a lot of very silly trade shows. My favorite trade show story was one of the last I did. In Newcastle, at 9:00 in the morning, we were doing our sales thing for about twenty-five men who didn't want to be there. They started with the sales director. He turns over a page and says, "Now, for my first set of figures," and out come the three dancing girls, and do a quick number. One of them was "Fraiche"; one was "Naturelle"; and the other "Au Delicate"—a vaginal deodorant. Something snapped. I just said, "Wait a moment. What am I doing? I do not believe this." And that was it. I had to stop doing that sort of thing.

The first show I did that really mattered was at the Old Vic, the Arrabel play, *The Architect and the Emperor of Assyria*. It changed me. It was a real benchmark. I learned to see on that show. Victor Garcia was such an odd animal. He spoke a funny French, and then only in metaphor. "Go away and rediscover light on the stage. When you've done so, come back and talk to me." We spent a month with four electricians in rehearsal trying things out on a small scale, exploring light—light sources, trying to start over again from scratch. By the time it got to the stage, one had a world in one's head with things to try. It was very interesting. I got Thorn to give us CSI's that had never been used on the stage before—sodium, mercury halide—we had all those things. If I hadn't been lucky enough to be with Theatre Projects, if there hadn't been some sort of retainer...there wasn't a lot of work around at the time. I could spend a month [in rehearsal]. I mean, today who could do that? It was just such a wonderful opportunity. That was the clear moment when maybe one was a lighting designer.

*Evita* was the first time I used beamlights as follow spots. Also, I began playing around with this thing we rather pretentiously call the "light curtain." The dynamic of the light in *Evita* was that we could do "white-outs" at the end of scenes. We are storytellers in what we do. As opposed to a collection of images, I am much more interested in the narrative side of lighting.

*Nickleby* was one of the most wonderful experiences I ever had in the theatre. It was very simple and very economical, very seamless. It was eight and a half hours long, and it was as if the entire creative team was tied together with an invisible umbilical cord. It was a wonderful voyage of discovery, too. I'd worked with John Napier before, but never with Trevor [Nunn], and I didn't even know who John Caird was. It was total chaos. Every man for himself. Amazing. We didn't have massive planning sessions; we just went with it. I mean, they were writing, and the ink was still wet. I would come out of the Aldwych Theatre having written eighty or ninety cues on the trot—kind of drunk with it in a way. I'd walk down the street, and think, "I've just written a hundred cues today. What have you done, mate?"

My favorite piece of kit is in *Cats* in London, the sweeping headlamp effect in the overture when the cat jumps up. It's a couple of Lekos with irises on a little bracket over the sound desk with a bit of string. They pull the bit of string, and the lights go across the stage. In New York, of course, it was this unbelievable machine, phenomenal cost, and it never worked very well either: wrong speed. I'm very pleased that the original piece of string is still in London.[3]

It's very different working in London and New York. The thing about England is that, by and large, people do what they do because they love doing it. It isn't just about money. I'm not saying that people in America only do it for the money, but it's gotten in the way a lot, creating attitudes toward working and penalties for infringing very rigid structures. Very often, in London, the lighting is allowed to develop and grow and nurture during the production process. Exactly the opposite in New York. The theatre is an empty box, and you start with nothing, partly because of economic pressure and partly because of interdepartmental disregard. It's a kind of anarchy—every man for himself. If you're not very organized and don't fight very hard for something very specific, you get steamrollered. If you want to put up a thousand-lamp rig in New York, no problem. It'll go up at a phenomenal rate. It's all labeled in the shop. But, once it's up, try moving a lamp! In England, you do your homework, but you have the luxury of allowing the design to grow as you work on it.

The most serious nasty was *Merrily We Roll Along,* which was a lesson on survival. (There was a lot of flack flying about. I was the first "wictim,"[4] we had badges made up for that show: "Wictim of the Day.") I was so thrilled to be asked to do a Sondheim musical on Broadway. The show opened cold in New York. The horror story was that when the show opened, half the audience left during the first preview. By the end of the show, half of the remainder left. The perception was that the show was perfect, except for the lighting. I had personally driven all these people from the theatre. Great screaming rows about what was the concept of the lighting. What do you want me to say? I light what I see on the stage, and if I don't see anything on the stage, I am in trouble. I feed off what the director and his actors are doing. This wonderful choreographer, Ron Field, came up to me and said, "I've just done you a great favor." I stepped back. He said, "I've just told everyone how terrible the lighting is. Now, you can get anything you want!" He went for everyone, the costume designer, the set designer, the cast...one day he went for Hal, and the next day Larry Fuller was the choreographer. Other people got fired, things got done, we did turn the corner, and eventually it did sort of get somewhere. We had just done *Nickleby* on Broadway, which had been a wonderful experience. I had begun to think about coming home, but after the *Merrily* wars I thought if this was what it was like at the top on Broadway, I'd be absolutely crazy to consider leaving London, where I had so many rich and varied sources of work.

*Les Miserables,* in many ways, was an extension of the form of *Nickleby.* What's interesting about a production like *Les Miz* is that when people that have spent most of their formative lives in classical theatre attack the musical, they bring on board something that is very different than if you've only worked in musicals all your life. It was an exciting working process. You have ingredients like the set and the music and a lot of revolve cues, which were worked out in advance but were changed in rehearsal. One of the highlights of the show was the suicide, and we didn't know until the last minute how we were going to do that. It was very late in the day when John [Napier] and Trevor and I had a session. It was actually John's idea, but it just clicked—simple and very obvious after the event. Those kinds of discoveries are wonderful. A lot of the drudgery, which is ninety percent of the time, seems worthwhile.

I don't turn down that many things that I am offered. Most of the things I get asked to do I'm interested in doing. And if I can fit it in, I do it. I'm protective about school holidays and family. I've been very lucky that I'm able to do that.

Theme parks, like expos, are sometimes exploring the sharp edge of technology. It's like a sandbox to experiment in. To take something very complex and really fine tune it to a quarter second; it's an exciting exercise. It's form, not substance. But, some of that feeds back when you do a play. We have a level of visual expectation, which is very different today than it was only quite recently. We are bombarded with videos, and the theatre can't be as complacent.

I don't see as much of other people's work as I should. I've always admired your work; I think you have a wonderful touch. Jules [Fisher] is a master of color, in a way that is breathtaking. *Grand Hotel* was magic. Jules is excellent, absolutely excellent. Andy [Bridge] does very good work—another one out of the stable. The TP lighting stable was a special experience. It worked because lighting was so embryonic, particularly in England. We were all a bit heady with the discovery of it. It was infectious. We'd go down to The Green Man[5] for a few hours, knock back a few pints, and talk about lighting. It was interesting how we could have so much ego under one roof and so little competition. I don't remember any backbiting or envy. I just remember the good times and the chats. Hardly any of us have had that sort of experience ever again. We don't sort of sit around and talk about the latest color, now do we? We were living it together and discovering it together. It was a very special time. Every single person in that group went on to do something important.

We used to do lots of angle calculations all the time. Geometry seemed very important. Now, one tends not to do that; one has an instinct what a lamp will do in a certain position. The rule is, surely, that there is no rule. You have to be able to gain control over the space, to allow the director to do anything he wants to do within that space. I do a two-pronged attack, on the text itself and on the space the design is offering. Sometimes you are able to influence that space and sometimes not. There is a curious duality. It's probably true that you do your best work when you are most invisible. When the lighting sticks out as an element in its own right, it's tricky. What you can do in one show is completely wrong in another. The rule is that every production is its own little universe. It has its own rules. Your job is to find out what those rules are for that particular show.

I suppose people can recognize my lighting. There are certain elements I tend to reach for. I don't consciously try to repeat myself. I try to start afresh. Repeating something never works. The curious thing is, it doesn't get easier—it actually gets harder. Maybe you become more self-critical.

I began using computers about five years ago for paperwork. In England there is never money for an assistant. If you have an assistant, you pay for it yourself, except in the very biggest spectaculars. In *Saigon* in London I had an assistant the management paid for and another that I paid for. In New York I had three assistants. Some of the assistants in America are wonderful. I'm a Macintosh person with my PowerBook at my side.

I have an agent. I've been very lucky and done some of the big, successful shows. I get a good fee and a royalty. I think the general situation of the profession must be very hard. If you are young and single, you can probably cope. How somebody who has to raise a family on it can manage, I don't know. In America if you hit it, it's okay—but there's so little work and so many good people.

*Stage Lighting Design*

All the advances in technology, computer control, et cetera, are, of course, very liberating. There are, of course, constraints of budget and time, but you do sit down with a white piece of paper. You can actually do almost anything you want to do. In a way, it was easier when you had built-in areas of limitation.

As far as the detail of control systems, they've all got their pluses and minuses. The fact is, the basic job they do is pretty amazing. Just like my PowerBook: unbelievable. How rapidly it's all changed—and God knows what will happen next. The repackaging of lightbulbs has actually not changed. There's not really been any serious revolution in that department. Wiggly, wobbly lights are fun to a point, but it's not an element that's going to take over everything. It allows you to delay a whole set of decisions. For me, the moment of truth is always the color call. I agonize and put it off forever. Something about actually saying this is the color, this is the lamp...it's an absolute commitment. Of course, the plotting process is very different now. It's not just marshaling groups of lights. It's marshaling whole groups of motors and very often means three or four systems all coming into one control. The need to rough things in and then clean them up later is paramount. It's now like the offensive/defensive specialists on a football team. You need the specialist to control the moving lights. Somehow, the whole thing must be integrated into a light board of the future.

Control system's unreliability is a nightmare. But at least now you can have the disk in your Mac under ExpressTrack and be able to reload. I think the totally unified control system must move closer. Whether there will be a serious improvement in light sources, I just don't know. I certainly hanker for greater extremes of contrast and brightness. Maybe things go in a cycle, and there'll be a revolt against whiz-bang spectacular shows, and we'll go back to something pure and unadorned. I have to say that the minute technology becomes an end in itself, I part company from it. I feel passionately that it's all only in support of what is, in the end, a very romantic idea.

I get asked all the time by students about a career in lighting. I tell them to go to the theatre, read as many plays as possible. I tell them a sense of literature is more important than electricity. You don't need to be able to mend a switchboard, and you shouldn't just go the technical route. People tend to think about lighting in just a technical way, and really, you should think about majoring in art history, not technology. You can learn all the technical stuff at any old time. There is no one way of doing it. I never really know what to say. If you really want to do it, you'll find a way.

# Chapter Twenty-one

# Pilbrow Story 4: Meeting "Sir"

The key stuck in the lock.

"Bugger."

Inside, the telephone was ringing. How could any idiot expect an answer when I was meant to be light years away in the Isle of Coll? Boxes under my right arm dropped, the key fiddled. I burst in and grabbed the phone.

"Hullo," yelled quietly but louder than necessary.

"Is Dickie Pilbrow there?"

"Yes." (Exasperated, I loathe being called Dickie.)

"May I speak to him please?"

"You are."

"Dickie, this is Larry Olivier."

"Oh, yes," leaving unsaid, "pull the other one."

"I'm calling you from Chichester. Where have you been?"

"On holiday...the Isle of Coll...the Hebrides...Sir!" the last word added because, although I was skeptical, that voice did have an exceptional sonority about it.

"I've been trying to find you. Can you come to Chichester?"

"When?"

"Right away."

"Sir...I've just driven over five hundred miles."

"Dickie, it's very urgent. Won't you come, please?"

Well, now it was obvious. It was Him. I'd only met him twice before, and then very fleetingly indeed, but that especially persuasive note of pleading was famous and quite irresistible.

"Well, I think I could come in the morning. I'll try."

"Please do, dear boy, as early as possible. I'll be rehearsing."

I put the phone down, rather awestruck.

A voice yelled stridently, "Come and get these bloody bags!"

"Yes, dear."

I settled in, basset hound and cat fed and whisky at hand, to fend off the rigors of miles down traffic-laden roads. Reality, after four weeks in the most isolated peace-ridden Hebrides, began to surface.

Viki said, "Who on earth was that?"

"Laurence Olivier."

"You're joking."

"No, I think it was him. It sounded like him anyway."

"How the hell would you know?"

"Well, it was sort of regal...like God...you know."

Very early next morning I was on the road. The beauties of Sussex flashed past as I wondered what on earth might have led to this summons. Chichester. I knew it had a new theatre with a thrust stage, based on the Guthrie Stratford, Ontario, model, and it was soon going to open under Sir Laurence's direction. That was about all I knew. Four weeks in the Islands was good insulation from the gossip of showbiz, or even theatre.

Well, the place was easy to find. It was impressive from outside, sitting in rolling parkland, still surrounded by a motley of builder's huts. I wondered when the place was meant to open. I should have checked.

Picking my way through frantic activity, I walked up a scaffold board right onto the back of the stage. Rehearsal was in progress. So was everything else. Hammering, sawing, fixing seats, shouting, beams of light piercing darkness: chaos as usual, except worse. A typical new theatre.

The stage manager found me and brought me into the presence. The image had been awesome; the reality, surprisingly scruffy, unshaven—and real.

"Dickie," (instantly, but with charm) "I've a desperate problem with the bloody lighting; you can't see anyone. Fellow lights garages, I think. Wait a moment." All the lights came up—and light dawned. It was *not* good.

I'd never worked a thrust stage, where the audience sits all around three sides, but the lighting problem was obvious. I saw that all of the lighting came from positions all round the stage from over the audience, like lighting in a football stadium. But light for actors has to surround them, it must clad them in light, as it does in nature. Most particularly, it must light their faces, so the audience can see. If the audience sits all round, then light must reveal the actor's face all around.

Here we had light coming from all around the edge, toward the stage.

Actors facing outward were well illuminated, but as soon as they turned inward, their faces were in darkness. The only way to light them was to raise the lights on the other side of the theatre, which then would shine straight into the eyes of the audience beyond. To light actors on a three-dimensional stage, half the lighting had to be above the stage, shining down at a steep—but not too steep—angle, to light the faces of all the actors around the edge of the stage as they faced toward the center, without blinding the audience.

"Sir Laurence, there's a straight answer. The lights are in the wrong place."

"I knew it," he said with some glee. "Where should they go?"

"Well, about half of them should be rehung over the stage, to light actors facing onstage."

"Right, we'll do it." And orders were issued.

I retired to the bowels of the theatre to consult with the chief electrician.

"Fucking impossible," was the response from him. "There's no way to mount them, no way to plug them in. The fire people won't allow anything temporary anyway." (That seemed likely, as new types of theatre do give fire authorities apoplexy.)

"Well, how long will it take?" I asked.

"At least three days and we bloody open tomorrow!"

My heart straightway nosedived. That was news, the one piece of information that I didn't have.

I knew that, with the best will in the world, the changes that were essential would take days. The building, being unconventional, had no means of hanging anything over the stage, and moving half the lighting rig was a huge task. I anticipated Sir's intense question.

"So, what else can we damn well do?"

"I'm sorry, Sir, I don't believe there is any alternative. You can't have a light hit an actor's face at the right angle unless it's in the right position to start with."

Well, that conversation went on for a long time.

Finally I left. Sir Laurence was somewhat less than gracious, clearly bitterly disappointed at his new (temporary) lighting consultant. Driving back through the surrealistically beautiful countryside, my thoughts were black: abject failure.

My first chance to work for the man who had been an idol since childhood. How many times had I sat through *Henry V,* hiding in the cinema while the house changed; how many times played the William Walton record and thrilled to "Once more unto the breach, dear friends"; how often relived a black-and-white *Hamlet* and a hypnotizing *Richard III*. My mother took me to many performances of the Old Vic at the New Theatre where, for six shillings, we were spellbound by pinnacles of performances of the English theatre.

I had met the man twice, first after a performance of *Venus Observed* at the (later lost) London's St. James Theatre. As a teenager I waited at the stage door after a performance. Seemingly hours went by. Everybody else drifted off. At last after midnight the great couple emerged, sweeping by. Speechless, I watched. Vivien Leigh stopped and turned.

"Hullo," she said. "You're late."

"I'm sorry."

"Where are you going?"

"Victoria Station," I stuttered.

"Come along then," she laughed. In a dream—and a very large black car—I was wafted to my suburban train and deposited with two autographs.

The next time I was a twenty-three-year-old assistant stage manager in my first West End job. My old drama school, Central, was organizing a benefit, and I was drafted to help (despite my recent departure from the establishment in some disgrace). My first task was to deliver a package to the stars, the Oliviers. I rang the bell to a small house near Eaton Square. Angry voices were raised inside and there was a long wait. As I was about to sneak away, the door opened and Olivier stood there. I stammered out my mission and passed over the goods. The door shut.

My next contact was the phone call from Chichester.

Driving away, it seemed like the whole world had come to an end...never again. I would probably never work again.

# Chapter Twenty-two

# Peter Maradudin

*ince 1984, when he designed his first professional production (*Ma Rainey's Black Bottom *on Broadway), Peter has designed the lighting for more than 150 productions at most of the major regional theatres in the United States, including the Kennedy Center, The Guthrie Theatre, The Mark Taper Forum, Seattle Repertory Theatre, The La Jolla Playhouse, The Alliance Theatre Company, Berkeley Repertory Theatre, The Repertory Theatre of St. Louis, The Denver Center Theatre Company, The Old Globe Theatre, Milwaukee Repertory Theatre, South Coast Rep and The American Conservatory Theatre in San Francisco, where he is currently designer in residence. His most recent Broadway effort was the Pulitzer Prize–winning American epic,* The Kentucky Cycle.*

Seventeen productions is a pretty average year, which is something ridiculous like a show every three weeks. I would like to do it less, because I'm finding that, after a certain point, there are all of these other things you'd much rather do with your life than sit in a theatre.

I just love to travel—I always have. I grew up in a traveling family and I don't get to do it as much anymore, at least not for fun. I've realized I enjoy days where I don't have to do anything. They're starting to get more valuable as I'm getting older. The other thing is that when you do seventeen shows a year, you find that most of them aren't going to be special, and most of them are just jobs. It doesn't mean they can't be fun, but as an artist, you start to thinking, "Boy, I'm not doing art seventeen times a year." It would be great to start to really select the projects that I really wanted to do.

I just want to do stuff that pushes me. I don't want to do, say, a *Philadelphia Story*—how many can you do with the same sunlight coming through the window in act 3? I would much rather do a really rock-'n-roll *King Lear*. I would love to do something—you're starting with the *text* first of all. I want to push my boundaries. I want to see things that no one else has ever done before. Finally, I'm probably getting those things. I've said this to a bunch of my artistic directors—I said, give me, next year, the biggest, nastiest, ugliest, hardest, most impossible show in your season. There are some plays I'll make exceptions for, like *A Long Day's Journey into Night*. I've done that now four times in my life and I'll do it forever, because every time you do it, it's a test of where you are as a lighting designer: some plays are like that.

Someone asked me, "For someone being interested in becoming a lighting designer, what course of study would you recommend?" And I said, "Well, I would study anything but lighting design." I was an engineering major with a minor in music; I ultimately took a degree in history. But, I said, "Study a foreign language. Read as much as you can get your hands on. Go to Europe, go to the Orient. See whatever. All of that is going to make you a much better designer than what makes a Leko tick or how to program a Light Palette." The most interesting people I work with are the people that have that philosophy. What I'm finding, is the more I end up working, the more...you do twenty shows a year, you find that you're removed from all the things that originally made you a good designer. I would really love to go back and do all those things that got me interested in art in the first place, and interested in culture, and made me realize how good it is to be alive in the first place; otherwise why am I doing this? Otherwise, I'm spending thirty weeks a year in dark rooms.

When I get angry is when I'm dealing with producers who don't take good care of the people who are working with them. I'll say, "Now why are you...?" Or [if there's] a director who's yelling at somebody, it's like, "Why are you yelling at that person?" We're about—not necessarily making people happy—but bringing them together. And we're doing this for people, we're not doing it for money. Unless you recognize that this is humanistic, that this is about good things for the soul, then why are you doing it?

I started with music. Going through high school, I was in rock-and-roll bands, and when I went to Stanford as an undergraduate, I was trying to figure out how to combine music and math and physics. I grew up in a household with a physicist father, a historian mother—both of whom were incredibly cultured people. I wanted to be a musician very badly, but I recognized that that was an impossible life choice. It's so hard to make a living as a musician. But I remember being struck at a rock concert how a band could extend itself visually through the lighting. I thought, this is great. If I'm going to be a musician, it'd be fun to know how to do that just for the heck of it. The theatre department had a class in lighting design. I had no idea that you could teach such a thing! I was that ignorant about it. Michael Ramsaur was teaching it, and it was one of those things where you're in the room and someone is telling you things and you're talking about things that you have absolutely no experience with before and it all makes perfect sense. I understood it really well. Although, when it came to dimming, it still confused me at the time—where the electricity came from—but in terms of, you have a light here to do such and such, all that made perfect sense. So, I took it for the second quarter for the fun of it. By the end of that, I was completely hooked. Michael gave me a tremendous amount of encouragement; I think I was the first student he'd had in a long time that was that interested and pursued it that religiously. I would get my friends together and we would put together our own shows. During my sophomore year, we did *Hair*. We took an abandoned lecture hall and built the stage in it. We took out all the seats. It was complete guerrilla theater. I was also the music director for the show, so I was in the band. We would set aside one evening when I would sit and write all the cues, and then I would have to get back on the stage and play in the band.

So, that's how it got started. I just kind of fell in love with it, because it really was a marriage of all the things I'd been interested in doing, and also the thing I loved about it was that so few other people understood it at all. I mean, I was the one person studying lighting at Stanford. I figured, sure, there are lots of people studying English. But on top of that, you can't touch it. You can't eat it. You can't smell it. Well, you can sometimes. I thought, there's something really wonderful and mystical about all this. And a number of times people would come up and say, "How do you figure all this out?" And I would say, "Well, you can draft it out. You can punch in the numbers, or you can see it in your head." And I would actually do all three. But I could *see* it, and that's something I realized that not many people can do. You think, this is great. I'm doing something that very few people know about—and even to this day, when I'll go out and meet a group of people and everyone else starts asking, "What is it that you do? You're a lighting designer? You work in the theater?" It's always, "Oh, that sounds fantastic." They see the drawings sometimes and they have no idea what a light plot means. It's just like anything else where you feel that you have something in your pocket that nobody else does. And that's fun.

I went straight to Yale. I'm really baffled as to why they took me. Jennifer [Tipton] once did say, "Well, we could tell that you were about ideas." And I think that might have been true. That was a fantastic experience.

Jennifer was an interesting surprise. I had never thought of lighting in the terms she does. I mean, to her it really is quite a mystical thing, and it's such an intellectual process as well. It's wonderful—when I was first being exposed to that, she would ask questions that I had never been asked in the four years I had been studying. It had everything to do with what the play was about, and she just made me think in ways I'd never thought before. I assisted for the first time at Yale, and had a terrible experience doing that and swore never to assist again. I was dealing with a third-year student who decided that I should learn to be the perfect assistant immediately and take the abuse that assistants should learn to take. I learned a lot from that experience, because to this day I challenge you to ask anybody who has ever assisted me—I am the sweetest man to my assistants. I take such good care of them. I give them a tremendous amount of slack, because I had a terrible time. I could not do it. First of all, I was just always distracted by other things. I always wanted to watch the stage. And the idea of number crunching and having that at my finger tips was just, at the time, not what I wanted to do.

But going to Yale was great because it was this incredible think tank. I learned more from my classmates than anything. Just being in an environment where everyone is challenging you all the time to justify what you're doing—why did you do it, design it like that? What did the director say? When you got together in the room, what did you say to each other and what were the *words* that you used? That, actually, was the biggest thing, learning to talk about something that you couldn't describe easily and that you couldn't necessarily draw, and so, often, discussions would be about what words did you use. What was the language that you used when you were talking this over? When you say soft lighting, and when a director says, what does that mean to you? I'll challenge directors and say, "What does that mean to you?" And then I'll say to the lighting designer, "Now, when he or she says that to you, what does that mean? And do you actually connect, or when he says 'soft' does that mean there are no edges, or does that mean that the light comes from everywhere, or does that mean there are no shadows, or the cueing is seamless?" It could mean any one of a number of things.

I think the first thing I ever saw Jennifer light, I did not like the lighting at all. But I saw her do some stuff that just was almost like seeing God. You're in the theatre and you're seeing light used in a way that you never thought you could do.

I knew immediately upon arriving on the East Coast that I did not want to stay. I just knew that New York was not for me, so when I moved back out here—which I knew I always would—it was fascinating to find out that nobody else had done that. I was the first Yale-trained lighting designer that I knew on the West Coast. I walked into South Coast Repertory [SCR] and within a couple of weeks of talking to Martin Benson and David Emmes—I went in and visited with Tom Ruzika and introduced myself— they hired me to do a show right off the bat and then hired me nonstop ever since. I do three to four shows a year for them. I suspect a lot of that had to do with them thinking, "Wow, we've got an East Coast designer that lives here. We don't have to fly him in. He lives down the street." That actually helped a lot. They take you seriously when you're a Yale graduate in a way that they might not otherwise. If people ask me, are you a Yalie,

I'll say yes. But if they don't ask me, I won't tell them, because I also know that there are a lot of people who resent that fact that there is that mystique and that cachet.

There is one thing that used to make me so mad—and still does. Jennifer and Ming Cho Lee—they're artists pure and simple. They're not even about talking about money. And that was one thing, that going through three years of school not having a clue as to what to do [about money]. We got out, and that was hard, in terms of getting work—negotiating a contract—you had no clue.

I think in my first year out, I did about ten shows. Sharon Ott was a new artistic director who saw my work at SCR, and that began another wonderful relationship. I started to do a lot of work in Berkeley. And so suddenly I had a whole new southern California and northern California circle, and from there it's just circles within circles. Each show you do someplace, you meet a new set designer, a new director, and then next time they think, "Well, gosh, Peter did a pretty job. Let's call Peter." I do remember pulling this great trick getting that resume to Berkeley Rep early on. I had just done my first show at South Coast Rep, so I would write to Berkeley Rep, send them my resume, and say, "I'm coming up for a meeting at ACT. May I talk to you and stop in?" Then I would write to ACT, and say, "I'm coming up for a meeting at Berkeley Rep, may I stop in and here's my resume." And I would write to San Jose Rep and I would say, "I'm coming up for meetings at Berkeley and ACT." So, I would set up all these appointments and meet them all, and it was true that at least if they would actually take the time to meet me, they would eventually hire me. As long as you do a good job—a good job being defined by doing it on time and under budget and doing it nicely and everyone getting along—then they'll ask you back.

Most of the people that I was working with were all so nice, but anybody I didn't like working with, I just didn't work with them anymore. So it was always easy to be nice and pleasant. I think I did get a reputation of being easy to get along with, and they would like that about me. A lot of it is just good professional behavior. And I'll go a little bit beyond that—try very hard to be kind to the people who are working for you, generous to the people who you're working with, and pace it with the people who you're working for. If you follow those rules, then, maybe that situation wasn't fun, but maybe the next time they'll ask you to do a show with other people that will be more fun.

I remember something Robert Moss from Playwright's Horizons said. He was one of the first directors I ever worked with, a fantastic, very sweet man. He would always tell me, "I always say to myself when I start rehearsals, this is the one where they find me out." I feel things that way every time I get ready to focus a show: this is the one where they'll find me out. They'll finally realize I have no clue what I'm doing. But I manage to pull it off. What's sort of nice is that, as the years go by, I realize that I actually sort of do know what I'm doing, and through time it's a little less unnerving. I still get nervous every single time. I don't know if other designers do or not, but I do. Every time, I go, "Oh God." I find it comforting to know that Jennifer does that too. She says, "Oh God. Can I do this?" I figure that means that we care.

I look at someone like Jennifer or Pat Collins and I'm amazed, inspired—and I think they're nuts. How do they do it? I mean, Pat does twenty-something shows a year. She's a maniac. But they must really love it and they thrive on it. And I don't think I could do it. When I'm fifty, I don't think I'll be doing this. Maybe I will be. I got to do a lot of the kinds of projects I've wanted to do at a really early stage in my career, and I'm spoiled. Where to from here? I ask myself that so much, and there are all these answers.

It gets hard because anything I've encountered outside of the theatre tends to be much more soulless. I did a project for Universal Studios in Orlando, "ET's Adventure." I was one of several in a chain of designers. It was one of the most disheartening experiences. The work actually looked pretty good, but the environment that I was working in was hopeless. I had two audiences: both the lowest common denominator. They would do tests and figure out that from these ride vehicles, the public could grab anything, break it off, throw things, and would redesign accordingly. Then you're designing for corporate vice presidents who wouldn't know art if it bit them on the butt. I mean, really. I was so frustrated. Also in theatre, when you show up and focus is postponed a day because the set is taking a long time to get loaded in, I mean, that's serious business. Heads are rolling. I showed up in Orlando to focus this thing on January 8th, and it was the 27th when we finally got started. I just said, "I'm not cut out for this." The income was fantastic. But the reason I took it in the first place was less for the money than just to do something different. Still, I do think about industrial work of all types, architectural work. There is something about lighting a building that's going to be around for awhile....

I was in La Jolla doing *The Glass Menagerie* when the Rodney King beating thing was just exploding, and I have to tell you it was such a strange feeling. I was so distracted, because I knew that we were working on this really beautiful little play out of harm's way, and as far as I was concerned, La Jolla was a very comfortable, beautiful community, very affluent, but the world as I knew it was blowing up outside. I thought, what am I doing and what does this all mean? I was able to reconcile it by saying, "Well, at least I am involved in a creative activity, and I am working on a beautiful, delicate play, and that's better than burning a house." I think there's still value in what I'm doing, but it made me think a lot about all the other things that I could or should be doing.

I really want to travel. Some of the most fun I've ever had was when I took two shows to Singapore for the 1990 Theater Arts Festival. That was a blast! I went across the way on opening night to see a Japanese company, Sankai Juku, perform. I was transfixed. It changed my life. I said, "This is what I want to be doing." You could tell that these people were so dedicated to this art that they were doing that it was something that transcended just theater or dance. It was visually fantastic, and showed imagination that I had just not seen in our country. I was thinking, "Oh, God, we've got this production of *You Never Can Tell* where they're all standing around in period clothes." I just thought, "Oh dear."

It's hard to define, but you feel it when you're in a preview or at a show that isn't challenging you—it's being done for reasons other than art. And I'm seeing that a lot now. You look at next season for so many theaters in this country, and it's all crowd-pleasing stuff. They're all the things that they know are going to sell tickets, and there's no sense of adventure what-soever. A big reason that I do this job is that every job is supposed to be different from the one before, and as soon as that is no longer the case, then why do it? I know Jennifer talks about going to Maine and just paint-ing. She says, "When I turn sixty, I'm just going to Maine and paint." And, I'm thinking, "Boy, when I turn forty, I'm going to Maine and paint." Or the south of France and paint. We all have our Maine or our south of France where we want to go and paint and read books and drink a lot of good wine. After that, I start getting hazy.

I do love what I do. I once said that as much as I hate it, I love what I do. I really feel that way. I mean, there are times when you just hate the fact that they're still giving you notes at one in the morning, and you just think, I'd rather be anywhere but here. But, there are some things I really love about it. I'll bang out every cue in the show that I think should be there. Just rough sketches. And then the fun part is to see how close I actu-ally got. And then there's the time when it's dead on and there's no more fun in the world. I mean, that's it. That's as fun as it gets. It's like, I nailed it! We talked about it, I plotted it, I focused it, I nailed it, and it feels right—and that happens once in awhile. And then it's all worth it—all the airplanes and hotels and all that.

I think about income all the time. That's another reason why I start thinking of applying what I do know about life to other fields, because I think I've maxed out what I can earn as a freelance lighting designer. I can now pretty much predict that I'm going to make a certain amount of money each year. Coming out of school, I always assumed that I could keep growing and keep getting more and more, and now I've realized there's a certain amount of work I can physically handle in a year. So I know what my limit is and I know what the fees are now. I'm lucky I get the good ones. Now what I want is that long-running Broadway musical. [Laughs.] Andy Bridge is the one I think about.

What I'm starting to do is say, "Well, maybe not that one, but what else are you doing this season? I'll tell you which ones I'm interested in." I don't know if people are thinking, well, that's just too much chutzpah, but I figure, there's no harm in asking. Give me the hard ones, or if you don't give it to me this year, give it to me next year.

Lately, I have to tell you the number of depressing designer get-togethers I've been at where we're all talking about, "Oh, did you hear where this theater just folded? I was going to do that show, but that theatre just collapsed in front of me. They just slashed their budget by so many thousands." It makes me so angry I cannot tell you. This is a scandal in this country that we spend so little on the arts, on education. It's like, California is facing a huge deficit all of a sudden, and the first things that are going are the educational programs. I keep thinking, "Wait a second! This is all so backward." The things that make life worth living—they're learning, they're being educated, they're being exposed to things—and it makes me so mad that communities can be so short sighted. I wish that students were better educated. If they're exposed to these things, they'll be better people. I just think about how much I enjoy life, and it's all because of the things I was taught to appreciate. I wish there was an awareness of all these cultures. I wish there was a blindness to color. I just wish people were more generous and more understanding. I was lucky when I went to high school. I had programs when we would go to the symphony and we would have classes: "You're going to listen to Mahler's something-or-other, and we'll listen to the movement and talk about it, and now when you hear this in the concert hall, you'll know what's going on." That was fantastic. You couldn't find a class like that now—in this state.

I figure anybody that has anything to do with theatre, it's self-preservation if nothing else. The audiences are going to start vanishing on you, because they're going to grow old and die. I want to address certain issues that are important to me and people like me at my age, and they're not going to the theatre. So, how does that make you feel? I say, it makes me feel like we should be doing videos for MTV. I don't know what; maybe. I wouldn't mind doing a video. It used to be guerrilla theatre at Stanford, and the energy was fantastic. I don't know how many days I'd go on four hours of sleep. I managed to do it, and am no worse for the wear now. I do miss that a lot. And now, it's much harder. Our visions have become more expensive. That's one of the things I've found. The things I want to do sometimes are more expensive than some theatres can afford. When we did the first production of *The Kentucky Cycle* at the Intiman, I just said, "The budget is meaningless." My electrician, we all just said, "The show's too important to be sitting here wondering if we're on budget. We'll do it. We'll go steal that lighting instrument from somebody." Well, thank God they did it and produced it.

I always love it when an audience...you can actually hear them think, "How did they do that?" That's wonderful. I love it when they really think they've been taken for a ride. They're exhilarated. That's what I want to do. What is driving me now is trying to find those projects and do them.

# Chapter Twenty-three

# Pilbrow Story 5: Hospitality

The production desk is the lighting designer's real home. When I began in the late fifties it seemed important to establish a proper base of operations. A dear friend from drama school, Nigel Birch, who sadly died of leukemia in his early twenties, custom built a lighting desk, which for many years traveled with me from show to show.

Laminated black Formica, it was adjustable in height to fit various conditions of theatre, and beneath its surface it contained a long drawer that held all the necessary accessories: lights, stationary, lots of papers, and other essential supplies. I personally always light using a lighting layout plan as my map, which, with the script, occupies most of the desk's surface. To the left was a recess that housed communications equipment and hospitality. We're talking of the days before talk-back systems were common place, and one of my first "innovations" was to buy two Pye radio walkie-talkies. To operate them, one needed a transmitting license from the government. The two radios' call signs were Projects Able and Projects Baker. These were the smallest walkie-talkies that money could buy and only measured eight by four by fourteen inches. Each was carried like a satchel on a strap over your shoulder; but when at the desk, they lived in the aforementioned recess. There was also room for a bottle of whisky.

Now there is some truth in the rumor that English lighting designers drink too much. Certainly the American taboo that forbids alcohol in the theatre is thought to be very bizarre in Britain. So a bottle of scotch and soda in the hinged section of the desk, which provided a flat surface for glasses, proved popular. Late into the night perhaps tensions could be somewhat mollified by a small glass of refreshment for the design team and their director.

I was somewhat taken aback when I first came to the United States to do the projection for *A Funny Thing Happened on the Way to the Forum*. The magnificent Jean Rosenthal was the lighting designer, who, at the load-in at the Shubert Theatre in New Haven, quickly introduced me to the idea that one had to go across the road to the neighborhood bar to learn that a screwdriver was not only a tool used to insert screws into wood. I always felt Jean was somewhat sympathetic to the idea that a little hospitality would ease the process, but tradition was too strong. Her first-night gift to me was particularly touching. Inside the package was a large American-style sandwich with layers of cheese and bologna and a large bite out of one end. But hang on! On closer examination, it turned out to be plastic, and this bite was a screw top. Dear Jean had decided that I needed an invisible aid: a flask disguised as lunch.

Lighting is after all just a job. No matter how seriously we take the art of it all, it isn't brain surgery! No matter the tensions, the frights, the ambition, we might as well try to enjoy it.

Success in lighting is also not only about one's skills in manipulating light; it's also about managing the politics of the situation. The enthusiasm and dedication of your crew has to be maintained. Your relationship with your design colleagues, your director and your producer has to be optimized. Almost every production is fraught with many tensions. There are heavy frustrations for almost everybody. Nothing ever seems to work the first time, and everyone is loaded down by all sorts of different problems. The director may scream at the lighting when in fact his worry is miscasting or an actor's temperament problem. Electrical hang ups may be tensions over collaboration between different department crew heads. Stage management may miss accurate cue placement by trying to simultaneously cope with a problem about dressers. The producer's nearly always more worried about money than you are.

So a cheerful demeanor can be quite an asset. There are some designers who get their way by shouting and tantrums, but I've never been able to do that. I'm always afraid if I tried it people would laugh. You have to follow your own temperament. But be warned, lighting is only half the job; living with your colleagues and making them want to employ you (or work with you) next time is a pretty high priority.

On my latest, *Show Boat*, it seemed a nice idea to offer a bit of hospitality. We decided upon a permanently overflowing bowl of M&Ms (Smarties for the English reader). It's a big show, and the production went on forever. While Garth Drabinsky, the producer, is a big spender, even he balked at $364 worth of M&Ms. The lighting designer had to pick up the tab. Was it worth it? You bet. The lighting production desk (only one of twelve desks in the auditorium—a big show!) made it as a social center. So perhaps a new slogan might be, *a pound of M&Ms a day, keeps the horrors away!*

# Chapter Twenty-four

# Luc LaFortune

*uc studied at McGill University in Montreal, Quebec. His design credits include lighting designer for the Gypsy Kings' 1991 European tour, the G-7 Summit in Halifax, June 1995, and many lighting designs for Cirque du Soleil; among them* Le Cirque Réinventé *North American and European tours;* Nouvelle Expérience *in Las Vegas and on tour;* Saltimbanco, *which toured North America and Japan, and was on tour in Europe in 1995-96;* Mystère *at the Treasure Island Theatre, Las Vegas (1993-98); and* Alegria, *on tour in North America 1994-95.*

I was studying psychology in university, but after the second year I knew that I wasn't going to be a psychologist. I had done some theatre in high school and that was fine, but making a living out of theatre, that was a whole different story. So to my parents' dismay and disapproval, I applied for the theatre program at Concordia University in Montreal. Originally it was set design that attracted me, but that didn't last. I did find out, though, that lighting played a big part in defining space, and I thought that was interesting.

I did the whole program, which lasted about three years. It really was a good program. The theatre had been completely rebuilt, because during the season before I entered there had been a fire. One of the plays may have been a bit too controversial. In any case, the theatre had been completely refurbished: new flying system, new spots, new everything. Also, because of the university setting, funds weren't so much of a problem—

which had nothing to do with reality, it is not the real world. [Laughter from Luc and Dawn.]

At the time that I was studying, I was also working in the industry as a stagehand, so I had an idea of how it was outside in the real world. Mostly I was working in the English theatre in Montreal. I was also a stagehand for loading in rock-and-roll tours that pulled into town.

The thing I liked about rock-and-roll gigs was that there were almost no sets. I was fascinated by how lights could completely redefine space. You pretty much decide the *image*—the vision the spectator is going to have. It's an incredible power—to take a complete space, a piece of scenery or an action, and decide that this is the *vision* that people are going to have, and this is how I am going to try to influence them. Because you are obviously trying to evoke something. And I thought that this was pretty exciting.

During shows I sat next to the board operators as much as I could to see what they were doing. When I started to design lights for Cirque du Soleil, I tried some of the things I had seen. I was surprised. I didn't think they'd go for a harder edge, for something along the lines of rock and roll, but they seemed to have enjoyed it. Of course I had to give it a bit of a twist because of the techniques involved out on the stage, but that was also interesting.

I did some straight theater, which I didn't really enjoy. I have a problem with "classics" being done over and over again. But then again, that's not fair, because there is always a new generation of theatergoers who want to see these plays in a more traditional way. But I think when you have done *King Lear* once, you kind of go, "Well, heck," unless you have the opportunity of working with a director who really wants to give it a twist. I'd like to do dance, though; but the dance, the technique of lighting dance, I'm not very familiar with. So I would have to study that. I enjoyed musicals a lot. The combination of action, in the stage sense, and music, I find very interesting. Also in musicals everything is so big.

But the moment that I got out of university, I went to work for Cirque du Soleil. What happened was that I graduated in 1984, which coincided with the 450th anniversary of the discovery of Canada, by the French at least. The government at the time was looking for ways to mark these celebrations and was open to suggestions. The founders of Cirque du Soleil, who had been doing some theatre on stilts for some time, applied for a grant and—poof—voila. One of the guys who had been working with them was also studying with me at university. He asked me if I wanted to go out and tour with them. I had already sent out a few applications but had gotten no response, so I said, "Sure, why not!"

Of course this was the cherry on the cake for my parents—initially, their son dropped psychology to go do theater, and the first job that he gets upon graduation is to tour with a circus, pitching a tent in the Quebec countryside! What happened?! You know, it was funny, because the first few years while I was working in the industry, I remember my dad kept on saying, "What about psychology?" Keep in mind that the first Cirque tour was only three months. In any case, at one point, I had to put my foot down as they say, and that was the last we heard of it. That also coincided with my first lighting design. It was really important to my parents that I not just be...I want to be careful, because I don't want this to sound...how do you say, *perjoratif*....They didn't want me to be pitching tents or pushing road cases around too long. There needed to be some creativity involved. I tried to get them interested in my lighting. I guess when they saw it for themselves, things changed. So, that worked.

When I started designing Cirque du Soleil, I had already been touring with them for two years as their board operator. They tried two designers initially. Both were from theatre, but every year they were considering new designers, because I guess they weren't happy. So I told them, "Look, you're not going to find a circus designer in Montreal, and the person who's got the most experience in circus is me." I said, "Why don't you let me try it?" And they said, "OK."

We opened the show in Vancouver in '86, and we got really good reviews. The '86 tour was also the tour that put us in contact with the people at the Los Angeles Art Festival, which was our first show in the U.S. We took a gamble with the Art Festival, because we told them, "We'll go, but there is only one condition—we want to do the opening night, the gala." And they agreed. We took all the money that we had and bought airline tickets. If it didn't work, there was no money left to bring people back home. We would have all been stuck. So that is why the gala opening was so important.

The Festival was great. We were headlining with acts such as the *Mahabarata* and the Lyons Opera Ballet, and a bunch of companies like that. So all of a sudden, it took circus and elevated it. And it worked, it just sold out. From that moment on, it was sold out for a year and a half. We toured places like New York and San Francisco, and everywhere it was the same story, sold out. Then in '89, we made a mistake. We went out with the same show in places where we'd already been, with a new cast, and that didn't work. The show had been developed around the personalities of the actors and the acrobats. They had been as much a part of the creative process as the designers. I don't think you can substitute actors so easily.

About one year before *Nouvelle Expérience* opened we started talking about the show. We wanted to do things differently than we had, but we also wanted to maintain some of the circus tradition.

I feel that with working with Cirque du Soleil, I am one of the luckiest designers around, because it allows me that flexibility. The artistic director and I talk about the show a lot. We don't talk about scenario or blocking or anything like that. We talk about the action. We talk about the intention. We talk about our motivation, what it is we are trying to say. What's our gut feeling about the show. And once we share a clear vision we go into rehearsals. The rehearsal process is a bit ad hoc, it's very intuitive. We still don't have any idea about who is going to enter at what time, on stage right or stage left. We still don't know that. We know what the set is going to be, we know who the characters are going to be and how they relate to each other, but that's it. All that's left is to write the show.

It's also interesting, because we try not to confine ourselves to a scenario. So we don't have the obligation of justifying a scenario or an action throughout the whole show. You know, as you walk into a theatre and your characters inhabit the set for the first time, you start finding out things that otherwise you never would have known. When we first go into rehearsals, there are a few lights hanging. I prefer to just sit in the house and look at what's happening, and then make *propositions* to the artistic director: "Well, I could do this, or I could do that, and then that would give you the possibility of doing something else." The thing that happens though is that during the day I just sit there and let the director do his thing, and try to get a sense of where all this is going and design as we go along. It makes for rather long days, though, because of course while the director is working, we can't really go onstage and start hanging. So instead we wait and hang at night, a little here and a little there, and eventually things fall into place.

Of course there are drawbacks in the way we work, because we are always up against impossible deadlines. *Nouvelle Expérience* was rough. One week before we opened we still had problems taking what we had discussed as our intentions and translating them onto the stage. It got really tense at one point. You could feel the tension and the pressure, but eventually things fell into place. When the show opened, it wasn't quite ready, but it evolved quickly. I guess opening night was no longer a concern. It seems that our shows constantly evolve, from the moment they open to the moment they close, which is very exciting. It would be difficult for me as a designer not to be able to move and change things around. You know, whether we're designing lights or costumes, it seems we're always thinking, "Oh, I could do this or I could do that, or I do could something different." I have been adding cues and updating things. It keeps the show fresh. And I have a very tolerant crew—they don't mind that too much.

Also if everything is canned and cued, it can create a problem because of the nature of the show. We need to be able to override real quick. People onstage get hurt and, because we do up to ten shows a week, some of the acts move around. The actors don't just do their act, they also participate in the action and they will maybe personify three or four characters, so that there is quite a lot that's asked of them. But it's also very exciting.

I look at black-and-white photographs and look at the play of light, which is the reason why I like black-and-white photography. I don't want to fall into the pattern of being too concerned with colors, at least not in the initial stages of design. I think that could be a mistake. Colors tend to be very suggestive, sometimes too suggestive.

I like to look at artwork and go see shows...just go see shows. You have to feed from something. I hate to say this, but there are too many shows that I saw that I was disappointed with. You can't let the technology influence your design, whether you're doing lights, or sets, or whatever. When you have huge effects where people just see the effect and not see what the effect is doing to the action—whether it is supporting it or taking it in a new direction—forget it, you know. Why are you doing that? What's the point?

I see a danger in having a set and lighting designer in one person. In Montreal there was a show where the artistic director also did the set and lighting design. I have a bit of a problem with that, because it reflects a limited vision. The reason I have a problem with that is that you are appealing to a lot of people. People need to go and see a show and at least be able to recognize something in there, something that's personal to them. If they can't associate with anything, then they're just sitting in the audience and they're...witnessing a show, and that's different.

With Cirque du Soleil we all contribute to the show through our lighting, costumes, sets and music, and choreography. We all write the show together. Our shows really are a succession of images. The downside of having so many contributors is that at one point you have to make it all fit, to blend all these elements together. The "filtering," as we call it, allows me to go up to the musical director and say, "Well, that's not quite the vision I had" of this act—and we discuss it and start moving things around. And it's not to say that it's necessarily the lighting that's going to be the last to adapt to the music or to the scenery. It's pretty flexible.

We choose to play inside a tent in order to maintain an intimacy, so the audience can feel that they are part of what's going on, that they're not just distant viewers, or mere observers. When I walked into the new tent I said, "This is...we've got a problem." It was huge. But there was no seating, there was no set—it was empty. Then I went home and relaxed [laughter from Luc and Dawn], and the elements started falling into place. I had to ignore the things I thought were going to be a problem, and look at what I had and how I could exploit it. So we use lots of projections on the tarp, and we light the masts, and we do that stuff from underneath the seating, and all that works to our advantage—and in any case, it couldn't have been any other way. Had I let the difficulties rather than the possibilities dictate my design, things wouldn't have come out so well.

With *Nouvelle Expérience*, the latest show, I found out that first day that I started hanging and firing up the instruments, that I was doing what I had done two years ago. Basically, I had the same images, the same colors, the same angles, everything. I told the guys to strike everything! [Laughter from Luc and Dawn.] They're cool! My crew's great, I'll tell you! And everything just came down. Then one night, I stayed alone inside the tent, kept the dimmers running, and started hanging myself. I moved things around, didn't want to be hampered by anything or anyone. I needed to do things at my own speed, I didn't want to be bothered by, "OK, time for a break." I had no patience, but most of all, I had no clear vision. I ended up hanging less than I had hoped but at least I got a clearer vision.

Of course in the real world, that won't work. So when I go out and do another gig, I better know what I'm doing. Because things are not going to go "up and down." I've been working on trying to visualize a little better. I find that renderings help a lot, and not being too concerned, at least initially, with who stands where at what time. I don't think that's the best way to do it. Unless you have a clear vision, your design will lack intention, and you'll be doing nothing more than illuminating the action.

When I was in university I took an art class, which I thought I wasn't very good at. Most of my drawings were very dark, very somber. I found out, though, that by taking away some of the darkness, I could create different images. So already I was going into the direction of the play of light. I find that I design lighting in the same way, starting with a dark stage and slowly chipping away at the darkness with what I guess could be thought of as strokes of lighting. I haven't really worked with any way other than my own. But I've also paid the price, because my approach doesn't really require that I come up with a lighting plot and with specific dimmer numbers, channel numbers and all that. So when I'm in a situation where I need to do that I stress out completely. Not because I can't do it, but because I feel that I'm going about it all wrong. It got to the point where my producer thought I couldn't draft and hired someone to do it for me.

I like the minimalist approach to lighting, with fewer fixtures and more limited budgets. It forces you to really think things out and question every decision you make. You can't base your design on the amount of projectors that you have, or the amount of money you have or the things you don't have. I'd rather not know what's available and what's not. I'd rather take these details and put them in a drawer and then say, "OK, what's this space like, what am I trying to say, what can I do with this space?" and then go ahead and design. Once you're comfortable with your vision and your images, see how you can translate them onto the stage given what you've got. You see, if your starting point is the logistics of lighting, then you've missed the point.

I get very nervous about hanging things and then turning them on and going, "OK, what's this thing going to look like?" And then realizing that the greatest fear I have is realizing that what I have done is...not right, that the vision I thought of is not there. The other fear I have is not having any ideas. That's always very present, whether it's for Cirque du Soleil or whether it is the Gypsy Kings or lighting cars—not having any ideas. I guess you can call it the white page syndrome. It seems that the best lighting is the one based on instinct, intuition. But it's also very...*risqué*. It can be very vague. I'm not always as intuitive as I would want to be. Some designers seem to have that sixth sense. I envy that.

In Europe they're less concerned with [Luc demonstrates with his hands a version of spectacle] and more about what it's going to look like on stage, the quality of the light. I find that more of them use moving lights in the blind—they never move when they are lit. That's interesting, because if at one point they decide to make it move while it's being lit, it has so much value. All of a sudden there is that element of contrast that is not there if you have a moving light cue every two minutes, or every minute. Moving lights are not the novelty they were. Movement for the sake of movement has lost some of its appeal.

Something else taught me things about making specific choices. For example about when to blackout, when not to blackout. Like the blackout at the end of the first act in *Nouvelle Expérience*. The last image just before the blackout is that of a motionless figure backlit by a huge white light. The source is a 1,200-watt HMI floodlight. As a matter of fact, it's a Pani projector with the lens taken out. In any case, the source projects a huge shadow on the tarp, filling the tent, and then we go to black. It's the first black since the opening and that gives it so much more value. Had we done, maybe, two or three blackouts prior to that, it would have been just another. It wouldn't have been as strong.

You're always wondering whether you made the right choice, and then you sign with someone and say, "Oh, but—yeah, now I've signed with this person for six months, and I am not going to be able to do anything else." The year after I decided not to be a board operator was a *lean* year. It costs a lot of money to promote yourself as a designer. You have to be around and you have to be seen at your shows and invite people. That's part of the investment you have to make.

In this business, as in any other I guess, if you do the same thing for too long, you become confined and, unless you go out and design shows, you'll never be perceived as a lighting designer. The first few years will be mean, but that's the nature of business. It's important as a designer to create trends, not to follow them. I can't remember who said that. You need to be able to find a company that will allow you to do that—that won't have pre-conceived ideas as to how the lighting should be.

Sometimes, if you see the show often, you get bored with it, because you see it regularly, and then you want to start changing things. But the people in the house who are seeing the show for the first time get that same feeling that you had when you saw it for the first time. You're getting used to it: habit. That can be a problem. You have to go away and say, "Well, I'd like to do things, but I'm not going to touch it for a while, I'm not going to see the show and then I'll come back." If you feel the change is justified, then do it.

I'd like to do architectural lighting—and that also comes from Cirque du Soleil, from lighting the space, the sets and the tents. I'd like to do a kind of architectural performance lighting, with huge cranes and movement that evolve—not just lighting a static building. I'd also like to go back to theater now—but something with an edge, something more experimental or avante-garde. I'd like to do it in a setting where people are not afraid of darkness. I find that darkness can be a very discomforting form of lighting: one can't exist without the other.

Lighting has gone in all sorts of directions. I think that we've gone as far as we can in terms of technological lighting—big moving lights and big effects. I think now we need to see what we have and what possibilities it gives us. But we also need to be able to put that aside and go back to the basics of lighting design, which are images, which are emotions and feelings, and translating an emotion onstage. And then go back to the technology and say, "OK, how can I do this now?" And I have this technology that's available to me—and it's cheaper, and maybe it's more effective.

But if you start doing a show with, "Well, I have sixty moving lights. Oh great! I'm going to have tons of moving light effects," already, forget it. As far as I'm concerned, you've already made a bad choice and you're letting a factor influence your design. I think I saw a lot of people designing because of what technology—toys—were available. I think we've done all we can with moving lights and things like that and effects. So I think at this point, if people are still going to be doing that, they are going to be copying what someone else has done. They're not going to be creating a new lighting trend. I feel that lighting design comes from within, not the rental shop.

That brings up another subject. What do you do? Are you at one point going to compromise your creativity so that you can have an incredible lifestyle? I think there's a choice that you have to make. And if you're lucky enough to be able to have an incredible creative output and to be able to buy an incredible house on that, Wow! Great!

Mind you it's a lot easier said than done. I did a car show once and didn't really like it. Still the pay was great: it can be tempting. But I also remember shows where at the end of the night, we passed the hat around.

I think if you're a designer, you're a creator to the same extent that the masters were, whether they are people like Mozart, whether it's Pissarro or anyone. You are a creator. And you have to make a choice as to whether you're going to compromise that creativity or not. And if you decide that you will compromise it because you have obligations or if you decide that you want to have this kind of a lifestyle, that's OK. I'm not passing judgement on those who have made that choice. Because there is also a market for that. You have to choose where you stand, and what it is that you want to do.

I remember on *Nouvelle Expérience* there was one period that I came home at night and just cried all the time. And I don't know how come it came to that, but that was it. That was the extent of my involvement in that production. And I don't know if that would happen working with other people.

I'm interested to see where the lighting is going to go in the next ten years. I'm interested to see if the turn of the century is going to affect our perception of lighting. It's going to be such a dramatic moment for everyone, the twenty-first century. And I wonder if it's going to have an influence on us.

# Chapter Twenty-five

# Pilbrow Story 6: Horror Stories

"There appears to be a new breed of specialist creeping into the West End theatre today: somebody called 'the lighting designer.' If last night's debacle is anything to judge by, this preposterous new fashion will not be with us long." This is a paraphrase of what Felix Barker (critic for London's *Evening News*) said about my work on an ill-fated production at the Cambridge Theatre in 1958. So slamming was the attack, so horrendous was the production, that I've blotted its name out of my memory and the cutting out of my scrapbook. Well, it was a pretty bad show. The quality of the lighting I'm less sure about, because just as the already chaotic production was about to get onstage, I was struck down by stomach trouble (which later led to the removal of my gall bladder) and spent the last week flat on my back in bed. I had asked that my name be removed from the program, but producers tend to forget that sort of thing. Anyway, as I sat up in bed reading the respected Mr. Barker, I was obviously certain that my career—then in its first year—was terminated.

Terrible things do happen. But soon after this, I was asked to light my first West End musical. Obviously the producer did not read the *Evening News*. It later turned out the producer probably couldn't read at all. The show was *Mr. Venus*, starring Frankie Howard. The phone call came on Friday afternoon: would I light this big new musical, bound for London's Prince of Wales Theatre, to open at the Opera House in Manchester on

Monday? "Which Monday?" I asked. "Next Monday," came the reply. "There's no budget for lighting, so you don't need any time. You must use what's in the theatre. Get up to Manchester tomorrow, see the last rehearsal, light the show on Sunday and we open on Monday." Always foolish, I accepted with enthusiasm.

That afternoon I went round to look at the model of the set. It was quite pretty, consisting of numerous backcloths and some small built pieces, all set in a quite elegant framework of bright blue floor, wings, borders and cyclorama. The following morning found me on the train to Manchester. Sitting in the same carriage was a familiar figure; it was the even-then famous comedian Frankie Howard. As I was drawing my light plot on my knee, we could hardly avoid striking up a conversation. He was very friendly, so much so that as we drew toward Manchester station, he was telling me his fears and phobias. "I'm a very easy person to get on with," he said. "I only have one absolutely immovable principle. I never, ever will walk on any stage on which there is anything *blue* anywhere in sight." The earth moved. I had a sixth sense that this was not going to be the easiest of weekends.

The Opera House, Manchester, in those days had one of the few three-valve thyratron control boards and a wonderful chief electrician named Wally Tomkins. I'd been there once before and he was a great man and supporter, even of a young upstart designer. We established the equipment that he had and agreed on the placement of his pitifully few spare instruments on two upstage pipes. At midnight on Saturday we began hanging the scenery and lights. Sunday morning we focused and at two o'clock Sunday afternoon the dress rehearsal began. By 3:30 Monday morning the dress rehearsal was not going well. Frankie had indeed become somewhat excitable and depressed when he walked onto the glacial icebox of a stage. A few lights, almost all in straw and orange, were not much compensation. Rehearsing the opening number took eight hours, the first scene change, four more. The fifteenth argument, the biggest, between producer, choreographer, director, designer and star took place at the aforementioned bewitching small hour of the morning. We were then two-thirds of the way through act 1. Could we open on Monday? I suspect the producer had no money left, so there was little to discuss. We would open come hell or high water.

There's not much high water in Manchester, the Ship Canal being a comparatively placid piece of wetness, but hell there certainly was on the stage of the Opera House that night. We never rehearsed past the opening of act 2. It was certainly not lit. I sat at the control board with Wally just above the prompt corner off stage left. I had what I thought were the scene by scene ground plans and I had seen the first half of the second act in a walk-through rehearsal on the Saturday morning. At intermission, after a catastrophic first act, with a third of the audience beginning to boo the ten-minute scene changes and the inept performance, the stage manager and I conferred. I said, "You have to tell me what happens in the last three scenes that I've never seen." He said, "What do you mean you've never seen them. I've never seen them either. We've never rehearsed them." Well, the curtain rose on act 2. I sat with Wally and read him a list of circuits that I thought might be appropriate for the next scene. The stage manager would scream, *"Blackout!"* and we'd blackout. On a *"Go"* from me, Wally would bring up what we hoped would be appropriate.

The end was not good, but most of the audience had left. Those that remained were voicing their displeasure at high pitch. The poor actors had little idea what to do next. The finale was a courtroom with Frankie in the dock. During the two-minute frontcloth scene, in which he was heroically ad-libbing on the forestage, we were setting up behind. Nobody had ordered benches or chairs for the jury and court spectators. Total panic! Chairs were rushed from dressing rooms and crew locker rooms and thrust higgledy-piggledy on the stage. The curtain rose; Frankie, in the witness box, had been placed in the wings, out of sight to most of the remaining audience. They were by now alternating between fury and hysteria. But Frankie climbed down with dignity and with the aid of two chorus boys pushed himself into greater prominence. The curtain fell to tears and hysteria. The choreographer punched the director. The stage manager joined in, and they all three became a pile of twisting, sweating, grunting bodies on the floor downstage center. The next day I resigned. I walked away from my first West End musical. *Mr. Venus* did, in fact, open at The Prince of Wales and ran for several months. My records don't show who lit it, but I know I didn't.

My next nasty was Peter O'Toole. Jocelyn Herbert asked me to light *Baal* at the Phoenix Theatre, directed by William Gaskell. The whole show took place on an open stage with small insets of scenery in front of a massive cyclorama. On this were a series of wonderfully provocative projections, designed by Jocelyn. The stage was wide open and bare in Brechtian style and there was literally nothing to capture acting-area spill light and stop it from diminishing the projections. These were pre-HMI days, and for projections to work, lighting had to be very tightly controlled. My only recourse was to use a lot of side light and as little as possible from the front. But these were the days before such things had become common. Our star, shall we say, was rather too nervous to appreciate this technique. He would have been happier with footlights and several follow spots. We lit through a very long technical that began, I remember, early on a Saturday morning and went through late into the night. There were many many scenes, and at every one Mr. O'Toole had a problem. Tension mounted. I tried to stay calm behind my production desk. The star was very unhappy and his principal peeve was obviously the lighting. Finally he snapped. With a hysterical scream, he advanced to the front of the stage. "Bill," he yelled, "this lighting is a fucking disgrace. Get this bloody idiot out of here and light me properly." Everyone froze. There was a very pregnant silence. Nobody drew breath for about fifteen minutes—but perhaps it wasn't that long. Finally, Bill stood up and said, "Richard?" I rose too. Trying to keep a steady voice, I said, "Bill, if Mr. O'Toole would concentrate on his fine performance and leave the lighting to those who know what they're doing, we might all be more confident of success." There was another pause. Steam could be seen rising. Finally, to his eternal credit, Bill said in a very loud and masterful tone, "Peter, for Christ's sake get on with it!" And he did.

Years later in the bar of the Chichester Theatre I accidentally overheard Peter haranguing Sir Laurence Olivier over my incompetence. Peter was to play Hamlet for the very first performance of the National Theatre Company at the Old Vic Theatre. Happily for me Sir Laurence, as director, obviously decided to stick to his guns—and me.

Those, I suppose are the spectacular stories. Although they were nasty at the time, time does solve all things, and they've been good tales ever since.

There are stories on a much smaller scale that were much more personal. I suppose there must be confident lighting designers, but I'm not one of them. The process of lighting a show—when all too often you're exhausted at the end of a long load-in and fit-up, a focus session fraught with frustration, followed by the start of cueing—is a pretty hellish thing. You have to perform in front of your peers. Surrounded by director, designer, perhaps the producer and numerous hangers-on, you have to turn the stage into magic. This is not good for the nerves. Even now, years later, I remember very well stealing away as the last lamp was focused, locking myself in a nearby toilet for a private bout of nausea. I don't think there's a theatre in Britain where I don't know which toilet is closest to the stage. Many have been private places where I've somehow had to get up the courage to go out there and do it. I've read about stage fright for actors. It must indeed be terrible. I found lighting fright to be pretty debilitating. However, you do go out there, get behind the production desk and the first cues seem absolute torture. How can anyone work more slowly than you do, you wonder. How can the stage look worse? How can everything you've thought of and painstakingly focused be just off its proper mark? Well with luck, one finally gets into a kind of rhythm. The actors come onstage and it half works. At long last the costumes are ready, and what seemed just a little dreary hopefully begins to sparkle into life. A tidge here and a tidge there on the focusing, a few quiet minutes with a tricky cue in act 2, the alteration by a fraction of a second of the stage manager's placement of a cue, and lo and behold, to your infinite surprise, things begin to look up. If you're really lucky, by first preview it's not too embarrassing and some of your colleagues start to smile. It is a nerve-racking business, but the horrors can sometimes be worth it.

# Chapter Twenty-six

# Anne Militello

A nne Militello's New York theater credits include the premieres of Sam Shepard's Simpatico *(Public Theatre)*, A Lie of the Mind *(Promenade Theater)*, Cuba and His Teddy Bear, *starring Robert DeNiro, David Lynch's* Industrial Symphony No. 1 *(BAM) and work for Mabou Mines, Richard Foreman, Squat Theater, Ping Chong, Eduardo Machada, John Vacarro, Tom Eyen, NYSF, LaMama, E.T.C. and Theatre for the New City. Her work with Maria Irene Fornes includes the premieres of* Abingdon Square, The Danube, Sarita, Conduct of Life, Mud *and* What of the Night. *Regional design includes the Mark Taper Forum, La Jolla Playhouse, A.R.T., Long Wharf and McCarter theatres. She has designed opera for director Christopher Alden at the Long Beach, Connecticut and Canadian Opera Companies. Concerts include* A Celebration of American Music *(for President and Mrs. Clinton) at the White House, the New American Music America Festival at BAM, Susan Deiheim at Carnegie Hall, and tours with Romeovoid, the Jim Carroll Band, Richard Hell, the Voidoids and the Cycle Sluts from Hell. She received an Obie Award for Sustained Excellence, a Dramalogue Award and an International Illumination Design Award and an Alpert Award in the Arts. She spent three years at Walt Disney Imagineering, where she designed the lighting for "Mickey's Toontown" and the "Roger Rabbit Cartoon Spin" at Disneyland.*

I walked into the theater when I was fairly young. I lived two blocks away from the symphony hall in Buffalo where I grew up, so being born restless and the whole bit, I started ushering there when I was twelve years old. Besides the symphony, there were a lot of touring companies that came through. It was a very important part of my growing up to be able to get away from the house, leave the chaos behind and escape and just be a part of this other world. I felt very at home immediately and I was comfortable there.

At the same time I was developing my love for art and music. As I entered high school, I started volunteering at the Studio Arena Theater, the local regional theatre. I did anything, even cleaned dressing rooms. I started working at the larger road houses, where concerts and Broadway tours would come in, and I got to see a lot more. I became friends with a guy that had come in with *Jesus Christ Superstar*. I went on the road with him to various cities and I couldn't keep my hands off moving road boxes. I wanted to be a part of it. The most interesting people that I met were the lighting people, and they seemed to be the most enlightened, or at least that was what I thought at that point.

Then I went to college as an acting major at the State University of New York at Buffalo and I met Ken Tabachnick, who was teaching lighting there. I talked to him at some cast party of a show that I'd been in. Again, it was like, these lighting people are the smartest ones and they know something the rest of us don't know, and I've got to find this out because I think there's something important going on here. I took a couple of lighting classes with Ken—he was a great teacher.

So after that, I immediately quit school [laughs] and moved to San Francisco so I could go and do it. I did a lot of lighting for rock bands at clubs in the beginning of the whole punk scene. I began volunteering at the Magic Theatre to try to work my way up into maybe running the light board. But in the meantime I was doing lights for these bands with all these kids who were my age. Everyone was a musician, everyone had a guitar—including me—so it was easy to get lighting work, as I was a part of that scene. For a while I took work as a roadie for a couple of San Francisco–based lighting houses and toured with various bands. I enjoyed the work and was good at it, but at that time females doing that type of work were rare, and I got a lot of flack. I won't go into detail, but some of it was pretty bad. I went back to working in clubs and at the Magic. I was there at a time when Sam Shepard and Michael McClure and Danny Glover and a lot of great people were there. I was talking to Sam one time—I didn't know he was a famous playwright. It was quick, quick, quick—I was trying to figure out things really fast by myself. I didn't want to sit in a classroom, as I was having the time of my life. Sometimes I regret that I didn't stick around to get more of a base of knowledge—I was too anxious. Sam was great. He gave me a play to read that he had just written, *Suicide in B-Flat*. It was pretty amazing and really inspiring—I thought OK, this is it. There's some substance here and that's kind of what I was looking for and what I needed. John Lyons, the artistic director at the Magic Theater, knew that I was interested and passionate about it and knew I was working my tail off doing lights for bands on the days I wasn't at the theatre, so he gave me a show. He tried me out on this new

Michael McClure play. I wasn't really sure what I was doing. It was wonderful—it just worked. I don't like to say that it was easy for me, but it was something I could do that I loved and I didn't have any turmoil over it.

Then Beverly Emmons came to town to light *Tongues* and *Savage Love* with Joseph Chaikin and Sam Shepard. Sam and John Lyons told me, "This New York designer is coming. We really have to hook you up. You'll like her, and you're going to be her assistant." You know, I didn't know what that entailed. The paperwork on the show that I designed at the Magic was make-shift—basic things I picked up from Ken, but I only took very beginning courses so I really didn't have it down. So I flipped through *Theatre Crafts* magazine and looked at plots and paperwork and bought as many books as I could—the Pilbrow book was so instrumental: all those little photographs of that man's head in different angles of light. I studied all these things to figure out what to do, but I still didn't know what being an assistant really meant. I worked on that show and kept track for her. I remember on one of the heaviest tech rehearsal days, I didn't come. I was goofing off or something. I didn't know it was an important day. I didn't realize it, and the next day when I casually came into the theatre, she said, "Where were you yesterday?" And I made up some outrageous excuse on the spot. And I realized, "Oh, my God, I think I should have been here." I was so green. She was really good about it. She really influenced me and inspired me.

I thought, this is a really serious profession. I've hit on something I love—and I got to see an example of someone who was successful and older, and her work blew me away. It made me cry when I saw what she had done with Joe Chaikin. This man had a halo around him, and what she did was just unearthly.

Fueled by my inspiration from Beverly, I left San Francisco, because I had to go to New York. There was so much happening in off- and off-off-Broadway in the late seventies, early eighties. It was pretty intense. I mean, I knew I had to do it, and I was daring enough or maybe naive enough and young enough that hardship didn't phase me. I didn't think about the fact that I had to make a living. I grew up poor, and there was always some way to get by, if I had to be on food stamps or sleep on someone's couch. It didn't enter my realm of thinking. So I was lucky enough to be daring and have the guts to get out there.

After I'd been in New York about six months I took a job at Production Arts cleaning lights and doing other assorted shop tasks. I went to Lester Polokov's to learn how to do proper paperwork. At Production Arts they first hired me to work in the office, and I didn't want to be in the office. I had to answer phones. It was like, "Please you guys, don't make me do that." I was getting Steve Terry's messages mixed up. I knew I was the worst possible office person they could ever have, and I said, "Please, just let me go into the shop." Finally there was an opening, and I got to go clean Lekos with the rest of the gals. It was mostly young women in the shop at the time that I was there—we had a great time. I got to play with the nuts and bolts. I continued to do rock shows at night.

I eventually quit Production Arts to do full-time night club work at the Rock Lounge, which was a nightclub with a New Wave, punk-type art scene. I lit many different bands a night for a couple of years and then got into the Studio 54 thing, where I was a lighting DJ; I was mixing lights for the dance floor. Pre-computer control, can you imagine? I didn't like that at all. If I didn't like the music I was not going to keep doing it. So I hit up Ellen Stewart, the head of LaMama Theater, on the street one day on Second Avenue in the Village. It was actually evening, and I was going back to the club after stopping home. I was a punk kid and I had the whole outfit: leather jacket, leather pants. And I said, "Oh, yeah. You're Ellen Stewart." I told her I had just moved there from San Francisco and Sam Shepard told me about her. And she said, "Oh yeah, Sam—OK." She said, "Well, you want some work?" And I said, "Yeah." And it was 9:00 at night, and she said, "What are you doing right now?" I told her, "Nothing," because I didn't know how to tell her I had to go back to work. She said, "Well, you come with me." She took me by the arm, literally, and walked me into the downstairs theater—and Tom Eyen was sitting there with Michael Bennett. He was doing a revival for their twentieth anniversary season, it was their opening show—*Why Hanna's Skirt Won't Stay Down*— it's a great, great play. And his lighting designer had just quit or something: two days to opening and they were stuck right then and there, and here I was just literally off the street. I remember Ellen said, "Tom, I got you a lightin' designer." And I was in teased up black hair and blue cat-eye makeup from my punk thing, and he knew better. He knew her long enough to know she was serious and he just looked at me like, oh great. And he just said, "Can you do it?" and I said, "Yeah, yeah, I can do it." And so I just stayed there and hung that show. And I remember working two or three days and nights in a row watching rehearsals, hanging it. And then Ellen gave me pretty much every show in that twentieth anniversary season. So I really got my foundation of getting shows back to back—left the rock world again, except for the occasional concert. I didn't live on much. I didn't think I had to. Ellen would occasionally bring me a tuna-fish sandwich, I guess if I was looking particularly bad! It was a really exciting time. There was a lot happening, and I was right in the middle and I got a nice foundation.

Then I met Maria Irene Fornes—who was someone else Sam Shepard had told me about—and I looked her up. She's amazing. I saw one of her pieces, *The Visit*, at Theater for the New City, and I was blown away, and I said, "Look, do you have anyone working with you?" And she said, "Not really." And I said, "Just let me do it please." She was wonderful. I got an Obie a couple of years later for the work that I did with her and the work at LaMama. I consider my collaborations with her as some of the most important work of my career. I quickly became established in those kind of

*Stage Lighting Design*

downtown Village venues. I didn't know about Uptown. I didn't know about much else outside of that world because I was submerged in it. There was this whole other theater world going on, and there were assistants that were working on Broadway, and I wasn't interested in any of this.

Four years ago, I moved to California to work for Walt Disney Imagineering, where I stayed for three years. I wanted to try something new and, in the meantime, see what it would be like to have a nice place and a few amenities like a fax machine and a computer. Working off-Broadway in New York or at regional theatres does not provide one with a nice income, or should I say barely an income. I always had a tough time with rent and health insurance. That's a stressful thought. It's been wonderful having the emotional support of a husband who's also an artist. The two of us have an understanding relationship when it comes to work and money.

The work at Disney was interesting and educational. I enjoyed many aspects of it and was able to see a few major projects that I designed through to completion. Lighting for theme parks has its unique challenges—the work will be seen for many years and must last. It requires different considerations. But working for a large corporation also has its drawbacks. For me, it was a struggle to maintain my identity in that environment. That wasn't so great. As I was leaving New York to take this full-time job, Ruth Maleczek from Mabou Mines wished me well by saying sarcastically, "Have a nice house, have a nice car!" I laughed because I wanted more experience, not a car—I wasn't leaving the theatre. But the experience that I gained there has helped me in my theatre work now and has given me the confidence to take on larger commercial jobs as an independent designer.

The other major reflection I've had about what I'm doing, is how I'm doing it. I neglected my health for a time because it didn't occur to me that I would have to take care of myself. I didn't get enough sleep, I didn't eat properly. I thought that I was indestructible. I worked on adrenaline, which I had plenty of, going nonstop. So, eventually, I got pretty sick! I am now more reasonable about how many hours I work in a row or how many jobs I take at one time or back-to-back, so that I can function properly. I never thought about the future impact of my behavior.

On architectural jobs, there's a great deal of time spent doing research on electrical codes, energy codes and construction procedures and things like that. It can get tiresome after a while. I don't care if the conduit is running in the same path as the water line. I just don't care! I know I should, but...well, I deal with it anyway, because it can be important. It makes those small amounts of time that you can actually sit down and think about the design, the look, real precious.

I've had a reputation in the past for staying within given budgets. I've been careful in that way—I sometimes enjoy the challenge of limitations, although I'm sure it stems from not wanting to argue with producers. I don't mean to imply that I wouldn't fight for more money if I felt strongly that the design must have certain things. It's hard to create when some-one's breathing down your neck, but when I have to do it, I do it. Sometimes having an agent has protected me from those confrontations. I find that more and more, as lighting technology becomes more sophisticat-ed and gives us more options, that most theatre companies haven't changed their budgeting structure enough to allow for this cost increase, and the lighting budget never seems to be enough. But let's face it, there's not much money circulating in the theatre in this country to begin with, and many companies are just barely surviving.

The reality in the commercial arena is different altogether. On these jobs, I think I've figured out a way to go into board rooms with suit-and-tie people and talk about budgets in a language they understand. As an artist, I've had to educate myself on how to work with the business people who hold on to the cash, so I can keep creating. It's not easy for me to talk about money. It's depressing to realize that profit drives just about everything.

I've neglected my family for birthdays and holidays. Oh my God, I've forgotten again. I didn't think about having children when I was at the right age. But my work just kind of took over, and nothing seemed more important. I don't want to get to the end of my life and realize there are things I haven't explored—like the outdoors—before it's too late. I now have these other goals to take time and smell the flowers a bit more.

Art and spirituality are, to me, tied so close together. I'm always looking to round out my life. I continue to seek out different experiences and to continue learning. That's my driving force instead of having the greatest car. I've learned to relax; hopefully that'll last! I think more about the importance of fulfilling myself as an artist and being able to appreciate the world around me as I get older. I think of other designers who are in their sixties who have been working so hard and I wonder, have they enjoyed their lives in between all that work? They seem pretty happy!

When I was doing the full-time company job, after a while, I was "allowed" the opportunity to go on leave and do an opera and a play. It was great. I needed that energy again, that injection of energy. It was like fresh air to someone who'd been stuck in a closet for years and finally got out. [Laughs.] I realized that I could only be happy as long as the structure of my life provided me with the freedom to continue to be a theatre artist.

# Chapter Twenty-seven

# Pilbrow Story 7:
# To Russia with "Sir"

T he following January after the Chichester debacle the telephone again rang. This time it was clearly Sir. "Dickie dear boy, it's January. We open Chichester again in June. Does that give you enough fucking time?"

I became lighting designer to the National Theatre and thus began a very golden period. In the 1960s the Old Vic Theatre had the best electrical crew in London. These were the early heady days of the National Theatre Company before their new concrete monolith was erected. The chief electrician was Lenny Tucker, his lieutenants were Ron Cox, Peter Radmore (a photograph of whom, seated at Lightboard, graced the cover of early editions of *Stage Lighting*) and Brian Ridley. The three of them were the core of an amazing team. By a strange and sad coincidence, Ronnie, Peter and Brian are no longer with us.

One day Ronnie, Viki and I set off for Moscow, where the National Theatre was to open its new production of *Love for Love* and Laurence Olivier's world-famous *Othello*. We were to play in a theatre actually in the Kremlin that had never been used before for live performance. It had apparently been built as Stalin's personal cinema. To overcome this horrendous prospect, we had been assured that the finest crew in all of Moscow had been pulled together to work with the National. We arrived. It was indeed impressive to drive through that famous gateway from Red

Square into the Kremlin itself. We took a hard right into a large courtyard, and there was the Kremlevski Theatre. We loaded in *Othello* first, since that was to be the opening production.

The difficulties began when the "skilled" Russian crew began to hang the scenery where they wanted to rather than where it was intended to go. To them it was quite obvious that every lighting pipe had to have a border hung immediately downstage of it, this despite the fact that half the overhead lighting was backlight. Heated arguments ensued. One kind Russian lady was doing all the translation and a protestation from us in English was followed by a fifteen to thirty minute argument in Russian.

Finally the lights were hung. Our hosts didn't understand the concept of focusing first. They wanted me to immediately go to the production desk and start lighting. I was assured that as soon as I called for the first cue, men all over the theatre would set any light I wanted in any direction. We explained that was not how we worked. With disbelief, they watched Ronnie focus every instrument.

Then we began to light. The first scene was at night, while the second—Olivier's famous entrance as the Moor, coming from upstage to down center, dressed only in a white loin cloth, holding a red rose—will never be forgotten. We lit conventionally, if slowly. Every socket outlet to which our equipment was plugged had a name that, in Russian, sounded much longer than "down right fly plug number seven." The control board was an ancient, manually operated tracker wire board controlling autotransformers. It was situated under the front edge of the stage. The chief operator had a view of the stage from under a hood, rather like a prompter in an old-fashioned opera house.

Curtain time, at which Mr. Bulganin was due to attend, was 7:30. At 6:10, with little time to go before the dinner break, we got to the end of plotting. I thought that we should just check the opening cue. I explained to my interpreter that I would call for cue one and when I said the words "Cue one GO," the switchboard crew would operate the first cue. "Certainly," she said, "All is understood."

I paused. "Standby for cue one. Cue one GO!" Nothing happened. Then one spotlight came on, then another, then some of the cyc, then another, then another. I said, "No, stop, stop! That's not right. When I say 'Cue one GO,' all the lights come on together and go to their predestined levels."

A conversation in Russian. The interpreter said, "Let's try it again."

"Standby cue one. Cue one GO!"

This time two lights came on, then another two, then one, then a random assortment.

"No," I said, "You don't understand. When I say 'cue one' *all* the lights must come together to their levels."

An extended conversation took place in Russian. In fact we tried it three more times with always similar results. Finally I started getting cross. "This is dreadful. We were assured these are the best operators in Moscow.

When they receive a cue, all the lights must move together."

A very angry shout came from the bowels of the stage. The hood was flung open and the senior Russian operator started to emerge, gesturing and shouting.

Finally he was translated. "This is ridiculous," he said. "I have only two hands. Only two lights can move at once. My assistant has two hands, that is four lights can move at once. These English do not know what they're talking about. This is not the way we work. This is crazy!"

The time was 6:35. Ron and I went to the edge of the stage and looked down into the pit and at the control board. It was indeed a relatively conventional Siemen's tracker wire board. I called the interpreter.

"Please explain that all the handles for the dimmers have a knob on the end, which, if you turn, locks them to the master, which, in turn, can be locked to the grand master in a direction that will take them either up or down. All the operator has to do is to set the upper limits for the dimmer movement, lock the handles in the right direction and turn the big wheel at the end." Again a translation.

"Impossible," exploded the electrician. "This is ridiculous," with much swearing, which thankfully we didn't understand.

Clearly we had a crisis. The audience would come in fifteen minutes. I said, "Ronnie, down the hatch. You'll have to work the board." Ever willing, he lowered himself through the trap door.

"What do you think," I said.

"My God, Richard, there's a real problem here."

"What's that?"

"The bloody board's marked in Russian. I can't read any of the names or the numbers."

"Christ Almighty!" In the remaining ten minutes before the house opened, we started to identify circuits. The top left-hand handle on the board was number 92, the next was circuit 2, the next was 109.

A crisis meeting: could we postpone the opening? Quick answer: Absolutely *no*. The head man of Russia was about to enter the lobby. By 7:30 we had about half the installation identified. Quickly we arranged that I would sit in a box with a walkie-talkie and Ronnie would work the board.

Before an audience glittering with medals and every display of pomp and ceremony allowed by the Communist system, the curtain rose. The first scene: night time. Suddenly all the lights came up. An urgent whisper into the radio, "Ronnie, what the fuck are you doing?" He said, "I can't stop them, they've locked everything on and turned the wheel!"

"Oh, my God!" I said. "Quick take 'em out, gently, one at a time. Yes, that's 73, yes, that's 110, no, leave that one, that's 98." So we gradually, while trying to minimize the catastrophic effect on the illumination of the stage, identified those circuits left to us to find.

Over the walkie-talkie, I said, "Ronnie, you've got to keep them away." He said, "I can't speak to them. They don't understand me. They keep on pushing me away." The first scene ended and on my instructions, Ronnie managed to ensure a fade to black. The next scene, Sir Laurence's famous entrance, was meant to be a bright interior. Ronnie took the cue and most of the lights did indeed appear miraculously. Sir Laurence entered up center in the arch to a huge standing ovation from the enthusiastic Russian audience. He began to stalk with menace downstage toward the audience. As he did so, every light faded to complete blackness. The audience went wild. They thought this one of the most exciting pieces of theatre they'd ever seen. Ronnie and I were less amused.

"Ronnie, 91 to 99 to full, 108, 171, get the bloody light on."

And so the evening progressed. In hindsight, I don't think the audience noticed. Perhaps they were used to odd illumination. By Act 2, we'd almost got things together. Sir Laurence was less amused. At almost every exit, he stalked into the prompt corner and swore most expressively at Diana Boddington, his wondrously reliable stage manager, who by this time was close to hysteria.

The end of the show was something else. Sir Laurence was a consummate professional and a stickler for every detail being exactly right. Just before he went on to smother Desdemona, he said to Diana, "Now at least get the damn curtain-call blackouts right, for God's sake!" In truth, Ronnie and I were pretty confident about that. They were simply up and down with all the lights locked to the grand master.

The play came to its tragic conclusion: blackout. No problem. Then a full up for the curtain call, perhaps the only truly correct cue of the entire evening. All the cast entered one by one, climaxed by Sir Laurence as the Moor. There was a tumultuous reception with every member of the audience on their feet cheering, flowers hurled from the galleries. What a sensation!

"Blackout," called Diana. Nothing happened.

"Blackout!" I screamed into the walkie-talkie, almost topping the audience applause.

A scream from Ronnie Cox came back, "I've blacked out!"

I looked up. Oh my God, so he had. Every light on the stage had gone off, but not even I had noticed as a huge bank of 10kW lights in the gallery had come up in all their blazing glory: lighting installed to film the production on stage. They had missed a pirate film of Sir Laurence's performance as *Othello*, but they were not going to miss the curtain calls.

"Blackout," screamed Diana.

"Blackout!" we all screamed to whomever we could find, without avail.

Sir Laurence was used to making a retreat in darkness. Finally with what dignity they could muster in the blaze of arc lights the cast did beat a retreat. Sir Laurence retired into the prompt corner. An angry Moor is a frightening sight, particularly when, instead of Shakespeare, the words are, "What the hell do you think you idiots are doing! That's the worst fucking lighting I've ever seen in my entire career!"

*Stage Lighting Design*

## Chapter Twenty-eight

# Jim Moody

*Jim Moody first received recognition in 1971 with the L.A. Critics Award for* The Glass
Menagerie. *In the same year he began to do concert lighting and has designed tours for The
Eagles, Frank Zappa, David Bowie, Linda Ronstadt, the Beach Boys and many others. He
received the first Concert Lighting of the Year Award from* Performance *magazine in 1980.
Jim is author of more than sixty technical articles and the 1990 textbook* Concert Lighting:
Technique, Art and Business. *He has designed lighting for many television shows and became
director of photography for* Entertainment Tonight *in 1987. He is currently responsible for the series
lighting of* Sightings, Hard Copy *and* Wheel of Fortune. *After founding and operating one of the first
concert lighting equipment companies, Sundance Lighting Corp., for more than ten years, he is now
CEO of Moody/Ravitz Design Partners Inc., with fellow designer Jeffrey Ravitz, working extensively
in architectural and theme-park lighting as well as all forms of theatrical design. He also operates
Production Resource Management, which provides below-the-line services and produces events. In 1993
he won the L.A. Drama-Logue Critics Award for* The Sicilian Bachelor. *He is staff designer for the
Telluride Repertory Theatre Company and in his free time sails his forty-two-foot Hunter.*

Diversity has always been my key. Because of my late entry into theatre,
I'm not one of those people who've dreamed about it all their lives. But
once I began, I was a sponge to learn all I could about lighting. I didn't
have the traditional theatre dislike for the other media. I've tried to stay in
touch with live theatre, but it's been limited to a few shows a year, usually

through art directors and scene designers I've worked with in the past. About three years ago I went to Telluride, Colorado, to do a theatre festival and became part of the town's repertory theatre company. Now I do five or six shows a year there besides some theatre design in the Los Angeles area.

I'd been involved in theatre as a kid by my grandparents via the local Catholic Children's Theatre program, so I had that interest, but I certainly didn't see it as a career. I learned from my grandfather to be open to life's unplanned opportunities. He believed in setting goals, but he would never let them stand in the way of an unexplored side path that seemed unique or interesting. Music was also a part of the home environment. They took me to recitals and plays in our town of Joliet, south of Chicago. Trips to Chicago were pretty special. I remember seeing the original touring productions of *Oklahoma*, *Brigadoon* and *Look Homeward Angel*. I was impressed and really loved going to the theatre, but pure music held a little more interest for me. I took lessons on several instruments and sang in the a cappella choir. I founded a folk group when that became the fashion. I even got a recording contract with Decca Records in my last year of undergraduate school.

The turning point for me came unexpectedly. I had returned from four years with the Air Force and Vietnam to finish college at Southern Illinois University in Carbondale. In school I was an English major with a theatre minor who expected to go teach high-school English and be involved in the school plays. Sam Seldon, who was the chairman of the theatre department at UCLA and, of course, an author, had just been hired for a semester at Southern Illinois to give some acting classes, and I was asked to be his assistant. At the time, I didn't see that I was lucky—I just needed the money. It was a wonderful experience.

One day Sam said, "You would do very well in theatre." And I kind of looked at him like, this guy is completely lost. I later said to him, "But what would I be good at?" He looked me straight in the eye and said, "Lighting." I went home to my wife and told her what he had said. I was convinced it was what my grandfather talked about in taking advantage of an unexpected opportunity.

I went back to him and said, "I can't start all over and go back to get a theatre major." And he just looked at me and said, "I can get you into the M.F.A. program at UCLA without a degree." And he did. I took that opportunity and ran with it. Two years later, in 1969, I graduated from the program with a specialty in theatrical lighting.

I was fortunate to meet a number of people outside the university community. One was Joseph Tawil. He'd just come to California to take over Berkey Colortran and he needed an assistant. I got the job and spent five years learning about specifications, manufacturing and R and D while doing plays at night and on weekends. Joe encouraged it. He is a great believer that there should be no sacred cows, so he encouraged people to bring any wild idea to the table. I was allowed to delve into a lot of nooks and crannies about lighting that my limited college time had not offered. Joe encouraged me to write technical articles and introduced me to a lot of directors of photography and some Broadway designers.

He was instrumental in getting Jules Fisher to take me on for the Los Angeles production of *Jesus Christ Superstar*. Jules's schedule was crazy. I was virtually handed the plot: "Here make it fit this theatre." The theatre was an outdoor amphitheater on a movie lot! So it couldn't be done with the usual Broadway plot. The show changed every day. It was a wonderful experience because I was living in one of the dressing rooms and at night changing the plots and cue sheets because it was such a helter-skelter kind of production. I was very appreciative of everything that Jules imparted to the people around him. He is a great teacher.

Jules was good about going to meetings and coming back with a list of things for you to do for the next day, and then he would go off. I remember having my list of things, and he got there the next day and went to his meeting after I'd seen him, and I had not told him that I did not get all of those things done. Whether it was my fault or not, it didn't make any difference. I had neglected to tell him everything. He walked into his meeting and told everyone that those things had been done, and a couple of them hadn't been. So, I got chewed out pretty good and rightly so. It was a good lesson. Jules wasn't interested in wasting time hearing about what had been done, he wanted to know only what had not been done. I never neglected to perform that seemingly minor but important job again. The best part was that Jules never made an issue of it. I knew I had screwed up; enough said.

I stumbled into the concert area. I received a call from the owner of a local lighting rental house saying some guy wanted to put on a concert in an old defunct theatre in the round and needed someone who knew how to light it. I had only been to a couple of rock concerts and none with any lighting effects. The bands turned out to be Fog Hat, Kansas and a piano player named Billy Joel. We all got ripped off. Nobody got paid. But the sound company took a liking to me and said, "Well, we have friends who just signed a contract to promote concerts at the Hollywood Palladium, and they're going to need some people." I got the job. It was certainly very simple. There weren't even PARs at that point. We were still using Fresnels and Lekos and beam projectors and a really weird little stage. But in a year and a half's time, I had done everybody that was touring as a musical act, including the Rolling Stones. That's how I met Chip Mounk, already a legend, even in the very young field of concert lighting.

In a short period of time, I was immersed in concerts. Out of that, I became known, because I had met so many people so quickly. Most of these acts had no idea—I mean, you went back stage and laid it out for the band and told them, "I'm the lighting director. Do you have a set list?" They'd go, "Set list? Oh, wow, man. We used to have one of those." You learned how pop music went together. It was fun because every night was a different experience.

These same promoters started promoting shows at the Hollywood Bowl. One of the acts to come in was "Small Faces, Featuring Rod Stewart." I was there to light the opening act. Well, the road manager walked in, and they'd fired the lighting designer the night before. So they came over and said, "We need a lighting director. Can you go on the road?" And I went, "Yeah." And they said, "Have you ever done this before?" And I went, "Sure." Lighting rig? I had never seen a truss. Nothing. The truth is I had no idea how to put that stuff together. I didn't have a clue. Bob See was the electrician. He and I had been friends for years. We had both been thrown into this, and this was his chance to move up to calling the show. So, we had a great time. Everything went fine. We literally went on the road the next night. It was just the circumstances that happened, being in the right place at the right time.

It was a wonderful, creative time because there were no limits—there were no guides. Everything you did was almost a first. Sometimes it worked and sometimes it didn't. Experimentation was the rule, because there were no rules. Along with a small group of people like Bob See, Chip Mounk, Bill McManus and Tom Field, I was at the center of a whole new medium while it was being born right in front of my eyes.

It is a very hard life. I am a big advocate, though, of people doing it, because short of going out with a dance company, there isn't another experience where you have to work so hard to be a problem solver. Every night has a new set of problems. If you really approach it in a good way, by "Can I accomplish this by solving these problems?" that makes you a better designer in whatever area you're going to end up designing. You're put on the spot and put under the kind of pressure that, as a professional, whether in theatre, architecture, television or film, you're going to be subject to. I don't think kids are put under that kind of pressure in college. Taking calculated risks was something I had never been afraid to do, largely due to my training as an air traffic controller in the Air Force.[6] I give a lot of credit to the training they gave me in handling stress and making decisions. I don't think I would have lasted very long, with the pressure to perform every night, without it. I believe that decision-making ability is one of my strongest points, far beyond any artistic ability I possess.

As a freelancer you've got to deal with the issue of paying the rent and taking care of yourself and possibly a family. Some people take the position, "I'll hold out for the few jobs that pay a lot of money." I'm the worker-bee type that says, "I need to be doing something all the time." So I never let the amount of the pay stand in the way of my wanting to work. I'm addicted to work, a workaholic. I tell the kids that I lecture, you've got to have goals. You've got to have that reach-for attitude to succeed professionally—but don't be blinded by it. Having the goal is something to strive for, but if you don't look down the other paths, I think you're missing something. You've got to have an open mind.

Suddenly television took notice of concert artists and created shows around their concert performances. *Don Kirshner's Rock Concert* tried to replicate the feel of a real concert. Since I had some TV experience as well as being a known concert designer, I got the job. We did five years of the show with almost every touring artist available. I was always proudest of my work when the group's lighting designer would come and thank me for making the band look like they did on tour.

Sundance was formed in 1975 because there were no lighting rental houses in L.A. or manufacturers willing to build equipment that would meet the demands of the touring designer. None of them saw this as a market. From Four Star we had boxes that you got splinters from. Since they wouldn't respond to your needs and you were the one on the road working twelve to sixteen hours a day and driving a bus, [and had] to do this all over again the next day, you were learning how to put this stuff together to make it work and to make it easier on your life. They didn't understand that, and they weren't willing to invest in it. I had a company that made the trusses, and we put them together in my front yard for the first tour. My neighbors hated me, as I had my lights on at night in the front yard. Every time you did it, you learned how to make it easier. People would call and say, "Oh, wow, man, I saw this lift that puts air conditioners in windows. Maybe we could use that." And that's how all that stuff came about. There were enough people like Bob See and Tom Field who were willing and wanted to do it.

I was probably the most vehement of them to say I was a designer. I am not a company owner or a mogul, who sits behind a desk and runs a rental house. I'm only doing this to accomplish what I want to in my design. And the day that that's not fun anymore, I'm not going to do it. And that's exactly what happened. I sold it when it wasn't fun anymore.

With this rock-and-roll equipment one of the best opportunities for us was in the corporate show area. Those were becoming very big multimedia shows. I could use my television skills, because there was large-screen video production; I could use my concert skills, because there was music and dance; I could use my theatre skills, because there were sketches and big dance numbers. And because of the rock-and-roll trusses and all that, it was very apropos, because a lot of industrials were done in marinas, convention-center settings, so you really could use those rigging skills. The background I had built in the years of touring fit the frenetic pace, and I believed I was prepared for the pressure. There was no margin for error, the financial stakes were too high. I loved it. But money got tight and the really big shows melted away.

How do you get work and how do you get paid? Everybody approaches it differently. My approach when we had the equipment company was to have someone in-house as a salesman. I'm not good at asking for money because I'm a workaholic. But I have to have a livelihood and pay for things. I used a colleague as a crutch, so it wasn't me who had to ask for the money. We as artists have a lot of trouble doing that because we take it personally, and it's very difficult to sit across the table from the producer, negotiate those fees, have those kinds of arguments and stand up for what really are your rights. I'm an advocate for getting paid for what you do. I think people in theater take terrible advantage of this in the area of designers and technicians—it's horrible, and done to them by fellow theater "devotees" and people who love theater. I just think it's abhorrent. That was why I had someone in-house negotiate those things so I could step aside.

Why did I call it Sundance, rather than by my name, which most people do? My feeling was if my name is attached to it, someone would come to me and say, "I really don't have a lot of money, and we're friends, and you own the equipment anyway. Can't you give me a deal?" I could hide behind the name and say, "I don't own the company guys. I'm one of the partners; I can't just give you this stuff." It also helped me to get the money I know I deserve and I know other people get. That's why a lot of designers hide behind the refuge of a Klages or a Fiorentino. They need that structure of someone else doing the negotiating. We are a business. We are a *creative* business, but a business. And as soon as students learn that what they're getting into is a business, the better off they'll be.

I feel I was very loyal to all the people that I used, but none of them were staff. You're using people from project to project. The one advantage was, you could go to them and say, "Look, here's what I need." If somebody said, "I can't do that project for that money" or "I don't have the time," I'd say, "Fine, I can use them later." Where if it's a staff person, they feel like you're making them do this cheapo show and they deserve better. Each of us has our own strengths. Jeff [Ravitz] has a lot more training in architectural lighting than I do, so he can lead in that area, and I can help him. My experience in television is a lot deeper, so I can do the same thing with him. It's funny because in theater we're trained that this is a cooperative art. And yet, when it comes down to doing our designs, we tend to be very individual. Even with Marilyn Rennagel [an early partner], I thought it was so good at that stage, years ago, that we could look over each other's shoulder and say, "God, why did you do that? Why didn't you put red here and do this?" And the other person goes, "Oh, yeah. That's good." And to be able to take it in the spirit that it was meant; not putting the other person down, but being able to add to [the project].

Without naming names, we all know some designers who are very headstrong, and, in fact, make their reputations on the fact that they are screamers and that, through tantrums, they must have things exactly their way. I can't do that—it's very much against my nature. Not that I acquiesce to people, but I'm not confrontational. I'm more the type that when I want something to go the way I want it, I wait for the right opening and right way to approach it to get it done. I've never really approached it to gain stardom as much as to be a creative part of the team and make my contribution. We're taught in theater, [that] the director is the final authority. When he says, "No, I want it my way," all the creative ideas you have in the world must come down to the fact that it's his show.

Solving problems and dealing with stage hands? Well, you're dealing with people and you're going into their home. They'll be there tomorrow. You won't. You have to learn how to cooperate with people and get people to work for you, to get what you need done in a way that you can come back in their house again. That to me is part of the training. It comes down to getting the job done the most expeditiously, so that it comes out the way you want it to be. My goal was always to be standing at the doorway when the artist came in for sound check and say, "Everything's great, and it's going to be the best show we've ever done." You're doing it so that actor or that singer doesn't have to worry about those things. He can put out to the audience what he has to do.

Who really is this someone you're meeting who is probably going to hire you? Is he the accountant, the group manager, the road manager, the group themselves, or the artist? Rarely will the artist get involved at that level. Either you're being called because the artist saw a show that you did or maybe a friend of theirs recommended you or another band did, which is how it happened for me in a couple of instances early on in my career. I was working for the Eagles and I got a phone call on the road from Linda Ronstadt saying, "Glen Fry talks really highly of you, would you do my tour?" I was thrilled because I was in love with Linda Ronstadt. So, that's how some of that happens. But, in most cases you're dealing with a road manager or a money person, and all those rules that we've learned in the union—that you don't do drawings and you don't give away ideas until the contracts are signed—they're out the window. You've got to sell yourself and you've got to know when to turn off the faucet and not give them any more information.

You can go through *Performance* magazine—for Paula Abdul's tour that's out right now, or U2, the Zoo Tour, it takes three pages to show you all the crew and designers that are out on that show. For every one of those, there are four hundred or five hundred acts that are playing clubs, on the road ten to twelve months a year playing the fairs, et cetera. That's where the real meat and potatoes of the business is. It isn't just the high-end people. There's very few of those. So there are a lot of opportunities out there to work—if you put your mind to it in the right way. Let's put on a show! [Laughs.] That to me is still to this day a lot of fun.

In the television and film area, you meet a wide range of people. If you go for an interview with a band, one thing to watch out for is wearing the T-shirt or jacket of a band that that artist or management may not like. Watch what you wear. You get into television and films and you've got a lot of people in coats and ties. So there's a certain image that's projected there. There are a lot of the film VPs and art directors that have a style or trademark. For example, Chip Mounk—he wore hockey jerseys all the time.

That was his trademark. Film people tend to be very formal on that level, until you get to the director and on down. Television people are the worst lot, because you never know what you're going to run into. I've walked into meetings with very big producers that are worse dressed than any electrician that I've ever met. Not putting down electricians, but, you know, torn jeans—not the kind in Beverly Hills—I mean, bad jeans. It's a very mixed bag and it's very difficult to know how to size yourself up in those situations. You have to play it how you feel most comfortable.

You come out of theatre school having some background in all areas. Even if you were just interested in lighting, you had to take some costume [classes], you had to take some scenic [design]. The one thing that still bothers me about education: drama departments ought to require a class in salesmanship and business. I'm very big on having a basic understanding of business, such as accounting, salesmanship, interpersonal relationships. It is very important, because most of the people around me that failed are the ones that cannot communicate with the other people of the creative team or the management. They may have the greatest ideas in the world but they can't communicate. And we also all know people who are great talkers, but who really can't produce. So it goes both ways. But that skill to communicate is the skill to get you the next job. It's also the salesmanship that sells your idea [and commitment] to do the best job you can on the production. You're in a creative team, you've got to communicate.

There's the old story that there's only one hundred people in Hollywood. It's true. Because what happens is, you get on a production, and if you're smart, the first thing you do, if there's a new person you don't know, you make sure you get their phone number. You network tremendously. If you surround yourself with people where you know their skills—they may not be the best person—but at least you know what they're capable of. That's very important in this town.

So is the ability to size things up when you walk through a door—what this means timewise, budgetwise, personnelwise, politically. There were times where you were hired by the accountant, but all of the real power could be the girlfriend of the lead singer. I can't tell you how many times there will be when you have dealt with someone who told you, "I have the power to make these decisions." And all of sudden you find out that this guy was completely off his rocker. Somebody else had all the authority. You've got to be smart enough businesswise to understand this is what happens and you have to see past all the smoke.

There's not only the personal part of making the contacts and finding the next job, but its also using those skills to draw out from the people that are in the show—whether that's the artist himself or management—what they're really saying, what they're really after. I don't think that's a skill that we're born with. That's a learned skill and very much a marketing type of business skill. I do a lecture called "Survival: The Business of Being a Designer." I try to explain to [students that] you are a business.

From the day you get out school, unless you're going to be a registered charity, you are a business, and these are the things you are responsible for and what you are not responsible for and what you must do to protect yourself as a business and the fact that one day down the line you're going to retire. If you're not going to work full time for the rest of your life for a school or for one employer, you better think about this on an individual basis and protect yourself.

That's why a basic course in business will help you to understand. We're lawyers every day. The fact is, every time we negotiate to do a show, even if it's a verbal contract, that is a legal document. And to know some of the basic things about law is important.

Students say: "When am I going to have time to learn all this?" The schools put so much onto kids. The best thing I can say to them is, as long as you understand that this is necessary—so that when you get out or when you have your free time in the summers, read books and learn. Pick this up on your own. It is going to be an asset that will stand you in very good stead throughout your career, because we are salesmen. We are creative salesmen, both for our ideas and for ourselves.

With an assistant, what I want is a person who comes to me with good basic skills and an open mind to learn what I can teach them. Because by the mere fact that I have hired them, I am saying, "I will teach you my job. You don't know my job. I don't care what school you go to. Having the specialized training turns out not to be the important thing. You don't know my field. So, spend your time getting that solid grounding, then you can build on it."

Kids coming out of school today can't come in thinking, "OK. Now I got hired. When do I start doing Michael Jackson, and when does my vacation start?" There's still dues to pay, and it's hard and it's not pleasant, but it's still there. There's hundreds and hundreds of paths. But if you go back to my initial premise, which was leaving all those doors open and keeping all your senses ready to take in anything that happens along the way, then it works.

I really enjoy a chance to get together with contemporaries and other people who are doing the work and talk about it. "Gee, I saw that show you did last month. How did you do that?" We've got magazines now that are giving us this information, but that interaction between the people is very good. Somebody years ago argued with me: "You're going to give your competitors all this information of how you do it." I don't care. Because by sharing it, I am going to learn more, and if someone takes a client because of information I've given them, I've got four more waiting, because I'm ahead of them. It helps me reinforce my own knowledge and grow in my knowledge when somebody asks, "How did you do that?"

Will Bellman argued design was a very individual thing and you really couldn't write a book about it. I understand what he was saying. Unfortunately, I think with Stanley McCandless we said: "This is how you design, that is the color combination, that is the angle." That is the Bible—

it was taught that way for many years. What I think books should now say is, "This is the design I did at that moment, under those circumstances, with that budget, with those people, on a Wednesday in the rain." You learn from that. You learn more from the mistakes than you learn from the successes. So, you read something like that and say, "Oh, that wasn't perfect. Oh, wait. I could have done this. Maybe that would have made it better." That's what it should be about.

Boy! I must admit I'm at a place in my life where I'm as much a workaholic as I've always been, and my wife will attest to that. I think one of the things that I did have to learn was that this couldn't be my whole life. I was introduced to boating and it worked for me. It was the release that I needed—a place to get away and forget about the business.

I get bored real easy, and that does come from doing concerts, I must admit. Once you've done touring, it's very difficult for a lot of people to slow down. The intensity is incredible. Sometimes it gets very difficult to sit through a tech rehearsal at a play. You go, we're scheduled for four days to do this? I could do this sucker in three hours.

Over the years I've written over sixty published articles and had a steady run of college lectures and artist-in-residencies at such schools as Carnegie Mellon and San Diego State. And I've written a textbook, *Concert Lighting: Techniques, Art and Business*. For the past three years I've been a lecturer in advanced lighting at Cal Arts in Valencia, California. I love teaching, and I welcome the opportunity to talk lighting with anyone.

What will be my next move? I'm always looking for new frontiers. I'm doing theme-park design and commercial property lighting now. My time is spent on a more diverse range of projects than at any other time in my career. To me that is what I love. I don't want to be pigeonholed. Keep the competition guessing and keep myself in love with what I do: that keeps the spark in my work.

# Chapter Twenty-nine

# Pilbrow Story 8: Darkness

I was asked to meet that very famous film director Ken Russell at seven o'clock one autumn evening at his house in Notting Hill Gate, London. Apparently an opera production was in the offing for him, and he wanted to talk about my lighting it. I was rather in awe of meeting this illustrious figure. Somewhat gingerly I walked up the steps to his front door and pressed the bell. It rang distantly.

After a pause a light inside the hall came on and the door opened. There stood the familiar, burly figure with a shock of white hair.

"Yes?" he said.

I replied, "Richard Pilbrow." As our fingers touched for the beginning of a handshake, the light went out. But not just the hall light, every light: the house, the neighbors, the street, every light....Pitch black.

"Ah ha, the Prince of Darkness!" came back the instant reply.

A few minutes later we were ensconced around a bottle of whisky and a candle—a pretty merry discussion. Sadly, the show didn't happen, so I never had a chance to work with this extraordinarily creative man.

*Darkness* is in fact terribly difficult. I remember when I began lighting in the fifties, shadows and the avoidance thereof were an obsession. With only twelve lamps on the first pipe and perhaps six in the front of house, together with the ubiquitous footlights, the avoidance of shadow was the highest priority. Nearly thirty years later, with the extraordinarily high light levels all too often found on the stage, real shadow becomes even more tremendously difficult. I think we all desire the bold stark dash of light that casts a strong shadow, but we hardly ever achieve it. Basically as we all know, we have to see the actors' faces as well as "paint the stage with light." Nine times out of ten, this means the softening of any stark shadows that one may have in stock.

Of course the director has to want to go for it. By coincidence, the production of *Show Boat* for director Hal Prince has—despite its six hundred lights, Vari*Lites, light curtains, color scrollers and countless special gizmos—a great dark moment, which demonstrates that *less is better*. I also have to admit this is totally Hal's doing. I have a tendency to turn on too much, too bright. The last scene takes place on the wharf outside the Cotton Blossom, which is just about to start its evening performance. Following a sensational Charleston dance number by choreographer Susan Stroman, which rises to a blazing climax, the stage darkens—the first time around certainly not enough for Mr. Prince.

"What are you doing, Richard?" Hal barks. Everyone who knows Hal will understand this is said in an extremely loud voice. "Dark. I want it dark," he yells by way of further explanation. So rather quickly I take everything out except the practical light fittings over the set and the Vari*Lite VL2s, which, with a leaf gobo and a pale blue-green color, cover all the key points of the stage with a dense, dark, dapple of moonlight as if through trees. Ravenal, after twenty-five years absence from his family, returns like a ghost, hardly discernible at the side of the stage in the broken moonlight. It's quite a good moment. Thank you, Mr. Prince.

I'm perhaps the last person who should write this paragraph. While my interest is in story telling rather than technology, I must admit that through my career I've always used quite a lot of equipment, and just like everybody else in these modern times, now use even more. What we do need to keep saying to ourselves is that *more is not better*.

Finally, on the absorbing subject of *darkness:* Tapas Sen, one of India's most revered lighting designers, was a speaker at the Showlight conference in Bradford, England, in 1993. With a short video of his work and a speech of such modesty, he became the star of the show. Here is an artist in light. With incredibly simple resources, one or two lamps, the most mundane ordinary objects, and shadow, he creates magic in light. The interplay of shadow and illumination and the absence thereof deceives the eye and most powerfully evokes emotion.

Dawn Chiang did a light show commissioned by the Whitney Museum of American Art in the spring of 1994. She, Eric Cornwell and colleagues created a program of great beauty, delicacy and mystery using, by happenstance, some of the approaches of Tapas Sen. The eye was continually delighted and the emotions provoked. The Museum had one stipulation: the whole show took place in a daylit gallery, and the power available was five 15-amp outlets.

Now that takes talent.

# Chapter Thirty

# Tom Munn

*om Munn serves as resident lighting designer and design consultant for the San Francisco Opera, a position he has held since 1976. He has created the lighting, projections and special effects for over 165 productions for San Francisco Opera, including televised productions of* Turandot, La Boheme, Aida, Mefistofele, Orlando, Capriccio *and* La Gioconda *(for which he received an Emmy Award). Other highlights include productions of* William Tell, Carmen, War and Peace *and* The Ring of the Nibelung. *He has also designed the scenery for a number of San Francisco Opera productions. His designs for other opera companies have been seen in New York, Houston, Dallas, Washington, San Diego, Minneapolis, Kansas City and Japan. At the Netherlands Opera he created the lighting and projections for* Macbeth, Lulu, Don Quichotte *and* Madama Butterfly. *Tom has also designed scenery and/or lighting for Broadway, off-Broadway, regional theatre, industrials, video, film, modern dance and ballet. Consulting projects have varied from a corporate board room for The Northface to the lighting systems for Het Musiektheater, Amsterdam, Holland.*

I knew by the time I was eight years old that I wanted to do something in the theatre or lighting. I was fascinated by it, I loved it, and that's all I could see myself doing. It came from seeing theatre.

By the time I got into seventh or eighth grade, all my extra time was spent backstage by the dimmer boards and experimenting with the lights. Every time I had an opportunity backstage, I was the first to volunteer.

At about this time my older brother and I began a marionette theatre.

My Uncle Hank built us an elaborate portable theatre. Our next-door neighbor was an electrical engineer for General Electric, who built us a dimmer board. We paid for the system by baby-sitting for his four young daughters at seventy-five cents an hour. It was one of my first experiences of bad business deals in the theatre. We were baby-sitting for that dimmer board until we went to college. We traveled about Connecticut presenting shows at birthday parties, fairs and church functions. I'm sure the puppet shows weren't very good, but the lighting and scenery were first rate!

As soon as I got to the Plainville, Connecticut, high school—a new high school with a brand new auditorium with flies—I was in heaven. I had a teacher (my high-school mentor) who recognized my love of theatre and introduced me to Leonora Merrick, who was then married to David [Merrick]. She took me down to the New Haven premiere of out-of-town previews for *A Funny Thing Happened on the Way to the Forum* and to meet Jean Rosenthal, who was lighting it. It was one of those unforgettable experiences. She was then going to do a season at the Stratford Connecticut Shakespeare Festival and offered me a position as lighting apprentice. I was on cloud nine! Much to my disappointment, I was not able to take up the offer because my father was transferred to Schenectady, New York.

Instead I went up to Saratoga Springs and knocked on a door at the Spa Music Theatre, and said, "Could you use somebody in lighting?" And the producer at the time said, "You do lights?"

I said, "Yes!"

They had just fired the lighting designer. The producer took me into the auditorium and said, "There is something wrong with this lighting. There's light everywhere; it doesn't look very good." The lighting was terrible. They had hung Fresnels out in front of the house, which were washing all over. I made a few comments, and he said, "You've got the job." So I started at the Spa Music Theatre for $50 a week, and never stopped working in one form of theatre or another.

That summer I attended St. Michael's College in Winooski, Vermont, but switched the following year to Boston University. They didn't have a lighting program, so they put me in the directing program. I took a year and a half of directing. I took a lot of art courses on the side, particularly design and painting. My second mentor, Harold Armistead (head of design) suggested I switch to a full design program. I ended up becoming a fairly proficient painter and scenic artist. So, all of a sudden, my career took a side step and I found myself working as a set designer and a painter.

I left BU before graduation. I had been secretly working professionally on the outside. Those were the days they were adamant about not working while you were in school. So I decided enough of this, I don't need any more school. I'll go work. I went up to Expo '67 and took a job as electrician and then came back to Boston and New York and worked as a design assistant to people like Marsha Eck, Doug Schmidt, Karl Eigsti and David Mitchell. I worked as a set design assistant for maybe four or five years in

New York and did more set design. Nobody would really consider me for lighting, except dance. I began doing a lot of dance lighting at the time—particularly with Mary Anthony. Through her I got to work with other choreographers such as Anna Sokolow, Charles Wydman and Pearl Lang.

Those early days in New York I did a lot of off-Broadway shows. Those I was able to light myself. When I conceived of a show, I always thought of it from the light first. When I did my first Broadway show, a play by Dore Schary called *Brightower,* the producers insisted upon another well known LD because I wasn't considered a lighting designer.

Around the edges I was teaching at Columbia. Doing whatever I could to make ends meet. Then I started doing industrial shows. With industrials I was able to design both the sets and lights and have decent budgets. A lot of companies wanted innovation. Fresh is good, new is good, as long as it works. There was always the pressure, because you only had the one shot. I got into projection on all levels, with video projection, using eidaphor projectors. They were just coming into use. So, again, my career took a slight turn and I ended up spending the next ten years doing industrials. It gave me the opportunity to use all kinds of equipment, develop special effects and experiment with everything from moving lights to lasers. I was able to apply a great deal of what I learned to another discipline or artistic area.

So from the work standpoint, all this was very exciting. But the pressure was starting to get to me. When I got to the point where I was doing an off-Broadway production that was opening in New York, and I had three industrials going, and I was commuting three days a week between Las Vegas and New York City, I said, "This is crazy. I can't do this. I don't want to work like this."

I was also working in Europe for the Netherlands Opera as a result of a collaboration with Bob Israel and the director Rhoda Levine. Rhoda had mentioned me to Kurt Adler, the general director of San Francisco Opera. He had seen a multimedia production of *Macbeth* we had done. He was looking for a lighting designer. So the opera called and asked if I would come out and interview. This was in 1966. I thought, "No, I can't do opera." I love music, yet I really always had fallen asleep. I had been to the Met a few times and every time I was bored to tears. I thought, "I love the music, but it is so dated, and the lighting all looks the same."

But the appeal of coming to San Francisco, and the thought of being in one place and only concentrating on one thing for a time (I had just recently got married) told me that this was the kind of break that I needed. At the very last minute I decided to take the job.

My first season I had something like three weeks to prepare ten operas, and the only one I had done before was *Tosca.* The first production I was to light was a revival of an old *Die Walkure.* I had never seen a Wagner opera. I told Adler this, and it worked in my favor, I guess. I was very honest with him, and I said, "You know you've got the wrong person, because I don't know the first thing about opera, I don't know about the tradition; I don't know about any of these things. All I have to go by is what the music says to me and instinct."

So he said, "Do what ever you can with it." Then he came in the middle of the sessions and said it was "much too bright, much too bright. It doesn't look like Wagner. You don't do this. You don't do this in opera." Because they had always done everything dark with straight-down follow spots for everything, and you never saw a face. I decided I wanted to see faces. I mean, watching opera I had never seen anybody's face. So I said, "Look, you hired me to do it. You gave me free reign. When it's done, if you don't like it, I'll go back to New York."

So the reviews came out and one of the first reviews said, the first time we'd ever "seen" (and the "seen" was in quotation marks) Wagner opera in San Francisco. Adler came to me afterwards and said, "Mr. Munn, you are right." That was all he said.

He was very innovative, and the company was very innovative. He was like a father. I had a crash course in opera. In those first three years I did forty productions with twenty-three different directors. I was spending all my time—when I wasn't learning on stage with one opera—glued to head-sets at home until the wee hours of the morning learning the next opera. It was crazy. But I actually ended up falling in love with it.

In my second season Adler asked me to design sets for *Pelleas and Melisande*, and I became sort of resident art director as well as lighting designer. I really started to settle in and enjoy working with the people from around the world. The resident staff became a wonderful team; not that we didn't have our problems, faults or differences; but we worked together, and I never felt alone.

I think the most difficult part of lighting is being away and alone so much. I love to travel and I like to meet new people. But you are always going your separate ways. By the time you get that working relationship established, poof, you are into the final dress rehearsals and it's over. That's why I think it's lonely.

When I got to San Francisco, what I found very appealing was the fact that I was working with a core of people over and over. And you could really begin to build on past experiences, explore possibilities, take chances, try new ideas. I like to work as part of a group. I think there is a tendency toward less collaborative effort lately, mostly due to time and money restraints.

When I say time, I'm referring to the production time a producer gives you. Often in opera the producer is bringing the director from one part of the world and the designers from another. All of a sudden, there are these individual personalities thrown together to do a new production. If you decide you want a particular look to a production, you'd better damn well get that designer who's going to give you that look immediately, because you aren't going to have time to change it. It's hard to change direction if you only have five hours to light an opera. It's easy to misinterpret. What a storm is to one person isn't necessarily what a storm is to another. If the director has a very strong or particular idea and you've missed the boat, so to speak, it's almost impossible to do anything about it. There's no time or money left to rethink, redo or make major alterations. Often you have to settle for a compromise.

The positive thing about all this is that it has opened the door, to a certain degree, to the use of technology—the electronic stuff, the high tech equipment, the moving lights, color changers, computers, CAD drafting. I think those are all beneficial and have grown out of the fact that time is money. Developing these things actually saves time in the long run. What it saves time for, hopefully, is for refining the artistic end. I am an idealistic person—enough to feel that all of these time-saving devices are there to allow me to refine the creative process. It really is just a means to an end.

The production of *William Tell,* particularly, was very visual. It was something that Lotfi Mansouri, the director, wanted to do right from the beginning. He was very excited by Gerard Howland's set design. This was a production that came out of economy. It was originally supposed to be a very high-budget production. One thing after another fell through in terms of the economic support, and we were faced with going from a $650,000 budget to a $200,000 budget. So the designer stripped away everything and we cut it down and the more we stripped away, the better everybody liked it.

It was an open stage with raked revolves, thirty-foot-high articulated mirrors perpendicular to the proscenium and a rear projection screen. When you are going to have a chorus of eighty on a fifty-foot-diameter circle, you've got to cover the area. There's not much question about where people are going to be. The principals are going to be downstage. I mean there are certain formulas from experience that you learn. To break up the huge space I decided that there would be very little unbroken light. Every fixture ended up with some form of gobo, and I used floor projections. The idea was to provide a heavily textured base with light and the look of painterly brushstrokes that were in the back projections.

We also had this surround of moving mirrors, so side light was restricted. I had worked with mirrors before, and I really wanted to use them. A lot of the light that is on the stage is actually reflected off mirrors; it's not focused directly on to the people. The little sidelight I was able to get in was through portholes between the mirrors. I used fixtures like 6x22s from two feet away from the singers, but it's actually over their head going to the opposite mirror and coming back to the mirror side. Now the mirrors are changing angle. That was tricky, but it worked out fine. I found that one way or another they were always reflective. It does make a wonderful blending quality, because of the reflective light—all the lighting is broken.

Once I realized I was going to stick with a mirrored box, then everything radiated out from the center. A lot of the standard things—bridge-ends, diagonal backlight, Fresnel and PAR washes—weren't going to work. I ended up with about eighty 6x12s that were just gobo patterns on the floor, cool and warm. I don't think there was one color that was the same in any instrument, and it radiated out. I did a color sketch and matched colors—the oranges and yellows—so that I had a purple against a yellow, or a blue-green against....I think we came up with about twenty-eight areas over the disk. That was the framework.

Careerwise, I think I made the choice to go into a fixed rep situation at the right time. You are still surrounded by total chaos at work, but my personal life is much more focused. I am enjoying the fact that I am able to have a family and a home life and still participate or be involved in what I love doing best. Still, the pressures are tremendous. Trying to have a career and a family in this kind of a situation, with the unscheduled hours and the crazy fourteen-hour, eighteen-hour days, the weeks on end where you are either at the drafting table or in the theatre—there is still the pressure.

When I was early in my career at San Francisco Opera, I was doing all of the productions all of the time and I only had one assistant. I think as I matured I found that I was much happier letting some of that control go and doing, maybe, seven or eight of the productions well. Once I was outside some of that pressure, I was actually able to do more for each individual production. We have been able to develop and see things over a longer period of time, so that we have a sense of building. I talk about this technology—for instance, motorized PAR-56 strips—which we had here years ago (1983) and have become part of the house system. Database and system management projects like that, which are long, ongoing and developmental, R and D, in a rep situation—I've had opportunities to experiment. In rep you've got to find ways to beat the system. So you look to, how can I bring to this production a special quality that is somewhat unique to it, and not have them all look the same?

If your angles and your focus and certain positions are fixed, and you are limited in certain respects because of time restraints, you look to things like color and intensity. One of the things I found most fun to work with is color. This is one of my basic philosophies about rep lighting—that the color has to be totally flexible. Personally, my choice would be to have fixed overhead positions as long as they have the ability to raise and lower and you can change the color and template on every instrument. Here I have eight bridges; I find that you can always get around the fixed positions—you can go to a system pipe—but I don't care what it is, as long as I can change the color on it. I keep coming back to the fact that I don't want to spend five hours or seven hours doing a major turnaround, changing every instrument in the house or changing a bridge from one position to the next. I'd rather have the instruments set. I can maximize my use of the equipment and find creative solutions that don't waste time on hanging and circuiting.

The technology of dimmer per circuit, which is finally taking hold in the U.S., does mean that there are a lot more possibilities. Today I think it is harder for a lighting designer to come to grips with the amount of possibilities. You have to know where to go and what you are doing so that if you are going to have a thousand circuits with a thousand lights ("thousand points of light!") in the air, you need a way to keep track of them. I would rather have an assistant who keeps track of that, freeing me up for dealing with any artistic choices, as opposed to having to make any kind of electrical choice. Once the planning is done, I want to let others, or somebody else, worry about the system. That's more and more difficult, I think, today as the systems get larger.

I think the biggest thing for an assistant is a knowledge of computers. I'm certainly looking for somebody who is computer literate, someone who is very capable of doing the paperwork. There is a sort of a right-hand or an artistic assistant who can deal with focus, deal with problems, be your second or third pair of eyes. I find, as production scale increases, you're overseeing a larger number of design and mechanical aspects, that is, color changers, moving lights, follow spots. All of these have become an intricate part of the production: having not just an assistant who can say the smoke is at fifteen percent, but someone who can look at it and say the smoke is too little at fifteen percent or it's too much, and deal with those aspects of production. [I want to find] somebody who has what I call theatrical common sense, someone who has a certain sensibility about what's happening on the stage in terms of the performers. They may not be so good at the computer, but they can be much more valuable. I think the training of that type of assistant is rare. A lot of people have this quality or they don't.

I started out as an assistant. I trained as an assistant at somebody's elbow, and I still personally think that's the best way. I think that's worth four times any formalized education. I get more conservative about that as I get older. I think there are an awful lot of designers, young people who are coming out, who don't want to take the time and feel they don't need to take the time to learn those kinds of subtleties to working as an assistant. I think they are in for a hard time. Traditionally ninety percent of the people who are lighting designers started because they were somebody's assistant and were handed the job or some one said, "I'm too busy, do this job." You succeed or falter. If you succeed, people recognize you and you are on your way. If you don't, you are out. I think that is still not a bad system. It's hard to go knocking on doors when you are unknown. But as soon as you work for somebody, you make the contacts. You learn the trade.

Somebody once said, with most job interviews in the business world, people make an impression in the first ten seconds of an interview. I do think that it is true. You have to be able to work with other people in a very high-pressure situation. You have to be able to produce under very difficult situations and maintain certain working relationships. As an assistant you must have an awareness, a sharpness, an alertness, a sensitivity to what is going on on the stage but also to whom you are assisting. The chemistry has to be there. That chemistry is established in the early meeting. I get calls from other designers for recommendations of assistants. There is a bigger, larger exchange of information in terms of who's coming up, who's available, than in terms of what colors did you use. Word of mouth is still the biggest plus; it's the biggest advantage that a young person has. If somebody screws up badly as an assistant to one person, it just doesn't take long; it's very hard for that person to overcome that.

The hardest thing for any of us is to also recognize or realize what we are really particularly good at—where we shine and in what area we shine—and to either stay or develop in that area, go in that direction. We do go in many different directions. I am a second-rate set designer. I like to think of myself as a first-class lighting designer. And recognizing that fact, I think, was certainly important in terms of developing a career. If you are an electrician, and that is really your strength, pursue that: there is a real need for first-rate electricians. It's recognizing where you want to go and not going off in too many directions early on.

I am also looking for somebody who has a goal when they come in. I want to know that the time I am spending isn't going to be wasted. I find that I'm not interested in somebody who comes in because they are not quite sure what they really want to do: "Maybe I want to be a lighting designer, maybe I want to be a set designer, maybe I want to be this, maybe I want to be that," "Well, I'll try this for two years, and see if it works," kind of thing.

I'm not particularly good at marketing myself. I was lucky to a certain degree. I fell into this niche with San Francisco Opera. It was probably just as well, because there is an aspect of my own personality that I recognized early on: that I'm not a "go-getter." I have been lucky, but I have not had to go knock on doors. I don't know how or what I would say to somebody who does have to go knocking on doors. When you knock on the door, if somebody offers you a job, be prepared to take it. That's about the only advice I can say. Don't hem and haw; if you get an opportunity, it doesn't matter who it's with, take it. I am going after the person who is decisive. To me the resume is way down at the bottom of the list.

# Chapter Thirty-one

# Pilbrow Story 9: America

My father was a fencer. He was British sabre champion both before and after World War II and was a member of the British Olympic team in 1936 and 1948. In 1936 he visited New York for an international fencing competition. He brought back with him a souvenir brochure of the city, with the Chrysler and Empire State Buildings looking as magnificent then as they do today. To a three year old (which I was at the time) this tourist brochure was a glimpse into a wonderland. In 1941 two of his fencing friends from New York came to visit us in London, then in the middle of the Blitz. One said he worked for the FBI and enrolled me as a "junior G-man." After their return to the States we corresponded. One day he sought my parents' permission to broadcast one of my letters on CBS: "News from London in Flames." Much later I was to do National Service in the RAF. By a stroke of good fortune I was one of the very few Englishmen posted to an American air base (in the U.K.) and spent two years as part of a small, privileged minority living in the PX on American rations (this at a time when many things in England were only to be obtained with food coupons).

So began my romance with America. Years later *A Funny Thing Happened on the Way to the Forum* paid my fare across the Atlantic. I remember my first night in an American hotel, the Taft, next to the Shubert Theatre, in New Haven. The room was steam heated, and I could find no way to turn it off. Finally I dragged the bed across to the window, opened it and laid a pillow on the window sill. That was more tolerable. The story at breakfast of how I awoke to find my head and shoulders covered in snow and the rest of me simmering gently below the boil got a ribald reception from the crew.

The top New York crews must be the best in the world. Yes, of course, they're unionized; of course they stop for lunch at exactly the allotted minute; but I've found their professionalism to be of an extraordinarily high order. The first edition of *Stage Lighting* was dedicated to both Lennie Tucker, my long-time chief at the Old Vic/National Theatre, and Herbie Anstett, who was my chief electrician in early forays on the New York scene. Herbie was a rock of good humor, patience, technical skill and thoroughness. He was one of the head men at Four Star Lighting, where the equipment for *The Rothchilds* came from. I had decided for the first time to use some low-voltage light curtains. These had to be custom built at Four Star and were shipped out to Detroit, where we were to open. It was an extraordinarily hot summer. The sunlight in Detroit was very bright and my assistant, Molly—whom I later married—was dazzling, so I invested in a pair of sunglasses. The load-in went reasonably well, although erecting the massive sets, by John Bury, took a bit of time. But finally we came to check-out. I said, "Let's try the light curtains," and on they came. My heart sank. They all seemed to be gelled with a rather chocolate neutral density filter, yet this was long before the days of the color scroller.

"Bring them up to full," I shouted up to the boards.

"They're at full," came back the reply.

This was depressing. The producer had been very reluctant to invest the money in this new-fangled equipment and it was certainly meant to be rather more effective. Out came the A-frame and up went the electricians to check the wiring of the transformers. Everything seemed to be correct. Damn. I rang Four Star in New York. Herbie had been supervising the preparation of the show and he came to the phone.

"Herbie, we've got a terrible problem. These light curtains are nothing like performing correctly. They must be wired wrong."

"Don't worry," came the reply, "I was just leaving anyway. Leave it until I get out there and I'll sort it out."

"Thanks, Herbie, see you soon."

I put the phone down. Back on stage the crew were in a huddle, staring upward, while debating what could have possibly been done wrong in building this crazy Englishman's esoteric device. It was hot and I was very concerned.

"Bloody hell," I thought, "I've really cocked this up!"

Fatigue or a stress headache made me slip off my glasses to massage the bridge of my nose.

"Whoops!" Somebody had turned the lights to full. My heart leapt.

There was a dazzling sheet of white light up which you could almost climb. The crew were looking at me like I'd lost my mind. I thought, "That'll teach me to buy a new pair of sunglasses."

Considerably embarrassed, I ran back to the stage-door telephone, dialed Four Star and asked for Herbie Anstett. "I'm sorry, he just left for the airport."

Thank you, Herbie, for diligence way beyond the call of duty.

I remember my first American memory board. This was for the New York production of *Rosencrantz and Guildenstern Are Dead*, several years before *A Chorus Line* and the first electronic memory board on Broadway. After several weeks on the road before uncomprehending audiences, we got to New York. During every preview audiences stumbled out in droves, frustrated and quite bewildered by the play. It was at the Alvin Theatre, which for the first time had a bar serving alcohol in the theatre. The reception to previews was so disastrous I found myself invited for a drink by a man wearing a long raincoat, whom I'd seen hanging around the theatre quite a lot. I gradually realized it was David Merrick. He seemed to enjoy a drink every night during Act 2. The first night finally arrived—I was surprised that he had had the courage to stick with it.

I went back stage to wish the crew good luck. The chief was Donnie Stern, then one of the younger generation, now the head of Bash Stage Lighting. The show, with six piano boards and rather more preset auxiliary boards than was usual, was pretty complex. After hearing "beginners" called, I was about to go out front when I realized there were no board plots (cue sheets) in sight. I didn't say anything (well one doesn't, does one), but sort of stood around pretending to be thinking about something else, wondering if the guys had forgotten and left them all in their road boxes. My personal level of tension rose as "places" was called and finally couldn't bear it another minute.

"I say...don't you want your plots?"

"No," came back the cheerful reply, "We know them all by heart!"

They did too. (This was truly Broadway's memory board debut.) It's amazing what miracles can be wrought by three men, hands, feet, elbows, knees, short pieces of wood and a lot of handles. Those guys deserve most of the credit for one of the nicest reviews I've ever received from *Newsweek* magazine!

Lighting is such a wonderful mix of the magical and the mundane. The airiest of dreams come down to wires and devices. The physical installation, the organization of the paperwork, the skills of the crew operating controls or pirouetting with the performers on a follow spot all make up the exquisite detail of the end result. The concept of lighting in three dimensions, modeling the actor, and, in Jean Rosenthal's words, making him appear "jewel-like" has spread from America around the world. Fresh influences—the stark whiteness of Brechtian theatre, the bold strokes of light using nonincandescent sources in Europe, the kaleidescopic searching beams of rock and roll, and the success of the English megamusical—have all brought an invigorating freshness to lighting today. But America is still the country where lighting is taken most seriously and where the profession of the lighting designer is at its strongest. Its teaching infrastructure and its professionalism still stand as a beacon for lighting everywhere else.

# Chapter Thirty-two

# Tharon Musser

*On Broadway Tharon Musser has designed many productions including* Dreamgirls, Forty-second Street, The Goodbye Girl, Secret Garden, Brighton Beach Memoirs, Children of a Lesser God, They're Playing Our Song, The Wiz, A Chorus Line, Pacific Overtures, A Little Night Music, Follies, Applause, Mame, Golden Boy, Long Day's Journey into Night, *and* Once Upon a Mattress. *In repertory she has worked with the José Limón Dance Company, Phoenix Theatre Company, National Repertory Theatre Company, The American Shakespeare Festival, Lincoln Center Repertory Theatre, Dallas Opera, Mark Taper Forum, Miami Opera and Wolftrap Foundation, among others. Her international credits include productions in Paris, London, Beirut, Israel, Munich and elsewhere. Tharon has been the lighting design consultant to the Ford Theatre Restoration, Washington, D.C.; Radcliffe College; American Academy of Dramatic Arts, San Antonio, Texas; and Berea College, Kentucky. Her four Los Angeles Drama Critics Awards, and two Antoinette Perry Awards (for* Follies *and* A Chorus Line*) are accompanied by innumerable nominations. The magazine* Lighting Dimensions *awarded Tharon a Lifetime in Light Award in 1990 and in 1995 she received the Wally Russell Award for her Outstanding Lifetime Achievement.*

At a symposium I did this spring one of the kids asked, "Should I get a lawyer or an agent?" I suggested that she get a job first, and it would sort itself out.

Coming from the South in the early twentieth century, theatre was practically unheard of. There was just the senior play every year. I did learn in high school that the last thing in the world I ever wanted to do was be on stage. I found it a horrifying experience. I was fortunate to be accepted by Berea College, a work-study school, where I got a job as tech director in their theatre, and discovered that I loved it. When I decided to go to Yale to work on a Master of Fine Arts degree I suspected that it made no sense to specialize in scenic design. I didn't like to draw and I'm still not good at it. I studied with Don Oenslager. Little by little it narrowed itself down to lighting. I don't know if I thought of it really as a career then, because there was virtually no such field. Bill Eckart held my hand while I got something done to graduate.

While I was still at Yale I went to work at the 92nd Street Y, which was known as the modern-dance factory. We did children's shows, string quartets and poetry readings and usually about three or four dance concerts a week. I really loved it. I worked there for two years, and when I decided to leave everyone said I would starve to death. I took the chance that all the performers I had been working with who said they couldn't do a concert without me weren't just blowing smoke. We're talking about 1952. You know, there were these people, bless their hearts, they'd save their money all year to do this one concert. I think I did practically every modern dance concert in New York City. I'd charge them fifty bucks. I got every penny. Sometimes it would come in at five dollars a month over a year, but they always paid me. Then I tied up with José Limón and began touring with him and the Connecticut Dance Festival in the summer and this, that and the other, I was grossing about three thousand a year. Even in those days that wasn't very much. So I decided to look into television.

There were no positions open for lighting, so I became a floor manager—like a stage manager in the theatre. I hung around in various studios and I finally had an offer from, I think, CBS for seventy-five dollars a week. I knew at that time they were offering the boys a lot more than that, and that pissed me off—so *adios* TV. I thought about becoming a stage manager, but then it occurred to me that I might get one of those shows with a door bell, three telephone rings and four cues, and that would make me crazy. It seemed that my only option for survival was to join the union and thus be able to light shows on Broadway. Five long years later I was in.

In those days you had to take the whole exam; lighting counted ten points out of a hundred. Again with Bill Eckhart's help I finally managed to pass. The separate lighting section came after I'd been in for a while. There were a lot of lighting designers who had the same background that I had who either couldn't or didn't want to take the entire exam. That's when the IA entered the picture. They called for a meeting with Jo Mielziner, Howard Bay, Jean Rosenthal, Peggy Clark, Abe Feder and myself to discuss taking in lighting designers. Well, this didn't thrill [USA] 829, and we had reservations too. There's a fine line between how one functions as a designer and those who make it all work. Remember, we were still living in the era of the "designer" head electrician, who used basically the same plot for every show. We had tried before to get the union to have an associate membership for lighting designers, as with costumes, but they thought the union was too split up as it was. This threat of losing our membership forced them to reexamine the possibilities.

I'll never forget it: we were in a union meeting in which it was finally decided to explore how a separate lighting section could be formed. Abe turned around and said, "OK, kid, it's your turn." I worked for two years establishing the lighting exam committee and then decided it was all bullshit. I don't know how you put yourself in judgement on another designer. What really finished me was when we were looking at Nick Cernavitch's practical. He was a Canadian who did lighting for ballet, did beautiful work. One of his companies was coming into New York, so he wanted to get into the union so he could light them on Broadway without supervision. He did his practical at Hunter College. I had tears in my eyes—it was so beautiful. Peggy Clark was sitting next to me and I looked over and she had graded it very, very low. I had given it the highest grade. I asked her why and she replied, "Oh, terrible color." I said, "Peggy, that's none of our business. Look at the composition." That's when I decided I didn't want to have any more to do with the exam. I think it's better now than it's ever been. It's almost an open shop, which it should be. If you can get a job, you should be allowed to work.

The spring I got in the union I was in Connecticut with the Dance Festival. I got a call from José Quintero to light *Long Day's Journey into Night*. Well, the ink wasn't dry on my union card, and I was a little leery, as I'd seen some of my contemporaries go down the tubes because they didn't understand the New York system—truly a system of its own. José asked if I would at least read the play, and I said I would. I called him back. "What do you think?" he said. I said, "Too long." He asked if I would come into New York and talk with them, and I said, "I really can't, I've got a dance concert going on here and I can't get away." "Well, could we come and talk to you?" And I said, "Yes, if you can get here between twelve and one, which is my lunch break. That's all the time I have." I was just being so high and mighty. The day after it opened, I'd have jumped off Brooklyn Bridge if I hadn't done it. So that was the beginning. Brooks Atkinson's review sent me to the dictionary to see if it was complimentary or not. Thank God it was.

I thought I'd die of old age before I ever got a musical. You know how the world loves to put us in a mail slot: "Oh she does straight shows and Shakespeare." The first one—*Shinbone Alley* with Eartha Kitt and Eddie Bracken [laughs]—was a nightmare. It went down the alley. We did it in New York, no out of town tryouts. I had the best billing on the house boards of that show I've ever had. Every night another name was whited out. They were firing people left, right and center. Eventually I was the only one left.

Yeah, there are blood baths. I've gotten to the point where I don't like to touch a musical unless I like the people or the product very much. They all take a lot of blood whether they're good, bad or indifferent, but the bad ones take gallons.

The best experience was Michael Bennett. Without a doubt that was the luckiest thing that ever happened to me. I keep working with new people hoping to find somebody with that spark. The theatricality just oozed out of his pores. He was incredible.

We did a lot of homework on his shows, making sure we were all in sync. But in the theatre if Michael saw a picture he liked, he'd change the blocking or choreography to make it work. If it was something I had to make work, that was OK, too. There was so little ego involved. We all understood that the production took precedence. I think I can safely say that it was a continuing experience like no other. When we were planning *Dream Girls* we met two or three times a week in Robin's [Wagner] studio with the set and Michael just moving little people around the model and we'd suggest scenic or lighting modes. A week before first rehearsal Michael said, "I'm gonna to think my cast are idiots. I know where they're supposed to go, why don't they." Michael loved tech rehearsal and he really gave us time to explore. The Shuberts said that we had become unproducible as a result of the three or four days of tech, so Michael decided that he'd rather become the producer than present a half-done show to an audience. I think the important point here is that he was encouraging the best ideas to rise easily to the top. I can't tell you how many shows have had a first preview or an invited audience before anyone's even made it through the show once. That way lies desperation.

I watched rehearsal on all those shows, starting with *A Chorus Line*. As I watched rehearsal I'd mark my script for cues and counts. We taught Jeff Hamlin, the production stage manager, how to count with the dancers, and he was fantastic.

We opened *Chorus Line* downtown at the Public. They had a five-scene preset, and we rented a little auxiliary board for the Mondrian pattern, et cetera. When it was apparent we were going to move uptown, the Shuberts said we could have whatever we wanted in the way of control. So I called Frank DeVerna of Four Star and said we were going to skip preset boards and go directly to memory. Well, that started a panic, because nobody really knew what was available. Added to this was the fact that we weren't scheduled to move until the fall, but everyone realized how much money they were losing every week by staying at the Public, so they decided to move tooty-sweety. EDI was the one company that could meet the deadline, so Frank and I flew out to Hillsboro, Oregon. There was a prototype of the LS8 sitting in the front office, but it wasn't available as they hadn't gone into production on it. The best they could offer was some tape thing, I can't remember what it was called, and while I didn't like it, it seemed better than going backwards. The day we got back to New York, EDI called Frank to offer the prototype LS8. Well, Frank didn't know shit from shinola about any of the electronics then, so he called me, and I jumped at the chance to avoid that tape thing. Century wasn't able to make our deadline, and I knew that if we didn't get a memory board on that show, God knew how long it would be. This was a sure-fire production, as sure as Broadway can ever be, and we had carte blanche. Well, if my hair wasn't white then, it would be. Oh, that poor old thing, what we went through. A couple of years before we closed on Broadway, it got to the point where if you sneezed it went out to lunch.

We called the board Sam. Sam went down one day in previews. I'd asked for a voltage regulator, and the shop decided to install it between matinee and evening shows. The stupid asshole didn't turn the juice off and hit the side of the chassis and bingo! Our "backup" was two-scene presets. I'd been up to see the matinee and then went home, and I got this call: "Sam's blown up!" So I grabbed Marilyn [Rennagel] and Richard [Winkler] and got up to the theatre, put two guys on the upper set of the two scenes, Marilyn worked the bottom set between their legs. Richard and I ran through cue sheets—me deciding what cues could be done and Richard reading to the board setters. It was a madhouse: "Call that one, don't call that one, call that one." We got about seventy-five percent of the show with the presets. After a mild celebration we spent the night writing the backup Bible. Steve Terry spent a week with a soldering iron to get Sam back together. Every night we'd run into some of the dancers on the way to the theatre and they'd ask: "How's Sam?" "Nope, not tonight." Everyone was involved with each other's concerns on that show. Much later, Steve called me when Sam was going to be retired and asked if he could have him. I checked with Joe Papp, and he had no objections, so Steve picked him up, and he's now happily ensconced in the Computer Museum in Boston: a very respectable retirement.

The great designers when I started out were Jean, Peggy and Abe! Jo Mielziner was doing sets too. It seems so strange that once Jo and John Harvey split neither was able to light their way out of a paper bag. But the shows that they did together were gorgeous. Howard Bay said he did [his own lighting], but actually Ralph Holmes, his assistant, did it. Bill and Jean Eckhart tried to do it, went through the hinges of hell and got into all sorts of trouble. Mostly their electricians did it. The electricians were then part of the management team and they knew what was expected: mostly brighter and brighter. I remember the days of Al Alloy and George Gebhart. A lighting designer mixing with them could have a problem. Jean did a show with George. They were in Boston, and the manager asked her to check a rental bill. She looked at it and said she didn't know anything about it. George had brought along what he thought the show really needed and had it stored in the basement for when Jean got fired. She didn't, of course; neither did he. It was rough going in those days.

Abe became more involved in industrial and architectural lighting. He actually could be considered the first "lighting designer." One of my favorite Abe stories was during the era of the Federal Theatre. Of course they always worked round the clock and they'd run out of pipe to hang the instruments on. Abe had them ripping out the plumbing to get the needed pipe. He did some nice work even on inch-and-a-half pipe. Peggy's stuff I never really cottoned to very much. But Jean, of course, we all know the art that she did: real art.

I learned a lot at the American Shakespeare Festival at Stratford, Connecticut. Shakespeare and musicals have a lot in common. It's repertory all in one night. It was a great experience. John Houseman...I loved Houseman. He was a villain to work for. He thought nothing of leaning across a row of people and yelling something at you during previews. He's the most creative man cursewise I have ever known. I got so I'd sit in the balcony to get away from him. I felt so sorry for the people in the audience while John's yelling something vile at the designers, but he was a creative genius and somewhere we're told that aberrant behavior might possibly be excused.

Opera: I love to listen to opera. I used to think it was so marvelous to get paid to light opera. A major problem with opera is that the companies expect the same time commitment from their designers that they do from their singers. I found it difficult to promise to light a production two years in advance when I might be offered a Broadway musical in the same slot. While I love opera, I'm a Broadway baby at heart.

At some point David Hayes and I were consultants on some theatre, and I remember taking the architects around to several Broadway theatres pointing out the good things and the bad. Finally I said to David, "You know, we're wasting their money and our time. They don't give a shit what we think." Oh, I give advice once in a while, but real consulting...no.

I'm the world's worst at architectural interior lighting. Friends used to say, "Oh, we've got a new apartment, you must come and tell us what to do." I'd ask them to remember what my apartment looked like. The only place you can safely read is at my drafting table. I don't like lamps—so many of them are ugly. The lamps I do like are usually at their best with fifteen or twenty-five-watt bulbs in, so they blend with the surround. Obviously, I'm not the best choice for practical advice.

I'm a great believer in collaboration. I like to be very involved. I like early meetings with the set and costume designer. You never know when tidbits are dropped that have a lot to do with your thinking on the project. I don't draw it till the last minute. And then when I put it in the shop, I don't give them color till the last minute, because color is very difficult, yet my favorite thing. I tend to do it early in the morning, when I'm half asleep, otherwise I beat it to death. This blue, or that blue, or that blue or that blue...come on, just write one down! Color's the easiest thing to change once you're in the theatre, but nine times out of ten your first impulse will have been a good choice

I don't begin to use as much equipment as what is commonly used these days. I go in and look up and go, gasp, I wouldn't want to focus all that. We do overamplify and overlight now because of that box up there [TV]. Everybody's used to it. The computers have done it, and I don't know how they get the designers to give them the kind of space to hang the number of lights they hang. I have to fight for every inch. Sure one guy can run whatever you put up there. But he can't maintain it. And what I see—and I don't think I'm getting to be an old fuddy-duddy—but I see all of this equipment. I call it supermarket lighting. You see mush. You don't see a point of view on that stage, just mush. [They figure] fill up all the spaces and something must work for whatever they need. But there's no point of view. It's the result of too much equipment.

In the old days, when you had two boards and one man or three boards and two men, you really had to do your homework, and say, "I really *need* this." I know I used to do a one set show and they'd say, "Two boards, right?" And I'd say, "Does it have a cyc?" "Yes." "OK, it's three boards." Anyway, it caused you to really think your show through. Now the difference in cost of four hundred units or eight hundred units is not really that much. Compared to the cost of the rest of the production, it's peanuts. I don't know what the answer is. It's out of hand, and I don't know the answer, because I don't think the people who are working with that amount of equipment would know what I was talking about. I'm sure they think they've done their homework.

I used moving lights on *Dreamgirls*. With Michael you could always count on a dancer being in the same spot every night. Then I used the VL5s at the Manhattan Theatre Club for *Putting It Together*—a nightmare! They saved my life, but they almost killed me, programming those mothers. I couldn't convince the director that they weren't follow spots. I said, "They're moving specials." They're marvelous, but there I had no space for a follow-spot show. If this were a real theatre, it would be a piece of cake. Programming was just a nightmare.

There still can be a point of view in terms of the set and the costumes. It has to look like I've been there when I do a show. And that's not just, "Turn 'em on." *I* have to think I've been there. I'm not saying other people do. *I* have to look at a show and say *Yeah, that's me*. It's a big help, because when a cue is wrong or a color is wrong, it sends cold shivers up my back. No, no, no, *that's* not me.

I'm getting very picky in my old age. I don't want to quit, but I don't want to kill myself anymore. You quit, you die. You seldom say never in this business. There are a few people I say never about, but not too many. Mostly it has to do with the property, whether I'm comfortable with it. As much as I think you should sit in rehearsals, I don't want to be bored in rehearsals before I even get to the project. I just say, "Thank you very much, but no thank you." Ginger asked me the other day, "Why are you doing this show at Circle?" And I said, "So I won't mold."

I wouldn't change anything in my life, even a year in Alaska. I learned a lot doing soldier shows.

Everybody says I probably made more money off *A Chorus Line* than anything, but *Forty-second Street* is very close in there. Yeah, that's where the money is. But you can only live through a musical or two a year at the most. Stage shows—I remember one year I did nine—but there aren't that many shows any more. I remember a producer invited me to lunch once and offered me a show, and I'd been in the union two years or so, and I was pretty green. He made me an offer, moneywise. And I said, "Assuming that I could do X number of shows a year, how am I supposed to live? I'm better off selling shoes." No, I don't regret....

I've been lucky, very lucky. Without some of that dumb luck, what do you do? The union retirement plan [laughter], the pension will get you from here to New York—maybe once. I don't know, I really don't know.

When somebody asks, "Miss Musser, how do I survive?" I always say, "Thank God it's you and not me." I really don't know today what they do. I just think anything slightly artistic—there's always Jesse Helms, the son of a bitch. I really feel very sorry for young people starting out. Half the things I did when I was starting out are not even around now. I did ten years of summer stock. Those things are not there. So I don't know what to say. I'm not a pessimistic person. I've had a very good life. It's been wonderful and I've been very lucky. I used to say, "If you have talent, getting the first job many times is just luck, and whether you stay there is then up to you."

I miss David Merrick. I used to have terrible fights with David, but I miss him. We were doing *Mack and Mable* and we'd opened in San Diego, then went to L.A. And we were playing these monster houses, and they were packed. We'd been out for about eight weeks. And I was talking to Jerry Herman one night, and I said, "Jerry, have you gotten any royalties yet?" He said, "No." It usually takes two or three weeks for them to get going, but this was a little long. So I went to Jack Schlissel and I said, "What's with royalties?" "Oh, we're not paying them for this period, because the production costs have been too high." I said, "I beg your pardon!!" So I was back in New York, and I called my lawyer, and I said, "Would you call the Merrick office and tell them that unless my royalties are paid up to date, I won't be there to move the show to Washington." Boy, I think I was the only one on that show that got any royalties. [Laughs.]

Now the producers are people who have made it in the fashion world and they decide to come and play theatre. We were doing *Jerry's Girls*, and the producers were Seventh Avenue genius types, and it was like they'd bought a new yacht—bring along all the friends, et cetera. Finally the three girls in the show just put their foot down and said, "They can't come into the dressing rooms unless our agent is here." They wouldn't even knock, they'd just barge in the dressing room. After we opened, I went into Sam's one night, and one of the producers was sitting there and he said, "Did you really expect those notices?" And I said, "I'm afraid I did." "Well, I just don't understand," he said. We had a production meeting one Saturday morning—Klotzie [Florence Klotz] wasn't there, thank God! She had done "What a Little Christmas" like, they were on white chaise longues with gold bathing suits on and, you know, and these guys decided (they'd come with a shopping bag)—thank God Klotzie wasn't there. During the meeting he pulled out this bathing suit, and it was what I call a Florida Jewish bathing suit—big flowers, et cetera. And he said, "Don't you think that number would be better in suits like this?" Jerry Herman said, *"No!"* I thought, "If Klotz was here, she would throw something at this guy." It's incredible.

Other people always know a lot about our business, it seems. They are still leery about lights; they don't know other than it's too bright or it's too dark.

Each director has his own way. Preproduction—in trying to find out if we're on the same wavelength, I use art books a lot and show pictures in terms of texture or color. In the theatre, I have very little to say other than yes or no. It's all been discussed. You're bare assed up there. Whether I agree or disagree, I'm good at letting people know that. If it's something I have a note on and am going to fix, I tell them. If it's something I don't agree on at all, I say, "Let's talk about it later." It depends so much on who the person is. If a director has changed his mind, you have to assume the playwright and composer go along with him, so best you do that.

What I hate the most are the first five cues of a show. You're sure that nothing you've done is gonna work. Yeah, we all do. And if it's a show I care a lot about on opening night, I'm in the bar next door. I can't stand it, just don't want to know about it.

I'm probably not as good at checking a show as I ought to be. But I make it very clear to the electricians and stage managers that if they have any problem at all to call me. I go back if there's a change of cast or stage manager. Have a clean-up every so often—I go in for that. Yeah, because I worry. I would like to worry when shows are on the road, but I found that you don't get any sleep if you do that. You just have to let them go. You provide them with all the information you can and start them out as clean as you can and that's about all you can do.

What about assistants? What do I look for? A sense of humor! I've had a couple of duds. Electricians are my best friends. I love 'em. Particularly the Lynch family—I've been brought up by them, I feel. Brian was saying, "Don't worry, we'll loosen him up for you." No, you know, you sit beside somebody all those hours every day...a sense of humor! I like for them to know what they're doing, yes. But I'm not looking for advice. I do my own drawing and I'm meticulous about the records. I don't want to run off to a computer every time I change a color or something. I still use the pencil hook-up, I can erase and bring it up to date. When I finally xerox it, I ask the electrician for the old one before I give him the new one, because they mix them up.

I had a follow-spot man on *Forty-second Street*, Bobby Segal, and he was in charge of color. He would not give up his hook-up. That poor old hook-up had more gaffers tape on it....But as I keep telling assistants, I don't go home after a show has opened and read focus charts before I go to bed at night. I won't know if these are right until I have a clean-up on this show or a road company. So you'd better be sure they're right. On *Brighton Beach Memoirs* there was a focus note on that, and we could not figure this focus note out. I knew where the lamp went, but I couldn't figure out the focus note. So I went home and I called the assistant. And he said, "This is my worst nightmare come true; I knew I was going to have a phone call like this sometime in my life. *I don't know what it meant!*" Mainly I like for them to be pleasant and prompt and meticulous with records and to be sensitive enough to know when to talk and when not to talk.

I never assisted, but it's a good way to start. There isn't a school in this country that teaches the system that we use in New York. I'm sure it has faults, but it's one of the best I've ever run into. I think it's a matter of familiarizing yourself with the system. You need to know union rules, golden hours and that kind of thing, so you don't come across as a blithering idiot or make some terrible mistake. I think working one or two shows would certainly be helpful, unless you get an offer of a job of your own first—in which case, close your eyes and dive in.

Some of Ken Billington's work is excellent. His club work is magnificent. There, you're on your own. Early on, he was too scared of the director and said, "Yes, yes, yes." And you know as well as I do, you have to figure out what's bothering the director. You seldom do what they say. You figure out what's bothering him and then you fix it in your own way so they're satisfied. I had a feeling on some of Ken's first shows that he was doing exactly what the director said, and that'll get you in trouble every time. Bette Midler called me once, and I happen to adore Bette Midler. It wasn't her secretary, it was Bette herself. I nearly dropped the phone. "No, I'm not the right one, but boy, am I impressed that you called. Call Ken Billington."

I do see a lot of stuff. But I'm not as patient as I used to be. I used to think you could learn as much from something you didn't like as from something you did. Now I tend to go to dinner at intermission a lot. I don't have that kind of patience any more. I just don't.

I was entertained with *An Inspector Calls*. I know it's an old dog. I was talking to Neil about that. He said, "Yeah the only thing about that was, why was this ritzy house in the slums?" Don't be picky, Neil, don't be picky. [Laughter.]

# Chapter Thirty-three

# Pilbrow Story 10: Theatre Design

**M**uch of my life outside lighting has been spent as a theatre consultant—a theatre *design* consultant concerned not only with the stage and its technology but in every aspect of theatre for live performance.

In truth, it took me too many years to discover the ground rules of this fascinating profession. Lighting design makes a good training ground for the theatre designer—the need to know every aspect of stagecraft, to get under the skin of the inner thought processes and motivation of the production, the imperative that one is sensitive to the vibes between play and audience—are all helpful to your credentials. Lighting is the glue that helps to make theatre work. The theatre designer can benefit from being such an all-round "enabler."

But I started as a backstage person, and my first priority was the stage—its planning and equipment. Fortunate timing led to my promotion, at an early age, from Sir Laurence's lighting designer to the post of the National Theatre's theatre consultant. I brought in my long-time friend Richard Brett, then an engineer with the BBC, to help me cross the divide from short-term theatre to the more weighty responsibilities of long-term construction. Not even a Cameron Mackintosh show lasts as long as a building, and mistakes in construction are truly cast in concrete.

And what a century for mistakes this has been. Even the National

Theatre of Great Britain—a dream for one hundred years—is flawed, despite a scrupulously chosen illustrious architect, advised by a building committee consisting of the finest talents and minds of the British theatre. But even more seriously, the world is littered with truly awful twentieth-century buildings purporting to be theatres that are grossly inhospitable to actors and audiences alike.

What went wrong? In hindsight we think we have an inkling. For centuries theatres evolved from the Grecian hillside, via the Elizabethan courtyard, to the Victorian and Edwardian theatres that form most of the stock of the West End and with some variation, Broadway. All were designed around an essential principle: they clustered their audiences around the auditorium as close as possible to the stage. Without amplified sound and bright modern lighting, audiences had to be close to see and hear. Since the Middle Ages theatres had been multileveled to gain this intimacy. Balconies and boxes clustered their audiences in a tight and intimate three-dimensional relationship with the lively performer in their midst.

Several changes coincided. Richard Wagner—seeking concentration upon his mystical stage images—abolished distracting side-box seating. Searchers for greater social equality railed against class-divisive balconies. The modern architectural movement banished elaborate decoration. Finally, the cinema—with its overwhelming popularity and need for full-frontal sightlines to a flat screen—swept all before it. Theatres changed from being exciting intimate multilevel rooms to one- or two-level, usually fan-shaped "auditoria" that seated audiences in ever longer rows receding ever further into the distance.

In the 1960s our theatre building heritage was despised as old fashioned, cramped and outdated.

It was working on the reconstruction of the Victorian Theatre Royal Nottingham in 1968 that made me see the light. This beautiful old theatre was a place of magic. Its intimacy so potent that laughter, tears and emotion were easily evoked. It was not the gold decoration that made such old theatres work; it was their geometry.

Since that time my quest has been to rediscover in a modern architectural language the intimacy and excitement that our ancestors took for granted. As an antidote to the passivity of TV and film, live theatre can rediscover its uniqueness through the active participation of its audiences.

But modern production demands and modern theatre economics are different. So our new/old theatres must meet new challenges, requiring twenty-first-century flexibility to provide new opportunities for staging.

Audiences come first. What has been wrong with so many modern theatres has been the fact that theatre directors and designers always tended to look *toward* the stage. Only the actor got to look into the maw of the audience. Perhaps that is why actors were among the first to sense that too much was too wrong with modern theatre architecture.

*Stage Lighting Design*

## Chapter Thirty-four

# Michael Northen

**M**ichael Northen is one of Britain's leading lighting designers. Michael's career spans more than five decades of British theatre. His initial major credit was Gielgud's King Lear at Stratford-on-Avon in 1950, when he was the first lighting designer in Britain to receive billing as such. At Stratford he lit productions for such directors as Peter Brook, Tyrone Guthrie and Anthony Quayle, and he worked with many leading artists, including John Gielgud, Laurence Olivier, Vivien Leigh, Peggy Ashcroft, Ralph Richardson, Paul Robeson and Charles Laughton. He worked extensively at the Royal Opera House and at Glyndebourne Opera, The Old Vic, Aldeburgh and overseas. A highlight was the premiere of Britten's The Turn of the Screw at the Fenice Theatre in Venice.

Michael has lit shows in every West End theatre in London. Musicals include The Music Man, Bells are Ringing, The Canterbury Tales, Noel Coward's Sail Away (as well as his seventieth birthday celebration, Talent to Amuse), Charlie Girl and Cranks. He also lit many of Danny La Rue's productions and the spectacular Harold Fielding pantomimes at the London Coliseum. Plays include The Mouse Trap, which is still running at the St. Martin's Theatre after forty-three years. In Variety he lit Tommy Steele, Max Bygraves, Cilla Black and Frankie Howard; cabaret performers include Hermione Gingold and Eartha Kitt at the Cafe de Paris.

He designed the lighting for the Son et Lumiere at Caernarvon Castle after the investiture of the Prince of Wales, and for the exhibition at the Tate Gallery on the occasion of John Piper's eightieth birthday.

During his fifty-plus years in the theatre, Michael has been associated with more than three hundred productions. He is currently writing his autobiography.

*Michael:* Back in those days all directors were keen on doing was lighting the acting area. F... the scenery, the scenery can look after itself, as long as I can see Marie Löhr in the middle of the stage speaking. *Art* wasn't considered. So consequently a spot bar of twelve patt 43s was just plonked straight into the middle; number one batten above it in three colors, if you were lucky, and that was it. A flood bar of twelve patt 49s hung together and a ground row, and no side lighting. A pageant through a window. Never more than one.

*Richard:* Let me take you back a bit. What first interested you in lighting and theatre?

*M:* Well, stage managing, you see. Never a thought about lighting. Stage manager first. And lucky enough, I was taught at Q Theatre, to which my father paid a hundred pounds for me to do a year's apprenticeship.

*R:* What year was this?

*M:* 1938. We had to learn stage management. We learned everything—from ice cream trays up and down the isle, running the curtain up and down, taking the iron up—everything. Nobody can pull a fast one on me about stage management—"Oh, I can't do that." They can't pull that on me.

*R:* What happened to get you into theatre in the first place?

*M:* I was mad about it. The Theatre Royal Brighton. My grandmother lived in Brighton. And in those days people had permanent seats; my grandmother always had the same seat for the first night at the Theatre Royal. And I was besotted by it.

*R:* Do you remember a particular production?

*M:* Yes, Marie Tempest in *Dear Octopus* right at the very beginning. And I thought, "Oh, I must do this." I always remember the very first show I took to Brighton, which was a revue with the two Hermiones: Hermione Baddeley and Hermione Gingold, called *Rise Above It*. I was stage manager for that at the age of seventeen, coping with two of the most difficult ladies in the world. I loved stage management. I thought it was wonderful. I didn't start lighting until after the war.

*R:* You were at the Q Theatre for a year?

*M:* No, because I was a clever boy and they thought I was rather good, they took me into the Duke of York's as stage director for a farce called *High Temperature*. I skipped being ASM. It was extraordinary. I was very lucky. The next job was understudying James Mason in a play called *Jupiter Laughs*. And I was stage director for that as well. Thank God, I never had to go on for him. But I didn't do any lighting. I watched like a hawk though. Jack De Leon, who was a wonderful, inventive gentleman, [did the lighting] with no equipment at all. Everybody always laughs at my rigs, because they are very small. They always have been, even on musicals. But I've never wanted millions of lamps; it terrifies the life out of me. I learnt from Jack that one lamp positioned in the right place could often do a hell of a lot throughout a play.

So then I took to stage lighting. While I was with *Jupiter Laughs*, the well-known director Tyrone Guthrie said would I like to come and be stage director at the Old Vic for *The Cherry Orchard*. This was during the war and the Old Vic had moved to Burnley. So I became stage director for that. It was a lovely company. I was still very young then, about twenty.

Then war came. I went into the R.A.F. for about five years. I was supposed to be an armorer, winding up bombs and filling up guns. Then someone at the camp said, "Michael, I see from your records you've something to do with the theatre. Would you like to run the cinema?" And I said, "Yes, so long as I can eat in the sergeants' mess." Since it was just across from the cinema and I had to work at night. So I worked those old carbon-arc projectors. That was fun. The Air Ministry said I should join the R.A.F. Gang Show, which I did. We had thirteen units, twelve people in each unit, run by Ralph Reader. It was bloody hard work playing all those camps and doing one night stands. Then they said you've got to go to India. So I went all over India doing one night stands. The best background you could have. Some of those camps had no lighting equipment at all. You might have a biscuit tin with a bulb to try and do something with. That is why it's so interesting to me now when you've got everything you could want.

I came back [after the war] and did some stage managing. Then I built this enormous great model.

*R:* That's when we first met. Robert Jackson, an actor in *No Time For Sergeants*, brought me to see you and the model. It excited me a great deal.

*M:* That started everything off. I did lighting from then on.

*R:* What was your first proper lighting show?

*M:* It was the Serge Lifar Ballet Company at the Cambridge Theatre. When I look back: it had a couple of terrible pageants, a groundrow and a filthy cyc. Then I went on doing millions more from there. Then I went *arty* because my one joy was going to the opera. I was a production assistant at the Opera House [Covent Garden] for two years—right at the very beginning, 1948, when the Opera House reopened. So I was there with Oliver Messel. I learned a hell of a lot, because the Opera had been dark for so many years.

*R:* Let's take you back for a moment. What theatre did you see in the thirties? Did you see any memorable lighting? Did you see some of those great Basil Dean productions we all hear about?

*M:* Yes, yes, they were fabulous! And I can tell you why they were fabulous—because it had lighting, but you never saw where it came from. So it was magic. In *Johnson over Jordan* there was this wonderful set and this one man standing there, lit. And you didn't know how, because you never saw any of the equipment. This is my old battle. It's so boring seeing five million lamps. It kills it for me, because my eye is fixed on one lamp and I think, "Is it going to come on?" and at the very end, it comes up to point one and you think, "Oh, that's clever." It was to me *magic*. And the great things to me were the huge pantomimes at Drury Lane. Transformation scenes that *were* theatre. Wonderful things: gauzes by the million, the lifts all being used, the cyc and everything else. That really fired me. I remember being taken to that by another grandmother and I couldn't believe what I saw.

*R:* Basil Dean is someone we know about. Was he very special? He clearly cared a great deal about lighting.

*M:* I worked for Basil Dean. I did the first London production of *The Wizard of Oz.* We didn't get on at all.

*R:* He was a most unpopular man.

*M:* He was a terror, but he knew what he was after. And another one was Robert Nesbitt. Those reviews in the old days at the Hippodrome—the fabulous walk-downs of girls in wonderful dresses lit for the first time in surprise pink. The magic of that surprise pink color being used with no other color was extraordinary.

*R:* Is there any other outstanding figure we've forgotten?

*M:* Bill Lorraine, remember him, he was a Strand man. An interesting thing, nearly all the lighting designers were engineers in Strand. Darling Joe [Davis] started that way. He never did anything at the Opera House. I stopped lighting for a while, so I could work at the Opera House. I wanted to know the technique of that particular medium. I didn't do any lighting there at the beginning. Doing all those productions, I learned a hell of a lot. Enjoyed every minute of it. But that was *art.* Then I went to Stratford in 1950. I was there with all those wonderful people—Olivier, Anthony Quayle and all that lot. I learned a lot about lighting there too. If I showed one inch of the snout of a light in an alcove, I'd get hauled up. Now you go there and it looks like a very tired old TV studio.

*R:* Do you think the wheel's going to turn? It always does.

*M:* Yes, it is. There's no interest, there's no excitement [when you can see all the equipment]. I coped with that enormous, empty stage at the Coliseum with *Aladdin* when we flew the scenery to the grid and we had a cyc right around the outer ring of the old revolve. Nothing on the stage at all. Lit with a bash of patt 49s for a blaze of white side lighting. Ken Miller[7] was under the stage letting off smoke guns. The smoke came up through the three rings of the three revolves and there was one dancer in the middle. No visible lights. Real magic! It's boring now seeing the tie-offs of the cyc and the exit signs backstage and miles of cable. It's show-off time—how clever we are with so much equipment.

*R:* Basil Dean and reflected light? I used to take him around the National Theatre before it opened and have lunch with him and he used to go on to me about that whole thing of reflected light he used to do. Did you ever see any of that? He'd point a patt 44 into a bowl, so all the light was reflected, diffused and soft.

*M:* I never saw that.

*R:* I've tried to do it and I can't make it work at all. Being so soft, it lights up everything. You light into a curved reflector. The thing Louis Hartmann and Belasco used to do on a spotbar over the stage, with the lamps pointing downstage into the reflector, that then casts a totally shadowless light.

*M:* I remember the floats [footlights] being done that way. They would face into the audience, but were reflected on to a white curved surface. I never found that worked at all. It shot light all over the place. Very few theatres had it.

*R:* Right! Back to Stratford.

*M:* From there I went down to Glyndebourne. That was horrendous for me. I didn't like being stuck down there. All those f....... cows. I was down there for two years, but I did have fun with John Piper and Oliver Messel. We had that old German board and those German horizon lights—the conical ones.

Then I did *Turn of the Screw*. And then the bank manager said, "You're working awfully hard, but I don't see any money for it." It's all very well—art. So I decided to do commercial theatre. At that exact time, Harold Fielding started producing. I did Tommy Steele at the Dominion, then Howard and Wyndham took me up. One year I did six pantomimes. We used to do all their theatres. Ken would go in and set up and focus and I'd come in and he'd go off to the next theatre. I did the dress rehearsal, lit it and off to the next. That was wonderful experience. You didn't get much money. I don't know how I made a living. Well, you didn't. Luckily, I did have a few acres behind me. You were so wonderful—you started your firm.

*R:* I had to; I didn't know how else to exist.

*M:* But it's jolly hard now. What was interesting was when I decided to give it all up about ten years ago. I said, "Right, that's it, I'm going to breed donkeys and live in the country and forget it and have a wonderful life." About five years ago, I'm sitting out here and the phone went and it was Tony Quayle. "Michael, I'm starting a little company. I want my chums. Will you come?" I adored Tony, so I said, "Right, I'll do one show only." It was *The Clandestine Marriage*, which came into London and with Michael Northen's name on the bills. And people rang me up and said, "I thought you were dead." Then I went to a charity show at the Lane and went out to have a drink at the interval. When I came back there were two notes on my seat: "Will you ring me in the morning?" So I went back to work again. But I had such a shock coming back—what with electronic boards and all. And not knowing how the fees were going—I had an agent for the first time.

But going back, George Andrews at the Theatre Royal Brighton. He was a terror. He terrified the life out of me on my first shows. He'd say, "Why can't you make up your f...... mind? How many more times are you going to change your mind? Can't you get it right?" and "I don't do follow-ons and I'm not going to start now." The board originally was in the prompt corner. As stage manager, I was squashed into the corner with George nearly on top with his levers controlling the tracker wires to the pots under the stage—they were water dimmers. The blackouts were done with a knife switch, which had arced so many times that there was a blinding flash and blinding noise every time it was pulled. And my review, *Rise Above It*, was all blackouts at the end of each sketch. So I was permanently singed on one side. And I would edge further and further away, until I was almost on stage whenever George did a blackout. There were about six pots under the stage that the tracker wires went to. The major pot for doing a general dim was just outside the door where the orchestra entered the pit. The worst possible place. They would try to pee into the pot before going into the pit. Terribly dangerous—and the smell! There was so little equipment. And they never toured an electrician. The stage manager did the lighting. We were trained to do the lighting in those days.

*R:* That's an interesting thing: the background of stage management. That's how I arrived. I've always thought that was a better way than coming up as an electrician. Joe [Davis] was the other school. He was an electrician. All too many come up now as electricians. I think that's unfortunate.

*M:* I think you can get so immersed technically. I did a lot of work at Plymouth after I came back. And I was surrounded by brilliant kids who knew every microchip for miles around. I came in one day to do some lighting and on my lighting desk there was a monitor. And I said, "What's that?" and they said, "Why, its your monitor; you must see where all your lamps are and their levels." And I said, "If I want to know, I'll ask you." Of course another thing in the old days in Brighton: if you wanted to call up a circuit, you had to say, "OP flys, white, number two." There was never a circuit number. It's wonderful how things have changed. It's marvelous.

*R:* Yes, lighting on a memory board is so easy.

*M:* Yes, the only problem for oldies is that it's so bloody quick, you never have time to think about the next cue.

*R:* I remember in my early years, which were all on manual boards, half my life was spent on how they were going to do the cue—not what it looked like. Fifty percent of the time you compromised in order to make it workable. Now you don't even think about that.

*M:* I remember doing a show at the Strand Theatre, on a CD board. It had six cues in the first three minutes, and there was no way they could do it. Then the electronic boards . . .

*R:*...another set of problems.

*M:* All those bloody valves going. We've lived through the whole lot and its been wonderful from my point of view. I didn't do gas!

*R:* Michael, of all that fantastic career, what are the moments that stick out as the most satisfying?

*M:* I'll tell you one, it was a production of *Twelfth Night* at Stratford designed by a mad lady called Lila de Nobili. It was a set I shall never forget. More beautiful than words can express. It was entire gauze—something quite lovely. She was absolutely mad.

*R:* Yes, you could never get her off stage; she was always painting.

*M:* Well, I finished lighting it the afternoon of opening night. It had taken an enormous amount of time. You do it bit by bit. But we finished and went off to lunch and did the first night shopping. Later I walked into the auditorium, all dressed up for opening night. I looked at the stage. I looked at the gauze. When we had left the theatre, she had gotten a ladder out and gone and repainted the gauze. It hadn't been stretched; now it was the size of a pocket handkerchief. The heat from the lamps had made it go blowzy. It was a little thing in the middle of the stage.

R: I did *Love for Love* at the National and we finally had an ASM to guard her, because every time the stage manager would take the worklights out to take the curtain out, she'd get a pair of steps and rush on stage with a flashlight to paint.

M: She was a wonderful lady. *Twelfth Night* was such an exciting show. It brings me back to my old thing—*magic*. You wouldn't dream of hanging a large Strand lamp in the middle of that set—it was so delicate and soft. And the other highlight for me was doing *Turn of the Screw* with Benjamin Britten at the La Fenice Opera House.

R: Actually at La Fenice? The most wonderful opera house in the world.

M: Oh, yes. Now that's real magical theatre. The scenery arrived by barge. That was a lovely company. Absolutely splendid. Another highlight, I think, was doing a production of *Cinderella* at the old Alhambra in Glasgow, which in those days had fabulous theatres. I closed the theatre permanently with a lady called Betty Grable in *Belle Starr,* which came to the Palace. *Cinderella* had Berkeley Sutcliffe scenery and the most wonderful transformations, because we had the mechanics and lifts.

R: You've worked with some of the great designers who were great painters.

M: Now you've hit the nail—Leslie Hurry, John Piper, Dali.

R: For me, in my career, I find it very difficult doing those painted surfaces. I prefer more three-dimensional stuff. Scenery has changed. When you referred to the Lila de Nobili sets, did you spotlight bits?

M: Yes.

R: You do washes, then fill, then highlights?

M: Exactly. Because a lot of it takes care of itself from bounce off the floor.

R: I got great reviews on *Love for Love* for the sunshine, which was really painted on by Lila.

M: Some designs you just could do so much with in the way of lighting, you just filled it up and let it take its own, if the designer knew what he was doing. Oliver Messel, one of the great painters of the day—you don't do anything. With the pantomimes today, I keep asking, "Where are the backcloths?" I like to light them very softly, so it appears to go to infinity. It's my technique.

That's another thing I say to the boys and girls today, "You've got to have a technique." You have one, I have one. I can recognize your lighting. I know Ornbo's instantly, and Davis's instantly, especially the color.

*R:* Describe yours, Michael.

*M:* My lighting is utter romance. Very soft, very gentle, a lot of side lighting, little front. I won't have great bars out front. Not because they're unsightly, but I find the balance is wrong. So much overhead lighting kills actors. I know the floats are gone now, so I have to put lamps under the dress circle boxes just to give a certain lift. I lit and was always asked by those older ladies—Gladys Cooper, Evelyn Laye, Marie Lohr, Peggy Ashcroft—because I always looked after them and lit them from underneath. You can't use these terrible halogen lamps bashing down on these old girls—they'd look a hundred and ninety.

I love great bashes from the side. My other technique is different colors from each side: if I use 17 steel blue from one side, the other side is 40. Never the same from both sides, because otherwise you don't get any contrast. That's just simple. I'm an old romantic. I'm not a three-dimensional boy. I do it—but I love my wings; I love my borders and my house curtain. I like it hand-pulled, coming in with courtesy and not a machine going plonk. But that's an old-fashioned man talking. I try to get people to understand the romance of the theatre.

*R:* What do you say to a kid who wants to do it; what words of advice do you have?

*M:* I say: Get *into* the theatre. If you're really keen and you love it and you want to do it; get into the theatre—even if you're brushing the carpet or sweeping the stage. Learn what you can, get a job, get your foot in and if the management says, "My God, those carpets are beautifully done, what else would you like to do?" tell them you want to work with the lights. Always set your sights on something. Don't waffle—a bit of this, a bit of that—if you want to light, light.

You can't teach *lighting*, you know. You can teach basics: how to hang a lamp, wiring, et cetera. But you can't teach angles; you have to find that out yourself. I can't teach you color. You have to experiment—cut up some colors, take a light on a stand and play with it. It's no good sitting at a desk in school doing graphs. You're speaking to an oldie now. I can't do all those wonderful lines and things. But I know exactly what each lamp will do. If I go onto a stage and someone has put a piece of scenery in front of a lamp, I move the lamp. That is the sort of spontaneous thing you must be able to do. For kids to learn, they have to get in the theatre and get on the stage. If you're good, you'll get on; if you're no good, you'll be out. The best will come through.

# Chapter Thirty-five

# Pilbrow Story 11:
# Diversity and Proportion

Very early on, *The Stage* newspaper (the English version of *Variety*) did a story on me, the new lighting designer. In it I was quoted as saying that I thought British lighting and technology had much to learn from abroad, particularly the U.S.A. or Germany. The following week I was somewhat stunned to read in a letter to the editor that Frederick Bentham—then technical head of Strand, whom I had long worshiped from afar—thought my views rubbish and he said in particular he had never learnt anything from abroad and foreign ideas had had no effect upon Strand's superiority.

I was crushed. But two weeks later two more letters swelled the correspondence columns, from men I'd then never met. The first, a robust comment from Ed Kook—then head of Century Lighting—pointed out that the Leko (Ed Kook's co-invention) had surely had a strong influence in the U.K. The other from Basil Dean—doyen director of the British theatre through the twenties and thirties—stated that he had imported the first miniature spotlights to the U.K. from the U.S. after World War One and that the acting-area lantern (a sort of fixed-beam downlight, then in common use) was first imported by him from Germany in the twenties. I felt relieved and vindicated.

On my first trip to the U.S.A. in 1961 I met Ed Kook, a dynamo of a man. I thanked him for supporting me. He dismissed my thanks, muttering that he always supported lighting designers, and seizing my arm, he dragged me down the corridor. "Look! Look there...the future!" He was pointing to a Fresnel hanging from the ceiling. But a Fresnel with a difference: it had pan, tilt and focus control—remote control.

After *A Funny Thing Happened on the Way to the Forum*, Hal Prince invited Tony Walton and me to become his partners in London to produce his shows. This was a new world to me. To help in the daunting task of raising money, Bill Styles introduced me to Louis Dreyfus, millionaire owner of Chappells, the music publishers, and of Williamson Music, my first employers. Louis, even then in his eighties, agreed to help and became a silent partner and later friend and mentor. Whatever the problem, Louis would urge us to go for it.

Producing was a new world. I had not just the lighting to worry about but everything else. *Forum*, after some scary moments, was a big hit in London, too. Again, with no precedent to follow, we made up how to do it. We turned the lobbies and exterior of the Strand Theatre into a Roman town. We tried new approaches to advertising. We tried to introduce new standards of courtesy in the conduct of auditions. With incredible cheek, I said to Hal (who had already had *West Side Story* and *Pajama Game* in London), "This is the home of Olivier, Gielgud and Shakespeare. Musicals are not taken seriously. We don't want the stage manager just reproducing a Broadway hit, we want the original director to recreate it—better if possible." He didn't take offense, and George Abbott came—the real Mr. Abbott.

Many productions followed, many from Hal—some hits, some failures. At one time I was on the executive committee of the Society of West End Theatre, the theatre owners and producer's organization. This was a deeply depressing experience. The antediluvian attitudes of the theatre establishment were light years away from the idealism that continued to drive the designers and artists whom they employ.

But many inescapable perspectives emerged. Lighting is only a small part of a whole complex creation. While as a rental shop owner I could short circuit some budget problems for producers, they seldom cared anyway. Finally tickets sold paid for all our lives. The subsidized theatre, which was just emerging in the early sixties, was far and away the most momentous event that was shaping our careers and the theatre.

I like to think that these lessons informed my design work and my conduct. Certainly when theatre consulting opened up as a third career for me, the mixed perspective of designer and commercial producer shaped my work.

Balance became the most important word in my dictionary. Openness to new situations became another. Persistence, dedication, commitment, simply never giving up.

Robert Ornbo and I had a catchphrase: "If we can get through this weekend, we can get through anything."

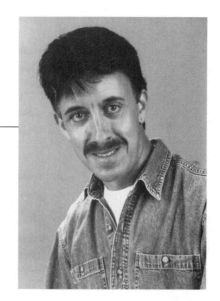

## Chapter Thirty-six

# Chris Parry

*C*hris Parry *is a transatlantic lighting designer originally from England and now resident in San Diego. He has designed eighteen productions for the Royal Shakespeare Company in England, including* The Blue Angel *for Trevor Nunn, and* Les Liaisons Dangereuses *for Howard Davies, which won him a Tony Award nomination and the New York Drama Desk Award for production design on Broadway in 1987. In 1993 he designed the lighting for* The Who's Tommy *on Broadway, for which he won the Tony Award, the New York Drama Desk Award and the New York Outer Critics Circle Award.*

*Other work includes the U.K. and U.S. touring versions of the RSC's* Nicholas Nickleby *and over forty British regional theatre and opera designs, as well as a growing number of designs for U.S. regional theatre, for which he has received several awards.*

*Chris is also a professor of lighting design at UC San Diego and now combines teaching with a transatlantic design career.*

My interest in lighting started in high school in England, with the school plays. The physics department had control of the lighting equipment, because it was technically oriented, and I liked the physics master, so that was fine. I didn't know you could do theatre lighting as a career or that there were such things as lighting designers.

When I left school I found myself in the post office telephone system as an engineer apprentice. I repaired people's phones. I was also a part-time movie projectionist, part-time taxi driver, part-time barman, part-time

341

everything, and I was still lighting little theatre shows. It wasn't until my early twenties that I realized I was in the wrong job. It wasn't a blinding flash or anything—but I realized, you only come this way once, and you better do what you enjoy doing. I began to evaluate what it was I really enjoyed doing, and that was lighting for the stage. I thought, "Is there a way that I can do this—work in theatre?" I wrote to Richard Pilbrow, which I know sounds completely bizarre—I still have his letter somewhere. I wrote to Richard, because I'd already bought his book by that stage and read it and thought, "This guy knows what he's talking about." So, I wrote and said I was very interested in theatre and lighting, and could he give me some advice. He wrote me this nice letter in return, explaining how his company worked, TP; that they used to take apprentices, but he advised me to take a job in regional theatre—start there. So, OK—I did. I got a job in small regional theatre companies as an electrician and went on from there. I eventually joined the Royal Shakespeare Company in 1976 as an electrician on the crew and worked my way up the RSC ladder.

My freelance lighting career really started about 1978, in a small way. The more I did, the more I became known. Eventually I found myself being asked by the resident directors to design things inside the RSC, which is strange—the RSC usually didn't use inside people. They always brought in outside designers. I started off by designing shows in The Other Place with the RSC, and it just went up from there. Howard Davies [the director] really put his faith in me in those early years. When I left them, I was assistant head of lighting for the main house in Stratford and a freelance lighting designer with a number of credits.

The RSC season would start in early March with two plays put on really quickly, one after another, so they could keep the turnover going. They would then, during the year, gradually add another four more—six altogether. By September you would turn over six shows in rotating rep. And those six could be a different show every day—and between a matinee and an evening, which is a killer because you've got to change the set and the lighting in two and a half hours. This is insane, but they still do it. After a while, there's no challenge to it anymore. You go in there, you've got the focus charts. The crew know the focus as well as you do, because they've done it so often. So it was just like an everyday job—punch in, punch out. It paid well. I had a very good standard of living, but the hours were insane. You'd be doing twelve-, fifteen-, eighteen-hour days for months: horrible. The older I got, the less I wanted to do that. I suddenly realized, here we go again—you don't want to do this for the rest of your life.

I suppose my choice was that my freelance work was getting to the point where it was interfering with my RSC work. I knew I was going to have to make a decision, and ideally my decision would have been to stay with the RSC, but to have more time to freelance. I went to talk to the management to see if we could arrange something, but they didn't seem to want to play ball at all, which was strange because by that time I designed award-winning plays. Just at that point, Richard Ridell met me and told me he was leaving UC at San Diego for a short time and was I interested in replacing him for three months? So I said yes, I would. (My first introduction to California was *Nicholas Nickleby*, when I took that over there for David Hersey.) While I was here, they said Richard was leaving permanently, and was I interested in applying for the job. So then I had a big decision. It's like one door closes, another one opens. I didn't see any benefits of me staying in England, either being tied to the RSC longer or to go freelance and be very insecure. I've been in California ever since—nearly six years.

My freelance career in England has continued all this time, and I thought it would stop. In fact, to my surprise, it's gotten slightly more busy. I live in a beautiful part of the world and working for the university is enjoyable—I like teaching, but not all the time, I have to say. Sometimes you have students that seem to make it hard for you. But most of the time I enjoy it, and it gives me a base income that allows me to pick and choose which shows I do. So in terms of a designer's lifestyle, I think it's fine.

I'm not the type of designer who can charge from one show to another, to another, to another. Peter Maradudin and I are great friends, and he describes himself as a workaholic. He just goes from one show to another. I can't do that at all. I realized many years ago that I wasn't built for that. So, for me to be completely freelance would be very dangerous. I need to spend time on a design—it doesn't come to me quickly. I think it's great that he can turn one out in three days. It takes me, generally, two weeks to plot it out. Part of it is, I can't just stand in front of a drawing board and let it all happen. I stand there for a while and a couple of ideas come. I go away and get a drink or a pizza or something. I sit down and read the paper. I go back to the drawing board, and do a bit more, and it kind of evolves. It's such an evolutionary thing for me, that it's only when it's all there, or all the ideas come and they're all on the paper, that I feel that I've got a design I can work with. Often I've got too many lights anyway, so now let's think, which are the really important ideas? That editing process starts. And it's only at that point that everything speeds up. The initial process is quite slow and drawn out. I try to make it faster and I can't.

Like most people, I have some shows that I feel have worked well and some shows I think, "Oh my God. Did I come up with that idea?" But just in terms of how designers feel about their work, to me it's often a nerve-wracking process. I don't know why. Maybe just because it's such an insecure thing. You have all these ideas. None of them are concrete. It's like this whole bag of untested ideas, which is terrifying. The bag of nothing. Here's a piece of paper. Where's the light? Well, we'll hang it up there and turn it on. I don't mean it to sound trite, but like many artists, I'm insecure about my art. I never know what people really think about it. People say, "Oh, it's wonderful. It's nice." In your heart of hearts, you know if you've done a good job or not for yourself, which I suppose, in the end, is the only person you're really trying to please.

It's an ongoing process of self-education as well. You keep thinking, "I've got a bag of things that work and a bag that doesn't." Next time you try it, some of those things that do work, don't work. I struggled for a long time before I decided to go into teaching. How can I teach what it is I do, because I'm not sure what it is I do myself? We all create in different ways, and I don't want people to turn out to be clones of Chris Parry. So I really question that I can teach them the "art." I can teach them the craft—no problem. But that's only half of what we do. I think I can teach them about my experience. I've been doing this for a long time now. The only other way I can teach them is, I try not to say, "If this were me, I'd do this." Often, I say, "Have you thought about this?"

In designing I find myself heavily influenced by the set—by what it can offer, by what atmosphere it is trying to convey—and also by the director—by what he tells me about the show, by what he can feed me. These days, if I haven't had a good conversation with the director, I'm really stuck. Some of the directors I work with, like Adrian Noble and Trevor Nunn, the trouble is you only get a very short space of time with them, so the meeting is short, but you gain such a lot of information in that time.

I don't consider myself to be a technician, but I have a grounding. You often read about designers who have been technicians, who use technology for the sake of it. If it needs to be created, let it be a technical effect. I don't like doing that at all, partly because it gives me a lot more work.

The one area I'm keen about telling people about—and I didn't realize this until I came over here to teach and work—is about the different types of instruments that people have to work with. They're like paintbrushes—different types of paintbrushes. If you're going to paint the side of a barn, you use an eighteen-inch paintbrush, you don't use a bunch of little two-inch paintbrushes tied all together to do the same job. So I was very surprised that in the U.S. the amount of instruments you're offered is much smaller than in England. You only have to look at the two rental catalogs between the two countries to see it. It's frustrating. It's true I was brought up and trained in the era of Fresnels in England; they are extremely popular and always will be as far as I can tell.

In some theatres you try getting a 5kW Fresnel and they think, "Why do you want one? Are we doing a TV show?" I think it's important to have that range of equipment as a tool to be used, not just for the sake of having a 5k, but because you'll use it to give you the quality of light you want to produce. I think Fresnels can save you instruments. I've just done *The Blue Angel* in London, and there's a lot of Fresnels; there are no PAR cans, partly because I didn't want to join together PARs to make a wash, and I knew I didn't need a huge punch. So I use a Fresnel and flood it wide. When you have an actor standing in this, you have a beautiful, single shadow, and it's very clean. The thing about joining together a million Lekos, there's no shadow left. There's fifty-three shadows, each badly focused. I like single-source lighting. HMIs and that kind of thing—I think they're fine, but I think it's a very specific style that the production needs to have. I don't think you can just lay an HMI on top of something that won't take it. I tried it once on *The Master Builder* in London. The set was designed by Richard Hudson and had very clean lines. There was this huge window in the back wall leaning at an angle toward the audience. I thought it'd be interesting—well, there's this Scandinavian world outside, cold and harsh, so it'd be interesting to use an HMI. We rigged one up. High technology, I suppose—and I had it track across the stage, so that the angle of light through the window could change as the play progressed. I found after the first day of trying to use this light that it was too big a statement. It was overpowering the rest of the lighting. The whole thing suddenly looked like it was a play about an HMI. You have to think, is it too attention catching? So, I changed it for a 5k Fresnel with a piece of Lee 201 in front of it, and that seemed much more in keeping.

Over the years I kind of look at the whole image or picture and see if anything is really jumping out at you, shouting and saying hello, when you don't want it to be—and sometimes you do want it to be. I certainly have done shows where a battle scene is all about the strength of light and how powerful it can be. Light through smoke—light as a physical element in the air. I love that. And that's really calling attention to itself too. I think that only works at certain times; you can't do that all the time.

Since being in the States, that's one thing you've taught me—have an assistant. Here's the plot, here's the ideas—go deal with it. The ideas are done. I'm bored with the rest of it. Go do the initial drawing. I love that help—I'm willing to pay for that.

I think designing should be fun. We don't get paid that much for it and it takes hours. If it's not fun, why on earth are we doing it? Why are we getting paid poor amounts to be miserable? I try not to let things get to me. I try to remain detached from it slightly. I remember, the first show I did on Broadway was *Les Liaisons Dangereuses*. I had an assistant Beverly Emmons recommended, Katy Orrick, who was a nice girl and incredibly efficient, and I had no idea how to use her. She was teaching me how to use an assistant. I was this strange English guy with all these ideas about what I wanted. She's a very calm person. She had a job doing voice-overs for the Muppets, and in the middle of a Broadway show tech we're doing Muppets. It was great. When the pressure is off, you can relax and tell a joke. It's not brain surgery, as I tell my students. Nobody dies. A designer in England called Robert Bryan (who used to design for the Royal Opera House in London)—I worked with him a great deal in Stratford—and part of his influence was to get me to relax and to just take it as it comes. Early on in my career I got very tense if I had pages of notes that weren't done. Bob would say, we'll do the important ones now or at lunchtime or whatever. By the end of the day, half of them would have fallen off the list anyway.

David Hersey was very influential. I assisted him when *Nicholas Nickleby* came out here. I learned that he doesn't like anybody that's not efficient—you have to be on top of what you're doing. In that respect, I became efficient. Working with David, you actually have to be one step ahead of him, because you have to be prepared for the next thing he'll ask for. But a lot of his techniques and ideas I became very familiar with through having to reproduce his lighting. You see the way he works. That's not to say he uses the same ideas—it's not that it's the same technique, the same style. Many lighting designers have a style of their own, which they may not be able to identify themselves. I think it's naive of directors and producers not to see that. If you want a set for a show, you don't use just anybody. If you use Richard Hudson, you know the kind of thing you're going to get—it's an angled, leaning piece of architecture, no right angles anywhere, no straight walls.

I really value the time I had with the RSC because it stage a very good training ground, and I would recommend anybody to do the same thing. The thing is, when you're learning it, you don't realize you're learning it until afterwards. It's not until you actually get out of there that you begin to realize how much you learned and how much you know and, therefore, how much you can use.

The one thing I think that's very important as a designer is learning to have to reproduce people's work every day. And not only to have to reproduce it in your own theatre, but to go relight somewhere else in a new space and to really look and remember the atmosphere that had been created with the original design. When you take it somewhere else, you start to learn to make very educated decisions about what needs to happen in order to create that atmosphere again.

It was quite interesting working with the same rig year after year at the RSC. You'd see a designer come in and use it a different way, you'd say, "Yeah, I never thought about that." Just going back to Bob Bryan again, he would come and the first thing he would do is say, "Show me the permanent focus." He'd run through it channel by channel and make notes of what he thought was useful in the permanent focus, that hit the set in an interesting way or whatever. So he would use what was there initially and then supplement that, whereas other people would come in and completely ignore the permanent focus and hang shitloads of specials and this cover and that cover, and you'd think, "We've got something almost like that up there already."

Most of the front of house is permanent focus in Stratford, so there's probably only about twenty percent left. The over stage is the most flexible. Very little on the over-stage pipes are permanently focused. But it's always a negotiating ploy with the master electrician as to what you can add on a tower or a ladder before he says, "No, you just ran out of time to focus the stuff."

I find myself these days becoming more intolerant of situations that I don't think are helpful to a working lighting designer, such as silly

*Stage Lighting Design*

things—like if the producing company is giving you accommodation, let's not make it fifteen miles away from the theatre; I'm cold and miserable. Otherwise, you're not going to get the best out of this artist. They're all little things that, when I was relatively young, I'd just ignore as part of the deal. It was so exciting to be doing anything, then fine, a little bit of hardship along the way just comes with it. If the producer feels that he can treat you that way, then he doesn't take your professionalism very seriously. We are all working professionals—we do this for a living. If you have a creative artist that is not happy, you're not going to get the best out of him. Some producers don't care about that.

Rather like over here, there are designers who will do fifteen shows a year in order to make a living. The RSC and the National Theatre at the moment pay a designer for their main house an average of £2,000, which sounds not bad when you convert it to dollars—it's like $3,800. But then we're talking of the biggest, major companies in England, and everybody else is below that, often considerably. Many regional theatres are paying £700 to £800 for a design, so it's hard. Also, the use of assistants in England is virtually unknown, so if you want an assistant, you have to pay for it yourself. It's very hard to get the producer or the theatre to pay for it unless it's a big West End show, and even then it depends on the producer.

I'm not going back to England—that's very clear! I like California a great deal. Part of what I like about it is that American theatre people take lighting more seriously than in England. The trouble is perhaps the American theatre is in danger of taking it too seriously and becoming too much a businesslike thing. What I like doing is working with a crew or a master electrician who wants to help me be creative. I find this is much easier in England than it is in America. Not everywhere—I have a very good master electrician here, John Stewart, at the La Jolla Playhouse, who I think is really excellent. He's learned to work with me and knows that I expect him to be involved in the production. I don't like the theatres where the master electrician says, "OK, your plot is due on August 12. I'll see you on August 12. Give me the plot, and I'll hang it, focus it, and that's the end of our relationship." I would much rather go to the master electrician and say, "Look, this is the kind of effect I'm trying to create. I can do it three different ways. Which one would you like? Which one would suit you, your house, your cabling arrangements, your ease of set-up, et cetera?" I want him to say, "I can do it that way, but it's going to take ten hours longer than if we do it this way." So, it's a balancing act. I'd much rather work like that. But it's hard to find people in the States that want to do that.

I know there are some designers who won't talk to the master electrician. They will do everything through the assistant. So the assistant becomes the go-between. I think that's terrible. You have to have a relationship with your crew, otherwise you're just fighting all the time. I think David Hersey talked about this in one of his articles years ago. When he moved to England from the States, one of the things he noticed was that the crew was much more willing to work with you to change a thing. If he came in the morning and said, "I need to take these down and put four of these up because I had a new idea overnight," they do it, no problem. I don't have a crystal ball, so I don't know how the production's going to go—if the requirements are going to change or not—but for some reason many electricians think I should know.

I don't like to be elitist—so precious about this whole thing. Many people will have a better idea than I will about things, so fine. I can use those ideas as well.

English and European designers—scenic designers especially and lighting as well—want the visuals to be much more strong, much more emblematic, much more poetic. That's kind of exemplified by John Conklin's approach more than anything else. I think in the States there has been a heavy focus on everything coming from the text, and scenery has just been a background for the stuff to happen in. I think that's changing now. I think that's true about lighting, too. Everything relates to nature all the time, but that's becoming less important. When you get into something much more expressionistic or emblematic, you can really use that as a tool.

## Chapter Thirty-seven

# Patrick Woodroffe

*P* *atrick has been lighting rock concerts for almost twenty years, and in that time has designed the lighting for many of the top names in the music world, including The Rolling Stones, Tina Turner, Rod Stewart, Roxy Music, Abba, Stevie Wonder, Cher, Robert Palmer, Bob Dylan, The Bee Gees, Depeche Mode, Bryan Ferry, Simply Red, Elton John and Phil Collins. He has also lit for industrial theatre (Mercedes Benz, Bordeaux Wines), musical theatre* (A Tribute to the Blues Brothers), *music festivals (Rock in Rio, Montreux Jazz Festival, Tokyo Music Festival), television shows ("A Tribute to Bob Dylan,"* Casta Diva, MTV Unplugged, *"The Brit Awards," "Golden Eye Awards") and has designed permanent lighting schemes for office buildings and residences in Europe and in the U.S.A.*

I never had any great aspirations to be a lighting designer when I was younger. My first real job was running a follow spot for David Cassidy. I thought it was all so exciting and glamorous at the beginning. I started to work full time for ESP in the days when people didn't have lighting designers. A job would come into the shop, and one of us would run the lights. I was offered a tour with the Pretty Things, who didn't have a lighting designer, and they just let me do it. My next job was calling the follow spots for the Osmonds. The first rig was just under a hundred lights— extraordinary. I went out as the third guy on the crew on an early Queen tour, the first tour in England to use a lighting truss, designed and built by Richard Hartman, that traveled in its own road box. Slowly but surely I started running the lights for other groups—Hot Tuna, Maggie Bell—and rather enjoyed it. Then I started working as a "proper" lighting designer for the Heavy Metal Kids, a theatrical punk group, traipsing up and down the M1 and on occasion doing tours of Spanish discotheques. So by the time I got my first big break, which was with Rod Stewart, I knew quite a bit about running light shows. Rod fired his lighting designer three days before the tour opened, and they looked around the place—I was up a ladder focusing at the time—and I got the job because I was the only one on the crew who'd ever "done the lights." That was it. I went all over the world—to Japan, to Australia, and to the States for the first time—a really fantastic experience for a young man who had only ever played places like Leeds, Brighton and Marbella.

I was brought up as an army brat, so I'd traveled all over the world, but never like this. I didn't really live anywhere until I was ten and ended up in Essex, by which time I was at boarding school. I was a bit of a dropout and ended up leaving public school under a cloud. I went on to a rather expensive private school for foreigners, where the education was poor but the lessons of life made up for it. I still stay in touch with some of the people: a Turkish arms dealer, a Japanese businessman....

After a couple of Rod Stewart tours I moved to California in 1979, where I lived for a couple of years. I picked up tours like Stevie Wonder, 10CC, the Tubes and Abba's last tour—a connection I've kept ever since. I also did a lot of Vegas shows for people like Cher, Raquel Welch and Donna Summer, where I learnt the discipline of having to actually plot things and plan ahead. At that time things in our industry were generally becoming more organized. You were expected to do rather more than just show up with some lights and make things happen. In 1982 I moved back to England and started Woodroffe Barnett Associates with Jimmy Barnett—a sort of rock-and-roll version of early TP, I suppose. We wanted to encourage young designers who would be our assistants so that we wouldn't have to travel so much. We landed some prestigious accounts, but neither of us were ever in the office as we were both touring so much, so a year or two later we split up quite amicably, and my career as a solo lighting designer slowly built up from then on.

Ten years ago I met and married my wife, Lucy, and started a family, so that was definitely the point at which I wanted to stop touring. It's worked out pretty well. We're lucky in the rock-and-roll business, where lighting designers are probably the only people on the touring scene who can spend less time traveling the more in demand they become, unlike even the best touring sound engineers or tour managers, who have to be with the tour every day to do their work. I have a loose group of people whom I always work with, and a lot of them have been around me for a long time. That way you can risk sending someone out with your show, knowing it will be exactly as if you were there yourself but having the additional benefit of their taste and technological know-how (they know far more about the technology than I do). I don't just run the show perfectly myself and then leave after few days. Dave Hill or Charlie Wilson or Vince Foster are all there right from the beginning of a project and they share in both the creative process and the credit.

The Stones are a favorite for a lot of people for many reasons. They are a pretty interesting bunch of people, and they have a great team of characters around them. There's no one on their level in terms of the excitement that they generate, and there's a perception in our industry that their shows always break the rules in terms of production. On the Steel Wheels tour they hadn't worked together live for eight years, so there was a danger that the chemistry just wouldn't work. But when they went out, it did work, and rather than being an old war horse, they were a current band with a record in the top ten and a show that was as good as any that had ever been. On this last Voodoo Lounge tour they've confirmed it again, and there's no reason why they shouldn't carry on next year and beyond.

Most of the shows I've done have turned out to my satisfaction and usually to the satisfaction of the client, but that doesn't mean that the journey there hasn't been difficult. There are always nights at the lighting board where nothing goes right. You're sure that your work has become dull and pedestrian and unimaginative; you have the certain knowledge that it'll never be right and you'll never work again and why are they paying you all this money anyway? The self-doubt is there. You're cold and tired and far from home. And then suddenly something will happen, some combination of cues, or some lateral idea, your own or someone else's, that just pulls it all together and makes sense of everything.

Even the arrogant, confident ones must have the self-doubt. Of course the better known you become, the more is expected of you. You have the advantage of being able to bluff things, because people assume that you're rather good at it, because you've been doing it for so long. So you can say with some confidence "Don't worry, it'll be OK." You'd have to be pretty bad to fuck it up completely. You also have a slight buffer in that your client assumes the same thing, and so when you say, "Don't worry, it'll be OK," they actually believe you.

I don't often run the board myself any more and I miss it in a way. There's an immediacy that's quite satisfying. But the advantage in not doing it yourself is that it gives you the space to sit back a bit and watch from the outside. Often Charlie or Dave or Vince or Mark will stay and program all night, and I can come in in the morning and spot very quickly where the changes need to be made—something I couldn't do if I was as closely involved in the technicalities as they are. The skill in running the new computerized boards is now very specialized and is something that I don't think I'll ever be able to master as well as the operators I work with. You can work with people who are technically very able, but the main characteristic they must have is an ability to work well under pressure.

I've done jobs other than rock shows. Keith Richards and Patti Hanson asked me to light their house in Connecticut a few years ago, which was an interesting departure, and I've lit a couple of big office buildings in Europe. These jobs are different, in that you can't just keep moving fixtures around if they're in the wrong place until you get it right, and a focus can take days rather than hours. I've done industrial shows, too, you know—speeches from middle management followed by a product reveal. The discipline and creativity are the same as a rock show, but, although you're still lighting to a musical track, there's ultimately an empty feeling at the end, because the final result is a truck coming out from behind a curtain, rather than the applause of thousands of people celebrating a great musical event.

Rock and roll has generally far more money to spend than any other field of lighting. Consequently we can build bigger and more exciting lighting systems. Because it's connected with a very live event that changes from night to night, the lighting is both instant and much more gratifying and emotional. The downside is that we don't have the control over what we're doing—the control and the planning in the design process that comes with other disciplines in the world of theatre, film or industrial presentation. To me the adventure in the next few years will be cultivating that sort of control, exploring ways that will allow you to have more of a handle on the run-up process until the moment you walk into the arena to start to program the show. At that point, of course, you're flying by the seat of your pants again, but anything that helps you get to that point with more of an understanding of what you're trying to do, the better. That was the reason that led me to set up the Four to One studio a few years ago.[8]

I've been very influenced by the development of the equipment that we use in the whole production industry. I've seen great lighting in tiny clubs, but that's more the operation than the design. I've always tried to be influenced by things outside pop music and rock and roll. The first time I used bulkhead lights, for example, was after seeing thousands of them on the runway at the Boston airport, and that's when we decided to scatter them all over the first big Stones show. It was those sort of obtuse connections— you see a building floodlit at night or you see a person silhouetted in a movie, and you think, "that'll be a good way to do it." There have been a lot of really good light shows, a lot of big light shows, but they all use much the same sort of equipment, and so one is constantly looking for new ways to mix it all up. You know, we always have to have trusses to hang the lights on, and PAR cans and Vari*Lites will always be around; you have to have follow spots to pick people out on the stage. So we're still pretty much working with the same sort of kit. Big, big sky trackers—that's different. But in terms generically, there's still only half a dozen different sorts of fixtures that exist. What I find quite interesting is taking something from a rock-and-roll show and putting it into a theatre show, or vice versa. That's a good way to mix things up.

David Hersey said to me [that] the biggest shows on the West End still only have a rental budget of £2,000 or £3,000 a week—£4,000 a week is his top show, but even a rinky-dink band would spend more. I'm doing a show now in America where our lighting budget is $12,000 a week, and I'm really having to think hard about what I can do with that. Can I actually afford Vari*Lites at all, or should I beef up the rest of the stuff? You know, if you want to use moving lights and maybe some projection and half a dozen follow spots—you're pretty much there with $12,000. Thirty thousand dollars a week for a decent system is about the norm, although I've just spent $120,000 a week for the last Stones tour. That buys us a couple of hundred Vari*Lites, a couple of dozen Telescans, some Skyarts, loads of follow spots, a lot of special effects and a crew of sixteen people. But to relate that to theatre people, we're traveling our own dimmers, trusses, rigging—everything.

It's the people that are more important, I think, than the music. If I'm asked by a band to light their show, I'll generally know who they are, but not always. So, the first question you ask is, "How do you want to appear to your audiences?" Do you want to be glamorous, exciting, high drama, or do you want to be seen as down-to-earth and rather simple and straightforward? Is your performance intrinsically exciting or not? Are you like Pink Floyd and just stand there, or are you Bruce Springsteen, who has this extraordinary energy and literally could do it with white lights on a bare stage? Not many people could do that. (Personally, I don't think it's a very good idea. [Laughs.] It's not in their best interest and certainly not in mine!) So, you try to find out what sort of people they are and then you have to translate that visually. There might be a set designer, costume designer, director in position—a manager with very strong ideas—or there might be nothing. Sometimes you're asked to pitch ideas first before you're hired, which is difficult—it's difficult to show people lighting in sketches or models, and if you do anything too elaborate then you've already given them the ideas. I think you have to show them you have sensitivity to them and to their music. Often I work closely with the set designer, and they will often come on board at the same time. I've worked a lot with Mark Fisher and Jonathan Park, and we have a sort of shorthand and a trust, which makes it easy to share ideas. They are as likely to come up with ideas for lighting as I am with ideas for scenic finishes, so you work very much as a team. Traditionally, lighting designers have also designed stage sets, because it takes a while for people to understand that you pay someone to design your lighting and someone to design your stage. I've done both a few times, and it's not as satisfactory as having a separate designer who takes on that responsibility and works together with you. I love jobs where there are also costume designers, choreographers and even directors, because if the chemistry is right, you can achieve so much more between you and you don't end up working in isolation.

Once there is a broad concept agreed on, I lay out the basic plan on my Macintosh, and that goes off to the lighting company, who usually have far more sophisticated programs, which they use to transpose my ideas. You start to get a feel for the budget, for the stage set, for the amount of crew, and once the show has gone to bid and the budget is approved, then you can really get down to the detail of designing the show. The second part of the design process comes after you get into rehearsal and you start to marry the lighting to the music—that's the really exciting part of the job, the most challenging of course, and the one that demands your taste, your imagination and your restraint. When it all works properly it's a wonderfully satisfying feeling.

I charge a fee for my time—a smaller fee and residuals for a smaller show, a larger single fee for big rock shows. The money is important because it dictates the amount of time I spend away from home—a couple of big jobs a year allow me to spend time on smaller, less lucrative, but just as creative projects.

There's probably another half a dozen of us who do the very big shows and, happily for us, we've been doing it for some time. It's a fairly limited market, I would say, but there's always room for other younger designers with smaller acts with smaller budgets to start making a name for themselves as well.

I really enjoyed my time on the road when I was younger. I loved that feeling of getting on a plane and landing in somewhere like Sydney or New York, the sun would be shining and you'd be there—single—and staying in a lovely townhouse and eating wonderful food and knowing that you had no responsibility to anything. I used to enjoy getting on a bus at three in the morning in Middle America with a bunch of guys that you'd become quite close to in the preceding two months, heading off down the road to some other city. But I certainly don't regret not doing that now. I still work hard, but the shared experience now includes my family, and the sound of gravel crunching under the car tires after the drive back from the airport is much more important nowadays.

I usually tell bright-eyed and bushy-tailed potential lighting designers who want a job to call Brian Croft. [Laughs.] I say, go be a lighting designer—go find a little band and do it. Charlie Wilson got the job because on the Stones tour he was one of the guys in the crew who used to come in in the afternoon when no one was looking and run the show. So one day I said, "You might as well do the real thing," and that night he ran a couple of songs and ended up running the board for the whole European tour. So you have to have that enthusiasm and you have to just get in there and do it, and there is no shortcut, really. Just do some lighting. You can start with tiny, little shows—I just did *The Nutcracker* at the primary school in the village with one Silhouette and an effects projector. I said to myself this is a very dangerous precedent you're setting....

# Chapter Thirty-eight

# Pilbrow Story 13: Money

Some people are good about money and some people are very bad. It must come in the genes. I don't even like to talk about money very much, and I've often wondered how many people really understand the hours of financial data that fills the media.

However, money matters to the lighting designer because even he—and this time a "she"—has to live. Some lighting designers even go so far as to want to make a career out of it, and in consequence perhaps marry, have babies or one day even retire with savings. (Well, that seems a little far fetched!)

Of course the lighting design profession now straddles many worlds. Thank God there are vastly more extended opportunities for the young lighting designer in so many spheres outside the theatre. Theatre opportunities are still very restricted. Some few designers get to the Broadway megamusical. That can pay well, and the biggest of successes can bring in royalties to a designer from productions around the world. There are rumors that there are even a few lighting design millionaires! But these opportunities are open to very few. Most theatre designers in America work outside New York, where royalties are unknown. Here, as in regional theatre everywhere, the fee structures are still low compared to the hours of work necessary. The perpetual problem remains for the successful designer: having to do far more work than he should just to make a living.

This is the endemic dilemma faced by every designer. It's one thing to be successful enough to get a job at all, but you then have to try to get enough work to live. That means almost certainly doing too much to allow a lifestyle with any sanity at all. Too many shows, too many week ends away from home, too much exhaustion—not good things for a family to live with. But also, too much work can mean too little attention; too little time spent getting one-on-one with your director and designer, too little time at rehearsals, too little time being creative. So it is a dilemma, and nobody seems to have the beginnings of an answer.

Heaven knows the costs of doing live theatre seem everywhere to be in excess of what the ticket-buying public are willing to support. Should theatres be considered like schools and libraries and therefore be beneficiaries of the public purse? Of course, having been brought up in a golden period, I think so, but many disagree. It's been fascinating for me watching how the theatre world has changed since I began in the 1950s. I would attribute an enormous part of that change, in Britain at least, to the intervention of government. The Arts Council of Great Britain grew from a body that in 1945 gave a few thousands pounds a year to live theatre to one giving over £120 million. Despite years under attack from the right wing of politics, what extraordinary benefits have accrued. All the English megamusicals that have had such a colossal effect revitalizing theatre in the West End, on Broadway, and around the world, owe their existence to the subsidized English theatre. The tourist industries of Britain (and New York), along with Andrew Lloyd Webber's and Cameron Mackintosh's wealth, attest that the seeds of subsidy can bear great fruit.

Can the "pot" be divided more fairly? How much should be spent on lighting? Modern lighting equipment certainly costs much more than did the candles of the past. Unionized crews are a great cost. But the designer, being an *artist,* is supposed to be cheap. Many antediluvian theatre producers are determined to keep it that way. Rock and roll, television and film seem to reward their lighting directors quite well. Perhaps theatre has to lose its brightest and best to architecture or theme parks. But wherever you, the lighting designer, work, light and its fascinations will draw you onward. But it does seem that the responsibility for control of everything our audiences see and how they see it should be a labor worthy of proper hire.

# Endnotes

1. A sad story—for your author! A postponement of *Phantom* for book rewrites led to a scheduling conflict for me. After four months of exciting preproduction work with designer Maria Bjornson, I had to withdraw in favour of Andy. Good for him though!

2. Decades later, working on the preplanning for *Phantom of the Opera* I remembered this ancient treasure house of antique theatre technology—and introduced it to Maria. Now go and see the show and watch modern/ Victorian technology.

3. So too is the Theatre Projects lighting equipment, supplied on a declining rental scale, which declined to zero—decades ago.

4. "Wictim": A derivation of "victim" coined by that wonderful designer— and human being—the late Boris Aronson, whose unique pronunciation of this word is the stuff of legend.

5. A pub on St Martin's Lane in London—popular with the lighting fraternity

6. Strange coincidence: Your author also did Air Force time in air traffic control—it does indeed help you to keep your head when all about you are losing theirs.

7. A great British production electrician.

8. Time passes, technology advances: now on CAD

9. Patrick has since sold the Studio.

# Part Four

# Mechanics

The following "notebook" covers some of the technical aspects of the designer's craft. It cannot claim to be comprehensive, and further information should be sought in more technical books on the subject (many of which are listed in the bibliography).

Technical information on equipment is taken from manufacturer's catalogues, which should be referred to for further detail. Some older equipment information has been retained for sentimental as well as practical reasons. You won't often find some of the antiques listed, but—let's face it—we sometimes get to work with yesteryear's kit.

# Chapter Thirty-nine

# Introduction

*Light and Electricity*

Mechanics provides a brief introduction to some of the technical factors that affect the lighting designer's job as a craftsman. Items of lighting equipment are to the designer what paint and palette are to the painter. They are simply the tools of the trade. A knowledge of the behavior of light and electricity, of reflection and refraction, of the design of fixtures and control consoles is not, in fact, essential to the lighting designer. What is absolutely imperative is that the designer's knowledge of these areas is sufficient to enable him to function with freedom as an artist. The designer must know what can be done with light and, if a problem should arise in any technical area, he must have enough knowledge to overcome it. The designer's know-how should enable him to choose a fixture and then ensure that it is func-tioning correctly; the designer should under-stand how much can be expected from the con-trol system he is employing. The designer's knowledge of electricity should be sufficient to allow him to plan the installation sensibly and correctly, and the designer must know how light behaves.

## LIGHT

Light is electromagnetic radiation visible to the human eye. We can only see because little blobs of energy zap into our eyes and excite all those rods and cones. For information about all that, go see your doctor—or read another book.

Light is usually measured in lumens per square foot (lm/ft.), alternatively known as foot-candles (f.c.). One foot-candle is approxi-mately the amount of light emitted by a stan-dard candle falling onto a surface one foot square, one foot away. The metric unit is known as a lux. This is a surface one meter square at one meter distance. A conversion *from foot-candles to lux* is made by multiplying foot-candles by a factor of 10.76.

1 Foot Candle = amount of light from 1 candle onto a surface, 1 foot square, 1 foot away.

1 Lux = amount of light from 1 candle onto a surface, 1 meter square, 1 meter away.

Conversions:   Y lux = X foot candles x 10.76

$$X \text{ foot-candles} = \frac{Y \text{ lux}}{10.76}$$

A photometer is an instrument that mea-sures light. It is calibrated to give a reading in foot-candles or in lux. This instrument is use-ful for checking fixture performance or for simply investigating relative brightness about the stage.

If our illuminated white card is moved from a distance of one foot to two feet from the candle, the light on the card will decrease, not to a half, but to a quarter of the original. The area now covered by the light at a distance of two feet is now four times the size of the original area and thus one quarter of the brightness. This is known as the **Inverse Square Law** and it should remind one of the golden rule that light spreads in three dimensions (Fig. 1).

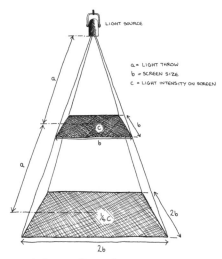

*1. Inverse Square Law*

### Brightness

What is bright enough? Well, how long is a piece of string? This is all so relative that talk of foot-candles is rarely useful. In the professional theatre 50 f.c. is not very much. For example a 6x9 Leko at 25-foot throw gives 140 f.c. and at 35 feet 77 f.c. I find that acting-area lighting for a Broadway show is often about 200-300 f.c. with frontlight at about 100 f.c. and accent and backlight at about two or three times that intensity. The full-up sunshine of *Four Baboons* was over 2,000 f.c. and seemed really bright—in part because of a low-key scene before.

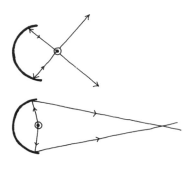

*2. Diffuse reflection*

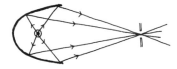

*3. Specular reflection*

### Reflection

Objects are only seen by the light they reflect. Black velour masking is often used to surround a set on stage. It reflects a minimum of light back to the audience and aids in maintaining visual focus on stage.

If an object has a matte, uneven surface, the light striking it reflects in many directions. This is known as diffuse reflection (Fig. 2).

If an object has a flat, shiny surface, the light is directly reflected. This is known as specular reflection (Fig. 3). The most familiar example of this is a mirror. In specular reflection the angle of incidence equals the angle of reflection. For example, if the light enters the mirror at an angle of 30° to an imagined perpendicular (angle of incidence), the light will reflect back at an angle of 30° (angle of reflection). This rule comes in handy when calculating how to keep

light out of the audience's eyes from say, a mirror on the set or a particularly reflective piece of flooring or scenery.

The principle of reflection is, of course, used inside a fixture to both control and collect the maximum possible amount of light emitted by the lamp. That is, a 1kW fixture with a reflector is more efficient and produces more light out the front end of the unit than a similar 1kW fixture without a reflector.

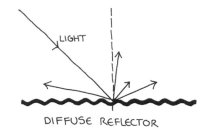

*4 and 5. Spherical reflectors*

For maximum efficiency the reflector has to be curved. The shape of this curve and the degree to which it surrounds the light source determines the amount of light collected and, in consequence, the efficiency of the fixture itself (Figs. 4 and 5).

The ellipsoidal reflector is used in most profile type instruments and collects the light and directs it to a point of second focus near the instrument's gate (Fig. 6).

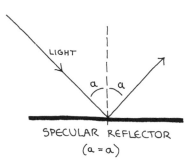

*6. Ellipsoidal reflector*

The parabolic reflector is that used in a beam projector—a little searchlight. It reflects the light into a virtually parallel beam from the instrument (Fig. 7).

*Stage Lighting Design*

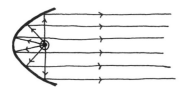

*7. Parabolic reflector*

A diffuse reflector is used for soft-edge beams such as those produced by scoops; specular reflectors are used in various types of ellipsoidals. Spherical, ellipsoidal and parabolic reflectors are the most common, but other more complex shapes can also be used.

### Refraction

When a light ray passes through any transparent material, it is bent or refracted. This happens at the join between two materials, for example between air and glass, or between one sheet of glass and another.

A lens is simply a piece of glass that uses this principle and bends the light passing through it in the direction required. The greater the curvature of a convex lens, the more the lens bends the light toward the focal point.

Rays of light from a single point source can be placed at the focal point of a lens, which will then refract them into parallel rays; the distance between the lens and this focal point is known as the *focal length* of the lens.

A description of a lens for an ellipsoidal gives its diameter first and then its focal length. For example, a 6x12 denotes a six-inch diameter lens, in which the beam converges twelve inches from the lens. The shorter the focal length, the larger the image projected. Such a lens is termed a wide-angle lens. The wide-angle lens is much closer to the lamp to bring the beam into sharp focus. Normal stage ellipsoidals use one or two lenses. However, when one enters the field of projection, complex lens combinations are employed (Fig. 8).

## ELECTRICITY

Electricity is dangerous—particularly since it can't be seen—and it should be treated with respect. The lighting designer must either have skilled help or must acquire sufficient knowledge of electricity to handle it by himself. The designer should always ensure that all wiring connections are neatly and firmly made. The designer should definitely know how much load can be applied to any particular circuit.

Ohms law, which is to be found in every electrical textbook, tells us that:

$$amps = \frac{volts}{ohms}$$

$$watts = volts \times amps$$

$$amps = \frac{watts}{volts}$$

The amp is a unit of the rate of flow of electricity used to describe the capacity of the outlet or cable; watts describe the amount of energy consumed by a lamp. The voltage is probably standard (in the U.S.A. 120 volts, in the U.K. 240 volts). The designer should be able to work out quite simply what load can be applied in what circumstances and what size cables are required to feed it.

The ampacity of a wire is determined by the insulation, how many current carrying conductors there are, and the ambient temperature. However a theatrical rule of thumb for cable ratings in the U.S. and U.K. are:

| U.S.A. | | U.K. | |
|---|---|---|---|
| Wire Gauge | Capacity (amps) | Wire Gauge | Capacity (amps) |
| 18 | 3 | | |
| 16 | 6 | 23/0076 | 6 |
| 14 | 15 | 40/0076 | 13 |
| 12 | 20 | 70/0076 | 18 |
| 10 | 25 | | |

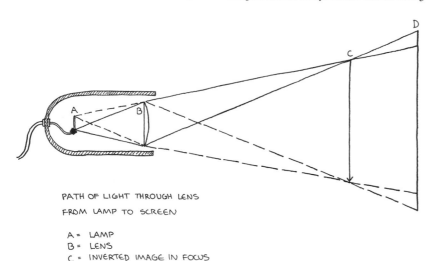

PATH OF LIGHT THROUGH LENS
FROM LAMP TO SCREEN

A = LAMP
B = LENS
C = INVERTED IMAGE IN FOCUS
D = OUT OF FOCUS SCREEN

*8. Path of light through lens*

# Chapter Forty

# Color

*Additive and Subtractive Mixing*

Color is perceived when we receive only part of the visible spectrum, which is in turn part of the electromagnetic spectrum from 380 to 770 nanometers. The spectrum, first studied by Isaac Newton (1666), breaks up a beam of white light into component parts (Fig. 9).

Note. In reality there are hundreds of pure (saturated) colors that blend imperceptibly, so the divisions to the right are arbitrary.

Beyond the red end of the visible spectrum is invisible infrared. Below the violet end is invisible ultraviolet.

Primary colors of light are *red, blue* and *green.*

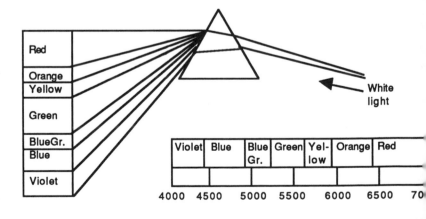

9. *True distribution of colors in spectrum*

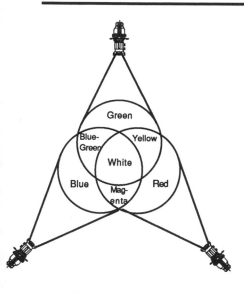

## ADDITIVE MIXING

If beams of red, blue and green light are mixed together the result will appear white.

$$\text{Red} + \text{green} = \text{yellow}$$
$$\text{Red} + 1/2 \text{ green} = \text{orange}$$
$$\text{Red} + \text{blue} = \text{magenta}$$
$$\text{Green} + \text{blue} = \text{cyan}$$

Secondary colors of light are *yellow, cyan* and *magenta*.

Each primary color is complementary to its opposite secondary thus:

$$\text{Red} + \text{cyan} = \text{white}$$

Additive color mixing chart with three primary color sources (double wattage of blue required):

| Red + | Green + | Blue = | White |
|---|---|---|---|
| Full | 1/3 | Out | Orange |
| Full | 2/3 | Out | Amber |
| Full | Full | Out | Yellow |
| 2/3 | Full | Out | Pea green |
| 1/3 | Full | Out | Light green |
| Out | Full | Out | Green |
| Out | Full | 1/3 | Deep green |
| Out | Full | 2/3 | Peacock |
| Out | Full | Full | Blue-green |
| Out | 2/3 | Full | Light blue |
| Out | 1/3 | Full | Mid-blue |
| Out | Out | Full | Blue |
| 1/3 | Out | Full | Violet |
| 2/3 | Out | Full | Mauve |
| Full | Out | Full | Magenta |
| Full | Out | 2/3 | Claret |
| Full | Out | 1/3 | Scarlet |
| Full | Out | Out | Red |

To achieve tints:

| Red + | Green + | Blue = | White |
|---|---|---|---|
| Full | 1/2 | 1/2 | Deep salmon |
| Full | 3/4 | 1/2 | Light salmon |
| Full | Full | 1/2 | Warm gray |
| 3/4 | Full | 1/2 | Green tint |
| 1/2 | Full | 1/2 | Pale green |
| 1/2 | Full | 3/4 | Steel gray |
| 1/2 | Full | Full | Steel blue |
| 1/2 | 3/4 | Full | Cold white |
| 1/2 | 1/2 | Full | Lavender |
| 3/4 | 1/2 | Full | Pale rose |
| Full | 1/2 | Full | Deep rose |
| Full | 1/2 | 3/4 | Pink |

Note: Color mixing with primaries is in practice extremely inefficient and wasteful of light unless one of the primaries themselves is actually required.

### Subtractive Mixing

The secondary colors of light are the primary colors of color filters (and photographic film): yellow, cyan and magenta. A yellow filter transmits only yellow, red and green light and subtracts the remainder. A blue filter transmits blue, blue-green and green light and subtracts the remainder. If a blue object is lit with a white or blue light it will appear blue. A red light that does not include any blue will make the blue object appear black.

Similarly, if yellow and blue filters are placed together in one frame in one instrument, the resultant color will be mixed subtractively. A yellow filter transmits yellow, red and green light. A blue filter transmits blue, blue-green and green light. Yellow and blue filters together transmit only common color, i.e. green.

Colors are identified in a lighting plot by their numbers. The manufacturer is identified by a letter as prefix, i.e. R20 = Rosco, G870 = Gamcolor, L196 = Lee.

Two or more colors in one frame mixed subtractively are described with a minus sign: e.g. L117-L138

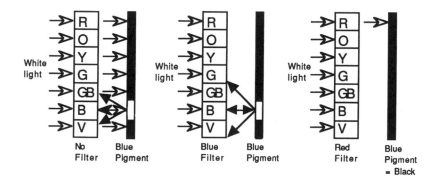

*Subtractive mixing*

# Chapter Forty-one

# Color Media

Color filters have been used in theatre at least since the Renaissance. Colored liquid filled the *bozze* to tint the candlelight, colored silk or glass was placed in front of the ancient oil lamp. Too many a fiery death originated from early attempts at color-changing gaslight battens.

At first electric lamps were dipped in colored lacquer, but the lacquer quickly faded due to heat. Then dyed gelatin sheets were used as color filters. The range of colors available was wonderful, but again heat quickly made the 'gels' brittle and faded. Only the word 'gels' has lasted to today. Then came cellulose acetate, such as Strand Lighting's Cinemoid or Rosco's Roscolene, each filter a thin shaving from a block of material that had been polished until transparent, but with the increase of lamp heat brought about by tungsten-halogen lamps this too fell by the wayside.

Color media today are principally plastic, either polyester or the more heat resistant poly-carbonate such as Lee HT, Roscolux Supergel, and Strand Chromagel.

Color manufacturers often differentiate between their regular colors and those intended for film or TV color correction. Both ranges are equally valuable to the theatre lighting designer.

Glass can be employed where exceptionally long life is required. Glass is still used more commonly in Europe (often as strips of glass in a frame to mitigate the heat problem), but the range is limited and colors are seldom consistent between batches.

With moving-light manufacturers leading the way, dichroic color filters have become common. Rosco manufacture a limited range of Permacolor glass filters. Dichroics utilize very thin layers of chemical on a sheet of glass that reflects selective wavelengths of light within the spectrum. Dichroics are effected by the angle of light to the filter, and color-changing devices have been made (for example by Vari*Lite) that, by turning the filters within the light beam, change the resultant color. Dichroics are found both in color filters as well as in reflectors, which will also tint the light.

The designer has at his disposal the whole range of colors from all the manufacturers. I think we probably all have our favorites. I tend to create a palette for each show, cutting up different manufacturers' swatch books and laying them out into groups and patterns from which I make my final choice. For me color selection is a very subliminal business, about which I fret and agonize a lot. Today those choices are more infinite with moving and color-changing instruments. Now a thirty-color scroller liberates times thirty, while a moving light may provide dozens, or hundreds, more choices. No wonder some resultant lighting looks like marmalade!! It's a matter of selection and TASTE. Every color is seen in elaborate and changing combinations and the totality has to **feel** right.

There follows an infinitely debatable color filter chart of all the principal makes of color filter. I owe a debt to Brian Fitt and Joe Thornley for their work in "Lighting by Design." Lucy and I have used this to up-date my earlier version, which was originally prepared by Molly, my wife, with designers from the TPL stable. Also thanks to Joe Tawil of Great American Market (who has the only set of sensible numbers) and Rosco for their help.

I've included "typical" names of colors. The names that manufacturers ascribed to colors vary from helpful to only poetic. But since print cannot reproduce colors correctly the names, which are commonly used, might be better than nothing.

The only way to pick or judge a color is to do it yourself. This list is a very rough guide to the parallels between the different brands largely available. See color *Color Comparison Chart*.

### Diffusion Material

I'm not an enormous proponent of diffusion material. I use it when I have to. Generally a well-focused instrument should do its job and, if required, blend unobtrusively with its neighbor. Ninety percent of all profiles (good ones at least) are used soft edged, and I usually find that even a light frost will often create too much scatter "glow" about the beam that diminishes the clarity of the effect you are seeking. But on occasion a light frost can be needed, and the heavier silks and frosts can have applications for special effects. The principal manufacturers of color media also produce ranges of diffusion material designed to alter the shadow characteristics and edge of a beam.

## COLOR COMPARISON CHART

| "Typical" name | Lee Filters | Lee HT | Cinemoid (Strand) | Chris James | Rosco Roscolux | Roscolene | Cinegel | Strand Chromagel | Strand Filter | GAM | Arri | Gelatran |
|---|---|---|---|---|---|---|---|---|---|---|---|---|
| 1/8 Antique rose | | | 279 | | | | 3318 | | | 108 | | |
| 1/4 Antique rose | 249 | | 249 | | | | 3314 | | | 107 | | |
| 1/2 Antique rose | 248 | | 248 | | | | 3313 | | | 106 | | 03 |
| Blush pink | | | | 333 | | | | | | | | |
| No-color pink | | | | | | 33 | | | | 155 | | |
| Antique rose | 247 | | | | | | 3308 | | | 105 | | |
| Pale-rose pink | | | | 37 | | | | | | | | |
| Light rose | | | | 38 | | | | 38 | | | | |
| Soft pink | | | | | | | | | | 135 | | |
| Lavender blue | | | | | | | | | | 101 | | |
| Blue rose | | | | | | | | | | 103 | | |
| Middle rose | 110 | | 10 | 110 | 337 | | | | 410 | 160 | 110 | |
| Light pink | 035 | 035 | | | 35 | | | 35 | | | | 05 |
| Flesh pink | 192 | | | | | | | | | 170 | | |
| Bright pink | | | | | | 827 | | | | | | |
| Dark pink | 111 | | 11 | 111 | | | | | 411 | | 111 | |
| Deep pink | | | | | 43 | | | 43 | | 150 | | |
| Rose | 022 | | | | 44 | | | | | 130 | | 83 |
| Follies pink | | | | 328 | | | | | 412 | | 328 | |
| Dark rose | | | | | | 828 | | | | 110 | | |
| Bright pink | 128 | | | 128 | 339 | | | | 428 | 120 | 128 | 13 |
| Rose pink | 332 | | | 332 | | 837 | | | | | | |
| Medium magenta | | | | | | 832 | | | | | | |
| Dark magenta | | | 12 | | 39 | | | | 449 | 140 | 332 | |
| Rose | | | | | 45 | | | 45 | | | | |
| Magenta | 46 | 46 | | | 46 | | | 46 | | | | |

| "Typical" name | Lee Filters | Lee HT | Cinemoid (Strand) | Chris James | Rosco Roscolux | Roscolene | Cinegel | Strand Chromagel | Strand Filter | GAM | Arri | Gelatran |
|---|---|---|---|---|---|---|---|---|---|---|---|---|
| Pale rose | 154 | | 53 | 154 | | | | | 454 | | 154 | |
| Pale salmon | 153 | | | 153 | | | | | 453 | | 153 | |
| Medium pink | 036 | 036 | | | 36 | 825 | | 36 | | | | |
| Light salmon | 109 | | 9 | 109 | 34 | 826 | | | 409 | | 109 | 15 |
| Cold pink | | | | | | 834 | | | | 190 | | |
| Light rose | 107 | | 7 | 107 | | | | | 407 | 195 | 107 | |
| Salmon pink | | | | | 31 | | | | | | | |
| Pale red | 166 | | | 166 | | | | | 466 | | 166 | |
| Cherry | | | | | | | | | | 180 | | |
| Cherry rose | | | | | 332 | | | | | | | |
| Bright rose | 148 | | 48 | 148 | | | | | 448 | | 148 | 09 |
| Rose pink | | | | | | 832 | | | | | | |
| Magenta | 113 | | 13 | 113 | 42 | | | | 413 | 220 | 113 | |
| | | | | | | | | | | | | |
| Pink | 157 | | 57 | 157 | | | | | 457 | | 157 | 17 |
| Rosy amber | 193 | | | | | | | | | | | |
| Pale red | 166 | | 66 | 166 | 32 | | | 32 | | | | |
| Light salmon | 008 | 008 | | | 40 | | | 40 | | | | 19 |
| Scarlet | 024 | 024 | | | 24 | 819 | | 24 | | | | |
| Flame red | 164 | | 64 | 164 | 25 | 818 | | 25 | 464 | 280 | 164 | |
| Fire | 019 | 019 | | | 19 | | | 19 | | | | |
| Light red | 182 | | | 182 | | | | | 482 | 270 | 182 | |
| Pink red | | | | | | | | | | 235 | | |
| Bright red | 026 | 026 | | | 26 | | | 26 | | | | |
| Primary red | 106 | | 6 | 106 | | | | | 406 | 245 | 106 | 08 |
| Medium red | | 27 | 14 | 321 | 27 | 821 | | 27 | | 250 | 321 | |
| Medium red | | | | | | 823 | | | | | | |
| | | | | | | | | | | | | |
| Ivory | | | | | | | | | | 435 | | |
| 1/8 CT orange | | | 73 | 223 | | | 3410 | | | 363 | 223 | |
| Warm straw | | | | | | 3115 | | | | 365 | | 32 |
| 1/4 CT orange | 206 | | | 206 | | | 3409 | | 206 | | 206 | |
| No-color straw | 159 | | | 159 | | | | | 459 | | | |
| Very light straw | 212 | | | 212 | | 805 | | | 440 | | | |
| Straw | 103 | | | 103 | 08 | | | | 403 | | 103 | |
| Straw | | | 3 | | | | | | | | | |
| Straw tint | 013 | 013 | | 308 | 13 | | | 13 | | | 308 | |
| 1/2 CT orange | 205 | | | | | | 3408 | | | 365 | | |
| Amber blush | | | | 205 | | | | | 205 | 360 | 205 | |
| Pale amber gold | 009 | 009 | | | 09 | | | 09 | | | | |
| Light amber | | | | | 16 | | 3102 | | | 385 | | |
| CT orange | 204 | | | 204 | | | 3407 | | 204 | 1543 | 204 | |
| | | | | | | | | | | | | |
| Pale honey | | | | | | | | | | 364 | | |
| Light bastard amber | | | | | | | | | | 340 | | |
| Bastard amber | 162 | | | 162 | 02 | | | | 462 | | 162 | |
| Light amber | | | | 311 | | 813 | | | | | | |
| Pale gold | 152 | | 52 | 152 | 304 | | | | 452 | 325 | 152 | |
| Rose tint | | | | | 05 | | | 05 | | | | |
| Bastard amber | 154 | | | 154 | 305 | | | | | | | |
| Gold tint | 151 | | | 151 | | | | | | 305 | 151 | 06 |

# COLOR COMPARISON CHART

| "Typical" name | Lee Filters | Lee HT | Cinemoid (Strand) | Chris James | Rosco Roscolux | Roscolene | Cinegel | Strand Chromagel | Strand Filter | GAM | Arri | Gelatran |
|---|---|---|---|---|---|---|---|---|---|---|---|---|
| Medium bastard amber | 004 | 004 | 75 | | 04 | | | | | | | 16 |
| Dark bastard amber | | | | 386 | 03 | | | 03 | | | | |
| Dark bastard amber | | | | | | | | | | 324 | | |
| Loving amber | 176 | | | 176 | 01 | 802 | | 01 | 476 | | 176 | |
| Rosy amber | | | | | | | | | | 260 | | |
| Light salmon pink | | | | | 30 | | | 30 | | | | |
| | | | 78 | | | | | | | | | |
| Mayan sun | | | | | 318 | | | | | | | |
| Peach | | | | | | | | | | 320 | | |
| Fluorofilter | | | | | | | 3310 | | | 323 | | |
| HMI to tungsten | 236 | | | 236 | | | | | 236 | | 236 | |
| Roscosun 85 | | | | | | | 3401 | | | | | |
| Flame | | | 47 | | 18 | 811 | | | | 375 | | |
| Apricot | 147 | | | 147 | 316 | | | | 447 | 343 | 147 | 30 |
| Light flame | | | | | 17 | | | | | | | |
| | | | | 313 | | | | | | | 313 | |
| CID to tungsten | 237 | | | 237 | | | | | 237 | | 237 | |
| Golden amber | 134 | | 34 | 134 | 321 | | | | 434 | | 134 | |
| CSI to tungsten | 238 | | | 238 | | | | | | | | |
| Sepia/chocolate | | | | | 99 | | | | | 330 | | |
| Super-white flame | 232 | | | 232 | | | | | | | | |
| Golden tan | | | | | | | | | | 380 | | |
| Chocolate | 156 | | | 156 | | | | | 456 | | 156 | |
| Walnut | | | | | | | | | | 390 | | |
| No-color straw | | | | | 06 | 804 | | 06 | | 510 | | |
| Pale yellow | 007 | 007 | 50 | | 07 | | | 07 | | 475 | | |
| Pale gold | | | | | | | | | | 470 | | |
| Daffodil | | | | | 310 | | | | | | | 40 |
| Mellow yellow | | | | | | | | | | 460 | | |
| Medium yellow | | | | | 12 | | | | | 480 | | |
| Medium yellow | 010 | 010 | | | 10 | | | 10 | | | | |
| Yellow | 101 | | 1 | 101 | 312 | | | | 401 | 450 | 101 | 41 |
| Medium yellow | | | | | | 806 | | | | | | |
| No-color amber | | | | | | | | | | | | |
| Deep amber | 104 | | 4 | 104 | | | | | 404 | | 104 | |
| Light straw | | | 49 | | 309 | 809 | | 11 | | | 309 | |
| Deep straw | 015 | 015 | | | 15 | | | 15 | | | | |
| Light amber | 102 | | 2 | 102 | | 807 | | | 402 | | 102 | |
| Medium amber | | | | | | | | | | 420 | | |
| Medium straw | | | 46 | | 14 | 810 | | 14 | | 410 | | |
| Golden sunset | | | | | | | | | | 395 | | |
| Yellow sun | | | | | | | | | | 455 | | |
| Chrome orange | 179 | | | 179 | | | | | 479 | 388 | 179 | |
| Brass | | | | | | | | | | 382 | | |
| Medium amber | 020 | 020 | | | 20 | | | 20 | | | | |
| Orange | 105 | | | 105 | | | | | 405 | 350 | 105 | |
| Golden amber | | | 33 | 315 | 21 | 815 | | 21 | | 355 | | 20 |

# COLOR COMPARISON CHART

| "Typical" name | Lee Filters | Lee HT | Cinemoid (Strand) | Chris James | Rosco Roscolux | Roscolene | Cinegel | Strand Chromagel | Strand Filter | GAM | Arri | Gelatran |
|---|---|---|---|---|---|---|---|---|---|---|---|---|
| Coral | | | | | | | 1540 | | | 335 | | |
| Golden amber | | | | | | | | 21 | | | | |
| Deep orange | 158 | | 5 | 158 | 23 | 817 | | 23 | 458 | 345 | 158 | |
| Autumn glory | 021 | 021 | 58 | | | | | | | 315 | | |
| Deep golden amber | 135 | | 35 | | | | | | 435 | | | 22 |
| Dark amber | 022 | 022 | | | 22 | | | | | 290 | | |
| | | | | | | | | | | | | |
| 1/8 Plusgreen | | | 77 | | | | 3317 | | | 1589 | | |
| 1/4 Plusgreen | 246 | | | 246 | | | 3316 | | | 1588 | | |
| New straw | | | | | | | | | | 520 | | 45 |
| 1/2 Plusgreen | 245 | | | 245 | | | 3315 | | | 535 | | 46 |
| White flame green | 213 | | | 213 | | | | | | | 213 | |
| Pale yellow green | | | | | 87 | | | | | | | |
| Light green | | | | | 88 | | | | | | | |
| Full plusgreen | 244 | | | | | | 3304 | | | 540 | | |
| Pale green | 138 | | 38 | 138 | | | | | 438 | | 138 | |
| Gaslight green | | | | | 388 | | | | | | | |
| Fluorescent 3600k | 243 | | | | | | | | | | | |
| | | | | | | | | | | | | |
| Light green-yellow | 121 | 121 | 21 | 121 | 86 | | | 86 | 421 | 570 | 121 | 47 |
| Yellow green | | | | 378 | | 878 | | | | | | |
| Moss green | 122 | 122 | 22 | 122 | 89 | | | 89 | 422 | | 122 | |
| Medium green | | | | | | | | | | 660 | | |
| | | | 23 | | | | | | | | | |
| Dark green | 124 | 124 | 24 | 124 | 389 | 871 | | 389 | 424 | | 124 | |
| Light green | | | | 371 | | | | | | | 371 | |
| Kelly green | | | | | 94 | | | 94 | | | | |
| Primary green | 139 | 139 | 39 | 139 | | | | | 439 | 655 | 139 | |
| Dark yellow-green | 090 | 090 | | | 90 | 874 | | 90 | | | | |
| Grass green | | | | | | | | | | 650 | | |
| Primary green | | | | | 91 | | | | | | | |
| | | | | | | | | | | | | |
| Turquoise | | | | | 92 | | | | | | | |
| Kelly green | | | | | | | | | | 680 | | |
| Pistachio | | | | | | | | | | 685 | | |
| Fluorescent 4300k | 242 | | | | | | | | | | | |
| Fluorescent green | 219 | | | 219 | | | | | 219 | | 219 | 49 |
| Blue green | | | | | 93 | | | | | | | |
| Fluorescent 5700k | 241 | | | | | | | | | | | |
| Plusgreen 50 | | | | | | | 3306 | | | | | |
| Light steel blue | | | | | | | | | | 720 | | |
| Nile blue | | | | | 70 | 849 | | 70 | | | | |
| Azure blue | | | | | 72 | 855 | | 72 | | | | |
| Sea blue | | | | | 71 | 854 | | | | | | |
| Princess blue | | | | | | | | | | 725 | | |
| Peacock blue | | | | | 73 | | | 73 | | | | |
| Peacock blue | 115 | 115 | | 115 | | | | | 415 | | 115 | |
| Blue green | | | | | | | | | | 710 | | 51 |
| Bluegrass | | | | | | | | | | 690 | | |
| Teal green | | | | | 395 | | | | | | | |
| Medium blue-green | 116 | 116 | | 116 | | 877 | | | 416 | | 116 | |
| Medium blue-green | | | | | 95 | | | 95 | | | | |

*Stage Lighting Design*

# COLOR COMPARISON CHART

| "Typical" name | Lee Filters | Lee HT | Cinemoid (Strand) | Chris James | Rosco Roscolux | Roscolene | Cinegel | Strand Chromagel | Strand Filter | GAM | Arri | Gelatran |
|---|---|---|---|---|---|---|---|---|---|---|---|---|
| Electric blue | | | | | | | | | | 790 | | |
| Water blue | | 45 | | | | 848 | | | | | | |
| Cool blue | | | | | 66 | | | | | | | 73 |
| Steel blue | 117 | | 17 | 117 | 363 | | | 66 | 417 | | 117 | |
| Shark blue | | | 40 | 350 | | | | | | 780 | 350 | |
| | | | 86 | | | | | | | | | |
| Azure blue | | | | | | | | | | 730 | | |
| Azure blue | 144 | | | 144 | | 853 | | | 444 | | 353 | |
| No-color blue | | | | | | 850 | | | | | | |
| Christel blue | | | | | | | | | | 770 | | |
| Pale navy blue | 143 | | 43 | 143 | | | | | 443 | | 143 | |
| Aqua blue | | | | | | | | | | 760 | | |
| Bermuda blue | | | | | 376 | | | | | | | |
| Light green-blue | | | | | 76 | | | 76 | | | | |
| Green-blue | | | | | 77 | | | | | | | |
| Green-blue moonlight | | | | | | 859 | | | | | | |
| Light blue | 118 | 118 | 18 | 118 | | | | | 418 | 740 | 118 | 76 |
| Bright blue | | | | 360 | | | | | | 750 | 360 | |
| Moonlight blue | 183 | | | 183 | | | | | 483 | | 183 | |
| Bright blue | 141 | 141 | 41 | 141 | | | | | 441 | | 141 | |
| Brilliant blue | | | 62 | | 69 | | | 69 | | | | |
| | | | | | | | | | | | | |
| 1/8 CT blue | 218 | | | 218 | | | 3216 | | 218 | 870 | 218 | |
| 1/4 CT blue | 203 | | | 203 | | | 3208 | | 203 | 885 | 203 | |
| | | | 67 | | | | | | | | | |
| 1/3 CT blue | | | | | | | 3206 | | | | | |
| 1/2 CT blue | 202 | | | 202 | | | 3204 | | 202 | | | |
| Clearwater | | | | | 360 | | | | | | | |
| No-color blue | 063 | 063 | | | 60 | | | | | | | |
| Tipton blue | | | | | 362 | | | | | | | |
| Booster blue | | | | | 62 | | | | | | | |
| Mist blue | 061 | 061 | | | 61 | | | 61 | | | | |
| North sky blue | | | | | | | | | | 830 | | |
| Full-light blue | | | | | | | | | | 820 | | |
| Pale blue | | | | | 63 | | | | | | | |
| Whisper blue | | | | | | | | | | 842 | | 72 |
| Blue belle | | | | | | | | | | 888 | | |
| Sky blue | | | | | | | | | | 860 | | |
| Tharon delft blue | | | | | 365 | | | | | | | |
| Full CT blue | 201 | | | 201 | | | 3202 | | 201 | 880 | 201 | |
| Southern sky | | | | | | | | | | 882 | | |
| Bonus blue | | | | | | | | | | 848 | | |
| City blue | | | | | | | | | | 847 | | |
| Alice blue | | | | | | | | | | 910 | | 66 |
| Double CT blue | 200 | | | | | | | | | | | |
| Trudy blue | | | | | 78 | | | 78 | | | | |
| Steel blue | | | | | | | | | | 840 | | |
| Blue bell | | | | | 364 | | | | | | | |
| Dark steel blue | 174 | | | 174 | | | | | 474 | | 174 | |
| Light steel blue | | | | | 64 | | | 64 | | | | 69 |
| True blue | 196 | | | | 65 | | | 65 | | 815 | | 65 |

# COLOR COMPARISON CHART

| "Typical" name | Lee Filters | Lee HT | Cinemoid (Strand) | Chris James | Rosco Roscolux | Roscolene | Cinegel | Strand Chromagel | Strand Filter | GAM | Arri | Gelatran |
|---|---|---|---|---|---|---|---|---|---|---|---|---|
| Slate blue | 161 | | 61 | 161 | 67 | | | | 461 | | 161 | |
| Moon blue | | | | | | | | | | 810 | | 71 |
| Daylight blue | 165 | | 32 | 165 | | 856 | | | 465 | | 165 | |
| Sky blue | | | | | 68 | | | 68 | | | | |
| Special medium blue | | | | 357 | | | | | | | 357 | |
| Medium blue | 132 | 132 | 132 | 132 | | | | | 432 | | 132 | |
| Urban blue | | | | | 81 | | | 81 | | | | |
| Alice blue | 197 | 197 | 63 | | 84 | | | | | 841 | | |
| Just blue | 079 | 079 | | | 80 | 857 | | | | 835 | | 64 |
| Bright blue | | | | | 79 | 861 | | 79 | | | | |
| True blue | | | | | | 862 | | | | | | |
| Dark blue | 119 | 119 | 19 | 119 | 82 | | | 82 | 419 | 845 | 119 | |
| Deep blue | 363 | 363 | | | 85 | | | 85 | | | | |
| Night blue | 195 | 195 | | 363 | 74 | 863 | | 74 | | 850 | 363 | |
| Medium blue | | | | | 83 | | | | | | | 60 |
| Dark sky blue | | | | | | | | | | 890 | | |
| Twilight | 85 | 85 | | | 383 | | | | | 915 | | |
| Deep blue | 120 | 120 | 20 | 120 | 385 | 866 | | | 420 | 905 | 120 | 61 |
| Congo blue | 181 | 181 | | | 382 | | | | 481 | | 181 | 62 |
| Real congo blue | | | | | | 846 | | | | 930 | | |
| | | | | | | | | | | | | |
| Pale lavender | 053 | 053 | | | 53 | | | 53 | | 920 | | |
| Lilac | | | 71 | | 55 | | | 55 | | | | |
| Special lavender | | | | 342 | | | | | | | 342 | |
| | | | 42 | | | | | | | | | |
| Special lavender | 137 | | | 137 | | 841 | | | 437 | | 137 | |
| | | | | | | 844 | | | | | | |
| Violet | | | | 344 | | | | | | | 344 | |
| Pale violet | 142 | | | 142 | | | | | 442 | | 142 | |
| Light purple | | | | | | | | | | 940 | | |
| Medium lavender | | | | | 356 | | | | | 960 | | |
| Surprise pink | 194 | | | | | | | | | | | |
| Lavender | | 58 | | | 57 | 842 | | 57 | | 950 | | |
| Dark lavender | 180 | | | 343 | 58 | 843 | | 58 | 480 | | 180 | |
| Rose indigo | | | | | 358 | | | | | | | |
| Gypsy lavender | | | 25 | | 56 | | | 56 | | | | |
| African violet | | | | | | | | | | 948 | | 88 |
| Cosmic blue | | | | | | | | | | 925 | | |
| Indigo | | | | | 59 | | | | | 945 | | |
| | | | | | | | | | | | | |
| Surprise pink | | | | | | | | | | 980 | | |
| Surprise lavender | | | | 340 | | | | | | | 340 | |
| Special lavender | | | | | 54 | | | 54 | | 970 | | |
| Pale lavender | 136 | | 36 | 136 | | | | | 436 | | 136 | |
| Light lavender | 052 | 052 | | | 52 | 840 | | 52 | 470 | | 170 | |
| Dark lavender | 170 | | | 170 | | | | | | 990 | | |
| Light rose-purple | | | | | 47 | | | | | | | |
| Rose purple | 48 | | | 381 | 48 | 838 | | 48 | | | | |
| Bright purple | | | | 339 | 349 | 839 | | | 469 | | 339 | |
| Mauve | 126 | | 26 | 126 | 49 | | | 49 | 426 | 995 | 126 | 81 |

# Chapter Forty-two

# Control Systems

The heart of every lighting installation is the control system. Primarily by means of dimmer controls, stage lighting is balanced to achieve the desired pictorial effect. All control boards provide this facility with various degrees of sophistication. But some instruments now allow "automated" remote control of focus and color. These use various forms of networked computer control. Sophisticated modern systems also allow the integrated control of other effects—smoke, slide-changers, and so on. Some allow interface with other controls or external sources such as MIDI.

In 1996 stage technology lighting is undoubtedly in a period of dramatic change. Moving lights are here to stay and will, one day quite soon, be part of every theatre's rig. We will look back at the twentieth-century lighting

with amused nostalgia. "How did those old fogies do it with fixed-focus lights?"

Control boards vary enormously in cost and complexity. Broadly speaking they may be categorized into three types: theatre controls, rock-and-roll controls, and automated-light controls. The boundaries between each, however, are falling—by the month.

The following is a brief summary of some of those systems that might be encountered by the designer. Obviously for operational information, more detail should be obtained from the appropriate manufacturer.

I haven't begun to attempt to list every feature of every board. Many share common features. For example, most keypad-driven controls share features such as "@" or "Thru," "+," "-"; many have some form of macro capa-

bility, and so on. I've attempted to touch on the highlights and to provide an overview of the broad spectrum of equipment.

## THEATRE CONTROLS
### ADB (Belgium)

*Vision 10:* The Vision 10 provides sophisticated integrated modular architecture control of intensity, motion, color or any other parameter;

*ADB Vision 10*

1,024 DMX 512 outputs and built-in compatibility to MIDI, SMPTE, DMX, RS 232 and RS 485.

*Vision Compact:* This is a smaller version of the above with DMX 512, internal card reader, VGA screen and 499 macros.

*Cantor:* Cantor has 24-way two-scene preset or 48-way single with soft patch to 512 dimmers and 12 submasters; operable in manual or memory mode. Green and red LEDs give indication of channels active in submaster, memories or effects and channels live onstage.

## Arri (U.K.; in association with ETC of the U.S.A.)

*Finesse:* Based on 32-bit RISC processors, the Finesse offers 1,024 dimmers on 300 channels with 600 cues and 2,000 macros. There are 24 simultaneous submasters or effects and options include SMPTE, MIDI, networking and remote control. I first saw the graphics tablet with Arri (with—as I understand it—inspiration along the way from Tim Burnham, Dave Cunningham and Eric Cornwall), which remains potentially a great way of handling lights.

*Imagine 3:* Designed for mixed rigs of conventional and moving lights, Imagine 3 features 1,536 dimmers with 300, 600 or 1,200 channels and up to 1,536 dimmers/parameters.

*Arri Imagine 2*

## AVAB (Sweden)

*Super Viking VLC:* This high-end (up to 4,096 channels) modular multitask system allows, for example, remote focusing concurrently with cue

*AVAB Viking*

operation. The board can simultaneously execute fades within fades, move remote-control instruments and color changers, even control mechanized scenery and issue verbal cues to spot operators! Utilizing Graphic User Interface (GUI) and multiple-monitor (up to eight) technology for control and display, it offers an intuitive and efficient interface for control of dimmers, automated fixtures and scrollers using drag-and-drop methods. Editing features allow the import or export of complete shows, individual cues, effects, channel groups and levels. A hand-held infrared control allows remote operation of any control from anywhere in the theatre. Viking employs "fields" to create lighting presets, which may be balanced on multiple mixer wheels. Any crossfade may contain up to 32 separate moving parts with separate delay and fade times. Viking utilizes high-quality wheels as faders with adjacent LED displays of direction and rate of change. Ethernet Local Area Networking (LAN) is available for multiple consoles and workstations.

*AVAB Lynx:* A smaller-scale software/hardware control for 512 DMX, the Lynx addresses on up to 128 control channels utilizing the VLC click-and-drag GUI interface of the Viking.

*AVAB 211:* This control is available in three versions: 24, 48 and 72 channels. Faders control channels or submasters with up to 150 recordable presets. Gang-loading function piles multiple presets and speeds onto submasters.

*AVAB 202:* AVAB 202 is available in 48, 96, 120, 192, or 240 channels. Twenty-four faders control channels or submasters. A joystick allows acceleration or slowing of any change.

The system also features integrated effects and chases.

*AVAB Expert:* Capable of communicating by DMX 512, MIDI or ASCII, the Expert can act as the heart of an integrated performance system. Twenty-four faders act as channel controllers or as submasters. A built-in electronic guidebook can incorporate operator's notes. Show information can be downloaded to a PC for off-line editing. Clear VDUs or flat-screen displays include pop-up menus for control alternates.

## Colortran (U.S.A.; now part of N.S.I.)

*Status 12/24 or 24/48:* These systems have compact consoles for simple operation, which can be operated in two-scene preset or multi-scene memory modes. There are 12 or 24 dedicated submasters with bump buttons. They have electronic patch for up to 512 dimmers with up to 120 cues. Cues, patch, submaster and effects can be stored on EPROM cartridges.

*Encore 24/48 or 48/96:* These controls operate either as two-scene preset or memory consoles with color monitor for up to 144 channels. Able to handle 512 dimmers they have 24 or 48 submasters (pile-on, timed, inhibitive and effects), with bump buttons and up to 300 or 350 multipart cues/groups per show. Data can be selectively retrieved from mixed shows.

*Encore XL:* This portable desk can be expanded from 512 channels to 1024 (the XL/2) with up to 600 cues/groups. With 48 programmable submasters with bump buttons, an additional 32 submasters may be added with an outrigger control. Alphanumerical labels can be added to name cues, groups, subs, effects or shows and named items can be called by name as well as number, i.e. cue "Intermission."

*Colortran Medallion*

*Medallion:* The Medallion is Colortran's top-of-the-line control. Its architecture is based upon an Intel 486™ processor with i960™ RISC coprocessor and it uses the OS/2 windowing operating environment. This allows customization of each of the two video displays, the assembly of cues and effects from different shows and on-screen selection of channels via a trackball. The control offers 1,000 cues per show, up to 1,536 control channels and dimmers, up to eight part cues, sophisticated macros and effects options and 96 submasters with individually programmable pile-on, timed, inhibitive and effects modes. There are eight playback masters, which clear automatically or manually and allow 32 simultaneous fades. An editable tracksheet allows easy cue editing. Optional extras include a third color monitor, off-line editing, Magic Sheet for alternate method of accessing any board function, 32 submaster outrigger and hand-held remote control. The Medallion can be part of a network on which multiple Medallions and other peripheral devices can share information while operating independently of each other.

## Electronics Diversified Inc. (EDI)

EDI built the first dimmers and computer memory system (LS-8) in the U.S.A. for Broadway's *Chorus Line* (see the Tharon Musser interview). The control, nicknamed "Sam," now resides in the Boston Computer Museum.

*EnAct 200/400/1000XL:* From the smallest, for 200 channels, up to 2,000, the EnAct series offer increasingly sophisticated facilities around a common control philosophy. Cursor control

allows positioning in screens and edit functions as well as recording information for cues, groups and submasters. Action can be by highest- or last-action takes precedence operation. Nine hundred ninety-nine user-addressable macros reduce keystroke operation. Eight principal faders as well as phantom faders allow flexible playback capability. Eight pages of 24 programmable linear playbacks can store channels, group and cue information, operated manually or with timed information consisting of up, down and dwell times. Channel tracking across cues allows global real-time editing.

*Omega 2:* Sixty or 120 channel controls with side panel of faders and LED indicators per channel are features on the Omega 2. The system has four independent faders for simultaneous playback, each with "Go" button and manual override. The Omega VDU has the unique capacity of displaying descriptive channel labels in addition to channel numbers on the screen. Channel location, focus area, type of fixture, color or special function can all be displayed in a range of easily identifiable colors—a really neat innovation.

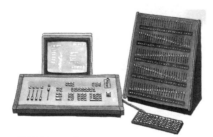

*EDI Omega 2*

## Electronic Theatre Control (ETC)

*Obsession, Obsession 3000 and 600:* A high-end tracking-style console using Intel 486™ electronics. The Obsession system can handle up to 3,072 DMX 512 dimmers and 3,072 control channels. One thousand cues, 250 groups, 100

*ETC Obsession*

effects, 2,000 macros, 48 overlapping submasters, 128 simultaneous fades (8 physical faders, 120 virtual faders) make up a lot of switchboard!! Channel levels may be displayed and edited in spreadsheet form or compressed in Flexichannel display mode. Any cue or submaster can be accessed as a group. "Sneak" allows subtle changes without disrupting the show, "Learn" records macros, profiles and fade rates, "Park" lets channels and dimmer levels remain independent of cues or submasters. Multiuser allows simultaneous multiple control positions and dimmer monitoring.

*Obsession ML:* Newest in the ETC stable is an Obsession with moving light control capability. Up to 500 fixtures may be controlled via a trackpad, VGA touch screed LCD display and six multifunction attribute encoders. The control offers built in support for many types of moving light including Vari*Lite, Clay Paky, Martin, Coemar, Wybron and High End Systems. It has gobo, color and position libraries.

*Concept 2x:* Concept 2x is a 1,536–dimmer and 1,000–channel control with new features for color changers and moving lights. An "X/Y Link List," grouping channels and groups, provides simultaneous control of pan and tilt or intensity and color position. A "Flip Attribute" provides simultaneous control of moving fixtures on opposite sides of the stage, while "Independent Attribute" prevents these devices reverting to "home" positions when the stage is faded out or channels released.

*Expression 2x:* Employing an Intel i960 processor this control handles 1,536 DMX 512 dimmers and 500 control channels for color changers and moving lights. "X/Y Link" with dual fader wheels allows linking of channels and groups so that pan and tilt or dimmer and color can be handled simultaneously. "Flip Attribute" allows moving lights facing in opposite directions to pan or tilt in the same direction when a wheel is moved. "Independent Attribute" separates a color or move attribute from moving under grandmaster or intensity level control. "Park" allows the setting of a channel independent of cues or submaster setting. A digitizer tablet described as a "Designer's Worksheet" is available.

*Insight 2x:* As above for 1,536 dimmers and 324 channels

*Impression 2:* As above for 1,024 dimmers and 250 channels

*Insight 2:* As above for 1,024 dimmers and 108 channels

*Idea:* Idea provides simple operation of a two-scene preset board combined with a 120-cue memory console for 512 dimmers and 12, 24, 36 or 48 channels. Faders double as channel or submaster faders.

*Microvision FX™:* This system has 120 channels for 512 dimmers with 200 cues. Two pairs of auto faders with pile-on interaction are supplemented by five pages of six pile-on submasters and an effects package.

*Acclaim™:* Acclaim is a two-scene preset board for 12, 24, 36 or 48 channels, with eight pile-on proportional submaster memories for the small theatre.

*The Express line:* Introduced in late 1995 the Express line has five different models, which all share common elements including:
- One CRT Monitor
- MIDI
- ETCNet (Ethernet peripheral devices)
- ETCLink (dimmer monitoring)
- 1024 DMX outputs
- Hundreds of recorded cues
- Two timed playback faders
- Remote macro inputs
- Printer output
- X/Y touch pad for moving light control

*The five models are:*

*Express 24/48*
- A two-scene version with 24-channels x 2 scene or 48 channels x 1 scene.

*Express 48/96*
- A two-scene version with 48 channels x 2 scene or 96 channels x 1 scene.
- An additional 24 dedicated submasters

*Express 72/144*
- A two-scene version with 72 channels x 2 scene or 144 channels x 1 scene.
- The same additional 24 dedicated submasters as the one above.

*Express 125*
- 125 channels
- 24 dedicated submasters

*Express 250*
- 250 channels
- 24 dedicated submasters

## Entertainment Technology (now part of the Rosco Group)

Entertainment Technology of Portland, Oregon, run by Gordon Perlman, with Steve Carlson, is one of the sources of invention in our industry. They were largely responsible for several innovative controls from Kliegl in their heyday, such as the Performer range and for controls for PanCommand Systems. ET developed the IPS non-SCR dimmer, which, due to its compact size and low noise, may be mounted adjacent to the instrument.

*Mac-360:* This is a 360-channel, multiple-attribute console, which transmits DMX 512 to dimmers and moving lights. Mac-360 is configurable to virtually any type of fixture with up to twelve attributes. Wheels and trackball give access to any attribute. Two independent time faders, six independent pile-on scenemasters and six assignable inhibitive submasters provide extensive facilities.

*Access and Access Pro:* Access and Access Pro are a very neat pair of low-cost controls marketed by the Great American Market. Forty-eight or 96 control channels for up to 256 dimmers. Proportional grandmaster, two independent dipless cross-faders, overlapping scene masters and soft-patch make up a flexible, all-purpose control

*ET Access Pro*

*ACE 240:* This is an inexpensive console for up to 512 dimmers on 240 channels. Three hundred seventy-five cues are available on X/Y faders with Go buttons, and 96 scenes on four pages of 24 scene masters. Cues have independent up, down, delay and wait times, and wait and next commands may be used to create automatic sequences and cue loops. The ACE 240 supports the IPS data return protocol to give feedback status reporting from IPS dimmers.

## Marumo Electrics Co. Ltd. (Japan)

*Sarius:* The system allows the designer to place his lighting plan on an overhead digital scanner

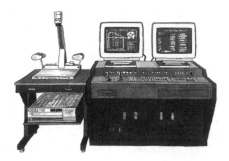

*Marumo Sarius*

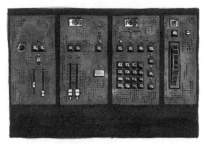

*Strand Tempus*

and then use a pen to move the beam of a spotlight in space. Pan, tilt, focus, color and barndoor shutter position are remotely accessible. One hundred twenty channels, 24 groups and 250 cues are available. Sarius also employs voice recognition: "Pan! Stop! Up! Left!" which is cool in any language.

*Marionet Lighting Control:* Marionet has 256 channels for 256 dimmers and 500 memories. The system uses a command keypad and wheel for channel and memory selection, has 10 submasters, three sub-crossfaders and an over crossfader and total crossfader that can operate simultaneously. Cues with time data may have delays and waits.

*File-IIEX:* A portable control originally intended for pop and rock and roll. It has 120 channels, with 50 pages of 20 scenes, 1,000 step effects on two chase panels, and 20 cue master faders, grand- and preset master, crossfader and cue master faders.

### Strand Lighting

*M24 and M24FX Tempus:* Simple to use memory desk, with up to 120 channels, 199 memories, and multiple fades. Effects and back-up are available with the optional M24FX desk.

*Mantrix LX:* The Mantrix comes with 12 and 24 channels. It is a two-scene manual preset control for small venues with split dipless

manual or timed crossfade. It has a slider per dimmer and bump button.

*Mantrix MX:* This control has 12, 24 and 48 channels for up to 512 dimmers. Two-scene manual preset control with memory is useful for small venues. Mantrix MX has an optional video terminal, manual, timed or recorded timed crossfades and slider per channel or memory scene masters and bump button. There are four pages of memories and 24 programmable effects, two proportional channel/dimmer patches; selectable dimmer protocols; MIDI interface and printer output.

*GSX with Genius:* GSX has 25, 50, 75, 100 or 125 channels and a hardware platform with application software packages for entertainment lighting and presentations. This is a modest entry-level board with channel quantity and feature upgrade paths. It has an integrated 3.5-inch drive and color monitor; command panel, two playbacks, and five pages of 24 submasters.

Genius, Kaleidoscope and Communique extension software is available (see below).

*LBX:* This system with 25, 50, 75, 100 or 125 channels is a rugged hardware platform with application software packages for concert lighting, multipurpose venues and touring. It is configurable as 96-channel single preset with five pages of 24 submasters, 48-channel two-preset desk or 36-channel two-preset desk with five pages of 24 submasters. It has an integrated

3.5-inch drive and color monitor, command panel, two playbacks, with five pages of 24 submasters.

Genius software for GSX and LBX systems controls up to 512 DMX dimmers and scrollers. It carries 200 cues in memory with numbers 0.1 to 999.9 available. Manual playback or recorded time with up to six simultaneous fades and separate fade and delay times, and chase effect with three effect memories. Optional Kaleidoscope extension software allows more complex special effects and advanced scroller control, allowing direct color selection from keyboard and intelligent control to avoid unwanted scroll resets. Optional Communique extension software allows use of various standard communications protocols, MIDI, DMX, RS232 ASCII remote control, and so on. Software is available in English, French and Spanish. Genius Off-Line Editor software allows off-line editing of the lighting on a PC.

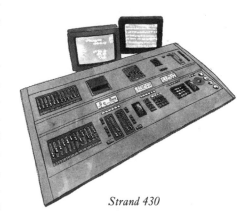

*Strand 430*

*Strand 430, 530 and 550:* This range of hardware, built to operate with a variety of applications software, was introduced in 1994. The user can choose between Light Palette or Genius operating software options. The boards are intended for professional theatre, concert halls, TV studios and touring. Subject to the chosen software, the Strand 430—in increments of 50 or 200 channels—has a maximum of 350 channels plus 250 attributes. The 530 has a maximum of 1,500 channels plus 500 attributes and 30 submasters. The 550 has a maximum of 1,500 channels plus 500 attributes and 54 submasters. There are six pages of individually controllable submasters and six user-programmable "Supermasters" for function mastering. With a single channel number selected, the user has instantaneous control of level, color device and any other moving-light attribute. A numerical keypad for channel, group or cue selection is accompanied by wheel, trackball (for moving lights) and three other attribute controllers. Two split cross-fade playbacks allow multispeed cues. The upgradeable software options provide a choice between Light Palette–style operation, with command-line and tracking or cue-only recording, or Genius style, with the more European direct action, move or cross-fade operation. Memories of cues or groups may be recorded, and single or dual, manual or timed crossfades operated with up to 128 simultaneous split fades. The programmable submasters may be configured for normal highest-takes-precedence, independent or inhibitive operation. Integrated special effects allow chase, build, cycle, flicker or random effects of 99 memories. Color channels may be linked to their instrument channels and can avoid unwanted scroll movement with any master action. "Automove when dark" instructs an automated fixture to move when the fixture fades out, to prepare for the next cue.

*Light Palette 90:* Wally Russell, during his tenure as president of Strand in the U.S., was inspired by the National Theatre's Lightboard to develop Light Palette as an American product. Designer David Cunningham utilized more economical microprocessor architecture and, with advice from Chuck Levy, employed an operating language that was more similar to the tracking method of plotting familiar to the American operators and designers from the

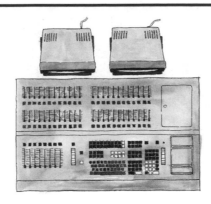

*Strand Light Palette 90*

days of the old-style manual piano boards. It combined this with a computer-style command-line method of inputting instructions. Over the years Light Palette has set the standard in the U.S., but along the way many improvements have also been made.

The most recent version is Light Palette 90. There are three versions, Mini Light Palette for 576 dimmers and 1,024 dimmers, Compact Light Palette for 1,152 channels and 2,048 dimmers and Light Palette 90 for 1,728 channels and 1,728 dimmers. Each have overlapping submasters, allow 128 simultaneous fades controlled by eight manual sliders, have effects with 99 steps, fade in, dwell and fade out times controlled by any cue or submaster. An integrated alpha keyboard allows written notes to be added. Off-line editing (on Macintosh or MS-DOS) is available, and a track-sheet allows the tracking and modification of channels across multiple cues. Multiple focus remotes and multiple control desks are available. This line of controls is superseded by the Light Palette version of the Strand 430, 530 and 550 (previous page).

*Galaxy Nova:* Galaxy Nova is the top of the line from Strand Lighting and successor to Lightboard. Modular construction allows different configurations. It features 999 channels patched to 1,536 dimmers and up to 249 remote fixtures. Two desks can operate in parallel on

*Strand Galaxy Nova*

latest-takes-precedence basis. There are keypad and wheel control levels of channel, group or cue. Multiple playbacks can "learn" a manual fade profile and repeat it automatically. Group master wheels allow the blending of different "pictures" of light prior to or after recording. An effects module handles up to 99 effects with 256 steps each. Integrated motion control and color change utilizes the instrument channel number for any attribute. Up to 24 simultaneous fades can operate from the playbacks. The EC90 MD plus allows dimmer status reporting to the console.

### Zero 88 (U.K.)

*Lightmaster XL:* This is a two-scene, twelve-channel console with 108 programmable level memories (twelve submasters of nine pages) with nine programmable chases. It has MIDI in and out, and is sound-to-light programmable.

*Linebacker:* An ingenious little device, Linebacker provides a handheld 60-memory DMX backup device, a DMX and cable test tool, a programmable scene/effect sequencer and a stand-alone very compact lighting desk.

## MOVING-LIGHT CONTROLS
### Compulite R & D

*Animator and Animator Plus.:* Animator is an integrated control of up to 72 Superscans, Goldenscans, Intellabeams, Syncrolites or Telescans using their own protocols as well as any DMX 512-compatible fixture and up to 512 standard dimmers or color scrollers. The editor enables spots, channels and parameters to be

*Compulite Animator*

selected and memories recorded. A keypad selection makes all possible functions available on an X/Y trackball, and there are eight wheels and individual keys for other parameters. Two manual or automatic cross-faders and eight controller faders may be used simultaneously as well as two independent chases. A grandmaster and two dimming submasters provide master control. Up to 15,000 libraries can be created for preset focuses of position, color and gobo. While running a preprogrammed move, a fixture may be directly controlled by trackball for follow-spotting. Animator Plus adds increased memory capability, 32-bit addressing and other enhancements.

*Photon:* A budget console with 120 dimmers plus 48 scroller channels to DMX 512 channels. 400 cues, dipless crossfade with manual override, grandmaster with blackout switch, optional 24 moving-light capability.

*Applause:* This system has 400 to 720 channels with two independent manual or automatic

playbacks, ten submasters, flash buttons, chases and soft-patch.

*Ovation:* Ovation is a control with a variety of configurations with 20 or 40 submasters, up to 1,024 channels, two independent manual or automatic playbacks, submasters with automatic timed playback facility, flash buttons, chases, programmable effects and soft-patch. Super Ovation also controls moving lights via MLA (Moving Light Adapter) and employs upgraded scroller management. The MLA has three wheels with six banks each and an alphanumeric parameter/editor function display.

### Flying Pig Systems

*Wholehog:* This control, which was revolutionary at the time of its introduction, has 6,000 channels preprogrammed for most "personalities" of moving light, accessing fixtures, colors and gobos through touch-sensitive displays and high-resolution encoders. Fixtures of different types may be programmed as one, while any parameter, sequence, cue, group preset or

*Wholehog*

palette may be named for identification. The control automatically generates sequences such as ballyhoos, circle movements or shutter chases. Any effect can be transferred from show to show, allowing multiple set-ups to be played back as one. Wholehog keeps track of fixtures in three-dimensional space; you can track a performer with every fixture in real time or point at a position onstage and immediately have

every light shining on it. Besides DMX, the control features MIDI, SMPTE and other fixture protocols. It is able to record in track or Cue Only modes. Each of twenty playback submasters have "Go," "Pause/Back," "Add/Swap/Bump" and "Select" buttons providing independent control of intensity, color, beam and focus. Every channel on every cue has independent timing settings. Up to 100 simultaneous playbacks of cue lists, chases or effects. Intensity is controlled on highest-takes-precedence and other parameters on latest-takes-precedence. It is an amazing device!!

*Wholehog II:* Wholehog II is a new, smaller and improved version of the Wholehog intended for intricate theatrical performances as well as the most unstructured TV or concert event. It features graphic displays and two touch-sensitive screens that allows access to focusing, movement and control of any attribute of a fixture. Wholehog II automatically generates sequences such as ballyhoos, circle movements or shutter chases. Eight playback masters each

*Wholehog II*

run the most complex cue lists and a single button can reload all masters. Multiple simultaneous running cue lists, unlimited cue parts and split fade times allow exceptional subtlety of light movement.

*WYSIWYG (marketed world wide by Flying Pig Systems):* This is software developed for CBC Television in Toronto by Robert Bell of CAST Lighting. Using a Pentium PC connected to a Wholehog II (or any DMX moving light console) it provides a "virtual" lighting system with full wire-frame rendering display of moving (or still) lights, colors, gobos and position on the computer's VDU in real time. This allows for the first time off-line programming and editing of moving lights. It works in three dimensions so that the rig can be viewed from any angle—useful for presetting lights upstage out of sight of the audience. AutoFocus generates focuses directly on WYSIWYG. Focus positions are recorded in three-dimensional space, so pointing at a position on the display will make every selected moving light immediately move to it. WYSIWYGLITE is designed for one 512-channel input for smaller projects and budgets.

### Jands

*Jands Event:* This two-scene console is available in 24, 36 and 48 channels. A one-scene mode doubles the available channels. (Jands Version III software extends channels to 120 or 252.) Twelve "assign" masters with programmable alpha-numeric labeling control scenes, chases and cue stacks. "Assign" and "File" add operator flexibility.

*Jands-Hog 250/500/600:* Marketed in collaboration with Flying Pig Systems, Jands-Hog is a 250-, 500- or 600-DMX-channel control with 12 or 24 submasters and four or six banks of 200 buttons and menus for parameter control.

*ESP II:* ESP II is a 48- or 96-channel control with proportional softpatch to 512 dimmers. It features ten pages of 12 or 24 submasters, ten pages of 50 step chases, 100 random accessible effects memories, and ten 100-entry cue stacks with dipless crossfade.

### Light & Sound Design

*LSD Ikon Control:* This system provides 1,000-channel software-driven control with consignable modular panels. Three hundred sixty-five backlit LCD buttons alter according to the function selected. All aspects of the Ikon and other moving-light instruments are individually controllable; ten matrix/chases may be run simultaneously with whatever lamp parameters desired. Different parameters may have different timing in each cue. The board may be programmed off-line from an Apple Macintosh with a 6802-plus processor. "Mock Icon" is a three-dimensional representation of lighting angles that runs on any Mac computer, which gives a front or side perspective of the stage to visualize cues off-line.

### Lightwave Research

*Status Cue:* A control for Cyberlight, Intellabeam, Trackspot and other moving lights, this is a 486-based system running on Windows software with menu-driven displays and off-line editing capability.

### L.S.C. Electronics Pty. Ltd. (Melbourne, Australia)

*Axiom:* Axiom is a 12-, 24- or 36-channel control, with two preset with wide-mode control, soft-patching, channel selection for highest- or latest-takes-precedence. It has twelve pages of memory with 1,022 total chases, cue stacks and two playback masters and grandmaster with DBO button.

### MA Lighting

*Scancommander:* Scancommander has up to 386 channels via DMX 512. Sixteen automated fixtures with up to 17 function each and 96 channels of dimmer or color changer are handled by this compact control. Up to 2,000 pictures are stored as memories and chaser steps. A graphic display offers direct access to preprogrammed values. When moving a show

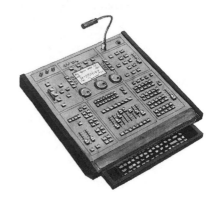

*MA Scancommander*

to a new venue, stage area limits can be set for a fixture, after which all others will adjust their position accordingly.

### Martin

*Case Professional 1 and 2 (N.V. R&D International of Belgium):* The Case Professional controls have from 512 to 2,048 channels with 2,000 memories and 350 preset focuses employing 16-bit fade calculation. Up to a dozen protocols can be supported simultaneously. An RGB library simplifies dialing in Lee, GAM or Rosco color on an automated luminaire with full color mixing.

### PanCommand

*LDS MP-100:* This controller employs user-programmable M-Cue library to preprogram common moving effects transferable from show to show. LDS uses a trackball for screen selection and fixture focusing with fine adjustment mode for pan and tilt. It provides easy access to groups of fixtures and a transferable color library.

### Seefactor

*Light Coordinator:* Light Coordinator is a control for up to 500 moving or fixed instruments with up to 127 attributes via DMX or instrument native protocol. Each instrument is considered as a unit, and at the touch of a button all attributes are assigned to digital encoders. Preset focus positions can be used to build cues, which can be readily updated from venue to venue. Color, speed and gobo attributes can be globally changed in programming. Cues may be stored as "go-cues," chases (up to 20 with 250 steps), or in 20 overlapping submasters, which operate on highest-takes-precedence for dimmers or dowsers, and latest-takes-precedence for all other attributes. A VDU screen provides a graphic layout. Automatic focus adjustment and performer tracking is to be available shortly.

*Vari\*Lite Artisan*

## Vari\*Lite

*Artisan:* Manual and programmed control for 1,000 channels and 1,000 cues per channel. A bidirectional digital link controls the computer in each fixture. Luminaires are selected individually or in groups via a push-button matrix, then intensity, color, pan, tilt and beam can be adjusted all together or separately and recorded per cue. Any function on any cue may be individually timed. Preset focuses assist faster programming and ease resetting from venue to venue. Eighty fixed preset colors may be supplemented by 160 chosen by the designer. Unlit luminaires are "marked" for prepositioning. Playback provides grandmaster, two random-access or sequential submasters, two chase subs, manual split-fade submaster and 20 matrix-assignable faders. Two hundred chases can be contained in any cue sequence.

*Mini-Artisan:* This is a small-scale version of the Artisan. Limited programming features make this a control suitable for running a show after it has initially been set up.

*Artisan VLQ Board Level Cueing Program:* This is a software program for the Apple Macintosh that allows you to record keystrokes from the Artisan or Mini-Artisan and play them back on command. It provides "Board Cues" to speed programming and simplify complex cueing sequences for both spontaneous and scripted events. A cue list displays a scrolling list of cues; wait times, loops or jumps out of sequence can be recorded.

## Wybron

*Autopilot:* Autopilot is an innovative control system for moving lights. Keny Whitright of Wybron developed this computer controller using an infrared trigger and ultrasonic pulse to allow a small transmitter/receiver to be worn by a performer, who is then followed about the stage by any selected lights with an incidence of error of only three inches. Amazing. Perhaps even more interesting is that the computer

provides focusing to absolute positions in three-dimensional space on the stage. Every "aiming" point is identified with "X, Y, Z" coordinates; "X" being across stage, "Y" up and down stage, and "Z" being height above the floor. The Autopilot control converts these absolute positions into pan and tilt instructions for each instrument, wherever it may be.

In January 1995 I had the idea to test a new version of Autopilot (known as Co-Pilot), in combination with an ETC control board with digitizer graphic pad and WYSIWYG to rapidly speed up prefocus and programming of moving lights. My suggestion was that by "capturing" the Autopilot data, any combination of moving lights could have their prefocus positions recorded simultaneously at the touch of a button as the operator walks from position to position across the stage, rather than laboriously having to set every prefocus by hand. On tour, moving to a new theatre, each instrument would have only three calibrations refreshed, upon which all the focus positions would be automatically revised.

Our tests were for the musical *Busker Alley,* on its way to Broadway. Coordinated by Steve

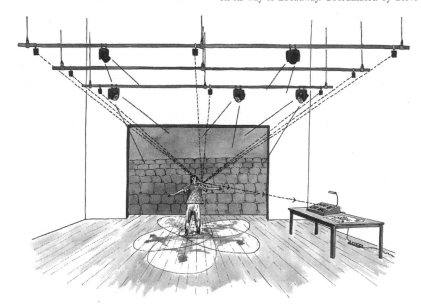

*Wybron Autopilot*

Terry of Production Arts, Keny Whitright (Wybron), Fred Foster (ETC) and Robert Bell (WYSIWYG) put together this new control combination with the new VL5 and VL6s. Co-pilot combines a really neat way to instantly prefocus moving lights and move those focuses from venue to venue, together with the spectacular Autopilot effect of having banks of dancing moving light chasing the star about the stage. The digitizer pad's instant access to any channel, group, attribute, color, gobo and prefocus X, Y, Z point is far faster than fiddling with endless buttons and wheels; and WYSIWIG's ability to give real-time graphic display of each moving light's focus as well as a highly accurate off-line editing capability provides a combination that is a glimpse of the future of moving-light control. Design in the studio—even with moving lights—can be seamlessly transferred from the studio to the stage. The laborious process of moving-light programming can be speeded up enormously.

The tests in principle worked. Sadly, there was no time to resolve the comparatively minor detailed "bugs," as the first production date was only a few weeks away. So this technology will be used next time. But aided by my manufacturing friends, who once again volunteered their services, I repeated this "experiment" as a hands-on demonstration at the Plasa 95 show in London, and yet again at the LDI show in Miami. Observers seemed to agree that here were the seeds of a new paradigm for lighting control.

## ROCK-AND-ROLL CONTROLS
### Avolites

*QM500:* QM500 has two or three preset consoles with lever-per-channel control and memory available on multiple faders. It has keyboard and alphanumeric display, three timed playbacks, and 20 memory chase programs on two simultaneous channels.

*Avolites QM500*

*QM500 -TD:* This system has 180 control channels and proportional soft-patch up to 512 dimmers. It also has three split-timed fade playbacks, 20 submasters, 600 memories, 720 steps, macros, bump buttons and manual override.

*Rolacue Sapphire:* Rolacue Sapphire provides control of 512 dimmers, color changers and moving lights with multiple chase playbacks. The board has 120 faders, but the fader-to-control mapping is paged, so that each fader controls several channels. Personality disks for different moving lights can preprogram the control. Editable preset focuses create building blocks for rapid working. Colors are called up by name (for example Lee 181) and personal color palettes may be saved. Copy feature allows copying of any channel attributes from cue to cue, channel to channel or page to page.

*Diamond II:* Diamond II has 1,024 control channels expandable to 6,000. One hundred eighty pageable channel faders with "add" and "swap" buttons and 30 submaster faders to control memories, chases and timed fades. It has 100 pages. Moving lights are patched as one instrument using Avolites Programmable Personality System, which assigns attributes to eight wheels and a keypad for control.

*Rolacue Pearl:* The Pearl is a smaller control for 512 channels, 450 memories, 30 pages, 60 faders and fifteen simultaneous active playbacks. Channels operate on highest- or latest-takes-precedence. Moving-light "personality"

*Avolites Rolacue Pearl*

may be patched from channel to channel. Preset focus buttons of position, color, gobo and intensity may be used to build a cue and are capable of subsequent editing. Moving lights may be required to track one another.

*Avolites 4D Track:* The Avolites Graphic Tablet provides an interactive stage plan on which any light or combination of lights, regardless of their position in the rig, may be moved in real time by tracking a stylus about the tablet. X/Y absolute positioning allows "follow-spotting," and if the performer moves off target a "nudge" mode moves the beams as required. A graphic color spectrum and gobo picker allows instant access to any color or gobo. The tablet works with the Pearl, Diamond II, and Sapphire. Avolites claims that the graphic tablet is at least thirty times faster than a conventional board. I can believe it. Very nifty indeed!!

### Axon Digital Design

*ShowCAD:* Powerful software enables an IBM 386 or above to become a 1,024 DMX 512 lighting and effects controller.

### Celco

*Aviator V2.0 R720/360/180:* The three versions of Aviator have 720 control channels and 2,048 DMX channels, 360 control channels and 1,024 DMX channels, and 180 control channels and 1,024 DMX channels respectively with multifader control for multipart cues, lists,

*Celco Aviator*

multimanual/timed playbacks and sequence playbacks. All three have the ability to program or edit via channel faders or keypad. The control uses scrolling techniques to handle multiple control channels on a fewer number of endless belt Penny & Giles faders.

*Navigator V3.0:* This version of Navigator has 240 control channels of 512 dimmer channels, usable on a highest- or latest-takes-precedence basis with 480 memories; up to 120 sequences each with its own speed in beats per minute; sound-to-light link capability and 36 preset focuses that allow rapid adjustment from venue to venue and customization to individual moving-light "personality." It has the ability to "Copy" attributes of one moving light to another, to "Gang" moving lights together and to "Include" multiple preset focuses in cues.

*Explorer EP:* The Explorer has 120 control channels for concert or theatre lighting, including comprehensive SVGA output and programming aids, with twelve submasters, comprehensive fade times for each and every cue, stack playback, sequence templates, assignable sound-to-light feature. The Pathfinder EPX has a similar specification with fewer control channels.

## Leprecon

*LM-850 MIDI Controller:* The LM-850 has 54 control channels accessed by eighteen faders, 100 programmable scenes, soft patch to 108 dimmers and 50 programmable chase sequences of 32 steps each.

*LP-1500 Control Console:* The LP-1500 is a two-scene preset with memory capability. It is available in 12, 24 and 36 channels with twelve pages of memory, twelve programmable effects, and a "Go" button with timed fades.

*LP-2000 Control Console:* This system is a two-scene preset with memory capability. It is available in 48, 72, 96 and 120 channels with 1,000 programmable scenes, eight programmable effects, built-in color control with 1,000 presets, soft-patch and optional Intellabeam control.

## NSI Corporation

*Melange:* Melange has 128 control channels, 200 cues expandable to 400, 512 dimmers with proportional soft patch, two independent cross-faders, and ten user-definable macros.

## Pulsar Light of Cambridge

*Masterpiece:* Masterpiece features 70 touch-pad controllers, 25 sliders, 108 LEDs, four-digit display and joystick to handle 216 scenes, 54 chases, 48 environments of scenes/chases and six environment chases.

## ADB

ISIS (Integrated Software for Intelligent Systems) for their *Phoenix* range of consoles, offers the same operating principles with integrated motion and color control, for a mid-range of consoles below their *Vision 10* system.

## AVAB Transtechnik

New top end control *Solaris* has modular construction, multiple touch screens and updated software.

## Avolites

The *Sapphire 2000* controls 2,048 channels with 400 moving light fixtures. It has a built-in graphics tablet and 'electronic legending' for memories and palettes. A *Visualiser* virtual

*Pulsar Masterpiece*

programming software package is accompanied by *Focus Finder*. This semi-automates the process of updating the positional data of an instrument relative to its preset focuses.

## Martin Professional

*Trackpod* is a move toward automating the follow spot process. A pointing device, like a small video camera, with which an operator can follow a performer and up to 64 moving light units will track along in real time as well.

## Rosco

The *Horizon* software to allow lighting control from any PC computer continues to grow in sophistication and interest. The interface for moving light control possesses a simplicity that more costly controls would do well to emulate, by seamlessly integrating WYSIWYG.

## Strand Lighting

The upgrades *500 series* consoles use Pentium II 233 MHz processors and offer up to 6,000 channels and 8,192 DMX outputs. The control can be partitioned so that up to five operators can work on the same show simultaneously. (How stimulating if potentially confusing!)

## Vari*Lite

At very long last the new Vari*Lite control system *Virtuoso*, to replace the Artisan has arrived. The big feature is that it now features an integrated 3D graphics interface which (it is promised) will offer visual information live or in preview and for off-line visual editing. It preserves all the multiple Artisan buttons of old, which will surely become an anachronism when the New World of full graphic visualization of lighting operation becomes commonplace.

## WYSIWYG

The new *WYSIWYG* has moved into full image rendering to step significantly closer to the day when lighting will be almost completely created in the designer's studio before the stage. The capability of simulating shadow, smoke and haze is fascinating and excellent light plot drafting and paperwork preparation tools accompany the software package.

# Chapter Forty-three

# Instruments

## PROFILE SPOTS

1. Data is based upon information published by the manufacturers. Omissions denote that information is not published or cannot be found. I must acknowledge here Robert C. Mumm, author of the amazingly comprehensive *Photometrics Handbook*. His sterling work prompted me to expand this survey of instruments.

2. Lamp stated is that in most common use.

3. Beam angle = 50% of maximum (Fig. 10).

4. Field angle = 10% of maximum.

5. Multiplying factor: multiply throw by this figure to obtain diameter of beam at any throw.

6. Peak candela is of interest for comparative purposes. (Profiles usually taken with peak field. Two figures denote spot/flood focus.) Divide the peak candela by the square of the throw at any distance to obtain the output, e.g. Patt. 23 with 17,000 candelas @ 5m throw: 17,000/25 (throw squared) = 680 lux

    Patt 23 with 17,000 candelas @ 15ft. throw: 17,000/225 (throw squared) = 75.55 f.cs

7. Dimensions key (Fig. 11): W = Width. L = Length. H = Height. HV = Height including yoke. HS = Height with stand (follow spots). Wt = Weight

8. MPF = Multiplying factor.

Note: These illustrations are not to scale—refer to dimensions.

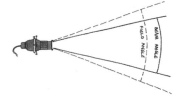

*10. Beam/field angle*

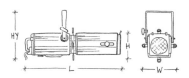

*11. Instrument dimensions key*

These instruments (Fig. 12) provide a beam of any profile, which is determined by the shape of the gate aperture (1) and by the use of either built-in shutters (2), an iris diaphragm, or a gobo (template). The maximum amount of light is collected from the lamp (3) by a reflector (4) and passed through the gate. The light from the gate is then brought into sharp or soft focus by a lens (5). The narrower the beam angle provided by the lens the greater will be the intensity.

The ideal ellipsoidal will provide an even beam that can be shaped easily and brought into hard or soft focus without undue alteration of beam size. The addition of a "tophat" on the front of an ellipsoidal will further reduce any stray light that might emanate from the beam (Fig. 13). A "half tophat" can also be useful. In an FOH situation the half tophat on the audience side masks the lens, but there is no bounce-back from the other missing side.

In the U.S. profile spots have been with us since the 1930s. A significant improvement in quality has been achieved with the new ETC 575-watt Source 4, providing greater efficiency with compact size and ease of handling.

250/500 watts = General usage in small theatres/onstage
575/1,000 watts = General usage
2,000 watts = Long range

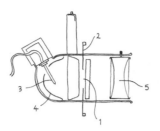

12. Section Leko

13. Tophat

14. Adjustment zoom profile spot

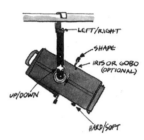

15. Adjustment profile spot

16. Strand patt 23

17. Strand patt 23/N

18. Strand T Spot

19. Colortran Ellipsoidal

20. Strand patt 765

21. 6" Leko

22. 8" Leko

23. Reiche & Vogel
650W ellipsoidal

24. Neidhammer
HPS 111

25. Pani HV 650

26. Reiche & Vogel Zoom
Optik 650W

27. Strand Cantata

28. Strand Alto

29. CCT Silhouette 19/45

30. CCT Turbo Silhouette

31. ADB DN101

32. Altman Shakespeare

33. ETC Source 4

34. Strand Lekolite

35. Teatro Comma 26

36. Robert Juliat
profile 614

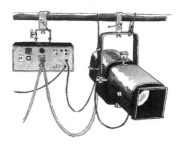

37. Robert Juliat
914 HMI profile

| Type | Manufacturer | Unit | B/A *=Approx | F/A | MPF | Lamp (or lampholder type) | Peak Candela *=math approx †=flat field candela | W in 0.04 | W mm 25 | L in 0.04 | L mm 25 | H in 0.04 | H mm 25 | HY in 0.04 | HY mm 25 | Wt lb 2.2 | Wt kg 0.5 | Other lamp |
|---|---|---|---|---|---|---|---|---|---|---|---|---|---|---|---|---|---|---|
| Zoom profile | ADB | DS 51 | | 18°–38° | 0.32–0.69 | CP 89 650W 220v | 38,000/23,200 | 8.6 | 220 | 17.3 | 440 | 7.1 | 180 | 10.2 | 260 | 7.9 | 3.6 | * |
| Zoom profile | ADB | DS 54 | | 18°–38° | 0.32–0.69 | CP 89 650W 220v | 38,000/8,500 | 8.6 | 220 | 17.3 | 440 | 7.1 | 180 | 10.2 | 260 | 7.9 | 3.6 | * |
| Zoom profile | ADB | DW 54 | | 30°–47° | 0.54–0.87 | CP 89 650W 220v | 14,500/7,000 | 8.6 | 220 | 14.5 | 370 | 7.1 | 180 | 10.2 | 260 | 7.1 | 3.2 | * |
| Zoom profile | ADB | A59 Z | | 16°–35° | 0.28–0.63 | CP 89 650W 220v | 41,400/10,900 | 9.4 | 240 | 20.2 | 515 | 7.5 | 190 | 13.0 | 330 | 12.8 | 5.8 | * |
| Zoom profile | ADB | DVW 104 | | 38°–57° | 0.69–1.08 | CP 90 1.2kW 220v | 36,500/17,500 | 13.4 | 340 | 23.6 | 600 | 11.4 | 290 | 16.5 | 420 | 29.8 | 13.5 | * |
| Zoom profile | ADB | DW 104 | | 15°–42° | 0.26–0.77 | GX 9.5 1.2kW 220v | 115,000/25,300 | 13.4 | 340 | 27.9 | 710 | 11.4 | 290 | 16.5 | 420 | 30.9 | 14.0 | * |
| Zoom profile | ADB | DS 104 | | 15°–31° | 0.26–0.55 | GX 9.5 1.2kW 220v | 167,000/67,000 | 13.4 | 340 | 27.9 | 710 | 11.4 | 290 | 16.5 | 420 | 30.9 | 14.0 | * |
| Zoom profile | ADB | DN 104 | | 9°–20° | 0.16–0.35 | GX 9.5 1.2kW 220v | 370,000/108,000 | 14.1 | 360 | 36.2 | 920 | 12.2 | 310 | 17.5 | 445 | 40.6 | 18.4 | * |
| Zoom profile | ADB | DSN 104 | | 11°–23° | 0.19–0.41 | GX 9.5 1.2kW 220v | 225,000/102,000 | 13.4 | 340 | 31.0 | 790 | 11.4 | 290 | 16.5 | 420 | 33.3 | 15.1 | * |
| Zoom profile | ADB | DS 201 | | 16°–38° | 0.28–0.69 | CP 79 2kW 220v | 350,000/40,000 | 16.5 | 420 | 28.8 | 732 | 14.1 | 360 | 19.7 | 500 | 45.4 | 20.6 | * |
| Zoom profile | ADB | DS 204 | | 13°–36° | 0.23–0.65 | CP 79 2kW 220v | 359,000/65,000 | 16.5 | 420 | 31.8 | 810 | 14.1 | 360 | 19.7 | 500 | 50.1 | 22.7 | * |
| Zoom profile | ADB | DN 204 | | 10°–20° | 0.18–0.35 | CP 79 2kW 220v | 570,000/198,000 | 16.5 | 420 | 36.7 | 935 | 14.1 | 360 | 19.7 | 500 | 50.5 | 22.9 | * |
| Zoom profile | ADB | DVW 204 | | 35°–54° | 0.63–1.02 | CP 79 2kW 220v | 68,000/33,500 | 16.5 | 420 | 27.5 | 700 | 14.1 | 360 | 19.7 | 500 | 47.0 | 21.3 | * |
| Zoom profile | ADB/Niethammer | HPZ 112 | 12°–27° | | 0.21–0.48 | GX 9.5 1.2kW 220v | 360,000/105,000 | 11.8 | 300 | 28.1 | 715 | 11.8 | 300 | 16.9 | 430 | | | * |
| Zoom profile | ADB/Niethammer | HPZ 115 | 15°–38° | | 0.26–0.69 | GX 9.5 1.2kW 220v | 235,000/65,000 | 11.8 | 300 | 25.3 | 645 | 11.8 | 300 | 16.9 | 430 | | | |
| Zoom profile | ADB/Niethammer | HPZ 211 | 11°–27° | | 0.19–0.48 | GY16 2kW 220v | 650,000/150,000 | 17.1 | 435 | 33.2 | 845 | 17.7 | 450 | 25.3 | 645 | 48.1 | 21.8 | |
| Zoom profile | ADB/Niethammer | HPZ 215 | 15°–40° | | 0.26–0.73 | GY16 2kW 220v | 400,000/80,000 | 17.1 | 435 | 31.0 | 790 | 17.7 | 450 | 25.3 | 645 | 49.0 | 22.2 | * |
| Micro-ellipse | Altman | MR-16 | 25° | 35° | 0.63 | EYJ MR16 75W 12v | 5,625 | 6.0 | 152 | 9.0 | 229 | 6.0 | 152 | 8.5 | 216 | | | * |
| Micro-ellipse | Altman | MR-16 | 42° | 64° | 1.25 | EYJ MR16 75W 12v | 3,375 | 6.0 | 152 | 9.0 | 229 | 6.0 | 152 | 8.5 | 216 | | | * |
| ERS 3.5x5 | Altman | 3.5 Q5 | 30° | 48° | 0.89 | EHD 500W 120v | 12,000 | 9.0 | 229 | 15.5 | 394 | 9.0 | 229 | 13.5 | 343 | 9.0 | 4.1 | * |
| ERS 3.5x6 | Altman | 3.5 Q6 | 21° | 38° | 0.69 | EHD 500W 120v | 15,000 | 9.0 | 229 | 14.5 | 368 | 9.0 | 229 | 13.5 | 343 | 9.0 | 4.1 | * |
| ERS 3.5x8 | Altman | 3.5 Q8 | 21° | 28° | 0.50 | EHD 500W 120v | 16,000 | 9.0 | 229 | 15.5 | 394 | 9.0 | 229 | 13.5 | 343 | 9.0 | 4.1 | * |
| ERS 3.5x10 | Altman | 3.5 Q10 | 21° | 23° | 0.41 | EHD 500W 120v | 17,300 | 9.0 | 229 | 16.5 | 419 | 9.0 | 229 | 13.5 | 343 | 9.0 | 4.1 | * |
| ERS 3.5x12 | Altman | 3.5 Q12 | 17° | 18° | 0.32 | EHD 500W 120v | 20,000 | 9.0 | 229 | 17.0 | 432 | 9.0 | 229 | 13.5 | 343 | 9.0 | 4.1 | * |
| Shakespeare | Altman | S650 | 23° | 50° | 0.93 | GE HX 600W 115v | 46,500 | 12.0 | 305 | 28.5 | 724 | 12.0 | 305 | 17.0 | 432 | 15.0 | 6.8 | * |
| Shakespeare | Altman | S640 | 20° | 38° | 0.69 | GE HX 600W 115v | 98,000 | 12.0 | 305 | 28.5 | 724 | 12.0 | 305 | 17.0 | 432 | 15.0 | 6.8 | * |
| Shakespeare | Altman | S630 | 13° | 28° | 0.50 | GE HX 600W 115v | 149,500 | 12.0 | 305 | 28.5 | 724 | 12.0 | 305 | 17.0 | 432 | 15.0 | 6.8 | * |
| Shakespeare | Altman | S620 | 13° | 20° | 0.35 | GE HX 600W 115v | 189,500 | 12.0 | 305 | 28.5 | 724 | 12.0 | 305 | 17.0 | 432 | 15.0 | 6.8 | * |
| Shakespeare | Altman | S610 | 7° | 12° | 0.12 | GE HX 600W 115v | 327,500 | 13.5 | 343 | 31.7 | 805 | 13.5 | 343 | 17.0 | 432 | 28.0 | 12.7 | * |
| Shakespeare | Altman | S61S35-Zoom | 9°–15° | 15°–35° | 0.26–0.63 | GE HX 600W 115v | 351,500/119,000 | 13.5 | 343 | 31.7 | 805 | 13.5 | 343 | 17.0 | 432 | 28.0 | 12.7 | *z |
| Shakespeare | Altman | S63Q55-Zoom | 13°–15° | 30°–55° | 0.54–1.04 | GE HX 600W 115v | 166,000/55,000 | 13.5 | 343 | 26.5 | 673 | 13.5 | 343 | 17.0 | 432 | 28.0 | 12.7 | * |
| ERS 4.5x6.5 | Altman | 360 | 25° | 56° | 1.06 | DNT 750W 120v | 24,000 | 13.3 | 337 | 17.5 | 445 | 13.3 | 337 | 16.8 | 425 | | | * |
| ERS 4.5x6.5 | Altman | 360Q | 22° | 55° | 1.04 | EHF 750W 120v | 51,000 | 13.0 | 330 | 18.0 | 457 | 13.0 | 330 | 16.3 | 413 | 13.5 | 6.1 | * |
| ERS 6x6 | Altman | 365 | 12° | 24° | 0.43 | DNT 750W 120v | 67,000 | | | | | | | | | | | * |
| ERS 6x8 | Altman | 365 | 11° | 21° | 0.37 | DNT 750W 120v | 85,000 | | | | | | | | | | | * |
| ERS 6x9 | Altman | 360 | 15° | 35° | 0.63 | DNT 750W 120v | 55,000 | 13.3 | 337 | 17.5 | 445 | 13.3 | 337 | 16.8 | 425 | | | * |
| ERS 6x9 | Altman | 360Q | 16° | 37° | 0.67 | EHF 750W 120v | 88,000 | 13.0 | 330 | 18.0 | 457 | 13.0 | 330 | 16.3 | 413 | 14.0 | 6.4 | * |
| ERS 6x12 | Altman | 360 | 15° | 25° | 0.44 | DNT 750W 120v | 70,000 | 13.3 | 337 | 19.5 | 495 | 13.3 | 337 | 16.8 | 425 | | | * |
| ERS 6x12 | Altman | 360Q | 11° | 26° | 0.46 | EHF 750W 120v | 154,000 | 13.0 | 330 | 20.0 | 508 | 13.0 | 330 | 16.3 | 413 | 15.0 | 6.8 | * |

| Type | Manufacturer | Unit | B/A (*=Approx) | F/A | MPF | Lamp (or lampholder type) | Peak Candela (*=math approx, †=flat field candela) | W in (0.04) | W mm (25) | L in (0.04) | L mm (25) | H in (0.04) | H mm (25) | HY in (0.04) | HY mm (25) | Wt lb (2.2) | Wt kg (0.5) | Other lamp |
|---|---|---|---|---|---|---|---|---|---|---|---|---|---|---|---|---|---|---|
| ERS 6x16 | Altman | 360 | 14° | 21° | 0.37 | DNT 750W 120v | 96,300 | 13.3 | 337 | 22.5 | 572 | 13.3 | 337 | 16.8 | 425 | | | * |
| ERS 6x16 | Altman | 3600 | 8.5° | 19° | 0.33 | EHF 750W 120v | 188,000 | 13.0 | 330 | 22.5 | 572 | 13.0 | 330 | 16.3 | 413 | 15.0 | 6.8 | * |
| ERS 6x22 | Altman | 3600 | 8° | 11° | 0.19 | EHF 750W 120v | 219,000 | 13.0 | 330 | 30.5 | 775 | 13.0 | 330 | 16.3 | 413 | 15.0 | 6.8 | * |
| ERS 8x8 | Altman | 365 | 10° | 18° | 0.32 | DNT 750W 120v | 99,000 | | | | | | | | | | | * |
| ERS 8x8 | Altman | 366*Old model | | 24° | 0.43 | T12/9 750W 120v | 101,200 | | | | | | | | | | | |
| ERS 8x8 | Altman | 366 | 8° | 19° | 0.33 | DNT 750W 120v | 164,000 | | | | | | | | | | | * |
| ERS 8x11 | Altman | 365 | 9° | 14° | 0.25 | DNT 750W 120v | 110,000 | | | | | | | | | | | * |
| ERS 8x11 | Altman | 366 | 7° | 14° | 0.25 | DNT 750W 120v | 173,000 | | | | | | | | | | | * |
| ERS-Zoom | Altman | 4.5-1530Z | 8°–13° | 15°–30° | 0.26–0.54 | EHF 750W 120v | 88,000/55,000 | 11.0 | 279 | 24.0 | 610 | 11.0 | 279 | 10.3 | 260 | | | * |
| ERS-Zoom | Altman | 4.5-2550Z | 17°–22° | 25°–50° | 0.44–0.93 | EHF 750W 120v | 80,000/40,000 | 11.0 | 279 | 19.0 | 483 | 11.0 | 279 | 10.3 | 260 | 25.0 | 11.3 | * |
| ERS-Zoom | Altman | 4.5-3060Z | 17°–23° | 30°–60° | 0.54–1.15 | EHF 750W 120v | 50,000/26,250 | 11.0 | 279 | 19.5 | 495 | 11.0 | 279 | 10.3 | 260 | | | * |
| ERS 8x11 | Altman | 367 | | 25° | 0.44 | T24 1kW 120v | 174,000 | | | | | | | | | | | * |
| ERS 4.5x6.5 | Altman | 1KL6-50 | 16° | 50° | 0.93 | FEL 1kW 120v | 98,000 | 17.0 | 432 | 23.0 | 584 | 17.0 | 432 | 19.0 | 483 | | | * |
| ERS 6x9 | Altman | 1KL6-40 | 14° | 40° | 0.73 | FEL 1kW 120v | 148,000 | 17.0 | 432 | 23.0 | 584 | 17.0 | 432 | 19.0 | 483 | | | * |
| ERS 6x12 | Altman | 1KL6-30 | 11° | 30° | 0.54 | FEL 1kW 120v | 195,000 | 17.0 | 432 | 20.5 | 521 | 17.0 | 432 | 19.0 | 483 | | | * |
| ERS 6x16 | Altman | 1KL6-20 | 9.5° | 20° | 0.35 | FEL 1kW 120v | 258,000 | 17.0 | 432 | 23.0 | 584 | 17.0 | 432 | 19.0 | 483 | | | * |
| ERS 6x22 | Altman | 1KL6-12 | 10° | 12° | 0.21 | FEL 1kW 120v | 343,000 | 17.0 | 432 | 25.5 | 648 | 17.0 | 432 | 19.0 | 483 | 24.0 | 10.9 | * |
| ERS 8x14 | Altman | 1KL8-10 | 7.5 | 12° | 0.21 | FEL 1kW 120v | 490,875 | 17.0 | 432 | 28.5 | 724 | 17.0 | 432 | 19.0 | 483 | 26.0 | 11.8 | * |
| ERS 10x24 | Altman | 1KL10-5 | 5° | 6.9° | 0.12 | FEL 1kW 120v | 801,250 | 17.0 | 432 | 35.5 | 902 | 17.0 | 432 | 24.0 | 610 | | | * |
| ERS-Zoom | Altman | 1KL6-2040Z | 9.5°–19° | 20°–40° | 0.35–0.73 | FEL 1kW 120v | 275,000/85,000 | 17.0 | 432 | 27.0 | 686 | 17.0 | 432 | 19.0 | 483 | | | * |
| ERS-Zoom | Altman | 1KL8-1424Z | 8°–14° | 14°–24° | 0.25–0.43 | FEL 1kW 120v | 490,000/262,0000 | 10.5 | 267 | 32.0 | 813 | 10.5 | 267 | 17.0 | 432 | 34.0 | 15.4 | * |
| Minuette 26 | CCT | Z0611 | 19° | 26° | 0.46 (FMR 600W in USA) | T27 650W 240v | 32,500 † | 12.3 | 314 | 14.2 | 362 | 12.3 | 314 | 10.1 | 258 | 7.9 | 3.6 | * |
| Minuette 30-48 | CCT | Z0603P | 28°–40° | 30–48° | 0.54–0.89 | T27 650W 240v (FMR 600W in USA) | 13,000/8,000 † | 12.3 | 314 | 14.2 | 362 | 12.3 | 314 | 10.1 | 258 | 7.9 | 3.6 | * |
| Minuette 17-36 | CCT | Z0602P | 15°–35° | 17–36° | 0.30–0.65 | T27 650W 240v (FMR 600W in USA) | 24,400/7,000 † | 12.3 | 314 | 17.3 | 440 | 12.3 | 314 | 10.1 | 258 | 8.8 | 4.0 | * |
| Minuette 21-36 | CCT | Z0602 | 17°–25° | 21–36° | 0.37–0.65 | T26 650W 240v (FMR 600W in USA) | 30,000/20,000 † | 12.3 | 314 | 17.3 | 440 | 12.3 | 314 | 10.1 | 258 | 7.9 | 3.6 | * |
| Minuette 6-10 | CCT | Z0608P | 5°–12° | 6–14° | 0.10–0.25 | T27 650W 240v (FMR 600W in USA) | 216,000/130,000 | 12.3 | 314 | 31.8 | 808 | 12.3 | 314 | 11.5 | 292 | 17.6 | 8.0 | * |
| Silhouette Turbo | CCT | Z001TWW | 18°–38° | 28–58° | 0.50–1.11 | T29 C13D 1.2kW 240v | 75,000/18,800 † | 14.5 | 370 | 20.6 | 525 | 14.5 | 370 | 15.7 | 400 | 23.7 | 10.8 | * |
| Silhouette Turbo | CCT | Z001TX | 11°–22° | 15–32° | 0.26–0.57 | T29 C13D 1.2kW 240v | 217,300/65,800 † | 14.5 | 370 | 27.1 | 690 | 14.5 | 370 | 15.7 | 400 | 25.4 | 11.5 | * |
| Silhouette Turbo | CCT | Z001TY | 10°–21° | 11–26° | 0.19–0.46 | T29 C13D 1.2kW 240v | 239,000/74,000 † | 14.5 | 370 | 29.9 | 760 | 14.5 | 370 | 15.7 | 400 | 27.0 | 12.3 | * |
| Silhouette Turbo | CCT | Z000WW | 17°–59.5° | 28–59.5° | 0.50–1.14 | CP91 C13D 2.5kW 240v | 107,000/14,400 † | 14.5 | 370 | 24.2 | 615 | 14.5 | 370 | 20.6 | 525 | 39.9 | 18.1 | * |
| Silhouette Turbo | CCT | Z000DX | 12.5°–33° | 13.5–33° | 0.24–0.59 | CP91 C13D 2.5kW 240v | 219,700/36,000 † | 14.5 | 370 | 30.7 | 780 | 14.5 | 370 | 20.6 | 525 | 42.1 | 19.1 | * |
| Silhouette Turbo | CCT | Z000DY | 9.5°–27° | 10.5–27° | 0.18–0.48 | CP91 C13D 2.5kW 240v | 283,800/60,700 † | 14.5 | 370 | 33.4 | 850 | 14.5 | 370 | 20.6 | 525 | 43.4 | 19.7 | * |
| Silhouette Turbo | CCT | Z000DS | 7.5°–20.5° | 8.5–21.5° | 0.15–0.38 | CP91 C13D 2.5kW 240v | 479,100/107,700 † | 12.5 | 317 | 38.5 | 980 | 12.5 | 317 | 21.0 | 535 | 48.5 | 22.0 | * |
| ERS 4.5x6.5 | Capitol | 6504/24/34/44 | | 46° | 0.85 | DEB 500W 120v | 12,500 | | | | | | | | | | | * |
| ERS 6x9 | Capitol | 650 | | 38° | 0.69 | T12/8 750W 120v | 27,200 | | | | | | | | | | | * |
| ERS 8x8 | Capitol | 851 | | 20° | 0.35 | T12C13D 1kW 120v | 128,400 | | | | | | | | | | | * |
| ERS 10x14 | Capitol | 1059 | | 25.5° | 0.45 | QT16-CL 1kW 120v | 220,000 | | | | | | | | | | | * |
| ERS 3.5x6 | Century | 1215/2115 | 25° | 32° | 0.57 | EHR 400W 120v | 8,700 | 9.0 | 229 | 11.5 | 295 | 9.0 | 229 | 10.8 | 273 | | | * |
| ERS 3.5x8 | Century | 1217/2125 | 18° | 24° | 0.43 | EHR 400W 120v | 13,500 | 9.0 | 229 | 12.5 | 318 | 9.0 | 229 | 10.8 | 273 | | | * |

| Type | Manufacturer | Unit | B/A (*=Approx) | F/A | MPF | Lamp (or lampholder type) | Peak Candela (*=math approx †=flat field candela) | W in 0.04 | W mm 25 | L in 0.04 | L mm 25 | H in 0.04 | H mm 25 | HY in 0.04 | HY mm 25 | Wt lb 2.2 | Wt kg 0.5 | Other lamp |
|---|---|---|---|---|---|---|---|---|---|---|---|---|---|---|---|---|---|---|
| ERS 3.5x10 | Century | 1219/2135 | 16° | 20° | 0.35 | EHR 400W 120v | 16,650 | 9.0 | 229 | 13.5 | 343 | 9.0 | 229 | 10.8 | 273 | 2.2 | 0.5 | * |
| ERS 4.5x3.5 | Century | 1586/7/8 | 32° | 42° | 0.77 | DEB 500W 120v | 20,000 | | | | | | | | | | | * |
| ERS 4.5x6.5 | Century | 1581 | 36° | 50° | 0.93 | DEB 500W 120v | 12,800 | | | | | | | | | | | * |
| ERS 4.5x6.5 | Century | 1580 | | 50° | 0.93 | T12/9 750W 120v | 9,500 | | | | | | | | | | | |
| ERS 6x9 | Century | 1590/1/2 | | 43° | 0.79 | T12/9 750W 120v | 26,450 | | | | | | | | | | | * |
| ERS 6x6 | Century | 2343/4 | 16° | 28° | 0.50 | EHG 750W 120v | 46,500 | | | | | | | | | | | * |
| ERS 8x9 | Century | 1575 | 16° | 20° | 0.35 | T12/9 750W 120v | 92,250 | | | | | | | | | | | * |
| ERS 10x12 | Century | 1521/2 | 8° | 14° | 0.25 | T12/9 750W 120v | 259,200 | | | | | | | | | | | * |
| ERS 8x9 | Century | 1567/8 | 18° | 23° | 0.41 | 2M/T30/1 2kW 120v | 158,400 | | | | | | | | | | | * |
| ERS 4.5x6.5 | Century Strand | 2211 | 38° | 50° | 0.93 | EGE 500W 120v | 13,250 | 11.5 | 289 | 16.0 | 406 | 11.5 | 289 | 24.3 | 613 | | | * |
| ERS 6x9 | Century Strand | 2321/2 | 24° | 40° | 0.73 | EGG 750W 120v | 37,800 | 11.5 | 289 | 16.0 | 406 | 11.5 | 289 | 24.3 | 613 | | | * |
| ERS 6x6 | Century Strand | 2341/2 | 18° | 28° | 0.50 | EGG 750W 120v | 58,800 | 11.5 | 289 | 16.0 | 406 | 11.5 | 289 | 24.3 | 613 | | | * |
| ERS 6x8 | Century Strand | 264W | 26° | | 0.46 | Q1000T12/4CL 1kW 120v | 30,000 | 9.5 | 242 | 22.2 | 565 | 11.0 | 280 | 15.5 | 395 | 16.5 | 7.5 | * |
| ERS 6x8 | Century Strand | 264 | 17° | | 0.30 | DNV 1kW 120v | 75,000 | 9.5 | 242 | 22.2 | 565 | 11.0 | 280 | 15.5 | 395 | 16.5 | 7.5 | * |
| ERS 6x6 | Century Strand | 2347/8 | 12.5° | 22.5° | 0.40 | EGJ 1kW 120v | 175,200 | | | | | | | | | | | * |
| ERS 8x9 | Century Strand | 2457/8 | 7.5° | 15° | 0.26 | EGJ 1kW 120v | 307,500 | 12.0 | 305 | 38.0 | 965 | 12.0 | 305 | 27.5 | 699 | | | * |
| ERS 10x12 | Century Strand | 2567/8 | 7.5° | 10.5° | 0.18 | EGJ 1kW 120v | 415,000 | 12.0 | 305 | 38.0 | 965 | 12.0 | 305 | 27.5 | 699 | | | * |
| ERS 12x12 | Century Strand | 2667/8 | 7.5° | 10.5° | 0.18 | EGJ 1kW 120v | 465,000 | 14.0 | 356 | 38.0 | 965 | 14.0 | 356 | 28.5 | 724 | | | * |
| ERS 3.5x6 | Colortran | 212-002 | 18° | 30° | 0.54 | EHD 500W 120v | 19,060 | | | | | | | | | | | * |
| ERS 3.5x8 | Colortran | 212-012 | 14° | 28° | 0.50 | EHD 500W 120v | 21,250 | | | | | | | | | | | * |
| ERS 3.5x10 | Colortran | 212-022 | 10° | 22° | 0.39 | EHD 500W 120v | 24,375 | | | | | | | | | | | * |
| ERS-Zoom | Colortran | 213-152 | 11°/22°/22° | 30°/40°/50° | 0.54/0.73/0.93 | EVR 500W 120v | 58,000/31,0006/19,476 | | | | | | | | | | | * |
| ERS 6x9 | Colortran | 212-042 | 23° | 40° | 0.73 | EHG 750W 120v | 30,000 | 15.0 | 381 | 24.0 | 610 | 25.0 | 635 | 16.0 | 406 | 20.0 | 9.1 | * |
| ERS 4.5x6.5 | Colortran | 650-012 | 17.5° | 50° | 0.93 | FEL 1kW 120v | 68,800 | | | | | | | 16.0 | 406 | | | * |
| ERS 6x9 | Colortran | 213-052 | 15° | 40° | 0.73 | FEL 1kW 120v | 112,000 | 15.0 | 381 | 24.0 | 610 | 25.0 | 635 | 16.0 | 406 | 20.0 | 9.1 | * |
| ERS 6x9 | Colortran | 650-022 | 15° | 40° | 0.73 | FEL 1kW 120v | 112,000 | 15.0 | 381 | 28.0 | 711 | 25.0 | 635 | 16.0 | 406 | 21.0 | 9.5 | * |
| ERS 6x9 | Colortran | 213-062 | 11° | 30° | 0.54 | FEL 1kW 120v | 154,000 | 15.0 | 381 | 24.0 | 610 | 25.0 | 635 | 16.0 | 406 | 20.0 | 9.1 | * |
| ERS 6x9 | Colortran | 650-032 | 11° | 30° | 0.54 | FEL 1kW 120v | 145,000 | 15.0 | 381 | 28.0 | 711 | 25.0 | 635 | 16.0 | 406 | 21.0 | 9.5 | * |
| ERS 6x9 | Colortran | 650-042 | 8.3° | 20° | 0.35 | FEL 1kW 120v | 224,000 | 15.0 | 381 | 28.0 | 711 | 25.0 | 635 | 16.0 | 406 | 21.0 | 9.5 | * |
| ERS 6x16 | Colortran | 213-072 | 8.3° | 20° | 0.35 | FEL 1kW 120v | 224,000 | 15.0 | 381 | 24.0 | 610 | 25.0 | 635 | 16.0 | 406 | 20.0 | 9.1 | * |
| ERS 8x9 | Colortran | 212-082 | 7.5° | 15° | 0.26 | EGJ 1kW 120v | 312,000 | 15.0 | 381 | | | | | 16.0 | 406 | | | * |
| ERS 8x14 | Colortran | 213-102 | 5.8° | 10° | 0.18 | FEL 1kW 120v | 563,000 | 15.0 | 381 | 28.0 | 711 | 25.0 | 635 | 16.0 | 406 | 20.0 | 9.1 | * |
| ERS 8x14 | Colortran | 650-072 | 5.8° | 10° | 0.18 | FEL 1kW 120v | 563,000 | 15.0 | 381 | 30.0 | 762 | 25.0 | 635 | 16.0 | 406 | 21.0 | 9.5 | * |
| ERS 10x15 | Colortran | 212-092 | 6.5° | 9° | 0.16 | EGJ 1kW 120v | 550,000 | | | | | | | | | | | * |
| ERS 10x23 | Colortran | 213-112 | 3.3° | 5° | 0.09 | FEL 1kW 120v | 939,000 | 15.0 | 381 | 37.0 | 940 | 37.0 | 940 | 16.0 | 406 | 25.0 | 11.3 | * |
| ERS 10x23 | Colortran | 650-082 | 3.3° | 5° | 0.09 | FEL 1kW 120v | 939,000 | 15.0 | 381 | 37.0 | 940 | 37.0 | 940 | 16.0 | 406 | 25.0 | 11.3 | * |
| ERS-Zoom | Colortran | 213-302 | 17°–27° | 40°–65° | 0.73–1.27 | FMR 600W 120v | 32,160/89,000 | | | | | | | | | | | * |
| ERS-Zoom | Colortran | 213-312 | 9.5°–18° | 25°–50° | 0.44–0.93 | FMR 600W 120v | 49,000/18,275 | | | | | | | | | | | * |
| ERS-Zoom | Colortran | 213-322 | 9°–11° | 15°–30° | 0.26–0.54 | FMR 600W 120v | 61,600/44,500 | | | | | | | | | | | * |

| Type | Manufacturer | Unit | B/A *=Approx | F/A | MPF | Lamp (or lampholder type) | Peak Candela *=math approx †=flat field candela | W in 0.04 | W mm 25 | L in 0.04 | L mm 25 | H in 0.04 | H mm 25 | HY in 0.04 | HY mm 25 | Wt lb 2.2 | Wt kg 0.5 | Other lamp |
|---|---|---|---|---|---|---|---|---|---|---|---|---|---|---|---|---|---|---|
| ERS-Zoom | Colortran | 213-002 | 14°–21° | 24°–43° | 0.43–0.79 | FEL 1kW 120v | 140,000/100,000 | 15.0 | 381 | 27.0 | 686 | 24.0 | 610 | 16.0 | 406 | 21.0 | 9.5 | * |
| ERS-Zoom | Colortran | 213-162 | 7.5°–14° | 15°–35° | 0.26–0.63 | FEL 1kW 120v | 270,000/136,000 | | | | | | | | | | | * |
| ERS 4.5x7 | Electro Controls | 3345 | | 34° | 0.61 | EVR 500W 120v | 27,200 | | | | | | | | | | | * |
| ERS 4.5x7 | Electro Controls | 7345AF 33 | 16.4° | 33° | 0.59 | EVR 500W 120v | 23,200 | | | | | | | | | | | * |
| ERS 4.5x9 | Electro Controls | 7345AF 29 | 15.6° | 29.6° | 0.53 | EVR 500W 120v | 28,000 | | | | | | | | | | | * |
| ERS 4.5x3.5 | Electro Controls | 7345AF30 | 16° | 29.8° | 0.52 | EVR 500W 120v | 25,200 | | | | | | | | | | | * |
| ERS 4.5x9 | Electro Controls | 7345AF 28 | 12.8° | 28.2° | 0.50 | EVR 500W 120v | 35,200 | | | | | | | | | | | * |
| ERS 4.5x9 | Electro Controls | 3345 | | 27.5° | 0.48 | EVR 500W 120v | 43,200 | | | | | | | | | | | * |
| ERS 4.5x3 | Electro Controls | 3345 | | 26.5° | 0.47 | EVR 500W 120v | 25,200 | | | | | | | | | | | * |
| ERS 4.5x9 | Electro Controls | 3345 | | 21° | 0.37 | EVR 500W 120v | 68,000 | | | | | | | | | | | * |
| ERS 8x4.5 | Electro Controls | 3201/2 | | 36° | 0.65 | PAR64 NSP 500W 120v | 11,400 | | | | | | | | | | | * |
| ERS 6x16 | Electro Controls | 3207/8 | | 26.7° | 0.47 | PAR64 NSP 500W 120v | 17,100 | | | | | | | | | | | * |
| ERS 8x8 | Electro Controls | 3205/6 | | 24.8° | 0.44 | PAR64 NSP 500W 120v | 22,500 | | | | | | | | | | | * |
| ERS 6x20 | Electro Controls | 3211/2 | | 20.6° | 0.36 | PAR64 NSP 500W 120v | 27,200 | | | | | | | | | | | * |
| ERS 8x11 | Electro Controls | 3209/10 | | 20° | 0.35 | PAR64 NSP 500W 120v | 40,000 | | | | | | | | | | | * |
| ERS 6x18 | Electro Controls | 3213/4 | | 12° | 0.21 | PAR64 NSP 500W 120v | 67,500 | | | | | | | | | | | * |
| ERS 4.5x7 | Electro Controls | 7363AF 56 | 27° | 56° | 1.06 | EGG 750W 120v | 45,200 | | | | | | | | | | | * |
| ERS 4.5x9 | Electro Controls | 7363AF 45 | 22° | 45° | 0.83 | EGG 750W 120v | 49,600 | | | | | | | | | | | * |
| ERS 4.5x9 | Electro Controls | 7363AF 39 | 21° | 39° | 0.71 | EGG 750W 120v | 51,200 | | | | | | | | | | | * |
| ERS 6x9 | Electro Controls | 3365 | | 34.7° | 0.62 | EGJ 1kW 120v | 82,000 | | | | | | | | | | | * |
| ERS 6x9 | Electro Controls | 3366 | 17.5° | 34.7° | 0.62 | EGJ 1kW 120v | 83,000 | | | | | | | | | | | * |
| ERS 8x4.5 | Electro Controls | 3386A/4.5 | 18° | 29° | 0.52 | EGJ 1kW 120v | 101,600 | | | | | | | | | | | * |
| ERS 6x6 | Electro Controls | 3365 | 9.3° | 24.8° | 0.44 | EGJ 1kW 120v | 180,000 | | | | | | | | | | | * |
| ERS 6x6 | Electro Controls | 3366 | | 24.8° | 0.44 | EGJ 1kW 120v | 180,000 | | | | | | | | | | | * |
| ERS 8x8 | Electro Controls | 3386A/8 | 13° | 23° | 0.41 | EGJ 1kW 120v | 155,700 | | | | | | | | | | | * |
| ERS 6x16 | Electro Controls | 3365 | 13° | 20° | 0.35 | EGJ 1kW 120v | 167,435 | | | | | | | | | | | * |
| ERS 6x8 | Electro Controls | 3365 | 6.9° | 18.4° | 0.33 | EGJ 1kW 120v | 290,000 | | | | | | | | | | | * |
| ERS 6x20 | Electro Controls | 3365 | | 16° | 0.28 | EGJ 1kW 120v | 208,000 | | | | | | | | | | | * |
| ERS 8x11 | Electro Controls | 3386A/11 | 11° | 15° | 0.26 | EGJ 1kW 120v | 347,400 | | | | | | | | | | | * |
| ERS-Zoom | Electro Controls | 7331A | 5.4°–7.5° | 10.9°–15.4° | 0.19–0.27 | EGJ 1kW 120v | 470,000/397,000 | | | | | | | | | | | * |
| ERS-Zoom | Electro Controls | 7367A | 12°–18.6° | 23°–33.4° | 0.41–0.6 | EGJ 1kW 120v | 164,000/97,600 | 12.8 | 325 | 24.8 | 630 | 12.8 | 325 | 20.0 | 508 | 13.6 | 6.2 | * |
| Source 4 | ETC | Source 4 450 | 33° | 50° | 0.93 | HPL575/115 575W 120v | 34,866 | 12.5 | 318 | 22.5 | 572 | 12.5 | 318 | 20.8 | 527 | 14.0 | 6.4 | * |
| Source 4 | ETC | Source 4 436 | 24° | 36° | 0.65 | HPL575/115 575W 120v | 84,929 | 12.5 | 318 | 22.5 | 572 | 12.5 | 318 | 20.8 | 527 | 13.6 | 6.2 | * |
| Source 4 | ETC | Source 4 426 | 17° | 26° | 0.46 | HPL575/115 575W 120v | 138,079 | 12.5 | 318 | 22.5 | 572 | 12.5 | 318 | 20.8 | 527 | 13.5 | 6.1 | * |
| Source 4 | ETC | Source 4 419 | 13° | 19° | 0.31 | HPL575/115 575W 120v | 167,435 | 12.5 | 318 | 22.5 | 572 | 12.5 | 318 | 20.8 | 527 | 14.0 | 6.4 | * |
| Source 4 | ETC | Source 4 410 | 6.9° | 10.3° | 0.18 | HPL575/115 575W 120v | 800,300 | 12.4 | 315 | 29.6 | 752 | 12.4 | 315 | 20.6 | 523 | 15.3 | 6.9 | * |
| Source 4 | ETC | Source 4 405 | 4.6° | 6.8° | 0.12 | HPL575/115 575W 120v | 996,000 | 14.2 | 361 | 37.9 | 963 | 14.2 | 361 | 21.4 | 544 | 25.8 | 11.7 | * |
| Profile condensor | Robert Juliat | 611S | | 8°–17° | 0.14–0.30 | 6X9.5 1.2/1kW 220v | 920 Lux at 3m⌀ beam † | 12.2 | 310 | 31.8 | 810 | 9.4 | 240 | 16.1 | 410 | | | |
| Double condensor | Robert Juliat | 611 SX | | 11°–26° | 0.19–0.46 | 6X9.5 1.2/1kW 220v | 1400 Lux at 3m⌀ beam † | | | | | | | | | | | |

| Type | Manufacturer | Unit | B/A (=Approx) | F/A | MPF | Lamp (or lampholder type) | Peak Candela (*=math approx, †=flat field candela) | W in 0.04 | W mm 25 | L in 0.04 | L mm 25 | H in 0.04 | H mm 25 | HY in 0.04 | HY mm 25 | Wt lb 2.2 | Wt kg 0.5 | Other lamp |
|---|---|---|---|---|---|---|---|---|---|---|---|---|---|---|---|---|---|---|
| Profile condensor | Robert Juliat | 612S | | 10°–21° | 0.18–0.37 | 6X9.5 1.2/1kW 220v | | 12.2 | 310 | 27.5 | 700 | 9.4 | 240 | 16.1 | 410 | 24.3 | 11.0 | * |
| Profile condensor | Robert Juliat | 613S | | 58° | 1.11 | 6X9.5 1.2/1kW 220v | 450 Lux at 3m∅ beam † | 12.2 | 310 | 20.6 | 525 | 9.4 | 240 | 16.1 | 410 | 19.8 | 9.0 | * |
| Double condensor | Robert Juliat | 613 SX | | 30°–53° | 0.54–1.0 | 6X9.5 1.2/1kW 220v | 2250 Lux at 3m∅ beam † | | | | | | | | | | | |
| Double condensor | Robert Juliat | 614S | | 13°–42° | 0.23–0.77 | 6X9.5 1.2/1kW 220v | 900 Lux at 3m∅ beam † | 12.2 | 310 | 25.2 | 640 | 9.4 | 240 | 16.1 | 410 | 24.3 | 11.0 | * |
| Double condensor | Robert Juliat | 614 SX | | 15°–38° | 0.26–0.69 | 6X9.5 1.2/1kW 220v | 1900 Lux at 3m∅ beam † | | | | | | | | | | | |
| Profile condensor | Robert Juliat | 710S | | 6.5°–12° | 0.11–0.21 | 6Y16 2kW 220v | | 14.5 | 370 | 36.2 | 920 | 13.4 | 340 | 25.9 | 660 | 44.1 | 20.0 | |
| Double condensor | Robert Juliat | 710 SX | | 9°–26° | 0.16–0.46 | 6Y16 2kW 220v | 3000 Lux at 3m∅ beam † | | | | | | | | | | | |
| Profile condensor | Robert Juliat | 713S | | 58° | 1.11 | 6Y16 2kW 220v | 770 Lux at 3m∅ beam † | 14.5 | 370 | 21.6 | 550 | 13.4 | 340 | 21.6 | 550 | 30.9 | 14.0 | * |
| Double condensor | Robert Juliat | 713 SX | | 30°–53° | 0.54–1.0 | 6Y16 2kW 220v | 4300 Lux at 3m∅ beam † | | | | | | | | | | | |
| Profile condensor | Robert Juliat | 714S | | 12°–43° | 0.21–0.79 | 6Y16 2kW 220v | 1550 Lux at 3m∅ beam † | 14.5 | 370 | 29.1 | 740 | 13.4 | 340 | 21.6 | 550 | 39.7 | 18.0 | * |
| Double condensor | Robert Juliat | 714 SX | | 15°–38° | 0.26–0.69 | 6Y16 2kW 220v | 2800 Lux at 3m∅ beam † | | | | | | | | | | | |
| Profile condensor | Robert Juliat | 914 | | 11.5°–34° | 0.20–0.61 | HMI 1200GS 1.2kW 220v | | 14.5 | 370 | 30.3 | 770 | 13.4 | 340 | 21.6 | 550 | 52.9 | 24.0 | * |
| Double condensor | Robert Juliat | 910 SNX | | 9°–26° | 0.16–0.46 | HMI 1200GS 1.2kW 220v | 2400 Lux at 3m∅ beam † | | | | | | | | | | | |
| Double condensor | Robert Juliat | 913 SNX | | 30°–53° | 0.54–1.0 | HMI 1200GS 1.2kW 220v | 3300 Lux at 3m∅ beam † | | | | | | | | | | | |
| Double condensor | Robert Juliat | 914 SNX | | 18°–36° | 0.32–0.65 | HMI 1200GS 1.2kW 220v | 2400 Lux at 3m∅ beam † | | | | | | | | | | | |
| Double condensor | Robert Juliat | 930 SNX | | 9°–26° | 0.16–0.46 | HMI 2500G38 2.5kW 220v | 4700 Lux at 3m∅ beam † | | | | | | | | | | | |
| Double condensor | Robert Juliat | 933 SNX | | 30°–53° | 0.54–1.0 | HMI 2500G38 2.5kW 220v | 6600 Lux at 3m∅ beam † | | | | | | | | | | | |
| Double condensor | Robert Juliat | 934 SNX | | 18°–36° | 0.32–0.65 | HMI 2500G38 2.5kW 220v | 4800 Lux at 3m∅ beam † | | | | | | | | | | | |
| ERS 3.5x? | Kliegl | 1340 | | 46° | 0.85 | EHR 400W 120v | 6,900 | 5.5 | 140 | 15.0 | 380 | 5.5 | 140 | 16.5 | 420 | 9.0 | 3.8 | * |
| ERS 3.5x? | Kliegl | 1343 | | 19° | 0.33 | EHR 400W 120v | 18,000 | 5.5 | 140 | 17.5 | 440 | 5.5 | 140 | 16.5 | 420 | 9.0 | 3.8 | * |
| ERS 5x? | Kliegl | 1163 | | 27° | 0.48 | T14/8 500W 120v | 46,875 | | | | | | | | | | | |
| ERS 5x? | Kliegl | 1163W | | 53° | 1.00 | T14/8 500W 120v | 25,000 | | | | | | | | | | | |
| ERS 6x? | Kliegl | 1165 | | 23° | 0.41 | T14/8 500W 120v | 93,700 | | | | | | | | | | | |
| ERS 6x2 | Kliegl | 1165W | | 44° | 0.81 | T14/8 500W 120v | 56,250 | | | | | | | | | | | * |
| ERS 8x2 | Kliegl | 1165/8 | | 14° | 0.25 | T14/8 500W 120v | 143,750 | | | | | | | | | | | * |
| ERS 6x? | Kliegl | 1365 | | 17° | 0.30 | T14/8 500W 120v | 60,000 | | | | | | | | | | | * |
| ERS 6x? | Kliegl | 1365W | | 34° | 0.61 | T14/8 500W 120v | 24,300 | | | | | | | | | | | * |
| ERS 8x? | Kliegl | 1365/8 | | 13° | 0.23 | T14/8 500W 120v | 96,000 | | | | | | | | | | | * |
| ERS 6x8 | Kliegl | 1355 | | 18° | 0.32 | EH6 750W 120v | 126,000 | 9.0 | 230 | 22.0 | 560 | 9.0 | 230 | 19.5 | 495 | 14.0 | 6.4 | * |
| ERS 8x12 | Kliegl | 1355/8 | | 12° | 0.21 | EH6 750W 120v | 246,000 | 9.0 | 230 | 26.5 | 675 | 9.0 | 230 | 19.5 | 495 | 16.0 | 7.3 | * |
| ERS 4.5x? | Kliegl | 1555 | | 55° | 1.04 | FEL 1kW 120v | 88,000 | | | | | | | | | | | * |
| ERS 6x9 | Kliegl | 1554 | | 40° | 0.73 | FEL 1kW 120v | 103,000 | | | | | | | | | | | * |
| ERS 6x9 | Kliegl | 1553 | | 30° | 0.54 | FEL 1kW 120v | 169,000 | | | | | | | | | | | * |
| ERS 6x16 | Kliegl | 1552 | | 20° | 0.35 | FEL 1kW 120v | 266,000 | | | | | | | | | | | * |
| ERS 8x20 | Kliegl | 1550/8 | | 10° | 0.18 | FEL 1kW 120v | 420,000 | | | | | | | | | | | * |
| ERS 6x8 | Kliegl | 1357/6 | | 18° | 0.32 | DWT 1kW 120v | 120,000 | 10.0 | 250 | 26.0 | 660 | 10.0 | 250 | 27.3 | 700 | 21.0 | 9.4 | * |
| ERS 6x3.75 | Kliegl | 1357/6W | | 27° | 0.48 | DWT 1kW 120v | 58,500 | 10.0 | 250 | 26.0 | 660 | 10.0 | 250 | 27.3 | 700 | 24.0 | 10.8 | * |
| ERS 8x12 | Kliegl | 1357/8 | | 13° | 0.23 | DWT 1kW 120v | 249,600 | 10.0 | 250 | 31.5 | 800 | 10.0 | 250 | 27.3 | 700 | 24.0 | 10.8 | * |
| ERS 10x15 | Kliegl | 1357/10 | | 9° | 0.16 | DWT 1kW 120v | 411,600 | | | | | | | | | | | * |

| Type | Manufacturer | Unit | B/A (*=Approx) | F/A | MPF | Lamp (or lampholder type) | Peak Candela (*=math approx †=flat field candela) | W in | W mm | L in | L mm | H in | H mm | HY in | HY mm | Wt lb | Wt kg | Other lamp |
|---|---|---|---|---|---|---|---|---|---|---|---|---|---|---|---|---|---|---|
| ERS 12x16 | Kliegl | 1357/12 | | 9° | 0.16 | DWT 1kW 120v | 417,600 | 10.0 | 250 | 37.0 | 940 | 10.0 | 250 | 27.3 | 700 | 28.0 | 12.6 | * |
| ERS 6x? | Kliegl | 1164 | | 27° | 0.48 | 1M/T24/12 1kW 120v | 75,000 | | | | | | | | | | | |
| ERS 6x? | Kliegl | 1164W | | 53° | 1.00 | 1M/T24/12 1kW 120v | 62,500 | | | | | | | | | | | |
| ERS 6x? | Kliegl | 1167 | | 27° | 0.48 | 2M/T30/1 2kW 120v | 150,000 | | | | | | | | | | | * |
| ERS 6x? | Kliegl | 1167W | | 53° | 1.00 | 2M/T30/1 2kW 120v | 62,500 | | | | | | | | | | | |
| ERS 8x? | Kliegl | 1366 | | 28° | 0.50 | 2M/T30/1 2kW 120v | 108,800 | | | | | | | | | | | * |
| ERS 8x? | Kliegl | 1368 | | 18° | 0.32 | 2M/T30/1 2kW 120v | 180,000 | | | | | | | | | | | * |
| ERS 8x? | Kliegl | 1358/6 | | 22° | 0.39 | BWA 2kW 120v | 85,500 | | | | | | | | | | | * |
| ERS 8x12 | Kliegl | 1358/8 | | 19° | 0.33 | BWA 2kW 120v | 169,600 | | | | | | | | | | | |
| ERS 10x15 | Kliegl | 1358/10 | | 12.5° | 0.22 | BWA 2kW 120v | 410,625 | | | | | | | | | | | * |
| ERS 12x? | Kliegl | 1358/12 | | 12° | 0.21 | BWA 2kW 120v | 450,000 | | | | | | | | | | | |
| ERS 8x? | Kliegl | 1375 | | 18° | 0.32 | 3M/T32/2 3kW 120v | 350,000 | | | | | | | | | | | * |
| ERS 6x? | Kliegl | 1374 | | 27° | 0.48 | 3M/T32/2 3kW 120v | 175,000 | | | | | | | | | | | |
| ERS 8x? | Kliegl | 1373 | | 14° | 0.25 | 3M/T32/2 3kW 120v | 350,000 | | | | | | | | | | | |
| ERS-Zoom | Kliegl/CCT | 1010 Aimslite | 5°-8° | 9°-14° | 0.16-0.25 | FEL 1kW 120v | 605,000/361,250 | 12.4 | 315 | 36.5 | 930 | 9.8 | 250 | 15.5 | 395 | 43.4 | 19.7 | * |
| ERS-Zoom | Kliegl/CCT | 1015 Aimslite | 7°-10° | 11°-16° | 0.19-0.28 | FEL 1kW 120v | 396,000/304,000 | 12.4 | 315 | 28.1 | 715 | 9.8 | 250 | 15.5 | 395 | 22.9 | 10.4 | * |
| ERS-Zoom | Kliegl/CCT | 1030 Aimslite | 12°-15° | 21°-40° | 0.37-0.73 | FEL 1kW 120v | 125,000/96,800 | 12.4 | 315 | 20.7 | 527 | 9.8 | 250 | 15.5 | 395 | 15.2 | 6.9 | * |
| ERS-Zoom | Kliegl/CCT | 1040 Aimslite | 15°-16° | 27°-44° | 0.48-0.80 | FEL 1kW 120v | 101,250/80,000 | 12.4 | 315 | 20.7 | 527 | 9.8 | 250 | 15.5 | 395 | 15.2 | 6.9 | * |
| ERS-Zoom | Kliegl/CCT | 1990 Silhouette | 6°-9° | 10°-22° | 0.18-0.39 | FEL 1kW 120v | 592,000/313,000 | 12.4 | 315 | 36.5 | 930 | 9.8 | 250 | 15.5 | 395 | 43.4 | 19.7 | * |
| ERS-Zoom | Kliegl/CCT | 1991 Silhouette | 7°-11° | 12°-26° | 0.21-0.46 | FEL 1kW 120v | 354,000/230,000 | 12.4 | 315 | 28.5 | 725 | 9.8 | 250 | 15.5 | 395 | 22.9 | 10.4 | * |
| ERS-Zoom | Kliegl/CCT | 1992 Silhouette | 10°-12° | 20°-31° | 0.35-0.55 | FEL 1kW 120v | 271,000/203,000 | 12.4 | 315 | 26.5 | 675 | 9.8 | 250 | 15.5 | 395 | 22.9 | 10.4 | * |
| ERS-Zoom | Kliegl/CCT | 1993 Silhouette | 12°-15° | 22°-38° | 0.39-0.69 | FEL 1kW 120v | 141,000/106,000 | 12.4 | 315 | 20.7 | 527 | 9.8 | 250 | 15.5 | 395 | 15.2 | 6.9 | * |
| ERS-Zoom | Kliegl/CCT | 1994 Silhouette | 15°-20° | 31°-47° | 0.55-0.87 | FEL 1kW 120v | 87,000/66,000 | 12.4 | 315 | 20.7 | 527 | 9.8 | 250 | 15.5 | 395 | 15.2 | 6.9 | * |
| ERS-Zoom | Kliegl/CCT | 2010 Aimslite | 8°-14° | 10°-20° | 0.18-0.35 | BWA 2kW 120v | 470,500/168,200 | | | | | | | | | | | |
| ERS-Zoom | Kliegl/CCT | 2015 Aimslite | 10°-15° | 13°-27° | 0.23-0.48 | BWA 2kW 120v | 320,000/174,000 | | | | | | | | | | | |
| ERS-Zoom | Kliegl/CCT | 2030 Aimslite | 14°-31° | 21°-44° | 0.37-0.81 | BWA 2kW 120v | 135,200/45,000 | | | | | | | | | | | |
| ERS 4.5x6.5 | L & E | 61-04 | 38° | 50° | 0.93 | DNS 500W 120v | 14,500 | 7.8 | 197 | 17.8 | 451 | 7.8 | 197 | | | 18.0 | 8.2 | * |
| ERS 4.5x6.5 | L & E | AQ61-04 | 22° | 55° | 1.04 | EHG 750W 120v | 38,250 | 7.8 | 197 | 17.8 | 451 | 7.8 | 197 | | | 18.0 | 8.2 | * |
| ERS 6x9 | L & E | 61-06 | 32° | 40° | 0.73 | DNT 750W 120v | 35,000 | 7.8 | 197 | 17.8 | 451 | 7.8 | 197 | | | 18.0 | 8.2 | * |
| ERS 6x9 | L & E | AQ61-06 | 16° | 37° | 0.67 | EHG 750W 120v | 66,000 | 7.8 | 197 | 17.8 | 451 | 7.8 | 197 | | | 18.0 | 8.2 | * |
| ERS 6x9 | L & E | 61-12 | 20° | 30° | 0.54 | DNT 750W 120v | 60,800 | 7.8 | 197 | 19.5 | 495 | 7.8 | 197 | | | 18.0 | 8.2 | * |
| ERS 6x12 | L & E | AQ61-12 | 11° | 26° | 0.46 | EHG 750W 120v | 115,500 | 7.8 | 197 | 19.5 | 495 | 7.8 | 197 | | | 18.0 | 8.2 | * |
| ERS 6x16 | L & E | 61-16 | 12° | 19° | 0.33 | DNT 750W 120v | 78,300 | 7.8 | 197 | 21.5 | 546 | 7.8 | 197 | | | 18.0 | 8.2 | * |
| ERS 6x16 | L & E | AQ61-16 | 8.5° | 19° | 0.33 | EHG 750W 120v | 141,000 | 7.8 | 197 | 21.5 | 546 | 7.8 | 197 | | | 18.0 | 8.2 | * |
| ERS 6x22 | L & E | AQ61-22 | 7° | 11° | 0.19 | EHG 750W 120v | 164,300 | 7.8 | 197 | 28.0 | 711 | 7.8 | 197 | | | 18.0 | 8.2 | * |
| ERS-Zoom | L & E | AQ61-2M | 9°-18° | 20°-40° | 0.35-0.73 | EHG 750W 120v | 93,450/48,100 | 7.8 | 197 | 25.8 | 654 | 7.8 | 197 | | | 19.0 | 8.6 | * |
| ERS 4.5x6.5 | Little Stage Ltg | E306 | 20.7° | 41.7° | 0.76 | EVR 500W 120v | 21,960 | | | | | | | | | | | |
| ERS 4.5x9 | Little Stage Ltg | E309 | 13.4° | 26° | 0.46 | EVR 500W 120v | 37,700 | | | | | | | | | | | |
| ERS 4.5x12 | Little Stage Ltg | E312 | 10.6° | 19° | 0.33 | EVR 500W 120v | 46,400 | | | | | | | | | | | |

| Type | Manufacturer | Unit | B/A *=Approx | F/A | MPF | Lamp (or lampholder type) | Peak Candela *=math approx †=flat field candela | W in 0.04 | W mm 25 | L in 0.04 | L mm 25 | H in 0.04 | H mm 25 | HY in 0.04 | HY mm 25 | Wt lb 2.2 | Wt kg 0.5 | Other lamp |
|---|---|---|---|---|---|---|---|---|---|---|---|---|---|---|---|---|---|---|
| ERS 6x9 | Little Stage Ltg | E109 | 14.7° | 30.2° | 0.54 | 1MT12/2 1kW 120v | 115,068 | | | | | | | | | | | |
| ERS 6x9 | Little Stage Ltg | E209 | 13.3° | 30.8° | 0.55 | 1MT12/2 1kW 120v | 100,202 | | | | | | | | | | | |
| ERS 6x12 | Little Stage Ltg | E112 | 12° | 22° | 0.39 | 1MT12/2 1kW 120v | 166,631 | | | | | | | | | | | |
| ERS 6x12 | Little Stage Ltg | E212 | 11.2° | 22.4° | 0.40 | FEL 1kW 120v | 143,724 | | | | | | | | | | | |
| ERS 6x16 | Little Stage Ltg | E116 | 10.1° | 16.3° | 0.29 | 1MT12/2 1kW 120v | 143,673 | | | | | | | | | | | |
| ERS 6x16 | Little Stage Ltg | E216 | 9.6° | 16.6° | 0.29 | FEL 1kW 120v | 129,739 | | | | | | | | | | | |
| ERS-Zoom | Little Stage Ltg | E509 | 12.5°–15.1° | 21.5°–36° | 0.38–0.65 | FEL 1kW 120v | 160,434/76,343 | | | | | | | | | | | |
| Ellips w/Fres lens | Marumo | EEQ III 120F | 20.1° | 36° | 0.65 | JPD B/6 1kW 100v | 47,000 | 11.6 | 295 | 21.0 | 535 | 9.8 | 250 | 19.5 | 497 | 15.4 | 7.0 | * |
| Ellipsoidal | Marumo | EEQ III 5C | 22.3° | 32° | 0.57 | JPD B/6 1kW 100v | 49,000 | 11.6 | 295 | 21.4 | 545 | 7.9 | 200 | 18.6 | 473 | 13.2 | 6.0 | * |
| Ellipsoidal | Marumo | EEQ III 7C | 17.2° | 24° | 0.43 | JPD B/6 1kW 100v | 78,000 | 11.6 | 295 | 23.1 | 588 | 7.9 | 200 | 18.6 | 473 | 17.0 | 7.7 | * |
| Ellipsoidal | Marumo | EEQ III 10C | 12.5° | 16° | 0.28 | JPD B/6 1kW 100v | 108,000 | 12.8 | 325 | 29.1 | 740 | 7.9 | 200 | 18.6 | 473 | 17.6 | 8.0 | * |
| Ellipsoidal | Marumo | ECLQ 8Z | 7.4°–11.5° | 8°–12° | 0.14–0.21 | JP G-0 1.5kW 100v | 265,500/118,500 | 16.7 | 426 | 41.1 | 1046 | 13.1 | 334 | 24.1 | 614 | 38.1 | 17.3 | * |
| Ellipsoidal | Marumo | ECLQ 10Z | 8.6°–9.7° | 10°–15° | 0.18–0.26 | JP G-0 1.5kW 100v | 231,000/150,000 | 14.8 | 376 | 41.8 | 1063 | 13.1 | 334 | 24.1 | 614 | 34.2 | 15.5 | * |
| Ellipsoidal | Marumo | ECLQ 13Z | 9.7°–11° | 13°–18° | 0.23–0.32 | JP G-0 1.5kW 100v | 212,500/112,500 | 14.8 | 376 | 37.2 | 947 | 13.1 | 334 | 24.1 | 614 | 32.2 | 14.6 | * |
| Ellipsoidal | Marumo | ECLQ 16Z | 12°–12° | 16°–20° | 0.29–0.35 | JP G-0 1.5kW 100v | 156,000/106,000 | 14.8 | 376 | 34.5 | 877 | 13.1 | 334 | 24.1 | 614 | 34.2 | 15.5 | * |
| Ellipsoidal | Marumo | ECLQ 8Z | 7.7°–9.7° | 8°–12° | 0.14–0.21 | JP G-0 2kW 100v | 450,000/212,500 | 16.7 | 426 | 41.1 | 1046 | 13.1 | 334 | 24.1 | 614 | 38.1 | 17.3 | * |
| Ellipsoidal | Marumo | ECLQ 10Z | 8.7°–8.9° | 10°–15° | 0.18–0.26 | JP G-0 2kW 100v | 378,000/250,000 | 14.8 | 376 | 41.8 | 1063 | 13.1 | 334 | 24.1 | 614 | 34.2 | 15.5 | * |
| Ellipsoidal | Marumo | ECLQ 13Z | 10.4°–10.5° | 13°–18° | 0.23–0.32 | JP G-0 2kW 100v | 278,000/156,000 | 14.8 | 376 | 37.2 | 947 | 13.1 | 334 | 24.1 | 614 | 32.2 | 14.6 | * |
| Ellipsoidal | Marumo | ECLQ 16Z | 13.5°–15.7° | 16°–20° | 0.28–0.35 | JP G-0 2kW 100v | 172,000/109,500 | 14.8 | 376 | 34.5 | 877 | 13.1 | 334 | 24.1 | 614 | 34.2 | 15.5 | * |
| Halogen profile | Niethammer | HPS 111 | 11° | 11° | 0.19 | 1kW 220v | 260,000 | | | | | | | | | | | |
| Halogen profile | Niethammer | HPS 130 | 30° | | 0.54 | 1kW 220v | 40,000 | 11.4 | 290 | 22.6 | 575 | 10.4 | 265 | 15.7 | 400 | | | |
| Halogen profile | Niethammer | HPS 209 | 9° | | 0.16 | 2kW 220v | 850,000 | 17.3 | 440 | 35.8 | 910 | 15.7 | 400 | 22.2 | 565 | | | |
| Halogen profile | Niethammer | HPS 212 | 12° | | 0.21 | 2kW 220v | 500,000 | 17.3 | 440 | 31.4 | 800 | 15.7 | 400 | 22.2 | 565 | | | |
| Halogen profile | Niethammer | HPS 217 | 17° | 17° | 0.30 | 2kW 220v | 280,000 | 17.3 | 440 | 30.5 | 775 | 15.7 | 400 | 22.2 | 565 | | | |
| Halogen profile | Niethammer | HPS 223 | 23° | | 0.41 | 2kW 220v | 165000 | 17.3 | 440 | 27.1 | 690 | 15.7 | 400 | 22.2 | 565 | | | |
| Halogen profile | Niethammer | HPS 230 | 30° | | 0.54 | 2kW 220v | 75,000 | 17.3 | 440 | 27.1 | 690 | 15.7 | 400 | 22.2 | 565 | | | |
| Zoom profile | Niethammer | HPZ 212 | 11°–27° | | 0.19–0.48 | 2kW 220v | 650,000/150,000 | 17.1 | 435 | 33.2 | 845 | 17.5 | 445 | 25.3 | 645 | | | |
| Halogen profile | Niethammer | HMS 109 | 9° | | 0.16 | HMI 1.2kW 220v | 1,400,000 | 17.1 | 435 | 47.6 | 1210 | 17.5 | 445 | 25.2 | 640 | | | |
| Halogen profile | Niethammer | HMS 112 | 12° | | 0.21 | HMI 1.2kW 220v | 800,000 | 17.1 | 435 | 43.4 | 1105 | 17.5 | 445 | 25.2 | 640 | | | |
| Halogen profile | Niethammer | HMS 117 | 17° | 17° | 0.30 | HMI 1.2kW 220v | 450,000 | 17.1 | 435 | 40.7 | 1036 | 17.5 | 445 | 25.2 | 640 | | | |
| Halogen profile | Niethammer | HMS 123 | 23° | | 0.41 | HMI 1.2kW 220v | 260,000 | 17.1 | 435 | 38.1 | 970 | 17.5 | 445 | 25.2 | 640 | | | |
| Halogen profile | Niethammer | HMS 130 | 30° | | 0.54 | HMI 1.2kW 220v | 120,000 | 17.1 | 435 | 37.7 | 960 | 17.5 | 445 | 25.2 | 640 | | | |
| Profile kondensor | Pani | HV 650 | 11/22° | 11/22° | 0.19/0.39 | 66.35 650W 220v | 305,000/125,000 | 13.5 | 345 | 31.4 | 798 | | | 14.1 | 360 | 28.6 | 13.0 | |
| Profile kondensor | Pani | HV 1000 | 10/15° | 10/15° | 0.18/0.26 | 66.35 1kW 220v | 375,000/225,000 | 13.5 | 345 | 31.4 | 798 | | | 14.1 | 360 | | | |
| Profile kondensor | Pani | HV 2000 | 11/22° | 11/22° | 0.19/0.39 | GY16 2kW 220v | | 15.1 | 385 | 41.0 | 1040 | | | 17.7 | 450 | 55.0 | 25.0 | |
| Kondensor | R & V | EL 650 | 18° | 18° | 0.32 | 6X9 650W 220v | 64,800 | 11.8 | 300 | 19.8 | 500 | | | 17.0 | 430 | 26.5 | 12.0 | * |
| Kondensor | R & V | KL 1200 MS/K | 27°–45° | 27°–45° | 0.48–0.83 | QH 650W 220v | 46,000/16,000 | 12.2 | 310 | 19.7 | 500 | 9.8 | 250 | 19.8 | 505 | 28.2 | 12.8 | * |
| Kondensor | R & V | KL 1200 MS/M | 14°–22° | 14°–22° | 0.25–0.39 | QH 1.2kW 220v | 220,000/72,750 | 12.2 | 310 | 24.8 | 630 | 9.8 | 250 | 19.8 | 505 | 28.2 | 12.8 | * |
| Kondensor | R & V | KL 1200 MS/L | 11°–30° | 11°–30° | 0.19–0.54 | QH 1.2kW 220v | 242,000/35,500 | 12.2 | 310 | 31.4 | 800 | 9.8 | 250 | 19.8 | 505 | 33.1 | 15.0 | * |

| Type | Manufacturer | Unit | B/A (*=Approx) | F/A | MPF | Lamp (or lampholder type) | Peak Candela (*=math approx, †=flat field candela) | W in (0.04) | W mm (25) | L in (0.04) | L mm (25) | H in (0.04) | H mm (25) | HY in (0.04) | HY mm (25) | Wt lb (2.2) | Wt kg (0.5) | Other lamp |
|---|---|---|---|---|---|---|---|---|---|---|---|---|---|---|---|---|---|---|
| Kondensor | R & V | EL 2000 | 17° | 17° | 0.30 | GY16 2KW 220v | 200,000 | 20.5 | 520 | 33.1 | 840 | | 360 | 25.6 | 650 | 62.0 | 28.0 | * |
| Kondensor | R & V | KL 2500 MS/M | 18°–26° | 18°–26° | 0.32–0.46 | QH 2KW 220v | 183,000/72,500 | 16.9 | 430 | 26.5 | 675 | 14.1 | 360 | 19.7 | 500 | 51.2 | 23.2 | * |
| Kondensor | R & V | KL 2500 MS/L | 12°–24° | 12°–24° | 0.21–0.43 | QH 2.5kW 220v | 430,000/93,000 | 16.9 | 430 | 33.2 | 845 | 14.1 | 360 | 19.7 | 500 | 53.4 | 24.2 | * |
| Kondensor | R & V | TKLL 12 | 7.5° | 7.5° | 0.13 | HMI/MSR 1.2kW 220v | 1,000,000 | 16.5 | 420 | 36.2 | 920 | 18.1 | 460 | 25.2 | 640 | | | * |
| Fixed spot | Selecon | Acclaim fixed | 40° | | 0.73 | T/26 650W 240v | 24,393 | 10.6 | 270 | 15.1 | 384 | 5.9 | 150 | 11.8 | 300 | 10.1 | 4.6 | * |
| Fixed spot | Selecon | Acclaim fixed | 25° | | 0.44 | T/26 650W 240v | 63,162 | 10.6 | 270 | 13.2 | 335 | 5.9 | 150 | 11.8 | 300 | 10.1 | 4.6 | * |
| Condenser zoom | Selecon | Accliam18-32 | 18°–32° | 18°–32° | 0.32–0.57 | T/26 650W 240v | 50,000/17,860 | 10.6 | 270 | 18.9 | 480 | 5.9 | 150 | 11.8 | 300 | 11.2 | 5.1 | * |
| Condenser zoom | Selecon | Acclaim wide | 24°–44° | 24°–44° | 0.43–0.81 | T/26 650W 240v | 25,004/10,716 | 10.6 | 270 | 18.9 | 480 | 5.9 | 150 | 11.8 | 300 | 11.2 | 5.1 | * |
| Zoomspots | Selecon | ZS 650 wide | 24°–40° | | 0.43–0.73 | T/26 650W 240v | 54,000/26,500 | 14.3 | 365 | 20.0 | 510 | 14.3 | 365 | 14.3 | 365 | 10.1 | 4.6 | * |
| Zoomspots | Selecon | ZS 650 | 16°–30° | | 0.28–0.54 | T/26 650W 240v | 55,500/35,600 | 14.3 | 365 | 20.0 | 510 | 14.3 | 365 | 14.3 | 365 | 10.6 | 4.8 | * |
| Zoomspots | Selecon | Acclaim 18-34 | 18°–34° | | 0.32–0.61 | T/26 650W 240v | 70,100/52,400 | 10.6 | 270 | 19.7 | 500 | 5.9 | 150 | 11.8 | 300 | 10.4 | 4.7 | * |
| Zoomspots | Selecon | Acclaim wide | 24°–44° | | 0.43–0.81 | T/26 650W 240v | 78,600/40,500 | 10.6 | 270 | 19.7 | 500 | 5.9 | 150 | 11.8 | 300 | 10.4 | 4.7 | * |
| Condenser | Selecon | Condensor 1200 | 12°–28° | | 0.21–0.50 | T/29 1.2kW 240v | 279,000/75,600 | 10.6 | 270 | 29.1 | 740 | 8.4 | 214 | 17.7 | 450 | 28.9 | 13.1 | * |
| Zoomspots wide | Selecon | ZS 1200 | 22°–40° | | 0.39–0.73 | T/29 1.2kW 240v | 160,000/95,000 | 10.6 | 270 | 28.9 | 735 | 8.4 | 214 | 17.7 | 450 | 24.3 | 11.0 | * |
| Zoomspots medium | Selecon | ZS 1200 | 18°–34° | | 0.32–0.61 | T/29 1.2kW 240v | 205,000/147,000 | 10.6 | 270 | 28.9 | 735 | 8.4 | 214 | 17.7 | 450 | 24.3 | 11.0 | * |
| Zoomspots narrow | Selecon | ZS 1200 | 8°–16° | | 0.14–0.28 | T/29 1.2kW 240v | 310,000/147,000 | 10.6 | 270 | 37.3 | 950 | 8.4 | 214 | 17.7 | 450 | 27.6 | 12.5 | * |
| Zoomspots wide | Selecon | Arena ZS 2500 | 20°–37° | | 0.35–0.67 | CP 91 2.5kW 240v | 298,900/98,000 | 14.3 | 365 | 37.7 | 960 | 11.7 | 297 | 19.3 | 490 | 43.4 | 19.7 | * |
| Zoomspots medium | Selecon | Arena ZS 2500 | 14°–32° | | 0.25–0.57 | CP 91 2.5kW 240v | 509,600/122,500 | 14.3 | 365 | 37.7 | 960 | 11.7 | 297 | 19.3 | 490 | 43.4 | 19.7 | * |
| Zoomspots narrow | Selecon | Arena ZS 2500 | 9°–18° | | 0.16–0.32 | CP 91 2.5kW 240v | 661,000/401,800 | 14.3 | 365 | 46.0 | 1170 | 11.7 | 297 | 19.3 | 490 | 44.8 | 20.3 | * |
| Zoom profile | Spotlight | SS 500 | 12°–29° | 12°–29° | 0.21–0.52 | T/26 625W 220v | 62,000/40,000 | 8.1 | 205 | 19.1 | 485 | 6.3 | 160 | 14.1 | 360 | 12.8 | 5.8 | * |
| Zoom profile | Spotlight | fi 05 ZW "Sintesi" | 23°–40° | 23°–40° | 0.41–0.73 | CP 89 650W 220v | 49,000/33,000 | 8.8 | 225 | 15.3 | 390 | 5.9 | 150 | 11.0 | 280 | 8.4 | 3.8 | * |
| Zoom profile | Spotlight | fi 05 ZS "Sintesi" | 14°–30° | 14°–30° | 0.25–0.54 | CP 89 650W 220v | 80,000/44,000 | 8.8 | 225 | 19.7 | 500 | 5.9 | 150 | 11.0 | 280 | 10.1 | 4.6 | * |
| Zoom profile | Spotlight | SS 1000 | 12°–27° | 12°–27° | 0.21–0.48 | CP 63 1kW 220v | 200,000/90,000 | 10.6 | 270 | 25.5 | 650 | 7.7 | 195 | 17.1 | 435 | 19.4 | 8.8 | * |
| Zoom profile | Spotlight | fi 12 ZW "Sintesi" | 24°–50° | 24°–50° | 0.43–0.93 | CP 90 1.2kW 220v | 168,000/48,000 | 10.2 | 260 | 22.6 | 575 | 7.9 | 200 | 14.9 | 380 | 15.4 | 7.0 | * |
| Zoom profile | Spotlight | fi 12 ZS "Sintesi" | 13°–35° | 13°–35° | 0.23–0.63 | CP 90 1.2kW 220v | 180,000/72,000 | 10.2 | 260 | 28.5 | 725 | 7.9 | 200 | 14.9 | 380 | 22.1 | 10.0 | * |
| Zoom profile | Spotlight | SS 2000 | 11°–26° | 11°–26° | 0.19–0.46 | CP 72 2kW 220v | 330,000/150,000 | 12.6 | 320 | 39.1 | 995 | 10.2 | 260 | 20.8 | 530 | 37.0 | 16.8 | * |
| Zoom profile | Spotlight | fi 25 ZW "Sintesi" | 17°–36° | 17°–36° | 0.30–0.65 | CP 91 2.5kW 220v | 260,000/130,000 | 13.4 | 340 | 43.6 | 1110 | 11.5 | 293 | 21.6 | 550 | 52.9 | 24.0 | * |
| Zoom profile | Spotlight | fi 25 ZS "Sintesi" | 9°–25° | 9°–25° | 0.16–0.44 | CP 91 2.5kW 220v | 580,000/200,000 | 13.4 | 340 | 43.6 | 1110 | 11.5 | 293 | 21.6 | 550 | 52.9 | 24.0 | * |
| ERS 3.5x5 | Strand | Patt 23 | 17° | 30° | 0.54 | T17 500W 240v | 18,000 | 11.2 | 285 | 13.9 | 355 | 9.3 | 235 | 12.2 | 310 | 6.8 | 3.2 | * |
| ERS | Strand | Patt 23W | 37° | 37° | 0.67 | T1 500W 240v | 6,500 | 11.2 | 285 | 13.9 | 355 | 9.3 | 235 | 12.2 | 310 | 6.8 | 3.2 | * |
| ERS | Strand | Patt 23N | 11° | 11° | 0.19 | T17 500W 240v | 52,000 | 11.2 | 285 | 19.6 | 500 | 9.3 | 235 | 12.2 | 310 | 12.3 | 5.6 | * |
| ERS | Strand | Patt 823 | 11° | 22° | 0.39 | T17 500W 240v | 55,000 | 11.2 | 285 | 17.5 | 445 | 9.3 | 235 | 12.2 | 310 | 12.3 | 5.6 | * |
| Profile | Strand | Minim 23 | 18° | 28° | 0.50 | RSE/18 500W 240v | 23,000 | 6.5 | 165 | 12.2 | 310 | 6.3 | 160 | 9.6 | 245 | 8.5 | 3.9 | * |
| Zoom profile | Strand | Prelude 16/30 | 16.5°–33.5° | 28°–40° | 0.50–0.73 | RSE/26 650W 240v | 36,500/15,500 | 9.0 | 230 | 20.6 | 525 | 7.3 | 185 | 13.4 | 340 | 14.3 | 6.5 | * |
| Zoom profile | Strand | Prelude 28/40 | 16.5°–33.5° | 28°–40° | 0.50–0.73 | RSE/26 650W 240v | 36,500/15,500 | 9.0 | 230 | 17.1 | 435 | 7.3 | 185 | 13.4 | 340 | 13.9 | 6.3 | * |
| ERS | Strand | 2275 Quartet 25 | 11° | 19.4° | 0.34 | FRE 650W 240v | 40,958 | 9.5 | 243 | 16.7 | 424 | | 260 | 11.3 | 288 | 9.7 | 4.4 | * |
| ERS-Zoom | Strand | 2274 Quartet 22/40 | 11.3°–12.8° | 24.4°–30.6° | 0.43–0.55 | FRE 650W 240v | 42,031/24,868 | 9.5 | 243 | 18.6 | 474 | | | 11.3 | 288 | 10.6 | 4.8 | * |
| Ellipsoidal | Strand | Patt 264 | 17° | 17° | 0.30 | T4 1kW 240v | 62,500 | 9.5 | 242 | 22.2 | 565 | 11.0 | 280 | 15.5 | 395 | 16.5 | 7.5 | * |
| Ellipsoidal | Strand | Patt 764 | 14° | 20° | 0.35 | T11 1kW 240v | 82,000 | 12.4 | 315 | 24.0 | 610 | 8.5 | 220 | 16.3 | 415 | 17.8 | 8.1 | * |

| Type | Manufacturer | Unit | B/A (*=Approx) | F/A | MPF | Lamp (or lampholder type) | Peak Candela *=math approx †=flat field candela | W in 0.04 | W mm 25 | L in 0.04 | L mm 25 | H in 0.04 | H mm 25 | HY in 0.04 | HY mm 25 | Wt lb 2.2 | Wt kg 0.5 | Other lamp |
|---|---|---|---|---|---|---|---|---|---|---|---|---|---|---|---|---|---|---|
| Ellipsoidal | Strand | T spot 64 | 16° | 30° | 0.54 | T9 1kW 240v | 58,000 | 12.2 | 310 | 22.0 | 560 | 7.4 | 190 | 18.1 | 462 | 22.0 | 10.0 | * |
| Profile | Strand | Harmony 12 | 10.5° | 11.5° | 0.20 | RSE/18 1kW 240v | 145,500 | 11.6 | 295 | 25.3 | 645 | 9.0 | 230 | 19.7 | 500 | 25.4 | 11.5 | * |
| Zoom profile | Strand | Harmony 15/28 | 9.5°–27.5° | 15°–28° | 0.26–0.50 | RSE/18 1kW 240v | 145,000/34,500 | 11.6 | 295 | 25.3 | 645 | 9.0 | 230 | 19.7 | 500 | 25.8 | 11.7 | * |
| Profile | Strand | Harmony 22 | 9.5°/20° | 23° | 0.41 | RSE/18 1kW 240v | 109,000 | 11.6 | 295 | 22.6 | 575 | 9.0 | 230 | 19.7 | 500 | 24.5 | 11.1 | * |
| Zoom profile | Strand | Harmony 22/40 | 14°–36.5° | 22°–42° | 0.39–0.77 | RSE/18 1kW 240v | 94,000/23,250 | 11.6 | 295 | 22.6 | 575 | 9.0 | 230 | 19.7 | 500 | 24.9 | 11.3 | * |
| ERS-Zoom | Strand | 2271 Cantata | 10.9°–13.5° | 11°–26° | 0.19–0.46 | FEL 1kW 120v | 248,000/134,000 | 11.8 | 300 | 36.1 | 917 | 9.5 | 240 | 16.5 | 420 | 28.2 | 12.8 | |
| ERS-Zoom | Strand | 2272 Cantata | 12.5°–17.1° | 18°–32° | 0.32–0.57 | FEL 1kW 120v | 171,000/80,000 | 11.8 | 300 | 30.4 | 772 | 9.5 | 240 | 16.5 | 420 | 26.4 | 12.0 | |
| ERS-Zoom | Strand | 2273 Cantata | 18.3°–23.4° | 26°–44° | 0.46–0.81 | FEL 1kW 120v | 88,000/48,000 | 11.8 | 300 | 26.3 | 420 | 9.5 | 240 | 16.5 | 420 | 24.2 | 11.0 | |
| Ellipsoidal | Strand | Leko 2215 | 8.5°/12.5° | 14°/15° | 0.25/0.26 | FEL 1kW 120v | 192,000 | 11.7 | 300 | 26.7 | 680 | 11.7 | 300 | | | 13.2 | 6.0 | |
| Ellipsoidal | Strand | Leko 2220 | 11.5°/13.5° | 21°/21° | 0.37 | FEL 1kW 120v | 186,000 | 11.7 | 300 | 22.2 | 565 | 11.7 | 300 | | | 12.8 | 5.8 | |
| Ellipsoidal | Strand | Leko 2230 | 12.5°/15.5° | 23°/30° | 0.41/0.54 | FEL 1kW 120v | 150,000 | 11.7 | 300 | 21.0 | 535 | 11.7 | 300 | | | 12.3 | 5.6 | |
| Ellipsoidal | Strand | Leko 2240 | 14.5°/15.5° | 28°/38° | 0.5/0.69 | FEL 1kW 120v | 118,000 | 11.7 | 300 | 18.7 | 475 | 11.7 | 300 | | | 12.3 | 5.6 | |
| Ellipsoidal | Strand | Leko 2250 | 23.5°/24.5° | 39°/53° | 0.71/1.0 | FEL 1kW 120v | 63,000 | 11.7 | 300 | 17.2 | 435 | 11.7 | 300 | | | 11.9 | 5.4 | |
| ERS-Zoom | Strand | Leko 2206 | 10°–24° | 15°–40° | 0.26–0.73 | FEL 1kW 120v | 204,000/50,000 | 12.3 | 311 | 27.0 | 686 | 7.5 | 191 | 18.0 | 457 | 23.7 | 10.8 | * |
| Zoom profile | Strand | Optique 8/17 | 6.6°–11.1° | 6.9°–17° | 0.12–0.30 | T29 1.2kW 120v | 394,900/114,520 | 11.8 | 300 | 29.7 | 755 | 11.8 | 300 | 16.1 | 410 | 34.0 | 15.6 | |
| Zoom profile | Strand | Optique 8/17 | 6.7°–11.9° | 11.7°–17.7° | 0.21–0.31 | T29 1.2kW 240/220v | 334,000/103,550 | 11.8 | 300 | 29.7 | 755 | 11.8 | 300 | 16.1 | 410 | 34.0 | 15.6 | |
| Zoom profile | Strand | Optique 15/42 | 10.7°–22.3° | 17.7°–41.2° | 0.31–0.75 | T29 1.2kW 120v | 121,690/25,860 | 11.8 | 300 | 25.5 | 648 | 11.8 | 300 | 16.1 | 410 | 34.0 | 15.6 | |
| Zoom profile | Strand | Optique 15/42 | 10.8°–22.7° | 14.9°–41.2° | 0.26–0.75 | T29 1.2kW 240/220v | 120,500/24,860 | 11.8 | 300 | 25.5 | 648 | 11.8 | 300 | 16.1 | 410 | 34.0 | 15.6 | |
| Zoom profile | Strand | Cadenza 9/15 | 8°–13.5° | 9°–15° | 0.16–0.26 | RSE/79 2kW 240v | 565,000/248,000 | 14.5 | 370 | 38.7 | 985 | 14.5 | 370 | 19.1 | 485 | 52.9 | 24.0 | |
| Zoom profile | Strand | Cadenza 12/22 | 7°–16.5° | 12°–22° | 0.21–0.39 | RSE/79 2kW 240v | 432,000/180,000 | 14.5 | 370 | 34.6 | 880 | 14.5 | 370 | 19.1 | 485 | 50.3 | 22.8 | |
| Zoom profile | Strand | Cadenza 19/32 | 17°–26° | 19°–32° | 0.33–0.57 | RSE/79 2kW 240v | 382,500/184,400 | 14.5 | 370 | 31.0 | 790 | 14.5 | 370 | 19.1 | 485 | 49.0 | 22.2 | |
| Zoom profile | Strand | Alto 8/16 | 6°–6.5° | 8°–16° | 0.14–0.28 | 2kW 240v | 584,000/544,000 | 14.1 | 360 | 41.1 | 1045 | 11.4 | 290 | 18.1 | 460 | 52.0 | 23.7 | * |
| Zoom profile | Strand | Alto 14/32 | 8°–16° | 14°–32° | 0.25–0.57 | 2kW 240v | 328,000/124,000 | 14.1 | 360 | 39.1 | 995 | 11.4 | 290 | 18.1 | 460 | 53.0 | 24.0 | * |
| Zoom profile | Strand | Alto 20/38 | 12°–19° | 20°–38° | 0.35–0.69 | 2kW 240v | 158,000/54,000 | 14.1 | 360 | 31.6 | 805 | 11.4 | 290 | 18.1 | 460 | 47.8 | 21.7 | * |
| Zoom profile | Strand | Toccata 10/26 | 7.6°–17.4° | 10°–26° | 0.18–0.46 | CP91 2.5kW 240/230v | 641,000/125,000 | 14.9 | 380 | 35.0 | 890 | 14.9 | 380 | 24.0 | 610 | 45.2 | 20.5 | * |
| Zoom profile | Strand | Toccata 15/38 | 13°–26° | 15°–38° | 0.26–0.69 | CP91 2.5kW 240/230v | 334,000/70,000 | 14.9 | 380 | 30.7 | 780 | 14.9 | 380 | 24.0 | 610 | 43.7 | 19.8 | * |
| ERS – Zoom | Strand Century | 2205 Leko | 16°–20° | 25°–50° | 0.44–0.93 | EVR 500W 120v | 26,000/14,000 | 8.8 | 222 | 20.5 | 521 | 8.8 | 222 | 15.0 | 381 | 15.0 | 6.8 | |
| ERS 4.5x6.5 | Strand Century | 2204 Leko | 21° | 44° | 0.81 | FEL 1kW 120v | 82,400 | 12.0 | 305 | 18.0 | 457 | 12.0 | 305 | 24.0 | 610 | 15.5 | 7.0 | |
| ERS 6x9 | Strand Century | 2209 Leko | 17° | 31° | 0.55 | FEL 1kW 120v | 151,800 | 12.0 | 305 | 18.0 | 457 | 12.0 | 305 | 24.0 | 610 | 17.0 | 7.7 | |
| ERS 6x16 | Strand Century | 2216/7 Leko | 7° | 17° | 0.30 | FEL 1kW 120v | 314,400 | 12.0 | 305 | 19.3 | 489 | 12.0 | 305 | 24.0 | 610 | 16.0 | 7.3 | |
| ERS 10x23 | Strand Century | 2123/4 Leko | 6° | 9° | 0.16 | FEL 1kW 120v | 878,000 | 12.0 | 305 | 36.0 | 914 | 12.0 | 305 | 25.0 | 635 | 24.5 | 11.1 | |
| ERS 8x13 | Strand Century | 2113/4 Leko | 7° | 12° | 0.21 | FEL 1kW 120v | 585,400 | 12.0 | 305 | 29.0 | 737 | 12.0 | 305 | 24.0 | 610 | 17.0 | 7.7 | |
| ERS 6x12 | Strand Century | 2111/12 Leko | 9° | 14° | 0.25 | FEL 1kW 120v | 303,500 | 12.0 | 305 | 23.8 | 603 | 12.0 | 305 | 24.0 | 610 | 15.5 | 7.0 | |
| ERS 6x12 | Strand Century | 2212/213 Leko | 11° | 25° | 0.44 | FEL 1kW 120v | 271,000 | 12.0 | 305 | 18.0 | 457 | 12.0 | 305 | 24.0 | 610 | 16.0 | 7.3 | |
| Profile | Teatro | Comma 26 | 12.8° | 28° | 0.50 | T27 650W 220v | 45,937 | 14.3 | 365 | 16.5 | 420 | 14.3 | 365 | 14.9 | 380 | 9.9 | 4.5 | |
| Zoom profile | Teatro | Comma 16/28 | 10°–16° | 16°–28° | 0.28–0.5 | T27 650W 220v | 39,000/38,300 | 14.3 | 365 | 22.0 | 560 | 14.3 | 365 | 14.9 | 380 | 10.1 | 4.6 | |
| Zoom profile | Teatro | Comma 22/35 | 14°–17° | 22°–35° | 0.39–0.63 | T27 650W 220v | 36,000/23,700 | 14.3 | 365 | 19.7 | 500 | 14.3 | 365 | 14.9 | 380 | 9.7 | 4.4 | |
| Zoom profile | Teatro | Comma 37/48 | 16.2°–18.6° | 36°–47° | 0.65–0.87 | T27 650W 220v | 25,725/20,212 | 14.3 | 365 | 16.5 | 420 | 14.3 | 365 | 14.9 | 380 | 10.4 | 4.7 | |
| Zoom profile | Teatro | Tipo 15/28 | 7°–12° | 15°–28° | 0.26–0.5 | CP70 1kW 220v | 203,200/58,400 | 13.9 | 354 | 32.6 | 830 | 13.9 | 354 | 16.7 | 425 | 26.9 | 12.2 | |

| Type | Manufacturer | Unit | B/A (*=Approx) | F/A | MPF | Lamp (or lampholder type) | Peak Candela (*=math approx, †=flat field candela) | W in (0.04) | W mm (25) | L in (0.04) | L mm (25) | H in (0.04) | H mm (25) | HY in (0.04) | HY mm (25) | Wt lb (2.2) | Wt kg (0.5) | Other lamp |
|---|---|---|---|---|---|---|---|---|---|---|---|---|---|---|---|---|---|---|
| Zoom profile | Teatro | Tipo 22/40 | 13°–18° | 22°–44° | 0.39–0.81 | CP70 1kW 220v | 92,000/39,300 | 13.9 | 354 | 29.0 | 738 | 13.9 | 354 | 16.7 | 425 | 24.9 | 11.3 | * |
| Profile | Teatro | Tratto 2 12 | 7° | 12° | 0.21 | CP93 1.2kW 220v | 258,600 | 11.2 | 285 | 32.8 | 835 | 11.2 | 285 | 16.5 | 420 | 28.2 | 12.8 | * |
| Zoom profile | Teatro | Tratto 2 15/28 | 8.5°–12° | 15°–28° | 0.26–0.5 | CP93 1.2kW 220v | 239,700/68,900 | 11.2 | 285 | 32.8 | 835 | 11.2 | 285 | 16.5 | 420 | 28.0 | 12.7 | * |
| Zoom profile | Teatro | Tratto 2 22/40 | 13°–18° | 22°–44° | 0.39–0.81 | CP93 1.2kW 220v | 108,600/46,400 | 11.2 | 285 | 29.1 | 740 | 11.2 | 285 | 16.5 | 420 | 26.2 | 11.9 | * |
| Zoom profile | Teatro | Acuto 9/15 | 6.5°–9° | 9°–15° | 0.16–0.26 | CP72 2kW 220v | 401,200/325,900 | 14.3 | 365 | 44.9 | 1142 | 14.3 | 365 | 21.9 | 557 | 54.7 | 24.8 | |
| Zoom profile | Teatro | Acuto 12/22 | 8°–9° | 12°–22° | 0.21–0.39 | CP72 2kW 220v | 367,300/230,000 | 14.3 | 365 | 39.7 | 1010 | 14.3 | 365 | 21.9 | 557 | 50.3 | 22.8 | |
| Zoom profile | Teatro | Acuto 19/32 | 9°–12° | 19°–32° | 0.33–0.57 | CP72 2kW 220v | 312,800/181,000 | 14.3 | 365 | 30.5 | 776 | 14.3 | 365 | 21.9 | 557 | 45.9 | 20.8 | * |
| Low-volt profile | Times Square | MR 35 T | | 28°–50° * | 0.5–0.93 | MR 11 AK530 50W 12v | 900/500* | 5.0 | 127 | 6.8 | 171 | | | 7.0 | 178 | 1.0 | 0.5 | * |
| Low-volt profile | Times Square | MR 75 Z | | 28°–50° * | 0.5–0.93 | EYI 75W 12v | 6,300/5,400* | 7.2 | 182 | 8.8 | 222 | | | 10.5 | 267 | | | * |
| ERS 3.5 | Times Square | Q 325 | 30°–50° | | 0.54–0.93 | EHV 325w 120v | 36,000/27,000* | 10.0 | 254 | 12.0 | 305 | | | 10.8 | 273 | 5.0 | 2.3 | * |
| ERS 3.5 Zoom | Times Square | Q3Z | 25°–40° | | 0.44–0.73 | EVR 500W 120v | 33,000/26,800* | 12.5 | 318 | 18.0 | 457 | | | 13.0 | 330 | 8.0 | 3.6 | * |
| ERS 4.5 Zoom | Times Square | Q4Z | 30°–50° | | 0.54–0.93 | EVR 500W 120v | 28,000/17,500* | 15.0 | 381 | 19.0 | 483 | | | 13.0 | 330 | 8.0 | 3.6 | * |
| ERS-Zoom | Times Square | Q4W | | 32°/40°/48° | 0.57/0.73/0.89 | EVR 500W 120v | 40,400/29,500/26,000 | | | | | | | | | | | |
| ERS 4.5 Zoom | Times Square | Q4Z Narrow | 15°–30° | | 0.26–0.54 | EVR 500W 120v | 67,000/27,600* | 15.0 | 381 | 22.0 | 559 | | | 13.0 | 330 | 9.0 | 4.1 | * |
| ERS 3.5x6 | Times Square | Q3 Wide | | 40° | 0.73 | FAD 650W 120v | | | | | | | | | | | | * |
| ERS 3.5x8 | Times Square | Q3 Medium | | 30° | 0.54 | FAD 650W 120v | | | | | | | | | | | | * |
| ERS 3.5x? | Times Square | Q3 Narrow | | 13° | 0.23 | FAD 650W 120v | | | | | | | | | | | | * |
| ERS 8x? | Times Square | 8EPC | | 19° | 0.33 | T12/9 750W 120v | | | | | | | | | | | | * |
| ERS 8x? | Times Square | Q8EPC | | 15° | 0.26 | EH6 750W 120v | | | | | | | | | | | | * |
| ERS 6x9 | Times Square | 6E6x9 | | 42° | 0.77 | E6G 750W 120v | | | | | | | | | | | | * |
| ERS 6x9 | Times Square | 06E6x9 | | 44° | 0.81 | EH6 750W 120v | | | | | | | | | | | | * |
| ERS 6x12 | Times Square | 6E6x12 | | 30° | 0.54 | E6G 750W 120v | | | | | | | | | | | | * |
| ERS 6x12 | Times Square | 06E6x12 | | 30° | 0.54 | EH6 750W 120v | | | | | | | | | | | | * |
| ERS 6x16 | Times Square | 6E6x16 | | 17° | 0.30 | E6G 750W 120v | | | | | | | | | | | | * |
| ERS 6x16 | Times Square | 06E6x16 | | 20° | 0.35 | EH6 750W 120v | | | | | | | | | | | | * |
| ERS 6x9 | Times Square | 06x9 | | 30° | 0.54 | FEL 1kW 120v | 104,000 | | | | | | | | | | | * |
| ERS 6x12 | Times Square | 06x12 | | 30° | 0.54 | FEL 1kW 120v | 131,200 | | | | | | | | | | | * |
| ERS 6x16 | Times Square | 06x16 | | 18° | 0.32 | FEL 1kW 120v | 135,000 | | | | | | | | | | | * |
| ERS 6x22 | Times Square | 06x22 | 12° | | 0.21 | FEL 1kW 120v | 230,000 | 15.0 | 381 | 26.0 | 660 | | | 14.3 | 362 | 18.0 | 8.2 | * |
| ERS 6-Zoom | Times Square | 06Z | 20°–40° | | 0.35–0.73 | FEL 1kW 120v | 280,000/148,000* | 15.0 | 381 | 25.5 | 648 | | | 19.3 | 489 | 20.0 | 9.1 | * |
| ERS 6-Zoom | Times Square | 06Z35 | 30°–55° | | 0.54–1.04 | FEL 1kW 120v | 197,000/95,000* | 15.0 | 381 | 20.5 | 521 | | | 19.3 | 489 | 17.0 | 7.7 | * |
| ERS-Zoom | Times Square | 06V | 30°/40°/50° | | 0.54/0.73/0.93 | FEL 1kW 120v | 192,000/145,000/92,500 | | | | | | | | | | | |
| ERS-Zoom | Times Square | 06Z | | 20°–40° | 0.35–0.73 | FEL 1kW 120v | 280,000/91,200 | | | | | | | | | | | * |
| Fixed profile | Zero 88 | Focus 650 | 26° | | 0.46 | 650W/500W 240v | | 12.3 | 314 | 15.3 | 390 | 12.3 | 314 | 13.5 | 344 | 7.9 | 3.6 | |
| Zoom profile | Zero 88 | Focus 650 21-36 | 21°–36° | | 0.37–0.65 | 650W/500W 240v | | 12.3 | 314 | 17.4 | 442 | 12.3 | 314 | 13.5 | 344 | 7.9 | 3.6 | * |
| Zoom profile | Zero 88 | Focus 650 30-45 | 30°–45° | | 0.54–0.83 | 650W/500W 240v | | 12.3 | 314 | 14.1 | 360 | 12.3 | 314 | 13.5 | 344 | 7.1 | 3.2 | * |
| Source 4 jnr | ETC | 26°, 36°, 50° | 17° | 26° | 0.46 | HPL 575/115v | 92,000 | 9.6 | 240 | 19.2 | 490 | | | 13.6 | 350 | 9.3 | 4.2 | |
| Source 4 zoom | ETC | 15°–30° | 15° | 23° | 0.41 | HPL 750/115v | 202,000 | 13 | 342 | 29 | 749 | | | 18 | 455 | 21 | 7.6 | |
| Source 4 zoom | ETC | 25°–50° | 25° | 36° | 0.65 | HPL 750/115v | 96,000 | 13 | 342 | 29 | 749 | | | 18 | 455 | 21 | 7.6 | * |

Follow spots are effectively very long throw profile-type spots primarily used to follow artists about the stage. The big brutes are used from the rear of a large auditorium or around a stadium in a music concert, the short stubby ones are used for small theatres, from sides of the auditorium or onstage. Note that low-voltage beam projectors, such as those manufactured by Reiche & Vogel, are also an excellent soft-edge follow spot, particularly for side and back follow-spotting.

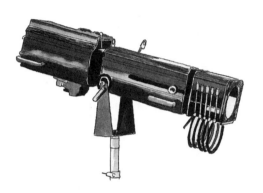

*38. Teatro Talento 1200MSR*

*39. Robert Juliat HMI 2,500W*

*40. Strong Xenon Super Trouper*

*41. Strand 2kW Solo*

| Manufacturer | Type | min. spot with Iris (* = approx) | B/A (spot) beam spread (* = approx) | MPF | Lamp | Peak Candela (* = math approx) | W in (0.04) | W mm (25) | L in (0.04) | L mm (25) | H in not incl stand (0.04) | H mm not incl stand (25) | Wt lb lamphouse only (2.2) | Wt kg lamphouse only (0.5) | lamp type | color frames |
|---|---|---|---|---|---|---|---|---|---|---|---|---|---|---|---|---|
| ADB | PRH 12 | | 6.5°–10.5° | 0.11–0.18 | HMI 1.2kW 220v | | 14.1 | 360 | 48.5 | 1235 | 15.5 | 394 | 61.7 | 28.0 | discharge | |
| ADB/Niethammer | MVU 118 | | up to 18° | max 0.32 | HMI 1.2kW 220v | 520,000 | 14.9 | 380 | 38.1 | 970 | 27.5 | 700 | | | discharge | |
| ADB/Niethammer | MVU 113 | | up to 13° | max 0.23 | HMI 1.2kW 220v | 1,100,000 | 14.9 | 380 | 42.1 | 1070 | 27.5 | 700 | | | discharge | |
| ADB/Niethammer | MZU 106 | | 6°–17° | 0.10–0.30 | HMI 1.2kW 220v | 2,600,000/360,000 | 14.9 | 380 | 55.4 | 1410 | 27.5 | 700 | | | discharge | 4 |
| ADB/Niethammer | HVU 218 | | up to 18° | max 0.32 | GY16 2kW 220v | 320,000 | 14.9 | 380 | 38.1 | 970 | 27.5 | 700 | 79.4 | 36.0 | incandescent | 4 |
| ADB/Niethammer | HVU 213 | | up to 13° | max 0.23 | GY16 2kW 220v | 600,000 | 14.9 | 380 | 42.1 | 1070 | 27.5 | 700 | 86.0 | 39.0 | incandescent | 4 |
| ADB/Niethammer | HVU 208 | | up to 8° | max 0.14 | GY16 2kW 220v | 1,200,000 | 14.9 | 380 | 51.9 | 1320 | 27.5 | 700 | 99.2 | 45.0 | incandescent | 4 |
| ADB/Niethammer | HZU 208 | | 8°–17° | 0.14–0.30 | GY16 2kW 220v | 1,200,000/450,000 | 14.9 | 380 | 51.9 | 1320 | 27.5 | 700 | 100.8 | 45.7 | incandescent | 4 |
| Altman | Orbiter short throw | | 1.5°–18° | 0.02–0.32 | GE Marc HID 350W 120v | 1,200,000/240,000 | 14.5 | 368 | 44.0 | 1118 | 18.0 | 457 | 83.0 | 37.6 | discharge | 6 |
| Altman | MARC 350 | | 1.3°–18° | 0.02–0.32 | GE Marc HID 350W 120v | 2,480,000/400,000 | 20.0 | 508 | 29.0 | 737 | 20.3 | 514 | | | discharge | 6 |
| Altman | Orbiter long throw | | 1°–8° | 0.018–0.14 | GE Marc HID 350W 120v | 12,750,000/2,000,000 | 14.5 | 368 | 44.0 | 1118 | 18.0 | 457 | 83.0 | 37.6 | discharge | 6 |
| Altman | Comet | 2.3° | 7.2°–12.2° | 0.13–0.21 | FLE(MR16) 360W 82v | 800,000/330,000 | 17.5 | 445 | 34.5 | 876 | 17.0 | 432 | 91.5 | 41.5 | incandescent | 6 |
| Altman | Voyager short throw | 0.5° | 4°–9.5° | 0.07–0.18 | Osram HTI 400W 120v | 2,500,000/600,000 | 12.3 | 311 | 50.0 | 1270 | 15.5 | 394 | 85.0 | 38.6 | discharge | 6 |
| Altman | Voyager long throw | 0.5° | 4°–9.5° | 0.07–0.18 | Osram HTI 400W 120v | 8,500,000/2,500,000 | 12.3 | 311 | 50.0 | 1270 | 15.5 | 394 | 85.0 | 38.6 | discharge | 6 |
| Altman | Satellite 1 | 1.8° | 7.3°–20° | 0.13–0.35 | Osram HMI 575W 120v | 2,400,000/530,000 | 13.0 | 330 | 46.0 | 1168 | 16.0 | 406 | 69.0 | 31.3 | discharge | 6 |
| Altman | 1000Q | 1.5° | 8.5°–13° | 0.18–0.25 | FEL 1kW 120v | 412,000/215,000 | 17.5 | 445 | 42.0 | 1067 | 24.0 | 610 | 93.5 | 42.4 | incandescent | 6 |
| Altman | Explorer long throw | | 5.7°–7° | 0.10–0.12 | Osram HMI 1.2kW 120v | 7,500,000/6,750,000 | 18.0 | 457 | 50.0 | 1260 | 33.0 | 580 | 90.0 | 40.8 | discharge | 6 |
| Altman | Explorer medium throw | | 5.25°–10.9° | 0.09–0.19 | Osram HMI 1.2kW 120v | 1,170,000/275,000 | 16.5 | 419 | 50.0 | 1260 | | | 90.4 | 41.0 | discharge | 6 |
| Altman | Explorer short throw | 2.86° | 18.2° | 0.32 | Osram HMI 1.2kW 120v | 540,000 | 17.0 | 432 | 37.0 | 940 | | | 78.0 | 35.4 | discharge | 6 |
| Altman | 902lr | 1.9° | 23°–25° | 0.59–0.83 | DTJ 1.5kW 120v | 36,000/20,000 | 16.0 | 406 | 26.5 | 673 | 16.0 | 406 | 53.5 | 24.3 | incandescent | 1 |
| Altman | 902 | 1.9° | 23°–25° | 0.59–0.83 | DTJ 1.5kW 120v | 54,000/34,000 | 16.0 | 406 | 35.0 | 889 | 16.0 | 406 | 72.5 | 32.9 | incandescent | 6 |
| Altman | Dyna Spot | 1.5° | 14° | 0.33–0.41 | DTJ 1.5kW 120v | 137,500/103,125 | 16.0 | 406 | 35.0 | 889 | 23.0 | 584 | 74.5 | 33.8 | incandescent | 6 |
| AVAB | MZU256 | | 6°–17° | 0.10–0.30 | 2599 HMI | 4,375,000 | | | | | | | | | discharge | |
| Ariel Davis | 3100 | | 0.9°–12° | 0.21 | PAR64 NSP 500W | 55,000 | | | | | | | | | incandescent | 7 |
| Capitol | Mk 111 | | 8.5° | 0.15 | QT8 C13D 1.5kW 120v | | | | | | | | | | incandescent | 6 |
| Century | 1064 | | 11° | 0.26 | PAR64 1kW 28v | 193,500 | | | | | | | | | incandescent | 1 |
| Century | 4481 | | 7.5°–11.5° | 0.23–0.43 | FEL 1kW 120v | 379,800/181,800 | | | | | | | | | incandescent | 6 |
| Coemar | Testa 575W MSR | 1.6° * | 3.25° * | 0.13 | MSR 575W | 691,875 | 14.0 | 355 | 40.9 | 1040 | 16.7 | 425 | 60.6 | 27.5 | discharge | 1/multi |
| Coemar | Testa 1000W | 1.6° * | 3.25° * | 0.13 | Halogen 1kW | 669,375 | 14.0 | 355 | 35.8 | 910 | 16.7 | 425 | 59.5 | 27.0 | incandescent | 1/multi |
| Coemar | Testa 1200W MSR | 2.1° * | 6.4° * | 0.22 | MSR 1.2kW | 3,195,000 | 14.0 | 355 | 40.9 | 1040 | 16.7 | 425 | 40.1 | 18.2 | discharge | 1/multi |
| Coemar | Testa 2000W | 1.6° * | 2.1° * | 0.9 | Halogen 2kW | 1,366,875 | 14.0 | 355 | 40.9 | 1040 | 16.7 | 425 | 45.2 | 20.5 | incandescent | 1/multi |
| Coemar | Testa 2500W HMI | 2.1° * | 6.4° * | 0.26 | HMI 2.5kW | 8,145,000 | 19.7 | 500 | 54.2 | 1380 | 24.0 | 610 | 91.1 | 41.3 | discharge | 1/multi |
| Colortran | LQFS-1 | | 0.9°–13.4° | 0.017–0.24 | BPS10-32 1kW 120v | 290,000 | | | | | | | | | incandescent | |
| Colortran | 210-011/12/17 | 0.72° | 9°–9.9°20° | 0.16–0.16±0.35 | FEL1kW 120v | 800,000/280,000 | 32.0 | 810 | 35.0 | 890 | | | | | incandescent | 1 |
| Colortran | 210-200 | 1.03° | 6.9°–22.6° | 0.12–0.40 | Xenon 2kW 120v | 3,460,000/316,000 | 20.0 | 508 | 66.0 | 1676 | 21.0 | 533 | 240.0 | 108.9 | discharge | 6 |
| Colortran | 210-100 | 0.53° | 3.5°–8° | 0.06–0.14 | Xenon 2kW 120v | 13,770,000/2,400,000 | 20.0 | 508 | 66.0 | 1676 | 21.0 | 533 | 240.0 | 108.9 | discharge | 6 |
| Robert Juliat | Pixie 1010R | | 8°–13° | 0.14–0.23 | HMI GS 575W 220v | 1500 Lux at 3m∅ beam | 13.6 | 345 | 31.4 | 800 | 13.0 | 330 | 46.3 | 21.0 | discharge | 6 |
| Robert Juliat | Korrigan 1011 | | 5°–9° | 0.09–0.16 | HMI GS 1.2kW 220v | 2300 Lux at 3m∅ beam | 14.7 | 375 | 47.2 | 1200 | 13.8 | 350 | 63.9 | 29.0 | discharge | 6 |
| Robert Juliat | Puck 1012 | | 15°–30° | 0.26–0.54 | HMI GS 1.2kW 220v | | 14.7 | 375 | 37.1 | 945 | 13.8 | 350 | 63.9 | 29.0 | discharge | 6 |
| Robert Juliat | Ivanhoe 1039 | | 9.5°–20.5° | 0.17–0.35 | HMI G38 2.5kW 220v | 4600 Lux at 3m∅ beam | 14.9 | 380 | 47.2 | 1200 | 17.7 | 450 | | | discharge | 6 |

| Manufacturer | Type | min. spot with Iris (*=approx) | B/A (spot) beam spread (*=approx) | MPF | Lamp | Peak Candela (*=math approx) | W in (0.04) | W mm (25) | L in (0.04) | L mm (25) | H in not incl stand (0.04) | H mm stand (25) | Wt lb lamphouse only (2.2) | Wt kg (0.5) | lamp type | color frames |
|---|---|---|---|---|---|---|---|---|---|---|---|---|---|---|---|---|
| Robert Juliat | Aramis 1013 | | 4.5°–8° | 0.08–0.14 | HMI W/S 2.5kW 220v | 5000 Lux at 3mB beam | 17.7 | 450 | 57.0 | 1450 | 12.6 | 320 | 114.7 | 52.0 | discharge 6 | |
| Robert Juliat | Heliose 1439 | | 16°–29° | 0.28–0.51 | HMI G38 2.5kW 220v | 5000 Lux at 3mB beam | 14.9 | 380 | 39.1 | 995 | 16.7 | 425 | 70.6 | 32.0 | discharge 6 | |
| Kliegl | 1393 | | 6° | 0.1 | DWT 1kW 120v | 950,000 | | | | | | | | | incandescent | 5 |
| Kliegl | 1174/1175 | | 4°–13° | 0.07–0.23 | T30/G13D 2kW 120v | | | | | | | | | | incandescent | 1 |
| Kliegl | 1178/1179 | | 3.5°–11.5° | 0.06–0.20 | 3M T30/G13D 3kW 120v | 900,000/500,000 | | | | | | | | | incandescent | 1 or 5 |
| L & E | 64-10 Mini | | 17°–22.6° | 0.3–0.39 | DYS 600W 120v | 59,000/35,000 | 10.5 | 267 | 23.0 | 584 | 8.8 | 222 | 13.0 | 5.9 | incandescent | 1 or 6 |
| L & E | 64-10 Mini + charger | | 17°–22.6° | 0.3–0.39 | FLK 600W 120v | 105,000/67,200 | 10.5 | 267 | 23.0 | 584 | 8.8 | 222 | | | incandescent | 1 or 6 |
| L & E | 64-14 Commander | | 12°–18° | 0.21–0.32 | FEL 1kW 120v | 338,000/101,000 | 12.0 | 305 | 33.3 | 845 | 15.0 | 381 | 46.0 | 20.9 | incandescent | 7 |
| L & E | 64-14 Commander | | 8°–13.3° | 0.14–0.23 | FEL 1kW 120v | 414,000/291,600 | 12.0 | 305 | 33.3 | 845 | 15.0 | 381 | 46.0 | 20.9 | incandescent | 7 |
| Lycian | L1264 Superarc 350 | | 2.41°–21.24° | 0.04–0.38 | EZT (Marc 350) 350W 120v | | | | | | | | | | discharge 6 | |
| Lycian | L1262 Superarc 350 | | 0.86°–6.7° | 0.015–0.12 | EZT (Marc 350) 350W 120v | | | | | | | | | | discharge 6 | |
| Lycian | 1236 Clubspot | 0.95° | 7°–14° | 0.12–0.25 | FLE(MR 16) 360W 120v | 360,000/100,800 | | | | | | | | | incandescent | 6 |
| Lycian | 1266 Superarc medium throw | 1.2° | 17° | 0.02–0.30 | HTI 400/24 400W 120v | 13,950,000/12,500,000 | | | 32.5 | 826 | 17.0 | 432 | 86.0 | 39.0 | discharge 7 | |
| Lycian | 1267 Superarc long throw | 0.45° | 8.6° | 0.01–0.15 | HTI 400/24 400W 120v | 1,450,000/680,000 | | | 50.0 | 1270 | 17.0 | 432 | 104.0 | 47.2 | discharge 7 | |
| Lycian | 1209 Midget | 0.85° | 10.3° | 0.18–0.18x0.36 | MSR/HMI 575W 120v | 400,000/180,000 | | | 37.0 | 940 | 18.0 | 457 | 78.0 | 35.4 | discharge 5 | |
| Lycian | 1206 Midget | 1° | 9° | 0.16–0.16x0.33 | FEL 1kW 120v | 436,800 | | | 32.0 | 813 | 14.0 | 356 | 40.0 | 18.1 | discharge 6 | 6 |
| Lycian | 1271 Starklite short throw | | 23.3° | 0.41 | HMI/MSR 1.2kW 120v | 928,000 | | | 29.5 | 749 | 18.5 | 470 | 60.0 | 27.2 | discharge 6 | |
| Lycian | 1271 Starklite medium throw | | 10° | 0.18 | HMI/MSR 1.2kW 120v | 1,574,400 | | | 41.0 | 1041 | 18.5 | 470 | 65.0 | 29.5 | discharge 6 | |
| Lycian | 1271 Starklite long throw | | 6.5° | 0.11 | HMI/MSR 1.2kW 120v | 1,606,400 | | | 51.5 | 1308 | 18.5 | 470 | 75.0 | 34.0 | discharge 6 | |
| Lycian | 1272 Starklite II | | 11.94° | 0.21 | HMI/MSR 1.2kW 120v | | | | 48.0 | 1219 | 19.5 | 495 | 86.0 | 39.0 | discharge 6 | |
| Lycian | 1275 Superstar | 0.47° | 3.78°–9.15° | 0.06–0.16 | HB 1.2kW 120v | 11,240,000/960,000 | | | 32.0 | 813 | 14.0 | 356 | 46.0 | 20.9 | discharge 6 | 6 |
| Lycian | 1207 Midget | 1° | 11° | 0.2–0.2x0.33 | BWA 2kW 120v | 550,800/273,000 | | | 58.0 | 1473 | 27.0 | 686 | 236.0 | 107.0 | incandescent | |
| Lycian | 1278 Superstar | 0.62° | 12.44° | 0.01–0.22 | MSR/HMI 2.5kW 120v | 13,350,000/8,500,000 | | | 23.6 | 600 | 20.2 | 515 | 32.2 | 14.6 | discharge 6 | |
| Pani | HV 2002/20 | | 7.2°–18.5° | 0.13–0.33 | Rad RH 1003P 1kW 220v | 744,000/245,985 | 14.1 | 360 | 24.8 | 630 | 22.0 | 560 | 56.0 | 25.4 | incandescent | 1 |
| Pani | HMV 1202/20 | | 12.6° | 0.22 | HMI 1200-GS 1.2kW 220v | 600,000 | 14.1 | 360 | 24.8 | 630 | 22.0 | 560 | 55.1 | 25.0 | discharge 1 | |
| Pani | HMV 1200/20 | | 10.44° | 0.18 | HMI 1.2kW 220v | 800,000 | 14.1 | 360 | 32.8 | 835 | 22.0 | 560 | 57.3 | 26.0 | discharge 1 | |
| Pani | HMV 1200/35 | | 6.28° | 0.11 | HMI 1.2kW 220v | 1,650,000 | 14.1 | 360 | 32.8 | 835 | 22.0 | 560 | 58.9 | 26.7 | discharge 1 | |
| Pani | HMV 1202/35 | | 7.4° | 0.13 | HMI 1200-GS 1.2kW 220v | 2,000,000 | 14.1 | 360 | 23.6 | 600 | 16.3 | 415 | 28.2 | 12.8 | discharge 1 | |
| Pani | HV 1001/20 | | 8°–13.3° | 0.14–0.23 | Rad RH 2003P 2kW 220v | 602,640/214,946 | 20.0 | 510 | 47.2 | 1200 | 22.4 | 570 | 165.4 | 75.0 | incandescent | 1 |
| Pani | HMV 2500 700M-CID | | 6°–16° | 0.10–0.28 | CID 2.5kW 220v | 3,900,000/1,500,000 | 20.0 | 510 | 52.9 | 1345 | 22.4 | 570 | 172.0 | 78.0 | discharge 1 | |
| Pani | HMV 2500 700M-HMI | | 5°–14° | 0.09–0.25 | HMI2500-G38 2.5kW 220v | 4,840,000/2,400,000 | 18.5 | 470 | 31.5 | 800 | 20.0 | 508 | 75.5 | 34.2 | discharge 1 | |
| Phoebus | Ultra Quartz | 0.64° | 7.6°–18.6° | 0.13–0.33 | FLE (MR-16) 360W 120v | 455,000/125,500 | 22.0 | 559 | 40.0 | 1016 | 22.2 | 564 | 128.0 | 58.1 | incandescent | 6 |
| Phoebus | UltraArc II/S short throw | 2.13° | 7.38°–21.45° | 0.13–0.38 | HTI 400W 120v | 1,020,000/230,000 | 19.5 | 495 | 33.0 | 838 | 22.5 | 572 | 97.0 | 44.0 | discharge 6 | |
| Phoebus | Mighty Arc II/S | 0.57° | 3.55°–7.25° | 0.06–0.13 | HTI 400W 120v | 3,650,000/1,350,000 | 22.0 | 559 | 56.0 | 1422 | 22.2 | 564 | 143.0 | 64.9 | discharge 6 | |
| Phoebus | UltraArc II/S long throw | 0.48° | 2.86°–9.15° | 0.05–0.16 | HTI 400W 120v | 6,500,000/720,000 | 22.0 | 559 | 56.0 | 1422 | 22.2 | 564 | 93.0 | 42.2 | discharge 6 | |
| Phoebus | UltraArc Titan long throw | | | | HMI/SE 1.2kW 120v | 7,500,000/1,600,000 | 22.0 | 559 | 40.0 | 1016 | 22.2 | 564 | 75.0 | 34.0 | discharge 6 | |
| Phoebus | UltraArc Titan short throw | | | | HMI/SE 1.2kW 120v | 1,200,000/280,000 | 22.0 | 559 | 40.0 | 1016 | 22.2 | 564 | | | discharge 6 | 1 |
| Selecon | Chorus 1200 | 0.9° | 8°–16° | 0.14–0.28 | T/29 1.2kW 240v | 310,000/147,000 | 10.6 | 270 | 40.5 | 1030 | 8.4 | 214 | 28.7 | 13.0 | incandescent | 4 |
| Selecon | Performer 1200 | 0.8° | 5.5–9.2° | 0.09–0.16 | HMI/MSR 1.2kW 240v | 3,335,175/1,603,800 | 13.5 | 344 | 46.0 | 1170 | 14.7 | 373 | 59.5 | 27.0 | discharge 6 | |
| Selecon | Performer 1200 short throw | 1.25° | 10°–15° | 0.18–0.26 | HMI/MSR 1.2kW 240v | 1,512,900/907,740 | 13.5 | 344 | 41.3 | 1050 | 14.7 | 373 | 59.5 | 27.0 | discharge 6 | |
| Seleco | Performer 2500 | 2° | 8°–14° | 0.14–0.25 | CP 91 2.5kW 240v | 504,700 | 13.5 | 344 | 43.2 | 1100 | 14.7 | 373 | 56.2 | 25.5 | incandescent | |
| Spotlight | MIP Iride (also a projector) | 2.2° | 20° (or 9° or 39°) | 0.35 | CP70 1kW 220v | 28,000 | 7.9 | 200 | 17.5 | 445 | 12.6 | 320 | 8.6 | 3.9 | incandescent | 6 |

| Manufacturer | Type | min. spot with Iris (* = approx) | B/A (spot beam spread) (* = approx) | MPF | Lamp | Peak Candela (* = math approx) | W in (0.04) | W mm (25) | L in (0.04) | L mm (25) | H in not incl stand (0.04) | H mm not incl stand (25) | Wt lb lamphouse only (2.2) | Wt kg lamphouse only (0.5) | lamp type incandescent / discharge | color frames |
|---|---|---|---|---|---|---|---|---|---|---|---|---|---|---|---|---|
| Spotlight | Vedette AS | 1.5° | 12° | 0.21 | CP63 1kW 220v | 150,000 | 7.7 | 195 | 24.4 | 620 | 7.7 | 195 | 16.5 | 7.5 | incandescent | |
| Spotlight | Vedette AP 1000 | 1.5° | 11°–19° | 0.19–0.33 | CP63 1kW 220v | 185,000 | 10.0 | 255 | 29.5 | 750 | 7.7 | 195 | 23.2 | 10.5 | incandescent | 4 |
| Spotlight | Vedette CID | 1.5° | 11°–19° | 0.19–0.33 | CID 1kW 220v | 600,000 | 10.0 | 255 | 32.2 | 820 | 7.7 | 195 | 30.9 | 14.0 | discharge 4 | |
| Spotlight | Vedette 1200 | 1° | 10°–18° | 0.17–0.33 | MSR 1.2kW 220v | 1,150,000 | 10.2 | 260 | 35.4 | 900 | 7.9 | 200 | 35.3 | 16.0 | discharge 6 | |
| Spotlight | Vedette AP 2000 | 0.8° | 10°–18° | 0.17–0.32 | CP72 2kW 220v | 325,000 | 15.7 | 400 | 43.2 | 1100 | 10.2 | 260 | 44.1 | 20.0 | incandescent | 4 |
| Spotlight | Vedette 2500 | 0.7° | 6°–14° | 0.10–0.25 | MSR 2.5kW 220v | 4,000,000 | 11.8 | 300 | 61.3 | 1560 | 11.5 | 293 | 66.2 | 30.0 | discharge 6 | |
| Strand | Solo CSI/CID | n/a | 6.5°–10.25° | 0.16–0.26 | CSI/CID 1kW 240v | 1,700,000/1,020,000 | 18.1 | 460 | 49.7 | 1265 | 18.9 | 480 | 93.7 | 42.5 | discharge 1 or 6 | |
| Strand | Solo 2kW | n/a | 8°–13.5° | 0.16–0.26 | RSE/79 2kW 240v | 660,000/285,000 | 18.1 | 460 | 41.9 | 1065 | 18.9 | 480 | 67.3 | 30.5 | incandescent | 1 or 6 |
| Strong | 45050 Super Trouperette | 0.77° | 4.27°–10.15° | 0.07–0.18 | HTI 400W 120v | 1,005,000/262,125 | 26.0 | 660 | 36.0 | 914 | 44.0 | 1118 | | | discharge 6 | |
| Strong | 18000 Roadie | 0.46° | 3.5°–9.32° | 0.06–0.16 | HTI SE 400W 110/220v | 3,045,000/544,000 | 45.0 | 1143 | 37.5 | 953 | 44.0 | 1118 | | | discharge 6 | |
| Strong | 41000 575 | 1.1° | 5.73°–17.1° | 0.10–0.3 | MSR 575W 120v | 2,553,000/260,000 | 45.0 | 1143 | 46.5 | 1181 | 46.5 | 1181 | | | discharge 6 | |
| Strong | 48050 Xenon Trouper | 1.07° | 6.8°–22.69° | 0.12–0.4 | Xenon 700W 120v | 2,287,500/165,000 | 45.0 | 1143 | 54.0 | 1372 | 47.5 | 1207 | | | discharge 6 | |
| Strong | 45003 Trouperette 3 | 1.4° | 7°–22° | 0.12–0.39 | FEL 1kW 120v | 387,500/80,000 | 26.0 | 660 | 33.0 | 838 | 44.0 | 1118 | | | incandescent | 6 |
| Strong | 83010 Super Trouper medium throw | 0.76° | 6.28°–14.58° | 0.11–0.25 | Xenon 1kW 120v | 4,300,020/500,040 | 45.0 | 1143 | 56.0 | 1422 | 53.0 | 1346 | | | discharge 6 | |
| Strong | 41050 Trouper 1200 | 1.25° | 4.58°–13.68° | 0.08–0.24 | MSR 1.2kW 220v | 4,108,000/481,500 | 45.0 | 1143 | 54.0 | 1372 | 47.5 | 1207 | | | discharge 6 | |
| Strong | 83060 Super Trouper short throw | 1.32° | 7.15°–23.17° | 0.12–0.41 | Xenon 1.6kW 120v | 3,096,000/324,000 | 45.0 | 1143 | 56.0 | 1422 | 53.0 | 1346 | | | discharge 6 | |
| Strong | 83016 Super Trouper medium throw | 0.76° | 6.28°–14.58° | 0.11–0.25 | Xenon 1.6kW 120v | 7,167,510/832,500 | 45.0 | 1143 | 56.0 | 1422 | 53.0 | 1346 | | | discharge 6 | |
| Strong | 83050 Xenon Super Trouper long throw | 0.84° | 3.58°–7.96° | 0.06–0.14 | Xenon 1.6kW 120v | 10,540,080/2,419,200 | 45.0 | 1143 | 77.5 | 1969 | 53.0 | 1346 | | | discharge 6 | |
| Strong | Super Trouper 2 | 0.96° | 4.12°–12.41° | 0.07–0.23 | Xenon 2kW 120v | 1,800,000/30,000 | 45.0 | 1143 | 58.0 | 1473 | 56.0 | 1422 | | | discharge | |
| Strong | 83080 Super Trouper short throw | 1.32° | 7.15°–23.17° | 0.12–0.41 | Xenon 2kW 120v | 3,833,600/389,120 | 45.0 | 1143 | 56.0 | 1422 | 53.0 | 1346 | | | discharge 6 | |
| Strong | 83070 Xenon Super Trouper long throw | 0.84° | 3.58°–7.96° | 0.06–0.14 | Xenon 2.5kW 208/230v | 12,226,800/3,886,480 | 45.0 | 1143 | 77.5 | 1969 | 53.0 | 1346 | | | discharge 6 | |
| Strong | 47050 Gladiator II | 0.6° | 3.27°–9.53° | 0.06–0.17 | Xenon 2.5kW 208/230v | 15,600,000/1,969,000 | 45.0 | 1143 | 77.5 | 1969 | 47.0 | 1194 | | | discharge 7 | |
| Strong | 47061 Gladiator III | 0.62° | 3.21°–10.29° | 0.06–0.18 | Xenon 3kW 208/230v | 21,270,100/2,527,000 | 45.0 | 1143 | 85.5 | 2172 | 47.0 | 1194 | | | discharge 7 | |
| Strong | Trouper (Arc) | 0.96° | 10°–28° | 0.18–0.50 | Carbons 120v? | 1,800,000/430,000 | 28.0 | 711 | 63.0 | 1600 | 47.5 | 1207 | | | carbon arc | 6 |
| Strong | Super Trouper (Arc) | 0.86° | 3°–14° | 0.05–0.25 | Carbons 120v? | 9,300,000/430,000 | 29.0 | 737 | 80.5 | 2045 | 53.0 | 1346 | | | carbon arc | 6 |
| Teatro | Talento 575 MSR | | 8°/12°/16° | 0.14/0.21/0.28 | MSR 575W 220v | 403,200/108,000 | 11.0 | 280 | 32.6 | 830 | 16.1 | 410 | 52.5 | 23.8 | discharge 1 or 6 | |
| Teatro | Talento 1200 MSR | | 6°/8°/12° | 0.10/0.14/0.21 | MSR 1.2kW 220v | 1,400,000/410,000 | 11.0 | 280 | 36.5 | 930 | 16.1 | 410 | 37.7 | 17.1 | discharge 1 or 6 | |
| Teatro | Talento 1200 TH | | 7.6°/14.8° | 0.14/0.26 | CP93 1.2kW 220v | 213,150/52,430 | 11.0 | 280 | 27.5 | 700 | 16.1 | 410 | 37.5 | 17.0 | incandescent | 1 or 6 |
| Teatro | Talento 2000 TH | | 8.5°–13° | 0.21–0.33 | MSR 2.5kW 220v | 240,000/147,000 | 15.3 | 390 | 45.0 | 1145 | 15.5 | 395 | 62.8 | 28.5 | incandescent | 1 or 4 |
| Teatro | Talento 2500 HMI | | 4.4°–7.5° | 0.07–0.13 | HMI 2.5kW 220v | 3,300,000/1,500,000 | 19.7 | 500 | 54.2 | 1380 | 24.0 | 610 | 78.3 | 35.5 | discharge 1 or 4 | |
| Times Square | QA 300 | 3° | 13.2° | 0.23 | EZM 300W 120v | | | | | | | | | | discharge 6 | |
| Times Square | IQ4ZMF | | 33° | 0.05–0.59 | EVR 500W 120v | 22,500 | | | 22.0 | 559 | 9.0 | 229 | | | incandescent | 1 |
| Times Square | 600S | | | | DYS 600W 120v | 155,000* | | | | | | | | | incandescent | 1 or 4 |
| Times Square | Q6MF | | | | FEL 1kW 120v | 300,000* | 15.2 | 386 | 27.0 | 686 | 7.5 | 191 | | | incandescent | 1 or 6 |
| Times Square | QF1000 | 1.1° | 10° | 0.02–0.18 | FEL 1kW 120v | 450,000/455,625 | | | 31.5 | 800 | 16.3 | 413 | | | incandescent | 6 |
| Times Square | QF1002 | 1.1° | 10° | 0.02–0.18 | FEL 1kW 120v | 185,625/202,500 | | | | | | | | | incandescent | 6 |
| Rocco Tool | Spot Dot | | Electronic red dot spotlight for Follow spot sight | | | | | | | | | | | | | |
| TTI | The Perfect Pick-up | | | | | | | | | | | | | | | |

The P.C. spotlight is back (Fig. 44). This was the spotlight in the days of my youth. Lamp (1), spherical reflector (2) and plano-convex lens (3) provide a clear-edged beam of light adjustable in diameter (4). Not as soft as the Fresnel, not as shapeable as the profile, it is still a useful workhorse instrument. The P.C. has remained the usual instrument of choice in Europe.

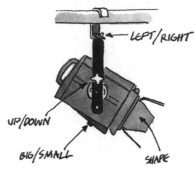
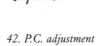

*42. P.C. adjustment*

*43. Strand Prelude P.C.*

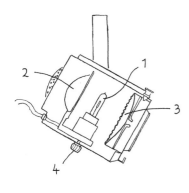

*44. Section P.C. Spot*

*45. Robert Juliat 1kW P.C.*

*46. Teatro Tratto P.C.*

*Stage Lighting Design*

| Unit | Manufacturer | Type | B/A | F/A | MPF | Lamp | Peak Candela (†=flat field candela) | W (in) | W (mm) | L (in) | L (mm) | H (in) | H (mm) | HY (in) | HY (mm) | Wt (lb) | Wt (kg) | Other lamp |
|---|---|---|---|---|---|---|---|---|---|---|---|---|---|---|---|---|---|---|
| Prism Convex Spot | ADB | C51 | 9°–51° | 15°–60° | 0.26–1.15 | CP 89 650W 220v | 50,000/7,000 | 8.6 | 220 | 12.2 | 310 | 7.1 | 180 | 10.2 | 260 | 7.7 | 3.5 | * |
| Prism Convex Spot | ADB | A56 C | 5°–63° | 9°–66° | 0.16–1.30 | CP 89 650W 220v | 120,000/5,250 | 8.8 | 225 | 11.4 | 290 | 7.9 | 200 | 13.0 | 330 | 9.5 | 4.3 | * |
| Prism Convex Spot | ADB | C103 | 4°–56° | 7°–61° | 0.12–1.18 | GX 9.5 1.2kW 220v | 266,000/9,300 | 13.4 | 340 | 18.9 | 480 | 11.0 | 280 | 16.5 | 420 | 23.6 | 10.7 | * |
| Prism Convex Spot | ADB | C203 | 4.5°–53.7° | 8.3°–57.5° | 0.14–1.10 | CP 79.22 2kW 220v | 280,000/20,800 | 11.4 | 290 | 21.2 | 540 | 11.4 | 290 | 16.9 | 430 | 27.8 | 12.6 | * |
| Plano-Convex Spot | Altman | 101 Box spot | 19.8°–46° | 27°–52° | 0.48–0.98 | 400G/FL 400W 120v | 2,670/1,323 | | | | | | | | | | | * |
| Plano-Convex Spot | Display | 816 | 17°–62° | | 0.3–1.2 | T-20 500W 120v | | | | | | | | | | | | * |
| Pebble Convex Spot | CCT | Minuette Z0644 | 7.5°–47° | 10°–58° | 0.18–1.11 | T27 650W 240v | 107,700/6,300 † | 7.9 | 200 | 12.0 | 305 | 5.6 | 142 | 10.1 | 258 | 5.5 | 2.5 | |
| Pebble Convex Spot | CCT | Starlette Z0052 | 7°–38° | 11.5°–47° | 0.2–0.87 | T19 1kW C13D 240v | 127,000/13,250 † | 11.2 | 285 | 15.7 | 400 | 9.8 | 250 | 17.7 | 450 | 21.6 | 9.8 | |
| Pebble Convex Spot | CCT | Starlette Z0052 | 7°–38° | 11.5°–47° | 0.2–0.87 | T29 1.2kW C13D 240v | 152,500/18,300 † | 11.2 | 285 | 15.7 | 400 | 9.8 | 250 | 17.7 | 450 | 21.6 | 9.8 | |
| Pebble Convex Spot | CCT | Starlette Z0082 | 5°–50° | 8°–55° | 0.14–1.04 | CP79 2kW C13D 240v | 440,250/24,000 † | 13.8 | 350 | 21.2 | 540 | 13.2 | 337 | 20.4 | 520 | 35.3 | 16.0 | |
| Pebble Convex Spot | Coemar | Corto E500 al | | 8°–50° | 0.14–0.93 | 500W 120v | 26,375 @ 8° B/A | 8.0 | 204 | 8.8 | 225 | 6.1 | 156 | 9.6 | 245 | 6.6 | 3.0 | * |
| Pebble Convex Spot | Coemar | Solar 1000al | | 10°–28° | 0.18–0.50 | 1kW 120v | 73,000 @ 10° B/A | 8.8 | 223 | 12.0 | 305 | 6.9 | 175 | 11.6 | 294 | 8.2 | 3.7 | * |
| Pebble Convex Spot | Robert Juliat | 305 HPB | 11°–60° | | 0.19–1.15 | GX 9.5 650W 220v | | 11.0 | 280 | 14.7 | 375 | 8.1 | 205 | 13.6 | 345 | 11.0 | 5.0 | * |
| Pebble Convex Spot | Robert Juliat | 306 HPB | 11°–60° | | 0.19–1.15 | GX 9.5 1kW 220v | | 11.0 | 280 | 14.7 | 375 | 8.1 | 205 | 13.6 | 345 | 12.1 | 5.5 | * |
| Pebble Convex Spot | Robert Juliat | 310 HPB | 6°–55° | | 0.10–1.04 | GX 9.5 1.2kW 220v | | 13.4 | 340 | 17.7 | 450 | 9.8 | 250 | 16.9 | 430 | 19.8 | 9.0 | * |
| Plano-Convex Spot | Kliegl | 53 | 22°–53° | | 0.4–1.0 | 400G/SP 400W 120v | | | | | | | | | | | | |
| Pebble Convex Spot | Kliegl | 5310 | 12°–62° | | 0.2–1.2 | 400G/SP 400W 120v | | | | | | | | | | | | |
| Pebble Convex Spot | Kliegl | 70 | 12°–44° | | 0.2–0.8 | 1000/G40/P3P 1kW 120v | | | | | | | | | | | | |
| Pebble Convex Spot | Kliegl | 71 | 12°–48° | | 0.2–0.9 | 1500/G40/15 1.5kW 120v | | | | | | | | | | | | |
| Plano-Convex Spot | Kliegl | 6N19 | 9°–48° | | 0.15–0.9 | 2M/648/4 2kW 120v | | | | | | | | | | | | |
| Plano-Convex Spot | Kliegl | 8N20 | 8°–65° | | 0.13–1.27 | 2M/648/4 2kW 120v | | | | | | | | | | | | |
| Plano-Convex Spot | Kliegl | 8N24 | 8°–70° | | 0.13–1.4 | 2M/648/4 2kW 120v | | | | | | | | | | | | |
| Pebble Convex Spot | Pani | LH-1000 | 6°–46.5° | | 0.10–0.86 | 6X9.5 1kW 220v | 221,250/12,500 | 12.0 | 305 | 14.9 | 380 | 9.8 | 250 | 14.1 | 360 | 16.5 | 7.5 | * |
| Pebble Convex Spot | Pani | LH-2000 | 3°–43° | 5°–48° | 0.09–0.89 | GP-79 2kW 220v | 667,000/23,325 | 13.1 | 334 | 19.8 | 505 | 11.8 | 300 | 18.9 | 480 | 32.0 | 14.5 | * |
| Plano-Convex Spot | RDS | AQS-5E | 4.5°–49° | 6.6°–54.7° | 0.11–1.03 | RT-12 650W 220v | 130,500/5,175 | 11.0 | 281 | 15.8 | 402 | 8.9 | 226 | 12.4 | 316 | 13.5 | 6.1 | |
| Plano-Convex Spot | RDS | AQS-10E | 4.2°–41.4° | 5°–45.8° | 0.09–0.84 | RT-11 1kW 220v | 270,000/11,525 | 13.1 | 333 | 19.5 | 497 | 10.7 | 272 | 14.6 | 372 | 21.2 | 9.6 | |
| P.k.-Scheinwerfer | R & V | L1200 MS | 5°–50° | 8°–70° | 0.14–1.40 | QH 1.2kW 220v | | 10.8 | 275 | 19.7 | 500 | 10.8 | 275 | 19.3 | 490 | 22.1 | 10.0 | * |
| P.k.-Scheinwerfer | R & V | L2500 MS | 4°–60° | 8°–80° | 0.14–1.66 | QH 2.5kW 220v | | 13.8 | 352 | 22.0 | 560 | 13.8 | 352 | 22.8 | 580 | 32.2 | 14.6 | * |
| Pebble Convex Spot | Selecon | Mini PC | 4.5°–54° | 12°–62° | 0.21–1.20 | T/26 650W 240v | 141,000/9,500 | 8.3 | 210 | 12.6 | 320 | 6.0 | 153 | 9.6 | 245 | 6.7 | 3.0 | * |
| Pebble Convex Spot | Selecon | Acclaim PC | 4°–60° | 7°–70° | 0.12–1.40 | T/26 650W 240v | 142,000/6,200 | 7.9 | 200 | 12.6 | 320 | 5.9 | 150 | 11.0 | 280 | 6.2 | 2.8 | * |
| Pebble Convex Spot | Selecon | Compact 6 PC | 5°–60° | 6.5°–66° | 0.11–1.30 | T/29 1.2kW 240v | 306,000/15,840 | 11.0 | 280 | 14.3 | 365 | 8.8 | 224 | 12.6 | 320 | 11.9 | 5.4 | |
| Pebble Convex Spot | Selecon | High Perf. 1200 | 4.5°–62° | 9°–65° | 0.16–1.27 | T/29 1.2kW 240v | 342,000/14,220 | 11.0 | 280 | 15.7 | 400 | 8.8 | 224 | 12.6 | 320 | 13.5 | 6.1 | |
| Pebble Convex Spot | Selecon | Arena PC | 4.5°–60° | 8°–70° | 0.14–1.40 | CP 91 2.5kW 240v | 546,350/38,220 | 14.3 | 365 | 18.7 | 476 | 11.7 | 297 | 17.7 | 450 | 22.6 | 10.2 | * |
| Pebble Convex Spot | Spotlight | va 05 "Sintesi" | 5.5°–58° | 10°–62° | 0.18–1.20 | CP 89 650W 220v | 90,000/8,800 | 8.8 | 225 | 12.6 | 320 | 5.9 | 150 | 11.0 | 280 | 7.1 | 3.2 | * |
| Plano-Convex Spot | Spotlight | QPS 500/AA | 3.7°–59° | 7°–64° | 0.12–1.25 | GY 9.5/CP 89 650W 220v | 100,000/4,500 | 7.1 | 180 | 11.6 | 295 | 6.3 | 160 | 10.4 | 265 | 7.1 | 3.2 | |
| Plano-Convex Spot | Spotlight | QPS 1000/AA | 8°–59° | 15°–75° | 0.26–1.53 | GX 9.5/CP70 1kW 220v | 148,000/9,000 | 8.6 | 220 | 14.9 | 380 | 7.7 | 195 | 13.0 | 330 | 11.7 | 5.3 | |
| Pebble Convex Spot | Spotlight | va 12 "Sintesi" | 3.7°–70° | 7.5°–76° | 0.13–1.56 | CP 90 1.2kW 220v | 300,000/12,000 | 10.2 | 260 | 16.3 | 415 | 7.9 | 200 | 13.8 | 350 | 13.7 | 6.2 | * |
| Plano-Convex Spot | Spotlight | QPS 2000/AA | 5°–64° | 10°–73° | 0.18–1.48 | GY 16/CP 72 2kW 220v | 390,000/14,000 | 11.8 | 300 | 20.0 | 510 | 10.0 | 255 | 18.9 | 480 | 21.6 | 9.8 | |
| Pebble Convex Spot | Spotlight | va 25 "Sintesi" | 3.6°–62° | 7.5°–68° | 0.13–1.35 | CP 91 2.5kW 220v | 700,000/30,000 | 13.4 | 340 | 21.2 | 540 | 11.5 | 293 | 19.7 | 500 | 28.7 | 13.0 | * |

| Unit | Manufacturer | Type | B/A | F/A | MPF | Lamp | Peak Candela | W in | W mm | L in | L mm | H in | H mm | HY in | HY mm | Wt lb | Wt kg | Other lamp |
|---|---|---|---|---|---|---|---|---|---|---|---|---|---|---|---|---|---|---|
| | | | | | | | | 0.04 | 25 | 0.04 | 25 | 0.04 | 25 | 0.04 | 25 | 2.2 | 0.5 | |
| Prism Convex Spot | Strand | Minim | 7.5°–52° | 13°–60° | 0.23–1.15 | CP81 300W 240v | 33,700/3650 | 6.8 | 174 | 8.5 | 216 | 6.3 | 160 | 8.1 | 205 | 5.0 | 2.3 | |
| Prism Convex Spot | Strand | Prelude | 7.5°–55° | 15°–60° | 0.26–1.15 | RSE/26 650W 240v | 54,500/7000 | 9.0 | 230 | 9.2 | 235 | 7.3 | 185 | 10.6 | 270 | 7.7 | 3.5 | |
| Prism Convex Spot | Strand | Quartet | 7.5°–55° | 12.5°–65° | 0.22–1.27 | RSE 26 650W 240v | 61,300/7000 | 9.5 | 243 | 11.2 | 286 | 6.3 | 160 | 11.3 | 288 | 7.3 | 3.3 | |
| Prism Convex Spot | Strand | Harmony | 3.75°–56° | 6.5°–60° | 0.11–1.15 | RSE/18 1kW 240v | 225,000/8,600 | 11.6 | 295 | 14.7 | 375 | 9.0 | 230 | 16.3 | 415 | 13.0 | 5.9 | |
| Prism Convex Spot | Strand | Cantata | 4.2°–49° | 8°–60° | 0.14–1.15 | RSE 29 1.2kW 240v | 206,000/14,300 | 11.8 | 300 | 16.1 | 410 | 9.4 | 240 | 16.5 | 420 | 15.9 | 7.2 | |
| Prism Convex Spot | Strand | Cadenza | 4°–61° | 7.5°–68° | 0.13–1.35 | RSE 79 2kW 240v | 570,000/28,000 | 14.5 | 370 | 18.7 | 475 | 11.0 | 280 | 17.7 | 450 | 33.5 | 15.2 | |
| Prism Convex Spot | Teatro | Punto 500 PC | 8°–50° | 13°–54° | 0.23–1.02 | T25 500W 220v | 57,600/6000 | 8.0 | 204 | 10.0 | 255 | 6.1 | 156 | 10.0 | 255 | 6.6 | 3.0 | |
| Prism Convex Spot | Teatro | Comma 650 PC | 9.5°–38.5° | 18°–50° | 0.23–0.93 | T27 650W 220v | 37,300/7,300 | 8.8 | 223 | 11.6 | 295 | | | 11.6 | 294 | 7.7 | 3.5 | |
| Prism Convex Spot | Teatro | Tipo PC 1000 | 5.5°–58° | 12°–66° | 0.21–1.30 | CP70 1kW 220v | 125,600/9,270 | 9.9 | 252 | 16.2 | 412 | 8.9 | 226 | 11.6 | 295 | 12.8 | 5.8 | |
| Prism Convex Spot | Teatro | Spazio PC1000/E | 10°–41° | 17°–50° | 0.30–0.93 | CP70 1kW 220v | 61,500/12,600 | 8.8 | 223 | 12.0 | 305 | | | 11.6 | 294 | 7.7 | 3.5 | |
| Prism Convex Spot | Teatro | Spazio PC 1000 | 5.5°–58.5° | 12°–66° | 0.21–1.30 | CP70 1kW 220v | 125,600/9270 | 11.4 | 290 | 17.1 | 435 | 9.4 | 240 | 15.7 | 400 | 13.7 | 6.2 | |
| Prism Convex Spot | Teatro | Tratto 2PC 1200 | 6.5°–48° | 10°–56° | 0.18–1.06 | CP93 1.2kW 220v | 134,800/11,500 | 11.2 | 285 | 19.2 | 488 | 9.0 | 230 | 16.5 | 420 | 18.7 | 8.5 | |
| Prism Convex Spot | Teatro | Spazio PC 2000 | 5°–60° | 11°–65° | 0.19–1.27 | CP72 2kW 220v | 213,000/17,400 | 11.4 | 290 | 17.1 | 435 | 9.4 | 240 | 15.7 | 400 | 13.7 | 6.2 | |
| Prism Convex Spot | Teatro | Acuto PC | 4°–57° | 7°–65° | 0.12–1.27 | CP72 2kW 220v | 432,700/21,800 | 14.3 | 365 | 22.7 | 578 | 14.0 | 356 | 21.6 | 550 | 24.5 | 11.1 | |
| Pebble Convex Spot | Zero 88 | Focus 650 PC | 10°–59° | | 0.18–1.13 | 650W/500W 240v | | 7.7 | 195 | 12.0 | 305 | 5.9 | 150 | 10.3 | 262 | 5.5 | 2.5 | |

These provide a soft edged spot (Fig. 47). Adjustable beam spread by movement of the lamp (2) and reflector (3) relative to the Fresnel lens (1). Barndoors can be fitted to give some shape to the beam and lessen stray light (Fig. 49).

250/500 watts=Small theatres onstage

650/1,000 watts=General onstage

2,000 watts=Special keylight for small theatres

5,000 watts & above=Special keylight for large theatres

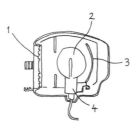

*47. Section Fresnel*

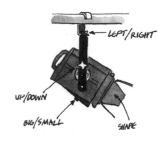

*48. Fresnel adjustment*

*49. Barndoors*

*50. Strand patt 23*

*51. CCT 2kW Fresnel*

*52. Century 8" Fresnel*

*53. Strand patt 243*

*54. Altman 2kW studio Fresnel*

*55. Arri 2kW studio Fresnel*

*56. Strand 5kW Bambino*

*57. Desisti/Desmar Leonardo 5kW*

| Type | Manufacturer | Unit | B/A | F/A | MPF | Lamp (or lampholder type) | Peak Candela † = flat field candela * = math average | W in (0.04) | W mm (25) | L in (0.04) | L mm (25) | H in (0.0) | H mm (25) | HY in (0.0) | HY mm (25) | Wt lb (2.2) | Wt kg (0.5) | Other lamp |
|---|---|---|---|---|---|---|---|---|---|---|---|---|---|---|---|---|---|---|
| Fresnel 4.5" | ADB | F51 | 9°–56° | 18°–65° | 0.32–1.27 | CP 89 650W 220v | 41,000/7,000 | 8.6 | 220 | 9.6 | 245 | 7.1 | 180 | 10.2 | 260 | 7.1 | 3.2 | * |
| Fresnel 4.75" | ADB | A57 F | 8°–51° | 14°–59° | 0.25–1.13 | CP 89 650W 220v | 71,500/8,300 | 8.8 | 225 | 11.4 | 290 | 7.9 | 200 | 13.0 | 330 | 8.8 | 4.0 | * |
| Fresnel 6" | ADB | F101 | 7.5°–52° | 13°–59° | 0.23–1.13 | GX 9.5 1.2kW 220v | 172,000/16,000 | 13.4 | 340 | 13.4 | 340 | 11.0 | 280 | 16.5 | 420 | 18.7 | 8.5 | * |
| Fresnel 8" | ADB | F201 | 6.5°–55° | 12.5°–61.5° | 0.22–1.19 | CP 79 2kW 220v | 440,000/27,500 | 11.4 | 290 | 16.7 | 425 | 11.4 | 290 | 16.9 | 430 | 21.2 | 9.6 | * |
| Fresnel 3" | Altman | 100 | 10°–34° | 23.5°–55° | 0.41–1.04 | ESP 150W 120v | 6,125/1,950 | 5.3 | 133 | 4.3 | 108 | 5.3 | 133 | 7.5 | 191 | | | * |
| Fresnel 3" | Altman | Location 300L | | 27°–77° | 0.48–1.53 | FKW 300W 120v | 15,000/4,200 | | | | | | | | | | | |
| Fresnel 4" | Altman | Location 650L | | 26°–79° | 0.46–1.65 | FRK 650W 120v | 55,000/9,000 | | | | | | | | | | | |
| Fresnel 6" | Altman | 650/165Q | 8.8°–59° | 16°–70° | 0.28–1.40 | BTN 750W 120v | 92,500/8,800 | 9.5 | 241 | 10.3 | 260 | 10.0 | 254 | 14.3 | 362 | | | * |
| Fresnel 7" | Altman | 65/165 | 10.4°–53° | 18.6°–64° | 0.33–1.25 | BFE 750W 120v | 67,000/10,500 | 9.5 | 241 | 10.3 | 260 | 10.0 | 254 | 14.3 | 362 | | | * |
| Fresnel 8" | Altman | 75/175 | 9.5°–40° | 18°–49° | 0.32–0.91 | 1MG40/23 1kW 120v | 110,000/18,500 | 13.5 | 343 | 11.0 | 279 | 13.5 | 343 | 19.0 | 483 | | | * |
| Fresnel 5" | Altman | 750/175Q | 6.7°–37° | 12°–45° | 0.21–0.83 | BVT 1kW 120v | 170,000/20,000 | 13.5 | 343 | 13.5 | 343 | 15.0 | 381 | 19.0 | 483 | | | * |
| Fresnel 6" | Altman | 1 KAF-MEBP | 6.4°–70.5° | 12.9°–76.5° | 0.23–1.57 | EGT 1kW 120v | 179,000/10,000 | 10.0 | 254 | 12.5 | 318 | 12.5 | 318 | 16.6 | 422 | | | |
| Fresnel 6" | Altman | 1 KAF-MEPF | 6.4°–69.2° | 12.2°–73.8° | 0.21–1.50 | BTR 1kW 120v | 179,000/12,000 | 10.0 | 254 | 12.5 | 318 | 12.5 | 318 | 16.6 | 422 | | | * |
| Fresnel 5" | Altman | Location 1000L | | 19°–69° | 0.33–1.37 | EGT 1kW 120v | 125,000/20,000 | | | | | | | | | | | |
| Fresnel 7" | Altman | Studio 1000S | | 18°–68° | 0.32–1.35 | EGT 1kW 120v | 175,000/18,000 | | | | | | | | | | | |
| Fresnel 7" | Altman | Location 2000L | | 22°–61° | 0.39–1.18 | CYX 2kW 120v | 325,000/42,000 | | | | | | | | | | | |
| Fresnel 10" | Altman | Studio 2000S | | 17°–73° | 0.30–1.48 | CYX 2kW 120v | 330,000/32,000 | | | | | | | | | | | |
| Fresnel 10" | Altman | Location 5000L | | 19°–63° | 0.33–1.23 | DPY 5kW 120v | 375,000/82,500 | | | | | | | | | | | |
| Fresnel 12" | Altman | Studio 5000S | | 18°–87° | 0.32–1.90 | DPY 5kW 120v | 464,00/56,000 | | | | | | | | | | | |
| Fresnel | CCT | Minuette 20642 | 8.5°–47° | 18°–57° | 0.32–1.09 | T27 650W (FMR 600W in USA) | 41,000/8,750 † | 7.9 | 200 | 9.8 | 250 | 5.6 | 142 | 10.1 | 258 | 4.9 | 2.2 | * |
| Fresnel | CCT | Starlette 20050 | 6°–57° | 10°–62° | 0.18–1.20 | T19 1kW 240v | 136,200/12,500 † | 11.2 | 285 | 12.2 | 310 | 9.8 | 250 | 17.7 | 450 | 17.6 | 8.0 | * |
| Fresnel | CCT | Starlette 20050 | 6°–57° | 13°–71° | 0.23–1.43 | T29 1.2kW 240v | 156,000/17,750 † | 11.2 | 285 | 12.2 | 310 | 9.8 | 250 | 17.7 | 450 | 17.6 | 8.0 | * |
| Fresnel | CCT | Starlette 20080 | 6°–50° | 12.5°–58° | 0.22–1.11 | CP79 2kW 240v | 295,250/31,000 † | 13.8 | 350 | 17.3 | 440 | 13.2 | 337 | 20.4 | 520 | 29.8 | ## | * |
| Fresnel 3" | Century | 1211 | 9°–35° | 16°–50° | 0.28–0.93 | 150G16-1/2 DC 150W 120v | 6,500/1,600 | | | | | | | | | | | |
| Fresnel 6" | Century | 500/550 | 9°–41° | 16°–52° | 0.28–0.98 | BFE 750W 120v | 75,000/12,000 | | | | | | | | | | | |
| Fresnel 6" | Century | 3312 | 8°–54° | 16°–60° | 0.28–1.15 | BTN 750W 120v | 102,150/10,200 | | | | | | | | | | | |
| Fresnel 8" | Century | 3413 | 9°–21° | 16°–33° | 0.28–0.59 | BVW 2kW 120v | 392,000/68,800 | | | | | | | | | | | |
| Fresnel | Coemar | Corto 300/500 al | | 11°–40° | 0.19–0.73 | 500W 120v | 25,200 @ 8° B/A * | 8.0 | 204 | 8.8 | 225 | 6.1 | 156 | 9.6 | 245 | 6.2 | 2.8 | * |
| Fresnel | Coemar | Solar 650 al | | 9°–27° | 0.16–0.48 | 650W 120v | 54,000 @ 9° B/A * | 8.8 | 223 | 11.6 | 295 | 6.9 | 175 | 11.6 | 294 | 7.1 | 3.2 | * |
| Fresnel | Coemar | Passo 650W | | 8.5°–50° | 0.15–0.93 | 650W 120v | 102,000 @ 8.5° B/A * | 11.4 | 290 | 17.1 | 435 | 9.4 | 240 | 15.7 | 400 | 13.2 | 6.0 | * |
| Fresnel | Coemar | Passo 2000W | | 11°–52° | 0.19–0.98 | 2kW 120v | 165,000 @ 11° B/A * | 11.4 | 290 | 17.1 | 435 | 9.4 | 240 | 15.7 | 400 | 13.7 | 6.2 | * |
| Fresnel 3" | Colortran | 214-002 | 10°–36° | 20°–48° | 0.35–0.9 | 176-188 150W 120v | 4,800/1,296 | | | | | | | | | | | |
| Fresnel 6" | Colortran | 214-012 | 7°–40° | 17°–53° | 0.30–1.0 | BTL 500W 120v | 60,075/10,800 | | | | | | | | | | | |
| Fresnel 6" | Colortran | 213-202 | 6.9°–61.6° | 13.9°–72.5° | 0.24–1.47 | BTN 750W 120v | 162,000/9,600 | 11.0 | 279 | 11.0 | 279 | 19.0 | 483 | 14.0 | 356 | 9.0 | 4.1 | |
| Fresnel 6" | Colortran | 100-412 | 10.5°–40° | 19°–54° | 0.33–1.02 | BWN 1kW 120v | 136,250/20,625 | 11.0 | 279 | 11.0 | 279 | 13.0 | 330 | 9.0 | 229 | 10.0 | 4.5 | |
| Fresnel 6" | Colortran | 213-512 | 6.1°–64.5° | 12.5°–74.6° | 0.22–1.52 | BTR 1kW 120v | 175,000/11,200 | 11.0 | 279 | 13.0 | 330 | 23.0 | 584 | 17.0 | 432 | 11.0 | 5.0 | |
| Fresnel 8" | Colortran | 100-362 | 6.5°–36° | 12.5°–44° | 0.22–0.81 | CXZ 1.5kW 120v | 336,000/38,000 | 12.0 | 305 | 11.0 | 279 | 19.0 | 483 | 11.0 | 279 | 19.0 | 8.6 | |
| Fresnel 8" | Colortran | 213-212 | 8.6°–50.8° | 15.3°–59.1° | 0.27–1.13 | BVW 2kW 120v | 355,000/40,500 | 13.0 | 330 | 13.0 | 330 | 25.0 | 635 | 17.0 | 432 | 20.0 | 9.1 | * |
| Fresnel 8" | Colortran | 213-522 | 8.4°–55.7° | 15.3°–63.5° | 0.27–1.23 | BVW 2kW 120v | 358,000/37,500 | 13.0 | 330 | 16.0 | 406 | 28.0 | 711 | 19.0 | 483 | 20.0 | 9.1 | * |

# FRESNEL TABLE

| Type | Manufacturer | Unit | B/A | F/A | MPF | Lamp (or lampholder type) | Peak Candela † = flat field candela  = math average * = math average | W in | W mm | L in | L mm | H in | H mm | HY in | HY mm | Wt lb | Wt kg | Other lamp |
|---|---|---|---|---|---|---|---|---|---|---|---|---|---|---|---|---|---|---|
| Fresnel 10" | Colortran | 100-182 | 3.2°–29° | 18°–62° | 0.32–1.20 | CYX 2KW 120v | 349,200/31,200 | 14.0 | 356 | 17.0 | 432 | 17.0 | 432 | 14.0 | 356 | 25.0 | ## | * |
| Fresnel 10" | Colortran | 100-392 | 3.2°–29° | 16.7°–66° | 0.29–1.30 | CYX 2KW 120v | 349,200/31,200 | 15.0 | 381 | 13.0 | 330 | 21.0 | 533 | 13.0 | 330 | 25.0 | ## | * |
| Fresnel 10" | Colortran | 100-242 | 12°–60° | 20.4°–73° | 0.36–1.48 | DPY 5KW 120v | 569,800/89,000 | 17.0 | 432 | 17.0 | 432 | 25.0 | 635 | 13.0 | 330 | 28.0 | ## | * |
| Fresnel 12" | Colortran | 100-402 | 9°–50° | 17°–57.6° | 0.30–1.10 | DPY 5KW 120v | 585,000/95,400 | 19.0 | 483 | 14.0 | 356 | 25.0 | 635 | 13.0 | 330 | 36.0 | ## | * |
| Fresnel 6" | Desisti/Desmar | Leonardo Studio F | 6°–53° | 13°–60° | 0.23–1.15 | 1kW Tungsten halogen | 170,000/14,000 | 12.2 | 310 | 11.7 | 297 | 10.8 | 275 | 22.2 | 565 | 16.3 | 7.4 | * |
| Fresnel 10" | Desisti/Desmar | Leonardo Studio F | 7°–53° | 16°–61° | 0.28–1.18 | 2kW Tungsten halogen | 350,000/27,000* | 16.5 | 420 | 14.1 | 358 | 15.2 | 386 | 26.9 | 684 | 28.4 | ## | * |
| Fresnel 12" | Desisti/Desmar | Leonardo Studio F | 8°–57° | 16°–65° | 0.28–1.27 | 5kW Tungsten halogen | 731,000/90,000* | 19.5 | 495 | 16.0 | 408 | 18.2 | 463 | 29.9 | 762 | 37.5 | ## | * |
| Fresnel 24" | Desisti/Desmar | SuperLee Studio F | 5°–30°approx. | | 0.09–0.54 | 20kW Tungsten halogen 220v | 2,760,000/560,000* | | | | | | | | | | | * |
| Fresnel 6" | Electro Controls | 3466+7466A | 8.5°–51° | 22°–63° | 0.38–1.23 | BTR 1kW 120v | 144,000/20,000 | | | | | | | | | | | * |
| Fresnel 6" | Electro Controls | 3467+7467A | 8.5°–51° | 22°–63° | 0.38–1.23 | BTR 1kW 120v | 144,000/20,000 | | | | | | | | | | | * |
| Fresnel 8" | Electro Controls | 3485+7485A | 5.4°–64.6° | 11.9°–71° | 0.21–1.43 | EGJ 1kW 120v | 180,000/8,000 | | | | | | | | | | | * |
| Fresnel 8" | Electro Controls | 3485A+7485B | 6.8°–59.7° | 14°–70° | 0.25–1.40 | BTR 1kW 120v | 200,000/14,000 | | | | | | | | | | | * |
| Fresnel 3" | Robert Juliat | 305 HF | 9°–52° | | 0.16–0.98 | GX 9.5 650W 220v | | 11.0 | 280 | 14.7 | 375 | 8.1 | 205 | 13.6 | 345 | 11.0 | 5.0 | |
| Fresnel | Robert Juliat | 306 HF | 9°–52° | | 0.16–0.98 | GX 9.5 1kW 220v | | 11.0 | 280 | 14.7 | 375 | 8.1 | 205 | 13.6 | 345 | 12.1 | 5.5 | |
| Fresnel | Robert Juliat | 310 HF | 8°–50° | | 0.14–0.93 | GX 9.5 1.2kW 220v | | 13.4 | 340 | 17.7 | 450 | 9.8 | 250 | 16.9 | 430 | 19.8 | 9.0 | |
| Fresnel | Robert Juliat | 329 | 7.5°–58° | | 0.13–1.11 | 2kW or 2.5kW 220v | | 17.7 | 450 | 18.7 | 475 | 12.6 | 320 | 19.8 | 505 | 26.5 | ## | |
| Fresnel 3" | Kliegl | 3603 | | 22°–64° | 0.39–1.25 | ESP 150W 120v | 6,700/1,637 | 5.8 | 150 | 5.0 | 120 | 5.0 | 120 | 7.5 | 190 | 3.0 | 1.4 | |
| Fresnel 4.5" | Kliegl | 3604 | | 18°–54° | 0.32–1.02 | BSP 500W 120v | 22,200/5,200 | 7.8 | 200 | 8.0 | 200 | 8.0 | 200 | 11.4 | 290 | 9.0 | 4.1 | |
| Fresnel 6" | Kliegl | 3606 | | 18°–62° | 0.32–1.20 | EHD 500W 120v | 46,000/11,000 | 10.0 | 250 | 13.5 | 340 | 10.5 | 270 | 15.3 | 390 | 13.0 | 5.9 | |
| Fresnel 8" | Kliegl | 3609 | | 14°–54° | 0.25–1.02 | DWT 1kW 120v | 118,400/14,500 | 13.0 | 340 | 15.0 | 380 | 13.0 | 340 | 20.4 | 520 | 20.0 | 9.1 | |
| Fresnel 8" | Kliegl | 3801 | 7.6°–54° | 13.3°–62° | 0.23–1.20 | EGT 1kW 120v | | | | | | | | | | | | * |
| Fresnel 8" | Kliegl | 3802 | 9.1°–54° | 15.7°–64° | 0.28–1.25 | CYX 2KW 120v | | | | | | | | | | | | * |
| Fresnel 10" | Kliegl | 3610 | | 18°–62° | 0.32–1.20 | CYX 2KW 120v | 290,000/37,000 | 16.0 | 41 | 17.0 | 43 | 23.5 | 60 | 28.5 | 73 | 30.0 | ## | * |
| Fresnel 10" | Kliegl | 3812 | 7.5°–50° | 9.5°–62° | 0.17–1.20 | CYX 2KW 120v | | | | | | | | | | | | * |
| Fresnel 10" | Kliegl | 3815 | 9°–50° | 15°–60° | 0.26–1.15 | DPY 5KW 120v | | | | | | | | | | | | * |
| Fresnel 12" | Kliegl | 3612 | 13°–59° | 27°–69° | 0.48–1.37 | DPY 5KW 120v | 550,000/100,000 | 17.3 | 44 | 18.0 | 46 | 24.5 | 62 | 29.5 | 75 | 38.0 | ## | * |
| Fresnel 3" | L & E | 60-03 | 10°–34° | 23.5°–55° | 0.42–1.04 | ESR 100W 120v | 7,000/1,800 | 4.0 | 102 | 4.5 | 114 | 5.0 | 127 | | | 2.5 | 1.1 | * |
| Fresnel 3" | L & E | 60-03 | 10°–30° | 21°–50° | 0.37–0.93 | ESP 150W 120v | 9,900/2,500 | 4.0 | 102 | 4.5 | 114 | 5.0 | 127 | | | 2.5 | 1.1 | * |
| Fresnel 3" | L & E | 60-03 High output | 9°–44° | 18°–64° | 0.32–1.25 | FEV 200W 120v | 19,400/4,900 | 4.2 | 105 | 4.8 | 121 | 5.0 | 127 | | | 3.0 | 1.4 | * |
| Fresnel 6" | L & E | 60-06/60-07 | 11°–38° | 17°–53° | 0.3–1.0 | BFE 750W 120v | 60,000/14,500 | 7.8 | 197 | 9.8 | 248 | 8.5 | 216 | | | 7.0 | 3.2 | * |
| Fresnel 6" | L & E | 60-06/60-07 | 7°–50° | 16°–64° | 0.28–1.25 | BTN 750W 120v | 83,250/13,500 | 7.8 | 197 | 9.8 | 248 | 8.5 | 216 | | | 7.0 | 3.2 | * |
| Fresnel 6" | L & E | 60-10 | 8°–57° | 10°–71° | 0.18–1.43 | BTR 1kW 120v | 134,000/23,400 | 7.8 | 197 | 12.0 | 305 | 9.0 | 229 | | | 12.0 | 5.4 | * |
| Fresnel 8" | L & E | 60-08/60-09 | 9°–52° | 19°–64° | 0.33–1.25 | BVV 1kW 120v | 136,800/29,760 | 10.3 | 260 | 12.0 | 305 | 12.5 | 318 | | | 25.0 | ## | * |
| Fresnel 6" | Marumo | FQ 500W | 7°–42° | 11.5°–51.5° | 0.20–0.97 | JPD 500W BT/6 100v | 72,250/7,000 | 9.9 | 252 | 8.3 | 212 | 8.6 | 220 | 14.7 | 375 | 7.1 | 3.2 | * |
| Fresnel | Marumo | FQ II 1000W | 7°–45.5° | 13.5°–57° | 0.24–1.09 | ESR 1kW G-D 100v | 158,000/15,750 | 12.7 | 322 | 11.0 | 280 | 11.9 | 302 | 17.4 | 442 | 13.7 | 6.2 | * |
| Fresnel | Marumo | LNH 120H 1000W | 7.5°–55° | 13.5°–68° | 0.24–1.35 | JP 1kW G-D 100v | 197,000/17,500 | 12.4 | 315 | 13.0 | 330 | 10.7 | 273 | 21.1 | 537 | 15.0 | 6.8 | * |
| Fresnel | Marumo | LNH 250H 1000W | 4.5°–41.5° | 7.5°–46° | 0.13–0.85 | JP 1kW G-D 100v | 275,500/17,000 | 12.4 | 315 | 18.1 | 460 | 10.7 | 273 | 21.1 | 537 | 17.4 | 7.9 | * |
| Fresnel | Marumo | LNH 350H 1000W | 2.5°–22° | 4.5°–25° | 0.08–0.44 | JP 1kW G-D 100v | 469,000/22,500 | 12.4 | 315 | 22.0 | 560 | 10.7 | 273 | 21.1 | 537 | 19.2 | 8.7 | * |
| Fresnel | Marumo | FQ II 1500W | 8°–45° | 16°–56.5° | 0.28–1.08 | JP 1.5kW G-D 100v | 186,750/24,750 | 12.7 | 322 | 11.0 | 280 | 11.9 | 302 | 17.4 | 442 | 13.7 | 6.2 | * |

| Type | Manufacturer | Unit | B/A | F/A | MPF | Lamp (or lampholder type) | Peak Candela †=flat field candela *=math average | W in (0.04) | W mm (25) | L in (0.04) | L mm (25) | H in (0.0) | H mm (25) | HY in (0.0) | HY mm (25) | Wt lb (2.2) | Wt kg (0.5) | Other lamp |
|---|---|---|---|---|---|---|---|---|---|---|---|---|---|---|---|---|---|---|
| Fresnel | Marumo | LNH 120H 1500W | 7.5°–55° | 14°–58.5° | 0.25–1.12 | JP 1.5kW G-D 100v | 284,000/26,000 | 12.4 | 315 | 13.0 | 330 | 10.7 | 273 | 21.1 | 537 | 15.0 | 6.8 | |
| Fresnel | Marumo | LNH 250H 1500W | 5°–42° | 8.5°–47° | 0.15–0.87 | JP 1.5kW G-D 100v | 389,000/26,000 | 12.4 | 315 | 18.1 | 460 | 10.7 | 273 | 21.1 | 537 | 17.4 | 7.9 | |
| Fresnel | Marumo | LNH 350H 1500W | 3°–22° | 5°–25.5° | 0.09–0.45 | JP 1.5kW G-D 100v | 577,000/34,000 | 12.4 | 315 | 22.0 | 560 | 10.7 | 273 | 21.1 | 537 | 19.2 | 8.7 | |
| Fresnel | Marumo | FQ 2000W | 5.5°–57.5° | 10°–62.5° | 0.18–1.21 | JP 2kW B/G 100v | 549,000/21,250 | 18.5 | 470 | 19.1 | 485 | 16.7 | 425 | 25.2 | 640 | 27.3 | ## | * |
| Fresnel | Marumo | FQ 3000W | 6.6°–58.5° | 10.5°–63° | 0.18–1.23 | JP 3kW B/G 100v | 472,000/27,750 | 18.5 | 470 | 19.1 | 485 | 16.7 | 425 | 25.2 | 640 | 27.3 | ## | * |
| Fresnel 6" | Mole-Richardson | Molequartz 4131 | | 27°–55° | 0.48–1.04 | CYX T10/4CL 2kW | 150,000/40,000* | 11.0 | 279 | 12.0 | 305 | 14.0 | 356 | 21.0 | 533 | 10.3 | 4.6 | |
| Fresnel 9.8" | Mole-Richardson | Molequartz 4191 | | 17°–61° | 0.3–1.18 | DPY T20/4CL 5kW | 580,000/96,000* | 18.0 | 457 | 16.0 | 406 | 19.0 | 483 | 30.0 | 762 | 26.0 | ## | |
| Fresnel 14" | Mole-Richardson | Molequartz 4181 | | 15°–63° | 0.26–1.23 | DTY 10kW 120v | 1,250,000/160,000* | 24.0 | 610 | 24.0 | 610 | 23.0 | 584 | 39.0 | 991 | 52.5 | ## | |
| Fresnel 24.75" | Mole-Richardson | Big Mole 4251 | | 21.8°–66.5° | 0.38–1.31 | KP200 20kW 220v | 2,780,000/428,000* | 33.0 | 838 | 30.0 | 762 | 32.0 | 813 | 47.0 | 1194 | 98.5 | ## | |
| Fresnel 6" | RDS | AQF-5E | 11°–36.2° | 20.3°–46.3° | 0.36–0.85 | RT-12 650W 220v | 45,000/10,000* | 11.0 | 281 | 11.2 | 284 | 8.9 | 226 | 12.4 | 316 | 10.1 | 4.6 | |
| Fresnel 6" | RDS | 0.5 KQS | 10.9°–50.5° | 17.6°–57.5° | 0.31–1.10 | RP 47 650W 220v | 82,250/10,625* | 10.4 | 264 | 9.9 | 253 | 9.4 | 240 | 13.0 | 330 | 8.4 | 3.8 | * |
| Fresnel 8" | RDS | AQF-10E | 6.4°–40.3° | 11.8°–47.1° | 0.21–0.87 | RT-11 1kW 220v | 122,000/12,225* | 13.1 | 333 | 15.8 | 402 | 10.7 | 272 | 14.6 | 372 | 15.7 | 7.1 | * |
| Fresnel | Selecon | Mini F | 8°–55° | 20°–68° | 0.35–1.35 | T/26 650W 240v | 58,357/13,018 | 8.3 | 210 | 10.5 | 268 | 6.0 | 153 | 9.6 | 245 | 5.9 | 2.7 | |
| Fresnel 6" | Selecon | Acclaim F | 6°–60° | 14°–70° | 0.25–1.40 | T/26 650W 240v | 58,000/7,000 | 7.9 | 200 | 11.0 | 280 | 5.9 | 150 | 10.6 | 270 | 5.3 | 2.4 | |
| Fresnel 6" | Selecon | Compact 6 F | 7°–50° | 14°–61° | 0.25–1.18 | T/29 1.2kW 240v | 165,600/17,640 | 11.0 | 280 | 12.6 | 320 | 8.8 | 224 | 12.6 | 320 | 9.9 | 4.5 | |
| Fresnel 7" | Selecon | Fresnel 1200 | 7°–56° | 13°–66° | 0.23–1.30 | T/29 1.2kW 240v | 228,939/27,158 | 11.0 | 280 | 12.6 | 320 | 8.8 | 224 | 12.6 | 320 | 11.0 | 5.0 | |
| Fresnel 7" | Selecon | Fresnel 2000 | 7°–60° | 13°–68° | 0.23–1.35 | CP 72 2kW 240v | 356,000/38,800 | 14.5 | 370 | 15.7 | 400 | 11.8 | 300 | 17.5 | 445 | 22.5 | ## | * |
| Fresnel 10" | Selecon | Arena High perf F | 8°–60° | 15°–70° | 0.26–1.40 | CP 91 2.5kW 240v | 418,950/44,100 | 14.3 | 365 | 15.7 | 400 | 11.7 | 297 | 17.7 | 450 | 19.2 | 8.7 | |
| Fresnel 10" | Selecon | Arena Theatre F | 7°–60° | 22°–70° | 0.39–1.40 | CP 91 2.5kW 240v | 338,400/34,560 | 14.3 | 365 | 15.7 | 400 | 11.7 | 297 | 17.7 | 450 | 19.2 | 8.7 | * |
| Fresnel | Spotlight | QPS 500/AF | 9°–58° | 18°–68° | 0.32–1.35 | GY 9.5/ T26 650W 220v | 100,000/10,800 | 7.1 | 180 | 11.6 | 295 | 6.3 | 160 | 10.4 | 265 | 7.1 | 3.2 | |
| Fresnel | Spotlight | ar 05 "Sintesi" | 6°–67° | 13°–75° | 0.23–1.53 | CP 89 650W 220v | 95,000/6,500 | 8.8 | 225 | 10.6 | 270 | 5.9 | 150 | 9.8 | 250 | 6.2 | 2.8 | * |
| Fresnel | Spotlight | QPS 1000/AF | 8°–50° | 17°–59° | 0.30–1.13 | 6X 9.5/ CP70 1kW 220v | 165,000/19,800 | 8.6 | 220 | 14.9 | 380 | 7.7 | 195 | 13.0 | 330 | 11.7 | 5.3 | |
| Fresnel 6" | Spotlight | ar 12 "Sintesi" | 7°–56° | 15°–65° | 0.26–1.27 | CP 90 1.2kW 220v | 180,000/8,000 | 10.2 | 260 | 12.6 | 320 | 7.9 | 200 | 13.0 | 330 | 9.3 | 4.2 | * |
| Fresnel 6" | Spotlight | QPS 2000/AF | 11°–62° | 25°–70° | 0.44–1.40 | GY 16/ CP72 2kW 220v | 210,000/30,000 | 11.8 | 300 | 20.0 | 510 | 10.0 | 255 | 18.9 | 480 | 21.6 | ## | * |
| Fresnel 7" | Spotlight | ar 25 "Sintesi" | 7°–65° | 16°–73° | 0.28–1.48 | CP 91 2.5kW 220v | 448,000/25,000 | 13.4 | 340 | 16.5 | 420 | 11.5 | 293 | 18.7 | 475 | 19.8 | 9.0 | * |
| Fresnel 3" | Strand | 3101 Mizar | 14°–43° | | 0.25–0.79 | FEV 200W 240v | 14,000/4,000 | 6.3 | 160 | 5.2 | 130 | 5.7 | 145 | 10.0 | 250 | 4.0 | 1.8 | |
| Fresnel | Strand | Minim F—current | 13°–40° | 27°–53° | 0.48–1.0 | CP 81 300W 240v | 17,630/6,570 | 6.8 | 174 | 8.5 | 216 | 6.3 | 160 | 8.1 | 205 | 5.0 | 2.3 | |
| Fresnel | Strand | Minim F—old | 12.5°–55° | 24°–65° | 0.43–1.27 | RSE/18 500W 240v | 25,000/6,000 | 6.5 | 165 | 5.5 | 140 | 6.3 | 160 | 7.7 | 195 | 4.0 | 1.8 | |
| Fresnel 6" | Strand | Patt 123 | 15°–45° | 26°–51° | 0.46–0.95 | T/1 500W 240v | 16,920/5,440 | 10.4 | 265 | 10.4 | 265 | 9.0 | 230 | 12.6 | 320 | 5.7 | 2.6 | |
| Fresnel 6" | Strand | Prelude F | 9°–40° | 17°–52° | 0.30–0.98 | RSE/26 650W 240v | 56,000/12,000 | 9.0 | 230 | 8.8 | 225 | 7.3 | 185 | 10.6 | 270 | 7.7 | 3.5 | * |
| Fresnel 6" | Strand | Quartet F | 10°–40.5° | 20°–54° | 0.35–1.02 | RSE 26 650W 240v | 54,500/11,400 | 9.5 | 243 | 11.2 | 286 | 9.4 | 240 | 11.3 | 288 | 6.8 | 3.1 | |
| Fresnel 6" | Strand | 3380 Fresnel | 6°–55° | 13°–65° | 0.23–1.27 | BTR 1kW 120v | 175,500/18,500 | 10.2 | 259 | 12.1 | 307 | | | 12.3 | 312 | 10.5 | 4.8 | |
| Fresnel 6" | Strand | Harmony F | 6.5°–52° | 13.5°–58.5° | 0.24–1.12 | RSE/18 1kW 240v | 121,000/13,000 | 11.6 | 295 | 11.4 | 290 | 9.0 | 230 | 16.3 | 415 | 13.0 | 5.9 | |
| Fresnel 8" | Strand | Patt 743 | 8°–57° | 15°–45° | 0.26–1.27 | T/11 1kW 240v | 110,000/10,300 | 13.6 | 345 | 12.6 | 320 | 11.0 | 280 | 15.5 | 395 | 15.0 | 6.8 | |
| Fresnel 8" | Strand | Patt 223 | 10°–60° | 18°–70° | 0.32–1.40 | T/6 1kW 240v | 92,120/10,000 | 13.6 | 345 | 12.6 | 320 | 11.0 | 280 | 15.5 | 395 | 15.0 | 6.8 | |
| Fresnel 10" | Strand | Patt 243 | 15°–50° | | 0.26–0.93 | 1kW 240v | | 15.9 | 405 | 16.9 | 430 | 14.9 | 380 | 19.7 | 500 | 30.9 | ## | |
| Fresnel 5" | Strand | 3201 Bambino | 9°–60° | 16°–68° | 0.28–1.35 | EGT 1kW 120v | 152,000/14,200 | 9.1 | 230 | 9.6 | 246 | 10.2 | 260 | 14.2 | 360 | 9.0 | 4.1 | * |
| Fresnel 6" | Strand | 3301 Polaris | 6.5°–57.5° | 14°–66.5° | 0.25–1.31 | EGT 1kW 120v | 126,000/10,800 | 11.8 | 298 | 11.5 | 290 | 10.2 | 260 | 20.0 | 508 | 11.0 | 5.0 | * |
| Fresnel | Strand | Cantata F | 7.7°–50° | 16°–58° | 0.28–1.13 | RSE 29 1.2kW 240v | 123,250/10,900 | 12.7 | 322 | 11.8 | 300 | 12.6 | 320 | 13.4 | 340 | 12.8 | 5.8 | |

| Type | Manufacturer | Unit | B/A | F/A | MPF | Lamp (or lampholder type) | Peak Candela † = flat field candela * = math average | W in | W mm | L in | L mm | H in | H mm | HY in | HY mm | Wt lb | Wt kg | Other lamp |
|---|---|---|---|---|---|---|---|---|---|---|---|---|---|---|---|---|---|---|
| Fresnel 10" | Strand | Patt 243 BP | 10°–40° | 10°–40° | 0.18–0.73 | G38 CP/41 2kW 240v | 280,000/41,500 | 15.9 | 405 | 16.9 | 430 | 14.9 | 380 | 19.7 | 500 | 30.9 | ## | |
| Fresnel 8" | Strand | 3480 Fresnel | 8°–62° | 14°–68° | 0.25–1.35 | BVW 2kW 120v | 412,000/35,000 | 12.7 | 323 | 14.5 | 366 | | | 16.7 | 424 | 17.0 | 7.7 | * |
| Fresnel | Strand | Cadenza F | 7°–62° | 13°–70° | 0.23–1.40 | RSE 79 2kW 240v | 350,000/28,000 | 14.5 | 370 | 14.9 | 380 | 13.4 | 340 | 17.7 | 450 | 26.9 | ## | |
| Fresnel 6" | Strand | 3302 Bambino | 11°–61° | 20°–72° | 0.35–1.45 | CYX 2kW 120v | 208,000/26,000 | 11.4 | 290 | 11.5 | 292 | 15.7 | 400 | 19.7 | 500 | 13.0 | 5.9 | * |
| Fresnel 10" | Strand | 3501 Castor | 11.5°–53° | 24°–64° | 0.43–1.25 | CYX 2kW 120v | 264,800/39,500 | 16.5 | 420 | 14.0 | 356 | 15.7 | 400 | 26.4 | 670 | 21.0 | 9.5 | * |
| Fresnel 12" | Strand | 3601 Pollux | 13°–59° | 27°–69° | 0.48–1.37 | DPY 5kW 120v | 550,000/100,000 | 20.0 | 508 | 14.2 | 361 | 19.7 | 500 | 28.5 | 725 | 26.0 | ## | * |
| Fresnel 14" | Strand | 3701 Vega | 13.5°–55.5° | 24°–65.5° | 0.43–1.28 | DTY 10kW 120v | 820,000/151,200 | 20.0 | 505 | 17.3 | 440 | 20.8 | 530 | 34.0 | 860 | 37.0 | ## | * |
| Fresnel | Teatro | Punto 500 F | 11°–40° | 23°–46° | 0.41–0.85 | T25 500W 220v | 25,200/8,760 | 8.0 | 204 | 10.0 | 255 | 6.1 | 156 | 10.0 | 255 | 6.2 | 2.8 | |
| Fresnel | Teatro | Comma 650 F | 9°–27° | 18°–40° | 0.32–0.73 | T27 650W 220v | 54,000/17,400 | 8.8 | 223 | 11.6 | 295 | | | 11.6 | 294 | 7.7 | 3.5 | |
| Fresnel | Teatro | Tipo F 1000 | 8.5°–50° | 15°–57° | 0.26–1.09 | CP70 1kW 220v | 116,200/13,600 | 9.9 | 252 | 13.4 | 340 | 8.9 | 226 | 11.6 | 295 | 10.4 | 4.7 | |
| Fresnel | Teatro | Spazio F 1000/E | 10°–28.5° | 20°–41.5° | 0.35–0.76 | CP70 1kW 220v | 73,000/24,300 | 8.8 | 223 | 12.0 | 305 | | | 11.6 | 294 | 7.7 | 3.5 | |
| Fresnel | Teatro | Spazio F 1000 | 8.5°–50° | 15°–57° | 0.26–1.09 | CP70 1kW 220v | 116,200/13,600 | 11.4 | 290 | 17.1 | 435 | 9.4 | 240 | 15.7 | 400 | 13.7 | 6.2 | |
| Fresnel | Teatro | Tratto 2 F | 8.5°–34° | 15°–45° | 0.26–0.83 | CP93 1.2kW 220v | 138,500/24,600 | 11.2 | 285 | 14.6 | 372 | 9.0 | 230 | 16.5 | 420 | 14.6 | 6.6 | * |
| Fresnel | Teatro | Spazio F 2000 | 11°–52° | 21°–60° | 0.37–1.15 | CP72 2kW 220v | 165,000/27,200 | 11.4 | 290 | 17.1 | 435 | 9.4 | 240 | 15.7 | 400 | 13.7 | 6.2 | |
| Fresnel | Teatro | Acuto F | 6°–53° | 12°–60° | 0.21–1.15 | CP72 2kW 220v | 245,250/25,000 | 14.3 | 365 | 18.2 | 462 | 14.0 | 356 | 21.6 | 550 | 23.8 | ## | |
| Fresnel 3" | Times Square | C3 | | 18°–60° | 0.32–1.15 | ETG 150W 120v | 4,200/1,050 | 5.4 | 137 | 5.3 | 133 | 4.5 | 114 | 6.6 | 168 | 2.3 | 1.0 | * |
| Fresnel 6" | Times Square | C6 | | 18°–60° | 0.32–1.15 | BTL 500W 120v | 68,000/10,250* | 9.0 | 229 | 8.8 | 222 | | | 12.0 | 305 | 6.0 | 2.7 | |
| Fresnel 6" | Times Square | O6P | | 33°–71.5° | 0.59–1.44 | EVR 500W 120v | 12,250/3,250 | | | | | | | | | | | * |
| Fresnel 6" | Times Square | 6PC | | 18°–60° | 0.32–1.15 | BTR 1kW 120v | 160,000/105,000* | 9.0 | 229 | 9.4 | 239 | | | 12.0 | 305 | 6.0 | 2.7 | * |
| Fresnel 8" | Times Square | O8PC | | 18°–49° | 0.32–0.91 | BTR 1kW 120v | 161,000/18,500 | 13.5 | 343 | 11.0 | 279 | | | 18.0 | 457 | | | * |
| Fresnel | Zero 88 | Focus 650 F | 18°–57° | | 0.32–1.09 | 650W/500W 240v | | 7.7 | 195 | 9.6 | 245 | 5.9 | 150 | 10.3 | 262 | 4.9 | 2.2 | * |

Basically the beam projector, or beamlight, is a small searchlight, providing a very narrow and intense beam of light with limited adjustability (Fig. 58). It uses a parabolic mirror (1) to focus the lamp (2). Spill rings, or baffle, spherical front reflector or sometimes a crown-silvered lamp (3) prevent stray light diverging to the side. This is the most useful instrument for shafts of sun or moonlight when used in multiple banks. Low-voltage beamlights remain my favorite instrument for that clean hard punch! More powerful xenon searchlights, which can also be automated (see Moving Lights, below), give a sensational beam of light useful for World War III or other wonderful effects.

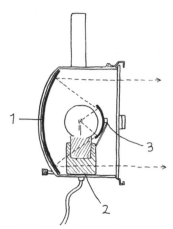

*58. Section beam projector*

*59. Century Beam Projector*

*60. Strand 500W Beamlight*

*61. Robert Juliat 843 Beam Projector*

*62. Reiche & Vogel Beamlight*

*Stage Lighting Design*

| Type | Manufacturer | Unit | B/A | F/A | MPF | Lamp | Peak Candela | W in (0.04) | W mm (25) | L in (0.04) | L mm (25) | H in (0.04) | H mm (25) | HY in (0.04) | HY mm (25) | Wt lb (2.2) | Wt kg (0.5) | Other lamp |
|---|---|---|---|---|---|---|---|---|---|---|---|---|---|---|---|---|---|---|
| Beam Projector | Altman | 660 | 8° | 18°–32° | 0.32–0.57 | BTN 750W 120v | 217,800/98,000 | 13.0 | 330 | 11.5 | 292 | 13.0 | 330 | 16.0 | 406 |  |  | * |
| Beam Projector | Colortran | 216-072 | 5.7°–14° | 11°–20° | 0.19–0.35 | BTL 500W 120v | 270,000/120,000 |  |  |  |  |  |  |  |  |  |  | * |
| Beam Projector | Century | 1515 |  | 15°–25° | 0.26–0.44 | T20/G13 750W 120v | 180,000/75,600 |  |  |  |  |  |  |  |  |  |  | * |
| Beam Projector | Century Strand | 4121 |  | 15°–25° | 0.26–0.44 | BTR 1kW 120v | 292,500/121,500 |  |  |  |  |  |  |  |  |  |  | * |
| Beam Projector | Electro Controls | 7701A | 9.5°–37° | 22.5°–47° | 0.4–0.87 | FEL 1kW 120v | 134,375/20,200 |  |  |  |  |  |  |  |  |  |  | * |
| Beam Projector | Kliegl | 3440 |  | 10°–22° | 0.18–0.39 | EGT 1kW 120v | 320,000/148,000 |  |  |  |  |  |  |  |  |  |  | * |
| Beam Projector | Kliegl | 1143 |  | 13°–20° | 0.23–0.35 | GWZ 1.5kW 120v | 480,000/123,200 |  |  |  |  |  |  |  |  |  |  | * |
| Beam Projector | L & E | 63-32 |  | 17°–23° | 0.3–0.41 | BFE 750W 120v | 88,000/81,000 | 9.0 | 229 | 9.8 | 248 | 9.0 | 229 |  |  |  |  | * |
| Beam Projector | Pani | P250 | 6°–14° | 10.5°–23.5° | 0.19–0.42 | E27 250W 24v mirror domed | 150,000/28,750 | 10.8 | 275 | 14.7 | 375 | 10.8 | 275 | 15.7 | 400 | 10.2 | 4.6 | * |
| Beam Projector | Pani | P500 | 5°–10° | 9°–13.5° | 0.16–0.24 | E40 500W 24v mirror domed | 480,000/150,000 | 12.6 | 320 | 16.9 | 430 | 12.6 | 320 | 18.9 | 480 | 35.3 | 16.0 | * |
| Beam Projector | Pani | P1001 | 5°–7.5° | 8°–12° | 0.14–0.21 | K39d 1kW 24v mirror domed | 1,300,000/560,000 |  |  |  |  |  |  |  |  | 17.8 | 8.1 | * |
| Xenon Searchlight | Phoebus | Silverbeam PSL-14 | collimated /1.5°/10° |  | 0/0.018/0.18 | 2kW Xenon 120v | 137,500,000/90,000,000/8,750,000 | 17.8 | 451 | 24.5 | 622 | 17.8 | 451 | 31.5 | 800 | 75.0 | 34.0 | * |
| Xenon Searchlight | Phoebus | Silverbeam PSL-20 | collimated/1.5°/10° |  | 0/0.018/0.18 | 3kW Xenon 120v | 127,500,000/80,000,000/16,250,000 | 25.5 | 648 | 33.0 | 838 | 23.8 | 603 | 40.0 | 1016 | 110.0 | 49.9 | * |
| Xenon Searchlight | Phoebus | Silverbeam PSL-20 | collimated/1.5°/10° |  | 0/0.018/0.18 | 4kW Xenon 120v | 175,000,000/135,000,000/28,125,000 | 25.5 | 648 | 33.0 | 838 | 23.8 | 603 | 40.0 | 1016 | 110.0 | 49.9 | * |
| Xenon Searchlight | Phoebus | Silverbeam PSL-20 | collimated/1.5°/10° |  | 0/0.018/0.18 | 7kW Xenon 120v | 262,500,000/202,500,000/42,187,500 | 25.5 | 648 | 33.0 | 838 | 23.8 | 603 | 40.0 | 1016 | 110.0 | 49.9 | * |
| Beam Projector | R & V | NS/250/T | 12° |  | 0.21 | 250W 24v | 480,000 | 12.4 | 315 | 16.3 | 415 |  |  | 17.5 | 445 | 26.5 | 12.0 | * |
| Beam Projector | R & V | NS/500/T | 8° |  | 0.14 | 500W 24v | 830,000 | 14.1 | 360 | 18.1 | 460 |  |  | 19.7 | 500 | 34.2 | 15.5 | * |
| Beam Projector | R & V | NS/1000 |  |  |  | 1kW 24v | 1,400,000 | 20.4 | 520 | 20.0 | 510 |  |  | 21.8 | 555 | 39.7 | 18.0 | * |
| Beam Projector | Robert Juliat | 843 | 7° | 12° | 0.21 | E27 250W 24v |  | 8.1 | 206 | 16.9 | 430 | 9.0 | 230 | 13.6 | 345 | 22.1 | 10.0 | * |
| Beam Projector | Robert Juliat | 845 | 7° | 12° | 0.21 | E40 500W 24v |  | 9.8 | 250 | 19.3 | 490 | 9.8 | 250 | 17.3 | 440 | 37.5 | 17.0 | * |
| Beam Projector | Strand | Beamlite 500 | 4.2° | 6.9° | 0.12 | 500W 24v | 672,000 | 13.8 | 350 | 16.5 | 420 |  |  | 15.1 | 385 | 28.7 | 13.0 | * |
| Beam Projector | Strand | Beamlite 1000 | 4.7° | 7° | 0.12 | 1000W 24v | 1,550,000 | 14.7 | 375 | 18.9 | 480 |  |  | 18.7 | 475 | 37.5 | 17.0 | * |
| Beam Projector | Strand Century | 4122 | 15°–25° | 15°–25° | 0.26–0.44 | BTR 1kW 120v | 292,500/121,500 | 14.5 | 365 | 10.5 | 264 | 12.0 | 305 | 15.5 | 394 | 13.5 | 6.1 | * |
| Beam Projector | Strand Century | 4125 | 9°–22° | 16°–30° | 0.28–0.54 | BVW 2kW 120v | 592,000/120,800 | 18.0 | 460 | 14.5 | 365 | 15.0 | 381 | 23.0 | 585 |  |  | * |
| Beam Projector | Spotlight | RP 1024 | 7° | 12° | 0.21 | K39j/592 1kW 220v | 1,008,000 | 16.3 | 415 | 15.3 | 389 | 14.5 | 370 | 18.5 | 472 | 25.1 | 11.4 | * |

Lamps with internal reflectors are an important part of the designer's armory. The ubiquitous PAR lamp, perhaps particularly in the 1,000W PAR64 size are an effective and low-cost substitute for the Fresnel and beam projector. The PAR can has become the instrument of choice for most of the concert world, being rugged in construction, economical and easy to troupe. Using these is like being back at school. A lamp in a tin can—but now it's really bright.

Low-voltage PARs, built as headlamps for airplanes can be very punchy and a good alternate to the beamlight. They can also be used in strips as light-curtains.

Most PAR lamps have an oval beam, which allows a variety of effects by rotating the lamp in the fixture.

The range of these lamps is enormous so only a selection are listed here (see Table A on opposite page).

A product new to the market at the end of 1995 is the ETC Source 4 PAR. This is a die-cast unit employing the 575W lamp from the Source 4 as a light source but now with a range of PAR-lamp interchangeable front lenses to provide a soft light with some of the beam characteristics (but with a circular rather than oval beam) of a conventional 1kW PAR (see Table B on page 415).

63. Section PAR can

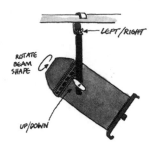

64. PAR can adjustment

65. CCT PAR head

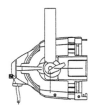

66. ETC Source 4 PAR

| Lamp | Type | B/A (W x H) | F/A (W x H) | MPF | Peak Candela | Voltage | Lamp Base Type | Color Temp |
|------|------|------|------|------|------|------|------|------|
| MR-11 | 20W Q20MR11/SP | | 17° | | 1,760 | 12 | 2-pin (GU4) | 3500°K |
| MR-11 | 20W Q20MR11/NSP | | 10° | | 5,500 | 12 | 2-pin (GU4) | 3500°K |
| MR-11 | 20W Q20MR11/NFL | | 30° | | 600 | 12 | 2-pin (GU4) | 3500°K |
| MR-11 | 35W Q20MR11/SP | | 20° | | 3,000 | 12 | 2-pin (GU4) | 3500°K |
| MR-11 | 35W Q20MR11/NSP | | 8° | | 9,000 | 12 | 2-pin (GU4) | 3500°K |
| MR-11 | 35W Q20MR11/NFL | | 30° | | 1,300 | 12 | 2-pin (GU4) | 3500°K |
| MR-16 | 20W VNSP ESX | 7° | 12° | 0.21 | 8,200 | 12v | 2-pin (GX5.3) | 2925°K |
| MR-16 | 20W NSP ESX | | 19° | 0.33 | 3,350 | 12v | 2-pin (GX5.3) | 2925°K |
| MR-16 | 20W FL BAB | 40° | 59° | 1.13 | 490 | 12v | 2-pin (GX5.3) | 2925°K |
| MR-16 | 35W NSP FMT | 12° | | 0.21 | 8,000 | 12v | 2-pin (GX5.3) | 3050°K |
| MR-16 | 35W SP | 20° | | 0.35 | 3,800 | 12v | 2-pin (GX5.3) | 3050°K |
| MR-16 | 35W FL FMW | 40° | | 0.73 | 1,100 | 12v | 2-pin (GX5.3) | 3050°K |
| MR-16 | 42W VNSP EZY | 7° | | 0.12 | 13,500 | 12v | 2-pin (GX5.3) | 3025°K |
| MR-16 | 42W NSP EYR | 11° | | 0.2 | 7,075 | 12v | 2-pin (GX5.3) | 3025°K |
| MR-16 | 42W SP EYS | 20° | | 0.35 | 2,800 | 12v | 2-pin (GX5.3) | 3025°K |
| MR-16 | 42W FL EYP | 36° | | 0.65 | 990 | 12v | 2-pin (GX5.3) | 3025°K |
| MR-16 | 50W NSP EXY | 14° | 24° | 0.43 | 9,500 | 12v | 2-pin (GX5.3) | 3050°K |
| MR-16 | 50W NFL EXZ | | 49° | 0.91 | 2,700 | 12v | 2-pin (GX5.3) | 3050°K |
| MR-16 | 50W FL EXN | 40° | 64° | 1.25 | 1,500 | 12v | 2-pin (GX5.3) | 3050°K |
| MR-16 | 50W NFL EXK | | 52° | 0.98 | 2,450 | 12v | 2-pin (GX5.3) | 3050°K |
| MR-16 | 50W NFL ENL | | 49° | 0.91 | 2,325 | 12v | 2-pin (GX5.3) | 3050°K |
| MR-16 | 50W WFL FNV | 55° | | 1.04 | 1,150 | 12v | 2-pin (GX5.3) | 3050°K |
| MR-16 | 65W NSP FPA | 14° | | 0.25 | 11,500 | 12v | 2-pin (GX5.3) | 3050°K |
| MR-16 | 65W NFL FPC | 23° | | 0.41 | 4,000 | 12v | 2-pin (GX5.3) | 3050°K |
| MR-16 | 65W FL FPB | 38° | | 0.69 | 2,000 | 12v | 2-pin (GX5.3) | 3050°K |
| MR-16 | 75W NSP EYF | 14° | 24° | 0.43 | 12,300 | 12v | 2-pin (GX5.3) | 3050°K |
| MR-16 | 75W NFL EYJ | 25° | 35° | 0.63 | 4,600 | 12v | 2-pin (GX5.3) | 3050°K |
| MR-16 | 100W EXV | 53° | | | 3,100 | 12v | 2-pin (GX5.3) | 3350°K |
| MR-16 | 75W FLEYC | 42° | 64° | 1.25 | 2,100 | 12v | 2-pin (GX5.3) | 3050°K |
| PAR 36 | 25 PAR 36 NSP | 8°x10° | 17°x19° | 0.30x0.33 | 4,500 | 12v | Screw terminal | |
| PAR 36 | 25 PAR 36 WFL | 26°x37° | 41°x49° | 0.75x0.91 | 500 | 12v | Screw terminal | |
| PAR 36 | 25 PAR 36 VWFL | 33°x40° | 80°x82° | 1.68x1.74 | 250 | 12v | Screw terminal | |
| PAR 36 | 50 PAR 36 NSP | 9°x11° | 17°x20° | 0.30x0.35 | 9,200 | 12v | Screw terminal | |
| PAR 36 | 50 PAR 36 WFL | 28°x36° | 41°x48° | 0.45x0.89 | 1,300 | 12v | Screw terminal | |
| PAR 36 | 50 PAR 36 VWFL | 37°x40° | 80°x80° | 1.68 | 600 | 12v | Screw terminal | |
| PAR 36 | 650W FGS/DWA | | 30°x20° | | 18,000 | 120v | Ferrule | 3400°K |
| PAR 36 | 650WQ650PAR36/2 DXK | | 40°x30° | | 28,000 | 120v | Ferrule | 3400°K |
| PAR 36 | 650W Q650 PAR36/3D FAY | | 25°x15° | | 36,000 | 120v | Ferrule | 3400°K |
| PAR 36 | 650W Q650 PAR36/3 FBJ | | 25°x15° | | 67,000 | 120v | Ferrule | 3400°K |
| PAR 36 | 650W Q650 PAR36/6 FCW | | 60°x55° | | 9,000 | 120v | Ferrule | 3400°K |
| PAR 36 | 650W Q650 PAR36/7 FCX | | 40°x30° | | 24,000 | 120v | Ferrule | 3400°K |
| PAR 36 | 650W Q650 PAR36/1 DWE | | 40°x30° | | 24,000 | 120v | Screw terminal | 3200°K |
| PAR 36 | 650W Q650 PAR36/5D FBE | | 25°x15° | | 36,000 | 120v | Screw terminal | 5000°K |
| PAR 36 | 650W Q650 PAR36/5 FBOE | | 25°x15° | | 67,000 | 120v | Screw terminal | 3400°K |
| PAR 56 | 120 PAR 56 VNSP | 6°x8° | 10°x15° | 0.18x0.26 | 60,000 | 12v | Screw terminal | |
| PAR 56 | 120 PAR 56 MFL | 9°x18° | 15°x29° | 0.26x0.52 | 19,00 | 12v | Screw terminal | |
| PAR 56 | 120 PAR 56 WFL | 18°x35° | 25°x50° | 0.44x0.93 | 5,625 | 12v | Screw terminal | |
| PAR 56 | 240 PAR 56 VNSP | 6°x9° | 10°x17° | 0.18x0.30 | 140,000 | 12v | Screw terminal | |
| PAR 56 | 240 PAR 56 MFL | 8°x19° | 15°x28° | 0.26x0.50 | 46,000 | 12v | Screw terminal | |
| PAR 56 | 240 PAR 56 WFL | 18°x35° | 27°x50° | 0.48x1.11 | 13,000 | 12v | Screw terminal | |

| Lamp | Type | B/A (W x H) | F/A (W x H) | MPF | Peak Candela | Voltage | Lamp Base Type | Color Temp |
|---|---|---|---|---|---|---|---|---|
| MR-16 | 150W FL EZK | 60° | | 1.16 | 3,600 | 120v | Oval 2-pin (GY5.3) | 3200°K |
| MR-16 | 250W FLENH | 32° | | 0.57 | 11,700 | 120v | Oval 2-pin (GY5.3) | 3250°K |
| MR-16 | 250W FL EXX | 57° | | 1.09 | 6,750 | 120v | Oval 2-pin (GY5.3) | 3300°K |
| PAR 36 | 30W PAR36 RAIN #79-04 | 5°x5° | | 0.087 | 55,00 | 5.5v | GE 4515 | |
| PAR 38 | 150W SP | | 28° | 0.5 | 11,500 | 120v | Medium skirted | 2750°K |
| PAR 38 | 150W FL | | 60° | 1.15 | 4,000 | 120v | Medium skirted | 2750°K |
| PAR 38 | 150W WFL | | 117° | 3.26 | 1,400 | 120v | Medium skirted | 2750°K |
| PAR 38 | 250W SP | | 24° | 0.43 | 28,000 | 120v | Medium skirted | 2900°K |
| PAR 38 | 250W FL | | 60° | 1.15 | 6,500 | 120v | Medium skirted | 2900°K |
| PAR 46 | 30W PAR46 RAIN #79-06 | 5.5°x4° | | 0.07x0.096 | 95,000 | 5.5v | GE 4535 | |
| PAR 46 | 150W NSP | | 22°x20° | 0.39x0.35 | 20,000 | 120v | Medium side prong | 2750°K |
| PAR 46 | 150W MFL | | 39°x25° | 0.71x0.44 | 8,000 | 120v | Medium side prong | 2750°K |
| PAR 46 | 200W NSP | | 23°x19° | 0.41x0.33 | 31,000 | 120v | Medium side prong | 2750°K |
| PAR 46 | 200W MFL | | 40°x24° | 0.73x0.43 | 11,500 | 120v | Medium side prong | 2750°K |
| PAR 46 | 200W WFL | | 120°x120° | 3.46x3.46 | 1,500 | 120v | Medium side prong | |
| PAR 56 | 300W NSP | 10°x8° | 20°x14° | 0.35x0.25 | 68,000 | 120v | Mogul end prong | 2750°K |
| PAR 56 | 300W MFL | 23°x11° | 34°x19° | 0.61x0.33 | 24,000 | 120v | Mogul end prong | 2750°K |
| PAR 56 | 300W WFL | 37°x18° | 57°x27° | 1.09x0.48 | 11,000 | 120v | Mogul end prong | 2750°K |
| PAR 56 | Q 500W NSP | 13°x8° | 32°x15° | 0.57x0.26 | 96,000 | 120v | Mogul end prong | 2950°K |
| PAR 56 | Q 500W MFL | 26°x10° | 42°x20° | 0.77x0.35 | 43,000 | 120v | Mogul end prong | 2950°K |
| PAR 56 | Q 500W WFL | 44°x20° | 66°x34° | 1.3x0.61 | 19,000 | 120v | Mogul end prong | 2950°K |
| PAR 64 | 500W NSP | 12°x7° | 19°x14° | 0.33x0.25 | 110,000 | 120v | Extd mogul end prong | 2800°K |
| PAR 64 | 500W MFL | 23°x11° | 35°x19° | 0.63x0.33 | 37,000 | 120v | Extd mogul end prong | 2800°K |
| PAR 64 | 500W WFL | 42°x20° | 55°x32° | 1.0x0.57 | 13,000 | 120v | Extd mogul end prong | 2800°K |
| PAR 64 | Q 1kW NSP | 15°x8° | 31°x14° | 0.55x0.25 | 200,000 | 120v | Extd mogul end prong | 3000°K |
| PAR 64 | Q 1kW MFL | 28°x12° | 45°x22° | 0.83x0.39 | 80,000 | 120v | Extd mogul end prong | 3000°K |
| PAR 64 | Q 1kW WFL | 48°x24° | 72°x43° | 1.45x0.83 | 33,000 | 120v | Extd mogul end prong | 3000°K |
| PAR 64 | 64/1 1kW VNSP FFN | 12°x6° | 24°x10° | 0.43x0.17 | 400,000 | 120v | Extd mogul end prong | 3200°K |
| PAR 64 | 64/2 1kW NSP FFP | 14°x7° | 26°x14° | 0.46x0.25 | 330,000 | 120v | Extd mogul end prong | 3200°K |
| PAR 64 | 64/5 1kW MFL FFR | 18°x12° | 44°x21° | 0.81x0.37 | 125,000 | 120v | Extd mogul end prong | 3200°K |
| PAR 64 | 64/6 1kW WFL FFS | 48°x24° | 71°x45° | 1.43x0.83 | 40,000 | 120v | Extd mogul end prong | 3200°K |
| PAR 64 | 1kW NSP Daylight | | 24°x12° | 0.43x0.21 | 200,000 | 120v | Extd mogul end prong | 5200°K |
| PAR 64 | 1kW MFL Daylight | | 43°x20° | 0.79x0.35 | 70,000 | 120v | Extd mogul end prong | 5200°K |
| PAR 64 | CP60 | 12°x6° | | | 400,000 | 240v | GX16d | |
| PAR 64 | CP61 | 13°x10° | | | 260,000 | 240v | GX16d | |
| PAR 64 | CP62 | 25°x14° | | | 110,000 | 240v | GX16d | |
| R 40 | 150W SP | 25° | | 0.44 | 4,500 | 120v | Medium screw | 2750°K |
| R 40 | 150W FL | 70° | | 1.4 | 1,230 | 120v | Medium screw | 2750°K |
| R 40 | 300W SP | 24° | | 0.43 | 8,900 | 120v | Medium screw | 2750°K |
| R 40 | 300W FL | 77° | | 1.6 | 1,950 | 120v | Medium screw | 2750°K |
| R 40 | 500W SP | 15° | | 0.26 | 45,000 | 120v | Medium screw | 3200°K |
| R 40 | 500W MFL | 60° | | 1.15 | 6,800 | 120v | Medium screw | 3200°K |
| R 40 | 500W FL | 90° | | 2 | 5,500 | 120v | Medium screw | 3200°K |
| R 40 | 500W 3 SP | 21° | | 0.37 | 21,000 | 120v | Mogul screw | 2800°K |
| R 40 | 500W 3 FL | 72° | | 1.45 | 3,800 | 120v | Mogul screw | 2800°K |

| Type | Manufacturer | Lens type used | B/A | F/A | B/A | F/A | Lamp (or lampholder type) | Peak Candela | W in | W mm | L in | L mm | H in | H mm | HY in | HY mm | Wt lb | Wt kg | Other |
|---|---|---|---|---|---|---|---|---|---|---|---|---|---|---|---|---|---|---|---|
|  |  |  |  |  |  |  |  |  | 0.04 |  |  |  |  |  |  |  |  |  |  |
| Source 4 PAR | ETC | Clear, flat | 8° | 14° | 0.14 | 0.26 | HPL575/115V 575W | 356,000 | 10.25 | 260 | 10.75 | 273 | 9.00 | 228 | 12.75 | 324 | 7.5 | 3.4 | HPL 575/230V or 240V lamp |
| Source 4 PAR | ETC | Very narrow spot | 8° | 15° | 0.15 | 0.26 | HPL575/115V 575W | 314,000 | 10.25 | 260 | 10.75 | 273 | 9.00 | 228 | 12.75 | 324 | 7.5 | 3.4 | HPL 575/230V or 240V |
| Source 4 PAR | ETC | Narrow spot | 10° | 19° | 0.17 | 0.33 | HPL575/115V 575W | 203,000 | 10.25 | 260 | 10.75 | 273 | 9.00 | 228 | 12.75 | 324 | 7.5 | 3.4 | HPL 575/230V or 240V |
| Source 4 PAR | ETC | Medium flood | 12°x19° | 21°x34° | 0.21x0.33 | 0.37x0.61 | HPL575/115V 575W | 104,000 | 10.25 | 260 | 10.75 | 273 | 9.00 | 228 | 12.75 | 324 | 7.5 | 3.4 | HPL 575/230V or 240V |
| Source 4 PAR | ETC | Wide flood | 16°x33° | 30°x51° | 0.28x0.59 | 0.53x0.95 | HPL575/115V 575W | 49,000 | 10.25 | 260 | 10.75 | 273 | 9.00 | 228 | 12.75 | 324 | 7.5 | 3.4 | HPL 575/230V or 240V |

When calculating the brightness of pipes of floods, light curtains and striplights or battens you must take into account the multiplication effect of adjacent lamps This can only be an approximate calculation without resorting to higher mathematics. The beam angle and candela distribution of each lamp must be assessed in gauging overlap and consequent total output (Fig. 68).

### ADB Lighting

*Svoboda Light Curtain:* Double-stacked light curtains named after their distinguished inventor: the original "wall" of light (Fig. 78). HT2251 and HT2500 are fitted with nine 24v 250W lamps at 220v or ten lamps for 240v.

### Mole Richardson Co

*Molequartz Moleeno:* Twenty-four 1,000W lamps individually rotatable through 90°. Also available in nine-light and six-light Molepar configurations

### Thomas Engineering

*Spot Banks:* PAR64 six-light and nine-lights. PAR36 in four, six, eight and nine-light configurations.

### Lighting and Electronics Inc.

*MR16 Mini-striplight:* Six feet long and 3½-inch wide miniature striplight, which can be extraordinarily useful for getting a lot of light into too small a space!

### Altman

*Zip Strip:* A miniature striplight employing MR16 lamps (Fig. 80). Strips can be double mounted on a single bracket for lighting cloths from top and/or bottom.

*MR-11 Micro-strip.* In addition to Altman's version of the Zip strip, their latest development is an even smaller striplight using the 20W or 35W MR-11 lamp. Available in three lengths and wired for one, two or three circuits.

67. Flood adjustment

68. Flood spread diagram

69. Strand patt 60

70. Strand patt 49

71. AC 1001

72. Kliegl scoop

73. Century scoop

74. Strand Iris 1

75. Strand Coda 500

76. Altman Sky Cyc x 4

77. Strand S-type batten

78. Svoboda Light Curtain

79. Strand PAR strip

80. Zip strip

# FLOOD LIGHTS AND STRIP LIGHTS TABLE

| Type | Manufacturer | Unit | B/A | F/A | MPF | Lamp | Peak Candela | W (in) | W (mm) | L (in) | L (mm) | H (in) | H (mm) | HY (in) | HY (mm) | Wt (lb) | Wt (kg) | Other lamp |
|---|---|---|---|---|---|---|---|---|---|---|---|---|---|---|---|---|---|---|
| Flood | ADB | LF 1000 | 90° | 90° | 2.00 | R7S 1kW 220v | 10,000/9,000 | 13.8 | 350 | 2.8 | 70 | 5.5 | 140 | 7.5 | 190 | 3.3 | 1.50 | * |
| Flood | ADB | HF 1000 | 90° | 90° | 2.00 | R7S 1kW 220v | 10,000/6,500 | 13.8 | 350 | 2.8 | 70 | 5.5 | 140 | 7.5 | 190 | 3.3 | 1.50 | * |
| Scoop—10" | Altman | 153 | 57° | 103° | 2.51 | 400G/FL 400W 120v | 3,025 | 11.0 | 279 | 8.0 | 203 | 11.0 | 279 | 14.0 | 356 | 5.5 | 2.49 | * |
| Scoop—14" | Altman | 154 | 47° | 90° | 2.00 | 1000IF 1kW 120v | 12,550 | 16.0 | 406 | 13.5 | 343 | 16.0 | 406 | 23.0 | 584 | 9.0 | 4.08 | * |
| Scoop—14" | Altman | 160 | 32°–70° | 84°–108° | 1.8–2.75 | EGK 1kW 120v | 25,000/8,750 | 16.0 | 406 | 19.5 | 495 | 16.0 | 406 | 17.0 | 432 | 9.5 | 4.31 | * |
| Scoop—16" | Altman | 161 | 43° | 90° | 2.00 | FCM 1kW 120v | 28,000 | 16.5 | 419 | 14.0 | 356 | 17.0 | 432 | 15.5 | 394 | 8.5 | 3.86 | * |
| Scoop—18" | Altman | 155 | 60° | 106° | 2.67 | DKX 1.5kW 120v | 17,200 | 19.0 | 483 | 14.5 | 368 | 19.0 | 483 | 24.5 | 622 | 8.0 | 3.63 | * |
| Scoop—16" | Altman | 261 | 12°–46° | 54°–100° | 1.02–2.38 | BWF 2kW 120v | 180,000/42,500 | 17.0 | 432 | 18.0 | 457 | 17.0 | 432 | 16.0 | 406 | | | * |
| Flood | Altman | Sky cyc | 100°x105° | 108°x107° | 2.75 | FDB 1.5kW 120v | 10,924 | 19.6 | 498 | 9.8 | 249 | | | | | | | * |
| Striplight | Altman | 520 | 50° | 75° | 1.53 | 75/A19 75W 120v | 294 | | | | | | | | | | | * |
| Striplight | Altman | SE | | 85° | 1.83 | 100A 100W 120v | 428 | 4.8 | 122 | | | 9.5 | 241 | 9.5 | 241 | varies | | * |
| Striplight | Altman | 528 | 52° | 80° | 1.68 | 150A/23 150W 120v | 903 | 9.2 | 232 | | | 9.0 | 229 | 13.3 | 337 | varies | | 8 Types |
| Striplight | Altman | R40 | 25° | 60° | 1.15 | 150R/FL 150W 120v | 1,040 | 7.5 | 191 | | | 9.3 | 235 | n/a | n/a | varies | | * |
| Striplight | Altman | 537 | | 65° | 1.27 | 300M/IF 300W 120v | 3,860 | 11.5 | 292 | | | 9.0 | 229 | 14.0 | 356 | varies | | * |
| Striplight | Altman | 600 | 20° | 48° | 0.89 | EHM 300W 120v | 7,720 | 10.5 | 267 | | | 9.0 | 229 | 13.8 | 351 | varies | | * |
| Striplight | Altman | PAR 56B | Depends | | - | PI | | 8.5 | 216 | to spec | to spec | 11.0 | 279 | 17.2 | 437 | varies | | 6 Types |
| Striplight | Altman | Ground cyc | 50°x65° | 70°x83° | 1.4 x 1.77 | FCM 1kW 120v | 81,000 | 8.5 | 216 | to spec | to spec | 10.0 | 254 | 16.8 | 425 | varies | varies | * |
| Striplight | Altman | PAR64B | Depends | | L | PI | | 10.0 | 254 | to spec | to spec | 12.0 | 305 | 18.0 | 457 | varies | varies | 10 Types |
| Scoop—14" | Century | 1313 | 64° | 110° | 2.85 | Q1000T12/4 1kW 120v | 16,837 | 18.5 | 470 | 15.5 | 394 | 16.0 | 406 | 18.0 | 457 | | | * |
| Scoop—18" | Century Strand | 1318 | 80° | 110° | 2.86 | 2M/PS52/34 2kW 120v | 13,400 | 19.0 | 483 | 15.5 | 394 | 16.0 | 406 | 18.0 | 457 | | | * |
| Scoop—18" | Colortran | 104-232 | 27.5°–50.8° | 60.5°–88° | 1.17–1.93 | EGJ 1kW 120v | 42,000/16,845 | 17.0 | 432 | 17.0 | 432 | 21.0 | 533 | 12.0 | 305 | 8.0 | 3.63 | * |
| Scoop—18" | Colortran | 104-202 | 50°–80° | 60°–90° | 1.35–2.0 | BWF 2kW 120v | 41,300/17,100 | 17.0 | 432 | 17.0 | 432 | 21.0 | 533 | 12.0 | 305 | 8.0 | 3.63 | * |
| Scoop—18" | Colortran | 104-242 | 28°–75° | 68°–103° | 1.35–2.5 | BWF 2kW 120v | 88,000/21,937 | 17.0 | 432 | 17.0 | 432 | 21.0 | 533 | 12.0 | 305 | 8.0 | 3.63 | * |
| Scoop—14" | Electro Controls | 7514A | 80° | 120° | 3.47 | 500IF 500W 120v | 3,200 | 18.0 | 457 | 18.0 | 457 | 20.0 | 508 | | | | | * |
| Scoop—14" | Electro Controls | 35145 | 45°–115° | 80°–150° | 1.68–7.6 | FEL 1kW 120v | 22,700/4,275 | 9.0 | 229 | 1.8 | 46 | 4.3 | 108 | | | | | * |
| Scoop—14" | Electro Controls | 7515A | 45°–115° | 80°–150° | 1.68–7.6 | EGJ 1kW 120v | 22,700/9,675 | 10.5 | 267 | 3.0 | 76 | 5.5 | 140 | | | | | * |
| Scoop—16" | Kliegl | 3451 | | 102° | 2.47 | FHM 1kW 120v | 14,850 | | | | | | | | | | | * |
| Scoop—16" | Kliegl | 3452 | 75° | 65°–102° | 1.53–2.75 | FHM 1kW 120v | 39,375/14,850 | | | | | | | | | | | * |
| Scoop—10" | L & E | 63-10 | 34°–68° | 108° | 1.27–2.47 | 4006/FL 400W 120v | 4,077 | 11.0 | 279 | 7.0 | 178 | 11.0 | 279 | | | 5.0 | 2.27 | * |
| Scoop—14" | L & E | 63-14 | 85° | 90°–105° | 2.0–2.6 | EGJ 1kW 120v | 23,500/18,500 | 16.0 | 406 | 19.0 | 483 | 16.0 | 406 | | | 14.0 | 6.35 | * |
| Scoop—14" | L & E | 63-15 | 78° | 125° | 3.84 | DKX 1.5kW 120v | 5,400 | 16.0 | 406 | 16.0 | 406 | 14.0 | 356 | | | 13.0 | 5.90 | * |
| Scoop—18" | L & E | 63-18 | 83° | 110° | 2.86 | DKX 1.5kW 120v | 12,000 | 18.0 | 457 | 18.0 | 457 | 20.0 | 508 | | | 9.0 | 4.08 | * |
| Flood | L & E | 63-60 Cranny fill | 66° | 121° | 3.54 | FCM 1kW 120v | 19,500 | 9.0 | 229 | 1.8 | 46 | 4.3 | 108 | | | 2.0 | 0.91 | * |
| Flood | L & E | 63-50 Mini-flood | 57.6° | 108° | 2.70 | FCM 1kW 120v | 18,500 | 10.5 | 267 | 3.0 | 76 | 5.5 | 140 | | | 5.0 | 2.27 | * |
| Flood | L & E | 63-51 Set light | 72° | 102° | 2.40 | FCM 1kW 120v | 13,250 | 11.0 | 279 | 3.0 | 76 | 7.3 | 184 | | | 5.0 | 2.27 | * |
| Cyclight | L & E | 65-71 Broad cyc | 25° | 95° | 2.19 | FFW 2kW 120v | | 11.8 | 300 | 8.0 | 203 | 10.3 | 260 | | | 11.0 | 4.99 | * |
| Striplight | L & E | 65-60 | 49° | 35° | 0.63 | MR-16 NFL 75W 120v | 4,600 | 5.5 | 140 | 75.2 | ### | 5.0 | 127 | | | 45.0 | 20.4 | 9 Types |
| Striplight | L & E | 65-50 | 20° | 72° | 1.45 | FCM 1kW 120v | | 10.8 | 273 | to spec | to spec | 14.0 | 356 | | | to spec | | * |
| Striplight | Phoebus | 916 MR-16 9 light | | | 0.35 | MR-16 SP 42W 120v | See MR-16 lamps | 6.3 | 159 | 25.0 | 635 | 3.8 | 95 | 6.5 | 165 | | | Many |

| Type | Manufacturer | Unit | B/A | F/A | MPF | Lamp | Peak Candela | W (in) | W (mm) | L (in) | L (mm) | H (in) | H (mm) | HY (in) | HY (mm) | Wt (lb) | Wt (kg) | Other lamp |
|---|---|---|---|---|---|---|---|---|---|---|---|---|---|---|---|---|---|---|
| Flachenleuchten | R & V | HV 1000 | 110°x95° | | 2.85x2.18 | R7 1.25kW 220v | 24,000 | 14.9 | 380 | 10.6 | 270 | | | 21.6 | 550 | 11.0 | 5.00 | * |
| Flachenleuchten | R & V | HV 2000 | 127°x105° | | 3.95x2.60 | Fa4 2kW 220v | 54,000 | 20.8 | 530 | 10.6 | 270 | | | 17.3 | 440 | 17.6 | 8.00 | * |
| Flachenleuchten | R & V | HV 5000 | 110°x95° | | 2.85x2.18 | K24 5kW 220v | 93,000 | 27.9 | 710 | 12.4 | 315 | | | 27.5 | 700 | 46.3 | ### | * |
| Flood | Selecon | Cyc 500 | 76° | 134° | 4.8 | P2/11 800W 240v | 14,040 | 10.4 | 265 | 5.9 | 150 | 10.6 | 270 | 15.3 | 390 | 6.6 | 3.00 | * |
| Flood | Selecon | Flood 500 | 76° | 134° | 4.8 | P2/11 800W 240v | 14,040 | 11.0 | 280 | 7.1 | 180 | 7.1 | 180 | 18.5 | 470 | 7.3 | 3.30 | * |
| Flood | Spotlight | RA 1 | | | | R75 800W 220v | 14,500 | 11.6 | 294 | 5.3 | 135 | 6.9 | 175 | 9.6 | 245 | 4.2 | 1.90 | * |
| Flood | Spotlight | Domino 1000 | | | | R75 1.25kW 220v | 16,200 | 11.6 | 296 | 8.3 | 210 | 10.6 | 270 | | | 9.7 | 4.40 | * |
| Scoop—14" | Strand | 4271 | 88° | 130° | 4.29 | E6K 1kW 120v | 11,500 | 16.0 | 406 | 14.0 | 350 | 16.0 | 406 | 16.0 | 406 | 9.0 | 4.08 | * |
| Scoop—14" | Strand Century | 4291 | 56°–100° | 100°–150° | 2.38–7.6 | E6K 1kW 120v | 17,800/7,200 | 16.0 | 406 | 20.0 | 508 | 16.0 | 406 | 14.5 | 362 | 11.0 | 5.00 | * |
| Scoop—18" | Strand | 4273A | 90° | 110° | 2.86 | Q2000/4/95 2kW 120v | 13,400 | 18.5 | 470 | 16.0 | 392 | 19.0 | 470 | 22.0 | 559 | 9.0 | 4.10 | * |
| Flood | Strand | 5276 Border light | Depends on lamp type— see PAR lamps | | | 75W/150W/300W PAR | See lamp | 7.0 | 178 | 72.0 | 1846 | 10.3 | 260 | 12.5 | 317 | 35.9 | 16.3 | 12 Types |
| Flood | Strand | Coda 500/1 Mk2 | 66° | 66° | 1.3 | FDN 500W 120v | 3,500 | 11.0 | 280 | 8.3 | 210 | 9.8 | 250 | 11.8 | 300 | 8.3 | 3.75 | * |
| Flood | Strand | Nocturne 500 | 66° | 66° | 1.3 | K1 500W 240v | | 11.0 | 280 | 8.3 | 210 | 9.8 | 250 | 11.8 | 300 | 8.3 | 3.75 | * |
| Flood | Strand | Coda 1000 | 84° | 84° | 1.8 | K4 1kW 240v | 5,800 | 13.8 | 350 | 8.3 | 210 | 9.8 | 250 | 11.8 | 300 | 9.5 | 4.30 | * |
| Flood | Strand | Nocturne 1000 | 84° | 84° | 1.8 | K4 1kW 240v | | 13.8 | 350 | 8.3 | 210 | 9.8 | 250 | 11.8 | 300 | 9.5 | 4.30 | * |
| Flood | Strand | Iris | | | | 625W/1kW/1.25kW | | 20.3 | 517 | 9.7 | 247 | | | 26.3 | 670 | 17.2 | 7.80 | * |
| Striplight | Strand | 5300 Zip strip | | 15° or 38° | 0.26 or 0.69 | MR-16 75W 120v | 11,500 or 2,000 | 7.5 | 191 | 73.8 | 1892 | 9.0 | 229 | | | | | 5 Types |
| Scoop—14" | Times Square | Q145 | 90° | | 2.00 | 1000IF 1kW 120v | 12,500 | | | | | | | | | | | * |
| Scoop—14" | Times Square | Q114PC | 81°–108° | | 1.71–2.80 | E6J 1kW 120v | 49,400/19,700 | 14.0 | 356 | 17.0 | 432 | | | 19.0 | 483 | | | * |
| Scoop—18" | Times Square | 185 | 106° | | 2.65 | DKX 1.5kW 120v | 17,200 | | | | | | | | | | | * |
| Striplight | Times Square | 701 | 24° or 49° | | 0.43 or 1.91 | 75 PAR16 CAP 75W 120v | 524,000/179,000 | 6.5 | 165 | to spec | | 4.0 | 102 | 8.0 | 203 | | | * |
| Striplight | Times Square | 702 | 60° | | 1.15 | 150I/FL 150W 120v | 1,040 | 7.5 | 191 | to spec | | 9.5 | 241 | | | | | 8 Types |

*81. Pani BP4*

## PANI

Pani of Vienna has emerged as the leading theatrical manufacturer of high-power projection equipment. Production Arts represents them in the U.S.A. and the U.K.

*82. Pani BP2.5*

*83. Pani 1.2 front elevation*

*84. Pani 1.2 side elevation*

*85. Kodak Carousel*

### Kodak

*Carousel:* Surely the world's most successful piece of lighting equipment. Many variations are available including special high-power versions. The basic units are for 80 2x2-inch slides. Interchangeable lenses 60mm, 86mm, 100mm, 150mm, 180mm, 250mm, 70mm to 120mm zoom. 150W/250W 24v tungsten halogen. The AV market has developed many brilliant devices to aid the preparation, control and performance of complex multimedia, multiscreen presentations.

*86. GAM Scene Machine*

### Great American Market

*The Scene Machine:* GAM market the RDS system (see below) in Europe, North and South America under this name.

### Pani/Production Arts Accessories

*AMD-15 Automatic Slidechanger:* Fifteen slides of film or double-glass 18cm slides

*A-32 Random Access Slidechanger:* Thirty-two slides of film or double-glass 18cm slides with random access on DMX 512. Remote real-time display.

*AS-100 Image Scroller:* One hundred feet (30.3m) of 7-inch (18cm) wide quick change scroll media to be precisely moved through the gate of a Pani projector. Variable speed from .001 inch (.025mm) per second to 7 inches (178mm) per second and stopping accuracy .020 inch (0.5m). Operable at any angle from horizontal to vertical. Integral rotating mask. This provides a great rain or snow effect, slow panoramic movement or just lots of still images.

*87. Xenon 7kW Titan*

### Hardware Xenon Inc.

French manufacturers of high-power Xenon projectors, from 600W to 7,000W, now with offices in the U.S.A. Remote slide changers, scrollers and double scrollers are available.

*88. RDS FX Projector*

**RDS**

*Effects Projection Systems:* Flexible system employing either a 1kW Quartz Halogen or CSI lamp. This can be mounted in the conventional horizontal arrangement or in a vertical projection unit. Primary effects units include slide carriage, disc machine, spiral and film loop machines. Secondary effects include flicker, prism, kaleidoscopic and rotating mirror devices. A wide range of variable slide or gobo, still or moving effects can be achieved.

*89. Reiche & Vogel 2kW*

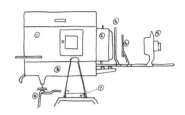

*90. Reiche & Vogel 5kW diagram*

**Reiche & Vogel**

*5kW Projector:* For 13x13cm or 18x18cm slides. Vernier adjustment of pan and tilt. Slide rotatable in holder through 20°. Vignette blades to facilitate joining adjacent images.

Key   1 Lamp housing
      2 Condenser lens
      3. Slide carriage
      4 Adjustable vignette blades
      5 Objective lens
      6 Vertical adjustment
      7 Horizontal adjustment
      8 Fans

*2kW Projector*

For 13x13cm slides or moving effects. Three element interchangeable lens assembly.

*91. Strand Cadenza 2kW*

**Strand Lighting**
*Cadenza™ EP*
2kW projector for 3.25x4-inch slides and moving effects.

**ETC Audio-visual (U.S.A. Supplier Production Arts)**
*PIGI:* Computerized projector combining slide projector with moving strip projectors to produce exceptionally complex computer-controlled moving and matte effects. Accurate to one hundredth of a millimeter with a speed range from one millimeter per minute to a practically instantaneous change.

| Manufacturer | Unit | Lamp | Initial lumens | Slide size | W mm (25) | W in (0.04) | L mm (25) | L in (0.04) | H mm (25) | H in (0.04) | f=13.5cm | f=18cm | f=22cm | f=27cm | f=33cm | f=40cm |
|---|---|---|---|---|---|---|---|---|---|---|---|---|---|---|---|---|
| Pani | BP2 | 2kW CP43 | 54,000 | 18x18cm | 650 | 25.5 | 520 | 20.3 | 445 | 17.4 | 10,850 cd / 60° | 18,760 cd / 46° | 31,960 cd / 39° | 39,940 cd / 31° | 66,420 cd / 24° | 87,480 cd / 20° |
| Pani | BP1.2 HMI | HMI 1.2kW | 110,000 | 18x18cm | 650 | 25.5 | 520 | 20.3 | 670 | 26.1 | | | | | | |
| | Ballast unit | | | | | | | | | | | | | | | |
| Pani | BP2.5 HMI | HMI 2.5kW | | 18x18cm | | | | | | | 14,240 cd / 60° | 23,180 cd / 46° | 36,750 cd / 39° | 46,750 cd / 31° | 96,400 cd / 24° | 121,050 cd / 20° |
| | Ballast unit | | | | | | | | | | | | | | | |
| Pani | BP4 HMI | HMI 4kW | 410,000 | 18x18cm | 720 | 28.3 | 715 | 27.9 | 910 | 35.5 | 24,190 cd / 60° | 45,360 cd / 46° | 63820 cd / 39° | 87,060 cd / 31° | 144,310 cd / 24° | 194,280 cd / 20° |
| | Ballast unit | | | | | | | | | | | | | | | |
| Pani | BP6 Gold | HMI 6kW | | 18x18cm | 720 | 28.3 | 1160 | 45.2 | 1454 | 56.7 | 59,830 cd / 63° | 90,980 cd / 48° | 124,490 cd / 40° | 149,020 cd / 33° | 174,070 cd / 27° | 255,880 cd / 20° |
| | Ballast unit | | | | | | | | | | | | | | | |
| Pani | BP12 Platinum | HMI 12kW | | 24x24cm | | | | | | | 89,000 cd | 135,820 cd | 207,000 cd | 243,330 cd | 308,800 cd | 453,040 cd |
| | Ballast unit | | | | | | | | | | | | | | | |
| Reiche & Vogel | 2kW projector | 2kW | | 13x13cm | 383 | 15.1 | 762 | 29.7 | 600 | 23.4 | | 185,560 cd | | 299,580 cd | | 557,320 cd |
| | 5kW projector | 1kW | | 18x18cm | 600 | 23.6 | 1110 | 43.3 | 864 | 33.7 | | | | | | |
| Great American | Scene Machine | 2kW | | | 368 | 14.5 | 483 | 19 | 483 | 19 | | | | | | |
| | | 1kW | | | 368 | 14.5 | 368 | 14.5 | 432 | 17 | | | | | | |
| Hardware Xenon | Titan | 7kW Xenon | 914,600 | 18x18.5cm | | | | | | | Images up to 50m (164ft) wide at 330m (1,082ft) distance | | | | | |
| | Titan | 5kW Xenon | 645,600 | 18x18.5cm | | | | | | | Images up to 50m (164ft) wide at 330m (1,082ft) distance | | | | | |
| | Titan | 2kW Xenon | 215,200 | 18x18.5cm | | | | | | | Images up to 16m (52ft) wide at 100m (328ft) distance | | | | | |
| | Titan | 1kW Xenon | 107,600 | 24x36cm | | | | | | | Images up to 10m (33ft) wide at 90m (295ft) distance | | | | | |
| | Titan | 600W Xenon | 43,040 | 24x36cm | | | | | | | Images up to 7m (23ft) wide at 60m (196ft) distance | | | | | |

A snapshot of moving lights will be out of date in a jiffy. They basically divide into two types: waggle mirror units and moving yokes. I am not attempting to cover the hundreds of moving-light machines primarily aimed at the Disco market. Some are miraculous in generating Star Wars effects into which you are encouraged to throw yourself with abandon. Yes, they still do that these days. It may seem curious to some of us who were too busy slaving away in some dark theatre in those ancient times, while all the others were having fun. Fun??

## MOVING-MIRROR UNITS

### Altman Lighting

*The Altstar:* Altman, long the stalwart reliable low-cost supplier of stage lighting instruments, have started to go high tech with the waggle-mirror Altstar. Prototypes have one unique feature of potentially great interest: remotely controllable shutters. Now that's a neat idea.

### Cameleon

This French company, founded by Didier Leclercq, was one of the pioneers of moving mirror fixtures.

*Telescan Mark IV:* Two point five kilowatt HMI modular unit 12-bit resolution mirror unit that incorporates a film-strip scroller with up to 50 color or black-and-white "gobo" images (capable of rotation with moving prism) and "trichromatic" color mixing. As seen used by Marc Brickman on the 1994 Pink Floyd tour and Patrick Woodroffe with The Rolling Stones.

*Telescan Mark II & III:* One point two kilowatt HMI modular unit 12-bit resolution 340°, 90° mirror unit that incorporates a "trichromic" mixing system, diffusion, four fixed and two indexable spinning gobos.

*Telejector:* Six kilowatt large frame projector with double scroller for 150 pictures and "trichromatic" color mixing system.

*Telespots:* A range of servo-controlled moving yokes for 2.5kW, 4kW and 6kW HMI Fresnels

### Clay Paky

*Superscan Zoom:* HMI 1.2kW. Two wheels of four interchangeable gobos each, three trioptic prisms with three, five and nine facets, dual color systems (RGB and color effects wheel for infinite color choice), and bicolor, rainbow or UV beam effects, variable frost, 8° to 16° zoom, with a field of 35° make this an amazing moving mirror device. Pan 150°, tilt 110°, and 1-7 flash/second strobe.

*Superscan:* HMI 1.2kW Indexable, bidirectional rotating mixable gobos, "four way" and "infinity" rotating prisms, dual color systems (RGB and color wheel for infinite color choice), and bicolor or rainbow beam effects. Pan 150°, tilt 110°, 1-7 flash/second strobe.

*Miniscan :* HTI 150W/1. Five gobos, eight standard and seven dichroic colors with continuous rotation. Pan 150°, tilt 110°, 1-7 flash/ second strobe.

*92. Clay Paky Golden Scan 2*

*Golden Scan "3" (Fig. 92):* HMI 1.2kW or 575W. Improved optics give performance 30% brighter than the Golden Scan 2. Zoom or adjustable aperture lens giving a sharp or diffused 11° or 16° beam (36° with built-in frost filter), with trichromatic color mixing system with selectable color temperature, fixed and rotating indexed-position gobos and prisms allow multiplication and separation of images and three dimensional effects. Pan 150°, tilt 110°. Strobe 1-7 flash/second. HMI 1200W 640,000 lumens, HMI 575W 266,000 lumens.

*Golden Scan:* HMI 1200 575W. Eight standard and seven dichroic colors with continuous rotation, two wheels of four interchangeable gobos each. Three interchangeable objectives lenses. Pan 150°, tilt 110°, strobe 1-7 flash/second. HMI 1200W 495,000 lumens, HMI 575W 205,000 lumens.

*Golden Scan HPE:* New from Clay Paky is this high performance HMI 1,200 discharge lamp unit. One hundred and thirteen combinations of color are available through three wheels of dichroic filters. One of the two separate wheels of interchangeable gobos allows indexable rotation at up to 150 revs per minute. A high-quality wide-angle lens covers 24°, which may be remotely changed to 15°. An optional lens modification kit provides 13° or 9°. There are five rotatable prisms and a frost effect that makes it possible to change gradually from concentrated beam to full diffusion.

*93. Coemar Nat tm 1200*

### Coemar

*Nat tm 2500, Nat tm 1200 (Fig. 93):* Coemar instruments boast a "total movement system," being a nifty rotating head on the end of the instrument that gives 360° movement in both axes, rotatable in all directions at a speed variable from 0.23 to 52 r.p.m. Ten interchangeable gobos give 36 image combinations, bidirectional at variable speed and able to provide a rolling gobo effect. Strobe shutter, full cyan, magenta, yellow color mixing, variable frost, color wheel with multicolored rotatable beam effects, multiprism wheel and iris...and more??

*Nat pc 1000:* 1,000W halogen lamp. Pulseable iris, zoom, adjustable frost and full color mixing.

*Microscan 3 575MSR:* Measuring only 11 feet 4 inches x 8.1 inches x 30.5 inches this is one of the smallest waggle lights on the market. It has nine interchangeable dichroic-colors and eight gobos (four of which are indexable and rotatable), strobe/shutter and 170° by 80° mirror movement. It has two lenses: 9° and 12°.

*Samurai Light:* One point two kilowatt MSR/ 1.2kW HMI moving light for TV and theatre. High lumen output and even field. Twenty-four interchangeable colors and gobos, strobe/shutter and 180° by 110° mirror movement.

### High End Systems
*Intellabeam:* Twelve colors, 12 gobos, strobe, iris, full dimming capability.

*Cyberlight™:* One point two kilowatt 5600° K light source with zoom, iris, dimming, variable-speed strobe, fixed and subtractive color system, fixed and rotating gobos and diffusion.

*Cyberlight™ CX:* One point two kilowatt 5600° K light source with zoom, iris, dimming, variable speed strobe, eight-position indexed dichroic color wheel, seven fixed and four rotating and mixable gobos, special-effects wheel with prism, diffusion and wide angle lens.

### Martin Professional
*Roboscan Pro 1220:* One point two kilowatt MSR intelligent light with four rotating and nine motorized superimposeable gobos. CMY color mixing system, variable-speed strobe, iris, focus, multiplying prisms, and so on.

*94. Martin Roboscan Pro 518*

*Roboscan Pro 518 (Fig. 94):* Two hundred watt MSD intelligent light with five rotating gobos, eighteen colors, three-facet prisms, frost filter and color temperature modifier.

*Robocolor Pro 400:* Two hundred watt MSD lamp in a compact 32-color changer spot. Motorized gobos providing 7°, 14°, and 21° beam angle and wash effect. Adjustable focus and strobe.

*PAL 1200:* One point two kilowatt MSR lamp moving-mirror unit with a notable innovation: a patented drive system that synchronizes a pair of stepper motors on each side of the frame to enable fully flexible control in any direction of shutters, with an accuracy of 1mm. The whole shutter assembly can also be rotated through 22.5° in either direction. The unit has remote zoom from 13° to 33°, rotating and interchangeable gobos, color dissolve and variable frost filter, 16-bit resolution DMX control.

### SGM Electronic Light
*Galileo II:* One point two kilowatt mirror light with eight interchangeable gobos (four rotating), eight colors with bicolor and rainbow beam effect. High-speed iris variable flash strobe.

### The Obie Company
*The Xescan (Fig 95.):* Developed for designer Marc Brickman, this moving-mirror spot uses a 2kW xenon lamp with a rhodium-plated, electro-formed parabolic reflector, through a dual scroll 25-foot-long Wybron color changer to large pan and tilt mirror. This very bright unit has a beam angle range from 1° to 20°. In

spot focus it gives 180 f.c. at 300 feet with a 5-foot diameter beam. At flood focus at the same throw it gives 40 f.c. with a beam diameter of 112 feet. This unit doesn't have all the bells and whistles of some of the other waggle lights, but it is bright.

## MOVING-YOKE INSTRUMENTS

### High End Systems
*Studio Color:* Fully automated color mixing, moving head wash luminaire with a MSR 575 discharge lamp. Using three wheels of cyan, magenta, and yellow with a fourth six-position selectable dichroic wheel, over 100 million color permutations may be obtained. The soft-edged beam from 8° to 22° may be shaped to provide variable horizontal and vertical width. A variable frost effect may be used, and optional PAR-type lenses can provide VNSP, NSP, WFL, and XWFL PAR beams

*95. Obie Xescan*

96. LSD Ikon

97. LSD Washlight

### Light & Sound Design

*LSD Ikon (Fig. 96):* Six hundred watt HTI light source with a 2:1 zoom lens 0.9° pinspot to 40° wash. Hard and soft edge focus. Variable speed shutter/strobe, seven indexable rotating gobos and seven fixed gobos, three wheel split and full color control, variable speed movement 360° pan and 270° tilt. Twelve degrees at 30 feet gives 1,003 f.c., 40° flood at 30 feet gives 69 f.c.

*LSD Washlight (Fig. 97):* A 575W automated 360° pan and 270° tilt soft-edge spot with two complementary graduated color scrollers to give subtle cross-fading of color.

### PanCommand

*P.C. Beam:* Soft-edged automated unit similar to a 1kW PAR lamp with an integral eleven-color scroller and FEL lamp. The circular beam may be manipulated remotely from the size of an ACL ray to the diameter of a PAR wide flood.

*Fader Beam:* Has an improved reflector and a color fader scrolling color changer, which using CMY color mixing gives any color including pastels.

*P.C. Spot:* Four-hundred-watt HTI lamp with a mechanical fader to adjust intensity. Zoom optics range from 2° to 35° with increased light output as beam size decreases. A patented full-spectrum dichroic color system allows bumps or fades to and from any color. A custom scroller allows special colors, correction filter, strobe, diffraction grating or other effect. Nine gobos including four rotatable gobos are provided. Three hundred sixty degree pan and 270° tilt (with -0.3° resolution) with independent variable-speed control on each feature.

98. PanCommand ProSpot

*ProSpot (Fig. 98):* Six-hundred-watt HTI lamp with configurable internal design capable of upgrading in features. Color options include single eleven-dichroic-color wheel or fading dichroic system with over 5,000 colors to choose from. Pattern options include either a wheel system with nine user gobos, or a rotating pattern system or soft-edge 3:1 zoom system. There is a single colorframe for color correction, frost, ultraviolet, and more.

### RDS Corporation

Technolite TV Automated system includes 1kW, 2kW, and 5kW Fresnels and 2kW soft-lights with servo driven X and Y motion, zoom focus, color scroller and dimming shutter.

99. Strand PALS Cadenza P.C.

### Strand Lighting

*PALS (Precision Automated Lighting Systems; Fig. 99):* Strand has developed this range of yokes that may be utilized to add remote focus capability to a range of their standard theatrical fixtures. They provide four functions, 360° pan and 120° tilt, focus (Fresnels and P.C.s) or iris (profile) or switch (softlights) and an optional eleven-color scroller. They may be operated through a stand-alone controller or the Galaxy control system. Instruments that can be utilized include the Cantata, Polaris, Castor, Pollox and Arturo range. Resolution is 0.36°.

*Hyperbeam 1200 and Hyperbeam 1288 (in alliance with Martin):* Moving-mirror luminaires with 1.2kW metal halide source. The 1228 has all the features of the 1220 but also has CMY full color mixing as well as nine-color wheels. The instruments are controlled via DMX from Strand 430 and 530 consoles running Tracker software. A trackball on the console gives control of the X-Y position of the beam, and four rotary controls can be paged to control the other attributes. With the "attribute channel" scheme used by Strand, up to 32 attribute channels can reside under a single channel reference number.

### Vari*Lite

*VL2B (Fig. 100):* Metal-halide 400W arc lamp with a 5600°K color temperature the VL2 is a remote-control focus instrument with nine

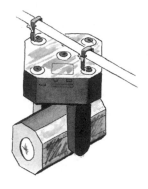

100. Vari*Lite VL2

interchangeable gobos on a wheel, dichroic color system with over 120 hues, soft or sharp edge focus. Beam size from 7° to 33°.

VL2C: As above but with 600W lamp.

VL3: A remote-control wash luminaire with a 475W 53v tungsten-halogen lamp with dissolving color cross-fading capability. Beam angle from 6° to 23° (now discontinued).

VL4: A remote-control wash luminaire with a 400W HTI metal halide lamp with dissolving color cross-fading capability. A shutter/dowser provides instantaneous blackouts, bumps or strobe effects. Beam angle from 4° to 14°.

101. Vari*Lite VL5

VL5 (Fig. 101): A silent remote-control wash luminaire with 1,000W tungsten lamp and cold mirror reflector. Cross-fadeable dichroic color

control. Interchangeable diffuser lens gives choice of beam angles. Clear lens initial candela is 420,000. Stipple lens initial candela is 250,000. Early models had limited tint colors available, particularly in the pale blue range, but new dichroics (the VL5B) have overcome this problem to provide a wonderfully versatile soft-edge instrument able to dissolve through the spectrum. A soft-edged delight.

102. Vari*Lite VL6

VL6 (Fig 102): A silent remote-control spot luminaire. MSR 400W short arc lamp with cold mirror reflector. Two wheels provide 22 options for laser-etched gobos or dichroic color filters. These gobos can provide what almost appears to be a half-tone gobo—much more subtle than the etched metal variety. Combinations can allow dissolve "morphing" from gobo to gobo as well as split-color effects. Two beam angles of 18° and 33° are initially available. An extraordinarily effective addition to the new Vari*Lite range: small, silent, accurate and very bright. I'd surmise that this instrument is a signpost to a new stage lighting.

Iridium AR5: Vari*Lite has a subsidiary company, Iridium, developing moving-light fixtures for the architectural market. Their first product was an outdoor version of the VL5, but this new miniature version, intended perhaps for display lighting, will find a lot of theatrical applications. Optional lenses give beam

103. DHA Digital Light Curtain

angles from 7.5° to 60° and full-range dimming and VL5-type color-dissolving capability will prove exciting in tight corners.

**DHA Lighting**

Digital Light Curtain (Fig. 103): Self-contained light curtains with built-in tilt and color controlled by Macintosh computer. Optional pitch ("Pilbrow's Pitcher") may be added to any unit. Twelve volt 240W PAR56 lamps in NSP, MFL or WFL angles. Tilt rotates through 320° with 0.1° resolution at speeds ranging from 60° per second to an hour. The pitching yoke attachment gives 30° of pitch in either direction with the same accuracy. Alignment of multiple units is achieved electronically. Curtains may be controlled by DMX or by special Macintosh software (Light Talk), which controls up to 99 units and enables versatile plotting, editing and execution of cues, on and off line. Color, tilt and pitch movement are independently timed. Light Curtains may be cued independently or in user-defined groups.

Digital Beamlight: Newly created by David Hersey for Martin Guerre is the Digital Beamlight. The R & V Beamlight has been a favourite of mine since 1960. Nothing else quite creates an "arrow" of light like it. In the old days TP Lighting often tried to copy its performance but never with any success. An instrument from the 1930s, it defies imitation. David Hersey has long shared my enthusiasm for the beamlight and pioneered their use as short-throw follow spots. Now he's gone one better. A very compact moving yoke improved beamlight with 19-color scroller. Control via DMX or Light Talk.

*104. Skyart*

**Theatre Projects Lighting**

Skyart(Fig. 104):This is the ultimate special. A real searchlight with 4kW xenon lamp and remote pan and tilt (accuracy of 1/280 of a degree) and color 16-frame scroller. Blisteringly bright (do you believe 325,000,000 candela?) and a great instrument for anyone thinking of competing with God. Used most effectively by Patrick Woodroffe for Voodoo Lounge.

**City Theatrical**

Now here's a neat device. An automated yoke for any ETC Source Four. It pans 360°, tilts through 180° and is controlled via DMX. An economical, quiet and effective solution.

**Clay Paky**

Two effect projectors and four washlight fixtures join the competition on the moving yoke scene. Washlites are *Stage Color 300, 575, 1000* and *1200* (with 3 levels of diffusion) and the projectors the *Stage Light 300 and Stage Zoom 1200*. The two types use identical yokes and can be interchanged. Four color mixing uses cyan, magenta, yellow and amber to give a wide range of tints. GTC (Gradual Temperature Control) provides gradual color temperature control from 6000 to 3200K from the desk. The projectors have rotating gobo and prism capability. Pan 450° and tilt 252°. All luminaires have a lock-down capability for transportation.

**Coemar**

The *CF 1200 Spot* (soft-edge 5° to 40°), the *CF 1200 HE* (hard-edge)using a Philips MSR 1200/SA light source, and the *CF Zoom* (500w halogen lamp) are useful additions to the moving yoke scene. All have 370° pan and 270° tilt. Bodies are constructed of very light carbon fiber.

**High End**

The *Studio Spot*™ is a hard edge partner to the *Studio Color*® washlight range (both with MSR 575W and 250W lamp). Moving yoke provides 370° pan and 225° of tilt. The spot has 13°, 18°, and 30° beam angle lenses, variable frost effect, variable speed iris, instant blackout and strobe capability.

**LSD/PRG**

The *Icon Series M* known fancifully as Medusa, is a glimpse of a new tomorrow. Using Texas Instrument technology, DMD (Digital Mirror Device)—previously found in video projectors—it presents video gobo capability instantly controlled from the console. It is in fact on the way to being a video light projector and introduces the possibility that the beam of light from any (or every!) luminaire in the 21st century will itself be "paint-able" in color, texture and definition.

**Martin Professional**

*MAC 250* and *Mac 500* moving head fixtures offer dichroic colors, rotating gobos and prisms and variable focus. The *MAC 600/600E* is a powerful washlight with variable beam angle and rich color range. The MAC 1200 is a powerful soft-edge spot with CMY subtractive color mixing as well as a separate wheel with 4 inter-changeable colors.

**Vari*Lite**

*VL6B*. This is a neat improvement of the VL6 with 3:1 zoom (12° to 36° field angles) and rotating, indexable gobos. The long awaited *VL7* is a bombshell of a light with an HTI 600W lamp. Big and powerful, it has an 8:1 zoom lens system to 40°, fixed and rotating indexable gobos and a brilliant new color dissolve system. The VL7B puts in place of the iris and fixed gobo wheel four remote controlled shutters! Each can rotate 50° to create a triangle and move all the way in to black out.

| Manufacturer | Unit | Moving Yoke / Moving Mirror | B/A (* = approx) F/A in italics indicates soft beam | MPF | Peak Candela (* =worked out by math average) | Movement Horizontal (pan) | Movement Vertical (tilt) | Lamp type | W in (0.04) | W mm (25.4) | L in (0.04) | L mm (25.4) | H in (0.04) | H mm (25.4) | HY in (0.04) | HY mm (25.4) | Wt lb (2.21) | Wt kg (0.45) |
|---|---|---|---|---|---|---|---|---|---|---|---|---|---|---|---|---|---|---|
| DHA Lighting | Digital Light Curtain | Moving Yoke | See PAR 56 spec, sheets: VNSP/MFL/WFL | | | pitch +/-30° | 320° | 8x PAR56 240W 12v | 10.4 | 265 | 75.8 | 1930 | 7.7 | 195 | 15.5 | 395 | 79.4 | 36 |
| LSD | Washlight | Moving Yoke | 13° or 26°x38°oval | 0.23 or 0.46x0.69 | 544,000 or 71,000* | 360° | 270° | Tungsten Halogen 575W 115v | 15.8 | 400 | 12.5 | 318 | | | 20.8 | 527 | 25.0 | 11 |
| | Icon | Moving Yoke | 0.9°-40° | 0.015-0.73 | 428,000/58,000* | 360° | 270° | HTI 600W 115v | 19.3 | 489 | 23.5 | 597 | | | 33.0 | 838 | 72.0 | 33 |
| Pan Command | Starburst | Moving Yoke | | | | 360° | 200° | PAR 36 | 20.0 | 508 | 10.3 | 260 | | | 36.0 | 914 | 75.0 | 34 |
| | PC Beam | Moving Yoke | variable | | approx. equal to PAR 64 | 360° | 245° | FEL 1kW | 20.0 | 508 | | | | | 24.0 | 610 | 35.0 | 16 |
| | Fader Beam | Moving Yoke | | | approx. equal to PAR 64 | 360° | 270° | FEL 1kW | 20.0 | 508 | | | | | 24.0 | 610 | 35.0 | 16 |
| | PC Spot | Moving Yoke | 2°-35° | 0.035-0.63 | | 360° | 270° | HTI 400W | 20.0 | 508 | | | | | 24.0 | 610 | 50.0 | 23 |
| | PC Soft | Moving Yoke | 2°-35° | 0.035-0.63 | | 360° | 270° | HTI 400W | 20.0 | 508 | | | | | 24.0 | 610 | 45.0 | 20 |
| | Pro Spot | Moving Yoke | | | | 360° | 270° | HTI 600W | | | | | | | | | 32.0 | 15 |
| Sky-Tracker | Sky-Tracker | Moving Yoke | | | 195,000,000 x 4 | | | 4 x 2kW Xenon Arc 240v | 94.3 | 2400 | 94.3 | 2400 | 74.7 | 1900 | n/a | n/a | 34.2 | 870 |
| T P Lighting Services | Sky-Art | Moving Yoke | 0.1°-15° | 0.0018-0.26 | 325,000,000 | 360° | 230° | 4kW Xenon Arc 240v | 39.7 | 1010 | 39.7 | 1010 | 51.5 | 1310 | 51.5 | 1310 | | 216 |
| Vari*Lite | VL1 | Moving Yoke | 27° | 0.48 | 200,000 * | 360° | 270° | HTI 250W 120v | 14.0 | 355 | 24.0 | 610 | 8.8 | 210 | 27.0 | 690 | 45.0 | 21 |
| | VL2B | Moving Yoke | 25° | 0.43 | 360,000/144,000 * | 360° | 270° | HTI 400W 120v | 17.5 | 445 | 17.5 | 445 | 10.8 | 275 | 32.8 | 835 | 58.0 | 27 |
| | VL2C | Moving Yoke | 6°-17° | 0.14-0.41 | 606,710/352,903 | 360° | 270° | MSR 600W 120v | 17.5 | 445 | 17.5 | 445 | 10.8 | 275 | 32.8 | 835 | 58.0 | 27 |
| | VL4 | Moving Yoke | 4°-14° | 0.19-0.42 | 876,000/81,200 * | 360° | 270° | HTI 400W 120v | 14.0 | 355 | 14.5 | 365 | 8.5 | 215 | 27.3 | 695 | 38.0 | 17 |
| | VL5 | Moving Yoke | Various lenses from 6° | 0.28/0.39 | 250,000/24,000 | 360° | 270° | Tungsten 1kW 120v ( &1.2kW) | 16.0 | 410 | 16.3 | 415 | 10.0 | 255 | 26.8 | 680 | 22.0 | 10 |
| | VL6 | Moving Yoke | 16° or 26° | 0.21-0.32 | 480,000/192,000 | 360° | 270° | MSR 400W 120v | 16.0 | 410 | 14.6 | 375 | 8.4 | 215 | 24.7 | 630 | 20.0 | 9 |
| Cameleon | Telescan Mark 2 | Moving Mirror | 12°-18° | 0.22 | 430,000/215,000 * | 180° | 90° | HMI 1.2kW 210-250v | 20.0 | 500 | 59.0 | 1500 | 18.0 | 450 | | | 99.0 | 45 |
| | Telescan Mark 3 | Moving Mirror | 12.5° * | 0.18-0.28 | 300,000 | 340° | 90° | HMI 1.2kW 210-250v | 19.0 | 480 | 43.0 | 1100 | 16.0 | 410 | | | 77.0 | 35 |
| | Telescan Mark 4 | Moving Mirror | 10.5°-16° * | 0.50/0.73/0.93/1.35 | 625,000/325,000 | 340° | 90° | HMI 2.5kW 210-250v | 18.0 | 470 | 54.0 | 1360 | 14.0 | 360 | | | 127.0 | 58 |
| | Telescan Mark 5 | Moving Mirror | 28°/40°/50°/68° * | | | 180° | 90° | HMI 2.5kW 210-250v | 18.0 | 470 | 54.0 | 1360 | 14.0 | 360 | | | 127.0 | 58 |
| | Teleprojector | Moving Mirror | | | | | | HMI 6kW 210-250v | 44.4 | 1130 | 61.3 | 1560 | 36.2 | 920 | | | | |
| | Telespot | Moving Mirror | | | | 340° | 180° | HMI 6kW 210-250v | 35.4 | 900 | 54.2 | 1380 | 27.7 | 705 | | | | |
| Clay Paky | Miniscan | Moving Mirror | 9°/15.2° | 0.16/0.26 | 205,000 | 150° | 110° | HTI 150W 200-240v | 9.4 | 238 | 22.9 | 582 | 5.9 | 150 | 11.0 | 280 | 18.7 | 8.5 |
| | Miniscan 300 | Moving Mirror | 9°/15.2° | 0.16/0.26 | 205,000 | 150° | 110° | HTI 300W 200-240v | 9.4 | 238 | 22.9 | 582 | 5.9 | 150 | 11.0 | 280 | 18.7 | 8.5 |
| | Golden Scan | Moving Mirror | 9.25°/11°/16° | | 266,000 | 150° | 110° | HMI 575W 200-240v | 16.9 | 430 | 39.9 | 1015 | 9.0 | 230 | 17.9 | 455 | 70.6 | 32 |
| | Golden Scan 2 | Moving Mirror | 9.25°/11°/16° | 0.16/0.19/0.28 | 495,000 | 150° | 110° | HMI 575W 200-240v | 16.9 | 430 | 43.4 | 1105 | 9.2 | 235 | 17.9 | 455 | 65.0 | 30 |
| | Golden Scan 3 | Moving Mirror | | | 495,000 | 150° | 110° | HMI 575W 200-240v | | | | | | | | | | |
| | Golden Scan | Moving Mirror | 9.25°/11°/16° | 0.16/0.19/0.28 | 640,000 | 150° | 110° | HMI 1.2kW 200-240v | 16.9 | 430 | 44.8 | 1140 | 9.0 | 230 | 17.9 | 455 | 98.1 | 45 |
| | Golden Scan 2 | Moving Mirror | 15°/23° or 8.5°/12.5° | 0.26/0.41 or 0.15/0.21 | | 150° | 110° | HMI 1.2kW 200-240v | 16.9 | 430 | 48.3 | 1230 | 9.2 | 235 | 17.9 | 455 | 86.0 | 39 |
| | Golden Scan 3 | Moving Mirror | | 0.18/0.28 | | 150° | 110° | HMI 1.2kW 200-240v | 16.9 | 430 | 48.3 | 1230 | 9.2 | 235 | 17.9 | 455 | 92.6 | 42 |
| | Golden Scan 'HPE' | Moving Mirror | | 0.14-0.28 | | 150° | 110° | HMI 1.2kW 200-240v | 16.9 | 430 | 48.3 | 1230 | 9.2 | 235 | 17.9 | 455 | 111.8 | 51 |
| | Superscan | Moving Mirror | 10°/16° | 0.16 | 790,000/270,000 | 150° | 110° | HMI 1.2kW 200-240v | 16.9 | 430 | 51.9 | 1320 | 9.0 | 230 | 17.9 | 455 | 97.0 | 44 |
| | Superscan Zoom | Moving Mirror | 8°-16° | 0.16/0.21 | 313,600 | 150° | 110° | HMI 1.2kW 200-240v | 16.9 | 430 | 57.8 | 1470 | 9.0 | 230 | 17.9 | 455 | | |
| Coemar | Micro Scan 2 | Moving Mirror | 9° | 0.12/0.16/0.21 | 592,900/382,200 | 80° | 170° | Halogen 1kW 120v | 11.4 | 290 | 30.5 | 775 | 6.3 | 160 | 8.1 | 205 | 24.7 | 11 |
| | Micro Scan 3 | Moving Mirror | 9°/12° | 0.18 | 391,050/269,100/191,925 | 80° | 170° | MSR 575W 120v | 11.4 | 290 | 12.6 | 320 | 5.7 | 145 | 7.5 | 190 | 28.4 | 13 |
| | Samurai Light | Moving Mirror | 6.8°/9°/12° | 0.18 | 672,000 | 80° | 170° | MSR 1.2kW 120v | 13.2 | 335 | 36.5 | 930 | | | 16.5 | 420 | 50.7 | 23 |
| | Nat 1200tm DX | Moving Mirror | 10.5° | 0.18 | 496,000 | 360° + | 360° + | HMI 1.2kW 120v | 22.0 | 560 | 39.3 | 1000 | 21.2 | 540 | 16.7 | 425 | 75.0 | 34 |
| | Nat 1200tm | Moving Mirror | 10.5° | | | 360° + | 360° + | HMI 1.2kW 120v | 22.0 | 560 | 47.2 | 1200 | 21.2 | 540 | 16.7 | 425 | 90.4 | 41 |

| Manufacturer | Unit | Moving Yoke / Moving Mirror | B/A (* = approx) F/A in italics indicates soft beam | MPF | Peak Candela (* =worked out by math average) | Movement Horizontal (pan) | Movement Vertical (tilt) | Lamp type | W in | W mm | L in | L mm | H in | H mm | HY in | HY mm | Wt lb | Wt kg |
|---|---|---|---|---|---|---|---|---|---|---|---|---|---|---|---|---|---|---|
| Ccemar | Nat 2500fm | Moving Mirror | 10.5° | 0.18 | 1,160,000 | 360°+ | 360°+ | HMI 2.5kW 120v | 22.0 | 560 | 53.8 | 1370 | 21.2 | 540 | 16.7 | 425 | 99.2 | 45 |
| High End Systems | Intellabeam 700HX | Moving Mirror | 10°/12.5°/17° | 0.18/0.22/0.30 | | 170° | 110° | MSR 700W 120v | 13.0 | 330 | 37.0 | 925 | 8.0 | 207 | 13.8 | 351 | 66.0 | 30 |
| High End Systems | Cyberlight | Moving Mirror | 12°–24° or 15°–28° | 0.21–0.43/ 0.26–0.50 | | 170° | 110° | MSR 1.2kW 200–240v | 13.0 | 330 | 42.0 | 1066 | 12.3 | 317 | 17.4 | 442 | 100.6 | 46 |
| High End Systems | Cyberlight CX | Moving Mirror | 12°/15°/17.5° | 0.21/0.26/0.31 | | 170° | 110° | MSR 1.2kW 200–240v | 13.5 | 339 | 42.0 | 1117 | 12.3 | 317 | 17.4 | 442 | 91.0 | 41 |
| High End Systems | Trackspot | Moving Mirror | 9°–15° | 0.16–0.26 | | 170° | 110° | QT8500 120v | 8.7 | 221 | 25.5 | 650 | 7.0 | 178 | 10.3 | 260 | 23.0 | 10 |
| Martin Pro | Roboscan 812 | Moving Mirror | 14.7° | 0.26 | | 180° | 90° | Arcstream/HTI 150W | 7.5 | 190 | 17.2 | 436 | 6.5 | 165 | | | 23.0 | 11 |
| Martin Pro | Roboscan 805 | Moving Mirror | 11.5°/16.5° | 0.2/0.29 | | 180° | 90° | HLX 150W | 5.0 | 130 | 22.0 | 560 | 4.5 | 110 | | | 19.8 | 9 |
| Martin Pro | Roboscan Pro 518 | Moving Mirror | 13.5°/17.5° | 0.24/0.31 | | 176° | 85° | MSD 200W | 11.0 | 280 | 20.9 | 530 | 7.3 | 185 | | | 31.0 | 14 |
| Martin Pro | Robocolor Pro 400 | Moving Mirror | 7°/14°/21° | 0.12/0.25/0.37 | (brighter than PAR 64) | | | MSD 200W | 8.9 | 225 | 12.0 | 306 | 7.8 | 198 | | | 26.5 | 12 |
| Martin Pro | Roboscan Pro 218 | Moving Mirror | 11.5° | 0.2 | | 180° | 90° | MSD 200W | 11.0 | 280 | 21.0 | 530 | 7.5 | 185 | | | 30.8 | 14 |
| Martin Pro | Roboscan Pro 1220 | Moving Mirror | 18.5°/13° | 0.32/0.23 | | 176° | 85° | MSR/HMI 1.2kW | 12.5 | 316 | 43.0 | 1107 | 11.5 | 285 | | | 117.0 | 53 |
| Obie Company | Xescan | Moving Mirror | 20° | 0.35 | 18,000,000 | 270° | 90° | Xenon 2kW 220v | 14.0 | 356 | 23.0 | 584 | 57.0 | 1448 | n/a | n/a | 95.0 | 43 |
| Pan Command | Pro Blaster 2500 | Moving Mirror | 3°–30° | 0.05–0.54 | | 360° | 120° | HMI 2.5kW | 11.0 | 280 | 38.7 | 985 | 8.3 | 210 | 11.1 | 283 | 65.0 | 29 |
| SGM | Galileo 2 575 | Moving Mirror | 4°–15° * | 0.07–0.26 | 78,000–90,000 * | 180° | 90° | HMI 575W | | | | | | | | | 66.2 | 30 |
| SGM | Galileo 3 575 | Moving Mirror | | | | 180° | 90° | HMI 575W | | | | | | | | | 70.6 | 32 |
| SGM | Galileo 4 575 | Moving Mirror | | | | 180° | 90° | HMI 575W | | | | | | | | | 50.7 | 23 |
| SGM | Leonardo 575 | Moving Mirror | | | | 180° | 90° | HMI 575W | | | | | | | | | | |
| SGM | Galileo 2 1200 | Moving Mirror | 4°–15° * | 0.07–0.26 | 202,000 | 180° | 90° | HMI 1.2kW | 11.0 | 280 | 43.4 | 1105 | 8.3 | 210 | 11.1 | 283 | 92.6 | 42 |
| SGM | Galileo 3 1200 | Moving Mirror | | | | 180° | 90° | HMI 1.2kW | | | | | | | | | 97.0 | 44 |
| SGM | Galileo 4 1200 | Moving Mirror | | | | 180° | 90° | HMI 1.2kW | | | | | | | | | | |
| Clay Paky | Stage Color 1200 | Moving Yoke | | | | 450° | 252° | HMI 1200W | | | | | | | | | | |
| Clay Paky | Stage Zoom 1200 | Moving Yoke | 12°–24° | | | 450° | 252° | HMI 1200W | | | | | | | | | | |
| Clay Paky | Stage Color 575 | Moving Yoke | | | | 450° | 252° | HMI 575W | | | | | | | | | | |
| Clay Paky | Stage Light 300 | Moving Yoke | | | | 450° | 252° | HMD 300W | | | | | | | | | | |
| Clay Paky | Stage Color 300 | Moving Yoke | | | | 450° | 252° | HMD 300W | | | | | | | | | | |
| High End | Technobeam | Moving Mirror | 11° | | 2,014,272 | 180° | 95° | MSD 250-2 | 13.4 | 341 | 34 | 864 | 9.6 | 244 | | | 35 | 16 |
| High End | Technobeam | Moving Mirror | 17° | | 1,162,080 | 180° | 95° | MSD 250-2 | 13.4 | 341 | 34 | 864 | 9.6 | 244 | | | 35 | 16 |
| High End | Technobeam | Moving Mirror | 32° | | 325,490 | 180° | 95° | MSD 250-2 | 13.4 | 341 | 34 | 864 | 9.6 | 244 | | | 35 | 16 |
| High End | Studio Spot | Moving Yoke | 18° | | 243,200 | 370° | 275° | MSR 575W-2 | 18.7 | 476 | 18 | 466 | 12 | 304 | 21.6 | 549 | | |
| High End | Studio Spot | Moving Yoke | 13° | | 342,000 | 370° | 275° | MSR 575W-2 | 18.7 | 476 | 18 | 466 | 12 | 304 | 21.6 | 549 | | |
| High End | Studio Spot | Moving Yoke | 30° | | 77,400 | 370° | 275° | MSR 575W-2 | 18.7 | 476 | 18 | 466 | 12 | 304 | 21.6 | 549 | | |
| High End | Studio Color | Moving Yoke | 17° | | 33,129 | 370° | 275° | MSR 575W-2 | 19 | 483 | 15 | 381 | 24 | 610 | | | 57 | 26 |
| Martin | MAC 1200 | Moving Yoke | 2°–32° | | | 440° | 306° | 1200W MSR | 19 | 480 | 22 | 575 | 39 | 1000 | | | 104 | 47 |
| Martin | MAC 600/600E | Moving Yoke | 18°–65° | | 722,000/34,500 | 440° | 306° | 575W MSR | 14 | 350 | 24 | 450 | 24 | 610 | 55.9 | 25.4 | | |
| Martin | MAC 500/500E | Moving Yoke | 17° | | | 440° | 306° | 575W MSR | 20 | 495 | 17 | 447 | | | | | | |
| Martin | MAC 250 | Moving Yoke | 14°, 17°, 21° | | | 540° | 289° | 250W MSD | 15 | 384 | 13 | 330 | 18 | 460 | | | 44 | 20 |
| Vari*lite | VL5B | Moving Yoke | 12°–30° | | | 360 | 270 | MSR 400W | | | | | | | | | 29 | 14 |
| Vari*lite | VL7/VL7B | Moving Yoke | 5° zoom | 0.08 | 2,308,000 | 370 | 270 | HTI 600W | 22 | 229 | 24 | 610 | 27 | 686 | | | 68 | 31 |
| Vari*lite | VL7/VL7B | Moving Yoke | 40° zoom | 0.7 | 69,200 | | | | | | | | | | | | | |

Color scrollers are a miracle. We used to have semaphore changers that laboriously placed up to five colors in front of an instrument. They were big and heavy and only used in FOH built-in situations. Then came the color wheel —a great improvement with five colors on an indexing wheel. Then came the scroller. Marvelous. Manufacturers include:

*105. Wybron Coloram*

### Wybron

Range of scrollers with from two to thirty-two colors (Fig. 105). Two-speed fan. Mounting plates of various dimensions and mounting for top hats and accessories. Optional three-speed operation. System operates on DMX 512 or analog. Twelve units on a single power supply may be separately addressed. Units may be daisy chained together.

### Rainbow

Range includes the Two16 for 1kW lanterns, the Alfresco (a weatherized 8-inch scroller for outdoor use), the 15-inch for larger luminaires, 2kW to 10kW including HMI and MSR, which includes the "PlusCard." The Cyc Rainbow fits cyc lights such as the Iris 1 and Orion, the 20-inch fits searchlights and cyclights, the eight-light for most Mole Fay units and other large luminaires. Rainbows are also made for 9 x PAR56 and 6 x PAR56 battens or striplights. Control is both DMX and analog with up to twelve Rainbows from a Maxi power supply

and twenty-four 8-inch using the 24-unit supply. The Two16 and Alfresco provide from two to sixteen colors and an end-to-end scroll takes 1.4 seconds. The 8-inch (optional), 15-inch and larger units have the "PlusCard" provides 12-bit resolution for very smooth scrolls (see table on page 430).

### Morpheus PanCommand

*ColorRanger* has two to eleven frames in 1.5 seconds for 7.5-inch or 10-inch frames. Variable-speed control capable of split frame color.

*XL Ranger* fits FarCycs, 2kW, 5kW and nine-lights. Two to eleven frames in 3 seconds.

*ColorFader* employs an innovative dichromatic color system to give unlimited color choice. Interchangeable for 7.5-inch and 10-inch color frames.

### Color Changing Spotlights

Finally in the color-changing department are a group of spotlights that, while they don't move focus, are built to change color remotely. These include:

### Fly srl

*Chroma:* One kilowatt G22 halogen color mixing spotlight with 24 dichroic colors CTO/CTB provided. It produces 7,000 lux at 6m with a 2m beam spread.

*Trichroma:* One kilowatt G22 halogen (also available with MSR 1.2kW lamp) color-mixing spotlight with RGB trichromatic color-fading system providing 9,500,000 colors. It produces 6,500 lux at 6m with a 2m beam spread.

### Clay Paky

*Combicolor 300:* HTI 300W lamp color-mixing spotlight with two independent combin-able color wheels with twelve colors plus thirty-seven combinations. Rainbow and bicolor beams, diffusion, a choice of five projection

widths, two interchangeable and one fixed gobo combine with an inbuilt mechanical dimmer.

### Color Kinetics

*Chromacore* variable-intensity LED lighting fixtures can be manufactured in a range of sizes and configurations from a small fitting, like the C-200 *WaterColor*, a MR 16 lamp-sized fitting to linear custom-built clusters. They prove to be surprisingly bright and effective, generating a wide range of colors and effects. Hewlett Packard are said to be about to produce LED's with ten times the present output so one can expect more surprises with this type of fixture.

### Wybron

The *CXI ColorFusion* scroller contains two scrolls with graduated frames of cyan, yellow and magenta to create a subjective color mixing system. With a single control channel, via the CXI menu, 255 preset colors matching popular colors from Rosco, GAM and Lee can be matched. A second channel provides an even greater range.

# COLOR SCROLLERS TABLE

**WYBRON**

| Model | Width inches 0.03930 | Width mm 25 | Height inches 0.03930 | Height mm 25 | Thickness inches 0.03930 | Thickness mm 25 |
|---|---|---|---|---|---|---|
| Coloram Head 7.5" aperture: PARs & 6" fixtures | 12.50 | 318 | 11.25 | 286 | 3.88 | 98 |
| Coloram Four 5.5" aperture: Source 4 & PAR 46s | 9.65 | 245 | 9.55 | 243 | 3.42 | 87 |
| 7" Scroller 11 colors in 2.2 secs | 11.72 | 298 | 10.00 | 254 | 2.55 | 65 |
| Coloram Head 10" aperture: 2–24 colors in 2.5 secs | 15.15 | 385 | 14.20 | 361 | 2.67 | 68 |
| Coloram Head 5kW model: 2–24 colors in 2.5 secs | 20.25 | 514 | 22.59 | 574 | 3.88 | 98 |
| Coloram Head Large Format: 2–24 colors in 5 secs | 22.62 | 575 | 25.00 | 635 | 6.65 | 169 |
| Eight Light Scroller 11 colors in 5 secs | 20.24 | 514 | 33.13 | 841 | 5.56 | 141 |

**RAINBOW**

| | Width inches 0.03930 | Width mm 25 | Height inches 0.03930 | Height mm 25 | Thickness inches 0.03930 | Thickness mm 25 |
|---|---|---|---|---|---|---|
| Two 16 8" Rainbow PAR to 1kW lamps | 11.79 | 300 | 12.97 | 330 | 2.55 | 65 |
| Two 16 Plus 8" Rainbow PAR to 1kW lamps | 11.79 | 300 | 12.97 | 330 | 2.55 | 65 |
| Alfresco 8" Rainbow | 11.79 | 300 | 12.97 | 330 | 2.55 | 65 |
| Rainbow LC9 Lightbatten scroller | 78.60 | 2000 | 9.83 | 250 | 8.25 | 210 |
| 15" Rainbow (2–10kW) | 20.24 | 515 | 22.40 | 570 | 3.34 | 85 |
| 8-light Rainbow | 18.98 | 483 | 32.62 | 830 | 6.01 | 153 |

# ULTRAVIOLET LIGHTING

UV light has improved in recent years. New and more powerful equipment allows UV effects to clearly be seen, even with quite a high level of other ambient light.

## Wildfire Inc.

*Wildfire 400 S/F:* High-intensity focusing UV 16.5° spot/44° flood designed to excite luminescent material at distances up to 150 feet. Optional barndoor. Eight inch (203mm) UV Fresnel lens. WF-L100 400W UV lamp, ballast, external dowser.

*Wildfire 400 F:* High-intensity focusing UV 80° flood designed to excite luminescent material at distances up to 100 feet WF-L101 400W UV lamp, ballast.

*Wildfire 400 E:* High-intensity focusing UV 20°/40° frameable projector designed to excite luminescent material at distances up to 75 feet. 20°-40° beam. WF-L102 400W UV lamp, ballast, external dowser.

*Wildfire 250 series:* WF-250 16° spot, 50° wide spot and 90° flood are designed to excite luminescent material at distances up to 10 to 150 feet. WF-L103 250W UV lamp, ballast.

Wildfire manufactures a full range of fluorescent materials, including custom fabrics, paints, make-up, water dyes and plastics. Blue-yellow and orange are supplied as "invisible" colors appearing as opaque white without UV light.

## ZC&R Coatings for Optics, Inc.

*250W MiniBlack and 400W Blackflood*

## Xenotech

*1kW to 7kW black lights*

## Fresnel S.A.

*400W Black Light STR-400 LN*

## ULTRAVIOLET LIGHTING TABLE

| Manufacturer | UV Unit type | Instrument | B/A | F/A | MPF throw ft/m | Maximum | Lamp |
|---|---|---|---|---|---|---|---|
| Altman | Blacklight tubelight | 701 | (wide flood) | | | short (10ft/3m) | F 40 B/LB 40W |
| Altman | Blacklight flood | 702 | 100° | | 2.38 | medium (20ft/6m) | H37 KB-250 250W |
| Spotlight | UV floodlight | code 135 | (flood) | | | short/medium | E 27 165–170W |
| Spotlight | Black Gun spot | code 510 | (parabolic spot) | | | | E 40 400W |
| Spotlight | Blacklight tubelight | code 529 | (wide flood) | | | short | RT20 20W |
| Spotlight | Blacklight tubelight | code 530 | (wide flood) | | | short | RT40 40W |
| Wildfire | UV spot/flood Fresnel | WF-400 S/F | 16.5°–44° | 26°–59° | 0.46–1.13 | very long (100ft/30m) | WF-L100 400W |
| Wildfire | UV floodlight | WF-400 F | 80° | 105° | 2.61 | very long | WF-L101 400W |
| Wildfire | UV ellipsoidal | WF-400E | 20°–40° | | 0.35–0.73 | long (75ft/25m) | WF-L102 400W |
| Wildfire | UV spot 20° | WF-250 S | 16° | 22° | 0.39 | very long | WF-L103 250W |
| Wildfire | UV wide spot 50° | WF-250 WS | 33° | 56° | 1.06 | medium/long (50ft/15m) | WF-L103 250W |
| Wildfire | UV flood 90° | WF-250 F | 64° | 96° | 2 | medium (25ft/7.5m) | WF-L103 250W |

# Chapter Forty-four

# Instrument Symbols and Drafting Technique

There are a number of conventions that should be observed when drafting up a lighting plot. These vary from country to country, but a discussion of the standard American approach recommended by the USITT will suffice. Plots in the U.S. are traditionally drafted in pencil, where in the U.K. ink stencils are more common.

The graphic representation of the lighting plot is realized primarily with a plan and section. These are drawn usually at 1/2- or 1/4-inch to the foot. Their purpose is twofold: first to provide the electrician and crew responsible for hanging the show a detailed set of instructions, and second, to act as the designer's map of the lighting installation that he'll use while lighting the show.

Obviously standard practices of drafting, neatness and clearly legible lettering are important. The outline of the theatre and the scenery should be shown first. It is important that some important conventions are followed. Every plan must have the "center line" of the stage clearly indicated. Also in a proscenium house the "proscenium line" or "plaster line" must be drawn. This is the line of the back of the proscenium or fire-curtain smoke pocket from which the stage dimensions are all measured. In the U.K. a second line: the "setting line" is common. This is the line from which all the scenery is set out. In the U.S. these measurements are usually taken from the proscenium line—there are seldom other obstructions upstage of that point, but in the U.K. there are often obstructions, such as perch platforms or permanently hung equipment that forces the set further upstage. Thus the second separate datum line in the U.K. (Fig 106).

Once the stage, the set and the critical setting-out points are shown, the exact location of all the instruments and mounting positions will be indicated utilizing scale symbols of each type of instrument. Some manufacturers issue stencils specifically for their own equipment (Fig. 107).

The plan should include a Key Block describing each of the symbols used, and a Title Block. The title block should state the title of the show, the name of the producing organization and/or theatre, a drawing title, number and date, name of designer, and drafter (if different) with dates of any revisions. It's useful to place these blocks in the same place on each sheet for a production.

*Mounting positions.* By convention, pipes over the stage are numbered from downstage to

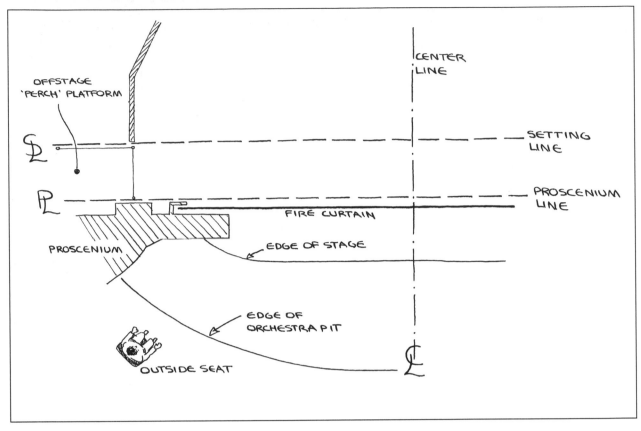

*106. Setting out the stage*

upstage; at the side, booms, ladders, tormentors, and so on, are numbered from downstage to upstage. Conversely, in a proscenium theatre, positions in the auditorium are numbered away from the proscenium, that is, the nearstage box boom and light bridge are number one. The only exception to this might be in a repertory situation utilizing "geographic" numbering. Then the rear of the house might be numbered 1–99, the next bridge and slots 100–199, and so on to the rear of the stage.

Each instrument symbol will need to be accompanied by information, which will vary from situation to situation (Fig 108).

*Instrument number.* Each instrument at each position is numbered. Instruments on pipes are usually numbered from stage left to right and vertical positions from top to bottom. Double-hung booms onstage number from downstage to upstage, and top to bottom. Box booms number away from the proscenium. This number is usually written within the instrument silhouette.

*Focus Area.* The intended focus or use of each instrument should be briefly described.

*Color.* The color number with letter prefix to denote the manufacturer should be noted.

*Channel Number.* This indicates the control channel that will be called for.

*Dimmer/Circuit Number.* This information as well as lamp wattage is best left to the written instrument schedule. When it comes to drawing booms and any vertically placed equipment, conventions vary. The ground plan should include a plan of the boom and its instruments as seen from above. In addition the boom should be drawn in elevation, so that all the instruments and their mounting heights are shown. These may be offset at an angle or shown vertically at the side of the plot.

*Dimensions.* Remember that your equipment will be rigged according to your drawings. All relevant dimensions should be clearly indicated. Pipe lengths and trim heights above the stage should be shown.

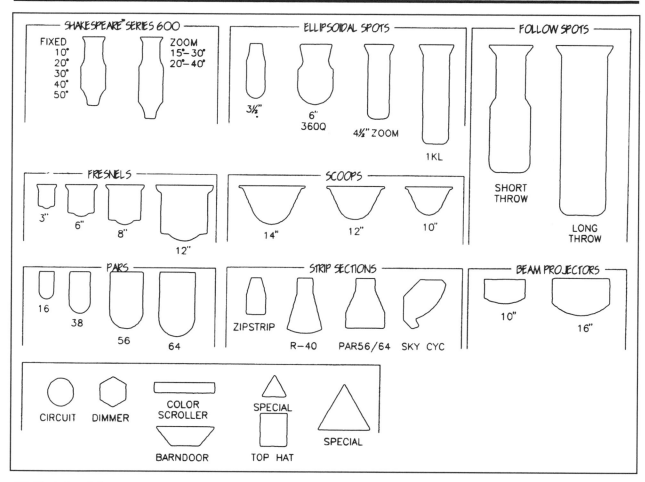

107. *Typical symbols*

## Marcplot

Lighting designer Marc Weiss has invented a neat package for aiding the conceptual design process before putting pencil to paper for serious drafting. This involves colored magnetized plastic light symbols that can be written on and placed on a magnetic board. By using these first to represent lighting functions, for example "front light," "acting area left" or "backlight," the colored symbols may be quickly and easily moved around the plot to build a design. After the initial concept has been roughed in, the symbols can be used to then actually represent each instrument in the rig. Only when the plot has been rationalized and duplications avoided is the design transferred into a conventional drawing.

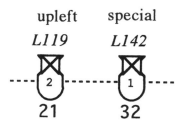

108. *Typical plot details*

# Chapter Forty-five

# Calculation of Lighting Angles

How do we start to place our light for actors? The acting area is first divided into modules of a chosen size. In this instance I have chosen 8'0" (2.4m). The most useful size is usually between 6'0" (1.8m) and 12'0" (3.65m; Fig. 109).

The actor is placed in the center of the acting area in position B. Assuming his eye level to be 5'6" (1.70m) above the floor, all angular calculations will be taken from this height. First we will draw in the vertical angle at which we want the lamp: I have called this angle X, and in this case we want it 45° from the horizontal. We then draw a line upward until we reach the rigging height, in this case at 20'0" (6.1m). This is the supposed level at which the instruments can be hung. We then draw lines to the up and downstage sides of area B; this gives an angle of about 54° at the front and about 38° at the back.

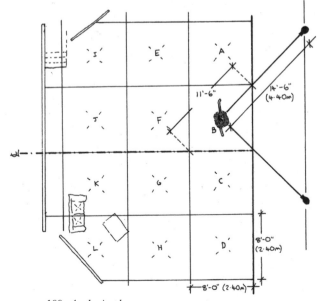

*109. Angles in plan*

436

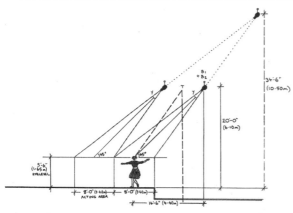

*110. Angles in section*

*111. Section through beam*

This exercise can be repeated for the other areas of the stage. The drawing, being a section through the stage center line, shows the spotlight beams as they would be if the instruments were going to be mounted directly to the actor's front. It would appear we need a beam of about 16° width (angle Y) and the instrument would be mounted (in plan) 14'6" (4.4m) away from the center point of the area. But we have already decided that we want to place the instrument not in front of the actor, but 45° to his side (Fig. 110).

If we move to the plan, we can first draw the acting areas and mark the actor at point B. We know that to achieve the angle X vertically, we have to place the instrument 14'6" (4.4m) away if the ceiling height is at 20'0" (6.1m). We can draw this in plan, not on the center line but at the required 45° angle to the side as shown. This will give the true position of instruments B1 and B2. Transferring this back to the section, we can mark this true position as position T. The last piece of information we can extract is the real beam angle that is required. We see from the plan that the actual area that the instrument has to cover is not 8'0" (2.4m) wide but 11'6" (3.5m) wide, being the diagonal across the square module. Accordingly, if we draw a section through the actual beam of the instrument, we find that the true beam angle required is about 25° (Fig. 111).

We can also see from the first section the effect of an increase in ceiling height. If we go up to a level of 34'6" (10.5m), we will see that the whole of the stage can be covered with the same angles from two positions instead of four. But it is probably undesirable to have such large areas. Furthermore, equipment needed for a long throw such as this would have to be more powerful and would consequently be expensive. A judgment call must be made.

We have noted earlier that the angle of 45°, used on its own, can be rather severe when lighting some actors' faces. Therefore we should also employ some lower lighting, at an angle of about 20° to 25° as a "fill-light" (Fig. 112).

We can see that a position that is lighting one part of the stage at one angle is very likely to serve, in another way, for another part of the acting area. Thus the 55° to 60° position provides crossed acting area lighting at 45° to the front edge of the stage but straight-in light at the 45° angle further back.

In conclusion it must be stressed that the angles we have been discussing are the basic ones for illumination. Any and indeed almost every other angle may be required for effect lighting.

What instrument to choose? This will depend on many factors. Usually lighting for the acting area from front-of-house or downstage pipes will employ Leko or profile spot-lights, which have a controlled, shapeable beam. Their power (and consequent brightness) will usually range upward from 500W—dependent upon brightness needed and throw available. How bright is enough? A tough question, the answer to which depends upon the circumstances of the production and the nature of the performance. A brightness of about 50 f.c. for the acting area may be minimum.

Of course with the computer many of these calculations about beam angle, spread and brightness can be easily obtained. A simple program such as Argus or MacLux Pro will instantly show an instrument's performance, allowing the designer to quickly try different mounting heights and angles and alternate instruments and wattages.

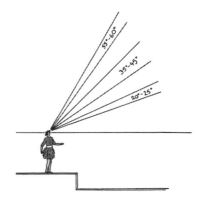

*112. Useful FOH angles*

# Chapter Forty-six

# Lighting Software

*by Eric Cornwell*

Specialized software has been developed, often by working designers, to assist in all phases of production. Programs are available for comparing photometric properties of luminaires, analyzing lighting angles within a theatre, drawing the light plot, preparing equipment schedules, tracking cues, editing console disks off-line, and even automating the process of reassigning control-channel numbers when a production is moved.

While the basic principles of lighting design remain fairly constant through the years, the specific tools used to achieve the design are improved constantly. From light sources to luminaires, color media, and control consoles, progress is continuous. Nowhere is this more evident than in the area of computer software.

Therefore this sample of currently available products should be taken as a guide to the types of tools available. One can expect that as computer power continues to increase and become more affordable to more designers, the products described will expand and evolve in ways unimaginable at present.

LightShop and LightCalc are databases of theatrical luminaires combined with photometric modelers that allow the designer to graphically and numerically compare light output and beam sizes of different fixtures at any location and angle. Beamwright is a simple utility that helps the designer choose the most appropriate instrument from a range of options, given the parameters of trim height, angle, throw and size of area to be illuminated. Projection Magic provides similar numerical calculations for motion-picture, slide, and scenic projectors.

Many programs are available for lighting equipment database management. Lightwright is probably the most popular in the U.S. It provides for speedy entry and editing of groups of lights as well as a great variety of customizable reports. Other lighting-specific databases include Laplight, XENON, Marcplot and The Lighting Technician.

Argus, MacLux Pro, MicroLux 1000, and LightsUp are multipurpose tools for analyzing beam angles and intensities, drawing light plots, and generating instrument schedules, hook-ups, color lists, and so on, all from one program. MacLux Pro can also create information that commercial imaging programs can use to render color images of scenes based on actual lighting angles, color, and intensities derived from the light plot and cue information stored in MacLux Pro. Candlepower produces light plots and paperwork, but lacks the more sophisticated photometric tools.

WYSIWYG is a program that provides a real-time emulation of moving and conventional lighting on a VDU. The program also can create the necessary plots and schedules and allows off-line set-up and editing of moving lights. The newest WYSIWYG is actually able to focus lights "on screen." Select a group of lights, touch a point on stage, and all those chosen instantly find the spot.

Perhaps the most sophisticated lighting simulator program is HighLight from Lighthouse Software BV of Holland. This program, using Microsoft Windows 3.1, provides a photo-realistic representation of the stage. Three-dimensional modeling in wire-frame or solid mode, with multiple views, realistic light performance including multiple reflection and transparency can be achieved. Instrument beam performance can be adjusted—indeed new theoretical instruments (or even colors) may be created.

Rob Shakespeare from the theater department at Indiana University has made extraordinary progress in photo-realistic rendering of stage and architectural lighting. This allows off-line creation of lighting images in great and realistic detail and will provide the ability to position and control lights—via the virtual model—during performance.

Virtual Lightlab is a program that allows the designer to experiment with color choices with an array of simulated instruments. A standard stage setting, geometric shapes, a performer in long shot or close-up are provided with a custom background, and up to thirty instruments can be placed to provide a variety of angles of illumination. Custom or standard manufacturers' colors may then be applied and the light intensity adjusted.

Bill Warfel is author of Gelfile—the color filter database. This allows you to examine over 1,200 color filters on a chromaticity and bright-ness plot and provides wavelength and saturation data. Touch any point on the color chart and the closest available color is shown.

Another ingenious and remarkably useful piece of software is "WinHook." Developed by Ashland Oregon Shakespeare's Stuart Cotts, this software allows a Windows-based computer to address any of the major consoles (Strand, ETC and Colortran). Instead of the usually extraordinarily unhandy handheld focus remote, any light (or up to six at a time) can be called up from your laptop and controlled. But this control uses the hook-up or instrument schedule to directly take control and thus focus notes, notes on "jobs to be done," can all be readily made or accessed live as the focusing proceeds.

Several programs provide cue tracking and off-line editing capabilities. ETCedit, from Electronic Theatre Controls, can translate disks amongst most of the ETC line of consoles, as well as allow editing of cue data on a PC. Obsession Off-Line reproduces all of the displays, controls and operations of the ETC Obsession on a PC. Express-Track offers a variety of cue-analysis and tracking tools, and provides translation to and from Strand Light Palette 90 disks. TrackMaster and PC Expert provide off-line editing for USITT ASCII Cue format files. These text files can be used directly with some consoles, like the AVAB Expert, while for other consoles translation programs like LightPort are needed to convert between show disks and ASCII cue files. ETCedit, Express-Track and TrackMaster also provide support for complete renumbering of channels when shows are remounted in different venues. Light-Cad provides off-line editing for and translation between Avolites and Celco consoles.

For designers who already have an investment in commercial database or drafting programs, there are various add-on libraries and templates available. Lighting Designer is a lighting database that interfaces with the popular and inexpensive Generic CADD drafting software. Autolight, Light "Works" and LightDoc provide similar links to the popular but more expensive AutoCAD. Freeman & Associates publishes libraries of lighting and scenic symbols in AutoCAD, Generic CADD and DXF formats.

Conventional word-processing, database and spreadsheet programs are used by designers as often as any of the specialized software. Equipment lists, cue synopses, rehearsal schedules, work notes, phone lists and the like are much easier to create and update on a computer than by hand. Regardless of how many specialized programs a designer may use, a simple word processor will always be required for the odd note or list.

Architectural lighting designers use computers to solve quite different problems than those faced by their theatrical counterparts. Programs like MICRO-EYE-LITE and CALA use IES format photometric data files provided by lighting fixture manufacturers, combined with fixture layouts and room-surface reflectance information, to calculate illumination levels within rooms. Lightcad, not to be confused with Light-Cad, also calculates power density and utility rebates, and the Advanced Graphics Interface can calculate outdoor lighting levels over uneven terrain. Beem is a lighting program that does not deal with lighting fixtures at all but helps designers assess the effect that sunlight through windows will have on energy costs for a building.

# Chapter Forty-seven

# The Lighting Installation

The permanent lighting installation in a performance space may be divided into four parts.

## 1. Production Lighting

This is the installation that controls the lighting for a show. It consists of the control system, the dimmers, wiring and instruments. An installation's complexity will depend on the size of theatre, its form, but perhaps most importantly upon the type of organization for which it's intended—and the budget. For example, a commercial theatre intended to receive long-run productions might be equipped on what is known as a "four walls" basis. This means that little is supplied other than the power for dimmer racks and control systems that are brought in by the production. On the other hand, a community arts center or college installation may

have a complete lighting layout including all the instruments necessary to light a wide range of productions. Between these two extremes lie many other alternatives.

## 2. Functional Lighting

An efficient theatre cannot rely only on the production lighting for every type of illumination. Functional lighting includes the worklight installation, which may be divided into two categories:

a. "High-key" worklight: These are bright work lights throughout the stage, backstage and auditorium roof voids that are used during the load-in and fit-up of a production and during the day when a performance or dress rehearsal is not taking place.

b. "Low-key" running light: This is controlled low-key lighting (usually blue in color) that is normally left on throughout a performance or rehearsal. This gives adequate illumination to every backstage space that might need to be accessed without being visible to the audience. Grids, galleries, lighting bridges and slots, sound and light locks immediately adjacent to the stage or auditorium will all have low-key lighting that will be maintained on to allow safe circulation by actors and technicians behind the scenes. When the production lighting is in a blackout condition, no spill light from the low-key worklight should be visible to the audience.

Other functional lighting might include special rehearsal light—to illuminate the actors in rehearsal when the production lighting is not in use; cleaners light—lighting for cleaners to be able to clean the auditorium between performances without the houselights on; and stage running worklights—lights on-stage or in the wings under the control of the stage manager that may be switched on to illuminate the stage during a scene change.

## 3. House Lighting

This is the architectural lighting that illuminates the auditorium. It has to illuminate the audience and the architecture in an appropriate and pleasing manner. Audiences want to look and feel good, and the architectural quality of the auditorium needs to be enhanced. The choice of lighting is again dependent upon the type of theatre. Most auditoria, before the production begins, should be lit in an attractive and atmospheric manner, if possible enhancing a sense of anticipation for the production that is about to begin. Some auditoria will be used for a wide range of functions. For example, a theatre used for conferences might need a higher level of illumination (for note taking) than that needed for a drama theatre, where more atmosphere might be more appropriate, calling for lower lighting levels. Houselights must always be dimmer controlled. The timing of house light fades can be an important preparation for the show to come. House lighting may be divided across a number of circuits so that different parts of the auditorium can be lit in different ways. For example, an unoccupied upper balcony might be left in darkness with a small audience, or circle-front sconces or other decorative lighting may fade out later than the general illumination to create a pictorial effect. Note that areas associated with the auditorium, such as sound- and light-lock lobbies, should have their high-key lighting controlled to fade out with the house lights, while a low-key lighting level should be maintained

## 4. Safety Lighting

Throughout the auditorium and stage safety codes require provision for lighting that is maintained on or brought on in the event of an emergency. Exit signs, which must always be illuminated, are the obvious example. However, a minimum level of illumination in the aisles, sound and light locks and exit corridors will certainly need to be maintained on and energized by a secondary power source in the event of a power failure. Local codes should of course be observed.

# Chapter Forty-eight

# Lighting Positions

The main lighting positions in a theatre will be primarily driven by the form of the auditorium and the shape of the stage. A proscenium or end-stage will broadly divide its lighting positions between FOH and stage. With an open, thrust, arena or space stage this division will not be so apparent.

To an extent, the architecture of the auditorium will dictate the availability of lighting positions. But each form of stage will demand that certain primary lighting positions be provided, and if the architect fails to make proper accommodation, the theatre electrician will soon rig lighting pipes where they are needed. It's far better that the architect supply appropriate lighting positions rather than have his architecture later compromised by scattered pipes and loose cable draped over his elegant interior.

Again, the placement of the lighting instrument depends on the positions of the actors and nature of the illumination at every moment through the production. In theory, we want to be able to aim a light at almost any angle to the actor on every part of the stage. But clearly this is impractical. The audience has to be seated somewhere, and the building has to be held up, with a roof to keep the rain out. The shape of the auditorium, the layout of seating, the number of levels, as well as other architectural considerations, will dictate where the principal lighting positions will be.

To light the actor's face, we've found that a considerable amount of light must come from above the actor to his front. We've seen that we need a series of vertical angles ranging from a quite low level through 45° to a fairly steep

level downward. Furthermore, while a proportion of the light will come from the front, some will come from the sides. A 45°–55° angle from the end of lighting bridges in the ceiling to the front of the stage, supplemented by sidelighting in the walls of the auditorium to give a cross-light to the front of the stage, will be needed. Consequently most well-organized proscenium theatres will have a number of lighting bridges in the auditorium ceiling and lighting slots or box booms in the side walls (Fig. 113).

All these positions should be accessed from catwalks behind the instruments for focusing and maintenance. It is perhaps desirable that lighting bridges in the ceiling run straight across the room, parallel to the front of the stage. But this can sometimes have a negative

*113. Auditorium production lighting*

impact upon the architectural design of the ceiling. An auditorium is, after all, a room: a room in which people are meant to feel comfortable and at home. Steel catwalks packed with lights overhead may be more reminiscent of a factory than a home. Therefore, the lighting designer should work with the architect to try to integrate, as far as possible, his lighting needs with the architectural form. If, as is often desirable, the room is to have some form of decorative ceiling, lighting positions can be integrated into that ceiling without necessarily destroying its visual strength. Catwalks can be integrated into coves in a visual ceiling or suspended below such a ceiling and architecturally integrated in some way. Sometimes a lighting bridge shaped to reflect the balcony and box configuration below can become an attractive architectural element, perhaps reflecting the feeling of a large chandelier integrating production lighting above and house lighting below.

Sidelighting will often be difficult to integrate architecturally. There's a widespread return to the use of boxes and side seating in per-

formance spaces to enhance the feeling of audience members' participation with the stage. This return to three-dimensional theatre design undoubtedly enhances the ambiance of theatre space. But it often makes the lighting designer's job more difficult, for sidelighting now has to be integrated with the side seating. Proscenium boxes may be called into double duty, providing vertical box boom positions.

The very phrase "box booms" reminds us how lighting in the auditorium began. Soon after the invention of the spotlight (and we're talking in oil lamp days) lighting designers began to fix their instruments to the balcony and box fronts. In the early days of electricity, this was followed by the box boom, which was a scaffold pipe fixed in the boxes adjacent to the stage, on which spotlights were hung to crosslight the downstage areas. There's no doubt about it that recent decades have made audiences everywhere familiar with the trees of lighting equipment standing in the boxes on either side of the theatre. In more recent times this is often accompanied by a truss hung over the front of the orchestra pit to provide an

overhead frontlight position that was not available in the theatres of yesteryear, with their decorative plaster ceilings. There's really little reason why production lighting should not be hung within the existing architecture, whether old or new. The only thing we have to try to improve upon is access. We have to be able to get to our lights, to focus and maintain them. Even if we're using remote-control focus instruments, the element of maintenance remains. Catwalk access is mandatory to the principal positions. What are these positions?

## 1. FOH Bridges

The quantity of FOH bridges will depend on the sophistication of the lighting installation. We certainly want to light the front of the stage with a vertical angle of approximately 45°–55°. This alone is really not satisfactory except in the simplest installations. After all, that angle will only be good for one position at the front of the stage, whereas further back the angle will be flatter, until it is taken over by light from the onstage lighting pipes. Two or three bridges are preferable. If two are used, one is hung at a steeper angle over the forestage (perhaps 85°); if three, there will be a steeply angled inner bridge with two further out at approximately 55° and 40°. The outermost bridge will give a lower frontlight angle, useful for front fill to the actor and color washes to the downstage area. Significant use of a large forestage may necessitate more bridges further out in the auditorium.

## 2. Box Booms

There need to be not less than two sidelighting positions at either side: one close to the proscenium to give crosslight to the front of the stage and the forestage and another further out to give good front/sidelight to the downstage areas. Some light from the side must be able to get into the near side of the stage, and the architectural design around the proscenium must take into account the need for a seamless transition from the FOH to onstage lighting.

### 3. High Side Walls

A side position high up on the walls of the auditorium, equipped with long-throw instruments, can give an excellent angle of light to the downstage areas. This position, which is usually easily accessible, might relieve pressure for instruments on transverse lighting bridges in the ceiling or obviate the need to hang an unsightly truss. In renovating a historic house (such as the Geary Theatre in San Francisco or the New Amsterdam in New York) a high side wall position can lessen the visual impact of equipment that would otherwise obscure the spectacular architecture. Of course, there will be shows where a steep front angle to the stage will require a truss, but sometimes it can be avoided.

### 4. Balcony Rail

The balcony rail will continue to be a useful lighting position. A high level will provide a good shot at a lower angle than the bridges. Upper-level balcony rails will be very useful for frontal fill light, often essential for lighting into the eyes of an actor. Front specials may be needed to pin-spot an actor or object on the stage. A lower level, while it only has limited use for actor illumination, may be needed to fill in deep-set eyes or get under the brim of a wide hat; more importantly, it might be needed for lighting scenery or for special effects. Cloths in the downstage area need to be lit from a low level, from below the top of the proscenium, so that light is not cut off the top of the cloth. Similarly, front-projection effects need an upward angle in many instances.

### 5. Follow Spots

Follow spots traditionally have been mounted in a room at the rear top of the auditorium. A vertical angle of between 30° and 40° is usually desirable. Any flatter light casts shadows of the actors over scenery behind them, and any steeper doesn't get well into the eyes to give that "star" sparkle. Follow spots in a large theatre will be large noisy pieces of equipment, and as the crew often have to talk to each other, the spots will have to be contained in a soundproof room. Theatres will usually use two or three follow spots from the front, but as many as five might be required on the largest productions.

Follow spots are increasingly used at a high position to the sides of the auditorium, particularly for big musicals. These usually use low-voltage beamlights or short-throw follow spots. A well-equipped theatre will make provision for a high side follow-spot position at roughly 45°–55° horizontally and vertically to the downstage center of the acting area. (Smaller follow spots may also be used onstage, either from "perch" platforms behind and to the side of the proscenium or from lighting or fly galleries above the stage. This traditional follow-spot position dates back to the days of limelight. Such acute angles to the performer can give a highly dramatic effect.)

### 6. Front Projection

Productions may employ front projection. Such projection might be a number of the ever popular Kodak Carousels mounted on the balcony rail but may be larger-scale front projection using HMI or xenon projectors. With a large-scale installation, a front projection room should be provided. Film projection will conventionally require a projection room at the rear of the top circle. But this must be not too high in the theatre. Front projection will usually require a fairly flat angle to the stage to avoid a shadow from the proscenium header at the top of the beam. Some stunning integration of film and live action, originated by Josef Svoboda, needed a stage-level projection position allowing a straight-on throw to the stage. Elaborate productions, such as the New York *Show Boat*, made provisions for Pani HMI projectors with moving effects to be built into a special balcony rail, which is separately air conditioned and acoustically isolated from the auditorium (Fig. 114).

*114. Rail—projection enclosure*

Opera often requires the projection of surtitles, a technique very popular with the public, that provides translation of the lyrics on a screen above the stage. Surtitles can be projected from the front with slide or video projection, and the employment of electronically generated signs is becoming viable. Screens are usually horizontal rectangles hung above the proscenium—but remember, Chinese characters are displayed vertically at the side! Hopefully, advances in computers will provide other, better solutions. For their 1995/6 season the Metropolitan Opera successfully installed surtitle screens on every seat back. Patrons have the option to turn them on or off individually.

### 7. Other Angles

Despite all the above, other more unusual angles may still sometimes be needed. I would advocate that, wherever possible, lighting suspension pipes be fitted around the face of each balcony and box front or immediately below. Particularly at the sides of the theatre, a low upward cross-light to the stage might be required for special effects, and an instrument fitted below a box can be ideally placed. Again a *Show Boat* example: both water-ripple and flame-flickering effects from below actor eye level at either side of the stage and from the orchestra pit are needed.

### On Stage

Flexibility must be the keynote for the production lighting installation on stage. Only the most modest installations, or one intended for use in circumstances where safety and permanence are paramount (such as a primary school), require fixed lighting positions around the stage. In all other circumstances the lighting should be able to be easily moved into new configurations.

Essentially, lighting might be placed anywhere in the stage area. A large proportion will come from overhead, where it will normally be hung on overhead pipes. A proportion will come from the sides, mounted on vertical booms (tormentors). Equipment may be hung on galleries at either side of the stage or placed on the stage floor on stands of variable height. All lighting pipes in the stage and auditorium should be standard 1²⁹⁄₃₂-inch (50mm) external 1½-inch (375mm) internal diameter steel pipe, to allow a lighting instrument to be fixed to them.

In a theatre with a permanently wired installation, circuits will be distributed around the stage in conduit or trunking to outlet devices. These may be connector strips (a strip with regularly spaced pigtails and connectors, usually mounted alongside a pipe), plug boxes (a multiplug box, fixed on the end of a multicore cable), or multicore cable to a "fan-out" (Figs. 115–117).

Outlets will normally be located above the stage on the grid or an upper fly gallery, from which the overhead lighting pipes are fed; on fly galleries to plug-in circuits for side lighting on booms, tormentors, or ladders; and at stage level.

The stage-level plug boxes are often placed in floor pockets ("dip traps," named after practice in the days of gas, when a water-filled trap would ensure a safe gas-plug connection). Today these are hinged traps in the stage floor that can be opened to access the outlets below. It is perhaps preferable to locate stage-level plug boxes around the walls of the stage, particularly in the rear of the proscenium wall and to the sides of the back of the stage. These positions are not likely to be covered by scenery or false floors. Wherever the stage plugs are located, it's a good idea to have covered troughs in the stage floor running from upstage to downstage and across the stage, both at the front and rear, to allow temporary cables to be placed out of harm's way below the floor. These troughs should connect through to the trap room below the stage, which will also require circuits for lighting equipment below the floor.

A theatre that is intended to accommodate long runs may not have wiring installed permanently on the stage. It is the custom for touring productions (particularly in the U.S.) to carry virtually all their own lighting equipment, including control boards and dimmer racks. The racks are placed on stage and all the wiring is temporary run-outs from the dimmers to the instruments. With variations of this technique, temporary wiring can be rigged neatly and efficiently and safety can be ensured (Figs. 118–120).

Getting power cables to overstage pipes must be considered. Sufficient length of cable must be allowed so that the pipe can be lowered to the floor for maintenance. This excess cable must be lifted when the pipe is flown out to its trim. Simply done, a hemp line to pull up the cable is usually sufficient. In the U.S. a cable cradle is often employed. In a repertory situation, a "windlass" or "dog's-leg" folding arrangement of flat multicore cable may be worthwhile.

Circuits in the auditorium, where temporary wiring would be impractical and unsightly, should be permanently wired back to a breakout panel onstage. From the panel, circuits can be connected to the in-house control or to any touring control that may be used.

115. Connector strip

116. Drop box

117. Multicable fan-out

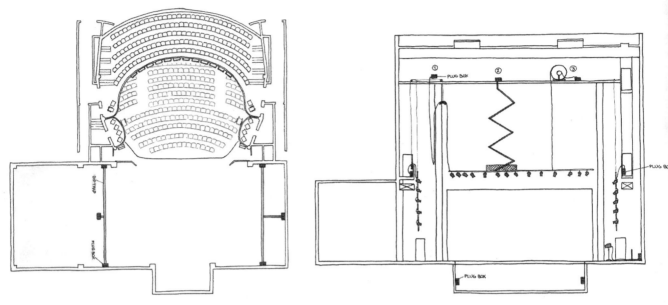

118. *Theatre in plan*

119. *Stage in elevation*
*Key:*
*1. Cable cradle on hemp line*
*2. "Dog's leg" cable trays*
*3. Windlass*

120. *Theatre in section*

# Chapter Forty-nine

# Production Lighting

*Scale and Power*

As we've observed, the scale of any lighting installation will depend on many factors. An international opera house or a large-scale Broadway musical might employ a thousand or more instruments. A giant casino showroom might increase this number to several thousand. A primary-school hall will be more modest. For every project the designer must decide on the appropriate scale. Whatever scale is chosen, we must consider the implications. The most obvious one is, of course, cost. Wiring is expensive to install and electricity costs can be significant. Lights emit heat, and a large lighting installation will significantly impact the cost of air-conditioning the auditorium.

Whatever scale is chosen, considerable diversity can be anticipated. In a manner that can often be confusing to the conventional elec-trical engineer, loads imposed by a production lighting installation can vary enormously. A production with a thousand lights will only very rarely, if ever, have all those lights on at the same time. Some shows will be much brighter than others. A musical set in the Arabian desert may be expected to be brighter than a production of Ibsen's *The Doll's House*. Many electrical engineers will hope for some rational balance between the three phases of the electrical supply. Such balance is never predictable. One production in one scene might use all the lights at one end of the theatre, perhaps the front of house, at full while nothing is used on stage; the next scene might be totally different.

It certainly can be assumed that the potential connected load will be much greater than the actual power required. In the U.S. theoreti-cally a fully loaded ninety-six dimmer rack could consume 800 amps. But 600 amps is sufficient, and most Broadway and touring theatres provide disconnects of 400 amps each for hook-up of temporary dimmer racks. Research by Con-Ed in New York in 1994 revealed that the maximum demand (including all electrical services and HVAC) of a range of Broadway theatres in 1994 was in the order of 512kW (Palace), 444kW (Shubert), 294kW (Imperial), to 149kW (Longacre).

## DIMMER QUANTITIES

The number of dimmers will depend upon the scale and complexity of the installation. Increasing availability of comparatively low-cost dimmers has encouraged the principle of dimmer per circuit. In the old days a comparatively small number of high-capacity dimmers might be installed with a patch panel to group individual circuits onto common dimmers. Now every outgoing circuit should, if possible, have its own dimmer. Infrequently used locations might share some dimmers with parallel-wired circuits. If in production many circuits are required to work together, these of course will be electronically patched onto a common control channel on the console.

A large majority of instruments use a 1kW lamp. Sometimes instruments might be used in pairs. This tends to make the 2kW dimmer a useful standard. However, the recently developed 575W lamp with the light output of the old 1kW lamp seems certain to become popular. In any event, the 1kW or 2kW dimmer is likely to be standard for most installations. However, larger dimmers are required for medium- or large-scale theatres. Five-kilowatt Fresnels are quite commonly used in the professional theatre. Cyclorama and backcloth lighting might require wattages in excess of 2kW. Large-scale incandescent projectors might need 5kW. So a number of circuits of this capacity should be prudently distributed around the theatre. The very large installation—for example, the opera house—might need to go even further and 10kW outlets might have to be made available.

However, in the professional theatre, where light sources of a greater intensity are needed, there's a trend toward employing non-incandescent light sources, for example, HMI, CSI or xenon. These lights do not work on a conventional dimmer, and they require nondimmable power to supply the lamp (and possibly fans), with a second connection to control the brightness. This will usually be some form of mechanical shutter and requires a control channel which will usually be the current international theatre standard DMX (digital multiplex).

Therefore, the modern dimmer installation needs to be supplemented by a variety of non-dimmable outlets and by a control channel network. The modern dimmer can be programmed to work either as a dimmer or as a nondim switchable circuit. DMX uses an internationally accepted five-pin XLR socket. One DMX socket can control 512 multiplexed devices. These devices include not only non-incandescent dimming shutters but also color scrollers, many types of remote control instruments (but not all), slide changers, smoke, fog and effects machines—indeed, almost any device that is amenable to remote control. So every permanently wired plug box around the theatre should have adjacent DMX sockets for control of devices in that part of the theatre.

The whole field of control interconnection is changing rapidly. As a standard, DMX has considerable limitations. Other standards such as Ethernet—common in the computer world—are increasingly found to allow multiple control locations and the interconnection of control equipment. Connection between multiple control boards and to other computers for off-line working throughout the theatre will become increasingly common. The increasing use of moving lights, with some manufacturers using proprietary control protocol, is a source of confusion in a permanent installation that hopefully will be resolved by the industry collaborating on new standards before too long. (Vari*Lite has developed standards for permanently wired installations for their own protocol.)

## CIRCUIT LAYOUT

There are no hard and fast rules as to how to lay out circuits around a theatre. Remember that it is almost always possible to rent additional dimmers for that once-a-year very-large-scale production. The permanent installation should be chosen bearing in mind the average use of the facility and with an eye to a healthy balance between economy and lighting enthusiasm.

| | Small | | Mid | | Large | |
|---|---|---|---|---|---|---|
| **Front of House** | | | | | | |
| Bridge 1 | 18 | | 30 | | 36 | |
| Bridge 2 | 12 | | 18 | | 30 | |
| Bridge 3 | | | 12 | | 24 | |
| Follow spot | | | 4 | | 6 | |
| Balcony Rail | 10 | | 20 | | 30 | |
| Projection Room | | | 4 | | 6 | |
| Mezzanine Rail | | | 8 | | 24 | |
| Box Boom L 2 | 6 | | 12 | | 18 | |
| Box Boom L 1 | 6 | | 8 | | 18 | |
| Box Boom R 2 | 6 | | 12 | | 18 | |
| Box Boom R 1 | 6 | | 8 | | 18 | |
| Boxes L | | | 4 | | 10 | |
| Boxes R | | | 4 | | 10 | |
| Subtotal | 64 | 33% | 144 | 37% | 248 | 32% |

| | Small | | Mid | | Large | |
|---|---|---|---|---|---|---|
| **Stage** | | | | | | |
| Overstage 1 | 24 | | 24 | | 42 | |
| Overstage 2 | 18 | | 24 | | 30 | |
| Overstage 3 | 18 | | 24 | | 30 | |
| Overstage 4 | 18 | | 24 | | 30 | |
| Overstage 5 | | | 24 | | 30 | |
| Overstage 6 | | | 24 | | 30 | |
| Overstage 7 | | | | | 30 | |
| Overstage 8 | | | | | 30 | |
| Overstage 9 | | | | | 30 | |
| Overstage 10 | | | | | 30 | |
| Flies Left 1 | 8 | | 12 | | 18 | |
| Flies Left 2 | 8 | | 12 | | 12 | |
| Flies Left 3 | | | 6 | | 12 | |
| Flies Left 4 | | | | | 12 | |
| Flies Left 5 | | | | | 6 | |
| Flies Right 1 | 6 | | 12 | | 18 | |
| Flies Right 2 | 4 | | 12 | | 12 | |
| Flies Right 3 | | | 6 | | 12 | |
| Flies Right 4 | | | | | 12 | |
| Flies Right 5 | | | | | 6 | |
| Stage DL | 6 | | 12 | | 18 | |
| Stage UL | 6 | | 6 | | 18 | |
| Stage DR | 6 | | 12 | | 18 | |
| Stage UR | 6 | | 6 | | 18 | |
| Orchestra Pit | | | 3 | | 6 | |
| Trap Room | | | 3 | | 6 | |
| Total stage | 128 | 67% | 246 | 63% | 516 | 68% |
| Grand Total | 192 | 100% | 390 | 100% | 764 | 100% |

# Chapter Fifty

# Control Rooms

A well-organized theatre should have control rooms with a good view of the stage positioned at the rear of the auditorium. Ideally, the rear of the orchestra stalls allows good communication to the production desk during rehearsals. The board operator should be able to see the lighting he is operating.

There are divergent views on this. On Broadway and with touring Broadway shows the control is usually placed offstage. It's felt that being near the stage and dimmer racks allows better control and efficiency for the crew. But even with color television monitors I personally think that a first-class view for the operator is preferable. This becomes even more important with moving lights, where the operator must see what he is doing to correct mishaps and overcome problems.

Particularly in a repertory situation, I've found that a sensitive operator with both a good view and an understanding of the idea of the lighting, can actually improve the timing and movement of light as a show matures. It might be anathema to some to imagine an operator changing anything, but under certain circumstances I disagree. A good operator can play his part and add to the sensitivity of the result.

During rehearsals it is always to be hoped that the lighting control, or part thereof, can be moved adjacent to the production desk. Again with moving lights this is almost mandatory. The good operator is a partner in the design process, and physical proximity can be of great value.

In these days of rigger's controls (handheld control keypads that can be carried about the theatre) focusing and focus checks can be carried out without the main board having to be manned.

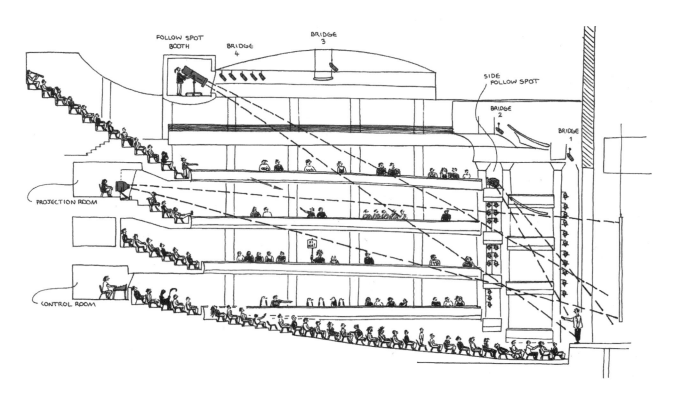

*The opera auditorium and typical control rooms*

# Chapter Fifty-one

# Rigging Techniques

## FRONT-OF-HOUSE LIGHTING POSITIONS

An electrician should have easy access to every position where lighting equipment is rigged. Front-of-house overhead lighting should, wherever possible, be positioned on bridges, running above the auditorium ceiling, along which the electrician can work. It must be remembered that these catwalk areas are workshops for the electrical crew. The electricians must be able to reach every instrument in dimly lit conditions, often during rehearsal or performance, without hitting their heads on any low beam or obstruction. Equipment has to be carried up to each lighting position, so access must be unimpeded (Fig. 121).

There should be separate access to the light bridge from outside the auditorium, and the electrician should be able to get up to the bridge during a performance without disturbing the

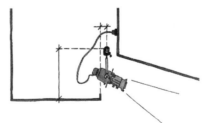

*121. Typical lighting bridge section.*
*Rail height 2' 4" (718mm) to 2' 10" (872mm)*
*Width 1' 9" (478mm) to 2' 4" (718mm)*

audience. The exact design of these positions has to be considered most carefully. Instruments there must not only light the front of the stage but should be able to cover the whole stage area. The adjacent areas of ceiling must not interfere with the beam, and it should be remembered that the electrician setting the instrument must be able to see the part of the

stage at which he is aiming. The ceiling around a lighting bridge must be finished in a dark non-reflective color. The same rules apply to slots in the side wall of the auditorium: the instrument fixing should be adjustable in height and a vertical ladder or staircase should give access to a series of levels about seven feet (2.1m) apart all the way up the slot (Figs. 122 and 123).

Instruments for low-angle light to the stage will be fixed around the front edge of any balcony in the auditorium. This position may be less commonly used, and the instruments can be fixed on a pipe cantilevered out from the gallery front (Fig. 124).

In the old days the instrument was usually concealed in some form of housing designed as part of the circle front; this was particularly

452

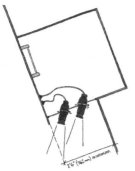

*122. Plan lighting slot*
*Width 2' 6" (769mm) minumum*

*124. Rail—underhung*

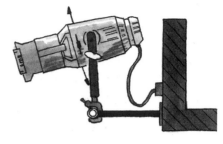

*125. Rail—overhung*

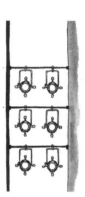

*123. Elevation lighting slot*
*Height 2' 0" (615mm) adjustable*

important if the instrument was used with any noisy color-change or moving effects equipment (which could be quite large). If the instruments are enclosed, the electrician, when focusing them, must be able to get at the locking nuts, masking shutters and focus. Similarly, a hinged access door over an instrument is useless if its open flap prevents the electrician seeing the stage. Such doors should hinge sideways.

Nowadays the public are so used to seeing equipment in the auditorium that it is usual to simply mount the instruments on a lighting pipe in full view. Instruments on the rail should generally be hung below their pipe, but in circumstances where the position is unlikely to be often used and where the downward sightline is critical, lamps can be overhung (Fig. 125).

## Proscenium—Downstage Areas

The area immediately behind the proscenium, both overhead and to the sides, is the most vitally important position. Although this statement may seem at first to conflict with what has already been said about the 45° angle, it does not, in fact, do so. The 45° angle is essential for lighting the face, but it is the light from more acute angles that produces the more dramatic and interesting lighting composition. Light coming from the proscenium zone itself is usually the most important in a proscenium production (Fig. 126).

The proscenium area is the place for the traditional first pipe, from which instruments are hung with a C-clamp, hook or barrel clamp (Figs. 127 and 128).

The pipe may be wired internally, or the feed cables may be strapped along it externally. The pipe will be hung below a counterweight

pipe, or instruments can be hung directly to the flying pipe.

A pipe stiffener may be employed to keep the pipe from pivoting along its axis if it is out of balance (Fig. 129).

On many productions it is common to find two pipes at the front of the stage stacked one above the other. The first is used principally for lighting upstage and the second for downlighting and crosslighting. In this position I usually prefer to use profile spots. Their wattage obviously depends upon the type of production and the height at which the pipe is to be hung (which in turn usually depends upon the proscenium height; Fig 130).

There are times when the set designer is simply unable to provide space for lighting behind the proscenium. The first time I met the problem was on Lionel Bart's *Blitz*, set designed by Sean Kenny. In this production moving scenery, which included a massive bridge span-

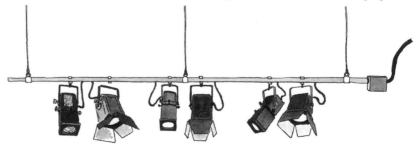

*126. Lighting pipe*

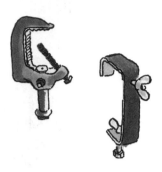

*left 127. C-clamp U.S.*
*right 128. G-clamp U.K.*

*129. Pipe stiffener*

*130. Stacked pipes*

ning the whole stage, came right down to the fire curtain. There was no question of hanging either a spot bar or booms within the stage area. We were able to rig a substitute for both outside the proscenium arch. These formed, in effect, an entire proscenium of lighting units. This was revolutionary in the sixties but is common prac-

tice today, with overhead advance trusses and box booms being practically ubiquitous. For access to an overhead truss a full catwalk is best, but if one is unavailable, access can be achieved by a focus track.

## Upstage Areas

The design of the top of the set, including any ceiling borders or top masking, will dictate how far upstage we can light from the number 1 pipe position. On a deep stage we will find that the upstage areas have to be lit from a second or third pipe hung farther back. If the angles to the upstage areas are very steep we may need further fill-light from the front. Any acting areas above the stage on platforms or rostra will need particular attention, and a section drawn through the set will help when working out lighting positions for these (Fig. 131).

If any action takes place beneath an upper level, the overhang may cut off the ordinary lighting, and it will be necessary to conceal some small instruments within the platform to light this "inner-stage."

## Backlight

Backlighting can present other problems, since we are even more dependent upon the top masking (Fig. 132).

No masking at all makes things much easier for the designer, since it imposes no limitation

on the angles at which he can focus his lamps. If borders or ceilings have to be contended with, we once again must sit down at the drawing board (or computer) and work out the problem in section. Particular attention must be paid to the bottoms of the borders if they are profiled in any way. The audience's sightline must be drawn not through the lowest point but through the highest, as this is the highest point they will be able to see. This forces the backlight position upstage higher, and yet at another point along the pipe we may have to light under the lowest point of the border. If this is really restricting, the instruments can be rigged at different heights under the pipe.

## Overstage Rigging

Overstage lighting is usually hung from lighting pipes. In Europe bridges to allow manual access for focusing and maintenance are still common. However these take up a lot of room and are probably only useful in the larger—and more old-fashioned—opera house.

It sometimes feels as if lighting pipes are only made to bounce scenery off. If the show has lots of tight flying it's prudent to make the lights stronger than the scenery. Scenery bumpers can be a good investment (Fig. 133).

## Touring Suspension

The music industry has taught us all about how to troupe large lighting rigs. The innovation was

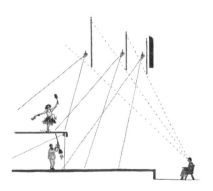

*131. Section with upper platform*

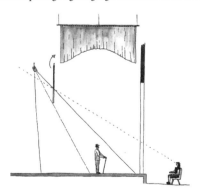

*132. Backlight and borders*

*Stage Lighting Design*

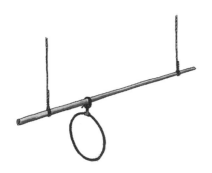

*133. Scenery bumper*

of course the truss. There is now an enormous range of truss types, broadly divided into triangular and square in section (Figs. 134 and 135).

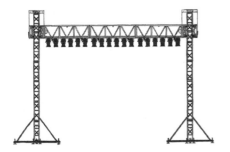

*134. Square truss*

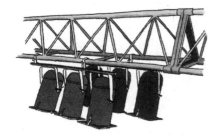

*135. Triangular truss*

These consist of welded aluminum frames, strong enough to allow for infrequent suspension points—often hung with chain hoists or stood on floor supports. Square-section trusses can have instruments permanently mounted within them. Some trusses allow the equipment to be lowered out of the truss when in use.

## Sidelight

The simplest way to sidelight is to put the instrument on a telescopic stand (Fig. 136). Such a stand can have a stationary base or be equipped with castors. The telescopic stand is easily movable and makes instruments accessible for color changing but, unless we are imitating an offstage low-level light source, there is rarely much need for such a low angle of light. Natural sunlight at an almost horizontal angle is very rare, only occurring at the last moments of dawn or sunset, and even then it is very often obscured by neighboring houses, trees and hills. Horizontal light brings other problems: actors cast shadows on one another, they get in one another's light, and as they exit towards the sunset they become strangely and suddenly brighter.

*136. Stand sidelight*

Sidelighting will usually be mounted mostly above head height, and the most practical method is to rig the instruments on a vertical boom or tormentor (Figs. 137 and 138).

This allows everything to be firmly fixed: the top of the boom can be suspended from the fly floor or grid under tension, and the bottom can be screwed or coach-bolted (lag bolted) to the stage floor. The boom must be securely fixed so it can't rotate. In England a large plate is usually fixed to the bottom of the boom and screwed to the deck. In the U.S. a smaller 6-inch diameter flange is accompanied by a short sidearm around the vertical pipe with a right angle elbow to a screwed down flange. This holds the boom tightly and has a smaller area base than the English model.

In England a boom is normally used with an 11-inch-long boom arm (Figs. 139 and 140).

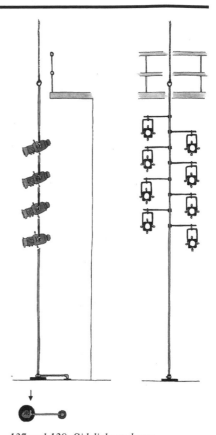

*137 and 138. Sidelight on boom*

I prefer the American rigging method, where a sidearm consisting of a standard C-clamp is used around the boom with an extension pipe that allows easy adjustment of the distance from the instrument to the boom (Fig. 141). Jules Fisher developed a neat way of

*139 and 140. U.K. boom arm*

*141. U.S. Sidearm*

rigging a "shin buster" for the Tony Walton–designed Christmas spectacular *A Christmas Carol*. Rather than mounting the bottom ellipsoidal horizontally, it points downward into a mirror, the "beam bender," that allows the light to skim the floor with minimum obstruction at the boom base.

If the vertical pipe to the ground is an obstruction the instruments will have to be suspended on a "ladder." This is a ladderlike frame that is suspended from two points above. A ladder cannot be made rigid very easily, although stiffeners can be used and fixed to any available firm surface. The advantage of a boom is that by careful arrangement of the boom arms more instruments can be fixed in a tighter space than on a ladder (Figs. 142 and 143).

If many instruments are needed and yet the boom cannot come down to the floor, a compromise can be achieved and the boom flown off the floor with suitable hanging irons and fixings to hold it rigid (Figs. 144 and 145).

The ladder allows sidelighting without obstructing the stage floor. It can be very useful in a repertory theatre because, instead of hanging it permanently, it can be suspended from a track that allows it to be moved up- and downstage from the grid or under the fly floors. It is an added help if, on an adjacent track, an access ladder for the electrician is provided. In a sophisticated installation ladders should be capable of separate movement up- and downstage, on- and offstage and should be capable of being used individually or all together.

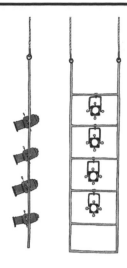

*142 and 143. Lighting ladder*

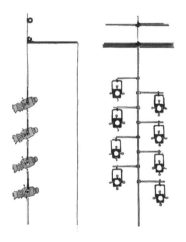

*144 and 145. Suspended boom*

On the larger stage in repertory, sidelighting can be fixed in rolling towers, which can easily be cleared out of the way for scene changes.

The world of dance has led the way in pioneering the use of the dance tower. This is effectively a vertical box truss in which sidelighting instruments can be mounted and then trouped without being dismounted. This is a useful device that's being increasingly used with every type of touring situation. It has the added advantage that the focusing electrician

can just climb up the truss for focusing and maintenance. (Fig. 146)

The fly gallery is, of course, a useful lighting position, and it, like all other galleries in the theatre, should be equipped with a lighting pipe in addition to the fly rail. The only problem with the fly gallery itself is, of course, that it is the place where the flymen work, and it does not help them if it is cluttered up with electrical equipment. Ideally, a theatre should be equipped with a separate lighting gallery on either side of the stage just underneath the fly gallery. In this way conflict between flymen and electricians can be avoided. In any event, the bulk of the electrical services should be kept on the non-working fly gallery side of the stage.

Side follow-spotting may be needed from the galleries or a special "perch" platform. Mounting the follow spot on a track can allow the operator to slide the instrument up- and downstage.

*146. Dance tower*

# Chapter Fifty-two

# Projection

Working out a projection scheme is relatively simple if the projector is placed square on to the screen: it is more complex if angular projection is called for, or if the screen is shaped in any way. However, all variables can be calculated in advance, and, with care and accuracy, slides can be predistorted to cope with all complications. It is sometimes possible to try out the projector in the theatre before the actual production and to reach a solution by a process of trial and error. If this is not possible, it may be best to take the problem to an expert or a company specializing in slide making (Figs. 147 and 148).

With straight on projection, we need to know the equipment to be used, the slide size and the desired distance between projector and screen. We will probably know the projector involved and the slide size. Thus we will know the beam angle that can be obtained with the widest angle lens. This will then show how close to the screen we can go to get the maximum brightness of picture.

We must be very careful to establish exactly how much of the slide is adequately illuminated. Some projectors, particularly those using larger slides, have a considerable fall-off of light toward the corners of the slide, and it is most unwise to try to use the whole slide right up to its edges. The performance of the projector to be used should be carefully checked before the work of calculation begins.

Simple formulae can be used to calculate such things as length of throw, desired size of slide or image size.

**Projection calculations**

$$\frac{d}{ES} = \frac{T}{SI} \quad \frac{1}{d} + \frac{1}{T} = \frac{1}{f}$$

$$\text{Tan } \tfrac{1}{2}\,BA = \frac{\tfrac{1}{2}\,ES}{T}$$

$$\frac{ES}{f} = \frac{SI}{T}$$

**KEY**

SI = image size

T = throw from projector to screen

Tan = throw angle

ES = effective slide size

d = distance of slide to optical center of objective

f = focal length of objective lens

BA = beam angle

# PROJECTION

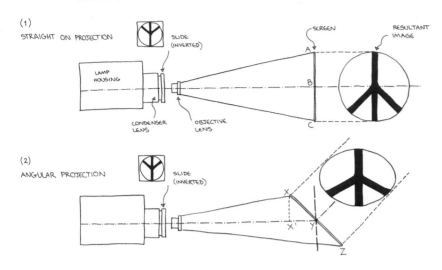

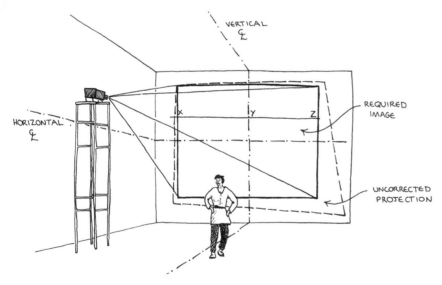

*147 and 148. Straight on projection and angular projection*

*149. Angular projection—view*

done about this loss of focus when projecting at an acute angle, and indeed it is the limit set by the depth of focus that probably dictates the maximum angle at which we can attempt to project (Figs. 150 and 151).

If we draw our beam angle of light in plan with the screen angled as shown, we get the picture as shown. However, we must always remember that the beam of light with which we are working is three dimensional. While we are covering the screen from X to Z in width, we must remember that only at Y will the picture be the same height as it was in our other example at position B. At Z the picture will be larger than at Y and at X the picture will be smaller. This might mean that the projector has to be taken farther away from the screen in order to get sufficient picture height at position X. If we are attempting to get a square image, the height of the picture will be dictated by the height that is possible at the point of the shortest throw, $X^1$. Once this principle has been established, it is possible to draw a series of sections through varying points of the beam to establish exactly how the picture shape changes as the relationship between the screen and projector changes due to angular distortion.

The effect of an irregularly shaped screen can be calculated in exactly the same way. If, for example, we are projecting on to a curved cyclorama, we first draw the beam in plan (from projector to cyclorama) at the height of the projector. We can mark the center line of the beam and draw sections through it to establish the exact size of the image. If we are projecting over or around scenery that might interfere with the projected image, this should be drawn in on the beam sections to establish the shape of possible resultant shadow.

Since it is likely that the projector will have to be placed as close as possible to the screen to secure maximum brightness, a wide-angle lens will have to be used.

Once we have established the beam angle of any particular objective lens and slide combination, we can begin to establish an angular projection set up (Fig. 149). We will see that when the screen is moved at an angle in any one plane the image becomes elongated. The greater the angle of screen to projector,

the greater this distortion will be. While this can be corrected in the slide, we must beware of another and sometimes greater problem: the depth of focus of the objective lens. We will see that not only is the image distorted but it also goes out of focus at its edges. There is virtually nothing that can be

*Stage Lighting Design*

However, the curvature of a wide-angle lens may distort straight lines on the slide: thus, if the straight lines are of great importance, a very-wide-angle lens should be avoided. A quick experiment will soon show how satisfactory the lens intended is actually going to be.

**Common slide sizes are:**

35mm, 2in., 3¼in., 5.2in. = 13cm, 7.2in. = 18cm. Note. Effective slide size is smaller than the actual slide by at least the width of slide bindings.

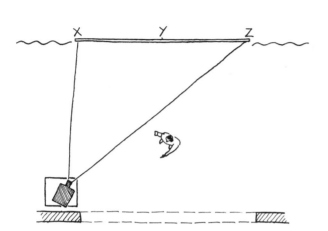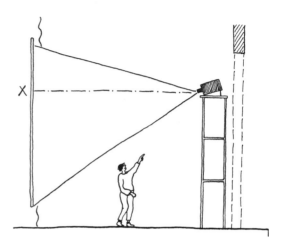

*150 and 151. Angular projection plan and section*

# Chapter Fifty-three

# Optical Effects

### Gobos

A very useful form of projection, which does not require a true projector, uses any profile spot in conjunction with a gobo. This is a piece of heat-resistant material—metal or heat-resistant glass—that is etched into a design or shape and placed in the gate of a profile spotlight. Wonderfully complex patterns can now be obtained via photographic processes onto glass to produce half-tone and even color images in gobos (Fig. 152).

The image can then be focused by the lens and projected onto any surface. A huge variety of stock gobos are available. A kit can even be obtained to make your own gobos "at home." Gobos are most suitable for providing any shadow-type effect, for example, a silhouette of light from a window offstage. They can be use-

ful for cloud effects and perhaps most particularly for the broken effect of light through the leaves of trees. An extensive use of gobo light can be extremely fascinating, and complex patterns of gobos built up from many spotlights can produce extraordinary break-up effects. Thus the designer can get away from the often ever present conical beam of the spotlight.

A doughnut mask in the color frame of the instrument can enhance the clarity of a gobo pattern if sharp focus is required.

An instrument that allows the gate to be rotated around the axis of the lamp makes focusing a gobo exactly as required an easier task. Alternatively, adjustable pattern holders that allow a degree of rotation of the gobo in the gate are available.

Many moving lights have changeable gobo

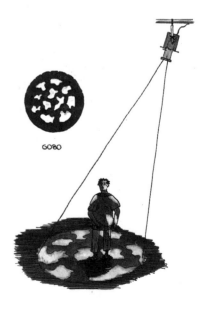

GOBO

*152. Gobo*

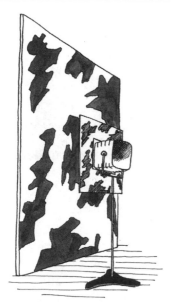

*153. Linnebach lantern*

wheels allowing multiple choices within one instrument. Some allow gobos to be rotated within the axis of the beam for all sorts of special effects.

Devices to rotate a gobo in a fixed spotlight can be very useful. The Rotator spins one gobo, while the twin-spin rotates two gobos in different directions with an optional fixed third gobo and gives wonderful animation effects to water ripple, flame flicker or undulating leaf shadow. A variation of this is the "yo-yo." This can oscillate a gobo for wave, flame and ripple effect, or may be indexed to give a "one-shot" movement; to open and close doors, venetian blinds or provide a rising or setting sun, etc.

An alternative form of animation is provided by the Animation Disk. This is a metal disk fixed to an animation motor unit on the front of an instrument—usually a Leko type. These variable-speed rotating disks break up and give movement to a gobo and are good for snow, flame, falling leaves or other effects.

Before we get too excited about these attempts to animate gobo projection, look at the behavior of real sunlight through real leaves fluttering in real breeze. Nature has still a significant edge!

## Linnebach Lantern

The Linnebach lantern is used to project large patterns or shadows at close range by direct light from a concentrated source. The beam spread will be very wide, possibly about 60° to 90°, and only a simple pattern can be used. The details of the slide must be larger than the filament of the light source. The edges of the picture will be blurred and the intensity irregular. The slide, which is a large one, has to be placed some distance from the light source, and the greater the distance, the more clearly defined will be the picture. Distortion can be corrected either by placing the slide parallel to the screen or by painting a distorted slide (Fig. 153).

## Projected effects

Projected effects should always be used with great discretion. While there are moments that require extravagant effect, these are rare, and the designer should beware of using any moving effect unless it is absolutely essential to the play. With almost all moving effects it is always better to use several projectors, overlaid one on another.

## Clouds

Projected clouds should usually remain stationary. It is better to use a slide, gobo or Linnebach projection of clouds to break up a sky surface without movement rather than use the all-too-familiar moving effect. But if movement is really called for, cloud effects are supplied on circular disks or short-loop film machines. These come in standard types: usually "stormy" and "fleecy." They should nearly always be used out of focus at a very slow speed. Only in the midst of a great storm or high wind do we normally notice clouds in movement. With multiple projectors one can achieve a break-up in the projected effect and suggest the difference in speed of various levels of cloud.

## Lightning

Sheet and fork lightning are the most commonly required on the stage. For the latter we actually project the fork of lightning itself and for the former we simulate the flash upon the stage.

Fork lightning can be done in a number of ways. An attachment that has a metal side on which the fork of lightning is cut can be fitted to the front of an effects projector. By operating the shutter very rapidly one achieves a realistic flash. (It should be noted that a steel-blue tint is valuable here.) Another method I used to like from Germany was a small handheld projector known as a "Blitz-gerat." This used an electronic flash gun for its light source. At the press of a button it emitted a very bright, brief flash of light through the objective lens system. A series of fork lightning slides could be slipped into the slide magazine and then projected in rapid succession (Fig. 154).

*154. Blitz-gerat*

A similar effect can be achieved with a Leko and lightning gobo equipped with a xenon flash lamp. The Diversitronics ESM-DMX replaces the lamp in an ETC Source 4 or an Altman 360Q spotlight with a xenon flash lamp and provides a dimmable strobe able to flash fifteen times per second. Control is via analog 0–10v or DMX 512. On the largest scale xenon flash tubes behind a full-scale fork-lightning-shaped cut-out provide a powerful effect.

The effect of sheet lightning or a lightning flash can be achieved by several (if possible) heavy-duty strobe lights or, most simply, by rapidly switching a cold or light-blue circuit of strip or floodlight. Rapid manipulation of strobes can produce blinding sheets of light that with effective thunder from the sound department, can make a great storm. In the old days lightning was produced with a stick of carbon and a steel file, a dangerous but undoubtedly spectacular method.

## Rain

Projected rain, in my opinion, has always been the worst effect in the catalogue. It was produced with a disc on which lines had been scratched and the resulting image was not only very dim, it was also extremely unrealistic, with rain coming down in curves. A new device, the 100-foot-long film scroller, produced by Production Arts for the Pani projectors, has at last allowed a higher-quality rain effect. With a film strip created by Wendall Harrington, a very realistic downfall can be produced. Used in such shows as the Disney production of *Beauty and the Beast* and also *Show Boat* an acceptable rain is back on the stage without getting everybody wet. Its effect is enhanced by subtly modulating the brightness of the projector as the effect runs. Once again, several projected effects tend to make the thing a little more acceptable.

The best way to produce rain successfully on the stage is with real water. This is not as difficult as one might imagine. The water is fed into a pipe above the stage that has tiny holes drilled along its length. From this pipe, the water should fall into a trough, the size of which will be determined by the length of pipe and the height at which it is hung. Great care must be exercised to avoid any danger of the water coming into contact with electrical equipment, and the effect should be operated well away from dip traps. Cross-lighting the water will produce the most marvelous effect (Fig. 155).

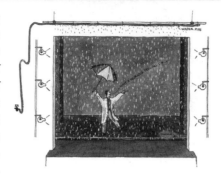

*155. Rain effect*

I lit *Singing in the Rain* with Tommy Steele at the London Palladium with six rain pipes across the stage and rain tanks in scenery all around. It truly poured, the water all being collected into a full-stage-size tank below a false floor of cobbled street and sidewalks. *An Inspector Calls* opens with the best rain storm I've ever seen. In New York the effect was created by Greg Meeh, Broadway's top special-effects expert.

## Snow

Effective projected snow is almost as unsatisfactory as rain. Snow does not all fall to earth in a regular mechanical manner. The long film strip referred to above for rain can also simulate snow much better than hitherto. But the same rules apply, and truly realistic snow can only be created by something actually falling from above. This can be confetti-like paper, fragmented polystyrene or even soap flakes. Trial and error will determine the best material to use. The snow is placed in a snow bag—which is traditionally made from a length of canvas in which a number of small holes have been cut—hung between two battens. The bag is hung on two separate sets of lines from the grid, and when these are moved gently the loose material finds its way through the holes and flutters down to the stage (Fig. 156).

*156. Snow effect*

## Suns and Moons

Because of its brightness, the depiction of the sun itself—unless seen through fog and mist—is virtually impossible. We can, however, represent the moon. A moon box, a metal box with some lamps inside it and with a cut-out shape of the moon on its front, can be hung behind a translucent cloth. Unless the cloth is a proper rear-projection screen, it may be necessary to have a diffuser over the face of the box to obscure the actual filament of the lamps. By hanging the box either very close to or away from the cloth, varying degrees of soft- or hard-edge images can be produced (Figs. 157 and 158).

*157 and 158. Moon box*

Such a light box can of course be made in any shape desired, and it is a very simple method of getting any lit shape in scenery (e.g. distant lit windows). Alternatively one can direct a profile spot with a mask onto a translucent cloth (see Chapter 6, the *Brand* set-up). A moon shape can also be projected with a profile spot from the front. To get a more exactly defined image, a projector with a moon slide can be used; indeed one of the most satisfactory of all optical effects is a "moon with passing cloud." This is produced by a moon slide and a cloud disc or film-strip in one machine and, when used with other cloud effects, gives the most extraordinarily realistic (and romantic) result. (Another technique was used in *Show Boat* to romantic effect).

## Stars

Most usually this used to be done with miniature Christmas tree lights that are poked through a cloth from the rear so that just their tips show through. A very tiny dab of blue or black paint on the lamps will reduce the light and give a most realistic impression. A gauze hung downstage of the effect will enhance it by creating a shimmering sensation. Stars can also be projected, but here great care must be taken, since even the smallest star painted on a slide can appear as large as a football on the screen. Another very simple method is to make tiny balls of silver paper and hang them on black thread downstage of the night sky cloth, then cross-light very carefully with a narrowly slotted profile spot.

Fiber-optics provide probably the best way of creating stars. A vast quantity of minute light sources from a programmable light source can subtly introduce the shimmer of starlight in the night sky. Fiber-optics can produce many other marvelous effects. Alan Ayckbourn's *Joking Apart* (Globe Theatre, London, 1979) used this device for distant fireworks bursting in the sky. A combination of small flash lamps, fiber-optics patterns with a manually operated punch-card pushed through the gate of the illuminator, giving changing color and moving fireworks "dross," all on a cloth moving behind a scrim, gave a super-realistic Guy Fawkes/Fourth of July impression.

## Flames and Smoke

Successful flame projection depends upon the number of projectors used and upon a sufficiently short throw to get a very bright image. A rotating disc mounted on the front of a small Fresnel can produce an acceptable substitute for the more expensive flame-effect projector. Twin-spin gobo rotators or animation wheels all create a good flickering effect. By muddling up the projected image with smoke and other means of producing flame effect, such as blown strips of silk or mylar, neon flicker lamps and so on, a marvelous conflagration can be produced.

*159. Rosco fog machine*

There are many types of smoke or mist, and several ways of producing them. Care has to be taken. Many stage smoke effects in the past used toxic chemicals, and this is clearly unacceptable today.

Dry ice can be used to produce a very heavy, white low-lying fog. A metal tank with a heating element will bring the tank water to boiling point. When solid carbon dioxide is lowered into the boiling water, a large volume of thick fog is produced, which can be directed around the stage by means of a hose.

Liquid nitrogen produces a thick white smoke effect that is nontoxic. With expert handling it can be used safely in a number of different ways to give differing effects.

But dry ice is costly and can leave a damp, slippery floor, so specially manufactured fog machines using a range of water-based fog fluids are preferable. Fog machines are manufactured in a range of sizes and types with ducting and remote control capability (Fig. 159). Different effects, from a soft mist to reveal the beams of light in the air to thick smoke or heavy low lying fog, can be obtained.

One of the problems of using live smoke or fog is controlling it and getting rid of it. It is absolutely essential to try the effect out when the theatre is at least partially full with a dress-rehearsal audience. The theatre's heating and ventilating system and the general condition of air currents can only be truly assessed when the audience is in the auditorium. The air-conditioning system for a new theatre should be designed to allow control by the stage manager or lighting operator. The first dress rehearsal with audience of the notorious production of *Blitz* was conducted in the presence of Princess Margaret. During the air-raid sequence, the smoke billowed in ever-increasing clouds from the stage, and the entire royal party (and auditorium) disappeared, only to emerge some scenes later.

A projected smoke effect is very similar to that of cloud, but is used traveling vertically rather than horizontally. It is a poor substitute for the real thing.

## Sea Waves and Water Ripple (Fig. 160)

The optical projected effect of sea waves is one of the most effective on the market. Instead of a circular rotating disc, this uses a fixed slide with vertically moving ripple break-up glasses. The result is the most extraordinarily accurate representation of a gently rolling seascape. This can be used not simply on a screen or backcloth but upon the floor of the stage to give an evocative undulating motion. The ripple of water in a river or stream or the effect of light reflected from rippling water can be done with a similar type of optical effect or with twin-spin gobo rotators or animation wheels. For short throws, a tubular ripple effect, which uses a

*160. Wave effect*

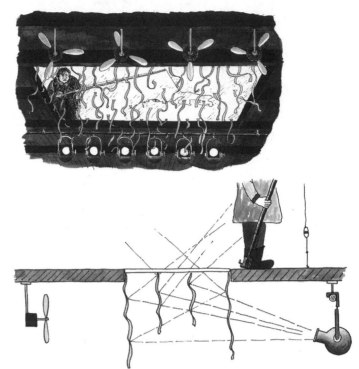

*162 and 163.* Show Boat *ripple*

lamp around which a perforated drum revolves, can be effective (Fig. 161).

Another way of producing the effect of reflected light from water is to put a tray containing water on the floor outside a window, for example, and to aim a spotlight into it. Gentle undulation of the tray will literally re-create the effect of light on water. Similarly, light reflected by a shimmering sheet of mylar (rippled by an adjacent fan) can be very realistic. Again, a mix of moving effects will add to their apparent realism. *Show Boat* uses large-scale Pani water-ripple effects, multiple twin-spin gobos with a variety of water-ripple and sparkle gobos, tubular ripples and multiple layers of moving mylar,

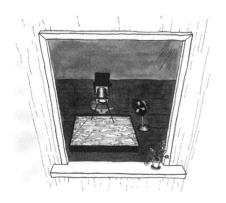

*161. Water ripple*

all to keep that "Ol Man River" rolling along. (Figs. 162 and 163).

If a distant view of the water is required, use can be made of projection onto a gauze ground row with layers of silver paper or aluminum foil carefully crumpled beneath the gauze. This gives the effect of sunlight glistening on the distant water.

### Candles, Torches, Oil Lamps and Gas

The only really effective way of producing candle- or torch-light on the stage is to have the real thing. Happily, fire authorities are now at last beginning to realize that times have changed since the demise of gas lighting, and that one or two naked candle flames are not a signal for the whole theatre to be burnt down. This is not to say that the danger should be ignored, however, and if real flame is used, the greatest possible precautions should be taken at

all times. If one has to produce an imitation candle, quite good electrical substitutes can now be obtained. A torch lamp concealed in a twist of tissue paper can provide an adequate substitute. A flickering candle or oil lamp can be assisted by connecting the lamp to a fluorescent lamp starter, which gives the light a good random flicker. This may often be too harsh on its own, so a second lamp, permanently on, will soften the extremity of the flicker. Electronic flicker controls are useful, providing a range of effects and control over speed of flicker or pulsing, and variable threshold and brightness.

A flaming torch is almost impossible to reproduce. Various attempts have been made with battery operated lamps, silk streamers, hidden fans and so on. None have been truly successful. Real flame is the best. Real flame—real moving light...perhaps we've come full circle, back to the cave with true, lively, moving light.

# Stage Lighting Bibliography

Bellman, Willard F. *Lighting the Stage: Art and Practice*. 2nd ed. New York: Crowell, 1974

Bellman, Willard F. *Scenography and Stage Technology*. New York: Crowell, 1977

Bentham, Frederick. *The Art of Stage Lighting*. 2nd ed. London: Pitman Publishing, 1968, 1980

Bergman, Gosta M. *Lighting in the Theatre*. Stockholm: Almquist and Wiksell Forlag, 1977

Bongar, Emmet. *Practical Stage Lighting*. New York: Rosen Publishing, 1971

Bowman, Wayne. *Modern Stage Lighting*. New York: Harper and Brothers, n.d.

Fitt, Brian, and Joe Thornley. *Lighting by Design: A Technical Guide*. London: Focal Press, 1992

Fuchs, Theodore. *Stage Lighting*. Boston: Little, Brown, 1929

Gillette, J. Michael. *Designing with Light*. Palo Alto, Calif.: Mayfield Publishing, 1978

Hays, David. *Light on the Subject*. New York: Limelight Editions, 1989

Jones, Robert Edmond. *The Dramatic Imagination*. New York: Theatre Arts Books, 1941

Keller, Max. *Buhnenbeleuchtung*. Cologne: DuMont Buchverlag, 1985

Kook, Edward. *Images in Light for the Living Theatre*. New York: Century Lighting, n.d.

McCandless, Stanley. *A Method of Lighting the Stage*. 4th ed. New York: Theatre Arts Books, 1958

McCandless, Stanley *A Syllabus of Stage Lighting*. New York: Drama Book Specialists, 1968

McGrath, Ian *A Process for Lighting the Stage*. Needham Heights, Mass.: n.p., n.d.

Moody, James. *Concert Lighting.* London: Focal Press, 1989

Morgan, Nigel H. *Stage Lighting for Theatre Designers.* London: Herbert Press, 1995

Mumm, Robert C. *Photometrics Handbook.* New York: Broadway Press, 1992

Ost, Geoffrey. *Stage Lighting.* London: Herbert Jenkins, 1957

Palmer, R. H. *The Lighting Art: The Aesthetics of Stage Lighting Design.* Englewood Cliffs, N.J.: Prentice-Hall, 1970

Parker, W. Oren, and Harvey K. Smith. *Scene Design and Stage Lighting.* 4th ed. New York: Holt, Rinehart and Winston, 1979

Penzel, Frederick. *Theatre Lighting before Electricity.* Middleton, Conn.: Wesleyan University Press, 1978

Pilbrow, Richard. *Stage Lighting.* London: Cassell and Co., 1970, 1979

Rees, Terence. *Theatre Lighting in the Age of Gas.* London: n.p., 1978

Reid, Francis. *The Stage Lighting Handbook.* London: Adam and Charles Black, 1976

Reid, Francis. *Lighting the Stage.* Oxford: Focal Press, 1995

Rosenthal, Jean, and Lael Wertenbaker. *The Magic of Light.* Boston: Little, Brown, 1972

Rubin, Joel E., and Leland H. Watson. *Theatrical Lighting Practice.* New York: Theatre Arts Books, 1954

Schivelbusch, Wolfang. *Disenchanted Light: The Industrialization of Light in the Nineteenth Century.* Berkeley: University of California Press, 1988

Selden, Samuel, and Hunton D. Sellman. *Stage Scenery and Lighting.* New York: Appleton-Century-Crofts, 1959

Sellman, Hunton D., and Merrill Lessley. *Essentials of Stage Lighting.* New York: Prentice-Hall, 1982

Streader, T., and J. A. Williams. *Create Your Own Stage Lighting.* London: Bell and Hyman, n.d.

Uum, Hugo van. *Tussen Licht en Donker.* Amsterdam: Uitgeverig International, 1991

Vasey, John. *Concert Sound and Lighting Systems.* Boston: Focal Press, 1989

Walne, Graham. *Projection for the Performing Arts.* Oxford: Focal Press, 1995

# Index

Abbott, George, xiii
Adler, Kurt, 309
agent, 212, 256, 319
Allio, Rene, 152
Altman, 158, 184, 233
American Shakespeare Festival, 324
*Angels in America,* 235
angle of light, 11
Anstett, Herbie, 316
Appia, Adolphe, 3, 8, 176
*The Architect and the Emperor of Assyria,* 253
architectural lighting, 222, 279
arena stage, 149
argand lamp, 173
*Armstrong's Last Goodnight,* 152
Aronson, Boris, 121
Aronson, Frances, 289
Aronstein, Martin, 121
Arrighi, Luciana, 101
Arts Council of Great Britain, 158
assistants, 211, 235, 248, 256, 303, 313, 327, 328, 345
Association of Lighting Designers, 34, 158, 184
Azenberg, Manny, 324, 326
*Baal,* 283
backlight, 448

Ball, Benny, 182, 248
Ballet Comique de la Reine, 170
Banbury, Frith, 189
Barker, Felix, 281
Barnett, Jimmy, 350
Barreca, Chris, 152
Bart, Lionel, 103
Bash Stage Lighting, 317
Bassey, Shirley, 207
Bastille Opera, 139
Bay, Howard, 320
Bayreuth, 127
beamlight, 158, 254
behavior of light, 107
    exterior night, 111
    exteriors, 110
    firelight, candle and oil lamps, 109
    interior artificial light, 108
    interior natural light, 107
    moonlight, 109
Belasco, David, 122, 175, 177
Bellman, Will, 303
Bennett, Michael, 322
Bentham, Frederick, xii, xxii, 159, 179, 190, 339
Bergman, Ingmar, xvii

Berkeley Rep, 267
Berliner Ensemble, 86
Bibiena, Ferdinando, 172
Billington, Ken, 182, 219–25, 328
Binkley, Howell, 182
Bintley, David, 123
Birch, Nigel, 271
Bjornson, Maria, 120
*Blitz,* 103
blood baths, 321
Boddington, Diana, 294
*bozze,* 167, 366
*Brand,* 89, 96, 248
Brandston, Howard, 183
Brechtian, 86, 87
Brett, Richard, 329
Brickman, Mark, 182
Bridge, Andrew, 38, 120, 121, 158, 181, 205, 248, 256
Brook, Peter, 127, 135
Brunelleschi, 166
Bryan, Robert, xii, 129, 181, 248, 345, 346
Bryden, Bill, 153
Bundy, William, xii, 126
Buontalenti, Bernardo, 169
Burnham, Tim, 370
Bury, John, 316
*Busker Alley,* 22, 154
cable ratings, 363
Caird, John, 254
calculation of lighting angles 431
Canadian Opera Company, 139
Carnegie Mellon, 232
*Carousel,* 157
*Cats,* 254
CCT, 136, 184
Central School of Speech and Drama, 217
Century Lighting, 180, 191
Chelton, Nick, 112, 181, 248
Chestnut Street Theatre, Philadelphia, 173
Chiang, Dawn, xi, xxiii, 141, 145, 156, 306
Chichester Festival Theatre, 135, 152, 259, 284
choosing a design program, 200
*Chorus Line, A,* 190, 322, 325
Cirque du Soleil, 274
Clark, Peggy, 120, 180, 220, 320
Cockpit, The, 170
Codron, Michael, 97
Cohan, Robert, 123
Collins, Pat, 182
Collison, David, 249
color, 364
    additive mixing, 89, 364
    broken color, 90

fluorescence, 90
    subtractive mixing, 89, 365
color scrollers, 87, 424, 428, 429
Comedie-Francaise, 173
computer-aided drafting (CAD), 44, 438, 439
control rooms, 445
control systems, 369
    moving light controls, 375
    rock-and-roll controls, 378
    theatre-based controls, 369
Copley, Peter, xi
Cornwell, Eric, xii, 145, 438
Cottesloe Theatre, 153
Craig, Edward Gordon, 3, 165, 176, 237
Croft, Brian, 249, 349, 354
cue sheets, 72
Cunningham, Dave, 158, 370, 374
cyclorama, 89, 92
Dachs, Joshua, 236
Davis, Joe, xii, 158, 180, 228, 334
De Loutherbourg, P. J., 172
Dean, Basil, xii, 177, 333, 334, 339
DeVerna, Frank, 322
Devine, George, 135
Dexter, John, 99, 104, 135
DHA, 253
dichroics, 366
diffusion material, 367
digital light curtains, 140
Dillon, Carmen, 56
dimmer quantities, 442
discharge lighting, 184
Di Somi, Leoni, 168
dominant key light, 28
D'Oyly Carte, Richard, 175
*Dream Girls,* 322, 325
dress rehearsal, 76
Dreyfus, Louis, 340
Dudley, Bill, 153
Eckert, Bill and Jean, 235
Eisenhauer, Peggy, 231, 237
electricians, 327
electricity, 363
Elliott, Michael, xii, 89, 90, 109, 135
Emmons, Beverly, 287, 289
ETC, 158, 184, 375, 386
*Evita,* 122, 253, 254
experiment in visibility, 11
fan-shaped auditorium, 147
*The Father,* 109
Feder, Abe, 120, 180, 183, 233, 320
Fedigan, Jimmy, 156
fees, 35

Feller, Pete, 221
Ferren, Bran, 103
fiber optics, 96, 248, 457
*Fiddler on the Roof,* 121
Field, Tom, 298, 299
Fielding, Harold, 335
59 Theatre Company, 248
film and video, 102
first night, 79
Fisher, Jules, xii, 103, 121, 182, 231–39, 252, 256, 289, 297
Fisher, Mark, 353
Fisher, Rick, 157, 182
Flying Pig, 379
focus schedule, 66
focusing, 59, 62
focusing moving lights, 68
follow spots, 76, 122
foot-candles, 361
*Forty-second Street,* 325
*Four Baboons Adoring the Sun,* 100, 110, 116, 152
Four Star Lighting, 316
front-of-house lighting positions, 446
functional lighting, 435
*Funny Thing Happened on the Way to the Forum, A,* xiv, 98
Furttenbach, Josef, 170
Gale, Brian, 159, 241–46
Gallo, Paul, 121, 182
Garnier, Charles, 175
Garrick, David, 172
Gaskill, Bill, 86, 135, 152, 283
gaslight, 173
gauzes, 94
Geddes, Norman Bel, 180
general indirect light, 3
Gentile, Douglas, 145
Gleason, John, 182
Glyndebourne Opera House, 134
God, 165
Goebbels, Wolfgang, 129
Goldby, Derek, 82, 88
*Golden Boy,* 122
*Good-bye Girl,* 324
grandmaster, 190
Great American Market, 367
Green Man, The, 256
Grey, Terence, 177
Grosser, Helmut, 139
groups, 138
Guthrie, Sir Tyrone, 85, 127, 147, 333
H. M. Tennent, 180
*Hair,* 235

Hall, Sir Peter, 99, 116, 135, 152
*Hamlet,* 152
hang/fit-up, 59
Harrington, Wendall, 100, 116
Harrison, John, 248
Hartmann, Louis, 177, 334
Hayes, David, 324
Heeley, Desmond, 82, 88
*Heliotrope Bouquet, The,* 152
Helmsley, Gilbert, 246
Henderson, Mark, 111, 182
Her Majesty's Theatre, 174
Herbert, Jocelyn, 86, 283
Hersey, David, xii, 4, 120, 121, 129, 140, 158, 181, 248, 251–57, 343, 346, 352
Hockney, David, 183
hook-up schedule, 44
house lighting, 4, 436
Houseman, John, 324
*How to Succeed in Business without Really Trying,* 103
Howard, Frankie, 281
Hudson, Richard, 345
Hughes, Mick, 182
Husinko, Greg, 145
*I and Albert,* 101
imagination, 206
Ingalls, Jim, 289
Ingeneri, Angelo, 169
*Inspector Calls, An,* 157
instrument schedule, 44, 46
instruments, 380
    beam projectors, 405
    floodlights and striplights, 411
    follow spots, 393
    Fresnels, 400
    moving lights, 417
    P.C. spotlights, 397
    PAR and reflector lamps (PAR cans), 407
    profile spots, 380
    projectors, 414
inverse square law, 362
Irving, Dennis, 183
Irving, Sir Henry, xviii, 174
Isle of Coll, 157, 259
Italian Renaissance theatre, 167
Izenour, George, 191
*Jelly's Last Jam,* 235
*Jesus Christ Superstar,* 235
job interviews, 313
Jones, Disley, 38
Jones, Inigo, 170
Jones, Robert Edmond, 113, 120, 180
*Jorrocks,* 38, 111

Joseph, Stephen, 181
*Juno and the Paycock,* 56
Kalman, Jean, 129, 182
Keller, Max, 185
Kendall, Brian, 228
Kenny, Sean, 181
*Kentucky Cycle, The,* 270
Kerr, Walter, 175
Kliegl Brothers, 179
Kliegl Performance, 193
Klotz, Florence, 140, 326
Kook, Ed, xii, xxii, 120, 180, 233, 339
Krauss, Marvin, 232
*Lady's Not for Burning, The,* 180
LaFortune, Luc, 273–84
Lam, William, 183
Lambert, Lindsay, 141
LaMama Theater, 288
LAMDA, 206
Larkin, Peter, 233
Lasdun, Sir Denys, 135
*Laterna Magica,* 102
*La Traviata,* 96
League of Regional Theaters, 35
Lee, Eugene, xv, 140
Lee, Ming Cho, 267
Levings, Nigel, 112, 183
Light Console, 180, 190
Light Palette, 136
Lightboard, 136, 159, 185, 194
lighting installation, 435
lighting layout plan, 41
lighting layout section, 41
lighting positions, 437
    balcony rail, 439
    box booms, 438
    FOH bridges, 438
    follow spots, 439
    front-of-house, 437
    front projection, 439
    high side walls, 439
lighting rehearsal, 68
lighting software, 433
limelight, 174
*Long Day's Journey into Night, A,* 111
Linnebach, Adolphe, 178
load-in/get-in, 59
Lorraine, Bill, 177, 334
*Love for Love,* 86, 291
*Loves Labour's Lost,* 90
lumens per square foot, 361
Lyceum Theatre, 173
Macintosh, 157, 159, 256, 353

Mackintosh, Cameron, 119, 157, 181, 206
Mackintosh, Iain, 135
Macready, Charles, 174
*Magic Flute, The,* 99
*Man of La Mancha, The,* 122
Mansouri, Lotfi, 311
Maradudin, Peter, 182, 263–70, 343
Marantz, Paul, 183, 236, 252
Marcplot, 435
Marshall, Norman, 135
May, Val, xxiii, 38
McCandless, Stanley, 12, 180, 303
*Measure for Measure,* 109
Merrick, David, 317, 326
*Merrily We Roll Along,* 255
Messel, Oliver, 333
"Method, The," 12
    blending and toning the acting area, 23
    lighting the acting area, 13
    lighting the scenery, 24
    motivated light, 25
    motivating light, 24
    special effects lighting and projection, 27
    special visibility, 27
    supplementary acting area, 22
Metropolitan Opera, 439
microwave lamps, 184
Mielziner, Jo, 120, 180, 233, 320, 323
Militello, Anne, 285–90
Miller, Ken, 334
Minnelli, Liza, 222
*Miss Saigon,* 69, 121
MMS, 194
Moiseiwitsch, Tanya, 135, 147
Moliere, 171
Moody, Jim, 183, 295–304
Morgan, Roger, 182, 234
Motta, Fabrizio Carini, 172
Mounk, Chip, 183, 297, 301
moving lights, 210, 236, 325
multiscreen projection, 100
Munn, Tom, 182, 307–14
Musser, Tharon, xii, 121, 182, 220, 319–28
*Mystery Plays,* 153
Napier, John, 38, 120, 254
Nash Gates, Sarah, 200
National Association of Boys Clubs, 216
National Ballet of Canada, 139
National Theatre at the Old Vic Theatre, 82, 90
National Theatre of Great Britain, 56, 104, 134
Negri, Richard, xxiii, 90, 248
Nelson, Richard, 182
Nesbitt, Robert, 334

Newton, Isaac, 364
Niethammer, 130
Nobili, Lila de, 86, 336
Northen, Michael, 158, 181, 228, 331–38
Nunn, Trevor, 120, 254, 344
O'Horgan, Tom, 235
O'Toole, Peter, 283
objectives of stage lighting, 6
    composition, 8
    information, 9
    mood, 9
    revelation of form, 8
    selective visibility, 7
Oenslager, Donald, 180
*Oh, Calcutta,* 253
ohms law, 363
Old Vic Theatre, 291
Olivier, Sir Laurence, 56, 90, 135, 259, 284, 291
*On the Level,* 101
*On the Twentieth Century,* 220
*One Over the Eight,* 97, 98
Opera House, Manchester, 282
optical effects, 103, 454
    candles, torches, oil lamps and gas, 458
    clouds, 455
    flames and smoke, 457
    gobos, 454
    lightning, 455
    linnebach lantern, 455
    projected effects, 455
    rain, 456
    sea waves and water ripple, 457
    snow, 456
    stars, 457
    suns and moons, 456
orientation control, 138
Ornbo, Robert, xii, 63, 101, 129, 181, 248, 340
*Othello,* 291
Ott, Sharon, 267
overstage rigging, 448
Palais-Royal Theatre, 171
Pani, 98, 100, 101, 130
PAR lamps, 91
Park, Jonathan, 353
Paris Opera, 174, 175
Parry, Chris, 182, 341–48
passion, 224
Perlman, Gordon, 372
*Phantom of the Opera,* 207
piano board, 190
Pilbrow's Philosophy, 27
    dominant lighting, 28
    fill lighting, 29

key light, 28
    rim lighting, 29
    secondary lighting, 29
    summary 29
Pilbrow, Daisy, xi, xxiv
Pilbrow, Molly, xi, 316
Pilbrow, Richard, xiii, xviii, 56, 82, 104, 116, 154, 234, 305, 342
planning
    analysis of the script, 36
    final rehearsals, 53
    obtaining the equipment, 46
    paperwork, plots and plans, 39
    planning the tour, 53
    rehearsals, 38
    shop orders, 46
    theatre and its equipment, the, 39
PLASA (Professional Lighting and Sound Association), 182
politics, 208
Pollock's Toy Theatre, 216
Polokov, Lester, 220, 287
Pressner, Stan, 156
Pride, Malcolm, 109
Prince, Hal, xii, xxiv, 119, 140, 220, 306, 340
problems in repertoire, 131
proscenium (downstage areas), 447
producing, 340
Production Arts, 101, 287, 378
production lighting, 435
    scale and power, 442
production schedules, 211
production team, 36
projection, 238, 451
"promenade" production, 153
prompt side, 82
properties of light, 4
    color, 5
    distribution, 6
    intensity, 4
    movement, 6
Pyant, Paul, 157, 182
Quaglio, Ferdinando, 173
Quayle, Anthony, 334
Quintero, José, 324
Radio City, 222
rainbow scrollers, 429
Ramsaur, Michael, 265
Rank Strand Electric, 136
Ravitz, Jeff, 183
Read, John B., xii, 122, 129, 152, 181, 248
rear projection, 100
Redgrave, Vanessa, 248

reflection, 362
refraction, 363
rehearsal light, 435
Reiche and Vogel, 97, 141, 158, 248
Reinhardt, Max, 178
Rennagel, Marilyn, 300, 323
*Richard III,* 86
Ridge, Harold, 178
rigging techniques, 446
Ritchie, Jack, 248
Robbins, Jerome, xiii, 119, 121
Robert Juliat, 130
rock-and-roll, 238, 299, 352
Rodgers and Hammerstein, 219
Rosco, 366
*Rosencrantz and Guildenstern Are Dead,* 82, 88, 317
Rosenthal, Jean, xii, xiii, 99, 119, 120, 180, 183, 185, 221, 233, 272, 308, 317, 320
*The Rothchilds,* 316
Royal Ballet, London, 122
Royal Court Theatre, 86
Royal Exchange Theatre, Manchester, 150
Royal National Theatre, 132, 182
Royal Opera House, Covent Garden, 126, 139
Royal Shakespeare Company, 86, 90, 132, 182, 342
Rubin, Joel, 228
Russell, Ken, 305
Russell, Wally, xii, 136, 183, 374
Sabbattini, 169
safety lighting, 436
San Francisco Opera, 309
saturation rig, 133, 136
Saunders, George, 173
Savoy Theatre, 175
Scales, Robert, 9
Scarfe, Gerald, 99
scenic projection, 97
Schlesinger, John, 101
scrims, 94
See, Bob, 298, 299
Seldon, Sam, 296
Sen, Tapas, 306
Serlio, 167
Servandoni, G. N., 172
Sharman, Jim, 112
*Shelter,* 101
*Show Boat,* xiv, 69, 110, 121, 122, 140, 306
shop orders, 46
sidelight, 449
Siegfried and Roy, 207
Siemens, 179, 192, 195
Simon, Neil, 324
Simonson, Lee, 120, 180

Skelton, Tom, 221
Smith, Oliver, 119
Sommi, Leoni di, 168
Sondheim, Stephen, 236
Sondheimer, Hans, 234
Source Four, 158, 224
specific direction light, 3
spotlight and the dimmer, xxvi
Stanbury, Robert, xxiii
Stanton, Robert, 217, 227
Stern, Donnie, 317
Stoker, Bram, 175
*Storm, The,* 99, 104
Strand CD Control, 191
Strand DDM, 193
Strand Electric, 179, 191, 228
Strand Galaxy, 139
Strand Lighting, xxi, 183
Strand LP (Luminous Preset), 192
striplight, 91
Stroman, Susan, 306
style in lighting, 111
Styles, William, 227
Sundance, 299
*Sunset Boulevard,* 38
surtitles, 439
Svoboda, Josef, 23, 96, 99, 102, 104, 185
Tawil, Joe, 296, 367
*Teahouse of the August Moon,* 217
Teatro Olympico, 169
technical rehearsals, 76
Tessin, Nicodemus, 171
Tetley, Glenn, 123
theatre consultant, 236 329
Theatre Projects, xxi, 101, 121, 181, 217, 227, 228
Theatre Projects Consultants, 135, 249
Theatre Projects Trust, 200
Theatre Royal, Brighton, 190, 332, 335
Theatre Royal, Nottingham, 330
Theatre Royal, Drury Lane, 172
Thomas, Anthony, 216
Thompson, Rob, 183
Thorn Q-File, 192
*Three Sisters, The,* 108
thrust stage, 147, 151
Tipton, Jennifer, 182, 265, 289
Tomkins, Wally, 282
Toms, Carl, 90
touring suspension, 448
TP lighting stable, 256
training, 200
translucency, 96
Tucker, Lenny, 291, 316

Tune, Tommy, 22, 154
TV lighting, 130, 149
twin-spin gobo rotators, 140
ultraviolet lighting, 426
United Scenic Artists, Local 829, 34 184
Universal Studios, 268
upstage areas, 448
USITT, 299
Vari*Lite, xxii, 121, 141, 154, 159, 184, 249, 366
Viki (Pilbrow), 217, 260, 291
Vivian Beaumont Theatre, 100
*Voodoo Lounge*, 103, 351
Wagner, Robin, 221, 235, 322
Wagner, Wieland, 127, 185
Walt Disney Imagineering, 241 243, 289
Walton, Tony, xii, xiii, 97, 98, 100, 101, 116, 152, 154,
      234, 252, 340
water dimmers, 190
Watson, Lee, 183, 228
Webber, Sir Andrew Lloyd, 38 119
Weiss, Marc, 182, 430
*West Side Story*, 119
Whitfield, Michael, 183
Wilson, Michael, 248, 252
*Wise Child*, 252
Wojewodski, Stan, 152
Wolfe, George C., 236
women designers, 213
Wood, J. T. (Woody), 191
Wood, Peter, 86
Woodroffe, Patrick, xxiv, 158, 182, 349–54
worklight, 138, 435
Wrede, Casper, 109
Wybron Autopilot, 68, 377
Wybron Scrollers, 429
WYSIWYG, 376, 377, 434
Yale University, 180, 266, 320
Zeffirelli, Franco, 127
zipstrips, 91

# Acknowledgments

Thank you to the following manufacturers for all their assistance:

| | | |
|---|---|---|
| A.D.B. Lighting Systems | Robert Juliat Semco S.A. | R.D.S. Corp. |
| Altman Stage Lighting Co. | Kliegl Bros. Stage Lighting Co. | Reiche & Vogel—B. Deltschaft |
| Avolites Ltd. | Lee Filters | Rosco Laboratories Inc. |
| C.C.T. Lighting Ltd. | Light & Sound Design Inc. | S.G.M. Elettronica Srl. |
| Cameleon Sarl. | Lighting & Electronics Inc. | Selecon New Zealand Ltd. |
| Celco | Lycian Stage Lighting | Spotlight Srl. |
| Clay Paky Spa | M. & M. Camelont Ltd. | Strand Lighting |
| Coemar U.S.A. | Martin Professional A./S. | Strong International |
| Colortran Inc. | Marumo Electric Co. Ltd. | Teatro Srl. |
| D.H.A. Lighting Ltd. | Mole- Richardson Co. | Theatre Projects Lighting Services Ltd. |
| Desisti Lighting/Desmar Corp. | The Obie Company | Times Square Stage Lighting Co. Ltd. |
| Electronic Theatre Controls Inc. | Pancommand Systems Inc. | Vari*Lite Inc. |
| Flying Pig Systems Ltd. | Ludwig Pani | Wildfire Inc. |
| The Great American Market | Phoebus Manufacturing | Wybron Inc. |
| High End Systems Inc. | Production Arts Lighting Inc. | Zero 88 Lighting Ltd. |

A special thanks to Andy Collier at Strand Lighting (now at Teatro Srl.) & Tom Littrell at Vari*Lite for their help and humor.

To Barry Norman at the Theatre Museum in London, John Offord, Pat MacKay and Greg Havas for their research and information.

Many thanks to the photographers who kindly let us reproduce their pictures:

| | | | |
|---|---|---|---|
| Catherine Ashmore | Joe Giannetti | Elaine McCarthy | Peter Angelo Simon |
| Clive Barda | John Haynes | Deen van Meer | Jerome Sirlin |
| Maarten Brinkgreve | Ken Howard | George Mott | Marty Sohl |
| Tessa Buchan | Imagination | Paul Natkin | Timothy Streeter |
| Sheila Burnett | Leendert Jansen | Moritz NauschŸtz | Martha Swope |
| Peter Cunningham | Kevin Kolczynski | Micheal Olich | Eric Thompson |
| Michal Daniel | Paul Kolnik | Robert C. Ragfdale | Tony Walton |
| Zoe Dominic | Ivan Kyncl | Carol Rosegg | Ruth Waltz |
| Joel Fontaine | Lewis Lee | Ron Scherl | |
| Adrain Gatie | Joan Marcus | Al Seib | |

And to the following designers for their time and generosity in letting us use these photographs of their beautiful designs:

| | | | |
|---|---|---|---|
| Benny Ball | Jules Fisher | Anne Militello | Hans Toelstede |
| Ken Billington | Rick Fisher | Jim Moody | Tony Walton |
| Hal Binkley | Brian Gale | Tom Munn | Michael Whitfield |
| Marc Brickman | Wendall K. Harrington | Tharon Musser | Hans Wolff |
| Andy Bridge | Mark Henderson | Robert Ornbo | Patrick Woodroffe |
| Bill Bundy | David Hersey | Chris Parry | Scott Zielinski |
| Heather Carson | Jean Kalman | Jerome Sirlin | |
| Dawn Chiang | Max Keller | Mark Stanley | |
| Pat Collins | Nigel Levings | Josef Svoboda | |
| Pat Dignan | Peter Maradudin | David I. Taylor | |

Richard Pilbrow is an award-winning lighting designer, theatre design consultant and author. He began work in the theatre in London as a stage manager and in 1957 founded Theatre Projects. He has also been a successful theatrical, film and television producer.

Retained by Lord Olivier to be theatre consultant to the National Theatre of Great Britain, he created Theatre Projects Consultants, a team of theatrical, architectural, management, and technical experts, who have been responsible for more than five hundred arts centers and theatre projects in forty countries worldwide. Richard Pilbrow has led many innovations in auditorium and stage design as well as in other technological developments.

He was a pioneer of modern stage lighting in Britain. His lighting designs of more than three hundred productions have been seen in London, New York, Paris, Berlin, Vienna and Moscow. Most recently he has been responsible for the lighting design of Cy Coleman's *The Life* (Tony Award and Drama Desk nominations, 1997), Harold Prince's *Show Boat* (Drama Desk Award, Outer Circle Critics Award), as well as other awards in Canada and British Columbia, the Lincoln Center Theatre Company's *Four Baboons Adoring the Sun*, directed by Sir Peter Hall (Tony Award nomination), and the Los Angeles Music Center Opera's *The Magic Flute*, also directed by Peter Hall.

As a theatre producer Richard Pilbrow has presented thirty West End productions, many in association with Harold Prince. Some of those include *A Funny Thing Happened on the Way to the Forum, She Loves Me, Fiddler on the Roof, Cabaret, Company, A Little Night Music,* the National Theatre's *The Mysteries,* and Herb Gardner's *I'm Not Rappaport.* He was the producer of the feature film of Arthur Ransome's classic children's book *Swallows and Amazons,* and coproducer with BBC-TV of two television series of further books in the series, *Coot Club* and *The Big Six.* He was also the executive producer of *All You Need Is Love—The Story of Popular Music,* a seventeen-part international television series.

His book *Stage Lighting,* with a foreword by Lord Olivier, was published in 1970, followed by a second edition in 1979 and reprinted in 1991. It has become a standard work used for teaching stage lighting worldwide. Richard Pilbrow is a resident of Ridgefield, Connecticut.